REG

Taxation & Regulation

CPA Exam Review

2025 Edition

Permissions

The following items are utilized in this program, and are copyright property of the American Institute of Certified Public Accountants, Inc. (AICPA), all rights reserved:

- Uniform CPA Examination and Questions and Unofficial Answers, Copyright © 1991 – 2025
- Audit and Accounting Guides, Auditing Procedure Studies, Risk Alerts, Statements of Position, and Code of Professional Conduct
- Statements on Auditing Standards
- Statements on Standards for Accounting and Review Services
- Statements on Quality Control Standards
- Statements on Standards for Attestation Engagements
- Accounting Research Bulletins, APB Opinions
- Uniform CPA Examination Blueprints
- Independence Standards Board (ISB) Standards

Portions of various FASB and GASB documents, copyright property of the Financial Accounting Foundation, 401 Merritt 7, PO Box 5116, Norwalk, CT 06856-5116, are utilized with permission. Complete copies of these documents are available from the Financial Accounting Foundation. These selections include the following:

Financial Accounting Standards Board (FASB)

- The FASB Accounting Standards Codification™
- Statements of Financial Accounting Concepts
- FASB Statements, Interpretations, and Technical Bulletins

Governmental Accounting Standards Board (GASB)

- GASB Codification of Governmental Accounting and Financial Reporting Standards and GASB Statements
- GASB Concepts Statements
- GASB Interpretations and Technical Bulletins

Published by UWorld
9111 Cypress Waters Blvd.
Suite 300
Dallas, TX 75019
accounting.uworld.com/cpa-review

Printed in English, in the United States of America.

Acknowledgments

Keeping the course materials updated and accurate would not be possible without the contribution of our team of content experts. Our team includes academics and professionals who have expertise and experience in their respective fields; several have had experience at the Big Four or have PhDs in areas related to the exam. All are passionate about helping candidates pass the exam and about UWorld's dedication to creating the highest quality materials.

Taxation & Regulation

Introduction

Introduction

Introduction

How to Best Use Your Course

Welcome to the UWorld CPA Review course! Our expert team is passionate about helping you succeed and has developed an award-winning program that is proven to yield results. Before you get started, please read through this guide on how to best use your course so that you can master all of the topics laid out for you in the AICPA Blueprints and ultimately pass the CPA Exam. At UWorld, our passion is to make the hard stuff easy to learn and understand.

Plan Your Studies

When preparing for the CPA Exam, half the battle is setting yourself up for success with a solid plan from the get go. This includes establishing short- and long-term goals to ensure you're staying on track.

To get started, use the Study Plan in your course. Start your plan by setting the beginning and ending dates for your schedule. Then select your pace (Fast Track vs Customize) and set the number of hours per day you will study. The system will create your plan based on your choices. It is important to follow your plan steadily so that you can ensure you hit your goals. If you miss a day, make it up!

Tip!

Download the app! This gives you access to everything your course offers while on the go.

Master the Concepts through Active Learning

With this program, you will build your foundational knowledge and mastery of core exam topics through **active learning**. This evidence-based learning methodology centers around the principle that students retain information best when they actively participate in answering questions.

- **Begin with the Representative Task.** Read through each representative task carefully. (The Representative Tasks are from the AICPA Blueprints and are presented in our books and videos to guide you through the materials.) Pay particular attention to the words at the beginning of the task; they provide guidance on level and focus
- **Scan the book chapter.** Do you feel confident with the material? If you do, you might want to move directly to the questions and begin to practice. If you find that you are hesitant about an area, read the book or watch the video to solidify your understanding before you practice on some questions
- **Watch the videos.** If you prefer to absorb material on video rather than by reading the book, you will notice that the videos are deliberately set up in small segments. Our team created these segments so you can review what you need, either as part of the whole topic or for specific review of a smaller area
- **Practice the questions.** In our question bank (our QBank) we have taken great care to provide you with very high-quality questions and explanations. Each explanation not only tells you why the concept tested is important to understand but also teaches you why the answer is correct and why the other answer choices are not correct. Images, tables, and links to definitions also help fill in gaps as you use the questions and explanations to learn by doing

Track Your Progress and Performance

As you complete each chapter, track your progress and performance using our signature **SmartPath Predictive Technology™**. SmartPath is a data-driven platform that provides recommended targets based on previous students who have passed the CPA Exam. This is an important tool to help you study efficiently and gauge whether you are *exam-ready*. Your goal is to hit both your progress target (Questions Attempted) and performance target (Score) for each chapter.

As you work through the material, don't worry about hitting your "Score" target right away and focus your efforts on hitting the "Questions Attempted" target first. This approach may feel uncomfortable, but trust that you are building your knowledge as you absorb the answer explanations.

Once you've completed all the topics in a chapter, you can go back and focus your efforts on hitting the "Score" target. If you are falling short, drill down in the Performance tab to see which topics need extra attention.

Tip!

Don't over-study. **SmartPath™** helps determine when you can move on to the next topic.

Solidify the Concepts

Need extra help mastering the concept? Take advantage of the additional learning tools that are integrated into your course. For example, you could be working through a difficult question and find you need further explanation. No problem! There's a link to the supporting lecture right there in the question. Want to remember something for later review? Easily transfer content directly from the question to a digital flashcard. These are just a few ways we make it easy to navigate to and access the right tools you need at the right time.

These additional tools are designed to enhance your studies—**you do not necessarily need to read or watch all of this material!** Rather, use these tools as a means to improve on weak areas:

- **Video Lectures** – From the Lectures tab or directly integrated in the link at the bottom of each practice question, you have access to the profession's most motivating and effective lecturers. Lectures break down difficult topics into simplified concepts and provide helpful memory aids. These are especially recommended for visual and auditory learners
- **Textbooks** – Digital eTextbooks are accessible side by side with the video lectures or in a printed format with some of our course packages. These can be used as a reference if you need further explanation of a concept. Many students also find it beneficial to follow along in the textbook while watching the lectures and either take notes directly in the physical books or by using the Notes feature and highlighting tool in the platform
- **Digital Flashcards** – Create custom flashcards directly from your practice questions by clicking on the lightning bolt symbol. Depending on your program package, your course may also be pre-loaded with an "Expert Deck" of flashcards covering the most heavily tested topics. You can review all your cards in Study Mode or using our **Spaced-Repetition Technology**. This is an evidence-based learning method that presents cards you've marked as *difficult* more frequently and cards you've marked as *easy* less frequently. The spacing of how and when the flashcards are introduced has been proven to increase retention and strengthen memory recall

Get Exam-Ready

The final days leading up to the exam are a critical time in which you're going to want to review your SmartPath data and ask, "Am I *exam-ready*?" If you have hit all the targets, you are in a really good spot. However, if any areas are still marked "Needs Improvement," now is the time to focus your efforts on meeting those targets.

Finally, we recommend you **take at least one full practice exam before exam day** (click on the "Exam Sim" tab in the QBank). This allows you to hone your test-taking skills in an exam-like environment that follows the same 5-testlet, 4-hour structure as the exam.

AICPA Blueprints

The UWorld CPA Review course is based on the AICPA Blueprints, which show candidates what skills and content topics will be tested on the CPA Exam. You don't have to make tough decisions about what concepts to focus on. If you follow our methodology, you will be well on your way to passing the exam.

Let's take a look at what we mean by starting with the AICPA Blueprints. The Blueprints have four levels:

- Area
- Group
- Topic
- Representative Task

Each Representative Task also has a Skill level.

- Remembering & Understanding
- Application
- Analysis
- Evaluation (used only in AUD)

Here is a snapshot of a Blueprint with the levels and skills marked.

Area I – Business Analysis (40–50%)

Content group/topic	Skill: Remembering & Understanding	Skill: Application	Skill: Analysis	Skill: Evaluation	Representative Task
A. Current period/historical analysis, including the use of data					
1. Financial statement analysis		✓			Determine attribute structures, format, and sources of data needed to prepare financial statement analysis.
			✓		Compare current period financial statement accounts to prior periods or budget and explain variances.
			✓		Interpret financial statement fluctuations and ratios (eg, profitability, liquidity, solvency, performance).
			✓		Use outputs (eg, reports, visualizations) from data analytic techniques to identify patterns, trends, and correlations to explain an entity's results.
			✓		Derive the impact of transactions on the financial statements and notes to the financial statements.

BAR
Area I: Business Analysis
Group A: Current Period/Historical Analysis
Topic 1: Financial Statement Analysis

The Table of Contents of the BAR book shows how each UWorld textbook is set up to follow the order of the AICPA Blueprints, with

- Area
- Group
- Topic

Business Analysis & Reporting

In the pages of each book, we provide the Representative Tasks from the AICPA Blueprints. We did that to make a direct connection between the exam and our content. Our team deliberately focused on what the Tasks say and wrote study materials that match with the Task. There is no closer connection between what will be tested and what you are studying.

1.01 Financial Statement Analysis

Overview

A company appraises the past, present, and future execution of goals and economic fitness by performing **financial statement analysis** on its results from operations in a given period. Refer to the financial ratios used in the FAR exam for this section.

The results are viewed in relation to prior periods, budgets, and key performance indicators (ie, benchmarks). Companies **make informed decisions** using this analysis. The analysis is often presented using summaries and visualizations that present the financial data in an easy-to-understand, meaningful report.

Attribute Structures, Format, and Sources of Data

Representative Task (Application): Determine attribute structures, format, and sources of data needed to prepare financial statement analysis.

Beyond connecting to the topics of the AICPA Blueprints, our team also differentiated the textbook content to match the skill levels of the Tasks.

- **Remembering & Understanding** tasks require you to understand the definitions and fundamentals of the topic. We have presented the information in these areas with an eye to creating clear explanations of the topics
- **Application** tasks are more about using your knowledge in scenarios to indicate that you understand the concepts. Our authors have therefore provided examples that show you how to apply your knowledge in specific situations. Many of these examples are similar to questions that you will find on the exam
- **Analysis** tasks require a higher level of thinking, many times leading you to choose one outcome over another or to make a decision. On the exam, these tasks will always be addressed in Task-Based Simulations, or TBSs. The AICPA intentionally makes these more challenging to determine if you really know the material and can work with it as a professional. In our materials, our authors often guide you through the critical thinking required to work with TBSs
- **Evaluation** tasks are only in the AUD section of the exam and are at the highest level of thinking. They go a step further than the Analysis level and require you to evaluate or judge different approaches or outcomes

The CPA Exam

Within the AICPA Blueprints, there is information about how much time candidates have for each section and how many questions by question type each section contains. Question types include Multiple-Choice Questions (MCQs) and Task-Based Simulations (TBSs).

Section	Section Time	Multiple-Choice Questions (MCQs)	Task-Based Simulations (TBSs)
AUD – Core	4 hours	78	7
FAR – Core	4 hours	50	7
REG – Core	4 hours	72	8
BAR – Discipline	4 hours	50	7
ISC – Discipline	4 hours	82	6
TCP – Discipline	4 hours	68	7

Scoring Weight by Exam Section

The AICPA also shows candidates how the question types for each section are weighted and account for their overall score.

	Score Weighting	
Section	**Multiple-Choice Questions (MCQs)**	**Task-Based Simulations (TBSs)**
AUD – Core	50%	50%
FAR – Core	50%	50%
REG – Core	50%	50%
BAR – Discipline	50%	50%
ISC – Discipline	60%	40%
TCP – Discipline	50%	50%

Skill Allocations

As mentioned earlier, each Representative Task is tested at a specific Skill Level, and each part of the exam has its own weighting of the Skill Levels, as seen here.

Section	Remembering & Understanding	Application	Analysis	Evaluation
AUD – Core	30–40%	30–40%	15–25%	5–15%
FAR – Core	5–15%	45–55%	35–45%	–
REG – Core	25–35%	35–45%	25–35%	–
BAR – Discipline	10–20%	45–55%	30–40%	–
ISC – Discipline	55–65%	20–30%	10–20%	–
TCP – Discipline	5–15%	55–65%	25–35%	–

Content Allocations

The AICPA Blueprints address how coverage of the various content areas is allocated in each exam. Using the UWorld system that ties directly to the Blueprint structure, it is easy to see which topics are covered to what extent.

AUD

Content Area		Allocation
Area I	Ethics, Professional Responsibilities, and General Principles	15–25%
Area II	Assessing Risk and Developing a Planned Response	25–35%
Area III	Performing Further Procedures and Obtaining Evidence	30–40%
Area IV	Forming Conclusions and Reporting	10–20%

FAR

Content Area		Allocation
Area I	Financial Reporting	30–40%
Area II	Select Balance Sheet Accounts	30–40%
Area III	Select Transactions	25–35%

REG

Content Area		Allocation
Area I	Ethics, Professional Responsibilities, and Federal Tax Procedures	10–20%
Area II	Business Law	15–25%
Area III	Federal Taxation of Property Transactions	5–15%
Area IV	Federal Taxation of Individuals	22–32%
Area V	Federal Taxation of Entities (including tax preparation)	23–33%

BAR

Content Area		Allocation
Area I	Business Analysis	40–50%
Area II	Technical Accounting and Reporting	35–45%
Area III	State and Local Governments	10–20%

ISC

Content Area		Allocation
Area I	Information Systems and Data Management	35–45%
Area II	Security, Confidentiality, and Privacy	35–45%
Area III	Considerations for System and Organization Controls (SOC) Engagements	15–25%

TCP

Content Area		Allocation
Area I	Tax Compliance and Planning for Individuals and Personal Financial Planning	30–40%
Area II	Entity Tax Compliance	30–40%
Area III	Entity Tax Planning	10–20%
Area IV	Property Transactions (disposition of assets)	10–20%

Exam Testlets

Each section of the exam is divided into five testlets. Two testlets cover MCQs, and three testlets cover TBSs. Not all sections have an equal number of MCQs and TBSs, as the following chart shows.

	Testlet					Total	
	1	2	3	4	5		
Section	MCQ	MCQ	TBS	TBS	TBS	MCQ	TBS
AUD - Core	39	39	2	3	2	78	7
FAR - Core	25	25	2	3	2	50	7
REG - Core	36	36	2	3	3	72	8
BAR - Discipline	25	25	2	3	2	50	7
ISC - Discipline	41	41	1	3	2	82	6
TCP - Discipline	34	34	2	3	2	68	7

Finally, to manage your time effectively in the exam, we recommend that you:

- Use 75 seconds per multiple-choice question as a benchmark,
- Allocate 15-20 minutes per task-based simulation, depending on complexity, and
- Take the standard 15-minute break after the third testlet; it doesn't count against your time.

To see the full AICPA Blueprints, visit
https://www.aicpa.org/becomeacpa/cpaexam/examinationcontent

Above all, start the study process with confidence! As Roger always says, "You do not have to be a genius to pass the CPA Exam. If you study, you will pass!" You've got this.

REG

Area I: Ethics, Professional Responsibilities, and Federal Tax Procedure

REG 1
Ethics and Responsibilities in Tax Practice

REG 1: Ethics and Responsibilities in Tax Practice

1.01 Regulations Governing Practice before the IRS

Regulations Governing Practice before the IRS

Representative Task (Remembering & Understanding): Recall the regulations governing practice before the Internal Revenue Service.

Representative Task (Application): Apply the regulations governing practice before the Internal Revenue Service given a specific scenario.

Circular 230 contains the IRS's rules of practice governing CPAs and others who practice before the agency. The government may censure, fine, suspend, or disbar tax advisors from practice before the IRS if they violate Circular 230's standards of conduct. "Practicing" entails primarily preparing and filing documents and communicating and meeting with IRS representatives on behalf of a taxpayer.

Circular 230 consists of 5 subparts. Within each subpart, certain sections are particularly applicable to CPAs. Below is a summary of the subparts and sections typically tested on the CPA exam.

Five Subparts of Circular 230	
Subpart A	Provides rules related to the authority to practice before the IRS • Sec. 10.3 – Who may practice • Sec. 10.8 – Return preparation and application of rules to other individuals
Subpart B	Describes the duties and restrictions of those authorized to practice before the IRS • Sec. 10.20 – Information to be furnished • Sec. 10.21 – Knowledge of client's omissions • Sec. 10.22 – Diligence as to accuracy • Sec. 10-24 – Assistance from the disbarred • Sec. 10.27 – Fees • Sec. 10.28 – Return of client's records • Sec. 10.29 – Conflicting interests • Sec. 10.30 – Solicitation • Sec. 10.31 – Negotiation of taxpayer checks • Sec. 10.34 – Standards with respect to tax returns and documents, affidavits, and other papers • Sec. 10.37 – Requirements for other written advice

Five Subparts of Circular 230	
Subpart C	Indicates sanctions for violations • Sec. 10.50 – Sanctions • Sec. 10.51 – Incompetence and disreputable conduct
Subpart D	Provides rules for disciplinary proceedings • Sec. 10.60 – Institution of proceeding
Subpart E	Relates to the availability of public records.

Section 10.3 – Who May Practice

Subpart A of Circular 230 sets forth rules governing authority to practice before the IRS. Examples of individuals who may practice before the IRS include attorneys, CPAs, registered tax return preparers, enrolled agents and enrolled actuaries, and enrolled retirement plan agents. Most importantly, Section 10.3 provides that in order for a CPA to practice before the IRS, the CPA must:

- **Not** currently be under **suspension or disbarment** from practice before the IRS
- **File a declaration** with the IRS indicating that the CPA is currently qualified as a CPA and **authorized** to **represent** the party

Although providing **written tax advice** (eg, tax opinion) is **considered practice** before the IRS, an exception is made for the written declaration requirement. Providing a written declaration for every instance of written tax advice would be too onerous for the CPA and IRS.

Although there are no minimum education requirements, practitioners must be competent, meaning that they possess the appropriate level of knowledge, skill, thoroughness, and preparation necessary. They may acquire competence by studying the relevant tax law or consulting with experts.

Circular 230 Requirements to Practice before the IRS

	Practice before the IRS	Provide Written Tax Advice
Be in Good Standing	✓	✓
Written Declaration	✓	✗

Practice before the IRS includes *all matters connected with a presentation to the IRS* or any of its officers or employees related to a taxpayer's rights, privileges, or liabilities under laws or regulations administered by the IRS. These presentations include but are not limited to:

- Preparing documents (eg, tax returns for compensation)
- Filing documents
- Corresponding and communicating with the IRS
- Representing a client at conferences, hearings, and meetings (eg, tax audit)
- Rendering written advice with regard to transactions having a potential for tax avoidance or evasion

A CPA prepares a tax return for a hair salon owner in exchange for free haircuts. While no cash has exchanged hands, this barter transaction is still considered *preparing a tax return for compensation*. Therefore, the CPA **is** practicing before the IRS.

A CPA, who normally does not prepare tax returns, agrees to prepare a tax return for her mother's hair salon because her mother's regular CPA was in the hospital and could not complete the return. No compensation was received for preparing the return.

Since this was a one-time situation to help a family member and no compensation was received, the CPA is **not** considered to be practicing before the IRS.

A CPA delivers a written tax opinion discussing the detailed tax implications her client is considering. Providing a detailed, written tax opinion to a client **is** considered practicing before the IRS.

A taxpayer may represent themselves or be represented by a family member (who is not paid to do so) or by the person who prepared the tax return. In addition, entities may be represented by the following: employers by a full-time employee, a partnership by a partner, a corporation by an officer, and a trust or estate by the trustee or executor.

Section 10.8 – Return Preparation and Application of Rules to Other Individuals

A preparer tax identification number (PTIN) is required to prepare a tax return or claim for refund in exchange for compensation (compensation is any value received). Only attorneys, CPAs, enrolled agents, registered tax return preparers, and annual filing season program participants may obtain PTINs.

Circular 230—PTIN Requirements

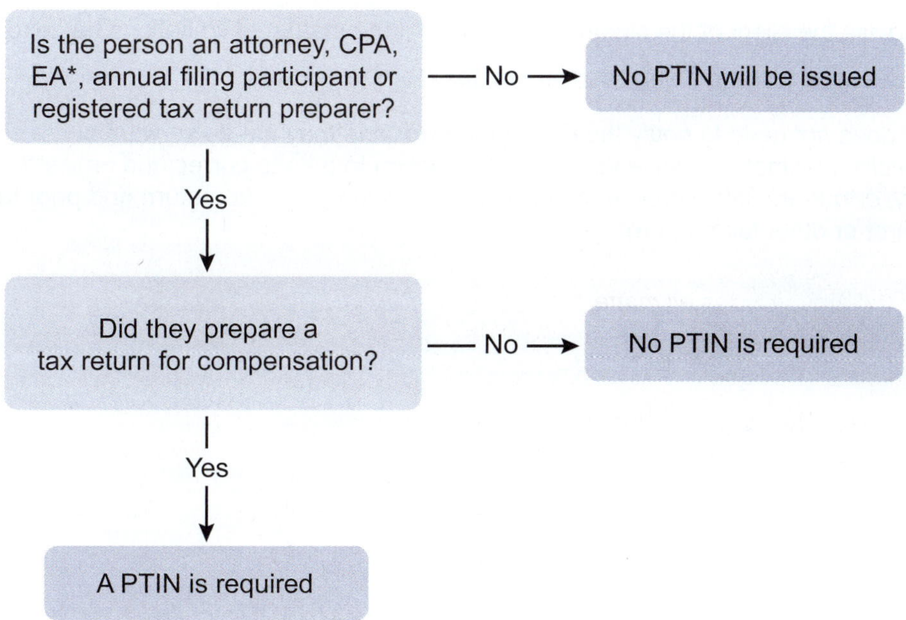

**EA is an enrolled agent with the IRS*

Section 10.20 – Information to Be Furnished to the IRS

A practitioner must promptly submit to the IRS any records or information that its agents and officers request properly and lawfully, "unless the practitioner believes in good faith and on reasonable grounds that the records or information are privileged." In other words, Section 10.20 requires prompt *cooperation* with all IRS requests for information.

When the IRS Requests Client Information from a CPA

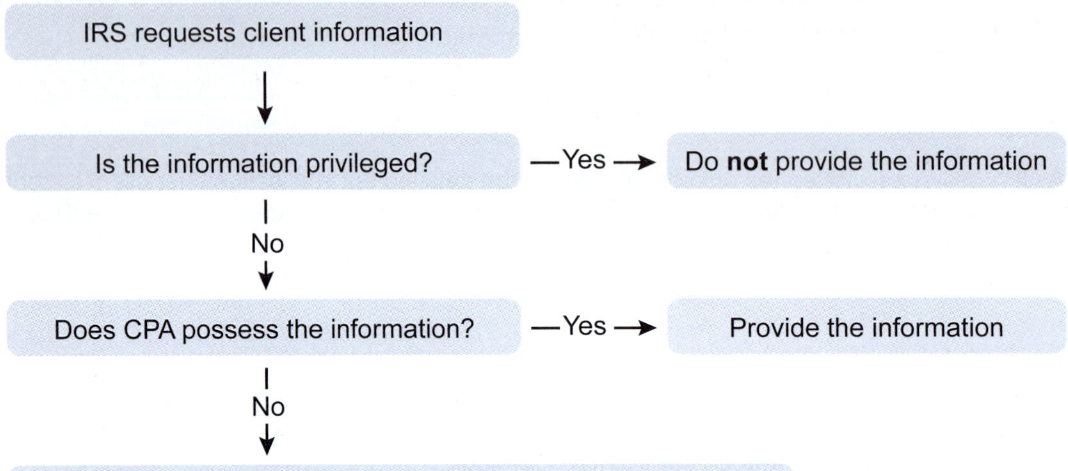

Section 10.21 – Knowledge of Client's Omission

If a practitioner becomes aware of an incident of a client's noncompliance with tax laws or of an error or omission on a filing with the IRS, the practitioner is required to:

- *Promptly advise* the client of the circumstance (even if the statute of limitations has expired); and
- Advise the client as to the *potential consequences*.

The practitioner does *not* need to notify the IRS of the error and may not do so without the client's permission. The *client* ultimately decides the course of action to take to correct the omission (eg, amend the return). Typically, errors are discovered when reviewing a recently filed tax return and prior tax returns filed by the tax preparer or other tax preparer.

Tax Practitioner Duty to Inform Client of Error

Section 10.22 – Diligence as to Accuracy

A CPA must exercise due diligence in preparing or assisting in the preparation of filings with the IRS and in determining the correctness of representations made by the practitioner to the IRS and to clients. The practitioner can rely on another person, provided that the practitioner has exercised reasonable care and due diligence in engaging, supervising, training, and evaluating the individual.

Section 10.24 – Assistance from the Disbarred

A practitioner should *not* knowingly accept even indirect assistance from any person disbarred or suspended from practice by the IRS.

Sam and Judy are partners in the S&J Partnership. Sam has violated regulations and been disbarred by the IRS. However, Judy (who is in good standing with the IRS) needed help during tax season and allowed Sam to work on tax returns. Judy signs off on all of the work completed by Sam. This arrangement involves accepting indirect assistance from a disbarred individual and violates Section 10.24.

Section 10.27 – Fees

Generally, a practitioner may **not** charge either an unconscionable fee or a contingent fee for matters before the IRS. However, there are *three exceptions* regarding **contingent fees**. Contingent fees may be charged for:

1. An administrative examination or a challenge to an original return, an amended return, or a claim for refund (not for preparing original return);
2. Services related to a claim for credit or refund in connection with statutory interest or penalties charged by the IRS; or
3. Services related to a judicial proceeding under the IRC.

Section 10.28 – Return of Client's Records

A practitioner is generally required to return any and all client records needed for the client to comply with tax obligations, although *copies may be retained*. Generally, a dispute over fees does **not** justify retention of client records.

However, the practitioner may temporarily withhold the records if the *practitioner's state law allows* the retention of client records as a result of a dispute over fees. When they are retained under such circumstances, the practitioner must:

- Return those that are required to be attached to the client's tax return; and
- Provide reasonable access to the client to review and copy records necessary to comply with the client's tax obligations.

Treasury Department Circular No. 230: Requirements for a Tax Practitioner to Return Client Records	
General Rule	• Must return all client records when requested by client • May retain copies
If There Is a Fee Dispute	• May temporarily withhold *some* records if state law permits • Must return any records necessary for client to comply with tax obligations and allow access to others
Types of Records	• Written and electronic documents from client • Material prepared by client or client's other representatives (eg, attorney) • Prior returns and refund claims • Other material prepared and used for client's tax matter (eg, appraisals)

Section 10.29 – Conflicting Interests

A practitioner may **not** represent a client before the IRS when there is a conflict of interest, such as when representation of one client would be adverse to another or when there is a risk that representation will be limited as a result of responsibilities to other clients or others.

A practitioner may represent a client despite a conflict of interest if **all** of the following apply:

- It is reasonable for the practitioner to believe that representation will be competent and diligent;
- Representation is not prohibited by law; *and*
- All affected clients waive the conflict of interest, by giving their written, informed consent.

In addition to Circular 230 guidelines on conflicts of interest, the AICPA has its Guidelines for Conflicts of Interest in the Performance of Tax Services, which add these additional responsibilities for practitioner management of conflicts of interest.

- The practitioner should adopt procedures to use in identifying and managing conflicts of interest
- The standard for evaluating whether a conflict exists is whether a reasonable third party evaluating the situation would conclude that the practitioner's integrity and objectivity are compromised

A practitioner has been filing a joint tax return for a married couple for 10 years. The couple is now going through a divorce. A conflict would exist if the practitioner prepared returns for each of the spouses separately because circumstances may find the spouses having different views on deductions. The practitioner would also have extensive knowledge of each spouse's financial position, which might affect the practitioner's objectivity in evaluating decisions about their returns.

Section 10.30 – Solicitation

A practitioner may **not** make false, fraudulent, or coercive statements or claims or misleading or deceptive statements or claims with respect to any IRS matter in any form of public communication or private solicitation. Nor may a practitioner make an uninvited solicitation to perform services in matters related to the IRS, whether written or oral, if doing so violates federal or state laws or another applicable rule.

Any *lawful* solicitation by or on behalf of a practitioner before the IRS must:

- Identify that it is a solicitation
- Indicate the source of information used to choose the recipient, if applicable

A practitioner may disseminate information about fees, including fixed fees for specific routine services, hourly rates, ranges of fees for particular services, and fees charged for an initial consultation. Fee information may be communicated in a variety of ways, including professional lists, telephone directories, print media, mailings, electronic mail, facsimile, hand-delivered flyers, radio, television, and any other method. Advertised fees must be honored for at least 30 days. Additionally, copies of the advertised communications must be kept by the practitioner for at least 36 months from transmission.

Practitioners may not use the term "certified" in describing their standing or experience with the IRS. However the following language may be used:

- Enrolled to represent taxpayers before the Internal Revenue Service
- Enrolled to practice before the Internal Revenue Service
- Admitted to practice before the Internal Revenue Service

Section 10.31 – Negotiation of Taxpayer Checks

A tax preparer may not endorse or otherwise negotiate a client's government check issued in relation to a federal tax liability (eg, a client's tax refund).

Section 10.34 – Standards with Respect to Tax Returns and Documents, Affidavits, and Other Papers

A **tax return** should not be filed with a tax position that *lacks* a *reasonable basis*, is an unreasonable position, or represents a willful attempt to understate the liability or constitutes an intentional disregard for rules or regulations. A practitioner may not willfully, recklessly, or through gross incompetence:

- Sign a tax return or claim for refund when the practitioner knows or should know that it contains such a position; or
- Advise a client to take such a position or prepare a portion of a return or claim for refund containing such a position.

A tax practitioner may not **advise** a client to take a *frivolous tax position* on a document, affidavit, or other paper submitted to the IRS. Nor may a tax practitioner advise a client to submit a document, affidavit, or other paper to the IRS if:

- It is intended to delay or impede administration of federal tax laws or is frivolous; or
- It contains or omits information indicating an intentional disregard for a rule or regulation, unless the practitioner also advises the client to submit a document indicating a good-faith challenge to the rule or regulation.

A practitioner is required to **advise clients regarding potential penalties** that are reasonably likely to be assessed, and the opportunity to avoid penalty through disclosure, when those penalties have the potential of arising from:

- A tax position taken if the practitioner either signed or prepared the return or advised the client relative to the position
- A document, affidavit, or other paper submitted to the IRS

A practitioner may, in good faith, **rely on information obtained from a client** without verification. If information furnished by the client appears incorrect, incomplete, or otherwise unsatisfactory based on information known by or furnished to the practitioner, that fact may **not** be ignored by the practitioner.

Ben, a tax practitioner, has been completing Xavier's personal and Subchapter S tax returns for 10 years. During that time, Xavier has always submitted mileage amounts for his vehicle used in his business. When Xavier submitted information for the sale of that vehicle and the purchase of a new one, Ben noticed that the odometer mileage on the vehicle documented by the dealership for the trade-in was 45,000 miles less than the total business mileage Xavier had submitted during the time he used the original vehicle. Ben has knowledge of an inconsistency and may not ignore it.

Section 10.37 – Requirements for Other Written Advice

Tax practitioners may give written advice if it is based on reasonable factual and legal assumptions and the practitioner reasonably considers all relevant facts and circumstances. A practitioner is prohibited from giving written advice that is based on unreasonable assumptions; unreasonably relies on representations, statements, findings, or agreements of the taxpayer or another; does not consider all relevant information that is known, or should be known, by the practitioner; or considers the possibility that the position, or the return on which it is taken, will not be audited or will be resolved through settlement.

A practitioner may rely on the advice of another, provided:

- The advice is reasonable; and
- Reliance is in good faith, considering all facts and circumstances.

Treasury Department Circular No. 230: Requirements for a Tax Practitioner When Giving Other Written Advice	
Required	• Basing advice on reasonable factual and legal assumptions (past and future) • Reasonably considering all relevant facts • Making reasonable efforts to identify facts for each tax matter • Relating applicable law to the facts
Prohibited	• Relying on the client's representations or documents (eg, appraisals) if reliance would be unreasonable • Taking into account the possibility that a tax return will not be audited

Section 10.50 – Sanctions

The Secretary of the Treasury has the authority to **censure**, **suspend**, or **disbar** a practitioner from practice before the IRS if the practitioner:

- Is shown to be incompetent or disreputable;
- Violates requirements either willfully or as a result of gross incompetence; or
- Willfully and knowingly misleads or threatens a client or prospective client with the intent to defraud.

The Secretary of the Treasury also has the authority to impose a *monetary penalty* on any practitioner who engages in the prohibited conduct indicated above. The maximum penalty equals 100% of the gross income derived from the misconduct.

Section 10.51 – Incompetence and Disreputable Conduct

Some of the actions or events that indicate incompetence or disreputable conduct include:

- Conviction of any crime under federal tax laws
- Conviction of any crime involving dishonesty or breach of trust
- Conviction of any state or federal felony that would render one unfit to practice before the IRS
- Giving false or misleading information to tax officials or attempting to influence an officer or employee of the IRS
- Soliciting employment in violation of Section 10.30
- Willfully failing to prepare a federal tax return or evading, or attempting to evade, an assessment or payment of federal tax
- Being disbarred or suspended from practice as a CPA or an attorney
- Willfully assisting, counseling, or encouraging a client or prospective client to violate a tax law or evade federal taxes or their payment
- Failure to promptly remit funds received from a client for the payment of taxes
- Contemptuous conduct, such as using abusive language, knowingly making false accusations, or circulating malicious or libelous material in connection with practice before the IRS

- Knowingly, recklessly, or as a result of gross incompetence giving a false opinion
- Willingly failing to sign a tax return when required
- Willfully disclosing or using a tax return or tax information inappropriately
- Willfully failing to file using electronic media when required to do so
- Providing covered tax services without a valid PTIN
- Willfully representing a taxpayer before the IRS when not authorized to do so

Section 10.60 – Institution of Proceeding

Any violation of laws relative to practice before the IRS may result in reprimand or a proceeding for sanctions. Instituting a proceeding requires that the respondent be advised in writing of the law, facts, and conduct warranting such action and given an opportunity to dispute facts, assert additional facts, and make arguments.

1.02 Internal Revenue Code and Regulations Related to Tax Return Preparers

Who Is a Tax Preparer

Representative Task (Remembering & Understanding): Recall who is a tax return preparer.

A "tax return preparer" (TRP) includes anyone who prepares **for compensation**, or who employs one or more persons to prepare, all or a **substantial portion** of any tax return or claim for refund. This includes a person who prepares a return or claim for refund *outside* the U.S. regardless of the person's nationality, residence, or the location of the person's place of business. The term *tax return* applies to **all** federal income tax returns, federal estate and gift tax returns, employment tax returns, and excise tax returns.

- The compensation received can be either explicit or implicit (eg, bartering)
- A person may be a TRP *without* regard to educational qualifications and professional status requirements
- A TRP does **not** have to be enrolled to practice before the IRS. An enrolled agent is anyone who has passed a comprehensive exam given by the IRS and has the right to represent taxpayers before the IRS and perform tax-related services (eg, prepare tax returns)
- TRPs must be competent, meaning that they possess "the appropriate level of knowledge, skill, thoroughness, and preparation necessary." They may acquire competence by studying the relevant tax law or consulting with experts

Performing the following acts does **not** classify a person as a tax return preparer:

- An individual preparing a return of a taxpayer, or an officer, a general partner, member, shareholder, employee, trustee, or executor of a taxpayer, by whom the individual is regularly and continuously employed or compensated
- Preparing a return for family or a friend free of charge or through a sponsored volunteer program (eg, IRS Volunteer Income Tax Assistance Program, tax counseling for the elderly)
- Simply typing, reproducing, or providing other mechanical assistance in preparing a return

CPA as Tax Return Preparer	
Qualifies If	• Prepares tax returns for compensation (eg, money or barter) • Employs others to prepare tax returns
Does Not Qualify If	• Prepares returns for friends or family free of charge • Provides tax return administrative tasks (eg, data entry) • Prepares entity's return as an employee of that entity
Other Elements	• Required to have a Preparer Tax Identification Number (PTIN) • Need not be enrolled to practice before the IRS (ie, enrolled agent)

Under the Internal Revenue Code, what is a person who is paid to prepare and file federal tax returns called?

The IRC uses the term a **tax return preparer** for anyone who prepares for **compensation**, or who employs one or more persons to prepare, all or a substantial portion of any tax return or claim for refund. The preparer may be a CPA or an enrolled agent. The terms "tax return professional" and "tax practitioner" are often used to refer to individuals who handle tax-related matters.

Signing and Nonsigning TRP

A TRP includes both **signing** and **nonsigning** preparers. A **signing** preparer bears the "**primary responsibility**" for the overall **accuracy** of the return or claim for refund even when the nonsigning preparer prepared all or a substantial portion of a return. However, in certain circumstances, a nonsigning preparer could *potentially* have the same level of responsibility (ie, be subject to preparer penalties) as a signing preparer.

- When there are multiple people working on a return, the person who is primarily responsible for the position giving rise to an *understatement* is the TRP punishable under the tax provisions
- If it is unclear who is responsible for the position taken by the taxpayer, the person with **overall supervisory responsibility** for preparing the return or for the position will be the TRP

A nonsigning TRP is any TRP who is **not** a signing TRP but who prepares **all or a substantial portion** of a return or provides advice (written or oral) to a taxpayer or to another tax return preparer when that advice leads to a position that constitutes a substantial portion of the return. Factors considered for determining whether a portion of a return is a *substantial portion* include:

- The size and complexity of the item relative to the taxpayer's gross income; and
- The size of the understatement attributable to the item compared to the taxpayer's reported tax liability.

Smith is preparing an income tax return for a client. He brings in his partner, Kahn, who is a tax expert and whose advice Smith uses to complete a major portion of the return. Smith signs the return. Although Kahn contributed substantially to the completion of the return, he is considered a nonsigning preparer.

There are **two exceptions** (ie, de minimis rule) when a **nonsigning** TRP will **not** be deemed as completing a substantial portion of a tax return and, therefore, not subject to any potential preparer penalties. A portion of the tax return is **not** considered to be a substantial portion if it involves amounts of gross income or amounts of deductions:

1. Less than $10,000; or
2. Less than $400,000, which is also less than 20% of the gross income indicated on the return.

Jessie, a partner in a CPA firm, reviews a tax return reporting $26 million in gross income and offers an opinion that the taxpayer may take a deduction of $300,000. Another partner in the firm signs the tax return. Because the $300,000 deduction is less than $400,000 (which is also less than 20% of $26 million), Jessie has not completed a substantial portion. However, if the deduction was $600,000 (ie, greater than $400,000), Jessie would now be considered a nonsigning TRP.

Tax Preparer Penalties

Representative Task (Remembering & Understanding): Recall situations that would result in tax return preparer penalties.

Representative Task (Application): Apply potential tax return preparer penalties given a specific scenario.

Overview

To encourage tax preparers' compliance with established responsibilities and with tax regulations, the IRS can assess numerous **monetary civil and criminal penalties** (eg, imprisonment) for violations.

When preparing a return, a TRP may, in **good faith**, rely on information provided by the taxpayer. However, the preparer is responsible for making **reasonable inquiries** about information that appears to be wrong or inaccurate (eg, lack of substantiation for travel or charitable contributions). Failure to do so may result in a preparer penalty for any understated tax liability.

Tax Preparers Duty to Verify Taxpayer Information

- May rely in good faith and without verification on information provided by taxpayer or third party (eg, advisor)
- Must make reasonable inquiries if information appears incorrect or incomplete
- Must inquire about appropriate documentation if IRC requires it (eg, travel and entertainment expenses)
- Not required to:
  - Audit the taxpayer
  - Review or examine books, records, or operations
  - Copy *all* underlying documents to independently verify the information

To be guilty of **misconduct**, a preparer must knowingly or recklessly:

- Understate the tax liability of a client (eg, overstating expense and/or credits)
- Give erroneous advice or fail to advise a client of tax elections available
- Endorse or negotiate a refund check for their own account (ie, to ensure that a client's tax refund is not commingled with the preparer's funds)
- Adopt a frivolous position on a tax issue (eg, lack substantial authority)

In addition, a preparer may be held responsible for errors in the preparation of the return but may escape liability based on exceptions for good faith or reasonable cause, when the error results from utilizing the services of a computerized tax preparation service, obtaining advice from another professional on tax questions, or following inaccurate IRS form instructions or advice from an IRS employee.

Preparer Penalties under Section 6695

When retaining records of client tax matters, preparers have the option of either retaining copies of completed returns or keeping a list of the names and taxpayer identification numbers for all returns prepared. The copies of the tax returns must be **kept for three years**. The list of names and taxpayer ID numbers must include all clients from the prior three years. Failure to do so will result in a preparer penalty.

The purpose of this rule is to allow the IRS to efficiently identify all the preparer's clients for the prior three years. This may be necessary if the IRS is investigating a preparer who might not be upholding professional standards (eg, filing frivolous or false returns). In addition:

- The preparer must **sign** the preparer's declaration on the tax return and provide their preparer tax identification number (ie, **PTIN**)
- The return must be timely filed, and a **copy** of the completed return must be **provided** to the taxpayer
- The preparer need not obtain from the taxpayer documentation of information provided to prepare the return but must make **reasonable inquiries** about the existence of such support where appropriate. For example, the preparer should ask the client if travel costs are supported by a log and if charitable contributions exceeding $250 are supported by receipts from the charities
- The preparer may not negotiate a check made out to the taxpayer (other than to deposit the full amount into the taxpayer's bank account)

When preparing a client's Form 1040 U.S. Individual Income Tax Return, a CPA determined that there was documentation supporting only $6,000 of the $15,000 business expenses claimed by the client. The CPA has a duty to inquire about information that appears wrong or incomplete. Filing a return using incomplete information without making appropriate inquiries violates this duty. There are no exceptions, even for tax returns with a small likelihood of being audited. As a result, the CPA is subject to a preparer penalty.

Which of the following situations could result in a preparer penalty assessed by the IRS?

- Taxpayer fails to inform the preparer that the taxpayer earned income from being a part-time Uber driver for one month during the tax year
- Preparer fails to provide the taxpayer with a copy of the tax return
- Preparer inadvertently transposes two digits on a return, and the error results in an understatement of income by $120
- Preparer takes an aggressive tax position that has substantial authority, which results in a decrease of tax

Tax return preparers may be subject to penalties for **failing** to **provide a copy of the tax return** to the taxpayer. However, no penalty applies to errors based on reasonable cause, aggressive tax positions with substantial authority, or relying on information provided by the taxpayer.

Penalties for Underpayment of Tax from Unreasonable Tax Positions and Willful and Reckless Conduct

Two common situations that result in preparer penalties from underpayment of tax are unreasonable tax positions and willful and reckless conduct by the TRP.

The *Statement on Standards for Tax Services (SSTS) No. 1* defines a **tax return position** as:

- A position reflected on a tax return on which a TRP has specifically advised a taxpayer; **or**
- A position about which a TRP has knowledge of all material facts and, on the basis of those facts, has concluded whether the position is appropriate.

Preparer penalties are incurred when a tax position results in an *understatement of tax liability* and there is no *appropriate authority* for the position and/or the position was *not adequately disclosed*. The expectation is that a TRP should have known or reasonably should have known whether a tax position is reasonable or unreasonable.

When a TRP adopts an "unreasonable tax position" or engages in "willful or reckless conduct" (ie, disregards an established tax rule or position) in the preparation of a tax return, Section 6694 imposes a preparer penalty if an **underpayment** of the tax liability results. An underpayment of a taxpayer's liability occurs when the reported liability on the tax return excludes income or includes excess allowable deductions and/or tax credits. These penalties are **not** the same as the accuracy-related penalties that apply to the taxpayer.

A tax position (other than a position with respect to a tax shelter or a reportable transaction) is **unreasonable unless:**

- There is **substantial authority** for the position; or
- The position was **disclosed** and there is a **reasonable basis** for the position.

The **substantial authority standard** is an *objective* standard involving an analysis of the law and application of the law to relevant facts. It is less stringent than the **more likely than not standard** (the standard that is met when there is a greater than 50% likelihood of the position being upheld) but more stringent than the **reasonable basis standard** (20% likelihood of the position being upheld). Generally, the substantial authority standard is considered to have a 40% likelihood of the position being upheld.

The standards for unreasonable positions are different depending on whether the position is **disclosed** or **undisclosed** on the tax return.

- If a position is **disclosed**, it is "unreasonable" unless there is a **reasonable basis** for the position. Because disclosure alerts the IRS to the position, a more lenient standard is applied in determining "unreasonableness." A position having a "reasonable basis" requires a 20% chance of successfully being sustained if challenged by the IRS
  - Form 8275 Disclosure Statement is generally used to disclose positions that lack substantial authority. However, Form 8275-R Regulation Disclosure Statement, is used to disclose a tax position that is contrary to Treasury Regulations
- An **undisclosed position** is "unreasonable" if there is **no** *substantial authority*. The **substantial authority** standard requires a **40% probability of being sustained** on its merits
- If the position relates to a **tax shelter**, it is "unreasonable" unless it is **more likely than not (> 50% chance)** that the position will be sustained

Amount of TRP Penalties

- If the TRP *knew* or *reasonably should have known* about the resulting understatement of tax resulting from the tax position, the penalty per violation is the **greater of $1,000 or 50%** of the income derived by the TRP with respect to the return
- The penalty per violation for a TRP's **willful or reckless conduct** resulting in an **understatement** (eg, < 20% chance of successfully being sustained) is the **greater of $5,000 or 75%** of the income derived by the TRP with respect to the return. For example, the TRP fabricates deductions or ignores information provided by the taxpayer:
    - If the willful and reckless conduct penalty and the unreasonable tax position penalty are imposed, the willful and reckless conduct penalty is *reduced* by the unreasonable tax position penalty

The preparer can **avoid** the penalties if:

- The tax position is adequately **disclosed** and has a **reasonable basis**;
- The position is **not disclosed** (and is not a tax shelter) but there is **substantial authority** for the position; or
- A position regarding a tax shelter or a reportable transaction is more likely than not correct (ie, > 50%).

In addition, if the TRP had *reasonable cause* for the position and acted in *good faith*, **no penalty applies**. Good-faith defense applies when TRPs can establish that they relied on taxpayer-furnished information believed to be true.

Position Standard	Threshold	Significance of Threshold
No reasonable basis (willful and reckless)	Less than 20% chance of being sustained	Penalty of greater of $5,000 or 75% of the income derived by the TRP applies (eg, frivolous tax positions)
Reasonable basis	Greater than 20% chance of being sustained	Positions meeting this threshold must be **disclosed** to avoid penalty
Substantial authority	About 40% chance of being sustained	Applies for **undisclosed** tax positions that do *not* meet this threshold Penalty of greater of $1,000 or 50% of the income derived by the TRP
More likely than not	Greater than 50% chance of being sustained	Penalty applies for **reportable transactions** and **tax shelters** that do not meet this threshold

Any additional taxes and interest owed due to an error are entirely the responsibility of the taxpayer and not the preparer. The taxpayer also may be subject to accuracy-related penalties, negligence, or fraud penalties in addition to any penalties the preparer is assessed if the taxpayer is determined to have committed a penalty offense of their own.

A tax return preparer filed a corporate tax return for a client. The return contained a disclosure tax position on Form 8275 for which there was a reasonable basis. The taxpayer was charged $8,000 for the preparation of the tax return. The return was audited, and although it had a reasonable basis, it was disallowed by the IRS, resulting in $6,000 in underpayment of income taxes. What amount is the tax preparer's penalty?

Since the tax position was disclosed and there was a reasonable basis, **no penalty applies**.

Assume instead that the tax position was *undisclosed* and there was *no* substantial authority to support the position.

The penalty depends on whether it is determined that the preparer knew or reasonably should have known about the resulting understatement of tax resulting from the tax position or that the preparer's conduct in taking the tax position was willful or reckless (eg, no research performed).

- If the TRP *knew* or *reasonably should have known* about the resulting understatement of tax resulting from the tax position, the penalty per violation is the **greater of $1,000 or 50%** of the income derived by the TRP with respect to the return. In this case, the penalty is **$4,000**, the greater of $1,000 or 50% of preparer's fee ($8,000 × 50% = $4,000)
- The penalty per violation for a TRP's **willful or reckless conduct** resulting in an **understatement** (ie, < 20% chance of successfully being sustained) is the **greater of $5,000 or 75%** of the income derived by the TRP with respect to the return. In this case, the penalty is **$6,000**, the greater of $5,000 or 75% of preparer's fee ($8,000 × 75% = $6,000)

  Note: *The $6,000 willful or reckless penalty is reduced by the unreasonable tax position penalty. The* ***total owed by the TRP is $6,000*** *[$4,000 unreasonable position + ($6,000 reckless penalty − $4,000 unreasonable penalty)].*

Due Diligence Preparer Penalties

A TRP must always exercise due diligence in preparing a tax return. However, the IRS has identified certain tax benefits (eg, credits, filing status) that are frequently abused. Therefore, a TRP must meet specific due diligence requirements (eg, make further inquiries, obtain documentation, file Form 8867 Paid Preparers Due Diligence Checklist) if they are paid to prepare a tax return or claim for refund claiming any of these tax benefits:

- Earned income tax credit (EITC)
- Child tax credit (CTC), additional child tax credit (ACTC), credit for other dependents (ODC)
- American opportunity tax credit (AOTC)
- Head of household (HOH) filing status

If a tax preparer does **not** meet the due diligence requirements, a **$635** (for 2024 returns filed in 2025) **per failure** penalty is assessed for a return or claim for refund filed. The maximum total penalty is $2,540 ($635 × 4) for 2024.

A tax return preparer failed to meet the due diligence requirements regarding the child tax credit and the head of household filing status on a taxpayer's return. What amount is the preparer penalty?

The penalty is $1,270 for the two tax benefits ($635 × 2).

Other Common Criminal Provisions

The IRC also contains other civil and criminal provisions to punish TRPs and others for various tax-related violations. In a criminal case, the burden of proof is on the government to establish the crime beyond a reasonable doubt, whereas the burden of proof in civil cases is a mere preponderance of the evidence.

Section 6701 penalties are assessed for aiding and abetting understatement of tax liability. The penalty is $1,000 for individuals and $10,000 for corporations.

Section 7201 punishes **tax evasion** and includes but is not limited to failure to file a return, falsifying income, and falsifying amounts that reduce taxable income. The person is subject to a fine of not more than $100,000 ($500,000 in the case of a corporation) or imprisoned not more than 5 years or both, together with the costs of prosecution.

Section 7206 penalizes TRPs for fraud and making false statements. The penalty is $100,000 ($500,000 in the case of a corporation) or imprisoned not more than 3 years or both, together with the costs of prosecution. Examples include:

- Willfully making and subscribing (ie, signing) any document made under penalty of perjury (eg, tax return) that the CPA does not believe to be true as to every material matter
- Willfully aiding the preparation of any tax-related matter that is fraudulent as to any material matter to evade tax
- Removing or concealing a client's property with intent to defeat taxes

Section 7607 penalizes any person (including a TRP) for filing or disclosing a tax return, statement, or other documents known to be fraudulent or to be false not more than $10,000 ($50,000 in the case of a corporation) or imprisoned not more than 1 year or both.

Summary of Common TRP Penalties

<table>
<tr><th>TRP Penalties Imposed For</th><th>Amount of Penalty</th></tr>
<tr><td>Understatement of tax caused by undisclosed position lacking substantial authority (unreasonable tax position)</td><td>Greater of $1,000 or 50% of return preparation fee</td></tr>
<tr><td>Understatement of tax caused by preparer's reckless or intentional disregard of rules or regulations</td><td>Greater of $5,000 or 75% of tax preparation fee (reduced by unreasonable tax position penalty if both apply)</td></tr>
<tr><td>Failure to furnish copy of return to taxpayer</td><td rowspan="5">$60 per return, up to $31,500 per year (2024)</td></tr>
<tr><td>Failure to sign return</td></tr>
<tr><td>Failure to furnish identifying preparer number on return</td></tr>
<tr><td>Failure to retain a copy of return for 3 years or maintain a list of names and ID numbers of the taxpayers for whom the returns were prepared</td></tr>
<tr><td>Failure to retain and make available a list of the tax return preparers employed</td></tr>
</table>

Summary of Common TRP Penalties

TRP Penalties Imposed For	Amount of Penalty
Endorsing or negotiating taxpayer's refund check	$635 per check (2024), unlimited
Improper use or disclosure of taxpayer return information	• $250 for each instance, up to $10,000 per year* • If minor criminal offense, $1,000 max penalty or 1 year in prison or both* • If identity theft related, $1,000 each instance, up to $50,000 per year*
Failure to be diligent in determining eligibility for certain tax benefits	$635 (for 2024 returns) per failure penalty, unlimited
Aiding and abetting understatement of tax liability	$1,000 ($10,000 for a corporate tax return)
Willfully preparing a fraudulent return	• Fined up to $10,000 ($50,000 for corporations) • Imprisoned up to 1 year
Committing fraud or making false statements on tax returns to evade tax	• Fined up to $100,000 ($500,000 for corporations) • Imprisoned up to 3 years • Required to pay for the costs of prosecution
Fraudulent or deceptive conduct, including misrepresentation of eligibility to practice before IRS	The courts may enjoin such person from further engaging in such conduct

**Not adjusted for inflation*

Comprehensive Example – Preparer Penalties

A CPA who is a tax return preparer prepared and filed a return for an individual client. The tax return had an undisclosed tax return position that reduced taxable income by $45,000. The CPA intentionally did not perform research to determine whether the position was reasonable. Also, the tax return had a disclosed tax position, and a Form 8275 Disclosure Statement was filed, which reduced taxable income by $5,000. The unmarried taxpayer told the CPA that he normally files as head of household. The CPA did not request any documentation to support the filing status. The CPA prepared and signed the tax return. The client was charged $3,000 for preparation of the return.

The client's tax return was audited by the IRS the following year. The audit findings included the following:

- The IRS disallowed the deduction for undisclosed tax position because it lacked substantial authority. Because the CPA was unable to find support for the position taken on the return, the IRS prevailed in court actions against the preparer for fraud
- The IRS disallowed the deduction for the disclosed position but stated that it had reasonable basis
- The IRS allowed the head of household filing status once the taxpayer provided supporting documentation during the audit

For the violations listed in the table below, enter the penalties that apply to the preparer. Evaluate each violation based on the facts provided when determining the penalty. In Column B, enter the *maximum* applicable penalty amount in dollars; in Column C, enter the *maximum* applicable term of imprisonment in years.

	Violation	Maximum Penalty Amount	Maximum Years of Imprisonment
1	Understatement of tax liability due to an undisclosed position that lacked substantial authority		
2	Understatement of tax liability due to a disclosed position that had reasonable basis		
3	Willful attempt to understate tax liability		
4	Failure to be diligent in determining eligibility for certain tax benefits		
5	Willfully delivering false or fraudulent returns		
6	Willfully subscribing a return under penalties of perjury		

Row 1: Understatement of tax liability due to an undisclosed position that lacked substantial authority

A preparer is subject to a penalty if any part of a taxpayer's understatement of liability is due to an **undisclosed tax position** on the return for which there is not a reasonable belief that the position is backed by *substantial authority*. The preparer can **avoid** the penalty if the undisclosed position has substantial authority. The penalty is equal to the greater of $1,000 or 50% of the income derived by the preparer (ie, preparation fee) with respect to the return. **No imprisonment** is associated with this penalty.

In this scenario, the TRP did **not** perform research to determine whether the **undisclosed** tax position taken was backed by substantial authority. Therefore, the preparer knowingly filed the return with a tax position that was questionable (ie, unreasonable until documented otherwise). The IRS later deemed that the position lacked substantial authority. Therefore, the penalty cannot be avoided. The preparer's maximum penalty is **$1,500**, which is the greater of $1,000 or $1,500 (50% × $3,000 preparation fee charged to the client).

Row 2: Understatement of tax liability due to a disclosed position that had a reasonable basis

Here the TRP used an "unreasonable tax position" in the preparation of the tax return, but the position was disclosed on Form 8275 Disclosure Statement. Although the IRS disallowed the position, it was deemed to have a **reasonable basis**. Because the position was disclosed and had a reasonable basis, the penalty is avoided.

Row 3: Willful attempt to understate tax liability

Understatement of a taxpayer's tax liability due to willful or reckless conduct by the tax preparer is subject to a penalty equal to the greater of $5,000 or 75% of the income derived by the preparer with respect to the return. **No imprisonment** is associated with this penalty.

In this case, the preparer's conduct that resulted in understatement of the taxpayer's liability was *willful* (ie, the preparer knowingly took but failed to research or disclose one of the tax positions). Accordingly, the maximum penalty is **$5,000**, which is the greater of $5,000 or $2,250 (75% × $3,000 preparation fee charged to the client). However if *both* the unreasonable penalty and reckless penalty apply (as in this scenario), the reckless penalty is *reduced* by the unreasonable penalty. The **penalty is $3,500** ($5,000 reckless penalty − $1,500 unreasonable position penalty).

Row 4: Failure to be diligent in determining eligibility for certain tax benefits

A TRP must meet specific due diligence requirements (eg, make inquiries, ask for documentation) if they are paid to prepare a tax return or claim for refund claiming any of these tax benefits:

- Earned income tax credit (EITC),
- Child tax credit (CTC), additional child tax credit (ACTC), credit for other dependents (ODC),
- American opportunity tax credit (AOTC), or
- Head of household (HOH) filing status

Here the CPA failed to inquire about the taxpayer's eligibility to file as head of household. It does not matter that the taxpayer was able to provide documentation to justify the filing status during the audit. The CPA's failure to be diligent in determining eligibility of the filing status when preparing the tax return results in a **$635 penalty**.

Row 5: Willfully delivering false or fraudulent returns

Any person who willfully delivers a tax return known to be fraudulent or false as to any material matter (eg, resulting in an understatement of the taxpayer's liability) is subject to a **maximum $10,000** ($50,000 for a corporate return) penalty or **imprisonment not exceeding** 1 year or both.

In this case, the CPA willfully delivered a fraudulent return and is subject to a **maximum fine of $10,000** and/or **1 year of imprisonment**.

Row 6: Willfully subscribing a return under penalties of perjury

A person who willfully prepares and subscribes (ie, signs) a tax return or other document that the person does not believe to be true—when it contains a written declaration that it is made under the penalties of perjury—is guilty of a felony. For a tax preparer, the maximum penalty is $100,000 ($500,000 in the case of a corporate return) and/or imprisonment not to exceed 3 years.

In this scenario, the CPA prepared and signed a return under penalties of perjury that included a tax position the CPA had failed to research and could not ensure was backed by substantial authority. Therefore, the CPA was aware that the information reported might not be true. The **maximum fine of $100,000** and up to **3 years of imprisonment** applies.

The completed table is below.

	Violation	Maximum Penalty Amount	Maximum Years of Imprisonment
1	Understatement of tax liability due to an undisclosed position that lacked substantial authority	$1,500	0
2	Understatement of tax liability due to a disclosed position that had reasonable basis	$0	0
3	Willful attempt to understate tax liability*	$3,500	0
4	Failure to be diligent in determining eligibility for certain tax benefits	$635	0
5	Willfully delivering false or fraudulent returns	$10,000	1
6	Willfully subscribing a return under penalties of perjury	$100,000	3

**Total penalty of $5,000 − $1,500 unreasonable penalty from Row 1.*

REG 2
Licensing and Disciplinary Systems

REG 2: Licensing and Disciplinary Systems

2.01 Licensing and Disciplinary Systems

Licensing and Disciplinary Systems

Representative Task (Remembering & Understanding): Understand and explain the role and authority of state boards of accountancy.

Overview

Professional licensing and oversight is a **state-based regulatory system** in the U.S. and its territories. To assist state governments in the licensing and regulation of the public accounting profession, each state has created a **state board of accountancy**. The board may be part of another state agency (ie, state licensing board) or independent. Currently, there are 55 U.S. licensing jurisdictions providing oversight regarding the practice of a CPA and public accounting.

Generally, the members of the board are appointed by the respective state's governor. A board member's duties, length of service, and qualifications are determined by each state. State boards of accountancy have explicit authority regarding the **granting, maintaining, and revoking** of a CPA's license.

Authority

State boards of accountancy have the authority to **license CPAs** (ie, issue a certificate) and can prohibit non-CPAs from performing attest functions. State boards also license CPA firms to practice public accounting. CPAs must adhere to the board's code of conduct and meet any requirements established by their state board regarding the right to practice in that state. Only a state board that granted a CPA their license may revoke it.

- This authority should *not* be confused with the AICPA and state societies of CPAs that grant **membership** (not licensure). The AICPA and some state societies of CPAs have their own professional and ethical standards and other membership requirements. Violation of certain membership standards of these organizations can result in automatic expulsion, revocation, or suspension of membership
- The AICPA in conjunction with the National Association of State Boards of Accountancy developed the Uniform Accountancy Act (UAA) to provide states with a model statute for regulating CPAs (eg, qualifications for a certificate as a CPA, unlawful acts, confidential communications). Most states have adopted some or all of the UAA, ensuring that most state rules for CPAs are identical or at least similar to AICPA rules. The rules of state societies of CPAs generally follow AICPA rules
    - For example, the UAA states that a CPA may not charge a contingent fee for any professional service, including audits, reviews, compilations, examination of prospective financial information, return preparation or claims for refund
    - This rule aligns with the requirements of the IRS Circular 230, which states that there can be no contingent fees for tax return preparation. However, the IRS does permit exceptions for an administrative examination or a challenge to an original return, an amended return or a claim for refund, and services related to interest and penalties assessed by the IRS or a judicial proceeding
- Because each state licenses CPAs, an individual must decide in which state they plan to practice and work. State boards require that if a CPA lives in the U.S., they are required to be licensed in the state where they live and practice

- The National Association of State Boards of Accountancy (NASBA) may assist state boards with licensing services such as determining eligibility, educational credits evaluation, and the application process. However, they do **not** license CPAs. In addition, NASBA serves in an advocacy role to assist state boards in carrying out their mission
- The U.S. Secretary of the Treasury is authorized by the Internal Revenue Code (IRC) to administer and enforce federal revenue laws. The IRS is the agency created to accomplish that purpose. The domain of the IRS covers all federal taxes, including income taxes, excise taxes, payroll taxes, and gift and estate taxes. Treasury Department Circular No. 230 contains the rules for practice before the IRS. Circular 230 has its own set of qualification and discipline rules for tax practitioners. For example, Section 10.51(a)(10) defines "Incompetence and disreputable conduct" to include suspension from practice as a CPA by the CPA's state board of accountancy. Therefore, any disciplinary action from a state board of accountancy will also disqualify the CPA from practicing before the IRS

Organizations Governing CPAs	
Organization	**Purpose**
American Institute of Certified Public Accountants (AICPA)	Provides auditing standards, accounting education, and CPA exam
State societies of certified public accountants	Provide accounting education at the state level
State boards of accountancy	License CPAs, enforce rules of conduct, set continuing education requirements
Public Company Accounting Oversight Board (PCAOB)	Oversees CPAs who audit publicly traded companies
National Association of State Boards of Accountancy (NASBA)	Serves as a forum for the state boards of accounting
Internal Revenue Service (IRS)	Oversees CPAs who practice before the IRS
Financial Accounting Standards Board (FASB)	Provides accounting standards and principles

Licensing

Just passing the Uniform CPA exam does not automatically result in receiving a CPA license. Generally, most state boards have **three requirements** to qualify to be licensed as a CPA: education, passing the CPA exam, and work experience.

- **Education:** Although the actual education requirements may vary from state to state, generally a candidate must have a bachelor's or master's degree for a total of 120–150 hours. In some states requiring 150 hours, a candidate is permitted to sit for the exam after the 120 hours (ie, bachelor's degree) has been fulfilled. Some states specify the number of accounting hours and the areas of accounting. In addition, a professional ethics course is required by most states. After licensure, a CPA is required to complete annual professional continuing education to maintain their license
- **Examination:** Individuals must successfully pass the Uniform CPA exam administered by the AICPA
- **Experience:** Generally, an individual must complete a *minimum* of one year of *professional experience* (at least 2,000 hours). The work experience may be in accounting, attestation services, management advisory, financial advisory, information systems management, and tax or consulting areas. Experience may be obtained by working for any employer (accounting firm, corporation, government agency, etc.)
- **International candidates:** Candidates who do not reside in the U.S. must apply to sit for the exam at a U.S. location (including Guam). A few state boards offer international testing sites. In addition, international candidates must find a state board that allows licensing without a state residency and U.S. citizenship if they do not plan to work in the U.S. after passing the exam

Once licensed by a state, a CPA must meet requirements to *maintain certification*. For example, a CPA must register annually with their board of accountancy, pay a fee for license renewal, adhere to the state board's established code of ethics for CPAs, and satisfy the annual professional continuing education requirements. Licensed firms may be required to conduct a peer review as well.

Attest-Related Functions

State boards monitor to ensure that only a licensed CPA performs attest-related functions, including:

- Any audit or other engagement to be performed in accordance with SAS (Statements on Auditing Standards)
- Any review of a financial statement to be performed in accordance with SSARS (Statements on Standards on Accounting and Review Services)
- Any examination of prospective financial information to be performed in accordance with SSAE (Statements on Standards for Attest Engagements)
- Any engagement to be performed in accordance with the standards of the PCAOB. A PCAOB-registered CPA firm that performs 100 or more public company audits per year receives an annual PCAOB inspection

Discipline

Only state boards have the authority to revoke CPA licenses and impose other penalties (eg, fines). Discipline from the state board generally requires some due process of law (eg, a hearing) and the more likely than not burden of proof standard to be met. Such punishable acts include:

- Fraud or deceit in obtaining a CPA certificate
- Cancellation of a certificate in any other state for disciplinary reasons
- Failure to comply with requirements for renewal (eg, not paying dues, not completing continuing education hours)
- Revocation of the right to practice before any state or federal agency
- Dishonesty, fraud, or gross negligence in performance of services or failure to file one's own income tax returns
- Violation of professional standards or code of ethics
- Conviction of a felony or any crime involving fraud or dishonesty

Reciprocity and Mobility

State boards also control **reciprocity** and **mobility** of a licensed CPA. Reciprocity between states allows a licensed CPA or CPA firm to get a reciprocal license in another state if they move there. Mobility between states allows a CPA who is licensed in one state to *offer services* (ie, the privilege to practice) in another state.

Section 23 of the Uniform Accountancy Act (UAA) has lessened the burden for CPAs in this area by introducing the concept of *substantial equivalency*. If a CPA license is in good standing and has met components of substantial equivalency (ie, degree with 150 hours, minimum one year experience, and passed Uniform CPA exam), permission may be granted to practice in another state or jurisdiction.

However, when a CPA works outside the state that issued their license (ie, principal place of business), it is their responsibility to contact that state's board of accountancy prior to performing any services, comply with any requirements, and pay any fees.

REG 3
Federal Tax Procedures

REG 3: Federal Tax Procedures

3.01 Audits, Appeals, and the Judicial Process

Audit and Appeals Process

Representative Task (Remembering & Understanding): Explain the audit and appeals process as it relates to tax matters.

Audits

It's estimated by the U.S. Department of the Treasury that the discrepancy between taxes owed and those paid is approximately $600 billion per year. New funding is aimed at closing this "tax gap" by focusing on new audits. Currently, less than 1% of all tax returns are audited, so the IRS must be selective about which returns it does audit.

While many tax returns are randomly selected for examination (ie, audits), tax returns may also be selected for examination due to the probability that they will have an understated tax liability.

- A high score on the IRS computerized Discriminant Inventory Function System not only will cause a return to be selected for examination but also indicates a high likelihood that the examination will result in a change in the tax liability
- Returns are selected when information does not agree with that received from third parties in the form of W-2s or 1099s via an information matching program
- Returns are examined when some source, including newspaper articles, public records, informants, and other public or private data, provides information to the IRS regarding potential noncompliance
- All returns are checked for mathematical and calculation errors (known as the document perfection program)
- Certain transactions trigger a closer look by the IRS, such as acquiring other companies or deducting certain expenses where abuse is prevalent, like home office deductions or charitable contributions

Some of the most common types of tax audits are:

- **Correspondence audit:** This is an audit conducted via mail. The IRS sends the taxpayer a letter requesting documentation to support the item(s) in question on the tax return (eg, proof of medical expenses deducted on Schedule A)
- **Office audit:** This is an audit that takes place in the IRS office. The taxpayer is required to bring specific documentation and records for examination by the IRS. These audits are typically broader in scope and more complex than correspondence examinations
- **Field audit:** This is a more in-depth review of a taxpayer's tax return. It is conducted at the taxpayer's residence or place of business. It usually involves reviewing multiple items on the taxpayer's tax returns and is generally the broadest in scope and more complex than correspondence or office audits
- **Taxpayer Compliance Measurement Program:** This type of audit is triggered based on a statistical sampling of tax returns to measure compliance with tax laws. Returns are selected for audit based on statistical criteria that may indicate noncompliance (eg, volatile year-to-year revenue fluctuations)
- **Criminal investigation:** This is an audit conducted when the IRS suspects fraud or tax evasion

After the Audit and the Appeals Process

After the Audit

After the examination, the taxpayer is provided with a list of proposed adjustments (if any) to review. If the taxpayer agrees to the proposed changes, the taxpayer signs an agreement form and pays the additional tax owed or receives the proposed refund.

If a taxpayer does not agree with a proposed adjustment that results from an examination of a return, alternatives include fast-track mediation, offers in compromise, trust fund recovery penalties, and other collection actions.

Offers in compromise can be filed by a taxpayer to obtain a reduction in the amount of tax owed. The IRS will consider an offer in compromise if one of the following applies:

- The amount owed, or whether it is owed, is in doubt
- The taxpayer's ability to pay the amount owed is in doubt
- The taxpayer would suffer an economic hardship if required to pay the entire amount
- The IRS determines that the case presents compelling reasons that are a sufficient basis for compromise

The IRS has a well-established process for settling tax disputes. After the IRS assesses a deficiency and the taxpayer disputes the proposed changes, it sends the taxpayer a **30-day letter** explaining its reasoning along with a copy of the audit examination report. This gives the taxpayer 30 days to **accept the proposed change**, skip the appeals process, and **wait for the IRS to issue a statutory notice of deficiency or request a conference with an appeals officer**.

- In order to request that the Office of Appeals review the dispute, the tax deficiency must be less than or equal to $10,000 and have resulted from a correspondence or office audit (an appeal hearing isn't an option for a field audit). The Office of Appeals is permitted to resolve the dispute until the 90-day letter is issued. The appeals officer generally considers the likelihood of the IRS winning if the claim goes to court

The Appeals Process

If the taxpayer and the IRS still do not agree with the appeal determination at the appeals conference or if the taxpayer does not respond to the 30-day letter, then the IRS issues a notice of deficiency (ie, a 90-day letter). The **90-day letter** gives the taxpayer 90 days (150 days for nonresident taxpayers) to either **pay the deficiency or file a petition with the U.S. Tax Court**.

Although *not explained* in the 90-day letter, there is an alternative to petitioning the U.S. Tax Court. Taxpayers can pay the deficiency and then file a claim for refund with the IRS. The IRS will invariably deny the refund claim. At this point, the taxpayer can sue the IRS for the refund in the U.S. Court of Federal Claims or U.S. District Court. By paying the deficiency and filing a claim for refund, a taxpayer stops interest from accruing on the unpaid tax deficiency.

IRS Tax Deficiency Appeals Process

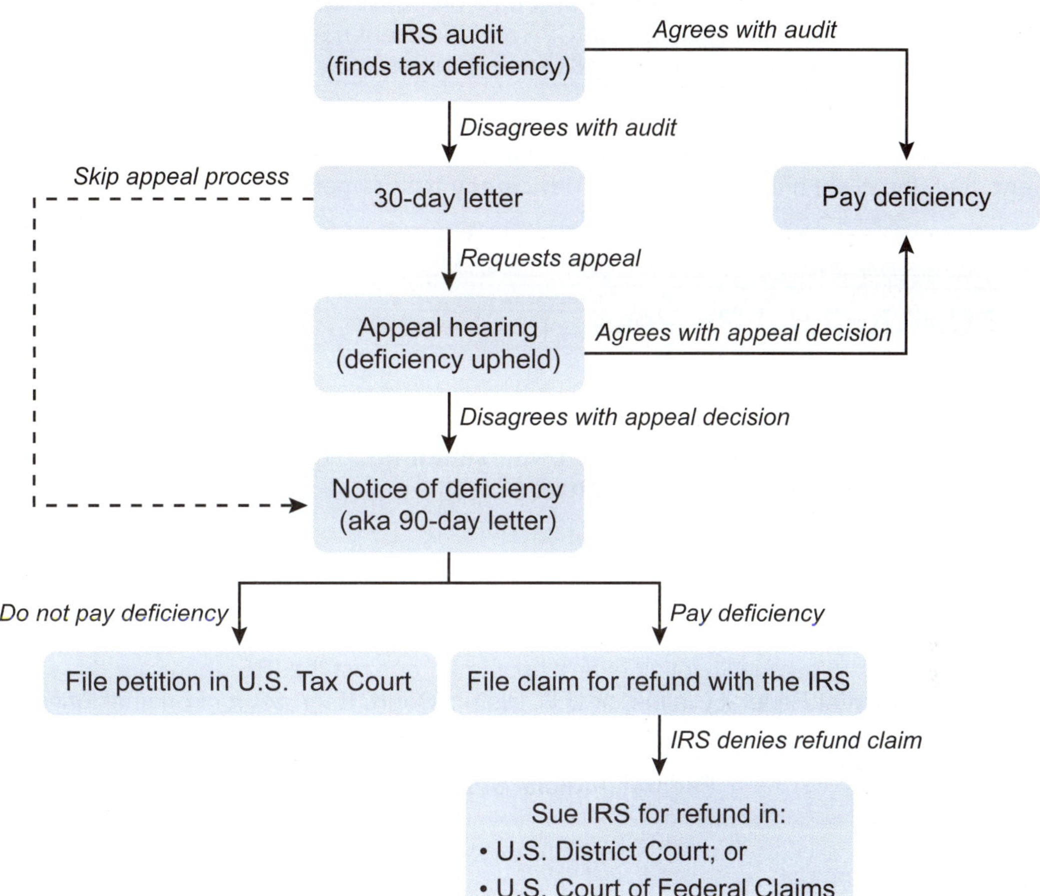

An individual taxpayer rejected the IRS examiner's findings in an audit of the taxpayer's tax return. What will the IRS do in response to the taxpayer's rejection?

- Issue a 30-day letter
- Begin immediate collection action
- Issue a statutory notice of deficiency
- Refer the case to the IRS Independent Office of Appeals

If the IRS assesses a deficiency and the taxpayer disagrees, **the IRS sends the taxpayer a 30-day letter explaining its reasoning along with a copy of the audit examination**. This gives the taxpayer 30 days to (a) accept the proposed adjustment and pay the deficiency, (b) skip the appeals process and wait for the IRS to issue a statutory notice of deficiency (ie, a 90-day letter), or (c) request a conference with an appeals officer at the IRS Independent Office of Appeals. This request by the taxpayer is necessary because the case is not automatically referred to the appeals office.

The IRS will not begin collection action until the taxpayer has exhausted, or failed to use, all appeals options. However, interest on the unpaid deficiency continues to accumulate during the appeals process.

An IRS agent has sent a 30-day letter reflecting a proposed adjustment to increase a client's taxable income in three prior years. The CPA and the client have reviewed the proposed changes and agree with the proposed adjustment. What would be the CPA's most appropriate recommendation to the client?

If a CPA's client (ie, **taxpayer**) receives a 30-day letter and **agrees** with the IRS's **proposed adjustment**, then the client should **accept the deficiency** assessment and **pay the additional tax**.

Levels of the Judicial Process

Representative Task (Remembering & Understanding): Explain the different levels of the judicial process as they relate to tax matters.

The Judicial Process

When a taxpayer decides to pursue litigation over a tax matter against the IRS, there are three choices: U.S. Tax Court, U.S. Court of Federal Claims, or U.S. District Court. Each court of original jurisdiction has unique characteristics.

Federal Judicial System

U.S. Tax Court is composed of tax experts and only hears tax cases.

- Hears cases related to income tax, estate tax, gift tax, and certain excise taxes
- Only court with a small claims division ($50,000 or less), but no appeals allowed
- Not required to pay the disputed amount before adjudication

U.S. District Courts are composed of generalists, not tax experts, and judges hear all types of legal matters.

- Only tax trial court where a jury trial can be requested
- Must pay disputed deficiency and sue for refund
- Many different district courts throughout the country

U.S. Court of Federal Claims is composed of generalists, not tax experts.

- Must pay disputed deficiency and sue for refund
- Will not hear a case involving a claim for refund of a penalty related to an abusive tax shelter or to aiding and abetting the understatement of tax on someone else's return
- Only one court of 16 judges located in Washington, D.C.

A taxpayer will consider which court would most likely rule favorably concerning their particular tax issue, or they might consider whether having a jury trial would benefit them. Taxpayers might not want to pay the disputed amount up front, and the U.S. Tax Court would give them that option.

In addition, a taxpayer may want to consider which appellate court would hear their case on appeal. Both U.S. Tax Court and U.S. District Court cases are heard by the U.S. Circuit Court of Appeals based on the taxpayer's residence.

U.S. Court of Federal Claims cases are heard by the Federal Circuit Court of Appeals based in Washington, D.C.

Finally, an unfavorable decision in any of the three courts of original jurisdiction and at the appellate level may be taken before the U.S. Supreme Court. The Supreme Court may or may not decide to hear the case (ie, grant certiorari). The U.S. Supreme Court usually grants certiorari when an issue has broad implications that are of national importance or when there has been disagreement among the circuit courts.

Federal Courts That Decide Tax Disputes

Federal Court	How Tax Dispute Gets to the Court	Decisions Have Precedential Value?
Supreme Court	Grant of certiorari (ie, court agrees to hear appeal)	Yes
U.S. Circuit Court of Appeals (regional)	Appeal from U.S. District Court or U.S. Tax Court	Yes
U.S. Circuit Court of Appeals (federal)	Appeal from U.S. Court of Federal Claims	Yes
U.S. Court of Federal Claims	Pay deficiency assessment and sue IRS for refund	Yes
U.S. District Court	Pay deficiency assessment and sue IRS for refund	Yes
U.S. Tax Court	Dispute tax assessed in 90-day letter	Yes
Tax Court (Small Claims Division) ($50,000 or less)	Dispute tax assessed in 90-day letter	No

A taxpayer was assessed a penalty by the IRS for failing to report certain foreign bank and financial accounts (FBAR). The taxpayer believes that the penalties were unlawfully calculated and that the applicable statute of limitations would bar the FBAR penalty from being imposed. The taxpayer's attorney researched similar court cases and found that the U.S. Circuit Court of Appeals representing the district had ruled favorably in a similar case, although the facts presented were not identical. The taxpayer is also nervous about interest charges accruing if the court's eventual ruling is unfavorable.

In this example, the taxpayer should consider paying the penalty and suing for a refund with the U.S. District Court. Although the taxpayer may eventually have to pay the FBAR penalties, interest will not accrue while the case is litigated, and the appellate court (the U.S. Circuit Court of Appeals) seems most likely to rule favorably on this particular issue.

A taxpayer received a 90-day letter proposing a deficiency of $28,000. The taxpayer's CPA said that a client with similar circumstances successfully sustained such a position in the Small Claims Division of the U.S. Tax Court. If the taxpayer decides to file a petition with the U.S. Tax Court, what is the significance of the success of the CPA's other client in sustaining the position in the Small Claims Division?

There is little significance since decisions in the Small Claims Division of the U.S. Tax Court lack precedential value.

Most court decisions involving tax disputes have precedential value, meaning that the legal decision made by a court functions as an authoritative rule in similar future cases. A taxpayer will seek favorable similar cases with precedential value to support their position. However, decisions by the Small Claims Division of the U.S. Tax Court **may not be used as precedent** because they are **not** considered **primary authority** and cannot be used as substantial authority. Whether the tax has been paid or the case is on appeal does not matter.

3.02 Substantiation and Disclosure

Requirements for Appropriate Disclosure of a Tax Return Position

Representative Task (Remembering & Understanding): Summarize the requirements for the appropriate disclosure of a tax return position.

Disclosure of a Tax Return Position

The Internal Revenue Code is lengthy and complex and does not specifically address the tax consequences of each transaction type or every possible variation of a particular transaction. Even when taxpayers and preparers are acting in good faith, application of the tax law is subject to debate and differing interpretations by the IRS, courts, tax practitioners, and taxpayers.

A tax practitioner is held to high standards of care and conduct and may only recommend a tax position or sign a tax return if the position is **reasonable**. A reasonable position taken on a tax return is rooted in fact; is supported by the law, rules, and other legal and administrative authorities; and satisfies the applicable standards of care.

To that end, the Code has provisions to punish **unreasonable positions** under preparer and taxpayer penalty rules and, conversely, to protect good-faith attempts at compliance with federal tax law. In addition, the **Statements on Standards for Tax Services in SSTS No. 1** provides that a tax professional must "determine and comply with standards, if any, that are imposed by the applicable tax authority with respect to recommending a tax return position or signing a tax return."

Additional requirements include:

- Advising the taxpayer, when a position is taken, of the potential penalty consequences and the opportunity, if any, to avoid such penalties through disclosure
- Not recommending a position or signing a return that exploits the audit selection process

Every tax position is **unreasonable unless:**

- There is substantial authority for the position; or
- The position was disclosed and there is reasonable basis for the position.

Substantial authority involves an analysis of the law and application of the law to relevant facts. The standard is satisfied if the weight of authorities supporting the position is substantial in relation to the weight of authorities supporting a contrary treatment. The weight given to an authority depends on its relevance and persuasiveness and the type of document providing the authority.

- For example, a revenue ruling is given greater weight than a tax article addressing the same issue, while more recent rulings or technical advice memorandums are generally weighted heavier than an older one. The following are some examples of authority for purposes of determining if there is substantial authority:
  - Internal Revenue Code
  - Proposed temporary and final regulations
  - Revenue rulings and revenue procedures
  - Tax treaties
  - Court cases

Conclusions reached in treatises, legal periodicals, legal opinions, or opinions rendered by tax professionals are NOT authority.

Both substantial authority and reasonable basis are conceptually a level of likelihood that the tax position will be upheld on its merits if the IRS challenges the position. The four different levels apply as follows:

Likelihood That the Position Will Be Upheld on Its Merits If It Is Challenged		Description
More likely than not	> 50%	Standard satisfied if it is reasonable to conclude in good faith that there is a greater than 50% likelihood of success if challenged.
Substantial authority	≈ 40%	Objective standard satisfied if the weight of the authorities supporting the position is substantial in relation to weight of authorities supporting a contrary treatment.
Realistic possibility	≈ 33%	Generally satisfied if there is approximately a one-in-three likelihood of success if challenged.
Reasonable basis	≈ 20%	Satisfied if position is reasonably based on one or more authorities, taking into account the relevance and persuasiveness of those authorities. Reasonable basis is significantly higher than not frivolous or not patently improper.

More Likely than Not

For a **tax shelter** or a **reportable transaction**, it is automatically unreasonable unless there is **more than** a 50% chance that the IRS would accept the position.

Substantial Authority

If a position has at least a 40% chance that the IRS would agree, the position is considered to have substantial authority and **does not** need to be disclosed, and the practitioner's standard of care is considered reasonable. Substantial authority is the threshold that Congress and the IRS have deemed reasonable.

Realistic Possibility

This is the level of likelihood required as reasonable according to **SSTS No. 1**. Congress is the overriding authority, though, so unless the issue is **not a federal tax issue**, the 40% rule of substantial authority would apply.

Reasonable Basis

Reasonable basis is satisfied if there's at least a 20% chance that the position would be upheld if challenged by the IRS and the position is disclosed so that the IRS can review it. Anything below this threshold would be a disregard of the rules, be considered unreasonable, and be punishable.

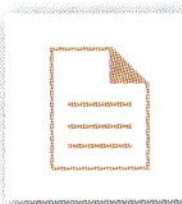

A CPA prepared a tax return that involved a tax position for a tax shelter that was disclosed on the return. When would the tax return position be considered reasonable?

To curb the use of abusive tax shelters, the IRS requires **disclosure** of **certain activities** (ie, reportable transactions). The disclosure requirements include all registered **tax shelters**.

Because of their aggressive nature, such activities must also meet the higher standard of **more likely than not** to succeed on their merits. More likely than not requires that the position have a **greater than 50%** likelihood of being sustained if challenged by the IRS.

Substantial authority has an approximately 40% chance of success on examination, realistic possibility has a one-in-three chance, and reasonable basis has roughly a 20% chance.

A tax preparer failed to disclose a tax position that had substantial authority. Can the tax preparer take the position if it's appropriately disclosed?

Tax positions based on substantial authority (ie, 40% chance of being sustained on the merits) do not have to be disclosed (ie, substantiated) on the tax return.

Determining whether the required reporting and disclosure standards have been fulfilled should involve:

- Establishing the relevant background facts
- Considering the reasonableness of the assumptions and representations
- Considering applicable regulations and standards regarding reliance on information and advice received from a third party
- Applying the pertinent authorities to the relevant facts
- Considering the business purpose and economic substance of the transaction, if relevant to its tax consequences (mere reliance on a representation that there is a business purpose or economic substance is generally insufficient)
- Considering whether the issue involves a listed or reportable transaction (higher 50% hurdle) as defined by the applicable taxing authority
- Arriving at a conclusion supported by the authorities

Situations in Which Disclosure of Tax Return Positions Is Required

Representative Task (Application): Identify situations in which disclosure of tax return positions is required.

Making Adequate Disclosure and Forms 8275 and 8275-R

When a tax position falls short of having substantial authority (ie, less than a 40% chance of success) but the position is reasonably based, making adequate disclosure can avoid certain penalties.

- **Form 8275**, *Disclosure Statement*, is generally used to disclose positions that lack substantial authority
- **Form 8275-R**, *Regulation Disclosure Statement*, is used to disclose a tax position that is **contrary to Treasury Regulations**

Disclosure is adequate with respect to an item or position on a return if the disclosure is made on a properly completed form attached to the return or to a qualified amended return.

Form 8275 and Form 8275-R shield a taxpayer from the portions of the accuracy-related penalty due to disregard of rules or to a substantial understatement of income tax for non-tax-shelter items *if the return position has a reasonable basis*. It can also be used for disclosures relating to the economic substance penalty and the preparer penalties for tax understatements due to unreasonable positions or disregard of rules. Filing either of these forms will have no effect on Section 6662 accuracy-related penalties if:

- The position does not have a reasonable basis (ie, > 20% chance of being sustained)
- It is attributable to a tax shelter
- It is not properly substantiated or the taxpayer failed to keep adequate books and records

Juan's tax preparer tells Juan that he can make a plausible claim to a particular deduction that will greatly reduce his taxes this year. A landmark case provides precedent for the claim, though the facts of the case are sufficiently different from Juan's that there's only a one-third chance that the position will be sustained.

Juan should disclose the position on Form 8275. Even if it is rejected, an understatement penalty will not be incurred because there's reasonable basis (≥ 20%) for the position. The amount of the understatement will be reduced by the amount at stake in this deduction.

Absent this disclosure, the 20% penalty would be applied once the deduction was rejected because it was not supported by substantial authority (≥ 40% chance of approval).

Sufficient substantiation for purposes of complying with SSTS No. 1 is as follows:

- Where the tax authority has a specific form for disclosure: The member should use the specific form of the tax authority for purposes of disclosure
- Where the taxing jurisdiction has administrative or judicial guidance with required contents for disclosure: The member should follow the procedures set forth in the administrative or judicial guidance
- Where there is neither form nor guidance: The member should disclose the position being taken, the amount of tax at issue, and the basis for the position

Reduction or Elimination of Accuracy-Related Penalty

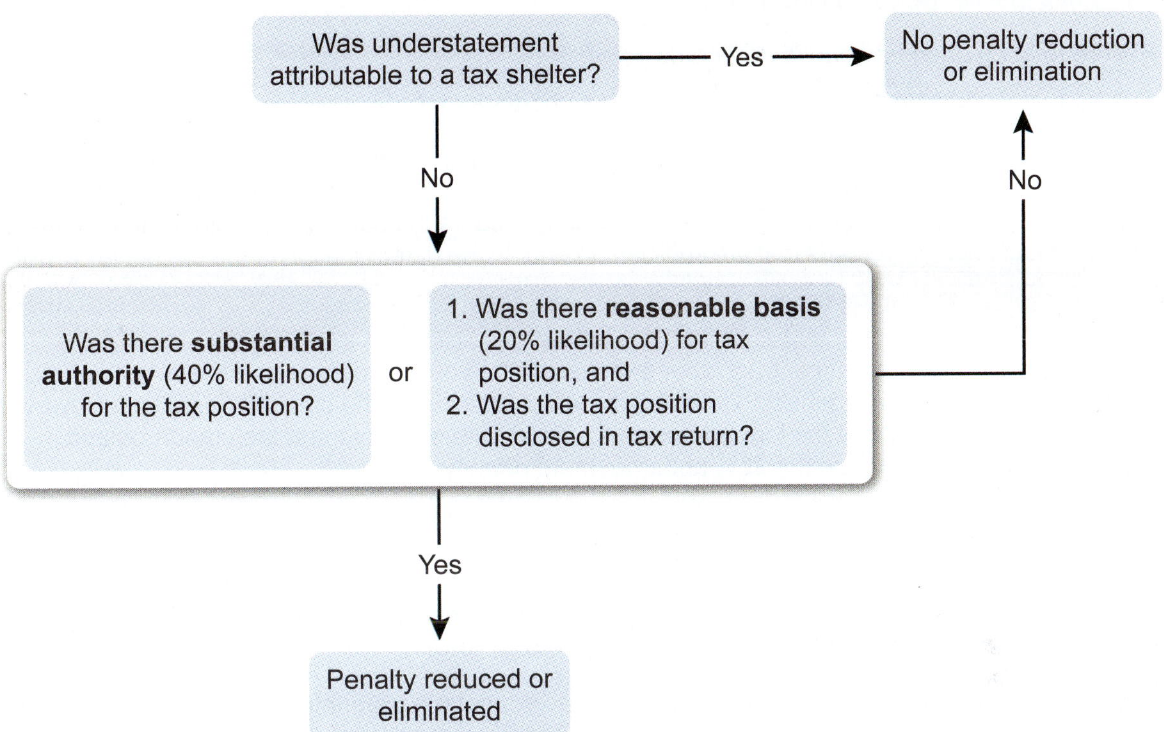

Schedule UTP Statement

Corporations that have at least $10 million in assets and uncertain tax positions must file Schedule UTP, *Uncertain Tax Position Statement*, using Form 1120 if the corporation or a related party has issued audited financial statements.

Schedule UTP was designed to increase transparency and efficiency in identifying audit issues by the IRS by reporting any federal income tax position for which an unrecognized tax benefit has been recorded in the financial statements. Disclosure requirements include a concise description of each UTP, which code sections relate to the position, and whether the position is a major tax position, among other things.

Sufficient Substantiation

Representative Task (Application): Identify whether substantiation is sufficient, given a specific scenario.

Substantiation is being able to provide the IRS with documentary proof of taxable income, deductions and credits, and tax positions taken on a return. It's important because upon examination, the proof can support the taxpayer's reported items and give the taxpayer a good-faith defense that they were trying to comply with tax law if deductions or credits are disallowed. As mentioned previously, tax positions need to be substantiated to show what authority the taxpayer and tax preparer relied on when taking the position.

Substantiation is also important because accuracy-related penalties can be imposed for underpayments caused by negligence, which can include:

- Failure to keep adequate books or records
- Failure to substantiate items that gave rise to the understatement

In general, the law does not require any specific type of record. Taxpayers may choose any suitable system that clearly supports an item of income, deduction, or credit (eg, receipts, canceled checks, logs). Taxpayers can keep hard copies or electronic records; however, the taxpayer bears the burden of substantiating the tax items reported and must maintain records that are sufficient to enable the determination of the correct tax liability.

A taxpayer kept a log of contract labor expenses. The court held that the log was not sufficiently detailed to meet the legal standards and therefore disallowed the claimed deduction. However, the court also held that the log represented a good-faith effort to meet the standards and therefore did not impose the 20% underpayment penalty.

Money amounts entered on tax forms must be verifiable. A number is verifiable if, on audit, the taxpayer can prove the origin of the amount (even if that number is not ultimately accepted by the IRS) and the taxpayer can show good faith in entering that number on the applicable form.

When the amount of an item is shown on a line that does not have a preprinted description identifying that item (such as on an unnamed line under an "Other Expense" category), the taxpayer must clearly identify the item by including the description on that line.

Examples of items that are often scrutinized and some of which require additional evidence include:

- Home office deductions
- Vehicle mileage/business use
- Gifts to clients
- Travel and meals
- Charitable contributions
  - Donations ≥ $250 must be documented with a receipt
  - Donations > $5,000 generally require a qualified appraisal

Records that should be retained:

- All tax returns for the previous seven years
- All records that pertain to a return for the previous three years
- Other records, no matter how old, that would be needed to support a tax position on a subsequent return

Requirements to Report Foreign Bank Accounts

Representative Task (Remembering & Understanding): Recall requirements to report foreign bank accounts.

Report of Foreign Bank and Financial Accounts

The Bank Secrecy Act requires U.S. persons to report information to the U.S. Treasury Department about their **financial interests in or signature or other authority over financial accounts** located outside of the United States.

To report foreign accounts, taxpayers must complete and file a Report of Foreign Bank and Financial Accounts (FBAR) using the Financial Crimes Enforcement Network (FinCEN) Form 114 if the aggregate value of **all foreign financial accounts exceeds $10,000** at any time during the calendar year. The value in the account(s) for FBAR purposes is determined by first identifying the maximum value of the account(s) during the year. Next, the foreign exchange rate at year end (12/31) is used to convert that account(s) balance to USD (eg, Japanese account valued in yen would need to be converted to USD). *Note that this is not the spot rate used on the highest balance day.*

- Taxpayers don't file the FBAR with individual, business, trust, or estate tax returns. The form must be filed electronically through the FinCEN website
- The deadline for filing the FBAR is April 15, with an automatic extension to October 15 for individuals

Foreign Bank Account Reporting

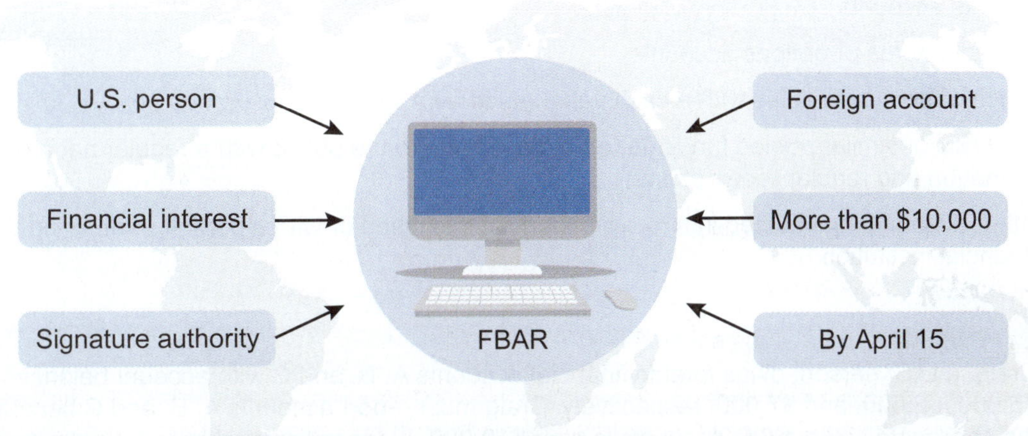

The U.S. government uses FBAR to identify or trace funds obtained through unlawful means or to pinpoint persons who may be using foreign financial accounts to circumvent U.S. law. A U.S. person is:

- A citizen or resident of the United States
- Any domestic legal entity, such as a partnership, corporation, limited liability company, or trust
- An estate formed under the laws of the United States
- U.S. persons who are disregarded entities for tax purposes

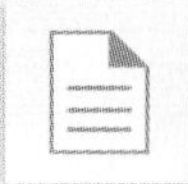

Marianela is a permanent legal U.S. resident. Marianela is a citizen of Spain. Under a tax treaty, Marianela is a tax resident of Spain and elects to be taxed as a resident of Spain.

Tax treaties with the U.S. do **not** affect FBAR filing obligations. Therefore, Marianela is a *U.S. person* for FBAR purposes and would **need to file Form 114** if the value of all her interests in foreign accounts **exceeds $10,000** at any time during the calendar year.

Foreign country: A foreign country includes any area outside the United States, the District of Columbia, all U.S. territories and possessions, and Native American lands. It is the location of the account, not the nationality of the financial institution, that determines whether an account is "foreign" for FBAR purposes. For example:

- An account maintained with a branch of a U.S. bank physically located in Italy is a foreign financial account
- An account maintained with a branch of a Mexican bank physically located in Texas is not a foreign financial account

Len, a U.S. citizen, purchased securities of a Canadian company through a securities broker located in Chicago. Len doesn't need to report these securities because he purchased the securities through a financial institution located in the U.S.

Financial accounts include:

- Bank accounts, such as savings accounts, checking accounts, and time deposits
- Securities accounts, such as brokerage accounts, securities derivatives accounts, or other financial instruments accounts
- Commodity futures or options accounts
- Insurance or annuity policies with a cash value (such as a whole life insurance policy)
- Mutual funds or similar pooled funds (ie, a fund available to the public with a regular net asset value determination and regular redemptions)
- Any other accounts maintained in a foreign financial institution or with a person performing the services of a financial institution

Craig, a U.S. person, owns foreign financial accounts A, B, and C with account balances of $5,000, $2,000, and $7,000, respectively. Craig must report accounts A, B, and C because the aggregate value of the accounts is over $10,000. It doesn't matter that no single account exceeds $10,000.

Eunice, a U.S. person, owns a foreign financial account with a maximum value of $15,000, but the account doesn't produce income. Eunice must file an FBAR to report the account. Whether an account produces income doesn't affect the requirement to file an FBAR.

Accounts Not Reported on FBAR

The following are not required to file an FBAR:

- Individual retirement account (IRA) owners and beneficiaries do not need to report a foreign account held by the IRA
- Participants of tax-qualified retirement plans do not need to report a foreign account held by the retirement plan
- A beneficiary of a trust, if the trust files an FBAR disclosing the trust's foreign financial accounts
- A spouse who jointly owns an account whose spouse files an FBAR reporting the account
  - If an account is jointly owned by nonspouses, then it must be reported by each person on their own FBAR
- Any governmental entity that owns foreign financial accounts (eg, a state-administered college or university)
- Any international financial institution of which the U.S. government is a member (eg, the World Bank)
- Any account located with a financial institution in a U.S. military installation
- A foreign account holding cryptocurrency unless it holds other reportable assets besides virtual currency

A U.S. taxpayer holds cryptocurrency in an offshore account, and the value of the cryptocurrency is greater than $10,000.

While the Financial Crimes Enforcement Network (FinCEN) seems intent on including virtual currency as a type of reportable account in the future, current FBAR regulations do not define a foreign account holding virtual currency as a type of reportable account.

If, however, the taxpayer exchanges some of the cryptocurrency for foreign currencies held within the same account, the taxpayer would be required to report the entire account value—cryptocurrency included—because it holds other reportable assets besides virtual currency.

Reporting of Foreign Financial Assets

In addition to the FBAR, U.S. taxpayers may be required to report the value of foreign financial assets on their tax return using Form 8938, Statement of Specified Foreign Financial Assets. This form is filed with the taxpayer's tax return and is due by the tax return deadline, including extensions.

- There are several important differences between the FBAR and Form 8938, including:
  - The FBAR and Form 8938 have different filing thresholds, with FBAR requiring reporting if the balance of foreign bank accounts reaches $10,000, while Form 8938 has varying thresholds based on filing status and location (although Form 8938 requirements are always higher)
  - FBAR requires reporting for various types of interest in a foreign account, including ownership, signature authority, and power of attorney, whereas Form 8938 only requires reporting for accounts where the taxpayer has a direct ownership interest
  - Differences exist in what qualifies as a foreign account: FBAR excludes accounts in U.S. territories, while Form 8938 includes them. Additionally, financial accounts held at foreign branches of U.S. institutions are treated differently between the two forms
- U.S. taxpayers with foreign financial accounts or assets may also be required to pay taxes on any income earned on those accounts or assets. This includes interest, dividends, and capital gains. Failure to report foreign financial accounts or assets can result in significant penalties, including fines and potential imprisonment

3.03 Taxpayer Penalties

Situations That Would Result in Taxpayer Penalties

Representative Task (Remembering & Understanding): Recall situations that would result in taxpayer penalties relating to tax returns.

Representative Task (Application): Identify taxpayer penalties given a specific scenario.

The U.S. income tax system is built on the idea of voluntary compliance. The IRS depends on taxpayers honestly reporting all their income, calculating their tax liability correctly, and filing and paying the tax due on time. The IRS can impose both civil and criminal penalties to "help" taxpayers comply with their taxpaying duties.

Civil penalties are much more common than criminal penalties, resulting in the taxpayer paying a monetary fine for the specific tax violation. Criminal penalties are commonly charged in tax-evasion cases, which include willful intent to defraud the government. Conviction in a criminal trial can only be imposed after a trial but can include hefty fines plus a prison sentence.

Delinquency-Related Civil Penalties

Penalties can be assessed based on the taxpayer being **delinquent in taking certain actions. Delinquency-related penalties** are:

- Failure to file a tax return (also called late filing penalty)
- Failure to pay tax owed (also called late payment penalty)
- Failure to make estimated tax payments

Late Penalties and Interest

Any balance due must be paid by April 15, the normal due date for the individual return. An individual can obtain an automatic extension of the due date for the return until October 15 (six months), but the *extension is only for the filing, not the payment* of the entire tax liability.

The **failure to file penalty** is based on how late a tax return is filed and the amount of unpaid tax as of the original payment due date, generally April 15 (not the extension due date). The penalty is 5% per month, or part of a month, that the return is late, up to a total of 25% of the unpaid tax. If the tax return is not filed within 60 days of the due date (including extensions), the *minimum* penalty is the **lesser of $510 (in 2024) or 100% of the unpaid income taxes**.

If the failure to file is fraudulent (intentional), the penalty is increased to 15% per month, up to a maximum of 75% of the tax due with the return.

A taxpayer files an income tax return two months after the deadline. The tax liability is $10,000. The taxpayer must now pay the $10,000 in taxes owed plus a $1,000 penalty ($10,000 × 5% × 2 months).

The **failure to pay tax owed penalty** (late payment) is half of 1% (0.5%) for each month, or part of a month, after the due date (April 15) that the tax is not paid, up to a total of 25% of the unpaid tax. This may reduce the failure to file penalty, if applicable.

If both penalties apply for any month, the failure to file penalty is reduced by the failure to pay penalty so that the maximum penalty is 5% per month, or part of a month. The minimum combined penalty if the tax return is not filed within 60 days of the due date (including extensions) is the lesser of $510 or 100% of the unpaid tax.

Interest is charged from April 15 to the date of actual payment, in addition to the penalties discussed.

Late Payment and Late Filing Penalties for Taxpayers

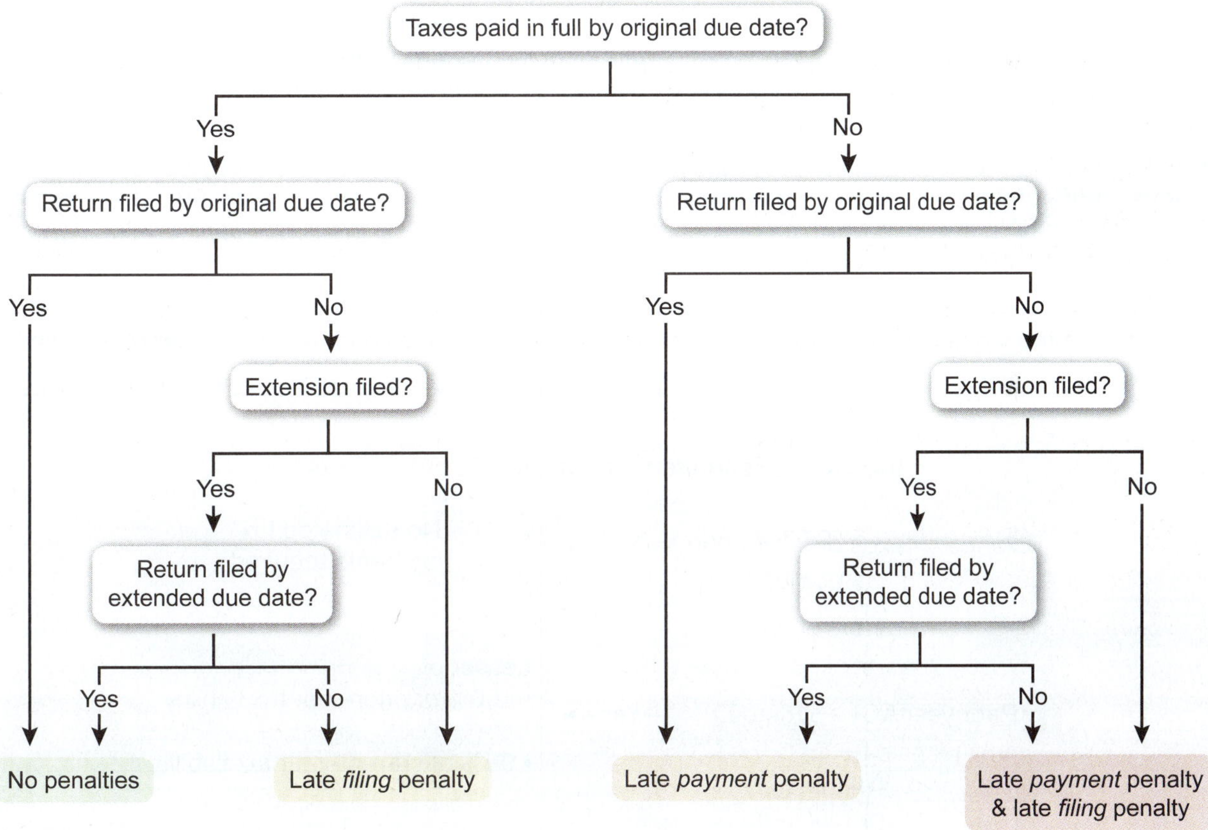

A taxpayer filed an income tax return after the due date but neglected to file an extension form. The return indicated a tax liability of $40,000 and taxes withheld of $35,000. What amount, if any, would be used to compute the penalties for late filing and late payment?

Taxpayers who fail to file their returns by the original or extended due date are subject to a late filing penalty (also called the failure to file penalty). An extension to *file* a tax return does not extend the time to *pay* the taxes. There is a late payment penalty (also called the failure to pay penalty) if any portion of the total taxes due is not paid by the original due date.

A taxpayer who files a **late tax return** and **underpays the taxes** due **is subject to both penalties**—late filing and late payment. Both penalties are calculated as a percentage of the *unpaid* taxes. The taxpayer paid $35,000 in taxes through withholding. Total taxes due was $40,000. Therefore, the amount of unpaid taxes is **$5,000**, which is the amount used to calculate both penalties.

Estimated Tax Payments and Underpayment Penalties

Individual taxpayers who have withholding on salaries and wages may not need to make estimated tax payments to the IRS during the year. If estimated tax payments are required, they are due by the 15th day of the *4th*, *6th,* and *9th* months of the taxable year and by *January 15* of the following year. An individual is only subject to an underpayment penalty if the balance due on the tax return is greater than **$1,000**. If the underpayment penalty applies, it is based on the amount of the underpayment, the period when due and underpaid, and the interest rate the IRS publishes quarterly. Even then, there are certain exceptions to the penalty that are available:

- Prior-year tax liability: No penalty is assessed if the withholdings and estimated payments totaled at least **100%** of the prior year's tax liability, unless the taxpayer had *more than $150,000 of AGI* in the previous year. In the latter case, payments must exceed **110%** of the previous year's tax liability to utilize this exception in the current year
- Annualized income method: No penalty is assessed if the cumulative payments for each quarter cover the tax on the income to date (assuming it continues at the same rate for the remainder of the year)
- Current tax liability: No penalty is assessed if the payments cover at least **90%** of the current tax liability

Individual Estimated Income Tax Requirements

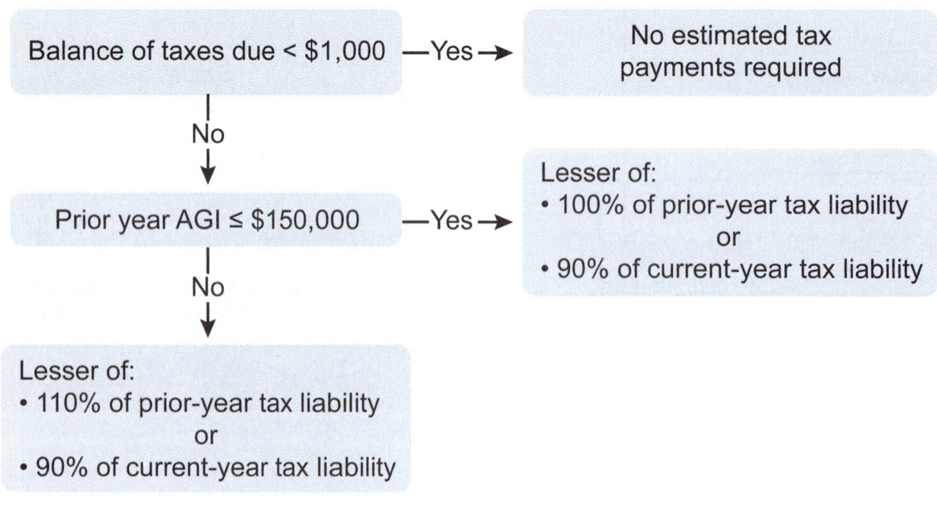

Note: Annualized method may be used

A taxpayer's Year 2 taxable income was $180,000, with a corresponding tax liability of $38,000. For Year 3, the taxpayer expects taxable income of $260,000 and a tax liability of $54,000. In order to avoid a penalty for underpayment of estimated tax, what is the minimum amount of Year 3 estimated tax payments that the taxpayer can make?

To avoid underpayment penalties, a taxpayer must pay a safe harbor amount. The general safe harbor amount is the lesser of **100%** of the **previous year's tax liability** (**110%** if the previous year's AGI is **over $150,000**) or **90%** of the **current-year tax liability**. There is **no penalty** if the balance due on the return is **less than $1,000**.

In this scenario, the Year 2 taxable income is greater than $150,000 ($180,000); therefore, the previous-year safe harbor must be computed at **110%** of the previous year's liability ($38,000 × 110% = $41,800). The current-year safe harbor is **90%** of the current-year liability ($54,000 × 90% = $48,600).

To avoid the penalty for underpayment of estimated tax, the taxpayer must pay either through withholding or estimated payments **$41,800** (the lesser of $41,800 or $48,600).

Delinquency-related penalties are **not imposed** if the taxpayer had **reasonable cause** for failing to file or failing to pay. Reasonable cause is cause outside of the control of the taxpayer and not due to neglect, such as irregularities in mail delivery, death or serious illness, unavoidable absence, or disaster. A taxpayer generally has the burden of proving that a failure was due to reasonable cause.

- For example, a taxpayer failed to file a timely return and pay taxes because the records were destroyed in a fire. This excuses both penalties but not the interest on the underpayment

Corporate Requirements

Estimated Tax Payments and Underpayment Penalties

Corporations are required to make quarterly estimated tax payments during the tax year and are subject to a penalty for underpayment of taxes if **100% of the current year's tax liability** has not been paid in four installments over the course of the tax year. The quarterly estimated tax payments are due by the *15th day of the 4th, 6th, 9th, and 12th* months of its taxable year (1120-ES). The penalty doesn't apply, however, if one of the following **exceptions** occurs:

- **Small balance:** The total underpayment is less than **$500**
- **Annualized income:** The installments each quarter cover the tax on the income to date, assuming total income will, for the full 12 months, be in proportion to the income to date (eg, the income for the first three months will be divided by 3/12 to estimate the full-year income in determining the first-quarter estimated payment)
- **Seasonal method:** The installments each quarter cover the tax on the income to date, assuming total income will, for the full 12 months, bear the same relationship to the income to date as it has, on average, in the previous three fiscal years. For example, if the income during the first quarter has averaged 40% of the total annual income over the previous three years, the income for the first three months of this year will be divided by 40% to estimate the full-year income in determining the first-quarter estimated payment
- **Previous year:** The payments equal at least **100% of the prior-year tax liability**

Note: This last exception may not be used to escape a penalty, however, if either:

- There was no tax liability in the previous year; or
- The corporation had taxable income exceeding $1 million in any of the preceding three tax years.

If the entire tax liability is not paid by the original due date of the return, interest will be owed to the IRS on the unpaid balance. If part of a tax underpayment is the result of fraud, there is an additional penalty equal to 75% of the portion of the underpayment attributable to the fraud.

A C corporation had a federal income tax liability of $36,000 for each of the last five years, each covering a full 12-month period. The tax for the current year is $38,000. What is the lowest amount that must have been paid as estimated taxes for the current year so that **no penalty** for underpayment is applicable?

Generally, a C corporation must pay estimated taxes equal to the lesser of 100% of the previous year's tax liability or 100% of the current year's tax liability. Since 100% of the current year's liability is $38,000 (ie, greater than the previous year's liability), the requirement will be 100% of the previous year's tax liability of **$36,000**.

Note: The previous year's liability amount would not suffice to eliminate an underpayment penalty if the corporation had no tax liability in the previous year or had taxable income exceeding $1 million in any of the preceding three tax years.

Accuracy-Related Civil Penalties

Accuracy-related penalties are assessed under IRC Section 6662 if a taxpayer's return includes an underpayment of tax due to negligent mistakes. The penalty is waived if there was substantial authority for the position taken or the taxpayer had a reasonable basis for the position taken and the position was disclosed on the return.

Taxpayers who omit income due to inadequate record keeping, erroneously classifying income, or filing an incomplete return *with notice to the IRS that it's incomplete* may be subject to an accuracy-related penalty if the error creates a substantial underpayment. However, these acts do not constitute a willful attempt to evade taxes (ie, fraud). Any of the following could subject the taxpayer to a **20% penalty** of the underpayment attributable to the inaccuracy:

- Negligence or disregard of the tax rules and regulations
- Any substantial understatement of income tax
    - Individuals: Substantial if the understatement of tax is more than the greater of 10% of the tax that should have been shown on the return or $5,000
    - Corporations: Substantial if the understatement of tax is more than the lesser of 10% of the tax that should have been shown on the return (or, if greater, $10,000) or $10 million
- Any substantial valuation misstatement for computing taxes (eg, inflating an asset's basis to reduce the gain on a sale)
    - Substantial if the value or adjusted basis of any property claimed is 200% or more of its correct amount
- Any substantial overstatement of pension liabilities
    - Substantial if the actuarial determination of pension liabilities is 200% or more of the amount determined to be correct
- Any substantial estate or gift tax valuation understatement
    - Substantial if the value of property claimed on a return is 65% or less of the amount determined to be correct
- Any disallowance of claimed tax benefits for transactions lacking economic substance
    - Economic substance refers to a transaction that has a purpose besides the reduction of tax liability
- Any foreign financial asset understatement

In certain circumstances, the accuracy-related penalty is **40%** of the portion of underpayment. These circumstances include:

- A gross valuation misstatement (400% or more)
- An underpayment attributable to *undisclosed* transactions lacking economic substance
- An understatement involving an *undisclosed* foreign financial asset

In Year 2, ABC Corp. files its Year 1 federal income tax return showing taxable income of $30 million and a tax liability of $6.3 million. The IRS examines ABC's return, resulting in a $35 million increase to taxable income and a $7.35 million increase to tax liability. Compute the understatement and penalty, if any.

	Amount Shown on Return	Amount of Increase Adjustment	Amount That Should Have Been Shown
Taxable income	$30 million	$35 million	$65 million
Tax liability	$6.3 million	$7.35 million	$13.65 million

The amount of understatement is **$7.35 million** ($13.65 million that should have been shown less the $6.3 million actually shown). A *substantial* understatement exists if $7.35 million exceeds the lesser of:

- 10% of the tax that should have been shown [ie, $1.37 million ($13.65 million × 10%)], or, if greater, $10,000; or
- $10 million.

Since $7.35 million exceeds $1.37 million (the lesser of the two amounts above), the understatement is deemed substantial, and the penalty is computed at 20%, or **$1,470,000** ($7.35 million × 20%).

A taxpayer incorrectly valued property donated to charity by more than 200%. Since the valuation is substantial (ie, > 200%), a 20% penalty could be assessed on the excess of the amount reported compared to the correct amount.

If the valuation was inflated by more than 400%, a 40% penalty could be assessed.

Erroneous refund claims under IRC Section 6676 assess a **20%** penalty of the "excessive amount" of a claim for refund or credit unless the claim can be shown to be due to *reasonable cause*. An excessive amount is defined as "the amount that the claim for refund or credit for any taxable year exceeds the amount of such claim allowable."

- Reasonable cause is not the same as reasonable basis, discussed earlier; it is a "facts and circumstances" test that looks to the taxpayer's good-faith efforts in their attempt to comply with the law

Civil Fraud

Taxpayers may legally seek to minimize their tax liabilities. However, a taxpayer may not willfully or deliberately attempt to evade tax. Doing so is considered **fraud**. **Taxpayers** who **attempt** to **evade taxes** (eg, maintaining false records, reporting fictitious transactions) may be **subject** to a **tax fraud penalty** equal to **75% of** the **tax underpayment**. This penalty applies to individuals and corporations for *any* tax underpayment attributable to fraud.

Tax Penalty Comparison	
Accuracy-Related Penalty	**Fraud Penalty**
• Encourages taxpayers to file accurate returns	• Deterrent for purposely evading taxes (ie, fraud)
• Applies to negligent mistakes and estimates that result in a *substantial* tax underpayment	• Applies to willful falsification of tax return amounts that results in *any* tax underpayment
• 20% of tax underpayment	• 75% of tax underpayment

Criminal Tax Culpability

Taxpayers who willfully attempt to avoid paying taxes that they rightfully owe are subject to criminal punishment under the following provisions, among others.

Tax Evasion

Section 7201 punishes tax evasion and has been used to prosecute, among other wrongs:

- Failure to file a return
- Falsifying income
- Falsifying amounts that reduce taxable income

The maximum punishment for individuals is a fine of $100,000 and/or five years in jail.

Tax Fraud

Section 7206 punishes fraud and false statements by taxpayers and others:

- Willfully making and subscribing to any document made under penalty of perjury that the taxpayer does not believe to be true as to every material matter
- Willfully aiding the preparation of any tax-related matter that is fraudulent as to any material matter
- Removing or concealing property with intent to defeat taxes

A taxpayer owned and operated a company that bought and resold copper metal for more than 10 years. For three years, the taxpayer directed customers on several occasions to wire payments to their personal bank account rather than the business account. The taxpayer intentionally did not record these payments as income in the corporate books, which were then provided to their accountant, willfully causing the accountant to prepare false corporate tax returns. As a result, the corporate tax returns underreported more than $2.5 million of gross income for these years.

Tax-evasion cases, which include willful intent to defraud the government, have higher penalties and can include prison sentences, if a taxpayer is found guilty. Criminal penalties can only be imposed after normal due process, including a trial. Guilt must be proven beyond a reasonable doubt (versus clear and convincing evidence for a civil tax fraud charge).

3.04 Authoritative Hierarchy

Appropriate Hierarchy of Authority for Tax Purposes

Representative Task (Remembering & Understanding): Recall the appropriate hierarchy of authority for tax purposes.

Tax Rules Hierarchy

Level	Authority	Binding status
1	**Internal Revenue Code**	Binding on IRS
2	**Treasury Regulations**	Binding on IRS
3	**Internal Revenue Bulletin** • Revenue rulings • Revenue procedures • Notices • Announcements	Binding on IRS
4	**Written determinations** • Private letter rulings (PLR) • Technical advice memorandums (TAM) • General counsel memorandums (GCM, no longer issued)	Binding on IRS to specific taxpayer only
5	**Other IRS publications and information** • Forms and publications • News releases and fact sheets • FAQs • Online help and resources • Videos	Not binding on IRS

Types of Tax Authority

There are two types of authority: **primary** and **secondary**. Primary authority consists of the original source of the law, whereas secondary authority is commentary on tax law, such as treatises, journals, and commentaries provided by editorial services.

Primary authority comes from each of the three branches of the federal government (executive, legislative, and judicial) and consists of:

- Legislative (statutory) authority
- Administrative authority
- Judicial authority

Legislative Authority

Tax law generated by the legislative branch consists of statutory authority from Congress. Sources of statutory authority include and are weighted from highest source in the following order:

- The U.S. Constitution (such as the 16th Amendment authorizing an income tax)
- The Internal Revenue Code statutes
- Treaties
- Committee reports of the House Ways and Means Committee, the Senate Finance Committee, and the Joint Conference Committee

The Internal Revenue Code (IRC) is the codification of the tax laws promulgated by Congress.

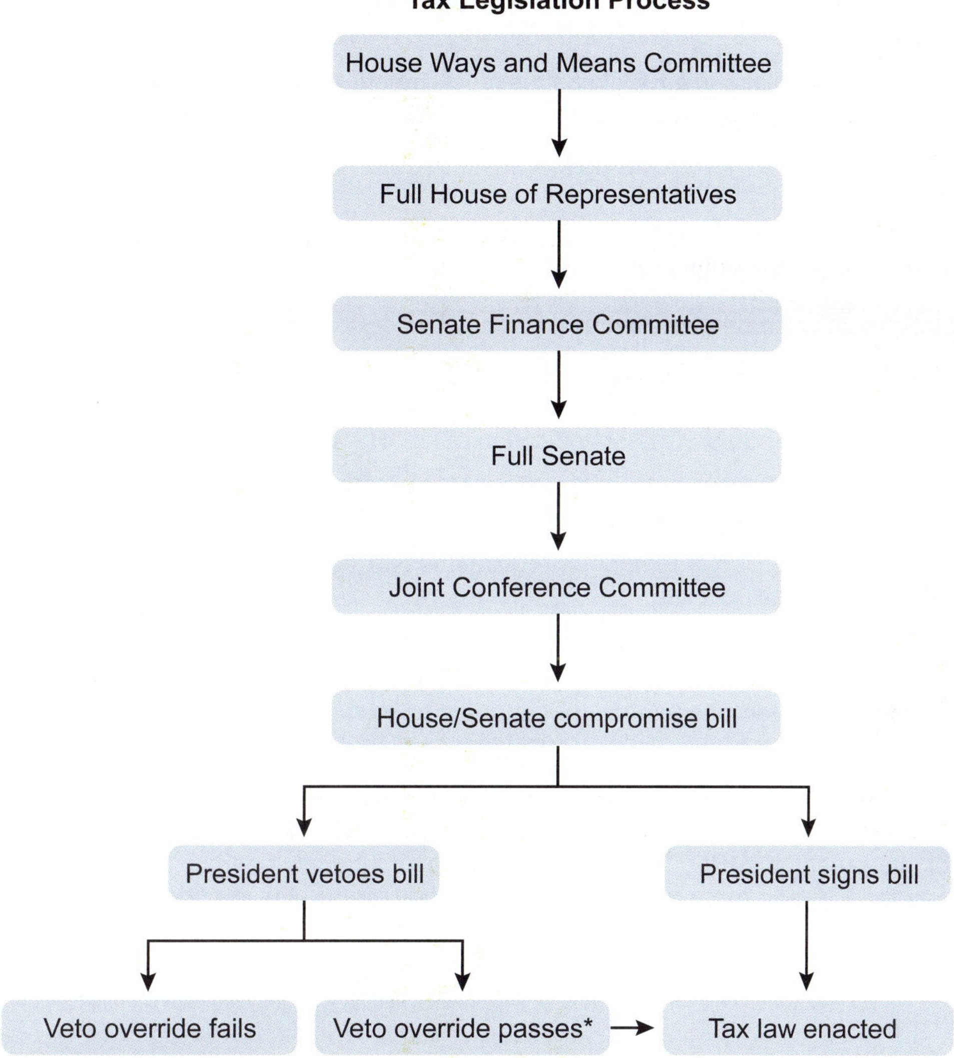

** Congress can override a veto with a two-thirds vote*

Administrative Authority

Administrative authority is the official source of law generated by the Treasury Department and IRS. The most common primary sources are:

- Treasury Regulations
- Revenue rulings: Limited to a given set of facts and more specific than regulations
- Revenue procedures: Internal management practices of the IRS
- Private letter rulings: Request by a taxpayer for the IRS to provide consequences on a specific transaction and only applicable to the taxpayer who made the request
- Technical advice memorandums: Requests made by the IRS field agents during an audit. They only apply to the affected taxpayer
- Other sources: Includes notices, announcements, and general counsel memorandums

Treasury Regulations are published in the *Federal Register* and later in the *Internal Revenue Bulletin*. Regulations can be classified as:

- **Legislative:** These regulations have almost as much weight as the IRC, since Congress has authorized the Treasury to develop regulations dealing with a specific issue
- **Interpretative:** These regulations are written under the general mandate given to the Treasury to develop regulations to interpret the laws legislated by Congress
- **Procedural:** These regulations apply to procedural issues, such as the information required to be submitted, the process for submission, etc.

Treasury Regulations can also be classified as:

- **Proposed:** Regulations must be issued as proposed regulations for at least 30 days before becoming final, although they may exist in a proposed form for many years. Proposed regulations do not have the effect of law, but they do provide an indication of the IRS's view on a tax issue
- **Temporary:** These regulations do have the effect of law but only for three years. Temporary regulations are usually issued when taxpayers need immediate guidance on a substantive matter of the law
- **Final regulations:** Proposed or temporary regulations can later be issued as final regulations, which have the effect of law until revoked

A taxpayer has located a regulation that appears to answer their tax research question. Which regulation should the taxpayer feel most confident about?

Legislative regulations are issued when Congress specifically directs the Treasury Department to issue regulations to address an issue in an area of law. In these instances, the Treasury is actually writing the law instead of interpreting the IRC. These regulations have generally been viewed to have almost as much weight as the IRC and more authoritative weight than interpretative and procedural regulations.

Judicial Authority

The weighting of a judicial decision depends on:

- Level of the court
- Legal residence of the taxpayer
- Whether the IRS has acquiesced to the decision (meaning the IRS has indicated that it will follow the decision in the future)
- The date of the decision
- Whether later decisions have concurred with the opinion

In researching a tax question, a tax practitioner finds only one authority (a trial-level court opinion) that is directly on point. Which court would the practitioner have least preferred to have heard this case and why?

U.S. District Court decisions are often considered to have the lowest authoritative weight compared to the U.S. Tax Court or the U.S. Court of Federal Claims because judges on these courts are generalists and deal with a broader spectrum of issues relative to those on the other courts. In addition, the U.S. Tax Court and the U.S. Court of Federal Claims have jurisdiction over all taxpayers, regardless of their residence. Conversely, a court opinion issued in a U.S. District Court must be rendered in the taxpayer's jurisdiction for it to hold authoritative weight.

REG 4
Legal Duties and Responsibilities

REG 4: Legal Duties and Responsibilities

4.01 Common Law Duties and Liabilities to Clients and Third Parties

Tax Return Preparer's Common Law Duties to Clients and Third Parties

Representative Task (Remembering & Understanding): Summarize the tax return preparer's common law duties and liabilities to clients and third parties.

Representative Task (Application): Identify situations which result in violations of the tax return preparer's common law duties and liabilities to clients and third parties.

Common Law Principles

A tax practitioner is expected to be competent, maintain objectivity and integrity, and properly administer the law when serving their clients. Many different statutes, rules, standards, and codes of conduct, including the AICPA's *Statements on Standards for Tax Services*, Treasury Department *Circular No. 230*, relevant penalty provisions in the Internal Revenue Code, and state licensing boards and other agencies must be adhered to.

In addition, tax professionals are also legally governed by **common law principles**. Many lawsuits against practitioners for malpractice are based on various "common law" causes of action created by the courts over the years (rather than by statute or code). The common law theories of practitioner liability are:

- **Breach of contract:** When a CPA does **not** fulfill the terms of an engagement contract (eg, tax practitioner did not file a tax return for the client despite having a signed engagement letter by both parties)
- **Negligence:** When a CPA fails to exercise due professional care (eg, tax practitioner filed a return in a timely manner but carelessly miscalculated the taxes)
- **Fraud:** When a CPA recklessly departs from the standard of due care expected of the profession when performing an engagement (eg, tax practitioner intentionally committed a reckless action in filing returns or giving tax advice)

Breaches of common law duties can also breach state and/or federal statutes. For example, a CPA provides certified financial statements that are used as part of a registration statement filed with the SEC for a security offering by a corporation. If the financial statements have omissions or inaccurate statements, the CPA will have liability under federal and state securities laws.

Accountant's Common Law Liability

	Contracts	Negligence	Gross Negligence or Fraud
Accountant's Error Resulting in Action	Breach of contract	Carelessness	Recklessness or intentional misconduct (scienter)
Who May Bring Action	Client or an intended (named) user	Client or a foreseen user	Anyone injured

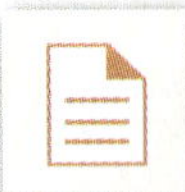

To which parties will a CPA be liable if the CPA fraudulently issues an unqualified opinion on a corporation's materially misstated financial statements?

Fraud is a common law principle of liability that can be asserted against a CPA by any party who used the financial information (eg, **shareholders** and **bondholders**). Fraud refers to the intent to deceive and takes two basic forms:

- Actual fraud: The CPA makes statements (eg, the audit opinion) knowing they are false. For example, an auditor performs an audit, finds material misstatements in the financial statements, and issues an unqualified (clean) opinion anyway
- Gross negligence (constructive fraud): The CPA makes false statements with a reckless disregard for the truth, not knowing if the statements are true or false. This usually occurs when the CPA recklessly departs from the standard of due care while performing an engagement

In ordinary negligence, only the foreseen users of the financial information can sue (ie, client and intended/foreseen third parties). For fraud, any party who used the financial information can sue whether or not these users were foreseen.

Breach of Contract

Accounting and tax services are performed under a contract between the CPA and client. An accountant who does not fulfill the terms of a contract or engagement will be held liable for **breach of contract due to nonperformance**. Since the CPA promises to perform the services in accordance with professional standards (eg, GAAS or Circular 230), a lawsuit charging breach of contract by the CPA must usually show violation of at least one professional standard.

The CPA's liability in this case is to the client (**in privity**) and any intended (**named**) third-party beneficiaries. Privity is a doctrine of contract law that says contracts are only binding on the parties to a contract and no third party can enforce the contract or be sued under it. Pay particular attention to who can sue under each cause of action presented.

To prevail in a breach of contract lawsuit, a plaintiff must prove the following four elements (**COBD**):

1. **A Contract must exist**
   a. Formation of an enforceable contract requires proper offer, acceptance, and consideration
   b. While some agreements must be in writing to be enforceable, most do not, so breach of an oral contract is typically actionable
   c. Obligations may be *expressly* spelled out (orally or in writing) but may also be *implied*. The law reads into professional contracts the obligation to perform to a professional standard
2. **One party fulfilled their Obligation**

3. **Breach of contract occurred**
    a. Defendant failed to perform and didn't meet their contractual obligation
    b. The breach may be intentional but need not be for this element to be satisfied
4. **Damages were caused by the breach**
    a. Plaintiffs may recover *compensatory* damages for losses (ie, injuries) sustained because of the breach
    b. Compensatory damages put the plaintiff in the same financial position the plaintiff would have been in if the accountant had not breached their contract
    c. *Punitive damages* are not recoverable in breach of contract claims

Examples of Breach of Contract

- Accountant failed to complete the tax return as promised due to lack of staff
- Accountant filed the tax return late
- Accountant filed the tax return filled with errors
- Accountant gave faulty tax-planning advice to the client

When a contract is breached, the victim of the breach is normally only entitled **to recover actual damages**. This includes damages directly caused by the breach and incidental to it but not unforeseen consequential damages. There are a few types of damages that may be awarded, depending on the specific contract and breach itself.

Remedies for Breach of Contract	
Compensatory Damages	Direct or actual losses
Consequential Damages	Indirect and anticipated losses
Liquidated Damages	Predetermined loss amount (eg, deposit forfeitures) agreed to by both parties
Nominal Damages	Trivial sum (eg, $1) to vindicate the plaintiff's rights when no actual loss or damage occurs
Specific Performance	Court ordering specific transfer of the contract's unique subject matter (eg, patents, works of art) when a monetary award will not suffice

Which penalty is usually imposed against an accountant who, in the course of performing professional services, breaches contract duties owed to a client?

An accountant who does not fulfill the terms of a contract or engagement will be held liable for breach of contract due to nonperformance. **Money damages** (ie, compensatory damages) are the most common type of penalty (ie, damages) an accountant will be required to pay for breach of contract. Compensatory damages are meant to reimburse an injured party for the economic loss suffered because of an accountant's breach of contract.

Specific performance is available in rare situations involving land and unique property (eg, art). It is not available for personal services contracts (eg, accounting services).

Punitive damages are not appropriate for breach of contract because they would enrich the injured party beyond the economic position of the original transaction in the contract. Punitive damages are used almost exclusively in tort cases (eg, bodily injury) to discourage extreme, harmful behavior.

Defenses for Breach of Contract

Common defenses for malpractice due to a breach of contract are:

- **Statute of limitation –** There are set deadlines for bringing a lawsuit. If too much time has passed since the breach occurred, then the client is prevented from bringing a lawsuit
- **Justifiable breach –** The client didn't provide documents, or documents provided were incomplete, inaccurate, or misleading
- **Substantial performance –** If a substantial amount of work was completed by the tax professional, yet, for example, they filed the return a few days late, the client may be compensated for penalties caused by the breach but would not be able to recover the full amount of fees
- **Legal incapacity –** A party may lack the legal capacity to enter a contractual agreement or is under duress to participate (eg, minor, persons with certain disabilities, coerced into agreement)
- **Statute of Frauds –** Certain contracts must be in writing (eg, real estate), and if not, then the contract is unenforceable
- **Mutual mistake –** If both parties are mistaken about the contract terms, then it is not a valid contract
- **Lack of consideration –** Without some sort of consideration, there is no contract
- **Illegality –** If the contract is for something illegal, the contract is unenforceable
- **Unconscionability –** If a contract is grossly unfair and/or manipulative, it may be deemed invalid

Mary and Larry hired CPA Dean to give them tax advice for setting up a trust to benefit their children, Ed and Molly. Dean did so, but after Mary and Larry died, a new CPA looked at the documents and realized that Dean had made many mistakes that resulted in substantial federal tax payments that could have been avoided.

Dean argued that Ed and Molly were not parties (in privity) to the contract he had with their parents, but the court allowed them to recover for breach of contract because Ed and Molly were donee beneficiaries (ie, intended third-party beneficiaries) of the contract for setting up the trust.

Negligence

The professional standard most often utilized is **due professional care**. This duty of reasonable care requires the accountant to exercise the degree of care, skill, and competence that reasonable members of the profession would exercise under similar circumstances. Thus, the most common lawsuit against a CPA will charge **negligence**, which is **an absence of due care**.

When negligent, the CPA's liability is to:

- The client (in privity);
- Any intended third-party beneficiary; and
- (In most states) any third party known or foreseen by the CPA.

Examples of Negligence

- Accountant carelessly neglects to file tax return on time
- Accountant carelessly fails to file documentation needed to support a tax position
- Accountant carelessly researches a tax issue and therefore erroneously advises the client to take a position that results in a substantial penalty
- Accountant carelessly fails to consider tax return options that would save the client a substantial amount of tax liability

To win a professional negligence malpractice case, a plaintiff must prove the following four elements by a preponderance of the evidence (**OBID**):

1. **Obligation of duty of care** owed by the accountant to the client plaintiff
   a. A contract between an accountant and a client typically includes a promise by the accountant to fulfill all professional responsibilities in a careful manner, but the law implies such a duty even if it is not spelled out in the engagement letter
2. **Breach of the standard of care** by accountant
   a. The essence of a negligence claim is carelessness, *not* intentional wrongdoing
   b. Accountants are not expected to be perfect but are expected to meet the standards of their profession in the relevant field—audit, tax, consulting, etc. Courts often say that accountants should act with the "skill and knowledge normally possessed by accountants in good standing in similar communities"
3. **Injury caused** by the breach
   a. The violation **proximately** causes an injury
   b. Causation has two components:
      i. Factual ("but for") causation, meaning that the courts can say that "but for" the accountant's breach of the duty of due care, the client's loss would not have occurred (ie, a *direct cause of the injury*); and
      ii. Legal ("proximate") causation, meaning that the injury was a reasonably *foreseen* result of the breach. Proximate cause places a limit on the possible negative consequences that could "flow" from an accountant's negligence
4. **Damages were caused/harm was suffered (ie, financial loss)**
   a. Plaintiffs are entitled to recover compensatory damages to compensate them for losses caused by the accountant's carelessness
   b. Generally, no punitive damages are allowed in negligence cases

Examples of Standard of Care Breach in a Negligence Claim

- Nondisclosure of information to the client (eg, internal control weakness)
- Errors previously discovered but not corrected
- Contract specifications not followed
- Professional standards not followed:
  - State and federal law
  - GAAS, GAAP, etc.
  - Customs of the profession

Lil People's Place, LLC, hired Serra & Company, LLLP, to file its tax return. Serra filed the return in a timely manner. However, Serra failed to obtain certain substantiation of expenses, which resulted in miscalculated taxes, causing Lil People's Place to pay a large tax penalty plus interest. Lil People's Place has a claim against Serra for negligence rather than for breach of contract (ie, performed the duty of preparing the tax return but failed to exhibit due professional care).

Which one of the following factors does a client suing a CPA for negligence not have to prove?

- Breach of duty of care
- Proximate cause
- Reliance
- Injury

Accounting services are performed under a contract between the accountant and the client. For this reason, the most obvious liability facing an accountant is for common law negligence due to breach of contract. To sue an accountant for common law negligence, the party suing the accountant (ie, plaintiff) must prove the following:

- The accountant's actions in performing the services must be the proximate cause (ie, main cause) of the plaintiff's loss
- The accountant must have performed the services in a careless manner (ie, absence of due care)
- The accountant's work (eg, financial statements) must have contained a material misstatement or omission
- The plaintiff must have suffered a financial loss or injury

Reliance on the CPA's acts (eg, providing an audit opinion) is a factor that must be proved when suing a CPA for **fraud**, **not negligence**.

Which of the following pairs of elements must a client prove to hold an accountant liable for common law negligence?

- Freedom from contributory negligence and privity
- Breach of the accountant's duty of care and loss
- Willful misrepresentation and breach of the accountant's duty of care
- Scienter and a violation of GAAP

To sue an accountant for common law negligence, the party suing (ie, plaintiff) must prove all of the following elements:

- The accountant's actions in performing the services must be the proximate cause of the plaintiff's loss
- Absence of due care – The accountant must have performed the services in a careless manner
- Material misstatement – The accountant's work (eg, financial statements) must have contained a material misstatement or omission
- Privity – The plaintiff must show enough of a relationship to the contractual arrangement that they are allowed to sue the accountant
- Suffered loss or injury – The plaintiff must have suffered a financial loss

Here the client must prove **a loss and an absence of care** (along with the three other elements) to win a negligence case against a CPA.

A plaintiff does not have to prove lack of contributory negligence. However, an accountant may use contributory negligence as a defense in a lawsuit. Willful misrepresentation and scienter are elements for proving fraud. They do not need to be proved when suing for common law negligence.

Privity

The privity requirement is often the biggest obstacle in a negligence suit. Parties that are not specifically cited as intended beneficiaries may attempt to prove they are foreseen beneficiaries in a negligence case. A **foreseen party** is:

- A third party or a member of a limited class that the accountant knew would be relying on their representations, for example, a tax return used to obtain a loan from a third-party lender

Foreseeable parties, meanwhile, are any party the accountant could reasonably foresee obtaining and relying on their work (ie, tax returns or F/S). The accountant is not usually liable for negligence to foreseeable parties.

The practitioner is generally liable to foreseen parties for negligence because most states have adopted the **Second Restatement of Torts**, which permits a user within a *class of people* **known or foreseen** by the tax practitioner to be relying on the tax return or tax advice to sue for negligence.

- Foreseen parties do not have privity to sue for negligence in a state that conforms to the *Ultramares* **decision**, however. The *Ultramares* doctrine holds that ordinary negligence is insufficient for liabilities to third parties because there is a lack of privity unless the third party is a primary beneficiary
- Thus, the scope of liability in *Ultramares* states is similar to the scope of liability for breach of contract (ie, limited to those in privity and intended (known) third-party beneficiaries). Accordingly, *Ultramares* states have a narrower scope of negligence liability as compared to states that follow the majority common law rule offered by the Second Restatement of Torts

Privity in Common Law Actions against a CPA		
Type of Party	**Common Law Negligence Majority Rule**	**Common Law Negligence Minority (*Ultramares*) Rule**
Client	Yes	Yes
Intended third party	Yes	Yes
Foreseen	Yes	No
Foreseeable	No	No
Unforeseeable	No	No

CPA Dolan carelessly recommended a tax position to his client, Fanny. Fanny told her neighbor, Dipson, about the tax strategy, and Dipson tried it on his own return. The IRS rejected the position as being without any reasonable basis, and Fanny was hit with tax penalties. She sued Dolan for negligence and won. Dipson also sued Dolan for negligence; he lost. Dolan could not have reasonably foreseen that Dipson would also rely on his advice, so he owed Dipson no legal duty of care.

Under the *Ultramares* rule, to which parties will an accountant be liable for negligence:

Clients, intended third parties, or foreseen parties?

Intended (ie, known) third parties are any specific parties that the CPA knew about. For example, if an audit's purpose was to provide audited financial statements (F/S) to a specific bank for a client's loan application, that bank is an intended third party.

Foreseen parties are any parties that the CPA either foresees or generally knows will rely on the CPA's services. For example, if the client told the accountant that the audited F/S would be submitted with a loan application but didn't name a specific bank, then any bank is a foreseen party.

Under common law, the majority rule for privity is that clients, intended third parties, and foreseen parties have privity and therefore can sue a CPA for common law negligence. The minority rule (ie, the *Ultramares* rule) is that **clients and intended parties have privity** but that foreseen parties lack privity and therefore cannot sue a CPA for common law negligence.

Distinguishing between Breach of Contract and Negligence (Tort) Claims

A tort is a wrongful or injurious act, other than breach of contract, that subjects the person who committed the act to civil liability. If the accountant did not do the job the client hired the accountant to do, there is a breach of contract. But, if the accountant did the job under the contract but did it carelessly, something that resulted in harm and costs to the client, there is a negligence claim. Some courts allow both a tort claim and a breach of contract action to proceed together. The distinction between a breach of contract claim and tort theory (negligence) is important in a procedural sense.

- The statute of limitations differs depending on the type of claim made (breach of contract suits often have longer statutes compared to negligence suits)
- The available defenses differ depending on the type of claim made
- In a negligence action, the defense of negligence by the plaintiff can bar or reduce any recovery; for example, the CPA could counter with claims of comparative or contributory negligence

Defenses for Negligence

- Statute of limitation passes – Too much time has passed
- Followed tax law – Showed due professional care
- Lack of privity – Cannot use against client or intended third party
- Comparative/contributory negligence – If the plaintiff was also careless and that carelessness contributed causally to the loss, the plaintiff's recovery will be reduced or potentially barred

A client approached a tax preparer a day before the tax deadline and asked them to prepare their tax return. The preparer agreed to the engagement but was unable to get the return done by the deadline. The taxpayer was assessed late filing penalties accordingly. If the client sues the tax preparer, the court will likely find that the preparer was negligent by accepting the engagement so close to the deadline. However, the tax preparer could counter with claims of comparative negligence on the part of the client since they waited so long to find someone to prepare the return.

Assume on the exam that negligence or carelessness is ordinary unless there is a clear statement in the problem that it constitutes gross or reckless behavior.

Fraud

A common law theory of liability that can be used by *any* party, including any third party (known or *unknown* to the practitioner), is **fraud**. The essence of fraud is intent to deceive and takes two basic forms:

- **Actual fraud** – Making false statements with knowledge of their falsity (ie, scienter)
- **Constructive fraud (gross negligence)** – Making false statements with a reckless disregard for truth, not knowing if the statements are true or false

A tax practitioner who *intentionally* or *recklessly* departs from the standard of due care when performing their duties faces liability for **fraud or gross negligence**.

A tax professional knowingly prepares and files a U.S. Individual Income Tax Return Form 1040 for a client that reports $12,300 in false medical and dental expenses and $8,500 in false charitable donations. By willfully acting in a way that is against the law, the tax preparer has committed actual fraud.

If a practitioner commits either actual or constructive fraud (ie, gross negligence), the practitioner can be liable to any party who used the financial information and can prove the fraud elements. For example, this applies if the tax return was used by a college to assess need-based financial aid awards.

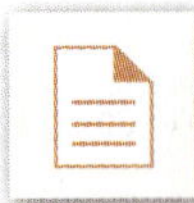

An accounting intern was hired to help ABC Co. during tax season. When they finished their first tax return, they handed it to the tax manager to review and sign. The manager signed it without looking at it, hoping that it was accurate. The return was inaccurate and contained inflated deductions, false credits, and other significant errors, including inventing the existence of a spouse. The manager was liable for *constructive* fraud because they did not verify a single detail on the return (ie, grossly negligent) and had no reasonable grounds to believe the return was correct.

The following are the general elements the plaintiff is required to prove in a fraud claim (**FMKID**):

1. **F**alse representation of fact (or omission to state a fact when there was duty to do so) is made by accountant
2. Misrepresented fact (or omission) was **M**aterial. Material in this context means that it is the type of information that would affect the client's decision to follow the accountant's opinion or move forward on a transaction
3. Accountant **K**new or recklessly disregarded the falsity
4. Accountant **I**ntended to induce the plaintiff to actually and justifiably rely on the misstatement or omission (scienter)
5. **D**amages were proximately caused by the false statement

Examples of Fraud

- Practitioner artificially reduces or omits income from a tax return
- Practitioner falsifies expenses and deductions to artificially lower the tax liability
- Practitioner promotes fraudulent tax shelter to help wealthy client avoid tax obligations
- Practitioner creates fake tax credits that are nonexistent
- Practitioner operates a tax preparer business and asserts that they are a CPA even though they have no license or accounting degree

Ford & Co., CPAs, issued an unqualified opinion on Owens Corp.'s financial statements. Relying on these financial statements, Century Bank lent Owens $750,000. Ford was unaware that Century would receive a copy of the financial statements or that Owens would use them to obtain a loan. Owens defaulted on the loan. To succeed in a common law fraud action against Ford, Century must prove, in addition to other elements, that Century was:

- Free from contributory negligence
- In privity of contract with Ford
- Justified in relying on the financial statements
- In privity of contract with Owens

Fraud is a common law principle of liability that can be asserted against a CPA. In addition to proving the other three elements of fraud, the party suing the CPA (ie, plaintiff) must prove it **justifiably relied on the financial information** audited or provided by the CPA. In this scenario, Century Bank relied on Ford & Co.'s unqualified opinion on Owens Corp.'s financial statements as part of its decision to make a loan to Owens.

When suing for fraud, the plaintiff is not required to prove freedom from contributory negligence. However, in this scenario, Century will have to refute it if Ford asserts contributory negligence as a defense.

Privity is an element necessary to prove a CPA's negligence. However, privity is not an element necessary to prove a CPA's fraud. In fraud cases, the CPA's liability extends to anyone who suffered a financial loss by using the financial information. This includes clients, intended third parties, and third parties known and unknown.

Defenses for Fraud

- Statute of limitations – The statute of limitations varies from state to state, but it is common to require plaintiffs to sue within four years of when they discovered (or should have discovered) the fraud
- Not grossly negligent – Showed due professional care
- Not material
- Lack of intent – Practitioner acted in good faith and had no knowledge of falsity (lack of scienter)

Keep in mind that the burden of proof is on the plaintiff to prove **all** the elements of the case (FMKID), while the defenses available for the defendant/practitioner are basically the opposite of what the plaintiff has to prove. They need to prove only one not to be liable for fraud.

Differences between Fraud and Negligence Causes of Action	Fraud	Negligence
Plaintiff must prove bad intent or recklessness	Yes	No
Plaintiff must prove carelessness	No	Yes
Plaintiff must prove proximate cause	Yes	Yes
Plaintiff can recover compensatory damages	Yes	Yes
Plaintiff can recover punitive damages	Yes	No
Comparative negligence is a defense	No	Yes
Burden of proof is on the plaintiff	Clear and convincing evidence	Preponderance of the evidence

Burden of Proof

The burden of proof in most civil cases, *including breach of contract and negligence cases*, is the **preponderance of the evidence** standard, meaning that the plaintiff need only establish that alleged facts are more likely true than not true (> 50%).

However, an accusation of fraud (and the damages that can result from proving it) is a more serious accusation. In most states, the burden of proof in fraud claims is raised slightly, requiring plaintiffs to prove their claims by **clear and convincing evidence**.

- Clear and convincing evidence is often defined as evidence that is "**substantially more probable to be true than not** and that gives rise to a firm belief as to its factuality in the mind of the trier of fact"
- Fraud, unlike mere negligence and breach of contract, often also constitutes a crime and is punishable under a wide array of state and federal statutes forbidding tax fraud, securities fraud, bank fraud, etc.

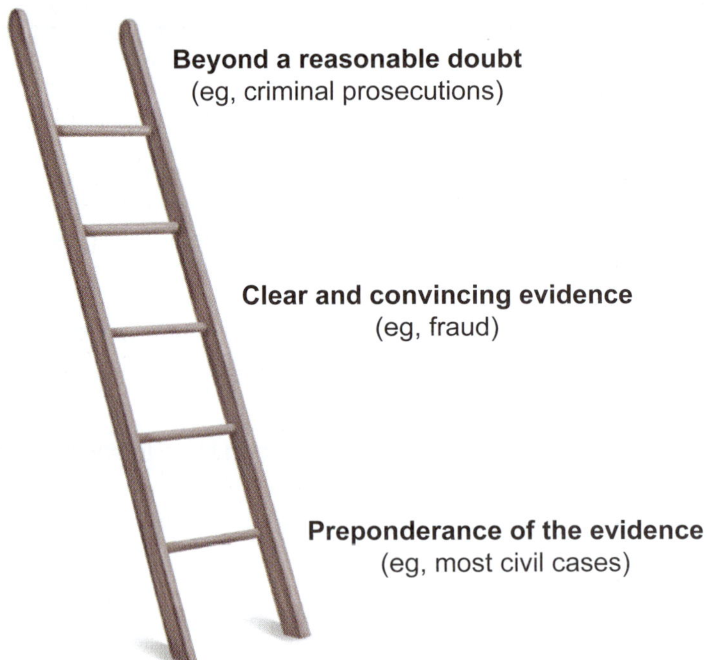

Note, the burden of proof in a civil case is on the plaintiff to prove all the elements of the case, so exam questions in which all points have not been established should be decided in favor of the preparer-defendant.

4.02 Privileged Communications, Confidentiality, and Privacy Acts

Privileged Communications as They Relate to Tax Practice

Representative Task (Remembering & Understanding): Summarize the rules regarding privileged communications as they relate to tax practice.

Representative Task (Application): Identify situations in which communications regarding tax practice are considered privileged.

Privileged Communications

Privilege laws prevent the party who received protected communications from using that information against the protected party in court. The most common examples would be attorney-client, doctor-patient, and priest-penitent privilege.

Different privileges are available under federal and, potentially, state law. With regard to federal law, IRC Section 7275 recognizes a limited accountant-client privilege (eg, a federally authorized tax practitioner providing tax advice to a client). It should be noted that federal courts have severely limited the scope of accountant-client privilege.

However, a small number of states have enacted privilege statutes. In those states:

- The privilege belongs to the client, not to the accountant
- The privilege can be waived by the client, either expressly or through voluntary disclosure of the relevant information
- Waiver of the privilege as to part of the communication is waiver as to all
- The privilege applies only in state court, where state procedural rules apply

Elements of Accountant-Client Privilege

- Only available in a small number of states
- Allows CPA to refuse to testify about a client
- Protects all nonpublic client information in the CPA's possession

Thorp, CPA, was engaged to audit Ivor Co.'s financial statements. During the audit, Thorp discovered that Ivor's inventory contained stolen goods. Ivor was indicted, and Thorp was subpoenaed to testify at the criminal trial. Ivor claimed accountant-client privilege to prevent Thorp from testifying.

In most states, communications between CPAs and clients lack the legal privilege that protects the privacy of attorney-client communications. However, a small number of states have **enacted privilege statutes for CPAs**. In those states, the privilege can allow a subpoenaed CPA to refuse to testify in state court. In addition, it applies to all confidential information the CPA possesses about the client and therefore is not limited to audit-related subjects.

The federal government recognizes workpapers developed in connection with the preparation of a tax return to be privileged in noncriminal tax disputes with the IRS. That privilege would not apply to this scenario, even if the case were in federal court.

Confidentiality of Workpapers and Client Information

Safeguarding clients' confidential information and communications is a high priority for all CPAs and tax practitioners (eg, enrolled agents). In general, when preparing a tax return, a CPA must have access to highly sensitive client information. The knowledge that this information is kept confidential encourages clients to be more forthcoming and provide all the financial information needed to complete an accurate tax return.

The AICPA's confidential client information rule states that "a member in public practice shall not disclose any confidential client information without the specific consent of the client." This means that absent client consent, no information can be disclosed that is not available to the public.

A CPA who prepares tax returns is not permitted to use client information for personal benefit or reveal this information to third parties without the consent of the taxpayer, except in limited circumstances. Client confidentiality does not preclude a CPA from providing confidential information access to other members of their firm.

A CPA is not obligated to inform the IRS or any other taxing authority of a client's failure to file a prior-year return without the client's permission, although there is an obligation to promptly inform the client upon becoming aware of such a circumstance. Also, a CPA must inform a client if there are material errors in a previously filed tax return so that the client may file an amended return.

The CPA, not the client, owns the workpapers that a tax professional creates during an engagement (eg, tax provision or tax return preparation). Nevertheless, the practitioner must maintain confidentiality and cannot provide the papers or information obtained during engagements to other parties without the permission of the client.

With regard to the confidentiality of workpapers:

- Tax return information includes returns, source documents, workpapers, and supporting schedules
- Noncompliance will subject the preparer to civil or criminal penalties
- The type of penalty applicable depends on whether the preparer unknowingly, knowingly, or recklessly disclosed the taxpayer's information

CPA Workpapers

- Are owned by the firm performing the accounting services
- Reflect compliance with professional standards (eg, GAAS)
- Document work performed and conclusions reached
- Must be kept confidential
- May be shared with others only with client consent or:
  - Based on a valid legal or administrative subpoena
  - Under court order
  - For quality-control peer-review purposes
  - For use by other members of the CPA's firm

Recognized **exceptions** regarding disclosing confidential client information for tax return preparers are summarized in the table below. For example, a CPA does **not** need the client's permission to turn over workpapers as part of a state CPA society voluntary quality-control peer review because the review board is subject to the same confidentiality requirements.

Exceptions to Rule on Confidential Client Information

- Comply with subpoena or summons*
- Comply with quality-control peer review (eg, peer review, review prior to potential sale of CPA practice)
- Comply with laws and regulations
- Initiate, pursue, or defend against actual or potential lawsuits
- Initiate or respond to complaints with AICPA ethics division or trial board
- Permit electronic preparation or submission of a client's tax return
- Secure legal advice from an attorney

**May refuse these in a state that has an accountant-client privilege statute*

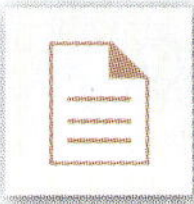

Which of the following statements is correct regarding a CPA's workpapers?

- Workpapers need not be disclosed under a federal court subpoena
- Workpapers must be disclosed under an IRS administrative subpoena
- Workpapers must be disclosed to another accountant purchasing the CPA's practice
- Workpapers need not be disclosed to a state CPA society quality-control review team

The CPA, not the client, owns and retains the workpapers. However, the CPA must maintain confidentiality and must obtain the client's permission before providing third parties with the workpapers or information obtained during an engagement.

The exceptions to confidentiality include:

- **Responding to a valid subpoena issued by a court or an IRS administrative subpoena**
- Providing the workpapers as part of a quality-control peer review
- Sharing the workpapers with other members of the CPA's firm

Therefore, a CPA must provide client information, including workpapers, when asked to do so under a valid subpoena issued by the IRS. Client permission is not needed.

Acquiring a CPA practice does not automatically authorize the purchaser to access client information. The client's permission is required before the selling CPA can share the workpapers with the purchaser.

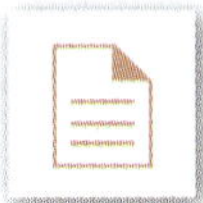

To which of the following parties may a CPA partnership provide its workpapers without being lawfully subpoenaed or without the client's consent?

- The IRS when the client is under investigation for tax fraud
- The SEC when the client is making a public offering
- A partner in the CPA's firm who is preparing the client's tax returns
- Another CPA who is considering purchasing a partnership interest in the firm

Workpapers must be kept confidential and may be shared only with the client's permission or under specific situations, such as a court order, subpoena, or peer review.

Because the CPA partnership owns the workpapers and all the partners are bound by the same rules of confidentiality, the papers can be shared with a partner in the firm without client approval.

Absent a subpoena, a CPA must not share workpapers with the IRS or the SEC. The severity and magnitude of the circumstances are irrelevant.

Workpapers may not be disclosed to an outside CPA without the client's consent. This restriction applies even if the disclosure is needed as part of a sale of the CPA's practice.

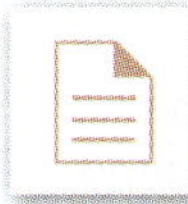

To which of the following parties is a CPA permitted to disclose confidential client information without the consent of the client?

- Another CPA firm if the information concerns suspected tax return irregularities
- The IRS so long as the information proves the client innocent of suspected tax return irregularities
- Another CPA who has purchased the CPA's tax practice
- A state CPA society voluntary quality-control review board

To protect taxpayers' personal information, CPAs are required to maintain the confidentiality of information obtained through tax return preparation.

However, **a CPA does not need the client's permission to share confidential information as part of a state CPA society voluntary quality-control review board**. The other CPAs involved in the peer review are required to keep the information confidential.

CPAs do **not** need the client's permission to discuss a client's confidential matter with other CPAs within their firm. However, a CPA must have the client's permission to discuss the matter with CPAs *from another firm*.

A CPA can disclose the client's information to the IRS without the client's permission only if the CPA receives a *valid order* (eg, subpoena) from the IRS.

Acquiring a CPA practice *does not* automatically authorize the purchasing CPA to have access to the client's information. The client must authorize disclosure to the purchasing CPA.

Jolene Griffith, CPA, prepares the Individual Income Tax Return Form 1040 for Fred Barker. Jolene received a request from Lender Bank asking for a copy of Fred's prior-year tax return. Lender Bank assured Jolene that the return would be used only to facilitate the bank's credit evaluation for a loan for which Fred was applying. After receiving a confidentiality agreement from Lender Bank, Jolene furnished the tax return without Fred's knowledge.

Under both the IRS and AICPA rules, with limited exceptions, a CPA is not permitted to provide a client's tax return information to third parties without the client's consent. This includes any financial institution, regardless of how the institution will use the information.

Internal Revenue Code Provisions

The IRC has several provisions dealing with confidentiality, including:

- Section 6713 imposes a **civil** penalty for each unauthorized disclosure or use of tax information by a tax preparer
- Section 7216 imposes a **criminal** fine and **potential imprisonment** for knowingly or recklessly disclosing any information obtained in connection with the preparation of a return or using such information for any purpose other than to prepare or assist in preparing a return

Joan Sims is an administrative assistant in the accounting firm of Tims and Brandt. Joan does not prepare tax returns, but she sees all tax returns as she scans them. Joan shared information about a political figure's income with a writer for a national business magazine. Joan can be charged criminally for revealing this client information.

A Broadway actress consulted an accountant managing the payroll for a play in which she was appearing. The accountant helped the actress with her return as a personal favor since he prepared several returns a year in his practice. The accountant then shared information about the actress's income with a television show focused on celebrity news. Even though the accountant was not paid, he still violated Section 7216.

Tax Practitioners' Privilege

Section 7525 of the Internal Revenue Code extends a modest privilege to clients of all tax advisors authorized to practice before the IRS, including accountants. The privilege does not apply to:

- Criminal matters
- Matters not before the IRS or federal courts in cases brought by or against the United States
- Tax advice on state or local matters
- Written advice in connection with promotion of a tax shelter

Jake Sullivan, a client of Marty Borgnine, CPA, told Marty as they were discussing Sullivan's federal tax return that he had engaged in insider trading during the last tax year. The IRC privilege does not apply to illegal (ie, criminal) stock trading.

Best Practices

The following are considered best practices regarding privacy and confidentiality for CPAs. They are based on the AICPA's *Privacy Checklist for CPA Firms* and the IRS Publication 4557, *Safeguarding Taxpayer Data*. Both documents set forth steps and actions the tax professional might consider taking to protect client data and mitigate significant threats.

- Notice: Provide notice about privacy policies and procedures and identify the purposes for which personal information is collected, used, retained, and disclosed
- Security for privacy: Protect personal information against unauthorized access (both physical and digital)
- Management: Define, document, communicate, and assign accountability for privacy policies and procedures
- Disclosure to third parties: Disclose personal information to third parties only for the purposes identified in the notice and with the individual taxpayer's implicit or explicit consent
- Use and retention: Limit the use of personal information to the purposes identified in the notice and to which the individual taxpayer has provided implicit or explicit consent; retain personal information only for as long as is necessary to fulfill the stated purposes

REG

Area II: Business Lav

REG 5
Agency

REG 5: Agency

5.01 Authority of Agents and Principals

Types of Agent Authority

Representative Task (Remembering & Understanding): Recall the types of agent authority.

Representative Task (Application): Identify whether an agency relationship exists given a specific scenario.

An agency relationship is one in which a party (principal) gives authority to another party (agent) to act on behalf of that principal. Agents undertake tasks or consummate transactions for their principals. A CEO is an agent of the corporation. A salesclerk is an agent of a department store. The authority to act on behalf of another is the central characteristic of an agency relationship. How that authority is given, how much authority is given, and when that authority ends are important legal issues in the principal-agent relationship. For CPAs, understanding these relationships is critical to understanding duties to clients.

For example:

- A corporation authorizes its CEO to negotiate a merger
- A real estate brokerage firm hires real estate agents to find property listings
- A college athlete hires a professional sports agent to serve as a representative in negotiations with professional sports teams

Types of Agents

There are several different types of agents that vary in terms of the scope of authority and time limitations on that authority. The labels for each of the types of agency help in recognizing those limitations on authority and how long that authority lasts.

Special Agent: An agent authorized to conduct a single transaction or series of related transactions on the principal's behalf.

A CPA is hired by a corporation to negotiate on its behalf a settlement of a dispute over depreciation formulas used by the company in preparing its tax returns. The CPA's authority is for one task, is limited in time, and is limited in authority and scope. The CPA would have no authority as an agent in any other corporate matters or even in any additional IRS matter.

General Agent: One agent authorized to conduct all necessary personal or business transactions for the principal.

A restaurant owner (principal) who owns a restaurant in another city hires a manager (general agent) to run that restaurant. Such an agent could hire and fire employees, purchase supplies, and deal with health inspectors.

Musicians and entertainers often have "managers." Their managers are general agents because they handle contract negotiations, finances, public relations, investments, budgets, and purchasing.

Power of Attorney: A common form of agency is a power of attorney, which is a written authorization for the agent to act on behalf of the principal for a specific or indefinite time. There are *two general* categories of a power of attorney:

- **General power of attorney** allows an agent to act on behalf of the principal on all matters affecting them
- **Limited power of attorney** gives the agent the authority to act only in certain matters on behalf of the principal. Examples include making health care decisions when the principal is unable to do so and executing a specific transaction (eg, sale of a house)
- The agent handles legal issues in all forms of powers of attorney
- The agent has authority to execute documents on behalf of the principal; therefore, any document signed by an agent with a power of attorney to act for the principal has *legally bound the principal* without the principal being there for the transaction
- Power of attorney may be created in anticipation of possible mental deterioration of the principal; therefore, it is often written with a specific provision keeping it enforceable in the event of the *insanity or incapacity* of the principal
- These relationships always terminate upon the death of the principal

Laura Olmstead is scheduled to have major surgery. Several property transactions Laura has pending are scheduled for closing during the two weeks of Laura's recuperation. Laura has given a power of attorney to her daughter to execute the documents in those closings for a period of two weeks. Laura's daughter can complete all of the closings for Laura, and the signature of Laura's daughter acting as Laura's agent is valid for purposes of accomplishing the transfers of the property.

Power of attorney is a name given to documents that authorize agents to act on behalf of their principals. "Power of attorney" is an abbreviated phrase used to describe both special and general agency relationships. The law of agency applies to powers of attorney just as it does to all agency relationships.

Independent Contractor: An independent contractor is someone who acts on behalf of a principal but whose day-to-day activities are not controlled by that principal, and the scope of the independent contractor is limited.

- An independent contractor is doing a *singular project* or executing a singular transaction and is not an employee of the principal. For example, auditors doing an audit for a company are examples of independent contractors. They work for their own firm and would be employees of that firm, but they are independent contractors when they are out working at audit client facilities
- Normally independent contractors are paid an agreed-upon amount and are responsible for paying their own taxes. Principals do not withhold taxes from payments to independent contractors but instead furnish their independent contractors with a Form 1099, indicating the gross amount received

David and Catherine Heighton have hired a lawyer to create a living trust for them. The lawyer is working for the Heightons on that limited activity. The Heightons do not control the lawyer's work hours or have liability for the conduct of the lawyer involving third parties. The lawyer is being paid a fee for doing the trust and is not an employee of the Heightons. The attorney is an independent contractor in relation to the Heightons. The lawyer's authority is limited to drafting and overseeing the execution of the trust.

Subagent: A subagent is an agent hired by another agent on behalf of the principal.

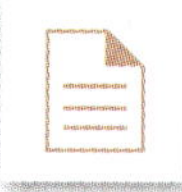

In the Multiple Listing Service (MLS) for real property sales, there is the real estate broker who lists the property as an agent of the property seller. But often there is a subagent broker of the listing broker. The subagent is not an agent of the seller of the property but has the authority to show the buyers the sellers' MLS properties. A subagent of the listing broker is entitled to earn a commission based on the subagency agreement with the listing broker.

Agency Coupled with an Interest: This is an agency in which the agent holds a property right in the subject matter of the agency. These types of agencies give the agent greater rights and protections (discussed later in these materials).

With this type of agency, neither the death nor incompetency of the principal terminates the agency relationship because of the property right the agent holds.

A book agent may have a property interest in the principal's book manuscript. The reason for this type of agency is because the book agent is generally paid a percentage of any future royalties from sales of the book (or movie rights, etc.).

Type of Agents	Definition
Special Agent	Authorized to conduct a single transaction or series of related transactions on the principal's behalf
General Agent	Authorized to conduct all necessary personal or business transactions for the principal
Power of Attorney	*General power of attorney* allows an agent to act on behalf of the principal on all matters affecting them *Limited power of attorney* gives the agent the authority to act only in certain matters on behalf of the principal (eg, health care decision, sale of a house)
Independent Contractor	Acts on behalf of a principal, but that principal does not control the agent's day-to-day activities; the scope of the independent contractor is limited (independent contractor is *not* an employee)
Subagent	Hired by another agent on behalf of the principal
Agency Coupled with an Interest	An agency in which the agent holds a property right in the subject matter of the agency

Creation of Agency Authority

Creation of agency authority includes the actual authority in agency relationships and the requirements for creating an express agreement. The principal is the party in an agency relationship who gives the agent the **actual authority** to act on behalf of the principal. Actual authority includes:

- **Express authority:** Authority that is in a written or oral agreement that outlines the responsibilities and authority of the agent
- **Implied authority:** Authority granted to an agent in the creation of an agency relationship as incidental and customary authority that is necessary for the agent to perform the outlined work and effort

A restaurant owner hiring someone as a bartender gives them the actual authority to sell drinks at the bar. *Express authority* exists when the owner of a tavern tells the bartender to order more bar glasses from a specific restaurant supply vendor.

Implied authority exists when the owner assigns the bartender the task of managing the bar operations at the restaurant. The bartender would then have authority that is customary for bar managers, which would include the authority to order glasses and other supplies from any vendor.

Requirements for **creating an express agency** agreement include:

- **Consent:** Both parties must consent to the agency relationship. There must be a meeting of the minds, as required for all contracts
- **Legal capacity:** The principal must have legal capacity to contract, but the agent does not. The principal is the party to the contract, not the agent. If a principal wishes to hire a 16-year-old minor (under the age of 18) to act as an agent, there is a valid agency relationship, and that 16-year-old can negotiate on behalf of and bind the principal
- **Writing or record:** The agency agreement itself need not be evidenced by a writing or record except under circumstances when the Statute of Frauds applies. Examples where the Statute of Frauds applies include:
  - An agency relationship to sell real property
  - An agency relationship that will run for more than one year
  - An agency coupled with an interest in which the agent is acting as a surety

WN Enterprises is a wholesale distributor of auto parts. WN is an authorized distributor for certain auto parts manufacturers and has 15% commission contracts with several of the parts manufacturers for all sales.

To become a distributor for the manufacturers requires submission of financial and other information before being permitted to distribute the parts. WN Enterprises is sold to Wegman Distributors. Wegman would need to negotiate new authorization and commission contracts with the manufacturers to continue acting as an agent for them.

Consideration is **not** a requirement for an agency relationship to exist. Known as gratuitous agencies, agency relationships in which the agent is not compensated are common. A member of the board of trustees of a university negotiating a land purchase for the university for no fee is still an agent for the university, and their agency relationship is legally established despite no fee being paid.

Royal Designers, LLC, hired Broadbent Recruiters to locate and hire interior designers for its expanding business. Broadbent Recruiters was in the process of incorporating but had not completed all the necessary statutory steps. However, Broadbent recruited three designers during this time with their contracts signed, "Broadbent Recruiters, Inc., for Royal Designers, LLC."

The contracts are binding for both Royal Designers and the interior designers. That Broadbent had no legal existence and, therefore, no legal capacity at the time the contracts were signed does not affect the validity of the agent's contracts for the principal.

The following chart summarizes the requirements for the formation of an express agency relationship.

Necessary to Form an Agency Relationship	
Required	• Mutual consent ("meeting of the minds") • Legal capacity of principal (only)
May Be Required	• Written agreement if Statue of Frauds applies, such as in: ○ Real estate ○ Agency relationship to exceed one year ○ Suretyship
Not Required	• Consideration • Legal capacity of agent

Creating an Agency Relationship through Apparent Authority

An agency relationship can be created by apparent authority. Apparent authority comes through agents acting as if they are agents of the principal and the principal permits that appearance of authority to occur. Because of the appearance of authority, the agent still has authority to act for a principal because the principal has allowed others to believe that there is an agency relationship. Apparent authority is authority based on circumstantial evidence such as an agent using a business card, stationery, or materials with the principal's name and knowledge of its use. Through the action or inaction of the principal, the third party concludes from how the agent appears that the agent has authority.

XYZ Corporation sells its custom-home division to Randy Eggerton, a former VP of XYZ. Eggerton continues to use office space at XYZ and even uses XYZ's custom home plans and letterhead. By not stopping Eggerton from using its name and office space, XYZ has allowed Eggerton to remain as an agent.

Customers of Eggerton would be led to believe that Eggerton was an agent of XYZ. It appears to the customers that Eggerton was XYZ's agent even though no actual authority or agency relationship exists. If Eggerton breached contracts with custom-home purchasers, those customers would have the right to bring XYZ into litigation as a principal through apparent authority. XYZ permitted the appearance by allowing Eggerton to continue to use its name, office, space, and plans.

Unknown Agent Limitations: There are times when principals place limits on their agents' authority. For example, a principal may authorize an agent to enter only into **contracts for $10,000 or less**. There is an express limitation. However, unless notified, a third party would not know of such limitation.

- Principals who have not told third parties about their agents' limitations will still be bound by their agents' contracts that exceed their maximum amount. The agent will be liable for breach of the agency contract, but the third party is protected because of apparent authority

Lingering Apparent Authority in Agency Relationships: Apparent authority also exists when a principal fails to give proper notice of the termination of an agency relationship. When an agency relationship is terminated, the principal is required to give two types of notice:

- **Actual notice** is direct notice to third parties who have dealt with the departing agent
- **Constructive notice** is published notice to the business world. Constructive notice generally comes through business publications that print formal announcements of departures of employees or the addition of new employees
- Without proper notice given, both actual and constructive, of the departure of an agent, the principal remains liable for the contracts the agent negotiates with third parties. Proper notice stops lingering apparent authority because third parties have actual or constructive knowledge of the termination of an agent's authority

Ralph and Nicholas were partners in an office supply and printing business, RN Printers and Supply. Ralph had always ordered the business supplies for RN. Ralph decided to retire, and Nicholas purchased Ralph's interest in the partnership. Nicholas notified RN's customers directly but did not notify other third parties who would have dealt with Ralph. After leaving, Ralph continued to place RN orders for paper and ink supplies.

Ralph would meet the deliveries behind RN's facility and sign the delivery documents. Ralph then sold the supplies to make extra money in retirement. The vendors continued to bill RN. Nicholas discovered the extra supply orders and refused to pay the vendors because Ralph was no longer a partner.

Nicholas will be required to pay for the supplies because of the failure to give notice to vendors—third parties who had dealt with Ralph and were entitled to be paid because of lingering apparent authority.

Agency by Estoppel or Ostensible Authority: For the purposes of the exam, this agency relationship is another form of apparent authority agency that is created when the principal acts as if another is their agent. Should the term "ostensible authority" be used, the term "apparent authority" can be substituted.

Agency Authority through Ratification: Agency authority obtained through ratification results when the agent does not have express, implied, or apparent authority but still enters into a contract on behalf of a principal. The principal is not bound but can use the process of ratification to retroactively approve the transaction, thereby providing the agent with ex post facto authority, or authority after the fact.

The principal has the choice to honor the contract or properly use the defense of lack of authority on the part of the agent. The requirements for a valid ratification are:

- Full knowledge about the agreement
- Some indication of the ratification either through written or oral statements or simply by going ahead with the contract
- Principal must ratify the *entire* transaction (no piecemeal)
- Ratification does *not require* consideration
- Principal is *not required* to notify third party of ratification

Hollywood Star P hires Ace Talent to handle public relations for P. Ace Talent's authority is limited to public relations. Ace Talent signs a contract for a movie for Hollywood Star P.

P need not honor the contract because Ace Talent was not given contracting authority, only public relations functions. P could still decide to honor the contract for goodwill or because the movie deal was a good one.

Existence of an Agency Relationship

Using the steps and information outlined above on how agency relationships are created, the following scenario illustrates how to determine whether an agency relationship exists.

Janeen is an agent for Xavier Fashions. Janeen's responsibility is the acquisition of fabrics for use in Xavier's clothing designs. In the agency agreement between Xavier and Janeen, there is a $100,000 upper limit on Janeen's authority. For fabric purchases above that amount, Janeen is required to obtain the CFO's approval. Janeen signed a contract with Taffeta, Inc., for $120,000 of fabric without obtaining the CFO's approval. Xavier has refused to honor the contract because of the limitation in Janeen's agency contract.

- **Is there an agency relationship between Janeen and Xavier?**
  Yes, the two parties have created an actual (express) agency relationship.
- **Is the agency agreement required to be in writing?**
  Yes—contracts for the sale of goods $500 or more must be in writing, so the agent's authority must also be in writing.
- **Can Taffeta enforce the contract for $120,000 against Xavier?**
  Yes, because Janeen had apparent authority to make the contract. Taffeta was not aware of the agency limitation.
- **Would the answer to whether there is a valid contract be different if Xavier's order form had the following appearing before the signature portion?**
  Note: All orders in excess of $100,000 require Xavier's CFO's approval.
  Yes, Xavier stops the apparent authority with the notification on its order form. Taffeta could not enforce the contract because Janeen would lack authority as an agent.

5.02 Duties and Liabilities of Agents and Principals

Duties of Agents and Principals

Representative Task (Remembering & Understanding): Explain the various duties and liabilities of agents and principals.

Duties of Principal to Agent

To Comply with Agency Agreement: As with any other contract, a principal must follow the terms of the agency contract.

Paula (principal) hired Alex (agent) to serve as her driver for two years. Alex is to secure parking permits and arrange for security details when necessary. Paula agreed to pay Alex $1,500 per month for that period. As the principal, Paula has the duty to pay Alex the $1,500 per month compensation promised under the agency agreement.

To Reimburse Reasonable Expenses: The principal must reimburse the agent for expenses incurred in carrying out the agency agreement. Absent contrary agreement, the principal is responsible for expenses the agent incurs in reasonably performing activities on the principal's behalf. The expenses must be related to performing duties and cannot be excessive. The principal would also be liable for any injuries the agent experiences in performing their duties for the principal.

Alyssa (agent) is a truck driver who delivers furniture for Pruitt's Furniture Store (principal). While doing deliveries for Pruitt, Alyssa uses all of the truck's gas and refills the truck so that she can complete the deliveries. Absent agreement to the contrary, Pruitt must reimburse Alyssa for the expense.

Duties of Agent to Principal

Duty of Loyalty: The agency relationship is a fiduciary relationship. Because an agent is a fiduciary, the agent owes a duty of loyalty to their principal. The agent cannot make a profit at the principal's expense. Subagents owe a fiduciary duty to the agent who hired them as well as to the principal of the agent. As a fiduciary, an agent acts in the best interest of the principal and does not make profits on transactions at the principal's expense. The duty of loyalty prohibits agents from competing with their principals. The duty of loyalty also prohibits conflicts of interest, appropriation of business opportunities, and the disclosure of confidential information about the principal.

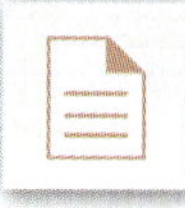

Rand Turner is the trainer for Cheshire Farms. Rand does not have an exclusive arrangement with Cheshire and also trains for Hillsbrook Farms. Rand arranged to have Cheshire sell two of its mares to Hillsbrook for a discounted price.

Rand had already pre-negotiated the sale of those mares by Hillsbrook to a third party for twice the amount Hillsbrook paid to Cheshire. Rand breached an agent's fiduciary duty because of the profit on the second sale without disclosing to Cheshire that the second sale, for twice the amount, was already pending.

Freda Payne is employed as an auditor at Magnum Software, Inc. Freda has access to the financial performance results for Magnum before those financials are released publicly. Freda is giving that advance information to several friends and family members so that they can take profitable positions in Magnum stock prior to the public release of the financials. Freda has breached her duty of loyalty by disclosing Magnum's nonpublic information.

Duty to Follow Instructions (Duty of Obedience): The agent should follow the principal's instructions unless those instructions call for illegal or immoral acts.

Duty of Reasonable Care: The agent must discharge all responsibilities carefully with the prudence of a reasonable person. Negligent conduct in the execution of duties allows the principal to recover from the agent. Agents, like all individuals in whatever capacity, are always liable for their negligence.

Todd Beecher is a real estate agent representing the Goodmans, who are looking for a home to purchase. In screening properties for the Goodmans to view, Todd neglected to check the county records that list properties designated as brown fields, or property that has environmental cleanup issues. The Goodmans purchased a home that had to be demolished in order to do below-surface cleanup.

Todd's failure to check the records falls below the reasonable standard for a reasonable professional, and Todd would be liable to the Goodmans for their resulting damage.

Liability of Principals for an Agent's Lack of Reasonable Care

Perhaps the greatest liability question principals face is whether they have liability for the actions (negligent and otherwise) of their agents. There are six ways in which principals can be held liable for the actions of their agents.

1. A principal is liable for the torts of agents if the agent was doing as the principal instructed or ordered.

Glencoe Delivery Services was engaged to deliver fruit on behalf of its principal, Reina Foods. Glencoe requested to delay its normal deliveries by one day because of a snowstorm along its route. Reina refused the request. The Glencoe truck slid on ice and ran into a local storefront, causing damage. Reina is liable to the local store owner (ie, third party) because Glencoe, the agent, was following the orders of the principal, Reina.

2. A principal is liable for the torts of agents if the principal hires an agent who is not qualified to perform the job assigned (sometimes called negligent entrustment).

Centene, Inc., a construction company, entrusts an employee, a high school student without a driver's license, to do pickups and deliveries with one of its large dump trucks. The student drives the truck at an excessive speed and runs a red light, causing injury to five members of a family in a compact car.

The family members can recover from both the high school student and Centene because Centene negligently entrusted the truck to an employee not trained or licensed to drive the large truck.

3. A principal is liable for the torts of an agent who was hired without doing an appropriate background check and pre-hiring screening (negligent hiring).

Jefferson's on Third hired Louise Freeman as its coat-check employee. Jefferson's was in a hurry to replace the former employee and did not check with Louise's former employers. Louise had been fired from two previous jobs for alleged embezzlement. During Louise's second week of work, two coats disappeared from the coat-check room after Louise had checked them. Louise never returned from her break following the second missing coat, and the two missing coats were never found.

Jefferson's would be liable to the customers whose coats were missing because of its failure to perform a complete background check.

4. A principal is liable for the torts of the agents if the principal failed to supervise properly (tort of negligent supervision and/or negligent in retention).

Samson Solar hired a sales agent who had a known history of aggression as a door-to-door sales representative. The sales agent was, however, very good at closing sales. Samson did receive several complaints from potential customers during the agent's first month about the agent's behavior while doing sales presentations in their homes. However, the sales agent was doing very well in closing sales. Samson took no disciplinary action against the sales agent after the complaints. While on a sales call at a potential customer's home during the second month, the sales agent assaulted the customer.

Samson would be liable for the injuries to the customer for its failure to provide better supervision of an employee who had a history indicating a need for tighter supervision.

5. Principals are also liable for any harm caused by the actions of their agents that involve inherently dangerous activities.

AllChem transports biohazardous waste. One of its drivers dropped three vials (containers) in loading the waste into the transport vehicles. The driver did not realize the vials were dropped. When the pickup logs are checked upon arrival at AllChem facilities, employees discover that three vials are missing. AllChem is not able to find the three vials.

AllChem would be responsible for any injuries that resulted from those who picked up the vials and any resulting injuries that resulted from improper disposal.

6. A principal is liable for the negligent torts of agents committed in the scope of employment. Even if the principal has not done anything wrong personally, they may be vicariously liable under the doctrine of **vicarious liability**, also known as the doctrine of *respondeat superior*. There are two requirements for imposing vicarious liability on principals for the negligent torts of agents:
   - **Existence of a master-servant relationship:** *Respondeat superior*, meaning "let the master answer," is a doctrine of vicarious liability based on a master-servant relationship between the principal and agent. A master-servant relationship is determined by the ability of the principal to control the activity of the agent. This relationship is different from an independent contractor relationship
   - **Agent is a servant:** The key to determining whether the agent is a servant (for whose torts the principal is liable) or an independent contractor (for whose torts the principal usually is not liable) is this question: Does the principal have the right to control the method and manner of the agent's work? If the answer is yes, then it is a master-servant relationship. If the answer is no, then it is an independent contractor relationship. Additional factors for determining whether an agent is a servant or an independent contractor are:
     - Does the agent work regular hours for the principal (eg, 9–5)?
     - Does the principal provide the agent's tools (eg, computer and cell phone)?
     - Is the agent paid by the hour or week rather than by the job?
     - Is the agent's major source of income or sole source of income from the principal? If the answer is yes, then it likely indicates a master-servant relationship. If the answer is no, then it likely indicates an independent contractor relationship
   - **Scope of employment** means that the agent (in the master-servant relationship) commits the tort while the agent is doing something for the principal related to the principal's business activities. The principal is less likely to be held liable for an agent's intentional torts than for an agent's mere negligence because it is more likely that the agent is not acting within the scope of employment when committing intentional torts. However, as noted above, if the agent is authorized to commit the tort, then the principal is liable. Deviations from the scope of employment will not alter the principal's liability if:
     i. They are minor; or
     ii. After deviation from the scope of employment, the agent is returning and "reasonably close" to returning to the assigned task from the principal.
        - Frolic and detour—Agent has diverted from the principal's business and is completing personal tasks while working on principal's business. There is no liability for principal during the agent's frolic and detour
        - Return from frolic and detour—This is the term for when an agent abandons personal activity and returns to the business of the principal. After personal business is complete, liability of the principal returns

Liability of Principal for Torts of Agents: Doctrine of *Respondeat Superior*

1. Master-servant relationship?

a. Degree of control
b. Method of payment
c. Other sources of income
d. Who furnishes tools and equipment

2. Scope of employment

a. Activity is related to business of principal
b. Not a frolic and detour (deviations from scope)

If Alden Welding hires attorney Joe Piedro from the Sapon and Partners law firm to handle its commercial litigation, Joe is an independent contractor.

If Alden Welding hires Joe as its general counsel, Joe is in a master-servant relationship.

If Joe is an independent contractor, Alden does not have vicarious liability for Joe's torts, even when Joe is driving to depositions for Alden's litigation.

However, if Joe is a general counsel for Alden, Alden would have liability for Joe's torts when he is driving to depositions on Alden litigation.

Tia Hales works for Excel Document Storage and Preservation picking up and delivering documents for shredding. While delivering documents to Excel's shredding facilities, Tia leaves the highway to get a soda at a fast-food restaurant just off the highway. Tia drives the Excel van carelessly in the fast-food restaurant's parking lot and injures a customer.

Both Tia and Excel are liable to the customer for any injuries and other economic damages.

Tia, again while driving for Excel, is driving two hours away from Excel headquarters to pick up some documents from an Excel customer. Tia's parents live at the one-hour point on the way to the location for the document retrieval. Tia exits the highway to stop and visit with her parents for half an hour. As Tia is leaving the driveway of their home, Tia hits another car with the Excel van and injures the driver of that car.

Tia, but not Excel, is liable to that driver because Tia was participating in a frolic and detour from the Excel document pickup assignment.

The tests for determining whether an agent is in a master-servant relationship or an independent contractor relationship are similar to the tests the IRS uses for determining whether an employee is a true employee (who will require payment of wages, taxes, and withholding) or an independent contractor (who receives a Form 1099 and files estimated payments to take care of the taxes on the payments received).

Tort Liability of Independent Contractors: Principals are liable for certain torts of independent contractors. If the actions of the independent contractor were authorized, then the principal is liable for the independent contractor's action (intentional conduct). When independent contractors (as well as agents) are engaged in inherently dangerous activities (eg, radioactive materials, toxic materials), they and their principals are both liable.

James Framer works for the law firm of Cutler and Willard and is doing corporate counsel work for Deluxe EVs, Inc. Framer is an independent contractor to Deluxe EVs. The CEO and CFO of Deluxe EVs instructed Framer to approve illegal sales of stock by officers of Deluxe EVs, which Framer then did. Framer is both civilly and criminally liable for doing so. Deluxe EVs is also civilly and criminally liable to those who were affected by the sales, including any fines, penalties, and costs.

Duties and Liabilities of Agents and Principals: Termination

Agency relationships require special steps and duties on the part of principals and agents when the relationship terminates so that certain third parties are not affected adversely through a lack of knowledge about those relationships. The means of termination controls the duties and liabilities of the principal and agent after termination occurs.

Termination by Actions of the Parties or Terms of Their Agency Agreement

Termination by fulfillment: An agency relationship is terminated when the conduct authorized under the agency relationship is complete.

Paul Purcell hired Alice Anderson (agent), a real estate broker, to sell a commercial parcel of land that Purcell owned. Once Alice has found a buyer and the sale closes, Paul's agency relationship with Alice terminates.

Termination by lapse of time: If an agency relationship is restricted in length and the authorized length of time ends, then the agency relationship ends.

Most real estate listing agreements, in which a homeowner (principal) hires a real estate broker (agent) to list a house for sale, are limited in length to 90 days. When the 90 days have ended, the listing agreement (agency relationship) also ends.

Termination by a specified event: An agency relationship established to accomplish an event ends when that event is done.

A wedding planner (agent) hired to negotiate contracts for venues, cakes, flowers, etc. for a wedding has no further agency authority once the wedding takes place.

Termination by mutual agreement: An agency relationship ends when the principal and agent agree to end their relationship.

When a company (principal) and an advertising agency (agent) agree that they no longer wish to work with each other, they have reached a mutual agreement, and the agency will no longer have the authority to negotiate ad contracts for the company.

Termination by unilateral act of one party: "You're fired" or "I quit." When the principal or agent fails to perform the duties under the agency agreement, the agency relationship ends, just as in any breach of contract. In addition, the principal can terminate an agent for business reasons. Absent a contract, the principal has the right to terminate an agent for cause or no cause. A principal cannot (ie, has neither the right nor the power to) terminate an agency coupled with an interest.

Paula (principal) hires Alex (agent) to serve as a driver for two years. Paula agrees to pay Alex $1,500 per month for that period. Either Paula or Alex can end the relationship at any time. However, the termination of the agency does not resolve the underlying issues of damages for breach of contract to the other party. Agency authority is ended, but the contractual obligations of the principal and agent survive unilateral terminations.

Remember: The termination of an agency relationship by actions of the parties (agent is fired or quits) or by their agreement does not end **all** of the agent's authority. Only the agent's **actual** authority (consisting of express and implied authority) is terminated by the act. Apparent authority continues unless the principal fulfills the duty to provide constructive and actual notice to third parties who have interacted with the agent.

Termination by Operation of Law

These types of agency relationship terminations are not achieved through voluntary agreements. These are legal events that cause the termination of the agency relationship. Termination by operation of law ends all authority: express, implied, and apparent. The duty of notice and risk of apparent authority do not apply because the law has ended all types of authority in the agency relationship.

Termination by death of either principal or agent: Death of the principal means that there is no longer a party to the contract. Death of the agent speaks for itself.

Termination by insanity of the principal: The insanity of the principal means that there is no party with capacity to enter into contracts. If there is no principal with capacity, there is no contract because the agent is not the party to the contract (living wills and health directives are an exception to the capacity requirement because they do not apply unless and until there is a lack of capacity).

Termination by bankruptcy: Bankruptcy of the principal is another event that triggers an operation-of-law termination of an agency. Some day-to-day activities can continue, such as the presence of salesclerks in stores that declare bankruptcy. Under bankruptcy court orders, stores may remain operational for 30–90 days to sell off merchandise. Bankruptcy of the agent terminates an agency relationship only if the agent's bankruptcy would impair the agent's ability to perform responsibilities.

Anissa (agent) has been working as the on-site leasing agent for Premiere Properties' (principal) apartment complex, Las Sendas. Premiere has declared bankruptcy. Anissa can continue with the day-to-day operations of Las Sendas. If, however, Anissa had been hired by Premiere to sell off some of its properties, the bankruptcy means that further sales would not be proper until the trustee has a chance to determine creditor rights and property transfers.

Termination by general contract law termination causes: As with all contracts, if the law makes the conduct of the agent or the subject matter of the contract illegal, the agency relationship ends. The loss or destruction of the property that is the subject matter of the agency relationship terminates the agency relationship.

Alan is hired to buy a dog racetrack for Peterson Entertainment, and dog racing is declared illegal. The agency relationship ends.

C Banana hires a mercenary group to provide protection for its employees in Colombia. The U.S. government passes a law that makes it illegal for U.S. companies to compensate groups that are listed as terrorist groups by the U.S. Department of Justice. C's agency relationship with the group terminates.

Anna is hired by Pearson Produce to sell one of Pearson's warehouses, which is destroyed by a tornado before Anna can sell it. Anna's agency relationship ends because the subject matter of the agency has been destroyed.

The following chart summarizes all the grounds for and effects of termination of agency relationships.

Grounds for Termination	Effect	Notice Required?	Example
Fulfillment of agency purpose	Agency ends	Actual and constructive notice	Agent has sold the property in a listing
Lapse of time	Agency ends	Actual and constructive notice	Agent listing agreement lasts only 90 days
Completion of specified event	Agency ends	Actual and constructive notice	Wedding that wedding planner was hired to stage has occurred
Mutual agreement	Agency ends	Actual and constructive notice	Principal and agent decide to end their relationship
Unilateral action	Agency ends except for an agency coupled with an interest	Actual and constructive notice	"You're fired" or "I quit"
Termination by Operation of Law			
Death of principal or agent	Agency ends	None	There is no longer a principal or an agent
Insanity of the principal	Agency ends	None	Court declaration of incompetency
Bankruptcy	Agency ends (with court order exceptions)	None	Petition for bankruptcy is filed
Failure to acquire a necessary license	Agency ends	None	Agent failed to promptly obtain a PTIN
Destruction of the subject matter	Agency ends	None	Tornado destroyed warehouse that agent was contracted to clean
Subsequent illegality	Agency ends	None	Materials banned by law that agent was contracted to procure

Contract Liability of Agents and Principals

The liability of the principal and agent to third parties for contracts and the ability of third parties to enforce contracts against principals and agents depend on two factors: the type of authority the agent had and whether the principal was disclosed to the third party. This section focuses on the disclosure issues in agency relationships.

Liability of Disclosed Principals: A disclosed principal is one in which the third party is aware that the agent is acting for a principal and the third party knows who that principal is.

A sports agent who is negotiating a contract for an NBA free agent is an example of a disclosed principal situation. The third party (the team) knows the identity of the player and knows that the sports agent is authorized to act on the player's behalf.

Disclosed Principal When Agent Has Actual Authority (Express or Implied): When there is a disclosed principal who has actual authority, the third party is liable to the principal, and the principal is liable to the third party.

- The agent has no liability on the contract that the agent obtained on behalf of the disclosed principal
- The authority of the agent can be expressly provided in the agency agreement (such as the authority to sell a car), or it can be implied authority that would include the customary authority of an agent acting as a landlord, a store manager, or an office manager

An antique dealer (agent) is hired by an estate executor (principal) to sell an armoire from an estate. The antique dealer discloses the executor's name to the armoire buyer (third party) and negotiates a contract for sale of the armoire for $1,700. The executor thinks the price is too low and refuses to honor the contract. The buyer can require the executor to convey title to the armoire, and the executor is liable for damages to the buyer if there is a failure to deliver. The antique dealer has no liability to the buyer even if the executor breaches the contract.

Contract Liability of Disclosed Principal

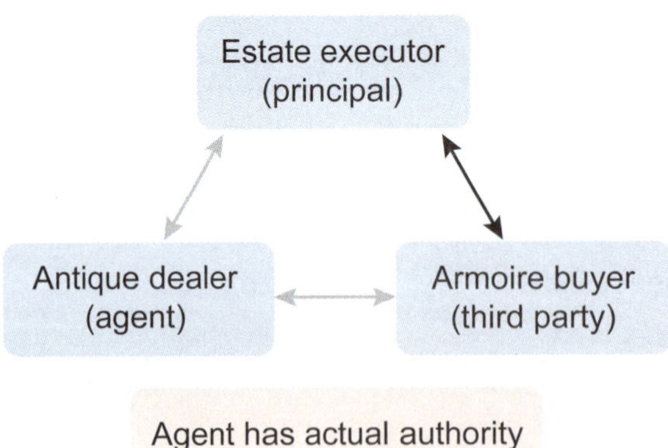

Disclosed Principal When Agent Has Apparent Authority: There must always be a disclosed principal under apparent authority because apparent authority can exist only if the principal has held out someone as an agent or has allowed a third party to believe that an agent has been given authority by the principal.

- In this situation, the principal *only* is liable to the third party. However, the agent is liable to the principal for acting as an agent without actual (express or implied) authority
- When an agent lacks actual (express or implied) authority, the principal is liable for contracts with third parties negotiated by the agent if:
  - The principal held the agent out as the principal's agent; that is, a third party reasonably believed that the agent worked for the principal and had the authority to enter into contracts;
  - The agent acted within the scope of apparent authority; *and*
  - The third party reasonably relied on the appearance of the agent's authority in entering into a contract.

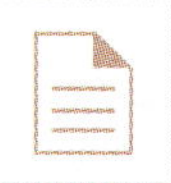

Rod has been a traveling sales representative for Portable Buildings, Inc., for 10 years. Portable fired Rod for dishonesty. Rod then contacts Scrapbookers, Inc., a longtime customer of Portable Buildings, to make a sale. No one at Scrapbookers had heard about Rod's firing. Rod and Scrapbookers negotiate a contract for a steel structure for $150,000. Rod accepts a down payment of $30,000, which Rod then absconds.

Rod has bound Scrapbookers to the contract, and Scrapbookers can hold Portable to the contract. Rod still had authority to act on Portable Buildings' behalf as an agent because of lingering apparent authority.

Portable Buildings has liability under the contract because of its failure to let third parties, such as its customer Scrapbookers, know that Rod no longer worked for Portable. Rod is liable to Portable for the deposit as well as any costs associated with fulfilling the contract with Scrapbookers.

Contract Liability of Disclosed Principal

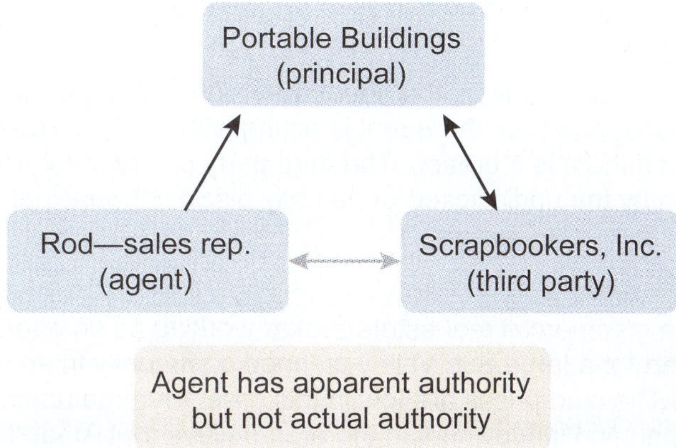

Disclosed Principal—Agent Has No Actual or Apparent Authority: In this situation, the agent only is liable to the third party; the principal has **no** liability.

Alex goes to a new town and negotiates, as a representative of the National Association of Realtors (NAR), with a hotel manager to book the hotel for the upcoming convention of the NAR. The hotel manager does not check with the NAR, and the manager reserves the hotel for the NAR.

NAR is not liable to the hotel for the deposits and damages if the convention is not held there, but Alex is.

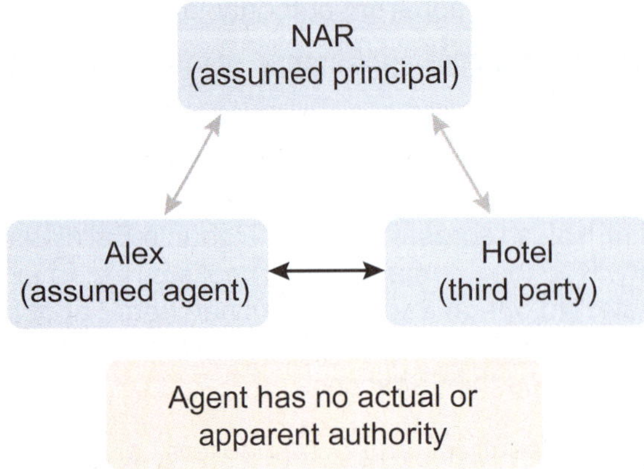

Liability of Partially Disclosed and Undisclosed Principals When Agent Has Actual Authority: If an agent is acting for a principal under actual authority but does not identify the principal, then both the principal and the agent are liable to the third party. There are other issues to be resolved between the principal and agent in terms of breach of duty.

- When real estate agents disclose that they are acting for a buyer but do not reveal the buyer, there is a *partially disclosed principal*. When the real estate agent does not disclose that there even is a principal, there is an *undisclosed principal*. In an undisclosed principal contract, only the agent's name is on the contract, so the agent is liable
- In a partially disclosed principal situation, the agent may sign, "Acting on behalf of an undisclosed principal." In both situations, however, the agent is acting with authority, so both the principal and agent are liable on the contract if there is a breach. The third party can recover from either the principal or the agent if there is a breach by the undisclosed or partially disclosed principal

Amanda Shields is a commercial real estate broker working as an agent for Sun Valley Homes, Inc., to purchase land for a large Sun Valley planned community in an undeveloped area 45 miles outside a city. The land prices are low in this area. Amanda has not disclosed that she is working for a principal, and landowners in the area believe that Amanda is the purchaser. Sun Valley, a major national builder, does not want its plans or name disclosed because of the effect such a disclosure would have on existing land prices. Amanda enters into a contract to purchase acreage for $12 million.

Both Amanda and Sun Valley are liable to the seller (the third party) for damages if Sun Valley breaches the purchase contract. A contract entered into with authority on behalf of a principal is the same as a contract of just the principal acting alone. If Sun Valley breaches the purchase contract, Amanda can identify Sun Valley if the seller/third party pursues the claim for breach of the contract. Amanda would be entitled to reimbursement from the principal if Amanda ends up paying the seller the damages.

Contract Liability of Partially or Undisclosed Principal

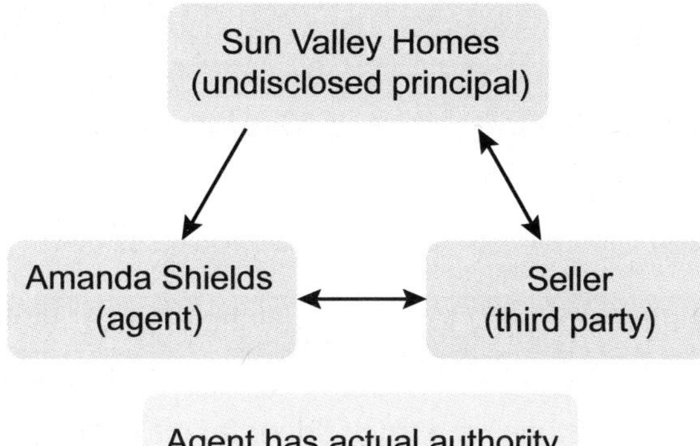

Liability of Partially Disclosed or Undisclosed Principal When the Agent Has No Authority: If an agent in a partially disclosed or undisclosed principal situation enters into a contract for which the agent had no authority, then only the agent has liability to the third party for breach of contract. In a partially disclosed or undisclosed agency relationship, there can never be apparent authority because the third party does not know of the identity or existence of a principal. An agent must, therefore, have actual authority (express or implied) to enter into the contract with the third party.

Contract Liability of Partially or Undisclosed Principal

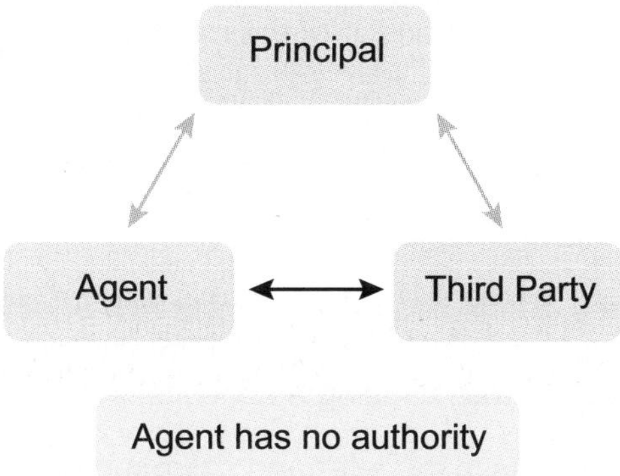

Identify the Duties of Agents and Principals

Representative Task (Application): Identify the duty or liability of an agent or principal given a specific scenario.

The following scenario provides an opportunity to analyze all the agency issues that can arise in the operation of a business.

Sanitary Dairies, Inc., employs Harold Stone as a truck driver for distribution of its dairy products. Stone's shift is daily from 7:00 a.m. to 5:00 p.m. Stone is paid by the hour and is given three weeks of PTO. Stone's employment contract limits Stone's job duties to loading, delivering, and shelf-stocking at Sanitary Dairies' customer stores. The contract prohibits sales activities by Stone.

While Stone is restocking the dairy cases at Super Dollar Grocery, the store manager approaches Stone and requests an additional allocation of chocolate milk. Stone tells the manager that what is in the truck is slated for delivery to other customers. Stone offers to shift that allocation to the Super Dollar store if the manager pays Stone $50 in cash. The manager agrees and receives the chocolate milk.

While Stone is restocking dairy cases at Thrifty Foods, the manager asks Stone if the next delivery could include buttermilk. Stone quotes the manager a price and commits to deliver the buttermilk.

While restocking dairy cases at Organic Farmer's Market, Stone argues with another dairy distributor, which results in a shouting match that requires intervention of the manager. The manager reports Stone's conduct to Sanitary Dairies.

While driving between Super Dollar Grocery and Thrifty Foods, Stone, driving above the speed limit, rear-ends Ronald Green's car. Mr. and Mrs. Green are both injured, their car has to be towed because of the extent of damages, and Stone has minor injuries.

During the following week's deliveries, Stone has an encounter with another dairy distributor at the Super Dollar Grocery Store in a dispute over space allocation for their products. Before the manager can intervene, Stone hits the other delivery driver, causing a concussion because of a fall to the floor.

Determine whether each of the statements in the left-hand column is correct or incorrect and then read the explanation for the answer.

Statement	Correct or Incorrect?	Explanation
Because Stone works so independently without supervision, Stone would be considered an independent contractor.	Incorrect	Stone's relationship has all of the trappings (hours of work dictated; route dictated; paid by the hour) of a master-servant relationship.
Sanitary Dairies is bound by the agreement Stone made for the delivery of buttermilk to Thrifty Foods.	Correct	Although Stone had no actual authority because of the contract limitations between Sanitary and Stone, Stone had either implied or apparent authority to take orders. Thrifty was unaware of Stone's contract limitations. Third parties must know of agent limitations before they are subject to them.

Statement	Correct or Incorrect?	Explanation
Sanitary cannot be held liable for the concussion injury because the third party did not work for Super Dollar Grocery store.	Incorrect	Principals can be held liable for intentional injuries committed by employees while they are working, even when the injuries result from intentional conduct, if the principal had prior knowledge of aggressive behavior. Liability would extend to employees of customers, customers of customers, and other distributors in the store at the time.
Stone would have apparent authority to negotiate contracts with the managers.	Correct	The store managers would not know of the limitations of Stone's authority, and it would appear to them that Stone had authority.
Stone's agreement with the Super Dollar Grocery manager for the chocolate milk is not a valid contract because taking the $50 was a breach of the duty of loyalty and terminated Stone's authority.	Correct	The breach of the duty of loyalty terminates the agent's authority. Payment of a bribe means that the third party does not have a contract.
If Stone had never had a previous accident, Sanitary Dairies would not be liable for the injuries to the Greens and their car.	Incorrect	Principals are liable for the harms caused by the negligence of their employees acting in the scope of employment. Stone was speeding, which is a violation of the law and qualifies as negligence. Stone was also in the scope of employment, driving between two delivery locations. Sanitary Dairies is liable to the Greens. Stone is also liable.
Stone can avoid liability to the Greens because Stone was engaged in the performance of Sanitary Dairies' business.	Incorrect	All agents are liable for their own negligence. The only issue is whether their employers will also be held liable.
Stone cannot use worker's compensation to have the injuries from the accident treated.	Incorrect	Stone was in the scope of employment. That an employee made a mistake or did not follow the rules does not preclude worker's compensation coverage.
Sanitary Dairies cannot be held liable for the concussion injury caused by Stone at the Super Dollar store because it was an intentional tort.	Incorrect	The reported aggression of Stone previously put Sanitary Dairies on notice that Stone required additional supervision, training, or some time away from deliveries to be sure such an incident did not happen again.
Stone has breached an agent's duty to follow the agency agreement with Sanitary Dairies by engaging in sales activities.	Correct	Stone's contract prohibited sales activities, so the agency contract has been breached.
Stone breached the duty to follow instructions.	Correct	The prohibition on sales activity was a written instruction in Stone's employment agreement.

REG 6
Contracts

REG 6: Contracts

6.01 Formation

Formation

The formation and performance of contract obligations have great significance for accounting purposes. Knowing that a contract has been properly formed means that both parties have financial commitments to the contract. The presence of a contract and its shipment and delivery terms determine the timing for booking revenues as well as the liability for losses of goods during shipment. Finally, a party who breaches a contract has liability exposure that requires disclosure. For example, an accountant must evaluate a company's ability to remain in business as a going concern. Significant liability for a breach of contract is material, and an auditor must be able to evaluate both when and if a breach has occurred and the extent of remedies that could be available to the nonbreaching party.

Contracts: Sources of Law

The two sources of contract law tested on the exam are common law and the Uniform Commercial Code (UCC).

Common law (ie, law derived from court rulings) applies to contracts with the following subject matters: real estate and services. A contract to sell a home, a contract with an employer for a new job, and a service contract (eg, providing a loan) are all governed by common law.

The **UCC**, which applies to the sale of goods, is a code that was developed by businesspeople, attorneys, and legal scholars to be adopted by individual states so that interstate commerce could be done more uniformly and easily. All states have adopted some form or portion of the UCC.

Most importantly, the exam tests knowledge of the UCC provisions because the UCC has been adopted in the majority of states to govern contracts for the **sale of goods**. The UCC, specifically Article 2: Sales, defines goods as **tangible personal property** such as cars, appliances, boats, airplanes, clothing, phones, bicycles, and pets.

When there is a **"mixed" contract** (ie, the buyer is purchasing goods but installation is included), the courts use **two tests** for determining whether the UCC or common law applies. What was the intent of the parties? What is the cost of the goods versus the cost of the services (ie, installation)?

A contract involves the sale of a refrigerator for $900 and a $50 installation fee. This contract is predominantly UCC. In other cases, this question is important: Was the buyer just buying the goods, or was installation critical to those goods? A water heater may be the predominant cost in a contract, but most buyers will need the water heater plumbed and installed. That expense may be slightly less than the water heater, so the service portion may be the most important factor in that contract.

The following chart provides examples of the application of UCC versus common law.

Contract Subject Matter	Common Law	UCC
Contract for the installation of carpet	✓	
Contract for the purchase of carpet		✓
Contract for the purchase of a car		✓
Financing contract for the purchase of a car	✓	

Because the common law of contracts differs from the UCC provisions, you should always ask: *Is this contract governed by the UCC or common law?* The failure to consider which source of law applies will result in a wrong answer in the areas of contract law in which the two sources take different approaches. You must know both sources of contract law, and you must be able to apply the correct law according to the subject matter of the contract.

Types of Contracts

Representative Task (Application): Identify different types of contracts (eg, written, verbal, unilateral, express, implied) given a specific scenario.

The types of contracts control the rights of the parties under those contracts.

Express vs. Implied Contracts

An **express contract** is a contract formed wholly by oral and/or written words. Some contracts are required to be in writing, but whether written or oral, they are called express contracts.

Assume that over the phone, an individual offers to sell a personal computer to another person for $400. Later that day, the person sends an email accepting the offer. The combination of the oral offer (by phone) and the written acceptance (by email) creates an **express contract**.

An **implied-in-law** or **implied-in-fact contract** is one that arises because of the circumstances created by the parties and because of their conduct. This type of contract results not from express language between the parties but through their actions and the surrounding circumstances.

When an owner takes a pet to the veterinarian, they have usually made an appointment. The owner provides information through paperwork. The staff at the vet's office explains to the owner that the doctor will see them shortly. No one discusses fees or charges. There is no signed agreement to pay. There is, however, an understanding that the owner expects treatment or services for the pet and the vet expects to be paid. Those expectations, unwritten and unspoken, create an implied contract.

Written vs. Verbal Contracts

Written or verbal contracts are a subset of express contracts. Certain types of contracts must be in writing under the Statute of Frauds, or they are not enforceable in court. However, verbal contracts not covered by the Statute of Frauds are valid and enforceable.

Unilateral vs. Bilateral Contracts

A **bilateral contract** is one in which both sides make a promise. Most business contracts are bilateral contracts.

Gausted & Freeland promises to do a 10-K audit for Jefferson Hitches, Inc., which promises to pay Gausted & Freeland a fee of $180,000 for the audit.

A car dealership offers to sell Brandon a car in exchange for Brandon's promise to make monthly payments for four years.

A **unilateral contract** is one in which one side makes a promise in exchange for an action or performance from the other side. This type of contract is formed by action required by one party in exchange for a promise by the other party. One side is not making a promise; that side simply accepts by performance. Once the party required to act begins that action, the contract has been accepted, and the promising party is bound to do as promised.

Alexis texts Danny, "Drive my car from New York to San Francisco, and I will pay you $1,000." If Danny gets the car to San Francisco, Danny collects the $1,000. The action or performance of driving the car is done in exchange for the promise to pay. In unilateral contracts, one side does not promise. One side must act to form a contract.

Void Contracts vs. Voidable Contracts

A void contract is one for an illegal purpose or that violates the law. A void contract cannot be enforced by the courts because enforcement would violate public policy and encourage illegal conduct. For example, a contract for murder for hire is void.

The accounting firm of White & Jackson agrees, for a fee of $10,000, to provide one of its clients with financial results for other clients before those clients' results are made public. The advance nonpublic information will allow the client to take a position in the stock of those companies that will produce a profit once the earnings are released to the public. Since the performance required under the contract is for an illegal purpose (insider trading, a crime), the contract is void.

A **voidable contract** is one that can be set aside because one party has protection under the law and thus has the right to opt out of the contract. Examples of voidable contracts include contracts that involved fraud in formation or where one party lacked the required legal capacity to form contracts.

Devon offers to sell a Picasso painting to Marie for $100,000. Devon knows that the painting is a forgery. Marie accepts the offer and buys the painting. Due to Devon's fraud, Marie can be relieved of any liability under this contract.

Jane, age 16 (a minor), buys a car from a car dealer using a fake ID. The contract is voidable because minors do not have the capacity to contract. The contract cannot be enforced against Jane, and Jane has the choice of honoring or disaffirming the contract.

Enforceable vs. Unenforceable Contracts

An otherwise valid contract that cannot be enforced because of a statutory or other legal defense is an unenforceable contract. The courts will not enforce the contract. Although an unenforceable contract is one that the courts will not enforce, the parties are still permitted to honor the contracts. These contracts are not void if the parties decide to proceed with performance.

DeAnne orally offers to sell Brenda her real property for $125,000. Brenda accepts. This contract is unenforceable because it is not in writing, as required by the Statute of Frauds. The courts cannot enforce the agreement because there is a legal defense of a lack of record of a contract that is, by law, required to be in writing. However, if the buyer and seller choose to honor their oral agreement, the courts do not prohibit this.

Executed vs. Executory Contracts

An **executed contract** is a contract that has been fully performed by both involved parties. Some of the rights in performance and remedies are affected by whether a contract is executed (ie, performed).

Al offers Pete a watch for $200. Pete accepts, and Al and Pete exchange the watch for $200 in cash. Since the contractual obligations of both parties have been completed, the exchange is now an executed contract.

An **executory contract** is a contract in which performance has not yet begun or has not yet been fully performed by the involved parties. An executory contrary is also one in which one side has completed performance but the other side has not.

Trina offers to sell a watch to Ray for $200, with the payment and transfer of the watch to take place in 10 days. Ray accepts. Since no performance has taken place but a valid contract has still been formed, their arrangement is called an executory contract. Once the money and the watch are exchanged, it is an executed contract.

A **partially executed contract** is a contract that has been performed in part. One side has performed all that was required under the contractual obligation. Contracts can also be labeled partially executed or partially executory—one side has done the work, but the other side has not paid. For example, suppose a CPA has agreed to conduct an audit and has completed the audit work but has not yet been paid. The contract is executed for the auditor but executory for the company. And it is a partially executed contract.

If in the Trina and Ray watch sale agreement, Ray pays Trina the sales price of $200 but Trina has not yet delivered the watch, the contract is a partially executed contract because one side has performed but the other has not. The buyer's side is executed, and the seller's side is executory.

A **quasi-contract** is a contract imposed by the courts or by law when some performance has gone forward or there has been a great deal of reliance, even though there is no express or implied contract. The law creates a quasi-contract for the parties in circumstances in which the failure to find a quasi- or implied-in-law contract would result in unjust enrichment of one party by the other.

A political campaign staff member goes to a copy center store to order posters for her candidate. The staff member asks the copy center employee to run 500 copies of the poster. That campaign staffer then resigns from the campaign. The posters are picked up by another staff member who directs the copy center to talk to someone else on the campaign staff about payment. Those at the campaign headquarters were not aware of the terms of the poster production, so they refuse to pay without a written agreement. The copy center is not paid even though it performed its part of the contract. The copy center would be entitled to payment under a quasi-contract or an implied-in-law contract. Allowing the campaign to place the large order, use the posters, and not pay would be unjust enrichment. There is no written agreement, but the cost to the copy center is great, the copy center relied on the actions of a campaign staffer, and the campaign benefited by having the posters to use.

The following chart summarizes the types of contracts and the effects of their creation.

Type of Contract	Effect
Express contract	Oral or written contract
Implied contract	Contract formed by the circumstances and conduct of the parties
Unilateral contract	Contract formed by an offer and accepted by performance
Bilateral contract	Contract formed by mutual promises of the parties
Valid contract	Valid formation (no defenses; form is correct); can be enforced by either party; courts are willing to resolve disputes
Void contract	Violates the law; caused by some defenses; neither party can enforce it; courts will not touch it
Voidable contract	One side has the choice to enforce the contract (capacity; misrepresentation); caused by some defenses
Unenforceable contract	Form violation (writing or record); rights that courts will enforce vary
Quasi-contract	Equitable right; courts decide a contract exists by circumstances, not by formal formation

Elements of Contract Formation

Representative Task (Remembering & Understanding): Summarize the elements of contract formation between parties.

Representative Task (Application): Identify whether a valid contract was formed given a specific scenario.

Formation of a contract can be compared to making something using a recipe. All the ingredients in the recipe must be brought together at the right time and without difficulties in circumstances for a valid contract to be formed. There must be an offer, acceptance, and consideration. In some cases, there must be writing or a record that documents the formation of the contract. And there cannot be any defenses to formation because those defenses would mean that there was not actually a valid offer or acceptance.

The following chart summarizes the elements required for formation of a contract.

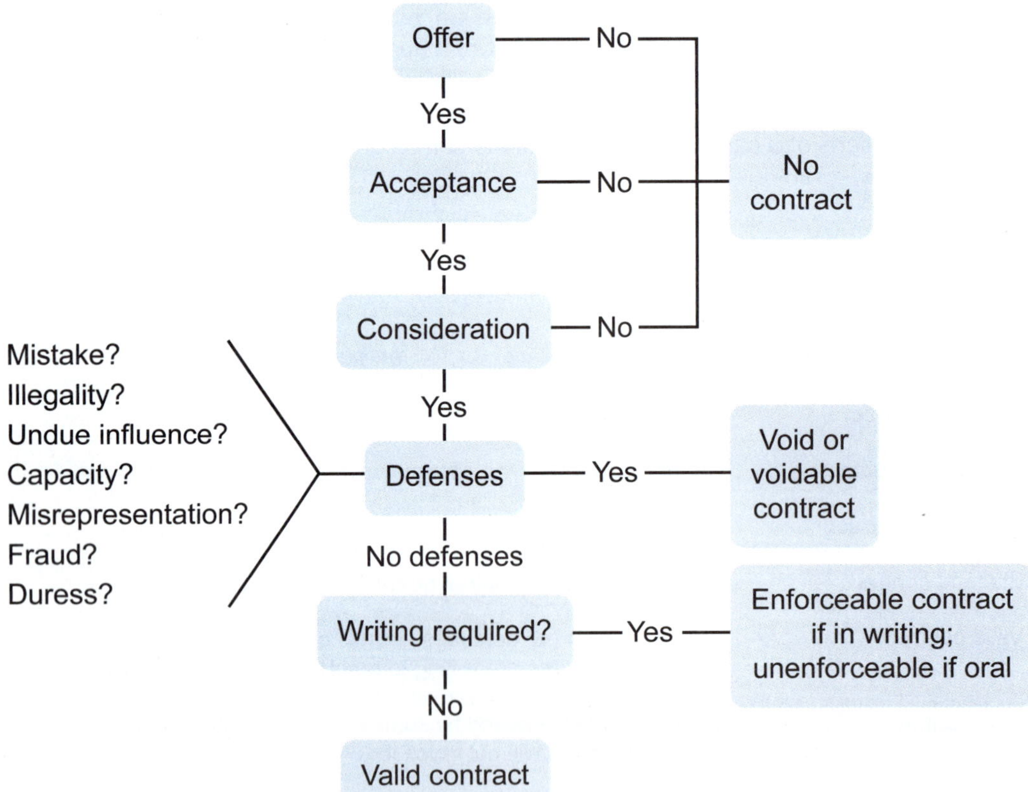

Offers: Requirements of a Valid Offer

For both UCC and common law, present intent to contract, definite and certain terms, and communication to the offeree are the same.

Present Intent to Contract

Present intent means that an offer does not exist if someone speaks of future plans. If someone writes, "When I retire, I think it would be great to sell this place and just buy a motor home and tour the country," there is no present intent to contract. This is just oral speculation about future plans.

The language must also show an objective observer that the offeror is serious about entering into a contract. Objective intent is measured by a reasonable person's interpretation of the acts, the language of the parties, and the circumstances surrounding the transaction. Humor, anger, and context are used to determine intent. Present intent also requires that the parties do something more than preliminary negotiations.

Statements, Actions, Circumstances	Intent to Contract?
A business owner who is having a tough day writes in an email, "Today has been so bad that I'd sell this business in a heartbeat to anyone with $50,000 in cash."	No present intent to contract; expression of future desire
Ad in newspaper from a clothier: "Dresses 50% off marked price"	Invitation for an offer; no present intent to contract
Ad by a dog owner with a photo of the dog: "$100 reward to the person who returns my lost dog, Lasso."	Valid unilateral offer
"I might consider selling it for the right amount of cash."	Negotiations; no present intent to contract
"When I am ready to retire, I will be selling my business."	Expression of future intent; no present intent to contract
"I will be mailing out an offer to sell my car next month."	No present intent to contract

Definite and Certain Terms

Terms of the offer must be definite enough to meet the minimum requirements under UCC or common law for formation.

Common Law: Under common law, definite and certain terms require identification of the parties, the subject matter, the price, and the time for and terms of performance.

UCC: The UCC relaxes the requirements for definiteness of terms. The UCC requires only that the offer identify the subject matter (and quantity if more than one is being sold). "I will sell you some Rolex President watches" is not enough for an offer under the UCC, but "I will sell you 100 Rolex President watches" is sufficient. The UCC also has a series of sections that supply any missing terms, including price, time of performance, delivery, and payment terms.

Open Price Term: A reasonable or market price at the time of delivery will apply, or if the price is to be fixed by either party, good faith is required in doing so.

Open Payment Term: Payment is due at the time and place the buyer is to receive the goods.

Open Quantity and Outputs and Requirement Contracts: Quantity is to be set by output (of the seller's factory) or needs of the buyer. This open-end quantity term is valid as long as there is a reasonable way to determine what is intended, such as the seller's past production records or the buyer's purchasing records.

- **Output Contract:** The buyer agrees to purchase as much as the seller is able to produce for a specific period of time, and the seller agrees to sell their entire output to the buyer
- **Requirements Contract:** The buyer agrees to purchase all that the buyer needs (requires) for a specified product for a specific period of time. The seller agrees to sell the buyer whatever that amount might be

Haul-It Switch agrees to purchase from a third party all the propane fuel it requires for heating its factory from November 1 through March 31. Even without a specific quantity of fuel, this contract is valid under the UCC because of the outputs or requirements exception under the UCC.

Open Place of Delivery Term: Delivery is at seller's place of business or, if the seller does not have a place of business, at the seller's residence.

Buyer Green is from New Orleans, and seller Smith is from Dallas. Smith offers to sell Green a watch for $100. Green accepts Smith's offer. The contract is silent as to the place of delivery, so delivery is **not** at the buyer's place in New Orleans.

In absence of agreement, delivery is at Smith's residence in Dallas. Green is required to "pick up" the watch or be in breach of contract.

Open Time for Contracted Performance: In absence of agreement, performance must be completed within a reasonable time.

Communication of Offer

To be a valid offer, the offer (meeting all the requirements for present intent to contract and sufficient detail for forming a contract) must be communicated to an offeree. If the offer is made to a specific person, a different person cannot accept it. If an offer is made to the public, such as a reward for information on a crime, it can be accepted by anyone who knows of the offer. Anyone who provides information without knowing of the reward offer is not entitled to receive that reward.

BonTon's CEO writes a letter offer to an MBA graduate offering her a position as director of credit at the store. However, the CEO never mailed the letter. There is no offer for the MBA to accept because it was never communicated. Even if the CEO's assistant found the letter on the CEO's desk and told the MBA of the letter, there is no power of acceptance unless and until the CEO communicates the offer or authorizes its communication to the MBA.

Irrevocable Offers: Options and Merchant's Firm Offers

Common Law: Options are offers related to a potential contract that are a separate contract for time. Offeree gives consideration (see the "Consideration" coverage), generally money, in exchange for the offeror's promise to keep the offer open (no revocation or lapse) for a specified period. Offeror must keep the offer open during the period specified for offeree who paid for it. The phrase "They have an option contract on that land parcel" is legally accurate because an option is a separate contract for time. This contract for time allows offeree's time to make a decision on whether to enter into the contract (eg, whether to enter into the contract to buy the land parcel).

A seller of land offers to sell a parcel of land to a school district. The school district is not sure whether it wants to buy this tract but does not want the seller to be able to withdraw the offer. The school district offers the seller $5,000 if the seller will keep the offer open for six months. If the seller agrees and accepts the payment, the school district has an option, and the seller must keep the offer open (not sell to someone else or revoke the offer) for six months.

Once a valid option contract is made:

- The offeror cannot withdraw the offer during the option period
- The offeree has the right to accept the offer during the option period but is not required to accept
- The offeree's rejection during the option period does not end the option. The offeree has the right to that offer during the full option period

UCC: UCC Article 2 has its own form of options called a merchant's firm offer. There are three requirements for a merchant's firm offer:

1. The offer must be made by a merchant. A merchant is a party who deals in goods of the kind being sold or someone who has knowledge or skill specific to the purchases or goods involved in the transaction (eg, Best Buy is a merchant of televisions; Home Depot is a merchant of lumber)
2. There is a signed writing or authenticated record
3. The offer states that it will be kept open or gives assurance that the offer will not be withdrawn for a stated period of time. The maximum length for a merchant's firm offer is three months. If, however, the parties need a longer period under the UCC, they can create a longer period with consideration (as under common law option requirements). If no time is given other than "This offer is to remain open," the offer is kept open for a reasonable time (an amount of time determined by the nature of the goods). Firm offers for produce that are left open-ended could be just days long, whereas firm offers for computers that are left open could be up to three months long

A valid firm offer is just like a common law option; it cannot be revoked, and it ends only upon the expiration of the stated time or three months, whichever is shorter.

Green, a retail seller of TVs, offers in a letter to purchase 500 Model X TVs from Vision, Inc. (a manufacturer of TVs), at the current Vision list price. In the letter, Green states that time is of the essence and that the offer is good for only 30 days from the date of the letter and will not be withdrawn during that time. A week later, Green decides to withdraw the offer and mails a revocation of the offer. Even if Vision receives the letter of revocation, Vision can accept Green's offer and bind Green to a contract during the 30-day period. Green's offer as a merchant, in a letter as a signed writing, gave Vision assurance that the offer would not be withdrawn for 30 days. Thus, Green made a firm offer, which was irrevocable for the 30-day period. Green cannot legally revoke the offer.

Irrevocable Offers under Common Law and UCC

Common Law	UCC
Options	**Merchant's Firm Offer**
Requires consideration	Does not require consideration if three months or less in length
Available to all types of contract parties	Must be made by a merchant
Can be oral	Must be in writing
	Must be signed by the merchant
Must have expiration date	Must state that it will be kept open
	Three-month maximum length unless consideration
Cannot be revoked	Cannot be revoked
Counteroffers during the time of the options do not end the option or underlying contract offer	Counteroffers during time of firm offer do not end the firm offer or the underlying contract offer

Offers: Termination of an Offer

Offers are terminated in a variety of ways—sometimes by the offerors, sometimes by various actions of the parties, and sometimes by operation of law.

Termination through Revocation

General Rule: An offer can be revoked at any time prior to acceptance. Revocations are effective when they are received, so they must be communicated. Revocation must be received prior to acceptance by the offeree.

Jane offers to sell Jim a textbook for $50. That evening, Jane mails Jim a letter of revocation. The next morning, Jim accepts Jane's offer. That afternoon, Jane's letter of revocation is received. Jane's revocation was not effective until received in the afternoon. Jim's acceptance in the morning binds Jane to the contract.

An ordinary offer that states that it will be kept open for a stated period can still be revoked at any time prior to acceptance.

Termination through Rejection

An offer is terminated, at any time prior to acceptance, by the offeree saying or writing something as simple as "Terms are not acceptable," "No thank you," or "Funds for purchase are not available at this time." An inquiry is not a rejection. Asking "Would you consider a lower price?" is not a rejection. Inquiries are not offers, and they are also not rejections. A rejection is effective when it is received.

Termination through Counteroffer

Common Law: A counteroffer made at any time prior to acceptance when there is a common law offer is a rejection. Under common law, an offeree makes a counteroffer when the response to the original offer contains changed terms or when the acceptance is conditional.

A counteroffer is a conditional acceptance. A conditional acceptance is a misnomer because it is never acceptance but rather a counteroffer under both common law and the UCC. Conditional acceptances involve the use of prepositional phrases, such as "but I must," "on the condition that," or "provided that." These terms in the offeree's response indicate conditional acceptance and, therefore, a counteroffer.

A counteroffer is not only a rejection of the original offer by the offeree but also a new offer from the original offeree to the original offeror.

David offers to sell a textbook to Doris for $60. Doris responds, "I will not buy your textbook for $60 but will offer to pay you $50 for it." Doris has made a counteroffer because Doris has made reaching an agreement conditional with the word "but," and thus David's offer for $60 is terminated. If Doris had responded, "I will buy your textbook for $60, but I must take delivery right now," Doris still made a conditional acceptance that is a counteroffer and a rejection even though David and Doris had agreed on the price.

Mirror Image Rule

Binding contract formed

Offer $150,000 = Acceptance $150,000

No binding contract formed

Offer $150,000 ≠ Counteroffer $145,000

Termination and UCC Rules on Differing Terms: The UCC does permit some modification of terms in acceptance. Those proposed modified terms do not result in a termination of the offer.

Termination of Offers through Lapse of Time

An offer automatically terminates at the end of a stated period for its existence, or, if no period is stated, it terminates after a reasonable period has lapsed.

Sally sends an offer to a real estate investor and offers to sell a house for $571,000 cash, stating that the offer will be kept open for 90 days. Sally sends another letter to the investor on Day 15 that states, "Never mind. I have decided to stay in my house and not sell." The offer is revoked. It is irrevocable only if the real estate investor pays for the 90-day period by creating an option contract.

Termination of Offers by Operation of Law

Certain events automatically terminate an offer by law.

1. **Death or Insanity of the Offeror or Offeree:** The exception is options. Because options are separate contracts to hold an offer open, they do survive the death of the offeror
2. **Destruction of the Specific Subject Matter of the Offer (General Rule):** If the specific object of the offer is destroyed prior to acceptance, the offer terminates (perishes) automatically with the destruction. If the items that are destroyed are fungible goods or commodities, the general rule does not apply because the offeror can easily obtain the same product to deliver to the offeree
3. **Illegality of the Subject Matter:** Sometimes the subject matter of the contract becomes illegal to sell. For example, in the United States, it is illegal to sell toys that contain lead paint. When lead paint was discovered on toys manufactured in China, all offers that toy companies had made for selling toys made in China were terminated by operation of law due to illegality

Name of Termination Method	Explanation
Revocation	• Offeror revokes the offer prior to acceptance
Rejection	• Offeree rejects the offer • Offeree makes a counteroffer • Offeree makes a conditional acceptance
Counteroffer	• Offeree proposes new or additional terms
Conditional acceptance	• Offeree makes a conditional acceptance
Lapse of time	• Time limit on offer expires • Too much time has passed (reasonable commercial standards)
Operation of law (automatic termination)	• Death of offeror or offeree • Insanity (declared incompetent in court) of offeror or offeree • Destruction of contract subject matter • Subject matter of contract becomes illegal

Acceptance

General Rules of Acceptance: There are two generally applicable rules of acceptance. The first is that the party accepting must have the power of acceptance. The party accepting must have had direct communication of the offer from the offeree. The second rule is that the offer must still be open; it has not been revoked.

Tyler sends an offer to Brooklyn, "I will sell you my iPhone for $550." Brooklyn is not interested in buying the phone but shows Megan the Tyler offer. Megan then emails Tyler, "I will buy your iPhone for $550." Megan cannot accept Tyler's offer because Megan does not have the power of acceptance. However, Tyler can accept what is an offer from Megan.

Acceptance of a Unilateral Offer: Acceptance takes place upon completion (total performance) of the act required by the offer. Generally, no notice to the offeror is required unless such is required by law or the offeror would have no means to know that the act has been completed.

If a housepainter paints a second home for someone who does not live there year-round, the owner would require notice because the owner would have no way of knowing that the painting was done.

Acceptance by Shipment of Goods: A seller can form a contract through action, that is, shipment of goods, as follows:

1. The seller ships conforming goods (goods that fulfill the buyer's order or offer) to a carrier
2. The seller can also accept an offer by promising to ship promptly
3. If the seller is shipping goods that are different from what the buyer ordered or offered to buy (ie, nonconforming goods), the seller must notify the buyer before shipping that the shipment is offered only as an accommodation. If the seller ships without advance notification of the nonconforming goods, then there is acceptance and an automatic breach at the same time

Acceptance of Bilateral Offers: Acceptance (promise) must be absolute, unequivocal, unconditional, and communicated to the offeror. Determination of acceptance is controlled by whether UCC Article 2 or common law applies.

Before answering any question on acceptance, be sure to determine whether the contract is governed by the **UCC** or **common law**. Then apply the appropriate rules for acceptance according to the source of law that governs the contract.

Acceptance under Common Law and UCC

Common Law	UCC
Communication of Acceptance	**Communication of Acceptance**
Offer must still be open	Offer must still be open
No conditional acceptance (counteroffer)	No conditional acceptance (counteroffer)
Mirror image rule: no contract if there are additional terms in the acceptance	Additional terms in acceptance: contract can still be formed if requirements are met

Common Law Acceptance and the Mirror Image Rule: An acceptance must be absolute, unequivocal, and unconditional, or it is treated as a counteroffer, not an acceptance. Under common law, which applies to contracts involving real property and services (eg, employment), any deviation in the terms of acceptance from those in the offer constitutes a counteroffer, not an acceptance.

Sally makes a written offer to buy a house for $571,000 from Bill. Bill reviews the offer and is fine with the price, closing date, and payment terms. However, Bill wants to take the storage shed in the backyard before the house closes. Bill writes back, "Will sell on your terms. Storage shed is not included." The storage shed may seem like an immaterial and negotiable item, but Bill has made a counteroffer and rejection because under the mirror image rule under common law, the acceptance contains different terms.

UCC Acceptance with Additional Terms: Under the UCC, a definite expression of acceptance followed by additional terms may or may not form a contract with the additional terms. For both merchants and nonmerchants, a definite expression of acceptance (not conditional acceptance) that does not change any terms results in a contract.

Whether the terms become a part of the contract depends on whether:

- The parties are merchants,
- The terms are material,
- The offer is limited, and
- The offeror objects upon receiving the additional terms.

There are UCC rules on what constitutes acceptance that are different when merchants and nonmerchants are involved in the formation process. As between a merchant and a nonmerchant, if there is a definite statement of acceptance (not conditional acceptance) followed by some additional terms, a contract is formed, but without the additional terms.

If there is a merchant-to-merchant formation (ie, for two merchants), if there is a definite statement of acceptance (not conditional acceptance) followed by additional terms, there is a contract with the additional terms unless:

- The additional terms are material, such as a waiver of warranties
- The offer specifically states, "This offer is limited to these terms." In this situation, a contract is formed, but without the additional terms in the acceptance
- The offeror objects within a reasonable time frame after receiving the acceptance to the additional terms

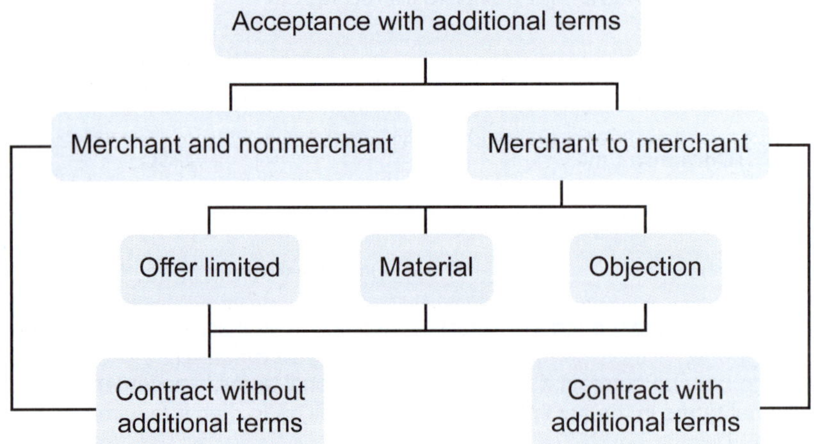

A seller offers to sell to the buyer 5,000 pounds of a "specific type" of chicken at 50 cents per pound. The buyer responds, "Accept your offer for 5,000 pounds (as certified by a public scale weight certificate) of a specific type of chicken at 50 cents per pound." Since this is a sale of goods (chicken) and the buyer gave a definite expression of acceptance ("Accept") without conditioning acceptance on the modification, a contract is formed, even though the buyer's acceptance with additional terms (public scale weight certificate) modified the terms of the seller's offer.

Since both parties are obviously merchants, the contract is formed on the offeree's (buyer's) terms unless the seller objects with notice to the buyer within a reasonable time frame. If the seller does object, the contract is formed on the seller's terms (delivery without a required public scale weight certificate).

Steib is a merchant of ribbon. Bold offers, "Will buy 50 spools of grosgrain blue ribbon for $4.39 per spool." Steib responds, "Will send ribbon. No warranty on color." The two have a contract without the warranty waiver because a warranty waiver is a material term.

Same parties, but Bold adds, "This offer is limited to these terms." Steib responds, "Will send ribbon. Terms are 2/10 net 30." The two have a contract for the ribbon without those payment terms because despite the fact that these types of terms are immaterial, Bold changed the terms of the offer that was expressly limited, and that requirement prohibits all terms proposed by the offeree—whether material or immaterial.

If the examples were changed and Bold and Steib were nonmerchants, then there would be a contract for the ribbon without the additional terms in both examples.

Timing of Acceptances: One of the critical aspects of forming a contract is determining when a contract is formed. The mailbox rule is the timing rule for determining when an acceptance takes effect and a contract is formed. The mailbox rule is as follows:

If the acceptance is sent by an authorized means (a proper means of acceptance), the acceptance is effective; that is, a contract is formed when the offeree delivers the acceptance to the authorized medium—even if it is never received by the offeror. **The mailbox rule of acceptances** provides that when there is a proper (authorized) method of acceptance used, the acceptance is effective when it is sent.

An authorized means is the same or a faster method of communication used by the offeror if no method of acceptance is specified in the offer.

If a means of acceptance is specified in the offer, the only authorized means is that specified means. If the offeree uses the specified means put in the offer, they accept when it is sent, regardless of any delays or nondelivery that happen after that.

If the offeree does not use the expressly stated means of acceptance in the offer to communicate acceptance, then the offeree has made a counteroffer and rejection because the offeree has violated the terms of the offer and the mirror image rule.

If the offer has no authorized (specified or stipulated) means and the offeree sends acceptance by an unauthorized means, such as using a slower method of communication than that used by the offeror, then the acceptance is effective only when received by the offeror.

The mailbox timing rule applies only to acceptance communication and not to offers, counteroffers, rejections, or revocations. Offers, counteroffers, rejections, and revocations are effective only when actually received.

Consideration

Consideration is a requirement for formation of a contract. Consideration is something of value given by one party to the contract to the other party. Consideration is required in contract formation because each party to a contract giving something of value is what distinguishes contracts from gifts. A promise to make a gift is not enforceable by law; a contract promise can be enforced.

Detriment and Benefit

Detriment (Tangible Property, Money, and Services): Each party to a contract must give up something of value for consideration to be present. Generally, the parties to contracts have detriment such as money, goods, services, or real property. Each party promises to give up something physical in exchange for something else physical. By giving up something, they are each doing something that they are free not to do. If a party does not give anything up, there is no detriment. Without that detriment, the parties are missing an element required for formation. They are missing the element of consideration; ergo, there is no contract.

Devon purchases a sofa from Maximum Interiors, LLC, for $850. Devon's detriment is the $850. Maximum's detriment is the sofa.

Starlight, Inc., engages Roswell Financial Advisors to prepare its registration statement for selling shares for its IPO for a fee of $500,000. Starlight's detriment is the $500,000. Roswell's detriment is the work and time required to prepare the registration statement.

Detriment (Rights): Legal detriment also includes giving up rights or not doing what you are free to do. You don't have to settle a lawsuit, but if you do settle it, giving up the right to have the case fully litigated is legal detriment for purposes of meeting the requirement of consideration. Both sides in such a settlement have legal detriment because both are giving up their right to go to court and have a court determine if there is liability, as well as how much that liability should be.

Jake is thinking of suing Vanessa because Jake believes Vanessa was negligent in preparing Jake's tax return. Jake and Vanessa reach a settlement agreement. Jake will not file suit against Vanessa, and Vanessa will pay the taxes Jake owes along with interest and penalties. There is legal detriment on both sides of this settlement contract. Jake is giving up the right to have a court determine that the damages are much greater than what Vanessa is offering to pay. Vanessa is giving up the right to have a court find that she was not negligent or that the damages are less than what Vanessa has offered to pay Jake.

Benefit: Each party must also have a benefit under a contract for consideration to be present. The legal benefit of one party to a contract is the legal detriment to the other party. Each party to a contract is a promiser of detriment and a promisee of benefit. Valid consideration for a contract exists when both sides have a benefit and a detriment.

Benefit Induces the Detriment: Consideration requires a bargained-for exchange. The reason a store is willing to turn over a refrigerator to a buyer is because the buyer is willing to pay for the refrigerator. The reason the buyer gives up the money (detriment) for the refrigerator is because the store will turn over the refrigerator to the buyer. Their mutual promises are induced by the benefit and detriment exchanged under the terms of their sale contract. Exchange of the detriment and benefit is called a bargained-for exchange.

Promisor
This promisor gives detriment that this promisee receives as a benefit
Promisee

Promisee
This promisor gives detriment that this promisee receives as a benefit
Promisor

Lisa does not have to buy a car, but if Lisa contracts to buy a car for $7,000, Lisa's detriment is giving up the money. Trevor does not have to sell a car, but if Trevor elects to sell a car to Lisa, Trevor has detriment because Trevor is doing what Trevor is free not to do. Lisa gives a detriment of $7,000 as promiser that Trevor receives as a benefit as promisee. Trevor gives the detriment of a car as a promiser, and Lisa receives the car as a benefit as promisee.

What Is Not Consideration

There are certain things that parties may try to use as consideration for forming a contract and that may seem to be consideration, but they are lacking the requirements of benefit and detriment on one or both sides.

Past or preexisting detriment is not consideration. Agreeing to be paid for something you have already done is not sufficient detriment for formation of a contract.

A company has a suggestion box to encourage employees to offer ideas that will benefit the company. Over the years, the company has received only a handful of useful suggestions, including one that suggested it start paying for useful suggestions instead of expecting them for free.

The board of directors likes this idea and offers to pay 10% of the savings that come from any implemented suggestion to the employee who made the suggestion.

The company is not required to pay those employees who have offered suggestions in the past that were implemented. They had contributed their ideas before the unilateral offer for a contract was made.

Promises to Pay Additional Consideration for an Existing Contractual Obligation: Parties to existing contracts cannot receive additional payment (detriment from the paying party) for what they were already obligated to perform under those contracts. In a bargained-for exchange, the benefit and the detriment must match. An agreement to do what you were obligated to do under an existing contract is not a contract because it lacks benefit and detriment on both sides.

Ace Painting signs a contract with a homeowner on November 1 to paint the owner's house by December 1 for $1,000. After signing the contract, Ace decides that the time estimates it gave the homeowner are unrealistic. Ace tells the homeowner that the job cannot be completed by December 1 unless Ace hires more painters. Ace tells the homeowner that either the job cannot be completed as promised or the homeowner needs to pay an additional $300 for a December 1 completion date because of Ace's recalculation of work time and resulting additional costs.

The homeowner agrees to pay $1,300, and Ace and the homeowner sign the contract on November 4. Ace finishes the job by December 1 with the help of the additional painters. Ace and the homeowner had offer and acceptance on their second contract, but the contract lacked the third part of formation: consideration. Ace cannot get more money for what it was already obligated to do for $1,000. The homeowner is legally obligated to pay Ace only $1,000.

The additional $300 demanded by Ace was not supported by any consideration. There was additional detriment on the homeowner's part—paying the extra $300. But there was no additional detriment on Ace's part. Ace was just doing what it was legally obligated to do under an existing and legally enforceable contract. Ace had a preexisting obligation to perform under a contract for $1,000.

Existing Duties with Third Parties: The preexisting duty rule also applies to legal obligations that a contracting party has from contracts with third parties or under the law. For example, a parent cannot enforce a contract with a child under the age of 18 to pay for room and board. All parents have an existing legal obligation to provide food and shelter for their children.

Police officers cannot claim a reward for catching criminals since their employment as police officers compensates them for their obligation through law and their oath's obligation to make their best efforts to carry out the duties of investigation, arrest, and testifying at trials. A parent cannot charge their minor child for room and board since the law mandates they provide it.

Legal Adequacy of the Amount of Consideration: Courts do not generally examine the amount of consideration as long as it is actually exchanged. There can be differences in values on each side because the value of the promises is not the key—what is controlling is whether the value promised is legally sufficient so as not to be considered a gift. This element distinguishes gifts from contracts.

Keystone Industries owns a parcel of land next to Kennesaw Community College. Keystone Industries wishes to support Kennesaw and signs an option agreement with Kennesaw for Kennesaw to have the right to purchase the land for six months as it determines if it can obtain the funding for the purchase. The consideration for the option is $1.00. Kennesaw does not pay the $1.00 called for under the option. A month later, while Kennesaw is exploring financing opportunities, Keystone receives an offer from a company to purchase the land for $11 million. Keystone accepts the offer and sells the land to the company. Kennesaw files suit to enforce its rights under the option and stops the transfer of the land to the company. The option contract between Kennesaw and Keystone was not a contract. There was offer and acceptance, but the failure to pay the consideration meant no contract was formed. Courts require actual exchange of the consideration.

Modifications of Contracts and Consideration

Common Law Contract Modifications: Parties to an existing contract for common law subject matter are always free to change the terms of that contract through a modification, as long as there is consideration for those changes (ie, new detriment).

J. Simmons, LLC, contracts to do an audit for Grace Steel Buildings for $150,000. J. Simmons cannot simply come back and say, "We really underestimated the work. We will need an additional $25,000." J. Simmons has no new detriment. However, if J. Simmons came back to Grace and said, "We think we are going to need to inspect another factory as part of this audit because of some serious issues we found at several other factories," that would be something that is required (in their professional opinion) that was not in the original scope. If Grace agrees to expanding the scope, there is new detriment, and J. Simmons could be paid the $25,000 for it because of an additional factory visit. Grace has the benefit of an audit that has covered all serious issues.

Contract Modifications under the UCC: The requirements for consideration under the UCC vary only slightly from common law. One of those areas is in contract modifications.

- Under the UCC, the parties are permitted to, in good faith, modify their contracts even without additional consideration (detriment) on both sides
- The parties are not required to agree to a modification, but if they do agree and the subject matter of the contract is under the UCC, then the modification is enforceable despite the lack of consideration
- The modification must also be in good faith. That is, one side cannot threaten the other side to stop performing on the contract unless there is a modification
- No one *must* agree to modify an existing contract. However, if they do agree to a modification under the UCC, the modification is enforceable despite the lack of new consideration

ABC Gas, Inc., has a requirements contract to furnish Green Industries with all the gas it needs to run its plants for 10 years at 50 cents per cubic foot of gas. Exploration and transportation costs will triple in the next three years, and ABC is starting to lose money on the contract. The current market price is 80 cents per cubic foot. ABC and Green agree in writing to raise the price of the gas supplied to Green to 60 cents per cubic foot for the rest of the term of the contract. Even though no consideration is given by ABC for the increase in price, the 60-cent price is now binding for both parties. Green is not required to agree to the price increase, but if Green does agree, the contract is enforceable despite no new detriment on the part of ABC.

Contract Modifications—Rescission and New Contracts: Rescission is the mutual rejection by both parties to a contract of their existing contract and then making a new one. The consideration consists of both sides giving up their rights under the original agreement in exchange for a new one. They are doing what they do not have to do by waiving those original contract rights. There is detriment on both sides—giving up the right to enforce the original contract.

Able contracts to build Westbrook a home for $950,000 according to a set of specific building plans. Westbrook then learns from the architect that the design may present drainage problems given the nature of the lot on which it will be built. The architect will redesign the home. The building plans will be different from the plans Able used in pricing the construction costs. Able and Westbrook agree to cancel the contract and negotiate a new one based on the modified design and building plans. Both Able and Westbrook have given up their rights to litigate the original contract. Their duties under that contract are discharged, and they are free to negotiate a new contact.

Contract Modifications—Accord and Satisfaction: An accord is an agreement to waive legal rights and release another party from legal obligations. Satisfaction is the actual payment of the amounts agreed to in the accord. The detriment on both sides of an accord is both parties agreeing to do something they are not legally required to do (settle a claim) or not doing what they could legally do (bring a lawsuit to recover on their rights). Whether an accord and satisfaction is valid depends on the nature of the underlying contract—whether the parties have liquidated or unliquidated obligations.

- **Liquidated Debts and Accord and Satisfaction:** A liquidated debt is one in which the amount owed is clear to both parties

Charlie owes Fred $5,000, plus 5% interest, and the amount is to be paid in monthly payments over a two-year period. Charlie and Fred have a contract for a liquidated debt. Charlie and Fred cannot create a valid accord because the amount due is fixed and certain. Charlie could not write "Payment in full" on his 20th monthly check and have the debt discharged. Charlie does not have detriment; only Fred would, as Fred would lose four payments.

The parties to a liquidated debt can always agree to an early payoff, and such an early payoff agreement is valid if there is detriment on both sides. If the debtor owes the creditor $5,000 on May 1 and the debtor offers to pay the creditor $4,900 on March 1, there is consideration because the creditor gets the money early and the debtor gets to pay less in exchange for paying early. There is a bargained-for exchange with both sides receiving benefit and giving detriment.

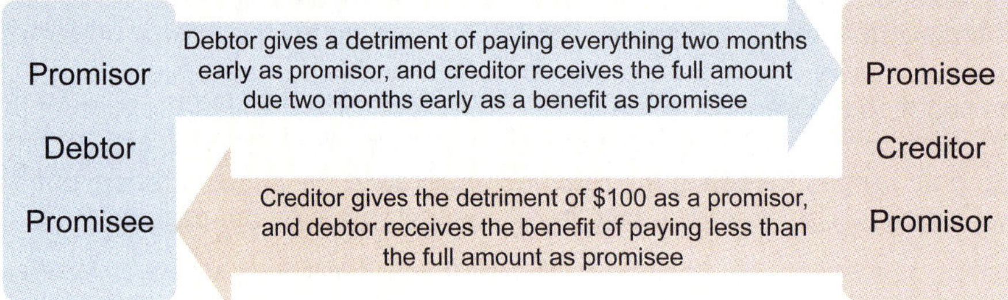

- **Unliquidated Debts and Accord and Satisfaction:** An unliquidated debt is one in which the parties acknowledge that money is due and owed, but they disagree on the amount. An agreement (accord) between the two parties on an amount and then payment of that amount is an accord and satisfaction because both are giving up their right to have the amount due determined by a court. The phrase "Payment in full" placed on a check for an unliquidated debt would discharge the debt.

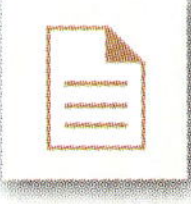

A client agrees to pay $2,000 to a financial planner for the development of a complete financial plan. The planner prepares a report which the client considers to be far less detailed and complete than was reasonable to expect and refuses to pay the planner, claiming that the financial planner didn't perform the work promised.

The planner agrees to reduce the fee to $1,000 if the client agrees no further services are required from the planner. This second agreement (accord) is a valid modification, even though the client is receiving a fee reduction, since it settles a dispute over the level of services required of the planner.

Sam negligently rear-ends John's car. Sam, in a signed writing, promises to pay John $1,000 if John will release Sam from any further property liability due to the accident. This accepted release by John is binding and bars John from any further recovery. Sam is giving up the right to have a court determine a level of liability, and John is giving up the right to have the court possibly determine damages, which may be greater than $1,000.

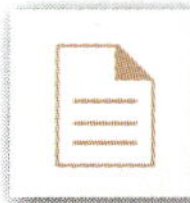

Jim borrows $100 from Joan, to be paid back without interest. Jim sends Joan a check clearly marked as "payment in full" for $90. Such an action would not serve to discharge the debt. Jim owes Joan $100, the debt is liquidated, and Joan can still legally pursue recovery of $10 from Jim.

Jim contracts to purchase from Joan a new file cabinet for $250. Upon delivery, Jim discovers that the cabinet is scratched. Jim tenders to Joan a check clearly marked "payment in full" for $200. Joan has no idea as to the cost of damage due to the scratches. Joan can avoid the issue and return the check (no accord), but if Joan cashes it (since reasonable persons could disagree as to the cost of damage), the purported debt is canceled because their agreement on what to do about the defective file cabinet (the scratch) is open for debate. It could cost $50 to fix it or $10 or something greater. The amount due is not liquidated (even though the original purchase price was) because they are now dealing with goods not delivered as promised. Joan does not have to accept the $200, but once Joan accepts (cashes the check), Jim's obligation is satisfied.

Exceptions to the Consideration Requirement

UCC Merchant's Firm Offer: While common law options require consideration, merchant's firm offers, as long as they meet the requirements (writing or record, by a merchant, states that it will be kept open), are valid even though there is no consideration.

Promissory Estoppel: A promise made by one party induces another party to rely on that promise. The result is that the party relying on the promise of another makes material financial and personal changes because of that promise. The party that made the promise is estopped from refusing to honor that promise based on a claim of no valid consideration.

Jim pledges (promises) $50,000 to the church for purposes of adding a child care room to the church. In reliance (induces church to change its position) thereon, the church contracts for the addition (changes substantially their position). In the interest of justice, the church can hold Jim to the pledge (sometimes referred to as charitable subscriptions) even though the pledge lacked consideration. Jim had the detriment of the pledge and the money, but the church had only benefit and no detriment. This exception provides protection for charities that rely on pledges of donations.

Promises Barred by the Statute of Limitations: The statute of limitations is the time the law imposes by statute for bringing a suit to enforce legal rights. For example, the general statute of limitations under the UCC is four years. Parties to a contract have four years from the time the contract is formed or from the time of the breach (depending on the reason for the suit) to enforce their rights. Once that time allowed under the statute passes, the contract is unenforceable. If, however, the party who owed money on that contract agrees to pay the amount due, the renewed promise to pay is enforceable because the party is agreeing to do something not required by law since the statute of limitations discharged the debt. Although the detriment is one-sided, these promise-to-pay agreements executed after the statute of limitations is expired are enforceable.

Promises to Pay Debts Discharged in Bankruptcy: A debtor need not assume responsibility for debts that could be discharged in bankruptcy, but if those debts are exempted from discharge prior to the discharge order, their payment can be enforced despite no new detriment on the part of the creditors who will be paid a discharged debt. Court approval is required.

The Statute of Frauds and the Writing or Record Requirement

There are some types of contracts that are not enforceable unless they are evidenced by a writing or record. For these types of contracts, formation of a valid contract does not occur until there is a writing or record. There could be offer, acceptance, and consideration, but if the Statute of Frauds applies to the subject matter of the contract and there is no writing or record, neither party to the agreement can enforce its provisions.

Contracts That Require a Writing or Record—Promise to Pay the Debt of Another: A contract that promises to pay the debt of another must be in writing under the Statute of Frauds. A party who guarantees a loan makes a promise to pay the debt of another. A surety or guarantor who agrees to pay a debt or complete a contract obligation if the primary party fails to do so is paying the debt of another. The Statute of Frauds does not apply to original promises, such as when someone takes out a personal loan.

Able is a commission agent selling Peter's products. Peter has a rule that agents sell only to customers who can pay cash. Able has determined that there are more commissions to be earned by selling to customers on credit. Able orally contracts with Peter, allowing Able to sell to customers on credit, and if any customer does not pay when due, Able agrees to pay Peter. Some customers who were sold Peter's products on credit fail to pay Peter. Peter demands that Able pay.

Does the Able-Peter contract allowing Able to sell on credit fall under the Statute of Frauds?

Yes. It is a contract (formed by words) between a guarantor (Able) and a creditor (Peter) creating a secondary debt obligation. Able is liable only if the customer, the principal debtor, fails to pay. In order to enforce the guaranty by Able, Peter must have a written agreement (record) signed by Able.

Contracts That Require a Writing or Record—Interests in Real Property: The general rule under the Statute of Frauds for interest in real property is that contracts involving an interest in real property, to be enforceable, must be evidenced by a writing or record and include:

- Real property purchase contracts
- Leases of real property (exceptions in most states apply to leases less than one year in length)
- Real property mortgages
- Easements
- Creation of any other real property interests
- Real estate broker contracts

Exception to Writing Requirement for Real Property Rule: There is a partial performance exception to the Statute of Frauds for contracts for real property interests. That exception applies when the parties have behaved in such a way and provided evidence beyond their own words that there was some kind of contractual relationship between them. The partial performance exception requires the following:

- Payment of some part or all of the purchase price,
- A buyer in possession of the land by living there (residential) or proceeding to develop it (commercial land), *and/or*
- The buyer has made valuable improvements. In some situations, the possession is simply whatever possession is necessary for making the improvements. Courts are looking for some proof beyond one person's word against another's

Mary orally contracts to purchase Jim's house and lot. Mary sends Jim a check for 5% of the purchase price, which Jim cashes. The closing (passage of deed and payment) will not take place for two months. Mary's lease has expired, and Mary and Jim agree that Mary can move into the house and pay Jim a rental payment. Mary moves into the house, plants a number of trees, and adds a deck to the back porch. Just before closing, Jim is offered $20,000 more than Mary's purchase price. Jim tenders return of Mary's down payment and claims the oral contract is unenforceable.

Does this contract fall under the Statute of Frauds?

Yes. A purchase of real property contract is an interest in real property.

Can Jim successfully claim that the oral contract is unenforceable under the Statute of Frauds?

No. The partial performance rule applies (in all states) because there was a payment, possession, and valuable improvements, which will not allow Jim to use the Statute of Frauds as a defense to the contract.

What if only the payment had been made (no possession or valuable improvement)?

This exception requires more than just payment to apply. Without more than payment, the exception does not apply.

Contracts That Require a Writing or Record—Contracts That Cannot Be Performed within One Year of Formation: Any contract that is objectively impossible to perform within one year from the date of contract formation (date of acceptance) without breaching the terms must be in writing or have written evidence of it to be enforceable. If the contract *could* be performed within one year, it need not be in writing to be enforceable. For example, ABC orally agrees to do an internal controls audit for XYZ Company. ABC does not know how long the audit will take. The oral agreement is valid because the audit could be done in less than a year. However, if ABC accepts a three-year engagement to do internal control audits each year, that contract must be in writing to be enforceable.

The one-year mark is measured from the date of acceptance; the time frame is not just the period of performance. For example, suppose Helen agrees to perform a nine-month consulting contract with Framery, Inc., to run from July 1, Year 3, until March 31, Year 4. Helen agrees to do so on February 1, Year 3. While the contract term is less than a year, Helen's acceptance is longer than a year out from completed performance, so the agreement must be in writing.

Contracts That Require a Writing or Record—UCC Contracts for the Sale of Goods and UCC Statute of Frauds: Any contract for the sale of goods priced at $500 or more must be in writing or record (memorandum or electronic communication such as email).

Do not mix together the provisions of the Statute of Frauds. The **UCC Statute of Frauds** applies only to contracts for the sale of goods. So, a contract for the purchase of an option in real estate for $450 must be in writing because it is a real property interest. But a contract for the sale of a refrigerator for $450 need not be in writing because it is covered by the UCC. The amount of the purchase price is irrelevant for real property contracts, which are covered under **common law Statute of Frauds** provisions. Under the UCC, the amount involved determines whether the contract must be in writing.

Exceptions to the UCC General Statute of Frauds Rule

Merchant's Confirmation Memorandum—between Merchants (Only): If two merchants have an oral agreement that must be in writing under the UCC Statute of Frauds, that writing requirement is met through a process referred to as a merchant's confirmation memorandum.

If one merchant sends the other merchant a written confirmation, and the other, after receipt, does not object in writing within 10 days, the oral contract is enforceable by either party, even though only one party actually signed the memorandum. The memorandum can be sent via letter, email, or fax.

ABC is an auto parts store. ABC orders by phone $10,000 worth of parts from Auto Warehouse. Auto Warehouse immediately sends ABC a fax covering the agreement made on the telephone. ABC receives the fax and reads it. Twelve days later, ABC learns it can buy all of the parts it ordered from another parts warehouse company for $9,500. ABC calls Auto Warehouse and tells Auto Warehouse not to ship the parts because it is claiming the Statute of Frauds as a defense. ABC and Auto Warehouse have an enforceable contract, even though it is an oral contract, for the sale of goods priced at $500 or more because both parties are merchants and Auto Warehouse sent by fax a written confirmation of the oral contract, which ABC read. Since ABC did not object to the contents of the written confirmation within 10 days of receipt, the oral contract is fully enforceable by Auto Warehouse. A merchant's confirmation memorandum that is not objected to becomes an enforceable contract, despite a lack of a written signature by one party.

Performance of the Contract Has Already Occurred: The UCC will enforce oral agreements that have already been performed. There may not be a written contract, but if the seller has already shipped goods and the buyer has accepted them, the buyer cannot then claim the Statute of Frauds applies. Likewise, if the seller has already accepted payment, then the buyer of the goods is owed the goods, and the seller cannot claim the Statute of Frauds as a defense. In these situations, the courts will enforce the contract for what has already been performed through acceptance of payment or goods.

Seller and Buyer have an oral agreement for the sale of 500 pounds of T-bone steaks at a price of $7.89 per pound. Seller sends Buyer 200 pounds of T-bone steaks, and Buyer resells the steaks. Buyer is liable for that amount of their agreement (200 × $7.89), but courts will not enforce the remainder of their alleged oral agreement. Likewise, if Buyer sends Seller a check for 200 pounds of T-bone steaks (200 × $7.89) and S cashes the check, S must deliver 200 pounds of T-bone steaks, but the remaining 300 pounds under their alleged oral agreement cannot be enforced.

Specially Manufactured Goods: Goods that a seller cannot resell in the ordinary course of the seller's business are known as custom or special-ordered goods. An oral contract for custom or special-ordered goods is enforceable if the seller has substantially begun performance or has made an irrevocable commitment to do so before the buyer cancels the order claiming the Statute of Frauds. An order for a custom-made suit would be an example.

Admission under Oath: Any admission under oath (deposition, testimony, or any other sworn document) that an oral contract was made removes the Statute of Frauds as a defense to formation.

Green, owner of ABC Television, orally offers to sell Red a TV for $600. Later, Red calls Green and accepts Green's offer. Later still, Red decides not to buy the TV. Because Red has not signed a written contract for the sale of goods priced at $500 or more and Red has neither taken possession of nor made a payment for the TV, Red can claim the Statute of Frauds, and Green cannot enforce the oral contract against Red.

Exceptions to Statute of Frauds:
Writing Requirement for Sale of Goods and Contracts (SPAM)

- **S**pecifically manufactured goods at buyer's request
- **P**erformance of contract already occurred
- **A**dmitted in court by defendant
- **M**erchant does not object to written confirmation within 10 days

Contracts That Require a Writing or Record: Standards for the Writing or Record

A record is tangible evidence of the existence of an oral contract. If the record meets all the standards and includes the necessary information, the requirements of the Statute of Frauds are met.

Signature (authentication in electronic records) of the party to be held liable on the oral contract is normally required.

Exception: Merchant's confirmation memorandum allows one party's signature to bind both parties (both are merchants) to the agreement.

Nature of the Record: A writing/record need not be in one document or formal in nature; emails, letters, and faxes can be grouped together to establish the written/record requirement for a valid contract. With the passage of the E-Sign Act, all states are required to accept electronic and fax communications as evidence of a written agreement.

The writing requirement is now referred to as a "record" because a writing includes the e-sign forms of communication. When these materials use the term "writing" or "written agreement," they are including "record," which can be electronic, as in an email, an electronic click agreement, a faxed document, or a PDF agreement.

Effect of the Statute of Frauds

The Statute of Frauds does not prevent parties with oral agreements from honoring them. There is nothing illegal about a contract that should be in writing but is not. Oral contracts are not void because they are not in writing. They are unenforceable by the courts—they cannot be civilly litigated.

Also, if the parties have behaved as if there is an underlying contract, then the courts will not allow unjust enrichment. In other words, an executory contract that is oral and required to be in writing cannot be enforced. However, if a contract is executed or partially executed, the courts will not punish the parties for falling short of the Statute of Frauds and will require payment, for example, for work already performed. The Statute of Frauds is not used to punish those who perform under an oral contract. However, for contracts that are executory, the Statute of Frauds prevents the use of courts to require performance of oral agreements that should have been in writing.

If ABC Corporation hired Bryce to complete a 14-month consulting contract for $140,000 in salary and a $20,000 bonus for on-time completion, the contract should be in writing. However, if Bryce completed the consulting agreement, ABC still would owe the salary and the bonus because the contract would be fully executed as of that time.

Interpreting Written Contracts: Parol Evidence Rule and Its Requirements and Effect

Application of the Parol Evidence Rule: Under the parol evidence rule, a fully integrated contract (one that is complete, unambiguous, and without defenses in formation) cannot be contradicted, varied, or altered by evidence of the parties' prior negotiations, prior agreements, or contemporaneous oral agreements. Once the parties reduce their agreement to a record, they are bound by those terms and cannot use the courts to rewrite their agreement with their contemporaneous oral agreements.

Without this rule, courts would always be dealing with who said what and when and whether what they said should be part of the contract. Remember the parol evidence rule by thinking, "If what you wanted is not in the contract but promised as an aside in negotiations or as you were signing the contract, you can't bring that up later and expect to get it." Sometimes parol evidence is permitted by courts, and the parties can introduce evidence about their contract during contract disputes.

Ambiguous Terms: If the record of a contract has ambiguities, it is not fully integrated, and parol evidence can be introduced only to clear up the ambiguity.

Obvious Clerical or Typographical Error: In reducing an oral contract to a writing or record, parol evidence can be used for obvious typos and clerical errors because, again, it is not fully integrated.

Subsequent Modification: If the parties to a contract later agree to modify their contract, evidence of the modification is admissible. If the modification is required to be in writing, the parties will need that record as proof of the modification. There must be additional consideration if common law applies.

Incomplete Contracts: Parol evidence can be admitted to "fill in" the gaps because an incomplete contract is not a fully integrated contract.

Contract Defenses: The parol evidence rule does not prohibit the introduction of evidence that shows a defense to formation, such as fraud or duress.

A CPA was conducting an audit of ABC, Inc. When reviewing the invoices issued by ABC, the CPA noticed that the invoice charged XYZ $600. However, the signed contract reflected a price of $500 per unit. When this was shown to ABC's CFO, the CFO said that before the contract was signed, ABC and XYZ orally agreed that the price should be $600. If ABC and XYZ had a legal dispute over the pricing issue in the contract, ABC would be prohibited from testifying in court about the pre-signing discussion to change the price to $600.

While signing a pest control service agreement, Gwyneth noticed that the contract provided for a $300 fee for early cancellation. Gwyneth objected to the fee because the sales representative for Zero-Pest had told her she could cancel at any time. The sales representative told Gwyneth that the $300 cancellation fee applied only to commercial customers, not residential. Gwyneth signed and then terminated the pest control contract six months later. Zero-Pest demanded a $300 cancellation fee from Gwyneth. Gwyneth could use misrepresentation as a defense to the contract, and parol evidence about the sales representative's representations would be admissible evidence.

Parol Evidence Rule

- When a written contract exists, the parol evidence rule bars the admission of the following evidence from contract litigation between the parties to the contract:
  - Prior written or oral contracts on the same subject
  - Concurrent (contemporaneous) oral contracts or promises
- The rule doesn't bar (still admissible):
  - Subsequent oral modifications
  - Incomplete contracts
  - Evidence to prove defenses to contract formation
  - Ambiguities in written contract

Defenses to Formation

Some actions during the formation stage of a contract result in the creation of defenses to formation of a valid contract. Offer, acceptance, and consideration must occur in a forthright atmosphere in which the parties agreed on a contract based on full and accurate information. If that voluntary and open atmosphere did not exist, there is a defense to the formation.

The following are types of defenses that can be used to invalidate the formation of a contract (under both the UCC and common law):

- Capacity
- Mistake
- Fraud (also called fraud in the inducement) or misrepresentation
- Duress
- Undue influence
- Illegality

Capacity Required for Formation of a Contract

Each party must be of legal age, and each party must have the mental capacity to enter into a contract. Mental capacity includes being free from a level of intoxication that results in mental incapacity.

Age Capacity Requirement (Minors): In most states and for most contracts, a minor is any person under the age of 18. A minor is not prohibited by law from entering into contracts, except for contracts that are illegal (eg, contracts for liquor or cigarettes). However, the law does provide protections for minors who do enter into contracts based on the public policy of protection for those who may not have developed the judgment or experience to enter into fairly negotiated contracts. Because of this public policy reason, the contracts of minors are voidable at their option.

- **Right to Disaffirm:** Minors are given the right to disaffirm the contract and avoid liability at any time before they reach the age of majority (18) and for a reasonable time thereafter. The contract is voidable at the minor's option. When a contract is voidable, it can be set aside by one of the parties by choice. If the minor wants to honor the contract, the minor can do so—the contract is not void because a minor is involved. The contract may or may not be performed—at the minor's option
- **How a Minor Disaffirms:** If a minor wishes to avoid liability (disaffirm), the minor must show intent to do so and must return any consideration derived from the contract that the minor still possesses or controls

- **Inability to Return Consideration:** The minor does not lose the right to disaffirm despite an inability to return the consideration given under the contract. If the minor does not possess or control the consideration, the minor still has the right to disaffirm the contract. The minor need only return what consideration remains. If all a minor has left of a purchased car is a hubcap, the minor can return the hubcap and be entitled to recoup any money paid to the seller of the car. Minors are entitled to receive back any consideration they have paid and cannot be held liable under the contract
- **Exceptions to the Minor's Right to Disaffirm—Necessities:**
  - Necessities are contracts for food, clothing, and shelter
  - Minors have limited liability for contracts for such necessities if they are under the care of a parent or guardian
  - The minor may disaffirm the contract, but the minor is still liable for the reasonable value of the goods used. Note: The contract remains voidable because of the lack of capacity, but courts allow recovery by the seller on the basis of reasonable value, not necessarily the negotiated contract price
- **Exceptions to the Minor's Right to Disaffirm—Ratification:** Any minor's contract that is ratified by the minor after reaching the age of majority (now an adult) results in the minor being fully liable
  - **Express Ratification:** This type of ratification occurs when the minor notifies the other party of the intent to honor the contract after reaching the age of majority
  - **Implied Ratification:** The minor continues to perform on the contract beyond reaching the age of majority and what would be a reasonable time for disaffirming

Able is a 17-year-old minor working his way through college (his parents are deceased). He leases an apartment from Sue for one year with rental payments of $400 per month. Able makes five payments, turns 18, and makes one more payment before Able and Sue have a dispute, followed by Able turning the apartment back over to Sue upon moving. What are the possible claims and results of liability for Able?

If Able can disaffirm (within a reasonable time after turning 18), Able (by majority rule) is entitled to the return of all six payments made to Sue and has no further liability (remaining six months' rent).

If a court determines that this is a contract for a necessity, Sue can keep the six payments made (reasonable value based on use) but cannot collect the remaining six months' rent.

Mental Capacity Requirement

Mentally Incompetent Persons—General Rule: Contracts made by a mentally incompetent person, but before a court has adjudged that person incompetent, are voidable by the person or legal guardian (the same as with a minor) during the period of incompetency and for a reasonable time after regaining competency. To avoid liability, however, the mentally incompetent party must be able to return the consideration received under the contract.

If the contract is made after the person has been adjudged incompetent by the court, the contract is void (the contract cannot be enforced by either side). The contracts of those who have been declared by a court to be incompetent are void. A person who is declared incompetent can make a valid contract only if the contract is entered into by the incompetent's legal guardian, who is appointed at the declaration of incompetency. The principles of necessity and ratification for voidable contracts after the contracting party regains competency are the same as for a minor.

Intoxicated Persons and Capacity—General Rule: Any person who becomes intoxicated can avoid any contract (the contract is voidable) made while intoxicated if the intoxication was to such an extent that the person did not understand the binding nature of the contract and did not understand what was actually being conveyed or purchased by the terms of the contract.

The person must be so intoxicated that their state is one of being mentally incompetent (not yet court adjudged) at the time the contract was made in order to have the contract be voidable. Courts are generally stricter on requiring restitution for contracts made voidable by intoxication.

The Defense of Mistake

Unilateral Mistake—General Rule: If only one of the parties makes a mistake, the mistake is binding on the mistaken party, unless:

- The other party knows or should know of the mistake, or
- The mistake is material and obvious, as when there is a transposition of numbers (eg, $501.20 versus $5,012.00); if the mistake is immaterial (eg, $501.20 versus $502.10), then the mistake is binding, or
- The error was due to a mathematical calculation (addition, subtraction, division, or multiplication), and the mistake was made inadvertently and not through gross negligence.

Jim is going to offer to sell Mary a laptop for $550. That evening Jim is typing up the offer to Mary and inadvertently types the price "$500" rather than "$550." Upon receiving Jim's letter, Mary writes back a simple "I accept" message.

Do Jim and Mary have a contract?

Yes.

What is the price in the contract?

$500. Jim made a typographical error, but on a resale computer, the $50 difference would not be obvious enough to Mary to alert Mary that there was an error. Even though Jim intended to sell Mary the laptop for $550, Jim made a unilateral mistake which Mary did not know had been made. Thus, the mistake falls on Jim, and the contract is for $500.

Would the answer be different if Jim had typed $5.50?

Yes, because in that case Mary would know Jim had made a mistake, and such cannot be held against Jim.

Bilateral (Mutual) Mistake—General Rule: If both parties are mistaken and the mistake is one that involves the identity, existence, or quantity of the subject matter, the contract cannot be enforced by either party.

John and Mary have negotiated an agreement for Mary to purchase John's office building for $787,000. Unbeknownst to both of them, the office building (which is located in another city) has burned down following a gas pipe explosion. Both parties are mistaken as to the existence of the subject matter and have the defense of mistake to the contract.

The Defense of Innocent Misrepresentation

Misrepresentation is deception about the subject matter of a contract that involves facts or promises of performance. There are four requirements for the defense of misrepresentation.

Statement of Fact: The misrepresentation must be based on fact-based statements, not sales puffing (the use of superlatives to describe products or property). Expert opinions on the contract subject matter are statements of facts (eg, an audit opinion or an appraisal). The opinions of nonexperts are treated in the same manner as puffing (eg, a nonaccountant who says, "This company's earnings are on track").

Statements of Fact	Puffing
"These bottles are made of 100% recycled materials."	"These bottles mean you are helping the environment."
"These shirts are 100% cotton."	"These shirts are soft and comfortable."

Misrepresentation is material to the contract. The deception must involve something material: Would the information affect the party's decision to enter into the contract?

Reliance: One party has relied on the deception. Parties in negotiations are permitted to rely on the factual representations and promises of performance made by the other parties.

Damages: The party claiming misrepresentation as a defense must be able to show the damages resulting from the misrepresentation.

The Defense of Fraud (Fraud in the Inducement or Fraud in Formation)

The defense of fraud is established when one of the parties to the contract has intentionally made false or deceptive statements about the subject matter. There are four requirements for establishing fraud.

Fact-Based Statement: A fact-based statement is one that is material about the contract subject matter or the kind of thing that would change someone's mind about entering into the contract.

Reliance: Just as in misrepresentation, one party has relied upon and been deceived by the other party's false representations.

Intentional Deception: This factor distinguishes misrepresentation from fraud. The party making the misrepresentation is aware that the information is false and is using it for the purpose of misleading the other party into entering into a contract.

Damages: The deceived party is entitled to damages (including punitive damages) or can rescind (cancel) the contract. Fraud in the inducement is one of the few times that punitive damages are available in contract suits. The basic differences between fraud and innocent misrepresentation are intent and a remedy of rescission for innocent misrepresentation versus punitive damages for fraud.

Jill is selling a home to Tanner. Tanner requires a termite inspection as a condition precedent to closing on the home. The first termite inspection by AAA Termite, Inc., results in a report that finds termites in the house. Jill does not turn the report over to Tanner; instead, Jill hires BBB Termite, Inc., to do a second inspection. BBB's report concludes that the house is clean, no termites. Tanner is pleased with the BBB report and closes on the house. Shortly after moving in, Tanner sees what appear to be termite tracks. Tanner happens to call AAA, and AAA discloses the report. Because Jill withheld the AAA report from Tanner, there is intentional deception, not misrepresentation. The defense of fraud or fraudulent misrepresentation applies here.

If Jill hired BBB first and BBB found no termites even though there were termites, then there would be misrepresentation. Jill, in that situation, would not have intended to mislead Tanner; she would have just hired a company that missed finding the termites.

The Defense of Fraud (Fraud in the Execution)

If a party enters into a contract without being aware of it, as a result of the other party getting them to sign an agreement without realizing they are signing a contract (deception), there has been fraud in the execution. The fraud does not involve the subject matter of the contract; the fraud involves deception about the nature of the document signed.

Jayson is a sales representative for Sunset Solar. Jayson is paid a flat fee for every in-home presentation completed and earns a commission on every solar system that he sells. Jayson does a presentation for Todd and Dolores at their home. Todd and Dolores decide that they do not want to purchase a solar system. Jayson presents them with a document and says, "Could you just sign this to verify that I did the presentation for you?" Todd reviews the presentation verification and agrees to sign. While Todd and Dolores are getting a pen, Jayson switches a contract for a solar system with the verification document. Todd and Dolores find out about the switch when the installers arrive one week later. Jayson orchestrated a fraud in the execution. Todd and Dolores will not be required to perform under the contract because there was fraud, and they can collect any damages for the fraud.

The Defense of Undue Influence

Undue influence arises when there is a special relationship, often called a confidential relationship. Because of this relationship, one party can exercise undue influence over the free will of the other when rendering decisions. Examples include lawyer/client, priest/parishioner, and child/elderly parent.

Undue influence exists when there is a relationship of trust and dependence and one party takes advantage of the other party because of the dependence. Contracts entered into under undue influence are voidable. The party who is unduly influenced is able to set aside the contract.

Brooke, who cares for her disabled brother, Randy, talked Randy into selling Randy's only asset, a house. The sale by Randy to Brooke is for 50% less than market value. This relationship of dependence allowed Brooke to overcome Randy's free will. Randy can set aside this contract because of undue influence.

The Defense of Duress

Duress is a defense that exists when one party to a contract has deprived the other party of free will or choice at the time they are entering into a contract. If duress is established, then the party who experienced the force or threat has a void contract. The party cannot be forced to perform under the terms of a contract that resulted from duress.

Duress in contract formation includes:

- Physical force or threat of physical force (that rises to the level of criminal assault or battery) to the party or to their family. Known as extreme duress, it occurs when a party enters into a contract as a result of a physical threat of force so great that it impairs any ability to exercise free will (eg, they sign the contract while a gun is being pointed at them). When there is this level of duress, the contract is void. The contract cannot be enforced
- The threat of physical force also constitutes duress
- Duress can also result because one party threatens to disclose private information about the other party
- Economic duress results when one of the contracting parties threatens a boycott of the business of that party

An employer threatens to fire and have an employee "blacklisted" in an industry the employer controls unless the employee contracts to sell the employer mineral rights to land the employee has just purchased. This threat of economic sanctions, loss of job, plus the employee not being able to work and apply their industry skills to earn a living, constitutes economic duress.

Voidable vs. Void Contracts	
Voidable	**Void**

May be voided by one party because of:
• Duress (social or economic threat)
• Undue influence
• Misrepresentation of a material fact
  ○ Unintentional misrepresentation
  ○ Fraud in the inducement
• Mistake
• Lack of capacity
	Cannot be enforced by either party because of:
	• Extreme duress (physical threat)
	• Fraud in the execution
	• Illegal subject matter
	• Incompetent party
	• Unconscionability

The Defense of Illegality

Contracts in Violation of Statutes: Contracts in violation of a statute are void. There may be offer, acceptance, consideration, and capacity, but if the subject matter is illegal, the contract is void, which means that neither side can enforce the agreement.

Assume Smith agrees to pay $20,000 to Jones in exchange for Jones's promise to steal trade secrets from Jones's employer and pass them to Smith. Smith gives Jones a $5,000 deposit at the time the contract is formed. The courts will not help Jones collect the other $15,000 if the secrets are actually stolen and will not help Smith recover the $5,000 deposit if Jones doesn't steal them. Of course, both persons are also subject to appropriate criminal prosecution.

Usury: Usury is charging a higher interest rate than permitted by law (maximum rate). Contracts for usurious loans are void. The remedy may be voiding the entire contract, the contract's interest, or the interest charged above the usurious rate.

Gambling Contracts: These contracts are illegal and void, but payment of the gambling debt may be only voidable.

Licensing Statutes: If the purpose of the licensing law is mainly revenue generation, the contract with the unlicensed person may be enforceable. If the purpose is to regulate public welfare (eg, a doctor or lawyer), the contract with the unlicensed person is void.

Real estate agents are required to be licensed in all states in which they are working. Even if an unlicensed agent has a listing agreement in writing, there will be no commission paid, nor will the listing contract be enforced by the courts because the licensing statutes are qualification statutes. To allow unlicensed agents to collect commissions would defeat the public purposes of having knowledgeable and trained agents.

Contracts Contrary to Public Policy: Contracts may be void not because they violate a statute but rather because enforcing them would undermine public policy goals and standards.

Unconscionable Contracts or Clauses in Consumer Contracts: Unconscionable contracts are those that impose such a burden on one party that the terms "shock the conscience."

A consumer credit contract under which the consumer is never able to repay the seller for the goods financed because the payments are spread among all the contracts the consumer has is unconscionable. The creditor, instead of paying off the debt one item at a time to provide the consumer with some paid-off debts, spreads payments across all the purchases so that the debtor always owes money on all the items purchased.

Exculpatory Clauses: A clause in a contract that disclaims any liability regardless of fault is unenforceable.

A clause in a sale-of-goods contract that eliminates all liability for personal injuries caused by a product is void.

Contracts in Restraint of Trade: Covenants not to compete are sometimes needed to prevent employees from leaving the business and using information and skills from the previous job to start a new, competing company. A covenant not to compete is enforceable if it is:

- Ancillary (a part of a larger contract), *and*
- Reasonable in restraint in length of time and geographic scope.

Charles contracts to sell his Italian restaurant to Susan. In the contract is a clause that prohibits Charles from starting an Italian restaurant in the city for six months. This clause is probably an enforceable covenant not to compete because it is ancillary (part of the business contract) and the restraint is reasonable in length and geographic scope.

6.02 Performance, Discharge, and Breach

Discharge of Performance Obligations

Representative Task (Remembering & Understanding): Explain the rules related to the fulfillment of performance obligations necessary for an executed contract.

Representative Task (Application): Identify whether both parties to a contract have fulfilled their performance obligation given a specific scenario.

A contract is a legal obligation to perform a given promise. However, implied in every contract are certain steps or conditions that must take place for performance to occur. The presence or absence of conditions controls the duty to perform the promises under a contract.

When Is Performance Due?

While a contract may have a date for performance, there are certain steps, known as conditions, that must be met before a party can begin performance. Without those conditions being met, the duty to perform does not exist, and there cannot be a breach of the contract when the conditions necessary for performance have not been met.

Types of Conditions for Performance

Conditions Precedent: A condition precedent is something that must be present or occur before a party has a duty to perform. An audit cannot begin until the audit client has given the auditor access. Without access, the auditor will not be in breach of the contract because the failure of the condition prevents performance.

Jane signs a contract for the purchase of her first home. The condition precedent for the purchase is that Jane must qualify for a home mortgage loan at a rate not to exceed 6%. If Jane cannot secure financing, the condition precedent is not met, and Jane is not required to perform under the contract. Jane's duty of performance did not exist under the terms of the contract.

Conditions Subsequent: A condition subsequent is something that must be present or occur after a duty to perform has arisen. A condition subsequent serves to discharge the ability to file suit for lack of performance. A condition subsequent that is not met serves to end the duty to perform.

A fire policy has a provision that requires the policyholder to submit a proof of loss by filing with the insurer within 60 days of the fire in order for the policyholder to recover for the fire loss. The requirement to submit a proof of loss to receive payment for the fire loss covered by the policy is a condition subsequent. If the condition subsequent of filing a proof of loss (also known as a proof of claim) is not met, then the insurer is discharged of its duty to perform (ie, pay the insured for the loss).

Conditions Concurrent: All contracts have conditions in the sense of the bargained-for exchange. Each party's duty to perform under a contract is dependent upon the other party's duty to perform at the same time. All contracts have some form of condition concurrent. At the grocery store, the customer pays as the groceries are being bagged. Simultaneously, the condition of turning over the food is met as the customer's condition to pay for that food is also met. The customer and the grocery store have conditions concurrent of payment and the store bagging the groceries for you to take with you as it passes title.

Jane is purchasing a home from Belmont Terrace Builders, Inc. An escrow is established for closing the sale. Jane must have her funds deposited with the escrow company, and Belmont Terrace must have a clean property title deposited with the escrow company. Those conditions concurrent must be met before Jane can close and obtain the title and before Belmont can obtain the amount of the payment under the contract.

Effect of Conditions on the Duty to Perform: When conditions are met, the duty to perform exists. If the conditions are not met, then the duty to perform is discharged.

If an author fails to complete a manuscript by the deadline provided in the publishing agreement, the author would be in breach of contract. However, the publisher must file suit within the statute of limitations (generally four years for breach of contract) in order to recover the advance paid to the author under the contract for the manuscript. If the publisher does not file suit within the four years, then the author's duty to return the advance is discharged.

What Constitutes Performance?

Common Law Standards and the Doctrine of Substantial Performance

Common law contracts involve complex issues such as the construction of homes, buildings, and freeways. Common law has a special doctrine for handling the standard of performance required for such contracts: substantial performance (ie, only minor items in the contract need to be performed). The requirements for substantial performance are:

- Is what was done, for practical purposes, just as good as what the contract required?
- Was the difference in what the contract required and what was actually provided done in good faith?
- Can the nonbreaching party be compensated for the nonperformance?

Common Law Performance: What Is It? When Is It Complete?

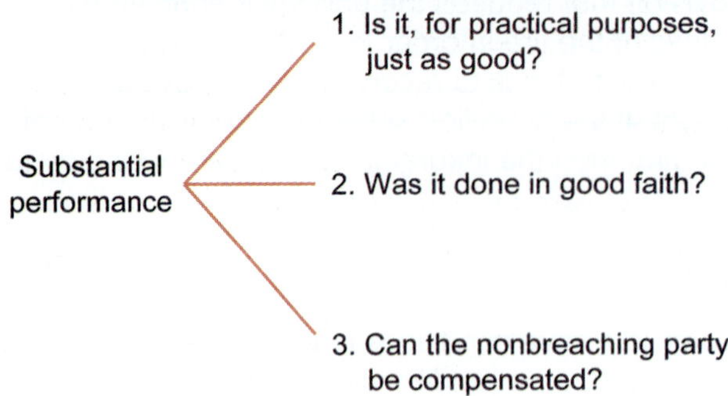

Geraldine Interiors hires Seismic Plumbing to install the bathroom fixtures in four model homes it is completing for a builder. The contract specifies the type of design and that the fixtures should be Kohldler fixtures. The contract also requires that the fixtures be installed by May 1 because the grand opening for the subdivision where the models are located is May 2. Seismic Plumbing is notified on April 29 that, due to supply chain issues, Kohldler cannot get the fixtures to Seismic until May 29. Seismic finds a nearly identical design available immediately from Crane Bathroom Fixtures. They are slightly less expensive than the Kohldler fixtures. Seismic installs the Crane fixtures, and all installation is completed by 11:00 PM on May 1. Seismic has substantially performed on the contract because the Crane fixtures are, for practical purposes, just as good as the Kohldler ones, Seismic made the substitution in good faith, using its judgment to complete the installation on time, and Geraldine Interiors can be compensated for the price difference.

What Constitutes Performance under the UCC?

At times, problems arise between the time the parties have their contractual obligations related to purchase and sale of goods and the actual delivery of the goods (performance of the contract). UCC Article 2 lists specific rights and steps for the parties during this interim period.

Heading Off Buyer or Seller Nonperformance—Right to Demand Assurances: The goal of UCC Article 2 is to have the parties do all that is possible to get the contract performance completed. To do that, both buyers and sellers have the right of assurance and the duty of cooperation.

Right of Assurance: If a party has "reasonable grounds" to believe that the other party will not perform as contracted, the concerned party may demand in writing that the other party give adequate assurance of due performance. If the party does not provide reasonable assurance as demanded within 30 days, the failure to provide those assurances is a repudiation of the contract and can be treated as an anticipatory breach.

- Once a party is entitled to and demands reasonable assurance, that party can suspend performance without liability until they receive the assurance requested
- Reasonable grounds for insecurity depend on the facts. Typical events that would trigger the right to demand assurances would be events like a strike at a seller's plant or news reports indicating that a buyer is considering bankruptcy
- The types of assurances would depend on the cause of the insecurity. If there are rumors of bankruptcy of the buyer, the seller could demand the assurance of a deposit or cash on delivery. If there is a strike at a seller's production plant, the buyer could demand assurances that the seller has a backup plan for production if the strike goes on too long
- Failure to provide assurances is a breach of the contract

Smith, Inc., has contracted to buy a specific piece of equipment from ABC. Smith believes that if it runs this piece of equipment at a certain speed, it will increase Smith's productivity by 5%. Smith learns from another buyer (Green) who has previously purchased a similar piece of equipment from ABC that, although Green seldom ran the equipment at that speed, whenever Green did do so, the equipment broke down. ABC's literature indicated the equipment could be run at a variety of speeds, including the speed Smith anticipated running the equipment.

Is Green's experience sufficient (reasonable) grounds for Smith to believe that ABC's equipment will not perform as contracted?

Most probably, yes.

What can Smith do before the equipment is delivered?

In writing, ask for reasonable assurances that the equipment will perform as contracted and for protection if it does not.

What reasonable requests for assurance could Smith seek?

Smith could ask for express warranties, money-back guaranty, or perhaps even replacement equipment if it is available. The point is that ABC must satisfy Smith's insecurity as long as it is reasonable.

Remember, the right to demand assurances exists only in UCC subject matter contracts. Common law contracts do not have an equivalent right to demand assurances.

Determining Seller Performance—Buyer Inspection: Under the UCC, upon delivery of the goods, the buyer has the right of inspection.

- Inspection need not be immediate. The buyer may receive the goods on a busy Friday afternoon but is not required to inspect them at that time. The buyer should have a reasonable time frame (at least through Monday) to conduct the inspection
- Inspection allows the buyer to open boxes, examine goods, and even conduct tests to see if the goods meet the buyer's needs as specified in the contract
- **COD (Cash on Delivery) Deliveries:** With COD deliveries, the buyer must pay before the carrier will turn over the goods, but the buyer does not lose the right of inspection. The COD payment does not waive that right. However, the seller will have the buyer's money, and COD makes it more difficult to get the seller to correct any problems. The buyer, however, does not accept by making the payment on a COD delivery

Failed Seller Performance under the UCC—Buyer's Right of Rejection: Under UCC Article 2, the seller has an obligation to deliver goods that conform to the contract specifications. This requirement is sometimes called the "perfect tender rule."

If the seller delivers goods that fall short of the contract requirements in any way (the shortfall need not be material because the perfect tender rule requires 100% compliance with the contract terms, including the correct goods, the correct color, and the correct amount), then the buyer has the following options:

- Reject the entire shipment,
- Accept the entire shipment, *or*
- Accept any commercial unit and reject the rest.

A commercial unit is determined by industry practices and custom for the particular good involved in the contract. For example, candy is often shipped in bags of one gross—144 pieces. The buyer would reject a shipment of candy by the bag, not by individual pieces of candy. The purpose of rejection in commercial units is to reduce confusion with partial packages and the breaking up of units (eg, envelopes come in boxes of 500 and thus should be rejected in boxes of 500).

The seller's contract calls for delivery of 100 cases of carrots. The seller tenders to the buyer 200 cases of carrots, a nonconforming goods tender. The buyer could reject the entire 200 cases, accept the 200 cases and pay for the additional 100 cases, or accept 100 cases and reject the other 100 cases.

Failed Seller Performance under UCC Article—Buyer's Responsibilities for Rejection of Nonconforming Goods: To reject and pursue remedies, the buyer must do so properly. The following are the requirements for rejection:

- Rejection must be within a reasonable time after tender of delivery or actual delivery
- Rejection is not effective until the seller has been notified
- The buyer must give specific reasons for rejection. The seller has the right to cure the problems with the goods that the buyer has found. The seller cannot cure defects if the buyer has not explained those defects. If the buyer fails to notify the seller or fails to give reasons for rejection, the buyer is not entitled to remedies if seller could have cured
- If the buyer has possession of the rejected goods, the buyer must act as a bailee (use reasonable care over the goods). If the buyer is a merchant, the buyer must follow any of the seller's reasonable instructions at the seller's cost
- If the seller does not give buyer instructions (and the goods are perishable or are rapidly declining in value, such as produce), the buyer can store the goods on the seller's account (storage charge), reship the defective goods back at the seller's expense, or sell the goods, deducting any costs and a sales commission from the proceeds of the sale of the defective goods

UCC Rights and Requirements in Determining Performance and Breach

Buyer's Rights in Determining Performance and Breach	When	How
Inspection	When goods arrive; before payment (unless COD)	Examination; lab test; samples
Rejection	Single delivery—fail to conform in any respect Installment—substantially impairs value of installment or contract (if rejection in full) Must reject within a reasonable time frame	Notification; nonuse
Acceptance	After inspection	Notification; use; failure to reject within a reasonable time frame
Revocation of acceptance	After acceptance; must materially impair value and either a defect nondiscoverable or a promise of cure	Notification; reshipment or nonuse

UCC Seller's Rights upon Buyer Rejection—Right to Cure: The reason that the buyer is required to follow certain steps in rejecting goods is because the UCC provides sellers with the opportunity to fix or "cure" the problems that the buyer has found upon inspection of the goods.

Fixing Seller Nonperformance—Right to Cure under UCC: A seller who has sent defective or nonconforming goods may still have the ability to cure and not be in breach of contract. Sometimes there is a casualty, partially or completely, to identified goods, or the seller is able to correct deficiencies and perform once the seller knows of the mistake.

If a seller tenders delivery of nonconforming goods prior to the contract date and the buyer rejects the goods, the seller can, with notice, indicate an intent to cure (ie, fix whatever problem the buyer has pointed out as the reason for rejection). The seller always has until the time that contract performance is due to get conforming goods to a buyer who has rejected the initial delivery.

Ribbon Warehouse has a contract to sell 500 spools of one-inch red satin ribbon to Crafter's Barn for delivery by June 1. Crafter's Barn receives the shipment on May 25, but the shipment contains 500 spools of green one-inch ribbon. Crafter's Barn has a duty to notify Ribbon Warehouse of the nonconforming goods. If Ribbon Warehouse has 500 spools of one-inch red ribbon and notifies Crafter's Barn, it has the right to cure performance. If the one-inch red ribbon arrives on or before June 1, then Ribbon Warehouse has fully performed under the contract.

UCC Seller Performance: When Is There Buyer Acceptance or Actual Seller Performance? Payment for the goods in and of itself is not acceptance. Under the UCC, acceptance can occur only after inspection and a determination by the buyer that the goods conform to the contract requirements and are not damaged. Acceptance occurs under UCC Article 2 when any of the following have occurred:

- After inspecting the goods, the buyer notifies the seller either that the goods are conforming or that the buyer will accept them despite the goods being nonconforming
- The buyer fails to reject the goods after inspection or after a reasonable opportunity to do so
- The buyer engages in any act that is inconsistent with the seller's ownership (such as knowingly using nonconforming goods)

UCC Seller Performance: When Can a Buyer Revoke Acceptance of Goods? Under the following conditions, buyers can revoke their previous acceptances:

1. The buyer was given reasonable assurance that the seller would cure a nonconforming shipment and the cure has not taken place

A buyer orders 100 barrels of Brand 52 cleaning solvent. The seller delivers Brand 50 cleaning solvent, a weaker but still usable solvent. The seller tells the buyer to use what it can of the Brand 50 solvent and an immediate corrected Brand 52 shipment (cure) will be made. The buyer's use of the Brand 50 cleaning solvent is technically an acceptance. If, however, the seller does not immediately deliver the corrected Brand 52 solvent, the buyer can revoke the acceptance of the goods and hold the seller liable for breach (same as if the original nonconforming shipment had been rejected).

2. The seller has assured the buyer that goods are conforming, but the buyer later discovers that goods are nonconforming

A buyer orders 20 cases of red pens. Each case contains 100 small boxes with a dozen pens in each. The cases arrive with the words "Green Pens" on each case. Without opening the boxes, the buyer calls the seller and tells the seller of the "Green Pens" notation. The seller assures the buyer that the labeling is a mistake and inside the case are red pens. The buyer stores the cases and pays the seller for the pens. When the buyer opens the cases six months later, the buyer discovers that there are, in fact, only green pens inside, not the red pens that the seller had assured the buyer. In this case, the buyer can revoke the acceptance.

3. The nonconformity of the goods was difficult to detect, even with an inspection

The buyer purchases a manufactured tiny home. The buyer had the tiny home inspected, and it received a clean inspection report. The tiny home is moved around the country by the buyer. As a result, the buyer is able to travel to avoid rainy and snowy weather. Six months after purchasing the house, the buyer experiences the first major rainstorm since living in the tiny home. The tiny home has serious roof leakage that has resulted in considerable water damage. Despite having lived in the tiny home for six months, the buyer can revoke acceptance because it would be difficult to detect the weatherproofing in the tiny home unless and until the tiny home experienced a rainstorm.

Discharge and Breach

Representative Task (Remembering & Understanding): Explain the different ways in which a contract can be discharged (eg, performance, agreement, and operation of the law).

Representative Task (Application): Identify whether a contract has been discharged given a specific scenario.

Representative Task (Application): Identify situations involving breach of contract given a specific scenario.

The obligations of a contract continue unless and until the events or steps taken work to provide a discharge of performance.

If a party to a contract is discharged from performance, then all legal obligations under the contract end, and the discharged party cannot be held liable for breach. Discharge can be accomplished by performance, agreement of the parties, operation of law, and a breach by the other party.

Universally Applicable Discharge Rules: UCC and Common Law

1. Discharge by Performance
   - If the contract is fully performed, the parties are discharged
   - If there is substantial performance (see earlier discussion under performance), there is also a discharge
2. Discharge by Agreement
   - **Rescission:** The parties agree to cancel the contract and are restored to their original position before the contract existed. The rescission is supported by consideration because both sides are giving up their rights to litigate under the contract to determine if there has been a breach
   - **Accord and Satisfaction:** See discussion under "Consideration"

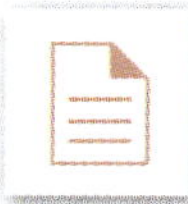

Kelly offers to give Connor a microwave oven (ie, the alternative duty) instead of paying $500 (ie, the original duty). If Connor accepts, then they have made an accord (ie, agreed) by accepting the alternative duty. When Kelly delivers the microwave (ie, satisfaction), the contract will be discharged just like it would have been had Kelly delivered the cash.

   - **Novation:** One party accepts the performance of a third party in place of the party obligated under the original contract. Both the original parties to the contract as well as the third party being substituted must be parties to the novation agreement

When forming a new corporation, a promoter often enters into contracts on behalf of the future corporation. The promoter is personally liable for the preincorporation contracts because the corporation is not yet in existence. Novation occurs when the newly formed corporation becomes liable for the preincorporation contracts and relieves the promoter from liability. The corporation, the promoter, and the third party that provided the services before the corporation was formed must all sign the novation agreement to substitute the newly formed corporation for the promoter.

Discharge of Contractual Duties by Agreement		
Discharge Type	**What Happens**	**When Original Duty Is Discharged**
Accord and satisfaction	One duty substituted for another	Performance of substituted duty
Mutual recission	Parties agree to end contract	At time of recission
Novation	New party substituted for an original party	At time of substitution of the new party

3. Discharge by Operation of Law
   - **Impossibility:** The objective of the contract becomes impossible (eg, under a contract for the sale of an office building, the destruction of the office building discharges the parties as an operation of law)
   - **Impracticability:** The UCC uses the term "impracticability" instead of "impossibility" for discharge under circumstances in which either the performance has become impossible or the expense of performing is something neither party contemplated when they entered into their contract
   - Death or incapacity of the party obligated to perform a personal service contract
   - Discharge in bankruptcy
   - Illegality of the services to be performed or contract subject matter

State A permits paralegals to draft and supervise the execution of wills under state law. Following a series of cases in which wills were not drafted or executed properly, the legislature passes a law prohibiting paralegals from drafting and supervising the execution of wills. Any agreement between paralegals and clients for such services (that had not yet been completed or started) would be void because of the new law. The parties to such agreements would be discharged from their responsibilities under the agreements.

4. Discharge by Breach by Other Party
   - Violation of contract terms
   - **Anticipatory Repudiation:** A breach of contract in advance of the time for performance; the nonbreaching party can choose from the following remedies:
     - Wait to see if performance is still possible
     - Cancel the contract
     - File suit immediately for compensatory damages

The decisions on actions to take when there is anticipatory repudiation are all left to the nonbreaching party (ie, they can choose which steps to take and when).

Discharge: UCC Rules on Allocation of Risk of Loss and Passage of Title

UCC Article 2 has specific provisions for transfer of title and risk of loss. There are times when the parties' rights on performance are affected by the passage of title and risk of loss. Title of goods refers to legal ownership and determines who records the goods as items in their financial records before or at year end and which creditors of which party will have rights to repossess the goods. Risk of loss deals with which party will bear the risk of loss if goods are damaged or lost.

The failure to deliver good title is a breach of contract, and the party who has the risk of loss at the time there is damage to the goods controls whether a party is excused from performance or must still perform on the contract and absorb the loss.

Discharge Issues in Passage of Title and Risk of Loss

Identification: Identification is a prerequisite to passage of title (which is a condition precedent to performance by buyers) and risk of loss (which determines who will pay for damaged goods). Before any interest in goods (title or risk of loss) can pass from a seller to a buyer, the goods must be in existence and identified to the contract. Before discharge or remedies can be determined under the UCC, there must be a determination of identification. Without identification, risk of loss and title passage also cannot be determined.

The key in most exams is whether identification has taken place because, in most cases, the answer to the question of whether goods are in existence is obvious. Some questions are tricky because they ask when risk or title has passed when the key to the question is knowing that the goods have not yet been identified.

General Rule on Identification: For goods in existence at the time the contract is entered into, identification occurs at the time the parties enter into the contract. If, for example, you are buying goods that have to be altered, they are not technically in existence at the time of the contract. A suit that you are having altered is not in existence at the time of the contracting. Once the goods are in existence, that is, your alterations have been completed, then title can pass because the goods are identified.

Fungible Goods: Fungible goods are those that either cannot be distinguished because of homogeneous qualities or are so mixed together that they cannot be distinguished by individual units (eg, grains, fruit, cases of canned goods). Identification occurs when the goods are shipped, marked, or otherwise designated for the buyer (ie, set aside in the warehouse).

Future Goods: For goods to be manufactured, such as when a company is manufacturing rocking chairs for a furniture store, identification occurs when those rocking chairs are shipped, marked, or otherwise designated for the buyer.

Green has 1,000 cases of peas in the warehouse, and Bryant has contracted to purchase 100 cases. Since the goods are fungible, the 100 cases must be identified (marked or separated from the mass) before title or risk of loss can pass.

Green and Smith have deposited wheat in a silo. Green's deposit is 5,000 bushels, and Smith's deposit is 10,000 bushels. Smith sells 2,000 bushels to Bryant. The wheat is fungible (mixture of like-kind goods with intent to become tenant-in-common owners) and is identified under the contract when it is shipped, marked, or otherwise designated for Bryant. Until then, the risk remains with the sellers, Green and Smith. If the wheat were destroyed, the loss would be prorated based on ownership (pro rata shares).

Once goods are in existence and identified, title and risk of loss can pass at the time the parties **expressly agree**, or, if there is no agreement, they pass according to UCC rules.

Seller contracts to sell 100 personal laptop computers to Buyer at a given price, with the FOB being the seller's warehouse via ABC Truck Lines. Until ABC Truck Lines picks up the 100 laptop computers, risk is on the seller. Once ABC Truck Lines has possession of the 100 laptop computers, the risk of loss is on the buyer.

The Rules for Passage of Title

When title passes is important for purposes of determining the rights of third parties with respect to the buyer and seller. For example, suppose that the IRS is about to levy a lien on the buyer's property. If the buyer has a contract that is FOB place of shipment and the goods are in transit, the IRS can seize the goods. If the IRS has seized the goods, there can be no performance by the seller. If, however, the contract was FOB place of destination, title to the goods still rests with the seller during transit. The IRS cannot seize the goods from the seller's warehouse or from the carrier. Title does not pass until the goods are tendered at their destination.

Passage of title occurs at different times depending on whether the contract is nondelivery or delivery.

Passage of Title in Nondelivery (Nonshipment) Contracts

- Determine whether there is a document of title involved with the goods and the contract
- If there is no document of title, title passes at the moment the contract is made
- If there is a document of title, and the document of title is nonnegotiable, then title passes to buyer upon buyer's receipt of the document
- If there is a document of title, and the document of title is negotiable, then title passes to the buyer upon the buyer's receipt of the document

Passage of Title in Delivery (Shipment) Contracts

If delivery is FOB place of shipment or FOB seller's place of business, warehouse, or residence, then title passes at the time and place of shipment or when the goods are delivered to the carrier.

If delivery is FOB place of destination or FOB buyer's city, business, warehouse, or residence, then title passes upon the seller's tender of conforming goods at place of contract destination.

Tender is the key. "Tender" means the goods have arrived, they are available for the buyer to pick up, and the buyer has been notified that the goods are there and available for pickup.

Bradford, a buyer in Norfolk, owes $210,000 to the IRS. The IRS has obtained a lien that allows it to seize any real and personal property owned by Bradford. Sanford, a seller from Los Angeles, agreed to ship 100 cases of plastic travel bottles to Bradford. The shipment term is FOB Norfolk. The 100 cases of plastic travel bottles arrive at the loading dock at Norfolk, and Bradford's receiving department is notified. The IRS seizes the 100 cases of travel bottles from the loading dock. Bradford objects on the grounds that the bottles still belong to Sanford, that title has not yet passed, and thus that the IRS cannot seize the goods. Bradford is incorrect. The 100 cases have been tendered and title passed to Bradford. The IRS can seize the goods.

Suppose Sanford is the party subject to an IRS lien, and Sanford is shipping the 100 cases to Bradford under an FOB Los Angeles contract. The IRS seizes the 100 cases at Norfolk. This time Sanford objects, claiming it was too late for the IRS to seize the goods. Sanford is correct. Title passed to Bradford when the goods were delivered to the carrier in Los Angeles. The IRS cannot seize the 100 cases as property belonging to Sanford because title has already passed.

Third-Party Rights and Title

Article 2 has special provisions to deal with situations in which a third party is affected by title issues related to the conduct of the original parties to the contract (ie, when there is some problem with perfect title as it relates to a third party). The problems result from there being an innocent third party known as a bona fide purchaser (BFP) for value.

Rights of a BFP When Void Title Has Been Transferred: A void title cannot be passed to anyone. The original owner has the best title.

Thomas, a thief, steals your bicycle and sells it to Smith. Smith has no knowledge that Thomas is not the owner or that the bike has been stolen. You discover Smith has the bike. You are entitled to return of your bicycle from Smith because Thomas had a void title (no title) to pass to Smith. Smith, however, can legally recover from Thomas (if Smith can find Thomas).

Rights of a BFP When There Is a Voidable Title: Although a voidable title, even though passed to a buyer, can be recovered, there is one exception—if the buyer in turn passes title to a BFP.

Mary is a minor who contracts to sell her bicycle to an adult, Jim, for $250. Mary transfers the bicycle and title to Jim. Since Mary is a minor, Jim receives a voidable title, and Mary can disaffirm the sale and recover her bicycle. If Jim sells the bicycle to Judy (a BFP for value) before Mary disaffirms the sale, Mary can still disaffirm the contract with Jim but cannot recover the bicycle from Judy. Judy's title is absolute and cuts off Mary's voidable title.

Rights of a BFP with Entrusting of Goods: Entrusting of goods to a merchant (person who deals in goods of that kind) by a buyer gives the merchant the power to transfer all rights (including the title) to a buyer in the ordinary course of business.

Harry took his TV set to ABC TV, Inc., for repairs. ABC sells both used and new TVs. The set is repaired but is sold by mistake to an ABC customer with no knowledge of Harry's ownership rights. Since ABC is a merchant (in the business of selling used TVs), ABC passed good title to Harry's set to the customer, and Harry cannot recover the set from the customer. ABC has committed a tort of conversion, however, and is liable to Harry in a civil suit.

The Rules for Passage of Risk of Loss

Passage of Risk of Loss in Nondelivery Contracts: Determine whether the contract is a delivery or nondelivery contract. Unless the parties provide for shipment/delivery, there is no delivery provided under Article 2.

Determine whether the seller is a merchant or nonmerchant.

- If the seller is a merchant, risk of loss does not pass until the buyer actually gets possession. For example, when you buy a sofa at The Room Store but agree to pick it up yourself, you do not assume the risk of loss until that sofa is in the back of your pickup truck
- If the seller is a nonmerchant, risk of loss passes upon seller's tender of the goods to the buyer. If you buy a sofa at a garage sale and leave to go get your truck to pick it up, the risk of loss has already passed to you. If the sofa is destroyed while you are procuring your truck, you absorb the loss
- If there are title documents, the risk of loss passes to the buyer upon the buyer's receipt of the documents

The determination of risk of loss is important because it controls which of the parties will be responsible for contract performance and which parties will not. If the seller has the risk of loss, the buyer need not pay. If the buyer has the risk of loss, the buyer must still pay the seller and will need to file a claim with their insurer to be able to buy substitute goods.

Passage of Risk of Loss When There Is Delivery (Shipment Contract): If delivery is FOB place of shipment (or ship point) or FOB seller's place of business, warehouse, or residence, then the risk of loss passes at the time the goods are delivered to the carrier.

If delivery is FOB place of destination or FOB buyer's place of business, warehouse, or residence, then the risk of loss passes at the time of tender.

Able Corp. sells 500 boxes of copy paper to Green Company. The 500 boxes were shipped to the Fox Warehouse Co. earlier, and Fox issues to Able a negotiable warehouse receipt representing the 500 boxes. Able endorses and delivers the warehouse receipt to Green at 4:00 PM on Friday. During the weekend, the warehouse burns down, and the 500 boxes are completely destroyed. Green suffers the loss because risk of loss passed to Green upon Green's receipt of the negotiable document of title.

Passage of Title under Article 2

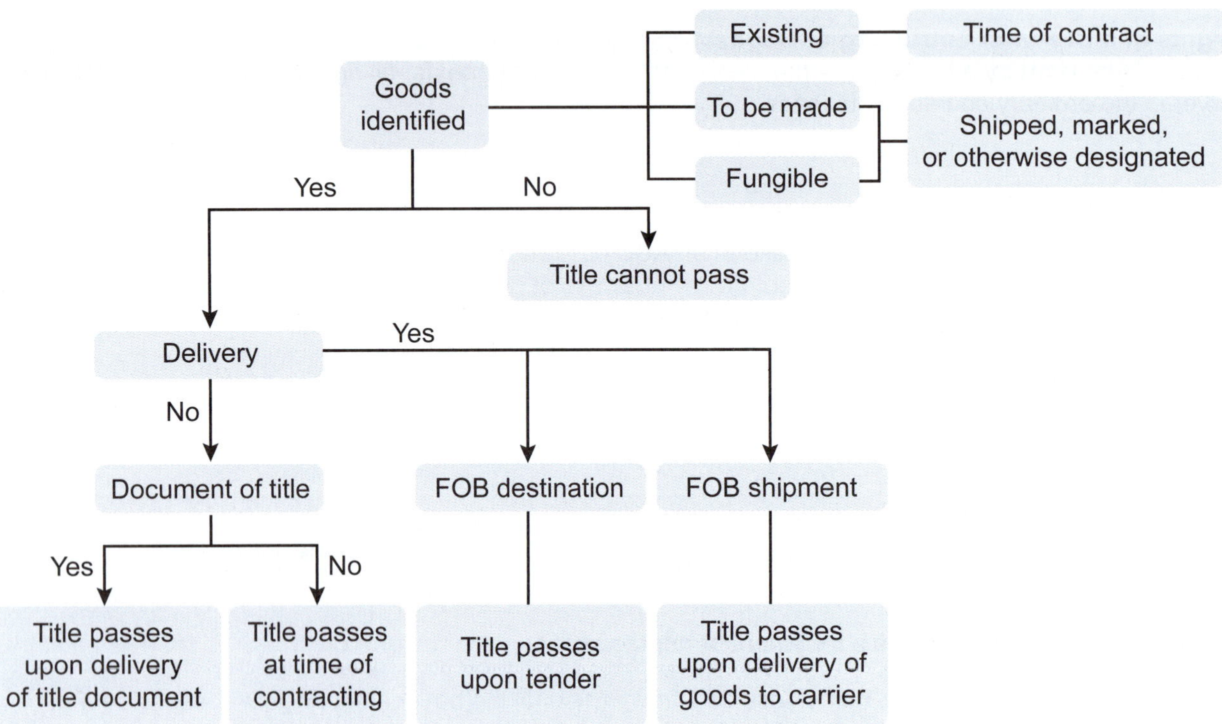

Effect of Breach on the Passage of Title and Risk of Loss (Nonconforming Goods): If the seller has breached and the buyer has a right to reject the goods, risk of loss does not pass to the buyer until the defects are cured or the buyer accepts the goods despite their nonconformity. The buyer does not hold the risk of loss for nonconforming goods in their possession or for their return to the seller.

In addition, if the goods are accepted and acceptance is revoked, risk of loss goes back to the seller, to the extent that the buyer's insurance did not cover the loss.

Breach affects risk of loss but not title. Title passes according to the rules **despite** the breach.

Special Issues in Title and Risk of Loss

Sale on Approval: The buyer is given a time period to try the goods. If the buyer does not want the goods and rejects them, risk of loss remains with the seller. The risk of loss does not pass until the buyer accepts the goods. The buyer can accept by:

- Notification to the seller (eg, "I accept")
- Failure to reject within a trial period (keeps the goods beyond the trial period)
- Performing any act inconsistent with seller's ownership (eg, buyer takes home lawn mower to try it out for two weeks; during the two weeks, buyer mows 15 yards for fees)

Sale or Return: This is an actual sale with title, risk of loss, and possession, with the buyer subject to the condition that the buyer can restore title and risk upon the seller via a proper return of the goods. Cost of return is on the buyer. Failure to timely return finalizes the sale. The UCC treats a consignment as a sale or return.

The following chart summarizes the time of transfer of title and risk of loss on goods that exist and are identified to the contract:

Situation	Passage of Title	Passage of Risk
Shipment contract	Placed with carrier	Placed with carrier
Destination contract	Tendered to buyer	Tendered to buyer
Pickup from merchant	Contract formed	Received by buyer
Pickup from nonmerchant	Contract formed	Tendered to buyer
Sale on approval	Accepted by buyer	Accepted by buyer
Sale or return	See normal sale rules	See normal sale rules
Buyer rejects goods	Reverts to seller	Reverts if proper
Buyer revokes acceptance	Reverts if proper	Reverts if proper

Once a breach of contract has occurred, the next step is to determine the appropriate remedy that will return the nonbreaching party to the same economic position (or as close as possible) as before the breach occurred.

6.03 Remedies

Remedies for Breach

Representative Task (Remembering & Understanding): Summarize the different remedies available to a party for breach of contract.

Representative Task (Application): Identify the remedy available to a party for breach of contract given a specific scenario.

Who Is Entitled to Contract Remedies?

Parties to the Contract Are Entitled to Remedies

The general rule is that those who are a party to a contract are entitled to collect remedies when that contract is breached. Those who are parties to a contract are referred to as having privity of contract.

There are exceptions to the requirement of privity of contract for entitlement to remedies. Assignments and delegations, as well as third-party beneficiary contracts, bring in third parties to contractual relationships who are entitled to remedies for breach of the underlying contract.

Third-Party Rights in Contracts

Assignments and Delegations: If parties transfer the rights they possess in contracts to a third party, the third party, also called the assignee, will be able to enforce the contract rights transferred to them.

Caldwell Properties contracted with Irrigation Specialists to install a sprinkler system at three of its apartment complexes. One of Irrigation Specialists' clients needed to expand the services Irrigation Specialists was providing. In order to take on the expansion of an existing contract, Irrigation Specialists assigned Caldwell's contract to Rain Systems, Inc. If Rain Systems is not paid, it has the right to seek remedies against Caldwell even though it was not an original party to the contract. Rain Systems steps into the same contract rights that Irrigation Specialists had.

Third-Party Beneficiary Rights

There are some contracts that benefit third parties even though those third parties were not parties to the original contract. Some of these beneficiaries are entitled to remedies for breach of a contract to which they were not a party (ie, they were not in privity of contract).

Donee (Intended) Beneficiary

Some contracts are made for the direct benefit of a named third party (the donee). The beneficiary and the donee's rights must be stated in the contract (ie, the donee beneficiary has a legal right to what is given by the two contracted parties).

A customer purchases a car from a dealer to be delivered to the customer's child as a birthday present. If the car is not delivered, the child can sue the dealer but not their parent. The consideration paid by the parent binds the dealer to the contract, and the dealer is obligated to deliver the car to the child per the agreement with the parent. The child generally cannot sue the parent for nonperformance of a gift promise.

If the contract explicitly or implicitly recognizes the child's right to benefit from the contract, the child may be considered an intended third-party beneficiary of the contract and be able to sue the dealer for breach.

Creditor Beneficiary

A creditor beneficiary is one that has a separate contractual relationship with one of the parties to the contract. Medical insurance is a classic example of a creditor beneficiary relationship. Individuals obtain health insurance. The obligation of the insurance company is to pay, according to the terms of the policy, the medical costs incurred by the individuals holding the medical insurance. If the medical insurance does not pay the medical providers as the policy provides, the insured can file suit to obtain payment. However, as a creditor of the insured, any medical provider has the right to sue to collect from the insurance company or the policyholder if the insurance company fails to pay. There must be a debtor-creditor relationship, and the debtor must make a contract that benefits the creditor with a third person.

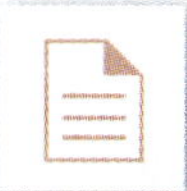

Hayden has a medical insurance policy and requires emergency room treatment at a hospital. The hospital is a creditor beneficiary of Hayden's insurance policy because Hayden owes the hospital for the emergency room treatment, even if Hayden's insurance does not pay. The hospital has the right to sue to collect from either the insurance company or Hayden because the hospital is one of Hayden's creditors.

Incidental Beneficiary

A third party who receives an unintended benefit has no legal rights to recover for breach or damages as a result of nonperformance of a contract between two other parties. A local city government chooses a contractor to design and build a city park. The residents of the city will benefit from such a contract, but they do not have a legal right to recover from either the contractor or the city if one of them breaches that contract.

A contractor has a contract with the city to build a swimming pool in a small neighborhood park. The swimming pool will increase the value of the homes in the neighborhood. The contractor breaches the contract. The city decides not to sue. The homeowners wish to file suits against the contractor as beneficiaries of the contractor-city contract. Since the homeowners are only incidental beneficiaries, they have no legal rights in the contractor-city contract. Incidental beneficiaries have no rights of enforcement against either party to the original contract.

What Are the Types of Remedies? Common Law and UCC

Compensatory Damages

Compensatory damages are economic in nature and compensate for direct losses and lost profits.

Jack signs a contract to supply bookkeeping services to AutoMat, Inc., for the month of May for $5,000 per month. On April 15, AutoMat lets Jack know that the bookkeeping services are no longer needed because a permanent bookkeeper has been hired. Jack is able to obtain another contract at another company for $4,200 per month. AutoMat owes Jack $800 in compensatory damages.

Consequential Damages

Consequential damages are also economic but restore the nonbreaching party's indirect costs and anticipated losses.

Government contracts generally carry a specified consequential damage amount (such as $500 per day) for each day that a service or goods are delayed. Consequential damages cover the costs the nonbreaching party experiences because of the breaching party's delay. In government contracts, the daily fee is to cover the government's costs in, perhaps, renting equipment temporarily until the goods can be obtained.

Incidental Damages

Under both common law and UCC contracts, incidental damages include the costs of rehiring or finding another job and the costs of searching for another piece of land or another buyer, as well as any expenses made in trying to close the sale or prepare the property. Under the UCC, the incidental damages for a nonbreaching seller would be the cost of reselling the goods as well as the costs, such as lawyer's fees, involved in bringing suit to recover the costs of reselling efforts. For a nonbreaching buyer, the incidental damages would be the costs of finding and securing substitute goods.

Nominal Damages

Nominal damages are appropriate when there has been a breach but there is no real, provable loss.

Nominal damages are those awarded to a nonbreaching party that has not experienced any compensatory or other damages. Nominal damages are known as principle compensation, or "It's the principle that matters, not the money." A party bringing suit is correct that there has been a breach of contract, but no one has experienced any harm. Sometimes a buyer will bring such a suit so that other sellers understand that the buyer is not difficult to do business with. A nominal damage award is admission that there was a breach and that one party is not at fault. Such damages are usually a small (nominal) sum such as $1.00.

A television news anchor is fired by a network and removed as a prime-time news show anchor. However, the anchor finds a new job immediately at a major corporation doing public relations. The new job pays more than the news anchor was earning as an anchor. The anchor may want to bring suit to have a court determine whether the firing violated the anchor's contract. Such a determination would help the anchor in securing another anchor position even though there are no compensatory damages owed.

Punitive Damages

Punitive damages are awarded to a party to a contract who has been harmed by the fraudulent acts of another in the formation of a contract. Punitive damages are rare in contract cases unless actual fraud is established.

Arctic Realtors sells a home to First Physicians, LLLP, for First Physicians to remodel into a medical office. Arctic furnishes a fraudulent termite report to First Physicians. First Physicians can recover compensatory damages for the cost of removing the termites, consequential damages for having to postpone the opening of its clinic while the extermination is completed, and punitive damages for the intentional and fraudulent act of Arctic falsifying the termite report.

Specific Performance

Specific performance is available for unique property (patents, real estate, art, rare antiques) but not for personal services or ordinary goods.

Circle G Properties has a contract to purchase a 1,200-acre ranch from Wyoming Cattle Company. Wyoming Cattle Company breaches the contract by refusing to deliver the title. Circle G Properties can request specific performance as a remedy. While there may be other ranches in Wyoming for purchase, there is only one with the right location and size for Circle G.

What Are the Formulas for Damages?

Now that the types of available damages have been defined, the next step is determining how much the nonbreaching party will recover. Because the types of damages can be combined in a recovery, formulas assist in the computation of how much the nonbreaching party can recover.

Liquidated Damages

Some contracts provide damage formulas as part of the parties' agreement. Such a provision could be a flat rate per day or a one-sum balance. Liquidated damage clauses are valid if they are established because of the difficulty in determining damages and are not a penalty to be awarded in addition to other legally provided damage formulas. The parties by agreement in the contract can predetermine the amount of damages in case of a future breach. The amount must be reasonable in anticipation of what the actual loss would be. This type of remedy is useful if there would be difficulties in the proof of loss and other adequate remedies probably would not be available. If the court holds the amount to be a penalty, the liquidated damage provision is void. If valid, the parties are limited to the liquidated damages stated in the contract.

Seller agrees to deliver certain inventory to Buyer, knowing that failure to deliver on time could result in Buyer having to shut down or limit production at its factory. Seller and Buyer agree that for every day Seller delays delivery, it will cost Buyer a loss of somewhere between $4,000 and $8,000. The contract contains a liquidated damage clause of $5,000 per day for each day's late delivery. This is a liquidated damage clause and is valid because it appears to be a reasonable amount in expectation of Buyer's loss, the proof of loss would be difficult to ascertain, and no other adequate remedy would be available.

Compensatory Damages

Service Contracts: When a service contract is breached by the party who hired or retained the other party, the compensatory damages are the compensation the nonbreaching party would have been paid, less any compensation the nonbreaching party earns by working elsewhere.

When the service contract is breached by the person hired, the damages will be the difference between what the hiring party would have paid and what they had to pay to find a substitute.

Daniel is hired as the head of marketing for Mr. Candy, with employment to begin on June 1 at a salary of $265,000. Daniel finds another job as director of marketing that pays $325,000 and tells Mr. Candy about the other job on May 25. Mr. Candy finds itself in a seller's market in terms of hiring and has to hire a new head of marketing for $350,000. Mr. Candy also has to pay a headhunter fee of $35,000 and $22,000 in moving expenses for the new head of marketing. Daniel did not have a provision for moving expenses in the Mr. Candy contract. Damages Daniel would owe to Mr. Candy would be as follows:

Compensatory Formula: Amount required to obtain a substitute employee − Amount under the breached contract + Incidental damages

$350,000 − $265,000 + $35,000 = $120,000

Real Estate Contracts: If the seller breaches the contract and refuses to convey title, the buyer has the choice of specific performance or the difference in cost of buying a substitute parcel.

Rodeo Properties, Inc., agrees to sell Falcon Farms, Inc., a 55-acre parcel in Pima County, Arizona, for $1.2 million. Rodeo Properties then refuses to sell. Falcon Farms finds another parcel in Pima County for a cost of $1.4 million. Falcon can choose specific performance (because the other property is not the same) or recover the $200,000 from Rodeo.

If the buyer breaches the real estate contract, the seller is owed whatever price difference results from the sale to another buyer.

Use the same facts as the Rodeo/Falcon example, but this time, Falcon refuses to close the sale. Rodeo is able to sell the property to Wild Boar Properties for $950,000. Falcon owes Rodeo the difference between $1.2 million and $950,000, or $250,000.

What Are the UCC Remedies for Sellers?

Identify Goods to the Contract

The seller can set aside the goods for the contract. If the seller is still in the process of manufacturing the goods when the buyer repudiates the contract or fails to respond to assurances, the seller can proceed to complete the manufacturing and resell the finished product rather than sell the unfinished goods as scrap. The seller can then proceed with the other remedies discussed below.

Withhold Delivery

If the buyer has repudiated the contract, has failed to provide assurances, or is insolvent, the seller can demand full payment in cash and withhold delivery if the assurances or payment are not given. The seller can then proceed with the other remedies discussed below.

Cancel and/or Rescind Contract

If the buyer is not performing or has failed to provide assurances, the seller can cancel or rescind the contract. The seller must notify the buyer of cancellation promptly and proceed with remedies below, or, if rescission is chosen, the seller is entitled to be indemnified to return to the original position before the contract was made.

Returning to the original position in cases of cancellations may require that the seller be given lost profits (the amount that the seller could have made had the goods been manufactured and sold). This remedy is available because the seller set aside its factory time for production and cannot make up for the loss of production time and the sale of the goods that could have been made.

Resell Goods

The sale must be conducted in a reasonably commercial manner (public or private sale).

- The seller must always give the buyer notice of private and public sale (except for perishable or rapidly declining value goods)
- The sale must be conducted at a reasonable time and place

Important: Any profit goes to the seller, but if there is a deficiency (proceeds of sale do not cover breach and sales costs plus contract price), seller is entitled to the amount not obtained through sale (ie, to obtain a deficiency judgment against the buyer).

If the goods are specially manufactured and cannot be resold, the seller's remedy is the full contract price.

File Suit for Breach of Contract

This option is used mostly if breach takes place before delivery or the buyer improperly rejects goods. There are choices for the seller:

- The measure of damages is the difference between the market price at the time and place of tender and the unpaid contract price, plus incidental damages
- The seller can resell the goods and recover the difference between the contract price and the resale price, plus incidental damages
- The seller has the choice to collect on the market price or resell the goods and collect the difference

- The statute of limitations for bringing suit for breach of contract under the UCC is four years from the time the breach occurs. The parties can agree to a period of less than four years but cannot agree to have less than a one-year statute of limitations
- For breach of warranty, the statute of limitations begins to run when the goods are tendered to the buyer

Joan and David order artificial turf from Turf Specialists for their lawn at a cost of $10,000. Joan and David pay a deposit of $2,000. The contract is formed on March 1, and the artificial turf is delivered by Turf Specialists on May 1. Joan and David reject the artificial turf because they say Turf Specialists delivered the wrong style. Turf Specialists delivered the type of turf that Joan and David specified in their contract. The market price on May 1 for the turf Joan and David ordered was $12,000. However, Turf Specialists has found another buyer for the turf for a price of $10,000. There will be delivery charges to that buyer of $500. The damages Turf Specialists is entitled to would be computed as follows:

Turf Specialists can sell the turf to another buyer and collect as follows:

Contract Price − Resale Price + Incidental Damages − Deposit

$10,000 − $10,000 + $500 − $2,000 = ($1,500), or the buyer owes no damages

Market Price − Contract Price + Incidental Damages − Deposit

$12,000 − $10,000 + $500 − $2,000 = $500 in damages under the market price formula

Again, the remedy chosen is the seller's choice.

Retain Buyer's Deposit

When the seller justifiably withholds delivery of goods and the buyer has made a deposit or payment and there is no liquidated damage clause, the seller may keep $500 or 20% of the purchase price, whichever is less.

If Buyer Is Insolvent

If the buyer is not paying debts when due or in ordinary course of business or insolvent under the Bankruptcy Act, the seller (upon buyer's repudiation) can stop any quantity shipped and can also recover goods from the buyer within 10 days after delivery. In addition, if the buyer misrepresents solvency within 90 days prior to delivery of goods on credit, there are no time limits on the seller's ability to recover the goods. Note that the rights for the seller to reclaim the goods when there is insolvency continue through delivery to the buyer (with the time limitations noted for insolvency events).

Stratford sells 300 flat-screen TVs to Kelvinator Appliance on a line of credit. There are rumors in the retail appliance industry that Kelvinator is struggling financially. Stratford demands assurances from Kelvinator that it will be able to pay for the TVs. Kelvinator sends an audited financial statement to Stratford on September 1 that indicates Kelvinator is in good financial condition and has a steady cash flow. Stratford ships the 300 TVs to Kelvinator on October 1. While the TVs are in transit, Kelvinator files for bankruptcy (on October 14). Stratford would occupy a position of priority above Kelvinator's secured creditors because of the misrepresentation of solvency, even though the goods would be reclaimed after 10 days. There is no time limit on a seller's right to reclaim the goods when there is a misrepresentation of solvency.

If the Buyer Is Not Insolvent

The seller can stop large shipments (carloads, truckloads, planeloads of goods). While sellers can stop any size shipment for insolvency (to prevent having the seller lose the goods when there can be no payment), stoppage of large shipments for other reasons is allowed because large shipments are easier to track and stop. Stopping any size shipment for any reason would result in a slowing of commerce.

This detailed concept, on insolvency and the recovery of goods, has been tested on the exam a number of times in the context of bankruptcy questions. Although the UCC is not currently a specific topic on the exam, its concepts show up in other areas. This concept of priority in goods upon insolvency is one of those concepts.

A contract calls for the seller's delivery of five cases of peas to the buyer's place of business. The five cases are loaded on ABC Truck Carrier's truck. The truck is also hauling products from five other sellers. The buyer repudiates the contract, claiming that the seller's peas are of poor quality. The seller cannot stop the goods in transit because the buyer's repudiation is not due to insolvency and the shipment (five cases) is not a truckload.

Remedies for the Seller If the Buyer Is Insolvent or Has Repudiated the Contract

The seller can stop shipment at any time (under the insolvency and repudiation rules just discussed). Until the buyer actually takes possession of the goods, there is a negotiation (formal transfer) to the buyer of a negotiable document of title or notification by a third party, such as a warehouseman or carrier, to the buyer that the goods are available for pickup.

Remedies for Seller If the Buyer Has Possession

- If the buyer received the goods on credit while insolvent, the seller may reclaim the goods within 10 days of receipt by buyer. If there has been misrepresentation of insolvency, then the 10-day time limitation does not apply
- The seller can seek to recover damages noted—the compensatory damages of the contract purchase price, plus any incidental damages incurred because of the buyer's failure to pay

The following chart provides a summary of the seller's remedies under Article 2 of the UCC.

	Stop Delivery	Resale Price	Market Price	Action for Price	Lost Profit
When Available	Insolvency*; advance breach by buyer	Buyer fails to take goods	Buyer fails to take goods	Specially manufactured goods	Anticipatory repudiation
Nature of Remedy	Stop delivery of any size shipment or recover goods if insolvent; stop delivery of large shipments for other reasons; reclaim**	K price*** − Resale price + Incidental damages − Expenses saved	K price − Market price + Incidental damages − Expenses saved	K price + Incidental damages − Expenses saved	Profits + Incidental damages − Salvage value

** Inability to pay debts*

*** Latest changes to UCC permit any size shipment stoppage*

**** K price = contract price*

What Are the UCC Remedies for Buyers?

Remedies When the Seller Fails to Deliver the Goods

- **Cancel and Rescind with Notice:** The contract is rescinded by the buyer with the effect of restoring both buyer and seller back to the positions they would have been before entering the contract
- **Cover:** Permits the buyer to make a reasonable substitute purchase (eg, on the open market) in good faith and within a reasonable time. The buyer can then recover the difference between the cost of cover and the contract price, plus incidental damages and consequential damages (foreseeable loss), less expenses saved in consequence of the seller's breach

Hartford School District orders 22 school buses from Educational Motors (EM) for delivery on August 3. Hartford's school year begins on August 15. On August 2, EM notifies Hartford that it cannot deliver the buses because of a shortage of materials. Hartford is unable to secure buses to cover for the EM breach until September 7. Hartford has to lease Greyhound charter buses at a cost of $1,000 per day per bus for the 15 school days until the alternative buses would arrive.

The new buses were purchased for $100,000 each. Hartford's contract with EM was for a cost of $90,000 per bus. Compute the damages Hartford could recover, listing the types of damages and amounts.

Compensatory Damages: 22 × ($100,000 − $90,000) = $220,000 (cost for covering to obtain substitute goods)

Incidental Damages: lease of 22 charter buses for 15 days at $1,000 per day = $330,000

Sue for Breach of Contract: The buyer can treat the nondelivery as a breach of contract and pursue a lawsuit to recover damages. The damages can include the difference between the market price at the time that the buyer learned of the breach (this time metric is changed to place of tender if goods are rejected or time of revocation of acceptance and at place of arrival) and contract price, plus incidental and consequential damages.

Specific Performance: Specific performance is available when the goods are unique or in other proper circumstances such as when the remedy to cover is not available (eg, rare goods, antiques). Specific performance is rare under UCC Article 2.

The seller agrees to sell the buyer an original painting by Picasso. Later, the seller refuses to deliver the painting even though the buyer has fully tendered the contract price. The buyer can in a court in equity file an action for specific performance (painting is unique—one of a kind) requiring the seller to transfer the painting to the buyer.

Replevin: If the seller refuses to tender delivery of identified goods to the buyer and the buyer cannot cover, the buyer can file a suit in equity requiring the seller to deliver the goods to the buyer. Replevin is also rare and would occur in those types of contracts where cover is not possible.

Remedies for Buyers If the Seller Tenders Nonconforming Goods (Buyer Rejects)

Some remedies that are available to buyers in the case of seller nondelivery are also available to buyers when sellers ship nonconforming goods, including:

- Cancellation
- Cover: If the seller was to deliver three-speed blenders, the buyer can go out and purchase substitute blenders to cover the breach by the seller. If all the buyer can find in the short time afforded for cover is five-speed blenders, that would be considered reasonable cover
- Treating the nonconforming goods shipped as breach of contract and pursuing suit for damages
- Keeping the goods and recovering damages for the value of the goods as delivered and as they should have been. (A price reduction for damages is typical)

Remedies for Buyers Who Accept Nonconforming Goods

The buyer can, with notice, pursue the following remedies. (Notice is important because failure to give notice bars the buyer from any remedies.)

Recover Compensatory Damages: These damages would include incidental and consequential damages.

Plessy College orders 2,000 picture frames from Advanced Frames for the members of the graduating class. Plessy had put together a photo collage of the events at Plessy over the past four years as a gift for the graduates. Advanced Frames sends Plessy 8 × 10" frames instead of the 11 × 13" frames Plessy ordered. There is not enough time to locate 2,000 frames and have the gift available for the graduating students. Plessy keeps the frames but has to have the photo collages reprinted to a smaller size at a cost of $1.50 per photo. Explain the damages Plessy could collect because of its need to keep nonconforming goods.

The reprinting of the pictures would be incidental damages and could be recovered. The amount would be the $1.50 reprinting costs for 2,000 photo collages, or $3,000.

Recover for Breach of Warranty: The buyer can recover the difference between the value of the goods accepted and the value the goods would have been, had they been as warranted (unless special circumstances show proximate damages of a different amount), plus, if appropriate, incidental and consequential damages.

An accounting firm purchases a computer warranted to be a $40,000 value for $30,000. Upon delivery, the computer (although usable) is found to be worth only $20,000 due to a defect. Unless special circumstances show proximate damages of a different amount, the buyer should recover $20,000, the difference between the value as warranted, $40,000, and the value of the computer as delivered, $20,000.

Deduction of Damages from Purchase Price (the "Self-Help" Remedy): The buyer can deduct all or any part of the damages from the price still due and payable to the seller. The buyer should note clearly to the seller that the amount tendered is in "Full Accord and Satisfaction" or "Payment in Full" and that the seller's acceptance of the deducted amount is considered full satisfaction of the debt.

The buyer has contracted for 10 new file cabinets priced at $300 each. The new file cabinets are tendered, but two are scratched, though still fully usable. With notice, the buyer can accept all 10 file cabinets and tender to the seller a check for $2,900 ($50 per scratched cabinet deduction to cover refinishing costs) and a letter, indicating clearly on both the check and the letter that the check is intended as final payment and it is in full accord and satisfaction of the contract price. If the seller cashes the check, the buyer has fully paid and has no further liability.

Buyer Can Seek Recovery of the Goods after Payment: If the buyer makes a payment and the seller is or becomes insolvent within 10 days of receipt of the payment and the goods are identified, then the buyer can tender the balance owed and is entitled to the goods.

Buyers' Remedies under Article 2

	Specific Performance (Replevin)	**Cover**	**Market**
When Available	Rare, unique goods	Seller fails to deliver	Seller fails to deliver
Nature of Remedy	Buyer gets goods (incidentals)	Cover price − K price + Incidentals + Consequential damages − Expenses saved	Market price − K price + Incidentals + Consequential damages − Expenses saved

REG 7
Debtor-Creditor Relationships

REG 7: Debtor-Creditor Relationships

7.01 Debtor-Creditor Relationship

Suretyship

Representative Task (Remembering & Understanding): Explain the rights, duties, and liabilities of debtors, creditors, and guarantors.

Representative Task (Application): Identify rights, duties, liabilities of debtors, creditors, or guarantors given a specific scenario.

Suretyship Terminology

A guarantor or a surety is someone who agrees to stand liable for the debt of another. A guaranty or suretyship is a way for a creditor to have another form of backup for payment of the obligation owed. A surety or guarantor can be in addition to any collateral the debtor might pledge to the creditor.

The Parties in a Suretyship

In a simple suretyship, there is a loan between a creditor and the principal debtor. The repayment of that loan is guaranteed by a surety or a guarantor.

- Creditor
- Principal debtor
- Surety or guarantor

There are additional terms that apply to suretyships that are different from the simple three-party model.

- **Guarantor of Collection:** The exam uses the terms "surety" and "guarantor" interchangeably. However, when the term "guarantor of collection" is used, the suretyship has an additional level of complexity. A guarantor of collection does not provide an immediate guarantee of the principal debtor's debt. A guarantor of collection only agrees to pay the principal debtor's debt *after* the creditor has exhausted all possible means of collection, including a suit to recover payment
- **Cosurety:** A cosurety is an additional surety on an obligation. Some creditors demand more than one surety as a protection. Cosureties can be sureties for the full amount of the debt. Cosureties can also be sureties for certain percentages of the debt
- **Subsurety:** A subsurety is a surety to a surety. There is a primary surety to step in when the debtor defaults, but if the primary surety also defaults, the subsurety steps in to pay. A creditor cannot turn first to a subsurety. The creditor must approach subsureties in the order in which they agreed to stand liable

Frank owes money to June. Dallan agrees to serve as a surety for Frank. Frank is the principal debtor, June is the creditor, and Dallan is the surety or guarantor.

Oscar made a $50,000 loan to Savannah but required that Savannah obtain at least two sureties for the loan. Hector has agreed to act as a surety for $50,000, and Emma has also agreed to act as a surety for $50,000. Oscar is the creditor, Savannah is the principal debtor, and Hector and Emma are cosureties.

First Consolidated made a $200,000 loan to Thesis Labs and required Thesis to obtain a surety. Thesis was able to obtain Quality Assurance as a surety for $200,000, but only if Thesis obtained a surety for Quality Assurance. Thesis obtained Fidelity as a surety for Quality Assurance. First Consolidated is the creditor, Thesis Labs is the principal debtor, Quality Assurance is a surety, and Fidelity is a subsurety for Quality Assurance.

Creation of a Suretyship

Writing Required

Because the suretyship is a relationship in which a third party agrees to stand liable for the debt of another, the suretyship contract must be evidenced by a record and signed by the surety (guarantor) for it to be enforceable against that surety. Suretyships are one of the contracts subject to the Statute of Frauds.

Consideration Is Not Required

A suretyship is created even when the surety is not compensated. However, there are different rights when there is a compensated versus an uncompensated surety.

Amount of Surety Pledge

Sureties, cosureties, and subsureties can pledge to back the debtor on 100% of the loan amount or any percentage thereof. When there are cosureties with unequal amounts pledged and the debtor defaults, the allocation of financial responsibilities among the sureties is computed on a pro rata basis. The creditor has the choice of cosureties. The creditor can demand payment from all of the cosureties (on a pro rata basis), or the creditor can choose to collect from a single cosurety for an amount that covers the full debt. The cosurety who pays the full debt can then recover the pro rata amounts due from the remaining cosureties.

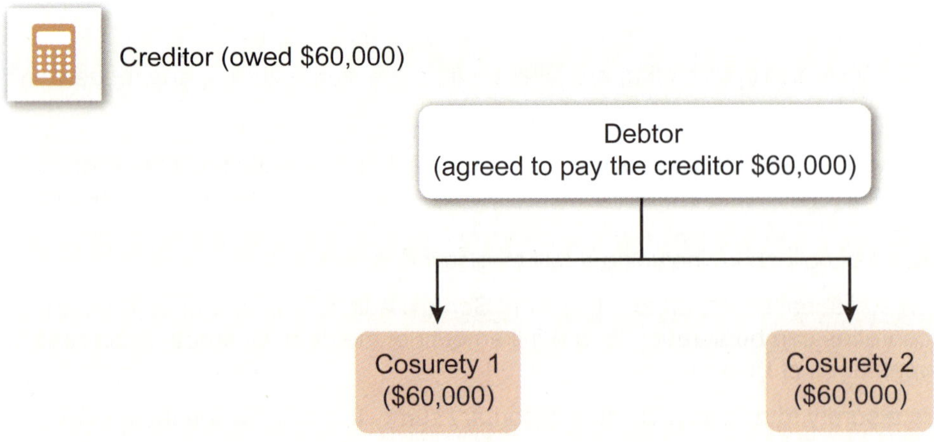

The creditor can turn to one or both of the cosureties for payment. If one cosurety has to pay the full amount due, then the other cosureties are liable for paying their share. Each surety is responsible for its share of the $60,000, determined by using a denominator of $120,000 and a numerator of their pledged amounts. If the debtor defaults owing $40,000, then Cosureties 1 and 2 each owe $20,000 ($60,000 / $120,000 × $40,000).

Creditor (owed $60,000)

Debtor (agreed to pay the creditor $60,000)

Suppose that a debtor owes the creditor $60,000. The debtor has three cosureties, as follows:

Cosurety 1: $30,000

Cosurety 2: $45,000

Cosurety 3: $15,000

If the debtor defaults owing $45,000, the cosureties' obligations are as follows:

Cosurety 1 owes $30,000 / $90,000 × $45,000 = $15,000

Cosurety 2 owes $45,000 / $90,000 × $45,000 = $22,500

Cosurety 3 owes $15,000 / $90,000 × $45,000 = $7,500

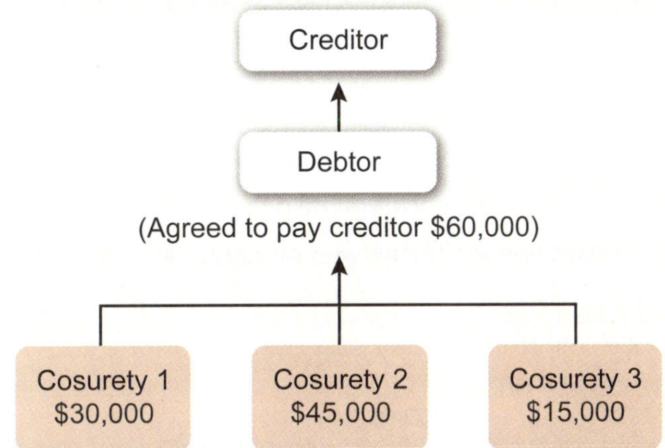

Suppose the same facts, but Cosurety 3 has declared bankruptcy.

The debtor has defaulted and still owes $45,000. To determine how much Cosurety 1 and Cosurety 2 owe, simply take Cosurety 3's pledged amount out of the denominator and continue to use the surety's share as the numerator. The original denominator was $90,000. With Cosurety 3 out in bankruptcy, the denominator is now $75,000; Cosurety 1 owes $30,000/$75,000, and Cosurety 2 owes $45,000/$75,000.

Cosurety 1 = $30,000 / $75,000 × $45,000 or $18,000

Cosurety 2 = $45,000 / $75,000 × $45,000 or $27,000

Be sure to know how to do these computations for surety liability, both with and without a surety bankruptcy.

Rights of the Creditor When the Principal Debtor Defaults

Generally, upon a principal debtor's default, the creditor has several choices in terms of how to proceed to collect the amount due:

- Recover from the principal debtor personally and/or the debtor's property
- Recover from the surety personally according to the surety contract
- Recover by proceeding against the collateral of the debtor held by either the creditor or the surety. The creditor can sell the collateral to satisfy the debt and default costs, and any balance must be turned over to the principal debtor

Rights of the Surety or Guarantor

Exoneration: This equitable right permits a surety to petition the court to order the creditor by court decree to exhaust recovery against the principal debtor before holding the surety liable.

Phillip is in default on a guaranteed loan made by West Bank. Phillip has numerous assets, but these are located in another state. Evans Assurance, the surety, has most of its assets tied up (such as in long-term CDs), to the extent that if Evans is required to pay now, it will suffer severe financial losses. Under these circumstances, Evans could petition a court of equity for exoneration, which the court may grant, thereby requiring the creditor to proceed first against the debtor.

Reimbursement and Indemnity: Whenever the surety has fully or partially fulfilled the debtor's obligation to the creditor, the surety has a right to seek reimbursement from the principal debtor. The right of reimbursement covers all costs that the surety has incurred because of surety agreement.

Subrogation: Upon payment, the surety steps into the shoes of the creditor and succeeds in any rights the creditor has. These rights include the following:

- Creditor's rights against the principal debtor, including the right to file a claim in bankruptcy
- Creditor's rights to the principal debtor's collateral held by the creditor or the surety
- Creditor's rights against third parties (eg, those who damage the principal debtor's collateral held by the creditor)
- Creditor's rights against a cosurety

Evans has guaranteed a loan made to Phillips by West Bank. West Bank has in its possession collateral owned by Phillips, some of which has been damaged due to the negligence of a third party, Green. Phillips files for bankruptcy, and the bankruptcy court, upon West Bank's petition, allows West Bank to collect from Evans.

What are Evans's rights in this situation?

Evans has the right of subrogation. This right allows Evans to file West Bank's creditor's claim against Phillips's bankruptcy estate, to sue Green for damage to the collateral due to Green's negligence, and to take possession of any remaining collateral held by West Bank.

Right of Contribution

The right of contribution applies when two or more cosureties are liable on the same obligation to the same creditor and, upon debtor's default, one cosurety pays more than their proportionate share of the obligation. The right of contribution entitles the cosurety who has paid to recover the amount paid above the pro rata share from the other cosurety or cosureties.

- **Joint and Several Liability:** Cosureties are jointly and severally liable. They can become cosureties by contract, can be bound as cosureties for different amounts, and can become cosureties even without knowledge of each other's existence
- **Release of Cosurety:** If the creditor releases a cosurety without the other cosureties' consent (or reserving rights in the release in the remaining cosureties), the remaining cosureties' liability is released to the extent that the right of contribution cannot be obtained

- **Reimbursement:** If a cosurety is fully reimbursed, there is no right of contribution
- **Collateral:** In the absence of another agreement, cosureties are entitled to share in proportion to their liability of a debtor's collateral in the hands of the creditor or acquired by a surety after the cosuretyship relationship was created

Able, Baker, and Carl are cosureties on Daniel's $50,000 debt. Able's maximum liability is $10,000, Baker's maximum liability is $16,000, and Carl's maximum liability is $24,000. Daniel is in default and still owes $40,000. The creditor collects the full amount from Carl, and Carl seeks the right of contribution from Able and Baker. Carl has these rights because Carl has paid more than his proportionate share of $19,200. Using the formula above:

Able: $10,000 / $50,000 × $40,000 = $8,000

Baker: $16,000 / $50,000 × $40,000 = $12,800, which means Carl's proportionate share owed is:

$24,000 / $50,000 × $40,000 = $19,200

Defenses of the Parties—Events That Do Not Release or Discharge the Surety from Liability

There are certain events that can occur as the principal debtor, the creditor, and the surety perform their obligations and exercise their rights.

- **Insolvency of the Principal Debtor:** Problems with the principal debtor's ability to pay is the reason for the surety agreement
- **Bankruptcy of the Principal Debtor:** Financial problems that the debtor might experience are among the reasons for having a surety agreement
- **Fraud or Misrepresentation by the Debtor:** The debtor fraudulently misrepresents their financial status in order to convince the surety to act as a surety for the debtor's obligation to the creditor. Unless the creditor participated with the debtor in perpetrating the fraud, the surety is not released because of the fraud. The surety has the usual contract defenses and resulting damage rights against the debtor, but the surety must still pay the obligation to the creditor
- **Principal Debtor's Incapacity:** Mental or age incapacity of the debtor does not affect the surety's obligation to pay the debt upon default

Daniel is the minor son of Emily, and Emily is the surety of a loan West Bank made to Daniel. Daniel, being a minor, has legally disaffirmed liability on the loan from West Bank. Although West Bank cannot hold Daniel liable, Emily cannot escape surety liability on the basis of Daniel's minority status as a defense.

Death of the Principal Debtor

The death of the principal debtor does not discharge the surety. The surety is there as a backup for payment to the creditor when unforeseen events occur.

Release of the Principal Debtor

Release of the principal debtor by the creditor, without the surety's consent and with the creditor reserving rights against the surety, automatically results in a release of the surety. There are circumstances when the release of the principal debtor makes no difference in terms of the surety's obligation. Also, when there is a guarantor of collection and the creditor releases the debtor, there is a release of the guarantor of collection because the guarantor agreed to pay only after the creditor exhausted all means of collection against the debtor. The creditor must fulfill the obligation of exhausting all means of collection from the debtor. Relinquishing that right gives a guarantor of collection a release.

If the creditor, in the release to the principal debtor, reserved rights against the surety, this is no longer a release but a covenant not to sue, which does not discharge the guarantor from liability.

There are times when the release of the debtor will not affect the surety's responsibility for payment. If the release does not affect the surety's rights, then the release of the principal debtor does not release the surety. For example, if the debtor is already in bankruptcy, the creditor's release does not affect the surety's rights. The surety will just be in line with other creditors in bankruptcy. If, however, the creditor released collateral and the debtor, the surety would be released to the extent of the amount of the collateral because the surety would have been a secured creditor in bankruptcy with a higher priority.

Changes or Modification

Changes or modification of the loan terms when there is a compensated surety may or may not discharge the surety. The surety is not released if the modifications make payments easier for the debtor. If the creditor has reduced the interest rate of the loan, such a reduction helps the debtor to pay and would not discharge the surety.

Phillips wants a loan to start a restaurant. West Bank will not make the loan to Phillips without a satisfactory surety. Evans, a financial entrepreneur, agrees with Phillips to be a surety if Phillips will turn over to Evans 5% of all gross proceeds for three years. Phillips agrees, and the guaranteed loan contract is made with West Bank. Later, Phillips and West Bank make a material, binding modification of the loan without Evans's consent. Upon Phillips's default, because Evans is a compensated surety, Evans can escape surety liability only to the extent of losses Evans can prove were suffered due to the modification. The key here is that the modification must affect the ability to collect the amount of the loan from the debtor.

Failure of Creditor to Give Surety Notice of Default

The creditor's failure to give the surety notice of the principal debtor's default does not result in a discharge. Unless the creditor agreed to give notice of the default, the creditor is not required to do so. The creditor is entitled to payment from the surety when there is default.

Failure of Creditor to Resort to Collateral First

Failure of the creditor to first resort to the collateral in order to satisfy the debt does not result in a discharge of the surety because it is the creditor's choice as to whether to proceed against the surety, against the collateral, or through litigation against the principal debtor.

Defenses of the Parties—Events That Result in the Release of the Surety

Principal Debt Paid: Once the principal debtor has satisfied the obligation to the creditor, the surety is released from the suretyship obligation.

Surety's Incapacity: Note that in some states a minor does not have capacity to contract as a guarantor or surety.

Surety's Discharge Decree in Bankruptcy: With certain exemptions discussed in bankruptcy, bankruptcy discharges all the debts of the bankrupt's estate, including surety obligations.

Statute of Limitations Expires: All contractual obligations are enforceable only if actions to enforce them are brought within the statute of limitations that applies to contracts. In a surety relationship, the statute of limitations for the creditor begins on the date the surety's liability kicked in (ie, when the creditor had the right to turn to the surety for payment).

Fraud or Misrepresentation by the Creditor: A surety is released from payment obligations to the creditor if the creditor participated with the principal debtor in committing fraud or misrepresentation that resulted in the surety's willingness to sign as a surety for the principal debtor. To be released for this reason, the surety must be able to show that the principal debtor and the creditor were working together to use false information to convince the surety to act as a surety.

Advance Mortgage works with Desmond Developers to create financial statements for Desmond that are fraudulent. Advance and Desmond also have an agreement with an appraiser on acreage to inflate the value of the land. Using those fraudulent bank statements and the falsified appraisal, Safety Surety agrees to act as surety for an Advance Mortgage loan to Desmond for $4 million for the purchase of acreage. Safety Surety is released from the suretyship for Desmond because of the joint fraud by Advance and Desmond. Note: This example is different from the debtor alone defrauding the surety.

Release of the Principal Debtor: If the principal debtor is released without the surety's consent, collateral of the principal debtor held by either the creditor or the surety can still be used by the creditor to satisfy the debt.

Refusal of the Principal Debtor's Tender: If the principal debtor tenders payment to the creditor under a surety contract, and the creditor refuses the proper tender, the surety is completely discharged from liability.

Peter has a loan from West Bank that is fully guaranteed by Susan. Peter sends a check for the full amount of the debt, including interest, to West Bank. Peter has more than sufficient funds on deposit at West Bank to cover the check, and the check clearly states that payment is in full accord and satisfaction of the loan. However, a bank officer mistakenly believes that the amount of the check is insufficient to cover both the principal and interest owed and sends the check back to Peter. Under these circumstances (proper tender refused), Susan is discharged from surety liability, and only Peter remains liable to West Bank.

Material Alteration by the Creditor: Any *material* alteration of the written loan or surety contract, such as the amount of the debt, by the creditor is a complete discharge of the surety's liability. The material alteration release includes situations in which the creditor substitutes a different principal debtor. A surety contract is personal to the principal debtor, and there cannot be substitution or assignment without the consent of the surety. Without consent, the surety is released from liability.

Gloria is the mother of Phillip, and she has guaranteed a loan made to Phillip by West Bank. Later, Phillip and West Bank, without Gloria's consent, raise the amount of the loan's interest rate and extend the loan period. This is a binding (with consideration) and material modification of the loan contract. Since Gloria is a gratuitous (uncompensated) surety, this modification completely discharges her surety liability.

Creditor's Failure to Disclose: A creditor's failure to disclose material facts that affect the risks of liability to a prospective surety is, in most states, presumed to be the defense of fraud and permits the guarantor to disaffirm the surety contract (complete discharge of liability).

Peter seeks a loan from West Bank. After a careful credit analysis, West Bank denies the loan because of two factors that West Bank feels would make the loan too risky to make. The next day, Peter goes to West Bank with a prospective surety, Gloria, who is a wealthy customer of the bank. Gloria tells West Bank to make the loan to Peter. Gloria also offers to sign a surety contract. In this case, if West Bank is willing to make the loan with Gloria as surety, the bank must tell Gloria of the material risk factors that caused it to deny the loan. Failure to do so is presumed fraud, and this failure allows Gloria, at any time, to disaffirm her surety liability.

Changes and Modifications Where There Is an Uncompensated Surety: A material and binding modification of the loan contract made between the principal debtor and the creditor without the consent of the surety results in a release of the uncompensated surety.

Evans is a gratuitous surety on a loan made for Erika, one of Evans's daughters, by West Bank. The loan is due in one month. Without Evans's consent, Erika and West Bank agree to extend the loan period for one month without interest or other fees charged. After the one month, Erika defaults. This type of change is not a change in the loan terms; it is simply an extension of time for the original terms (immaterial). The extension made no difference in the amount due or even the ability of the debtor to pay. Sureties are discharged when they are affected by a change, such as when collateral is released or the loan is restructured, but an added month on a loan that is already due does not change the loan contract in amount, interest, or terms.

Surrender or Impairment of Debtor's Collateral: If the creditor surrenders the debtor's collateral held in the creditor's possession without the consent of the surety or commits acts that impair the value of the collateral, the surety is discharged to the extent of loss suffered by the surety due to the surrender or impairment. The surety's obligation is reduced only by the amount of the collateral lost or released.

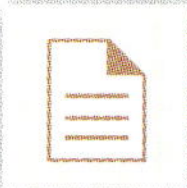

West Bank made a $100,000 loan to Phillip, with Phillip transferring to West Bank 5,000 shares of stock (value $25,000) and having Evans as a surety. Later, without Evans's consent, West Bank releases back to Phillip 3,000 shares. Upon Philip's default, Evans's surety liability on the $100,000 surety will be reduced by the value of the shares released to Phillip (or $15,000). If West Bank released all the shares back to Phillip, Evans would be released of $25,000 of the $100,000 surety obligation.

Special Release for Guarantor of Collections: Any failure of the creditor to give a guarantor of collection proper notice of the principal debtor's default, or any material delay in attempting to collect first from the principal debtor, discharges the guarantor of collection from liability to the extent of loss suffered by such failure.

A guaranty of collections is different from a surety or a simple guaranty, so this failure to give notice is different from an ordinary surety relationship, where the failure to give notice does not result in a release.

Lack of a Written Agreement—Complying with the Statute of Frauds: Surety contracts must be in writing. A surety is always released from liability under an oral suretyship agreement.

Secured Transactions

Representative Task (Remembering & Understanding): Explain the difference between a secured and unsecured creditor and the requirements needed to perfect a security interest.

A different method creditors use to reduce lending risks is to take an interest in collateral pledged by the debtor. The collateral can then be sold to satisfy the debt should the debtor not repay the loan. When goods, tangible personal property, fixtures, and some personal property rights are pledged as collateral, the process for doing so is covered under UCC Article 9: Secured Transactions.

Application and Basics of Article 9 Security Interests

Article 9 of the UCC is the uniform law that governs the rights of creditors and debtors for security interests in personal property and fixtures.

Application of Article 9

The general types of property that can be used for Article 9 security interests are personal property, fixtures, and goods. There are also types of property that exist through records and documents and include negotiable instruments, accounts, and some types of tort claims.

Article 9 does not apply to other types of interests evidenced by a record, such as some liens, some tort claims, judgments, leases, and real estate mortgages.

Basic Terminology of Article 9

There are some terms used in discussing the creation, perfection, and enforcement of secured transactions that are listed and defined in the table below.

Term	Explanation
Secured party	The creditor who has a security interest in the debtor's collateral; can be a seller or lender
Creditor	The party that lends money or extends credit to the debtor
Debtor	The party who is pleading property to secure a loan from a creditor/secured party
Security interest	The interest in the collateral held by the secured party and owned by the debtor that secures payment or performance of an obligation
Security agreement	The agreement between the debtor and secured party that creates or provides for a security interest
Collateral	The debtor's property that is the subject of the security interest
Financing statement	Referred to as a UCC-1 form, this document is the required written proof of the security interest and description of the collateral and is usually filed to give public notice to third parties of the secured party's interest

Collateral Terminology of Article 9

The rights of a secured party and creditors vary, depending on the type of collateral. The following table gives the classifications of collateral under Article 9. These classifications often control priority requirements and rights of debtors.

Term	Explanation
Consumer goods	Used or bought primarily for personal, family, or household purposes
Equipment	Used or bought primarily for use in a business and not part of inventory or farm products
Farm products	Crops (including aquatic goods) and livestock, or supplies produced in a farming operation, such as ginned cotton, milk, eggs, or maple syrup
Inventory	Held by a debtor for sale under a contract of service or lease, or raw materials held for production and work in progress
Fixtures	Personal property that becomes so attached or so related to realty that an interest in them arises under real estate law
Accessions	Personal property that is so attached, installed, or fixed to other personal property (goods) that it becomes part of the goods (other personal property)

Collateral Terminology of Article 9: Types of Intangible Goods

There are also forms of intangible property under Article 9 that provide for special rules and exceptions in the validity and priority of Article 9 security interests. For example, commercial tort claims can include organizational and individual tort claims but not tort claims for personal injury or death damages.

Basic Article 9 Security Interest Relationships

In an Article 9 debtor-creditor relationship, the creditor loans the debtor money, and the debtor agrees to pay back the loan but also pledges collateral under a security agreement as a means of reducing risk for the creditor. The collateral gives the creditor a fallback resource for collecting the debt. With an Article 9 security interest, the creditor is a secured party, which means that the creditor can repossess and sell the collateral and that the creditor takes a priority position in bankruptcy, with secured creditors being paid directly from the funds obtained through the sale of the collateral.

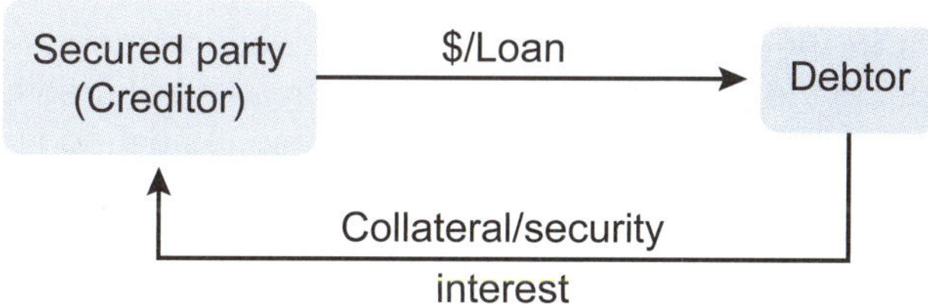

Creation of a Security Interest

A security interest is created by attachment. Attachment requires five steps: writing or record, signed or authenticated by the debtor, interest in the collateral, value, and underlying debt.

The Five Requirements for Attachment of a Security Interest

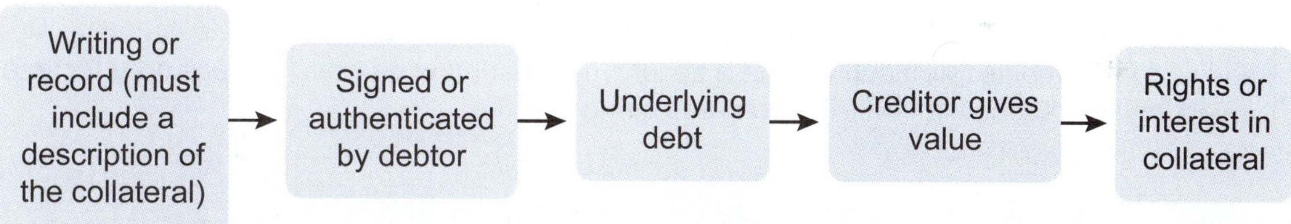

A writing or record: A "writing" is shorthand for all forms of tangible records, including electronic documents. Unless the collateral is in the possession of the secured party, there must be a written agreement creating a security interest, which is called a security agreement. Possession really is nine-tenths of the law and does serve as a substitute for a writing or record.

The security agreement must describe the collateral. Article 9 also gives examples of what constitutes a sufficient description of the collateral, such as "specified listing, category, quantity," and states that supergeneric descriptions, such as "all the debtor's assets" or "all the debtor's personal property" or similar words, are not a sufficient description.

The debtor must sign or authenticate the record: The writing must be signed or authenticated by the debtor. Authenticated includes any agreement or signature inscribed on a tangible medium or stored in an electronic or other retrievable medium.

There must be an underlying debt: There must be an underlying obligation between the debtor and the creditor; pledging collateral without an underlying debt is an illegal servitude.

The underlying debt can be preexisting. For example, a debtor may owe $500 to a creditor that has not been paid. In lieu of payment, the debtor can offer small payments and pledge some property as security for that repayment.

The creditor must give value: The creditor need not give present consideration, as is required with contracts, but there must be something of value underlying the pledge of the collateral. Value can be an unpaid unsecured debt or the creditor agreeing not to file suit for collection of an existing debt.

A creditor giving a debtor a credit line has given sufficient value to qualify for the security interest. The creditor could, for example, take a security interest in the debtor's equipment in exchange for the line of credit. As long as the credit line exists, the creditor qualifies for the value requirement. The security interest attaches immediately, even without a draw on the credit line, because the promise of the creditor in granting the credit line is sufficient value.

The debtor must have rights in the collateral: Rights in the collateral means some form of ownership interest. If the creditor is financing the purchase of inventory with a line of credit, the creditor will have an interest in the inventory (collateral) once that inventory is identified, as defined under UCC Article 2, which is that the goods are shipped, marked, or otherwise identified for the debtor.

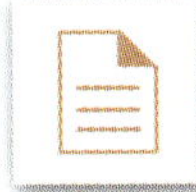

Safeco Production, Inc. (seller), and Bruce Equipment (buyer) sign a line of credit agreement as well as a security agreement (which meets all of the requirements under UCC Article 9) on December 1. The equipment is to be delivered FOB Bruce Equipment on December 15. The security agreement would attach when the goods are tendered at Bruce's place of business. If their contract terms were FOB Safeco Production, the security agreement would attach when the goods are shipped, marked, or otherwise designated for Bruce.

All five requirements for attachment of a security interest must be met. There is no attachment of a security interest until all five requirements come together.

The Meaning of Having a Security Interest

Once a creditor has a security interest in the debtor's collateral, the creditor gains the following rights:

- The right to repossess the collateral if the debtor defaults
- The right to sell the collateral to satisfy the debt if the debtor defaults
- The right to a top-priority position in bankruptcy proceedings
- The right to perfect the security interest against other creditors

Perfection of Security Interests: Additional Priority

Perfection is a means for the creditor to obtain priority over other security interests. There are four methods of perfection under UCC Article 9: Filing, Possession, Automatic, and Temporary.

Perfection by Filing

What Is Filed?

The creditor must file a record with the following information (if the debtor's authenticated security agreement meets these requirements, the security agreement can be filed):

- Names of both the debtor and the secured party and authentication or signature by the debtor
- Addresses of the debtor and the secured creditor. This information is critical for notification purposes, and notifications are critical in determining priorities of secured creditors
- A description of the collateral, which can be more general than the security agreement because the purpose of filing a financing statement is to let third parties know that the debtor has pledged property. The description for a financing statement can be a generic description, such as "all assets" or "all personal property." The standards for security agreement descriptions require greater specificity

Where Are Financing Statements Filed?

The place for filing is specified in each state statute. However, for the exam, the important information is that there are two generic places for filing: central and local. Local (which would be county recorder, land offices) filing is for fixtures and extractions (timber, oil, gas, and minerals). Central filing is for all other types of collateral. The important thing for central filing is to file in the state where the collateral is located.

When Can a Financing Statement Be Filed?

Once the debtor has authenticated the financing statement, it can be filed at any time by the creditor. However, perfection cannot occur until the security interest has attached. The financing statement is effective for five years from the date of filing and can be extended for another five years if a continuation statement is filed (only) during the six-month period prior to the expiration of the five-year period.

GEN Financing and Grayson Tools have entered into a security agreement for a $250,000 loan from GEN to Grayson. GEN has taken a security interest in the equipment Grayson will purchase with the loan funds. The paperwork for the security interest is signed on February 1. GEN files a financing statement for the collateral on February 2. The equipment is shipped to Grayson on February 24. The perfection is not effective until February 24—all requirements for attachment must be met for the financing statement to be effective.

Perfection by Possession

Article 9 also allows perfection by possession. Again, possession is nine-tenths of the law; for example, negotiable instruments, such as promissory notes, can be perfected by filing or possession of the note by the secured creditor. Creditors have 20 days from the time their security interest attaches to collateral to either take physical possession of the collateral or file a financing statement.

Field warehousing satisfies the possession perfection requirements. In field warehousing, the secured creditor has an agent at the debtor's place of business (warehouse), and the secured creditor's signature is required before the buyer can sell, pledge, or do anything with the goods subject to the secured and perfected-by-possession interest held by the creditor.

Automatic Perfection in Consumer Goods

Article 9 provides for automatic perfection in certain circumstances, which means that perfection is automatic upon creation of the security interest (no filing or possession required). One type of automatic perfection is when there is a purchase money security interest (PMSI) in consumer goods.

A PMSI is a security interest in which the creditor is providing the funds for the purchase of the collateral. PMSIs in consumer goods qualify for automatic perfection. Consumer goods are goods used or bought primarily for personal, family, or household purposes. (Note: Autos in which creditors hold security interests are administered under state vehicle registration laws.)

Type of Good and Use	Automatic Perfection?
Refrigerator for a home kitchen	Yes
Refrigerator in corporate office break room	No
Computer purchased for children to do homework at home	Yes
Computer purchased for administrative assistant's use	No

PMSIs can also be created in nonconsumer goods, such as inventory, fixtures, and equipment, and they carry special status in terms of priority. However, those PMSIs are *not* perfected automatically—only PMSIs in consumer goods are entitled to automatic perfection.

Beyer wants to purchase a large-screen TV from Sallor TV, Inc., for $1,500. Beyer pays $200 down and signs a security agreement giving Sallor TV a security interest in the set being purchased until the balance of $1,300 is paid. Sallor has an automatically perfected PMSI.

Beyer wants to buy a large-screen TV from Sallor TV, Inc. Beyer goes to West Bank seeking a loan to buy the set. West Bank loans Beyer the money, and Beyer signs a security agreement giving West Bank a security interest in the to-be-purchased TV set. If Beyer does purchase the set, West Bank has a PMSI in the set. (Note: If Beyer purchases a large refrigerator-freezer instead of the TV, West Bank would be an unsecured creditor.)

Automatic Perfection in Proceeds

A secured creditor's security interest can include proceeds from the sale of the collateral. When proceeds are included in the description of the security interest, the secured creditor can, even after sale of the collateral, be automatically perfected in any identifiable proceeds from the sale of the collateral.

The secured creditor can also file to create an additional security interest in proceeds following the debtor's sale of the goods. If the creditor has not perfected such a security interest in proceeds by filing a financing statement, priority in the proceeds extends for 21 days after the debtor's receipt of those proceeds. Unless the secured party perfects the proceeds by filing a financing statement within the 21-day period, the perfected status in proceeds is lost. There will still be a security interest in the proceeds but no perfection to gain priority over other secured creditors.

West Bank has a filed perfected security interest in all of Ralph's TV's present inventory, any after-acquired inventory, and the proceeds from any of these TVs. Able purchases a TV from Ralph's, signing a security agreement that requires monthly payments by Able. Ralph defaults on payments to West Bank. Although West Bank cannot repossess the TV sold to Able (Able is a buyer in the ordinary course of business), West Bank is entitled to the monthly payments by Able as identifiable proceeds.

Temporary Perfection

Temporary perfection is a status given under Article 9 to give creditors the time necessary to take additional steps for protection. For example, creditors have 20 days of temporary protection on negotiable instruments before they would be required to file a financing statement to achieve perfection without possession of the instrument.

Temporary Protection When Debtors Move to a Different State

If a security interest is perfected in one state (State A) and the debtor moves to another state (State B), the perfected secured party (located in State A) still has priority over a subsequent perfected secured party in State B for a period of four months from the date the debtor moved to State B. After four months, if the secured creditor has not also filed in State B, then the secured creditor is not a perfected secured creditor in State B.

West Bank has a perfected security interest in Wisconsin on Able's equipment. (Able is a sole proprietorship located in Wisconsin.) Able has built a new plant in Illinois, and on May 1, without West's consent, Able transfers some of the equipment from the Wisconsin plant to the Illinois plant and installs the equipment with some newly purchased equipment there. On June 1, Able gets a loan from East Bank in Illinois using all the Illinois plant equipment as collateral. Before making the loan, East Bank had checked for prior filings on the equipment in Illinois. If Able goes into default to both West Bank and East Bank on August 1, West Bank has priority over East Bank as to the equipment moved to Illinois because West Bank's perfection in Wisconsin still has priority over the equipment transferred to the Illinois plant until September 1.

Priorities in Security Interests

There can be more than one security interest and more than one *perfected* security interest in the same collateral. Article 9 provides priority rules that determine which secured creditors have priority and in what order in the same collateral. The factors that determine priority are whether there is a secured creditor, whether there is a perfected secured party, and the timing of perfection. There are certain exceptions to these general rules related to the three factors.

Priority of Security Interests under Article 9: General Rules	
Conflict	**Priority**
Secured party vs. secured party	If the secured creditors are secured by the same collateral, first to attach; for remaining debt, treated as general creditors (pro rata)
Unsecured party vs. secured party	Secured party
Perfected secured party vs. secured party	Perfected secured party
Perfected secured party vs. perfected secured party	Party who is first to perfect

Lienors in Secured Transaction Priorities

There are other types of interests that attach to the same types of properties under secured transactions. There are several types of liens that exist and often end up in conflict with secured parties. The law provides creditors with rights *similar to security interests* in various circumstances:

- Judicial lien (also known as a judgment lien): A court orders certain property to be made available to a party to satisfy a claim (judgment) the party has won in a case
- Statutory lien (mechanic's lien): Mechanic's liens are liens that provide contractors and suppliers for real estate projects to assess a lien against the improved *real property* for payment for their services or supplies
- Statutory lien (service or artisan's liens): A service person who repairs or improves *personal property* is given legal rights in the personal property that was repaired or improved property in the form of an artisan's lien until the owner pays for the repairs
- Garnishment: A garnishment is a sort of lien against a debtor's paycheck or financial accounts for payment of a judgment issued by court order. With this type of lien, the creditor is paid directly from the garnished funds before the debtor has access

The general rules for priority when there are various types of liens in the same property is that the priority of the liens is determined by the time of the filing of the lien. The following chart offers a summary of the priority rules on security interests versus liens.

Priority of Security Interests under Article 9: Lien Priorities	
Conflict	**Priority**
Secured party vs. lienor	Lienor because the lienor must file publicly to validate the lien claim
Unsecured party vs. lienor	Lienor
Perfected secured party vs. lienor	First to file for perfection or recording of the lien

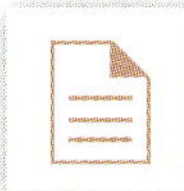

Compounding Labs, Inc., lost a lawsuit filed by a competitor, United Labs, and the court awarded a judgment to United on March 1. United filed the judgment lien on March 2. Compounding financed the purchase of new equipment through a loan from Commerce Bank. Compounding signed a security agreement for the equipment on April 1. The equipment was delivered on April 30. Commerce Bank filed its financing statement on May 1. Compounding failed to make payments on the judgment lien and to Commerce Bank. Both United Labs and Commerce Bank claim priority in Compounding's equipment. The following list summarizes the rights of the parties:

- United's judgment lien was perfected on March 2
- Commerce's security interest attached on April 30
- Commerce's security interest was perfected on May 1
- There are two perfected creditors in the same collateral; United perfected its interest first, so it would have first priority in the equipment

Exceptions to General Priority Rules

There are four exceptions to the general priority rule of "first in time, first in right," which means that the first to attach (in the case of competing security interests) or the first to perfect (in the case of perfected security interests) will take priority. These exceptions involve fixtures, equipment, inventory, and buyers of collateral subject to Article 9 security interests.

The Fixtures Exception: Real property owners need to replace equipment on their properties. A replacement of this nature, such as an HVAC unit, may need to be financed. Financing can come from a PMSI creditor who advances the money for the homeowner's purchase of a new air-conditioning unit. However, there may be a first and a second mortgage on the property. Mortgages are liens and are recorded. If the "first in time, right in right" rule were always followed, the mortgage company would always be paid, but those vendors who financed improvements that enhanced the value of the property would always have lesser priority.

Under the Article 9 exception, a PMSI creditor in fixtures will take priority over previous lien holders if the creditor perfects (files a financing statement) before the air conditioner is annexed or within 20 days after the air conditioner is annexed. The public policy reason is that repairing and replacing fixtures in real property benefits the owner and the lender. Giving creditors who finance the fixtures and replacement priority permits property owners to obtain financing (PMSI creditors) for those property improvements.

Lea has a home mortgage through Affiliated Finance that was recorded on October 1, Year 9. By Year 13, Lea needed a new HVAC system. Lea financed the $7,000 purchase and installation through Honorable Heating and Plumbing. Honorable took a PMSI in the system through a valid security agreement that Lea signed on June 30, Year 13. Honorable installed the unit at Lea's home on July 2, Year 13. Honorable also filed a financing statement on the HVAC system on July 15. Lea has defaulted on her mortgage as well as the payments to Honorable. Affiliated will be second in priority because Honorable perfected its interest within the 20-day exception requirement under Article 9.

The Equipment Exception: Business owners often have multiple creditors in their equipment. Under this exception, PMSI creditors for equipment purchases step to first priority position in perfection even though they file to perfect after other creditors, as long as they obtain that perfection within 20 days after the equipment is delivered to the debtor. The public policy reason is that it is in the interest of the debtor and all the debtor's creditors to continue to operate with efficient equipment. Without this exception, it would be difficult for businesses to obtain financing for new equipment purchases because the new creditors would always be in the lowest priority position.

Beatty Printing, LLC, began its business with a loan from Capital Advances to purchase its printing equipment. The security agreement was signed on August 1, Year 8. The equipment was delivered on August 14, Year 8. Capital Advances filed its financing statement on August 15. In Year 12, Beatty learned of some improvements in its printing systems that could increase production rates. Finova Capital agreed to finance the improvements. The security agreement was signed on August 1, Year 12. The equipment was delivered on August 14, Year 12. Finova filed its financing statement on August 15, Year 12. In Year 13, Beatty discovered additional computer capability for its printing system. First National financed the purchase to upgrade the system. The security agreement was signed on August 1, Year 13. The equipment was delivered on August 14, Year 13. First National filed its financing statement on August 15, Year 13. The order of priority of these secured creditors is First National, Finova, and then Capital Advances. This Article 9 priority exception permits businesses to more easily obtain financing for updates and upgrades to its equipment.

The Inventory Exception: A PMSI in a debtor's inventory will have priority over a previously perfected PMSI, provided that two events take place before the debtor takes possession of the collateral: the PMSI-secured party perfects *before the debtor takes possession* and the PMSI-secured party sends (and the non-PMSI party receives) written notice of the PMSI. This requirement is why addresses are required in financing statements. The filed financing statement is where creditors obtain names and contact information so that they can exercise their priority rights under Article 9. The notice before delivery permits other secured creditors to take steps to protect their collateral interests, such as securing other collateral. The public policy interest in this exception is that it permits businesses to replenish their inventory.

Ralph's TV, Inc., has a cash-flow problem. On May 1, Ralph secures a loan from West Bank, putting up Ralph's entire present inventory and any inventory acquired thereafter. This is a non-PMSI, and West Bank properly perfects its security interest with a filing on that same date. On August 1, Ralph's learns that the store can purchase 100 TV sets directly from one of its suppliers, Inter TV. Ralph's cannot pay cash but does pay 20% of the purchase price as a down payment and signs a security agreement giving Inter TV a security interest in the 100 TV sets Ralph's is purchasing. Delivery of the 100 TV sets is to be on or before September 1. Inter TV has a PMSI. On August 2, Inter TV perfects its security interest with a proper filing and on August 20 sends West Bank a fax, which is received, notifying West Bank of Inter TV's security interest. If Ralph's goes into default to both West Bank and Inter TV, Inter TV would have priority over West Bank's after-acquired collateral interest in the 100 sets purchased by Ralph's. This is because Inter TV has a PMSI properly perfected, and West Bank was sent, and it received, written notice of Inter TV's security interest prior to Ralph's possession of the 100 TV sets.

Buyers of Goods Subject to Security Interests: Under this exception, there is a general rule: if there is a buyer in the ordinary course of business, the buyer takes free and clear of all security interests, perfected and unperfected. Even when the buyer in ordinary course has knowledge about a secured creditor's interest in the collateral, the buyer takes free and clear of that interest.

Buyers in the Ordinary Course of Business: A buyer in the ordinary course of business is a buyer purchasing from a merchant who is in the business of selling the goods being purchased by the buyer.

On July 8, Ace, a refrigerator wholesaler, purchased 50 refrigerators. This purchase comprised Ace's entire inventory and was financed by Rome Bank, with Rome taking a security interest in all refrigerators on Ace's premises, all refrigerators acquired in the future, and the proceeds from sales. On July 12, Rome filed a financing statement for the refrigerators. On August 15, Ace sold one refrigerator to Cray for personal use and four refrigerators to Zone Co. for its business. Because Ace is a wholesaler, the purchase made by Zone, although for use in its business, was still a purchase in the ordinary course of business. All buyers in the ordinary course of business take free and clear of all security interests.

West Bank has a perfected security interest in a tractor owned by Dell Farms. After the harvest season, Dell sells the tractor to a farm implement dealer who buys and sells new and used tractors. Dell defaults, and West Bank claims priority to the tractor purchased by the farm implement dealer. The farm implement dealer claims it is a buyer in the ordinary course of business because it buys and sells used tractors. Here, West Bank has priority because the farm implement dealer is not a buyer in the ordinary course of business because Dell Farms does not regularly sell tractors and cannot make a sale of a tractor in the ordinary course of business.

Buyers Not in the Ordinary Course of Business: Buyers who do not buy in the ordinary course of business take free of the secured creditor's interest priority unless the buyer is aware of the creditor's secured interest. "Not in the ordinary course of business" means that the buyer has, for example, purchased books from a law firm going out of business or a delivery truck from a grocery store. The purchase is not from someone dealing in goods of that kind. Their business is not of selling the goods the buyer is purchasing. The condition of "awareness" can be met two ways: the creditor has filed a financing statement (perfected interest) covering the goods, or the buyer has personal knowledge of the creditor's security interest.

Buyers Not in the Ordinary Course of Business—PMSI Security Interests: This rule is an exception to the exception on buyers not in the ordinary course of business. A buyer not in the ordinary course of business of consumer goods will take free and clear of a previously perfected secured party who is perfected automatically, because consumer PMSIs are perfected without filing, if the buyer meets the following requirements:

- Buyer must give *value* to the seller-debtor;
- Buyer must *not know* of secured party's security interest;
- Buyer must buy for *personal use* (as consumer goods); *and*
- Buyer must buy *before* the *secured party perfects by filing a financing statement*.

A PMSI in consumer goods perfected automatically gives perfected secured status to the creditors as against all other subsequent parties *except* buyers of consumer goods not in the ordinary course of business. The secured creditor with a PMSI in consumer goods with automatic perfection can protect against consumer buyers by, in addition, filing a financing statement on the goods. The following diagram illustrates the exceptions for buyers in the ordinary course of business.

Buyers vs. Article 9 Secured Creditor

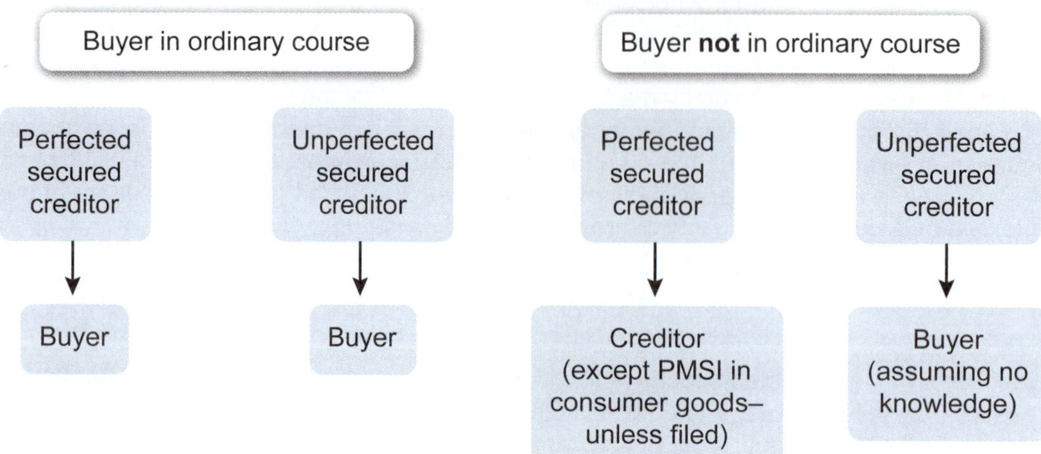

Beyer purchases a large-screen TV for personal use from Ralph's TV store. Beyer signs a security agreement giving Ralph's a security interest in the set purchased. Ralph's has a perfected PMSI without a filing (automatic perfection). Later, while still making payments to Ralph's, Beyer sells the set to a next-door neighbor, Sally Hawks. Hawks is not a buyer in the ordinary course of business. Due to some financial reversals, Beyer goes into default to Ralph's TV store. If Hawks did not know of Ralph's security interest at the time of sale and purchased the TV as a consumer good (for personal, family, or household use), Ralph's cannot repossess the set from Hawks. Had Ralph's TV store perfected its security interest (also) by filing before the sale to Hawks, it could have repossessed the TV from Hawks to satisfy the balance of Beyer's debt.

Exceptions to General Priority Rules of Secured Creditors under Article 9

Conflict	Priority
PMSI in fixtures vs. perfected secured party	PMSI creditor if perfected before annexation or within 20 days after annexation (PMSI will have priority even over prior perfected secured party)
PMSI in equipment vs. perfected secured party	PMSI if perfected within 20 days after delivery
PMSI in inventory vs. perfected secured party	PMSI if perfected before delivery and if perfected secured party gives notice to other secured creditors before delivery
PMSI in consumer goods vs. buyer	Buyer unless perfection is by filing before purchase
Perfected secured party vs. buyer	Buyers in ordinary course win even with knowledge

Rights of Secured Creditors and Debtors on Default

Self-Help and the Article 9 Right of Repossession: When a debtor defaults, the secured party can use judicial processes to collect. However, Article 9 also permits secured creditors to take peaceful possession of the collateral without the use of judicial process.

The UCC does not define "peaceful possession." The general rule is that the collateral has been taken peacefully if the secured party can take possession without committing any of the following acts:

- Trespass onto real property
- Assault and/or battery
- Breaking and entering

Process after Repossession: After the goods are repossessed, the secured creditor has the option to sell or keep the collateral. There are some restrictions on the creditor's choice.

Keep Collateral: The secured party must send notice of the intent to keep the collateral to the debtor and junior security interest holders.

When the Creditor Cannot Keep the Collateral: If the collateral is consumer goods and 60% or more of the purchase price has been paid, the creditor must sell it.

A debtor purchased an LCD television from Best Appliances for $1,000. Best Appliances financed the transaction. With finance charges, the total cost of the TV is $1,200. After paying a total of $600, the debtor defaults on the payment. Best Appliances repossesses the TV. Best Appliances has decided to keep the TV as a floor display model. The debtor believes it would be better for Best Appliances to sell the TV. Best Appliances must sell the TV because 60% of the $1,000 purchase price has been paid.

The creditor must sell the collateral *within a reasonable time, in a reasonable manner,* and only after giving notice to the debtor and other secured creditors in the property.

The Article 9 standard for conducting a sale is that it must be done in a "commercially reasonable manner." Once the sale is completed, the proceeds are distributed in the following order:

- **Expenses** incurred by secured party in repossession, keeping, and resale of the collateral
- **Balance of debt** owed to the first priority secured party
- **Junior lien holders**, including other creditors with security interests or other liens in the same collateral
- **Debtor** unless the collateral is accounts or chattel paper, then to secured party unless, to the contrary, provided to the debtor in the security agreement

Once the funds are exhausted, any debts owed to junior lien holders are discharged for purposes of the collateral. Whoever purchases the collateral takes that collateral free and clear of all liens and security interests. Creditors not paid in full are free to pursue deficiency cases against the debtor to collect those amounts.

Belmont Bank has repossessed Jake Smithfield's car. Belmont has conducted a proper sale of the car. The proceeds from the sale are $26,000. Expenses totaled $2,000. Belmont is owed $10,000. Five Star Finance, a second secured creditor, is owed $12,000. An auto mechanic has a $3,000 lien on the car for detail work completed for which there was no payment. The order of payment would be:

1. Expenses: $2,000
2. Belmont Bank: $10,000
3. Auto mechanic: $3,000 (these types of liens have priority in most states over secured creditors)
4. Five Star: $11,000
5. Jake receives nothing, and Five Star can file suit against Jake for the $1,000 deficiency.

Bankruptcy: Declaration, Processes, Distribution, and Discharge

Representative Task (Remembering & Understanding): Explain the rights of debtors and creditors and how property is distributed in bankruptcy proceedings.

There are times when debtors cannot pay their debts, and the collateral is insufficient to pay creditors. At that point, debtors declare bankruptcy, and the rights of debtors and creditors are determined under those federal proceedings.

Prebankruptcy Efforts by Creditors and Debtors

Before undertaking the bankruptcy process, debtors and creditors often try some alternatives to find a way to satisfy the debt obligations. These processes include garnishment, composition agreements, and assignments for the benefit of creditors.

Garnishment: A garnishment is a court order based on a judgment against the debtor that requires third parties (garnishees) to pay creditors directly certain amounts from the debtor's wages or accounts. A garnishment can be applied to the following:

- Bank accounts
- Wages

The amount is usually limited by federal or state law to 25% of take-home pay. An employer cannot discharge an employee because of a garnishment. The garnishment order cannot be applied to certain payments, such as Social Security.

Composition: A composition is a contract between the debtor and the debtor's creditors, whereby the creditors agree to discharge the debtor's debts upon a payment. Usually, all of the creditors have agreed to take a certain percentage of the total amount the debtor owes to them. The benefit to creditors is that they may be able to receive more in repayment because of the bankruptcy costs and priorities. Those creditors who do not agree to the composition are not bound by its terms.

Assignment for the Benefit of Creditors: This process involves an insolvent debtor voluntarily transferring certain assets to a trustee or assignee. The trustee or assignee liquidates the assets and tenders a payment on a pro rata basis in satisfaction of that debt to each creditor.

The amount of property turned over to the trustee or assignee, and thus the pro rata share, is entirely at the discretion of the debtor, and creditors are free to accept or reject the trustee's offer. This process is referred to as a "cram-down" or "take-it-or-leave-it" choice of the creditor.

If a creditor does accept the payment by the trustee, the whole debt is discharged. Those creditors that reject the cram-down can then pursue bankruptcy.

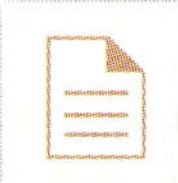

Debtor Smith has come upon difficult financial times and has 20 creditors who are not willing to accept a lesser sum in a creditor composition agreement. Smith's debts amount to $100,000. Smith turns $20,000 worth of property over to a trustee (Jones) and instructs Jones to sell the property and prorate the proceeds among the 20 creditors. Jones sells the property and then, on a pro rata basis, offers each creditor a sum. Creditors who accept the lesser sum discharge the debtor from the debt. If all creditors accept the sums offered by Smith, the entire $100,000 in debt is discharged. If none of the creditors accept, or if only some do so, Smith could do a voluntary petition into bankruptcy.

Forms of Bankruptcy

Chapter 7

The following are the general steps in a Chapter 7 bankruptcy, also known as a straight or liquidation bankruptcy.

Declaration That the Debtor Is Unable to Pay Debts as They Become Due: The standard for declaration of bankruptcy is not liabilities being greater than assets. The standard is the ability to pay debts as they come due. Known as the "means" test, this test is a formula that takes the debtor's monthly income, subtracts allowable expenses provided for under the bankruptcy law, and then determines whether the debtor has the means to pay off their debts.

A trustee is appointed, and the bankruptcy process begins.

Types of Chapter 7 Proceedings: There are two types of Chapter 7 bankruptcy proceedings: voluntary and involuntary.

In a voluntary petition, the debtor is filing for bankruptcy.

- Any person (individual, partnerships, or corporations) may voluntarily petition themselves into a Chapter 7 bankruptcy. It is possible that individual debtors or married couples may need to go through Chapter 13 instead of Chapter 7

In an involuntary petition, the creditors are asking that the debtor be brought into bankruptcy court.

Types of Entities Not Eligible for Involuntary Chapter 7: Anyone who would be ineligible for a voluntary Chapter 7 petition, as well as the following:

- Nonprofit (not for profit) corporations
- Farmers (except those who do not meet the Chapter 12 bankruptcy requirements)
- Stock brokerage firms (there is a special liquidation process for these firms)

Requirements for Creditors' Involuntary Petitions of a Debtor into Bankruptcy: If the debtor has *12 or more unsecured creditors*, the petition must be signed by three or more of these creditors whose aggregate claims are $18,600 or more.

If the debtor has less than *12 unsecured creditors with noncontingent claims*, the petition requires only one (more can sign) of these creditors with an aggregate debt of $18,600 or more to sign the involuntary petition.

Unger owes a total of $50,000 to eight unsecured creditors and one fully secured creditor. Quincy is one of the unsecured creditors and is owed $6,000. Quincy has filed an involuntary bankruptcy petition against Unger under the liquidation provisions of Chapter 7 of the Federal Bankruptcy Code. Unger has been unable to pay debts as they become due. Unger's liabilities exceed Unger's assets. Unger has filed papers opposing the bankruptcy petition. Quincy can establish that Unger meets the standard for granting a petition in bankruptcy of Unger being unable to pay debts as they become due. For an involuntary petition, when there are fewer than 12 creditors, one creditor can file the involuntary petition; however, that creditor must be owed at least $18,600. Quincy is owed only $6,000, so the petition will be dismissed.

Chapter 9

A Chapter 9 bankruptcy allows for the adjustment of debts of an insolvent municipality—a rehabilitation of municipalities, defined as any political subdivision, public agency, or instrumentality (includes any taxing unit) of a state.

- Permits *voluntary petitions* only by the municipality
- This chapter is rarely addressed on the exam
- Liquidation of the municipality's assets is not permitted

Chapter 11

A Chapter 11 bankruptcy allows for the *reorganization* of a business debtor to pay debts—a rehabilitation of a debtor.

- Permits *voluntary and involuntary* petitions
- Allows companies to restructure and be discharged from certain debts
- There is generally no trustee
- Court must approve a reorganization plan approved by half of the creditors with 2/3 of the total claims (includes shareholders)
- Savings and loans, banks, insurance companies, stockbrokers, and railroads are not eligible for Chapter 11

Chapter 12

A Chapter 12 bankruptcy allows for the *adjustment of debts of a family farmer or family fisherman*—a rehabilitation of a person (including a corporation or a partnership) who *meets the definition of a family farmer or fisherman* (rarely tested on the exam).

- Permits only *voluntary petitions* by the family farmer or family fisherman
- Chapter 12 is a more streamlined process than Chapter 11, which is used for other types of businesses
- The court appoints an interim trustee
- Debt adjustment plan is established at a meeting of the creditors

Chapter 13

A Chapter 13 bankruptcy, also called a wage earner's plan, allows for the adjustment *of debts of an individual with regular income*—a rehabilitation of only individuals (not partnerships or corporations) with limited total secured and unsecured debt amounts.

- Permits only *voluntary petitions*
- Less than $465,275 in unsecured and less than $1,395,875 in secured debt
- Always has a trustee
- Applies only to individuals (debt limits)
- Debtor's plan for repayment
- Court confirmation of the plan
- Three to five years for plan—discharged if payment is made

The debtor(s) must have undergone credit/debt counseling within the 180 days preceding the filing of Chapter 13 petition.

- The credit counseling must be from an agency approved by the U.S Trustee's office
- The agency gives debtors a certificate of completion that must be filed no later than 15 days after the bankruptcy is filed. The counseling service also provides a repayment plan that must then be approved by the court

Forms of Bankruptcy

	Chapter 7	Chapter 11	Chapter 13
Trustee	Yes	No	Yes
Eligible persons:			
Individuals	Yes	Yes	Yes
Partnerships	Yes	Yes	No
Corporations	Yes	Yes	No
Voluntary	Yes	Yes	Yes
Involuntary	Yes, except for farmers and nonprofits	Yes, except for farmers and nonprofits	No
Exemptions	S&Ls, credit unions, SBA, RRs, municipalities	Same as Chapter 7 plus stockbrokers and railroads	Only individuals allowed
Requirements: voluntary	Debts	Debts	Income + Debts < $465,275 unsecured and < $1,395,875 secured
Requirements: involuntary	< 12 = 1/$18,600 or ≥ 12 = 3/$18,600 + inability to pay debts as they come due	< 12 = 1/$18,600 or ≥ 12 = 3/$18,600 + inability to pay debts as they come due	N/A

Effect of Filing a Petition in Bankruptcy

Upon the filing of a *voluntary petition*, the court will grant an *order for relief*, or a stay. Upon the filing of an involuntary petition and following the determination that the debtor is insolvent (with insolvency being defined as the inability to pay debts as they become due), the order for relief is entered.

"Order for relief" or "stay" means that creditors must stop collection, all pending credit proceedings (lien foreclosure, judicial liens, litigation) are stayed (stopped), and the debts and payments will be handled through the bankruptcy court.

This stay sets in motion proceedings that lead to the discharge of the debtor's debts.

The Bankruptcy Process

There are steps in the bankruptcy process that must be followed in handling the collection of assets and making the distribution to creditors.

The following chart shows the collection-of-assets portion of the bankruptcy process. Beneath the chart is an explanation of each of the steps.

Anatomy of Bankruptcy Case

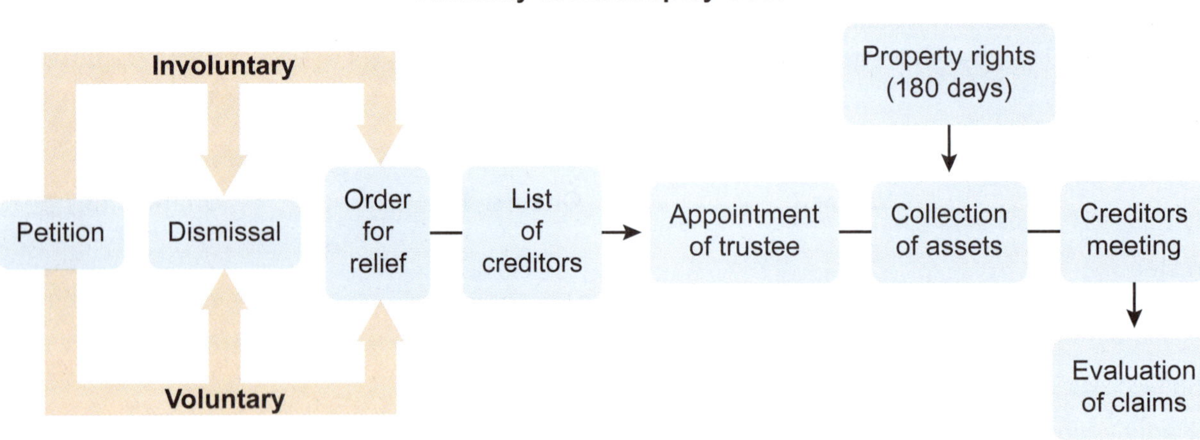

Collection of Assets: The Debtor's Estate

The trustee is responsible for bringing together all of the assets of the debtor. The debtor's estate includes all tangible and intangible property of the debtor held at the time the bankruptcy proceedings began. The debtor's estate also includes all property that the debtor acquires for 180 days following the filing for bankruptcy. This after-acquired property includes the following:

- Inheritances or gifts
- Divorce, separation, or property settlements
- Beneficiary proceeds from a life insurance policy

Powers of the Trustee

The trustee is given broad authority in collecting the assets of the debtor. These powers include:

- Bringing suits for collection
- Assigning leases of debtors to third parties
- Selling the debtor's property
- Completing or obtaining releases from contracts
- Evaluating existing contracts and professional fees of debtor

Property Exempted from Bankrupt's Estate (Property Not Included in the Collection of Assets by the Trustee)

There are some types of property that the trustee cannot seize as part of the bankruptcy estate. These exemptions from the reach of the trustee belong to the debtor. There are two lists of property exemptions for debtors: state and federal. Congress has authorized states to limit exemptions to those who are residents of the state, and a majority of the states have done so. However, if the homestead is acquired within three and a half years preceding the date of filing, the maximum state homestead equity exempted is $189,050, and the debtor must have been domiciled in the state for two years.

Other exemptions at the state and federal levels include one vehicle; household items, such as a computer or television; educational materials; clothing; animals; musical instruments; health aids; and appliances.

Debtors can keep their government benefits, such as unemployment compensation, Social Security, and veteran's benefits. Both traditional IRA and Roth IRA accounts up to $1,512,350 are also exempt. Debtors also retain the right to receive various private benefits, such as alimony, child support, pension payments, and disability benefits.

Voidable Preferences: Debtors sometimes try to conceal property through transfers. Such transfers will be examined by the trustee. The trustee has the power to set aside transfers of the debtor's property that occurred prior to the declaration of bankruptcy. These set-asides of transfers of property by the debtor are called voidable preferences.

There are two types of voidable preferences: transfers from the debtor to the creditor and transfers by the debtor to insiders of a business.

Voidable Preferences to a Creditor

- A transfer of the debtor's property to a creditor
- For an antecedent or preexisting debt
- Made within 90 days of the filing of the bankruptcy petition
- Made while the debtor was insolvent

Insolvency is presumed for any transfer made within 90 days of the petition being filed.

Insider Voidable Preference

An insider is an individual or business with a close relationship to the debtor. This could include a relative, a partner, or a corporation (board of directors of which the debtor is a member or is an officer of the corporation).

- A transfer of debtor's property to an insider
- For an antecedent or preexisting debt
- Made within one year from date of the filing of the bankruptcy petition

Exceptions to Voidable Preferences

There are several exceptions to a trustee's ability to claw back debtor property into the estate:

- Cash donations made to legitimate charitable organizations are not considered voidable preferences
- Contemporaneous transactions of goods in exchange for cash. Spending money on goods may not seem to be the best financial decision when a debtor is headed for bankruptcy, but it is permitted and not considered a voidable preference

- Employee retention bonuses (KERP or Key Employee Retention Program). These are bonuses paid to key employees (key employees are those who, if they leave the company, will result in financial harm to the company). These payments must meet the following requirements:
  - The KERP plan must apply to all key employees
  - The key employee must have other job offers
  - Those in key management (insider) positions cannot be paid more than 10 times the average KERP payment to employees in a calendar year. If the average KERP payment to employees is $35,000, the maximum payment to a management employee is 10 times that amount, or $350,000
- A consumer debtor's payment of up to $7,575 in consumer debt is not a preference
- Payments for paternity, alimony, maintenance, and child support are not preferences

On April 15, Year 3, Wren Corp., an appliance wholesaler, was petitioned involuntarily into bankruptcy under Chapter 7. The following transactions occurred before the bankruptcy petition was filed:

- On December 31, Year 2, Wren paid off a $5,000 loan from Mary Lake, the sister of one of Wren's directors
- On January 30, Year 3, Wren donated $2,000 to Universal Charities
- On February 1, Year 3, Wren gave Young Finance Co. a security agreement covering Wren's office fixtures to secure a loan previously made by Young
- On March 1, Year 3, Wren made the final $1,000 monthly payment to Integral Appliance Corp. on a two-year note
- On April 1, Year 3, Wren purchased from Safety Co. a new burglar alarm system for its factory, for $5,000 cash

Decide which of these actions were voidable preferences.

Wren Corporation and Voidable Preferences

Action	Voidable Preference	Explanation
Payoff of $5,000 loan from Mary Lake	Yes	Mary Lake is the relative of an insider (member of the board), so the payoff is a voidable preference; the timing was longer than 90 days, but there is a one-year cutoff for insider transfers
Donation of $2,000 to Universal Charities	No	Cash donations made to legitimate charitable organizations are not considered voidable preferences
Giving Young Finance a security interest on a previous loan	Yes	Voidable preferences occur when creditors are given a higher status (in this case becoming a secured creditor) than they would have had in bankruptcy
Final $1,000 monthly payment to Integral Finance	No	This would be considered a regular payment because Wren was paying what it would have paid in the ordinary course of business
Purchase of a new burglar alarm system for $5,000	No	Contemporaneous transaction. A firm going bankrupt may not need that much security, so the wisdom of the transaction may be in doubt; but it is still a transaction at the time and not a previous obligation

Distribution of the Debtor's Estate

Once the trustee has collected all the debtor's property, the time has arrived for distribution of the estate to creditors. The distribution is done according to a list of priorities.

Order of Priorities for Distribution

1. **Secured Parties:** Perfected secured parties have priority to the collateral or proceeds from the sale of that collateral over general creditors and the trustee. Unperfected secured parties are secured creditors who have rights in the collateral but are second to the rights of perfected secured parties. Once the collateral is sold and the perfected secured parties are paid from the proceeds, the remaining unperfected secured creditors drop down into the general creditor category for their unpaid balances due.

   The secured creditor has priority only for the amount provided by the collateral. Once the secured creditors receive that amount, the secured creditors with remaining portions due take the same position as the other unsecured general creditors.

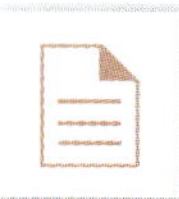

West Bank is a perfected secured party on a loan balance of $10,000 with a security interest in $14,000 of the debtor's equipment. The debtor is in default. West Bank has repossessed the equipment and stored it for $500, pending its sale. The debtor then declares bankruptcy. If the equipment is sold for $11,000 by either the debtor or trustee, West Bank would receive the entire $11,000 and would have to file a claim as a general creditor for the $500 storage fees.

2. **Domestic Support:** Claims for domestic support obligations include payments such as alimony and child support.
3. **Administrative Costs:** Administrative costs refer to the expenses of the bankruptcy, including trustee, attorney, appraisal, and accountant fees.
4. **Claims Arising in the Ordinary Course of Business:** In an involuntary bankruptcy proceeding, the debtor's challenges to the involuntary petition and any expenses incurred by the debtor in the ordinary course of business from the date of filing to the order of relief fall into this priority category. In a voluntary petition, there may be a court delay in appointing a trustee, and the debtor has the same authority to continue operating and entering into transactions with creditors.

   The reason for this priority is so that the debtor does not shut down in the time it takes to get the bankruptcy process moving forward. Those furnishing goods and services to the debtor during this court-induced waiting time are referred to as "gap creditors" or "interim creditors."

Three creditors whose aggregate unsecured, noncontingent claims are $50,000 sign an involuntary petition putting Elizabeth, the sole owner of a clothing store, into bankruptcy. Elizabeth immediately challenges the petition. A hearing is held two weeks later; when the court rules in favor of the creditors, an order of relief is issued, and a trustee is appointed. During the two-week period, Elizabeth has continued to do business and has incurred debts to ABC Wholesale Clothes and XYZ Janitorial Services. When distribution of Elizabeth's estate takes place, ABC and XYZ will be fourth in line to be paid under the bankruptcy distribution priorities.

5. **Employee Wages:** Employee claims for back wages, salaries, or commissions (including vacation, severance, sick leave, and other benefits) but limited to those earned within 180 days of the filing of the petition or cessation of business (whichever is first), to a maximum amount of $15,150.
   - Any amount of back wages etc. owed, regardless of when owed or amount owed above the $15,150 during the 180-day period, is still a claim but drops to the last category—general creditors

Clara is employed as the manager of a clothing store. She is paid $5,000 per month. The clothing store owner suffers financial reverses, and based on promises, Clara manages the store for four months without pay. The owner then goes into a Chapter 7 bankruptcy. Clara will file a claim for her entire $20,000 owed in back salary, with $15,150 (earned during the last 180 days) as a priority. The remaining amount (the amount above the maximum) is placed in general creditor status.

If Clara had worked one month without pay and quit, and the owner managed the store for six months before shutting down the business and then filed for bankruptcy, Clara would get employee priority only for what was earned within the 180-day period. For what was earned outside the 180 days (the one month before quitting), Clara would be treated as a general creditor because those wages would be outside the 180 days.

6. **Contributions to Employee Benefit Plans:** This priority is for any claim for contributions to an employee benefit plan arising from services performed within 180 days before the filing of the petition or cessation of business (whichever comes first) up to $15,150 per employee. However, whatever amount was claimed as an employee wage priority is subtracted from any amount due here. Any amount above the maximum is treated as a general creditor claim.
7. **Claims of Farm Producers and Fishermen:** Creditors who own or operate grain storage facilities or fish storage or processing facilities have a priority of up to $7,475 per creditor. Any amount above is treated as a general creditor claim.
8. **Consumer Creditors:** Consumers who deposit or prepay for the purchase, lease, or rental of goods or services for personal, family, or household have this priority position up to an amount of $3,350 per creditor. Any amount above $3,350 is treated as a general creditor claim.

John contracts with a yard fertilizer and maintenance company for weekly home yard mowing and home yard fertilizing eight times during the coming year. The price is $4,400, less 10% if paid in advance. John paid $4,000 to the company. Before any services were performed, the company filed for Chapter 7 bankruptcy. John has a priority claim of $3,350. Anything not received as a priority creditor drops down into a general creditor claim.

9. **Claims of Governmental Units for Various Taxes:** These claims are subject to time limits. For example, federal taxes for which the return was due longer than three years ago are discharged. The collection priority is only for the most recent years of taxes. Social Security taxes are never discharged.
10. **Claims for Death or Personal Injury:** Claims that result from the operation of a vehicle or vessel because the debtor was intoxicated from use of alcohol, drugs, or other substances enjoy priority at this level. Any amount of the judgment or settlement not paid would then fall into the general creditor category.
11. **All General Unsecured Creditors:** If, at any level of priority, there are insufficient funds to cover all the priority creditors, then the creditors at that level will share the proceeds in a pro rata distribution.

Ending the Bankruptcy: Discharges

The final portion of the bankruptcy is discharging the debts of the debtor so that the debtor begins again with a clean slate. However, the slate is not always completely free of debts. Some debts are dischargeable in bankruptcy, and some are not.

What Will Result in the Court Not Ordering Discharge of Debts?

Federal Laws on Discharge of Debts: The U.S. Bankruptcy Code has certain prohibitions on discharge. No debtor who has had a discharge in bankruptcy within eight years of the filing of the petition for the current bankruptcy can be given a discharge. A partnership or corporation cannot get a discharge decree under Chapter 7 (can under other chapters); only individuals can.

Conduct by the Debtor That Prevents a Discharge: Any intentional concealment or transfer of assets or records by the debtor that misleads creditors or the trustee will prevent a discharge. False claims, testimony, and statements by the debtor are also grounds for refusing a discharge. A debtor's refusal to follow court orders, refusal to furnish tax documents, failure to testify, or failure to explain the loss of assets are all grounds for denying a discharge. In consumer bankruptcies, the failure of the consumer debtors to complete the required consumer education course will preclude a discharge.

What Specific Types of Debts Will Not Be Discharged?

Apart from a court denying a general discharge, there are certain types of debts from which debtors will not have discharged under their discharge order. These debts continue to be due and owing, and following the bankruptcy discharge order, creditors can begin their collection processes anew.

1. Unpaid taxes, if:
    - The taxes were due at least three years before the filing of the bankruptcy petition;
    - The tax return for the taxes due was filed at least two years before the filing of the bankruptcy petition; and
    - The IRS assessed the liability for the taxes due more than 240 days before the bankruptcy filing.

If a debtor filed for bankruptcy in Year 5, the discharge for taxes would begin on taxes that were due at least three years before Year 5. Taxes for Year 2 are not due until Year 3, so those taxes would not be discharged. Taxes for Year 1 are due in Year 2, so the debtor might qualify for a discharge beginning with the Year 1 tax year if the bankruptcy petition was filed after April 15, Year 2, the due date for Year 1 taxes. If there is a dispute between the debtor and the IRS, the final determination of the amount of taxes due would need to be at least 240 days before the debtor filed for bankruptcy, regardless of the debtor qualifying under the three-year timing rule.

2. Debts incurred through fraud, larceny, or embezzlement
3. Judgments for willful and malicious injuries
4. Debts incurred (judgments against the debtor for injuries or wrongful death) as a result of the debtor driving while intoxicated
5. Unscheduled debts that the debtor failed to list as required upon filing for bankruptcy and not actually known to trustee
6. Alimony, maintenance, and child support
7. Debts resulting from fraud as a fiduciary (embezzlement)
8. Fines and penalties payable to a governmental unit

9. Student loan debts or benefits (there may be an exception if debtor can demonstrate undue hardship)
10. Sarbanes-Oxley bonuses and incentives awarded to executives of companies based on fraudulent financial statements (the obligation to repay these amounts cannot be discharged in bankruptcy)
11. Consumer debts: Debts incurred within 90 days of the bankruptcy filing by the debtor of $800 or less are exempted from this nondischarge. Anything that debtors spend over the $1,100 on luxury goods would be a nondischargeable debt—the debtor would emerge from bankruptcy still owing that overage amount to the creditor
12. Homeowners association fees

Debtors Who Choose to Pay Debts That Would Qualify for a Discharge: Reaffirmation Agreements

Reaffirmations: Agreements between a debtor and creditor that a debt will not be discharged in bankruptcy.

Debtors can choose to repay certain debts that would otherwise be discharged. Some debtors choose to do so in order to be in good standing with particular creditors. Some debtors choose this option because of their ethics. Whatever the reason, there is a process required for valid reaffirmation agreements that place otherwise dischargeable debts back in the hands of the debtor:

- The agreement must be entered into prior to the granting of the discharge decree in bankruptcy
- The agreement must be signed and filed with the court
- If the debtor is represented by an attorney, no hearing or court approval is required if the attorney files an affidavit or declaration that the debtor has been fully advised of the legal consequences of the agreement and that the reaffirmation is not a hardship on the debtor or the debtor's family. If not represented by an attorney, a hearing and approval are required
- The agreement must include a statement explaining the debtor's right to rescind the agreement at any time prior to the discharge decree being granted or within 60 days of the filing of the agreement, whichever is later. This statement must be clearly and conspicuously stated

REG 8
Federal Laws and Regulation of Business

REG 8: Federal Laws and Regulation of Business

8.01 Federal Laws and Regulation of Business

There are federal laws related to employment, health care, and bribery prohibitions that CPAs must understand because they have certain duties under these laws and are required to evaluate whether employers meet the compliance requirements for these laws.

The Patient Protection and Affordable Care Act (PPACA)

Representative Task (Remembering & Understanding): Summarize the federal laws and regulations for qualified health care plans, including required business mandates and premium tax credits.

Since the passage of the Patient Protection and Affordable Care Act (PPACA) in 2010, there have been many judicial and legislative changes. There are other issues and proposed modifications pending legislatively and judicially.

Introduction to the PPACA

Before the passage of the PPACA in 2010, most Americans had health care coverage either through insurance provided by their employers or through government programs such as Medicare, Medicaid, and CHIP (Children's Health Insurance Program). The PPACA extended coverage to approximately 20 million uninsured or underinsured Americans.

In 2021, Congress enacted the American Rescue Plan Act (ARPA) (also called the COVID-19 Stimulus Package or American Rescue Plan), which made several changes aimed at extending the PPACA's coverage, such as increasing government subsidies. These changes are temporary and expire in 2025, unless Congress acts to extend them.

PPACA Expansions of Health Care and Protections of Coverage

Coverage of Preexisting Conditions: The PPACA prohibits insurance companies from denying coverage on grounds of preexisting conditions. All health plans must cover preexisting conditions. Before the PPACA, those who had diabetes, cancer, or many other preexisting conditions often found it difficult to obtain health insurance.

Insurance companies are not permitted to eliminate benefits, refuse to renew coverage, or otherwise discriminate because of preexisting conditions. The PPACA also prohibits insurance companies from canceling coverage once an insured person become ill unless there has been a failure on the part of the insured to pay premiums or the insured failed to disclose preexisting conditions in obtaining the premiums (fraud).

Allison applies for health insurance through Safeco. Allison does not disclose on the Safeco application that she has received a diagnosis of diabetes. Allison feels that the diagnosis is new and that she would be able to bring the condition under control. Six months later, Allison requires dialysis because of complications from diabetes. Safeco notifies Allison that it is canceling the policy. Safeco has the right to cancel Allison's policy because of the failure to disclose a health condition. Allison's belief that the diabetes could be brought under control does not change the need to make the disclosure to Safeco.

Discrimination Issues in Health Insurance: The PPACA addressed certain discrimination in health care insurance pricing by insurance companies. The following table summarizes those issues and the requirements under the PPACA.

Type of Discrimination	PPACA Law
Gender discrimination	Before the PPACA, insurers could deny coverage to women or charge them more on grounds of gender. Insurance data showed higher health care costs for women. The PPACA prohibits gender-based premium differences.
Age discrimination	Senior citizens generally require more health care services than younger people, but under the PPACA they cannot be charged more than three times what younger people are charged for the same plan.
Geographic location	Because medical care is more expensive in New York City than it is, for example, in rural Kansas, health insurance premiums can differ geographically.
Tobacco use	Because people who smoke will generally have more health problems than those who do not, the PPACA permits insurers to charge up to 50% more for premiums paid by tobacco users for coverage.
Individual vs. family coverage	Because a family of four will use more health services than will a single individual, premiums for families will be higher than coverage for one person.

Extending Coverage for Children: Under the PPACA, parents can provide coverage for their adult children under age 26. The coverage is available even if the children are married, financially independent, not living with their parents, and/or entitled to purchase health insurance at their own work. This coverage is obtained through a family insurance policy.

Elimination of Lifetime Coverage Limits: Before the PPACA, insurance companies often placed caps on the total dollar amount they would spend on an individual. A cap such as $2 million for a lifetime was not unusual. The PPACA eliminates such lifetime dollar limits (as well as annual dollar limits) for "essential health benefits."

Essential Health Benefits	Nonessential Health Benefits
• Outpatient services (including diagnosis, observation, consultation, treatment, intervention, and rehabilitation services) • Emergency services • Hospitalization • Maternity and newborn care • Mental health and substance use disorder services • Prescription drugs • Rehabilitative services and devices • Laboratory services • Preventive and wellness services • Pediatric services	• Abortion • Dental care • Elective cosmetic surgery

The Computation of Coverage, Deductibles, Coinsurance, and Out-of-Pocket Expenses under PPACA

Deductibles and Out-of-Pocket Maximums: The PPACA provides a total annual maximum for out-of-pocket expenses. The total annual maximum is adjusted every year for inflation. The 2024 maximums under the PPACA are $9,450 for an individual plan and $18,900 for a family plan. The computation for reaching the maximum is done by taking the insured's expenses in the order in which the billing came.

The Smith family has a family insurance plan that covers two parents and two children. The family has had the following out-of-pocket expenses:

Prescriptions	$2,200
Physical therapy	$3,000
Doctor visits	$2,000
Hospitalization	$8,000

How much more do the Smiths need in out-of-pocket expenses before they reach the PPACA maximum?

$3,000. Their out-of-pocket expenses total $15,200. They need $3,700 more to reach the $18,900 maximum for families.

The deductibles that the insured pays are included in computing out-of-pocket expenses. The cost of the premiums paid is not included in computing out-of-pocket expenses.

Once the insured reaches the out-of-pocket maximums, all future covered costs will be paid by the insurer. Plans with higher premiums typically carry lower out-of-pocket maximums.

Coinsurance or Copayment: Coinsurance, or typically referred to as a copayment, is the amount the insured must pay on claims; it is also counted until the out-of-pocket maximum is reached. Some policies have a $10 to $30 copay on each claim. Other policies have a coinsurance or percentage copay, such as 20% of the claim. The insured must pay these copays until the out-of-pocket maximum is reached. The copays and deductibles are taken in the order that the claims are received.

Sam had surgery that had the following allowable costs under his health insurance.

Physician's fee for surgery	$5,000
Hospital costs	40,000
Rehab costs	7,000

Sam's insurance plan has a deductible of $2,000 and a coinsurance payment of 20%.

For the $5,000 physician's fee, Sam's $2,000 deductible must be taken out of what the insurer owes. So, Sam pays that $2,000 to the surgeon.

Sam's coinsurance payment is then 20% of the $3,000 that is left for insurance, so Sam will pay $600 more to the surgeon.

At this point Sam has met the insurer's deductible and has paid a total of $2,600 in total out-of-pocket costs.

Next is the hospital bill. Sam's coinsurance payment is 20% of $40,000, or $8,000. However, Sam has already paid $2,600 in out-of-pocket expenses. Taking the PPACA maximum of $9,450 and subtracting the $2,600, Sam will pay $6,850 of his hospital bill.

The total cost of Sam's $7,000 rehab will be paid by the insurer because Sam has maxed out on all out-of-pocket expenses. Sam does not owe the 20% copay, and Sam's deductible is satisfied for the remainder of all medical expenses during that year.

Employer Responsibilities under PPACA

The Employer Mandate: When the PPACA was enacted, approximately half of Americans received their health coverage via employer insurance plans. To ensure that employer coverage continues, the PPACA imposes a choice on "Applicable Large Employers" (ALEs):

- Offer "minimum essential coverage" to at least 95% of their full-time employees and nonspousal dependents, including their children up to age 26; or
- Pay a tax penalty (known as the employer shared responsibility fee).

This choice is known as the employer mandate. There is, however, no mandate for insuring employees because there is a choice to pay the penalty instead.

Determining Which Employers Are ALEs: To be an ALE for a particular calendar year, an employer must have had an average of at least 50 full-time employees (FTEs) (including full-time-equivalent employees) during the preceding calendar year.

An employer will use the size of its workforce during Year 3 to determine if it will be an ALE for Year 4.

The IRS does some aggregating of employers in determining whether the "mandate" applies. Business locations owned by the same company will be grouped together into one ALE.

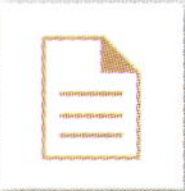

A group of smaller businesses has the same management team running four auto repair shops that operate under different names and are operated as separate LLCs. However, they will, in all likelihood, be treated, because of the common management team, as an ALE once the FTEs are aggregated.

Calculation of FTEs for Purposes of ALE Status

A firm's FTEs comprise:

- Actual full-time employees (employees who work at least 30 hours a week)
- Part-time employees who work less than 30 hours a week but more than 120 days per year (part-time employees are cumulated into FTEs by dividing the total number of hours they work in a week by 30)

ABC Co. tries to reduce its number of full-time employees by cutting Sam's and Tina's hours from 30 per week to 20 per week and hiring Tim to work 20 hours a week to make up for Sam's and Tina's reduced workload. However, the three of them now work, cumulatively, 60 hours per week. When that number is divided by 30, it indicates that Sam, Tina, and Tim constitute two FTEs. ABC has not reduced its FTE total and is therefore still an ALE if it has more than 50 FTEs, because coverage is required only for full-time employees. However, ABC has reduced the number of workers to whom it must offer coverage.

ALE Employer Penalties for Not Offering Health Insurance to 95% of Employees: If ALE employers choose not to offer health insurance to their employees, they have chosen to pay a penalty. The penalty employers pay for opting not to provide insurance will be used by the federal government for subsidizing health insurance for those who do not have insurance through their employers, because they either are not ALEs or have chosen not to offer insurance. The penalty is computed using this formula:

(Number of full-time employees − 30) × $2,970* = Federal penalty

**Figure for 2024 (adjusted annually for inflation)*

Granite Reef Industries, Inc., has 10,030 full-time employees. Granite Reef has chosen not to provide health insurance for its employees. Granite Reef's penalty is computed as follows:

(10,030 − 30) × $2,970 = $29,700,000

The Craftsman Guild, Inc., has 82 full-time employees. The Craftsman Guild has decided not to offer health insurance to its employees. Craftsman Guild's penalty is computed as follows:

(82 − 30) × $2,970 = $154,440

The two contrasting examples illustrate that it may be a cheaper option to have health insurance for employees in some situations, but in others it may be cheaper to have employees pursue government options (discussed below).

Type of Employer Coverage: The Definition of "Minimum Essential Coverage" (MEC) of Employer Policies: The government defines the components of MEC. A plan meets the minimum value requirement if it:

- Covers at least 60% of the cost of benefits
- Provides substantial coverage for inpatient hospitalization and physician services

The Department of Health and Human Services provides a minimum value calculator on its website for ALE employers to use to determine if their plans meet the 60% of costs test. ALE employers also have the option of using an enrolled actuary to calculate whether their plan meets the 60% test.

ALE Employer Coverage of Dependents of Employees: Spouses are not considered dependents, so coverage need not be offered to spouses. Coverage must be offered to employees and nonspousal dependents, primarily children. Stepchildren and foster children are excluded.

Cost Requirements for ALE Employers: The coverage provided by ALE employers must be affordable, costing less than 8.39% in 2024 of the employee's household income. However, employers may not know their employees' household income. The PPACA provides a "safe harbor provision" for employers in this regard. As long as the cost of health insurance obtained through an ALE employer does not cost more than a statutory percentage of the federal poverty level (FPL), then the employer will have met the affordability level.

A household's monthly income = $4,083 (or about $49,000 per year). 8.39% of the household's monthly income = $343. If the employer's cost given to the employee for obtaining health insurance is $300, the plan is considered affordable, and the employee would not qualify for coverage under the government Marketplace program. The employee would enroll in the employer's plan.

However, if the cost of coverage for the employee's family under the employer's plan is $450, the plan for family members is not affordable, and the employee and family members qualify for the government PPACA Marketplace program.

Marketplace Exchange for ALE Employees Priced Out of Employer Insurance: Employees who do not meet the income-level requirements of the PPACA are able to turn to the "Marketplace Exchange." These employees can obtain health insurance through the Exchange. However, because of their income levels, they are also eligible for subsidies from the federal government. Those subsidies are funded by their employers.

Employer Failure to Provide "Minimum Value" Health Insurance under the Mandate: There are also employer penalties for not offering "minimum value" plans, which results in employees resorting to using the Marketplace Exchange to obtain health insurance.

Also, those who are not covered by employers' plans, Medicare or Medicaid, Children's Health Insurance Program (CHIP), the Veterans Administration, or other government programs may buy policies from private insurance companies or the PPACA Marketplace.

The Marketplace Exchange is a one-stop, online location at HealthCare.gov where applicants may shop, compare options, enroll in an insurance plan, and determine whether they are eligible for federal tax credits, subsidies, or discounts that will help them cover their insurance costs.

This employer penalty is triggered if at least one employee of the non-minimum-value insurance of the employer, who is eligible for a subsidy, shops on the Marketplace. In 2024, the penalty for not offering minimum value coverage was $4,460 per full-time employee (excluding the first 30 employees). The following examples illustrate the differences in penalties for noninsuring employers and employers who have not offered minimum value insurance.

ABC Co. has 300 employees, 100 of whom work at least 30 hours per week. ABC does not offer health insurance coverage to any of its employees. At least one of ABC's full-time employees buys coverage on the PPACA Health Insurance Marketplace and qualifies for federal support. ABC would owe $207,900 ((100 full-time employees − 30 employee exclusion) × $2,970).

ABC has 300 employees, 100 of whom work at least 30 hours per week. ABC offers health insurance coverage to all its employees. Under ABC's plan, full-time employee Bill pays 15% of earned ABC wages for health insurance coverage (exceeding the 8.39% ceiling for the current year). Instead of accepting ABC's coverage, Bill goes to the PPACA Marketplace to buy more affordable alternative coverage and qualifies for federal support. ABC would owe $4,460 for the current year.

Penalties are referred to in the PPACA as "shared responsibility payments" because the penalty funds are used to subsidize the federal Marketplace.

Employer Penalty Type	Penalty Amount
Employer does not provide coverage to at least 95% of employees and their dependents	(Total full-time employees − 30) × $2,970*
Employer fails to provide health insurance to employees that provides "minimum value"	Lesser of: • $4,460* per full-time employee receiving Marketplace coverage subsidies; or • (Total full-time employees − 30) × $2,970*
Employer offers coverage, but it's not "affordable"	Lesser of: • $4,460* per full-time employee receiving Marketplace coverage subsidies; or • (Total full-time employees − 30) × $2,970* Funds are used to pay 60% to 90% of Marketplace insurance costs, depending on plan levels employees choose

**All figures are for 2024 and are subject to annual adjustments.*

Employer Disclosure Mandates: Employers must disclose the cost of health coverage (the cost to both the employer and the employee) on each employee's Form W-2 (though this does not mean that the coverage is taxable).

ALEs must provide Form 1095-C to covered employees and file both 1095-C and Form 1094-C with the IRS. The information disclosed on these forms enables the IRS to determine the employers that are required to offer minimum essential coverage to all their full-time employees but are not doing so. ALEs that fail to file may be penalized up to $310 in 2024 for each failure to file.

Non-ALE entities that provide minimum essential coverage to individuals (including health insurance issuers, self-insured employers, and government agencies) have similar filing requirements.

The Individual Mandate [Repealed]

Insurance works best if risk is spread over a large pool of people, and the PPACA originally required individuals either to pay to obtain coverage or to pay a tax. This imposition of a fine for the failure to obtain health insurance was known as the individual mandate. Congress effectively repealed the individual mandate (by making the penalty $0) following several judicial challenges but kept the employer mandate.

PPACA Revenue-Raising Provisions

The PPACA annually provides around $100 billion in subsidies to low- and middle-income Americans to help them pay for their new coverage. The PPACA provides employer tax credits and Marketplace subsidies and expands Medicaid and CHIP. The revenues for PPACA subsidies come from various sources including the additional Medicare taxes on higher-income earners and fees and taxes on insurance companies, some pharmaceuticals, and indoor tanning services.

Classification of Employee vs. Independent Contractor

Representative Task (Remembering & Understanding): Recall the factors used to determine classification of an employee versus an independent contractor.

The Reasons for Distinguishing between Employees and Independent Contractors

Independent contractors are often referred to as freelancers, consultants, contractors, temps, specialists, project workers, and so on. However, employees are referred to as "employees," with one label. They are very different in label but also in legal implications.

The classification of employees is important for the purposes of employer and employee taxes (statutory employees).

There are federal statutory and regulatory statutory issues related to whether a business has an employee or an independent contractor. Employers must pay FICA and FUTA taxes on employees and withhold taxes for everything reported on a W-2. Independent contractors are issued a 1099, and those independent contractors are responsible for their own federal taxes. For a common law employee, a business:

- Must withhold income tax and a portion of FICA (Social Security and Medicare) taxes;
- Is responsible for paying FICA and FUTA taxes on employee wages; and
- Must give employees a form W-2, showing taxes withheld.

However, the business that hires an independent contractor:

- Will give the independent contractor a Form 1099-NEC, Nonemployee Compensation to report what it has paid
- Does not withhold taxes or pay FICA or FUTA for the independent contractor

Independent contractors:

- Are responsible for paying their own income tax and self-employment (SE) tax (covering Social Security and Medicare);
- May need to make estimated tax payments during the year to cover their income tax liabilities; and
- May deduct business expenses on Schedule C of their tax returns.

Additional reasons a principal might prefer an "independent contractor" over an employee include:

- Not required to pay overtime and minimum wages under the Fair Labor Standards Act (FSLA)
- Not liable for employee discrimination under the Civil Rights Act of 1964, which protects employees against discrimination on the basis of race, gender, religion, color, and national origin
- Not liable for failure to provide leave and reinstatement under the Family Medical Leave Act (FMLA)
- Less likely to be held liable to third parties for injuries caused by workers' torts

Distinguishing between Employees and Independent Contractors

The Common Law Test: Many courts hold that workers are employees if their principals "control" or have the power to control the method and manner of their work but are independent contractors if not. This common law "control test" is typically supplemented by many additional factors, such as whether the workers:

- Are generally on the job 40 hours a week;
- Work primarily for one principal;
- Use the principal's tools; and
- Earn most of their income from this principal.

The more of the above factors present, the more likely it is that the worker is an employee rather than an independent contractor. The following chart compares employees and independent contractors through examples.

A Repairs Equipment in B's Manufacturing Plant	
A Is Most Likely an Employee If:	**A Is Most Likely an Independent Contractor If:**
• B supervises A's work • A works a regular, set schedule • A uses B's tools to make the repairs	• A works unsupervised • A is solely responsible for their work schedule • A owns the tools used to make the repairs

The IRS Test: The IRS test breaks down into three areas: behavioral control, financial control, and relationship type. The following diagram shows the three factors along with the issues that the IRS examines under each of the factors.

Factors to Consider When Determining Employee vs. Independent Contractor Status

Behavioral Controls	**Relationship**	**Financial Controls**
• Supervision • Instruction • Evaluation • Training	• Contracts • Benefits provided • Permanency • Crucial services	• Equipment ownership • Expenses • Profit or loss • Work for others • Payment

Employee? Independent contractor?

There are 11 components in this model that the IRS examines when distinguishing between employees and independent contractors. No single factor is conclusive. These factors are only for the IRS test.

Behavioral Control

Instructions: The more instructions given as to when and where the person works, what tools or equipment are used, what assistants to hire, where to purchase supplies, what sequence to follow, and so on, the more likely that control is being exercised and the worker is an employee.

Training: Independent contractors typically use their own methods. If they are trained in the principal's methods, workers are more likely to be employees.

Financial Control

Unreimbursed Business Expenses: Although employees often have unreimbursed business expenses, this component is more commonly a characteristic of independent contractors.

Worker's Investment: Often, though not always, independent contractors will tend to have significant investment in the tools or facilities they use to perform services for another. Employees are much less likely to make such investments.

Availability to Market: Independent contractors often advertise and seek to provide services to others in the marketplace.

Form of Payment: Employees are typically paid by the hour, week, or year. Independent contractors are more often paid a flat fee for a particular task or one narrowly defined job.

Worker Profit or Loss: Independent contractors typically have a chance to make a profit (or loss) from a job. Employees generally do not.

Type of Relationship

Written Contracts: If the parties have a written contract describing the worker as either an employee or an independent contractor, this component may be conclusive in a close case. But such a writing will be ignored if its characterization is clearly inconsistent with other factors because substance is more important than form.

Benefits: Independent contractors tend to provide their own medical plan, disability insurance, pension plan, and related benefits. If the business provides these to the worker, the worker is most likely an employee.

Permanency: Independent contractors are typically hired to complete a particular task. The longer a relationship lasts or is envisioned to last, the more likely it is an employer-employee relationship.

Regular Business of Company: If the worker provides services that are an integral part of the company's business, that worker is most likely an employee. If the services provided are more of a one-off for the company or tangential to its primary business, that worker is most likely an independent contractor.

A person who furnishes translation services for a law firm is most likely to be an independent contractor because the core business is the practice of law, not translation. If the translator works for several law firms, the translator is even more likely to be an independent contractor.

Department of Labor Economic Reality Test under the FLSA

In addition, the U.S. Department of Labor has provided guidance on how to determine who is an employee or independent contractor under the Fair Labor Standards Act (FLSA). Overall, the guidance provides that a worker is *not* an independent contractor (ie, they are an employee under the FLSA) if they are, as matter of economic reality, economically dependent on an employer for work.

In this framework, six economic reality factors are examined in determining whether a worker is an independent contractor or an employee. No factor (or set of factors) has a predetermined weight, and not all factors need to be satisfied to classify a worker as an independent contractor. Likewise, additional factors may be relevant if they in some way indicate the worker is in business for themselves, as opposed to being economically dependent on the employer for work.

In short, all factors should be examined, and a determination should be made based on the totality of the circumstances. The six factors include the following:

Factors	Independent Contractor	Employee
Opportunity for profit or loss depending on managerial skill	• Negotiates own pay • Chooses job order and timing • Engages in marketing efforts • Makes business-related decisions	• Exercises no business initiative or judgment • Decision to work more hours does not reflect the exercise of managerial skill
Investments by the worker and the potential employer	• Makes investments that support an independent business and increase work capabilities, reduce costs, or expand market reach	• Makes investments for specific jobs • Incurs costs imposed by the potential employer
Degree of permanence of the work relationship	• Performs work that is definite, nonexclusive, project based, or sporadic • Markets services to multiple entities	• Performs work that is indefinite, continuous, or exclusive of work for other employers
Nature and degree of control	• Controls own work performance and economic aspects of the working relationship, such as the prices or rates for services	• Employer reserves right to control the worker • Employer sets workers' schedules • Employer supervises work and has the right to discipline the worker • Employer limits other employment • Employer controls economic aspects
Extent to which the work performed is an integral part of the potential employer's business	• Function of work performed is not critical, necessary, or central to the potential employer's main business	• Function of work performed is critical, necessary, or central to the potential employer's main business
Skill and initiative	• Uses specialized skills in connection with business-like initiative	• Worker lacks specialized skills or relies on employer-provided training

Consequences of Misclassification

If an employee is miscategorized as an independent contractor without a "reasonable basis," there are several legal consequences for the employer.

Employees may file complaints and lawsuits to collect back pay and taxes or require that the employer pay what should have been its contribution if the proper "employee" classification had been applied.

Both the IRS and the Department of Labor (DOL) may become involved because the IRS wants to ensure that employers have paid their legally required share of taxes for what should have been an employee, and the DOL wants to ensure that workers who are truly employees receive their rights under various employment laws enacted over the years.

Employers who have misclassified employees and independent contractors may be liable for the following:

- Failing to withhold and pay state and federal payroll taxes
- Failing to make matching FICA payments to cover Social Security and Medicare contributions
- Back overtime and minimum wages under FLSA as well as fined (even criminally for "willful" violations)
- Missed FUTA contributions
- Wrongfully excluding the worker from benefit plans provided to employees

Specific Fines Levied on Employers for Misclassification

Unintentional Misclassification

If a misclassification is unintentional, the following penalties, among others, may be imposed:

- A $60 fine in 2024 for each Form W-2 that should have been filed
- Penalties of 1.5% of wages for income taxes that were not withheld, plus 40% of the FICA taxes that should have been withheld from the employee and 100% of the employer's matching FICA contribution
- A 0.5% penalty on the unpaid tax liability for each month, up to 25% of the total tax liability

Intentional or Fraudulent Misclassification

If a misclassification is intentional or fraudulent, the IRS may impose penalties up to:

- 20% of all wages paid
- 100% of both the employer's and the employees' FICA taxes
- Criminal penalties of up to $1,000 per misclassified worker and one year in jail

Safe Harbor Rule

The Internal Revenue Code provides a "safe harbor" allowing companies to classify workers as "independent contractors," even though the 11-part test indicates that they are employees, so long as a "reasonable basis" for the classification exists. A "reasonable basis" may result from any of the following:

- The classification is consistent with industry practice;
- A previous IRS or court ruling found the workers not to be employees; or
- An IRS ruling or opinion letter supports the classification.

The Statutory Employees Exemption: Employees Not Covered by Traditional Employee vs. Independent Contractor Tests

Certain workers are treated as employees for FICA purposes (Social Security and Medicare taxes), even though they may appear to be independent contractors under the 11-part control test, so long as they fall into one of the four following categories. By statute, they occupy a unique status.

The four categories are:

- A full-time traveling or city salesperson who solicits orders from wholesalers, restaurants, or similar establishments on behalf of a principal. The merchandise sold must be for resale (eg, food sold to a restaurant) or for supplies used in the buyer's business;
- A full-time life insurance agent whose principal business activity is selling life insurance and/or annuity contracts for one life insurance company;
- An agent-driver or commission-driver engaged in distributing meat, vegetables, bakery goods, beverages (other than milk), or laundry or dry cleaning services; and
- A home worker performing work on material or goods furnished by the employer.

Federal Laws and Regulations on Employment Taxes

Representative Task (Remembering & Understanding): Explain the federal laws and regulations related to employment taxes from both an employer and employee perspective.

Federal Insurance Contributions Act (FICA): Social Security and Medicare

Social Security: Benefits and Rights

Social Security benefits are aimed primarily at partially replacing earnings for workers who retire. Qualified individuals receive monthly benefits after they retire. A "fully insured" worker is entitled to payments that will vary in amount to account for inflation. To be "fully insured," a person must work a minimum of 40 quarters (10 years) and pay Social Security (FICA) taxes into the system during that time.

The original full-benefits retirement age under the Social Security system was 65. However, for reasons of fiscal solvency, the "full benefits" threshold has been changed and is now a sliding scale with full benefits determined according to date of birth.

Someone born in 1937 or before was entitled to full benefits at age 65. Someone born in 1938 was entitled to full benefits at age 65 and two months. Someone born between 1943 and 1954 is, or will be, entitled to full benefits at age 66. Someone born after 1960 will be entitled to full benefits at age 67.

Early Retirement: If people retire early, they will receive discounted benefits. Again, there is a sliding scale based on the age early retirement is taken.

If Sally was born after 1960 and retires "early" at age 62, she will receive only 70% of the full monthly benefit payments. If she retires at 65, she will receive only 86.7% of the full monthly benefits.

Additional Social Security Benefits: In addition to retirement benefits, "fully insured" workers earn survivor benefits for their widow/widower and dependents and disability benefits for themselves and their family.

A "currently insured" worker is one who has contributed to the Social Security system but has not yet contributed for 40 quarters. Such a worker is eligible for:

- Limited survivor benefits (usually limited to dependent minors or those caring for dependent minors);
- Disability benefits; and
- Lump-sum death benefits.

Medicare

Medicare covers much of the costs of hospitalization and medical benefits of insured workers (and their spouses) who are 65 and older. It can also cover younger disabled workers in some cases.

How Social Security and Medicare Are Funded: FICA

The Federal Insurance Contributions Act (FICA) imposes Social Security taxes on employers, employees, and the self-employed (under the Self-Employed Contributions Act Tax). FICA taxes fund Medicare but not Medicaid, which is paid for out of general government revenues. The FICA tax applies only to compensation deemed "wages."

Wages	Nonwages
Salary	Reimbursed employee expenses
Commissions	Interest on bonds
Bonuses	Dividends on stocks
Fees	Investment income
Tips	Other forms of passive income
Fringe benefits	
Other forms of active income	

FICA Rates

Rates are generally the same for employer and employees, who share responsibility. Rates change from time to time. However, for many years the rate has been 7.65% of the employee's wages, which is allocated 6.2% for Social Security and 1.45% for Medicare.

Social Security taxes are paid on only a base amount of income that is adjusted periodically for inflation ($168,600 in 2024). Medicare taxes are not similarly capped.

Ted made $195,000 during the current year. The last $26,400 ($195,000 − $168,600) of Ted's income would not be subject to Social Security tax but would be subject to Medicare tax.

Employers' Responsibilities under FICA

- Employer splits cost of FICA with employees (FICA total tax is 15.3%, with employer paying 7.65% and employee paying 7.65%)
- Employer withholds employee's equal share and remits it to the federal government in a timely fashion
- Employer must pay employee's share if there is a failure to withhold it
- Employer must furnish employee with a written statement of wages paid and contributions withheld
- Employer must supply taxpayer identification numbers when filing returns

Employers' Rights under FICA

- Employer collects employee's share from employee (though employer may voluntarily pay employee's share and deduct that amount as additional compensation, making it taxable to the employee)
- Employer may deduct as a business expense the contributions made on its own behalf to FICA

Federal Unemployment Tax Act (FUTA)

The purpose of FUTA is to provide unemployment compensation benefits to workers who lose jobs and cannot find new ones. FUTA is a joint federal and state tax program. There are both federal and state tax rates, and the administration of benefits is handled under both federal and state regulation.

The Federal Unemployment Tax: This tax must be paid by the employer with employees covered by FUTA legislation and regulation. Employers must file if they pay $1,500 or more in wages during any calendar quarter or have at least one full-time, part-time, or temporary employee during at least 20 different weeks during the year.

The employer must pay the federal rate—6% of the first $7,000 for each employee's wages—as its annual FUTA tax amount. This tax is deductible by the employer (who pays it), not by employees.

State Unemployment Tax: This tax must also be paid by the employer. The state tax rate may go up or down depending on unemployment claims made against an employer by former employees.

The federal government gives a credit for a low state tax rate to employers of up to 90% (or 5.4%) against the federal tax rate (6%). In other words, the federal tax rate decreases for employers the lower the level of unemployment claims the employer has. Many employers pay a federal tax of only 0.6% (on $7,000) after receiving credit for the state unemployment tax they pay. The state tax may be paid on higher amounts, beyond the federal $7,000.

Ryerson Co. has an excellent record in retaining its workforce. The general state unemployment tax rate in Ryerson's state is 5%. Ryerson is entitled to take a credit of 5% against the federal unemployment tax rate of 6%. Ryerson pays only 1% FUTA tax. The federal government rewards employers that reduce their unemployment rate by giving them a credit of up to their state's maximum rate.

FUTA Mandatory Unemployment Coverage

Employees are eligible for benefits if they have worked for a minimum specified period and earned a minimum amount of wages. The time and wage requirements vary from state to state. In addition to the minimum employed period and minimum wage, there are additional requirements.

The employee must have been terminated involuntarily and be currently available and seeking employment. The following chart offers examples of the types of terminations that qualify a terminated employee to receive benefits and the types of terminations that make the employee ineligible for benefits.

	Eligible	**Not Eligible**
Fired because of business reverses	X	
Quit because of boredom with job		X
Fired because of refusal to accept transfer to new department		X
Fired for embezzling from client		X
Laid off because of temporary decline in boss's contracts	X	
Seasonal worker paid on yearly basis (eg, baseball player)		X
Quit due to sexual harassment by co-employees	X	
Fired because of carelessness on the job	X	
Fired for repeatedly and vehemently arguing with boss		X
Quit because firing was imminent and didn't want bad mark on record		X

An employer and an employee get into a screaming match. The employee stalks toward the door, stops, and then turns around. The employer says, "Keep on walking." This action is held to be a termination, so the employee is entitled to recover unemployment compensation. If the employer had kept quiet, it probably would have been a "voluntary quit," and the employee would not have been entitled to unemployment compensation.

The following chart lists the types of issues that arise when determining availability for work and seeking work.

	Eligible	**Not Eligible**
Refused suitable job offer		X
Has not looked for new job		X
Enrolled full-time in school		X
Is taking a few night school classes	X	

Failure to Pay Federal Income Tax and Payroll Taxes

Most employers must withhold federal income taxes from employees' wages. The withheld taxes must then be deposited with the federal government. An employer's failure to withhold federal employment taxes and remit them to the federal government can result in a penalty.

Penalty for Failure to Pay Payroll Taxes: The penalty for an employer that fails to turn over to the federal government income tax withheld from employees is 100% of the amount not paid. The business entity is liable for not only payment of the taxes due but also any assessed penalty.

However, liability for the failure to withhold and remit income taxes withheld extends from the business entity to any responsible person who willfully fails to pay the tax.

Willful Failure: Willful failure is conduct that is not accidental or inadvertent. Willful does not require proof of intent to defraud the government. Willfulness means awareness of the obligation to pay and conscious and voluntary payment to someone else using funds owed to the federal government.

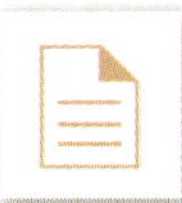

If ABC Co. lacks funds to both withhold taxes and pay its employees and its CEO chooses not to withhold taxes so that ABC can make its payroll that month, the CEO is acting willfully and is potentially personally responsible for paying those taxes to the federal government if ABC cannot do so.

Tibbs Call, Inc., uses payroll processing software to pay its employees. The software computes payroll and payroll taxes and provides a printout for Tibbs Call employees to issue checks and remit federal and state taxes. Tibbs Call has made the payments as directed by the software. After three quarters, the software company notifies Tibbs Call that there is an error in its program and Tibbs Call has underpaid its FICA and FUTA taxes. Tibbs Call has not acted willfully.

Responsible Persons: The FICA and FUTA penalty sections impose personal liability for the taxes due and any penalties assessed for "any person required to collect, truthfully account for, and pay over any tax."

There may be more than one "responsible party." Some courts hold that the key is whether the person had the "actual authority or ability" (ie, their assigned role within the corporation was to pay the taxes owed). There are seven factors used in determining individual liability for payment of the unpaid taxes and a penalty for failure to withhold and remit the taxes.

The seven factors are:

- Is the person an officer or a director?
- Does the person own part of the company?
- Is the person active in management of day-to-day affairs?
- Does the person have the ability to hire and fire?
- Does the person have discretion to decide which, when, and in what order debts or taxes will be paid?
- Does the person exercise control over daily bank accounts and disbursement records?
- Does the person have check-signing authority?

The CFO of St. Thomas Resorts has determined that the company does not have sufficient cash to meet its payroll requirements. The CFO discusses the lack of cash with his CEO, and they both agree to postpone remitting federal tax payments until their heavy tourist season begins in six months. There is a willful failure to pay, and both the CEO and CFO are responsible persons.

Accountants are considered "responsible persons" for purposes of personal liability if:

- They cosigned an entity's checks as representatives of third parties; and/or
- When they exercised a third party's authority to choose which creditors the entity should pay.

Accountants are *not* considered "responsible persons" for purposes of personal liability if:

- They were bookkeepers who neither were officers nor managed day-to-day affairs of the entity;
- They performed part-time accounting duties with check-writing authority but were not officers and wrote checks only as directed by superiors;
- They performed financial services and had signatory power for checks but in practice signed checks only as directed by superiors; and/or
- Their authority applied solely to preventing double payment of invoices.

Federal Laws and Regulations Prohibiting Bribery: The Foreign Corrupt Practices Act (FCPA)

Representative Task (Remembering & Understanding): Summarize the federal laws and regulations prohibiting bribery of foreign government officials, including payments made to generate preferential treatment from a foreign government.

The Foreign Corrupt Practices Act (FCPA)

The FCPA is a federal law that was passed in response to a series of reports on extensive bribery by businesses based in the United States in their efforts to gain contracts with foreign governments. The anti-bribery provisions were the first part of the FCPA. The second part of the FCPA, known as the Company Records and Internal Control provisions, focuses on placing internal controls in companies to prevent bribery. The U.S. Justice Department takes an active role in the enforcement of the FCPA.

The anti-bribery provisions of the FCPA apply to any companies whose securities are registered in the United States under the requirements of the 1934 Securities Exchange Act. The internal controls provisions apply only to those companies whose shares are traded on one of the U.S. national exchanges. These companies' employees, officers, directors, agents, and stockholders are also subject to the FCPA.

Under the FCPA, companies are prohibited from making, authorizing, or promising payments or gifts of money or anything of value to any foreign official, government party, candidate for office, or NGO with the intent to obtain, retain, or direct business opportunities. An NGO is a nongovernment entity such as the International Olympic Committee, FIFA (the world soccer league), the IMF, and other international nonprofit organizations that hold events that provide business opportunities.

The following chart provides a summary of what is considered "something of value" (and would be a violation of the FCPA) and what is permitted under the FCPA. These examples are from the U.S. Justice Department Guide for the Foreign Corrupt Practices Act.

Item Given	Something of Value?	Permitted under the FCPA?
Small gifts of diplomatic expression		X
Small gifts to local charities		X
Wedding gifts to local officials (small)		X
Hats, T-shirts, pens (marketing trinkets)		X
Bar tabs at group meetings		X
Jobs for children of government officials	X	
Donations to political campaigns of government officials	X	
Cab fare, transportation, travel for officials (for training)		X
Consulting fees to government officials or their family members	X	
Large charitable donation to nonprofit run by spouse of government official	X	
Paying for travel to the U.S. for training on company products being considered for a contract		X
Award of contracts to family members of government officials	X	
Loans to government officials	X	
Use of sham consultants to funnel money	X	

Whatever is being given to a government or NGO official that is of value must be done for a business purpose—trying to win a contract, retain a contract, or direct business opportunities to a particular company.

There is a distinction between this purpose and the action of paying additional fees for obtaining a license, securing a permit, having documents processed, or recording land records. Referred to as facilitation (or "grease") payments, giving additional fees or something of value for purposes of expedited processing or the ability to obtain a business license is different from giving something of value to win a business contract. The following chart reviews examples of bribes versus facilitation (or "grease") payments.

Description of Payment	Bribe	Facilitation/"Grease" Payment
Paying gratuity for getting to the front of the phone installation queue		X
Payment by a brokerage house to a government finance official to secure a bond offering	X	
Paying a clerk for fast processing of a visa application		X
Paying gratuity to government dock workers for rapid unloading of cargo		X
Paying gratuity to shipping employees for storing perishable goods in a refrigerated area		X
Paying a zoning department employee for processing a construction permit		X
Paying government customs agents to allow goods to enter the country	X	
FIFA officials accepting payments from broadcasting companies seeking to televise the world soccer championship	X	

Fines and Penalties under the FCPA: The FCPA carries fines of up to $250,000 and prison terms up to five years. In addition, the federal government can seek to recoup twice the amount of profits on the contracts awarded as a result of the bribes paid. If a company's profit on a $100 million contract was $10 million, the federal government could seek $20 million as a penalty.

The Accounting Provisions of the FCPA

Part two of the FCPA mandates that companies under the laws and regulations applicable to companies whose stocks are traded on a national U.S. exchange maintain a proper set of books and records that fairly and accurately reflect the issuer's transactions and disposition of assets.

These companies are also required to have an internal control provision requiring issuers to have internal control checks and balances that provide reasonable assurance that:

- Transactions are properly authorized and recorded
- Access to assets is restricted to only those authorized to use them
- Internal audits are performed to verify that accounting records correctly reflect the physical assets they claim to reflect, and then adjustments are made for discrepancies

The greatest percentage of the most recent FCPA prosecutions focus on the accounting controls of companies. One company was charged with falsification of its FCPA compliance system in reports to regulators. Practices such as off-the-books slush funds and disguising payments to foreign officials through false labeling of those expenses are typical violations of the FCPA accounting provisions.

Types of Bankruptcies and Requirements for Discharge

Representative Task (Remembering & Understanding): Recall the types of bankruptcy and the requirements for the discharge of bankruptcy.

Chapter 7 Bankruptcy: Chapter 7 is the liquidation type of bankruptcy. In a Chapter 7 bankruptcy, all of the debtor's assets are collected (with all exempt property being kept by the debtor), assets are sold, and debts are paid to the extent possible. If all debts cannot be paid, with certain exceptions, they will be discharged with the completion of the bankruptcy.

Major Steps in a Typical Chapter 7 Bankruptcy

Debtor needs debt relief → Petition filed for Chapter 7 → Collection efforts halted → Trustee gathers debtor's assets (ie, bankruptcy estate)

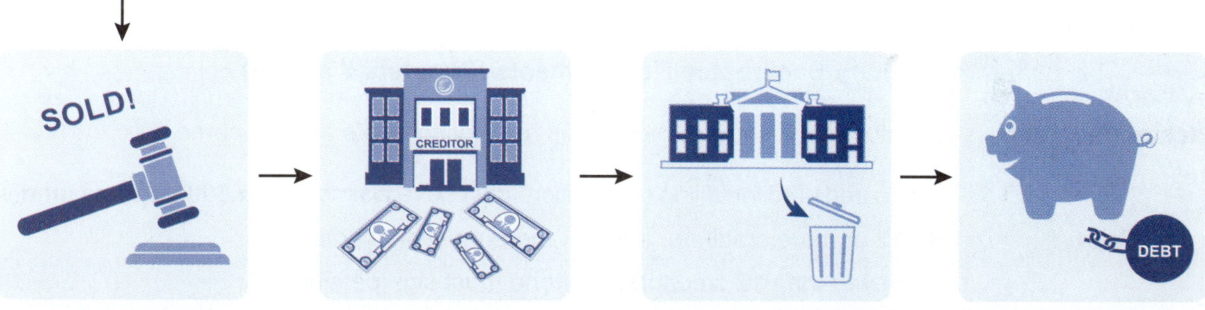

Trustee liquidates bankruptcy estate → Proceeds used to pay creditor claims → Unpaid creditor claims discharged by court → Debtor is relieved of discharged debt

Chapter 11: Reorganization Plan: Under a Chapter 11 bankruptcy, the debtor is seeking a restructuring of debt with the hope of continuing the business. Under Chapter 11, the debtor and creditors formulate a plan under which the debtor repays a portion of the debts owed and the remainder is discharged. The plan must be approved by a creditor vote of at least *2/3* of the *dollar amount* of all creditor claims and more than *1/2* of the *number of claims* in each class.

Not available to banks, savings and loans, insurance companies, and stockbrokers, Chapter 11 is typically for corporations or partnerships. Individuals, especially those whose debts exceed the limits of Chapter 13, may file Chapter 11.

Major Steps in a Typical Chapter 11 Bankruptcy

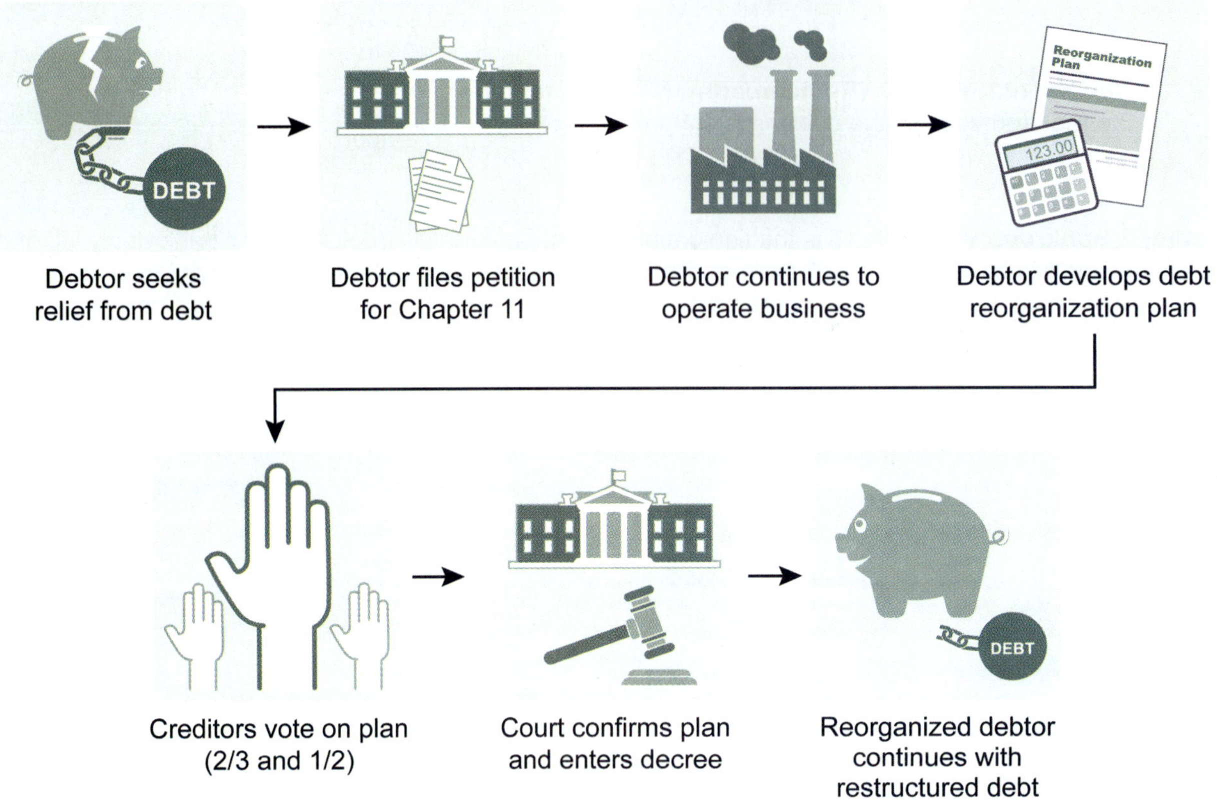

Debtor seeks relief from debt → Debtor files petition for Chapter 11 → Debtor continues to operate business → Debtor develops debt reorganization plan → Creditors vote on plan (2/3 and 1/2) → Court confirms plan and enters decree → Reorganized debtor continues with restructured debt

For Chapters 7 and 11 involuntary declarations, there are certain requirements, summarized below.

Involuntary Bankruptcy Requirements (Chapters 7 and 11)	
Lack of Payments	Creditors must show that debtor is not paying debts as they come due.
Debt	Unsecured creditors filing the petition must have claims of $18,600* or more, **and** if: • 12 or more creditors, three or more must sign petition; **or** • Fewer than 12 creditors, only one must sign petition.

**Amounts are cost adjusted every three years.*

Assume a debtor has four debts outstanding, all unsecured, which they are unable to pay as they come due. Creditors A, B, and C are each owed $3,000, while Creditor D is owed $20,500. In this case, Creditor D can satisfy all of the requirements for filing without any cooperation from the others, since D is owed more than the required amount and there are fewer than 12 unsecured creditors. A joint filing by A, B, and C, on the other hand, would be dismissed since the claims total only $9,000.

If, in addition to these claims, the debtor owed $100 each to eight other unsecured creditors, then D couldn't file alone, since the 12 unsecured creditors in total require three signatures on the petition. D may, however, file jointly if any two other creditors join the petition (the sizes of their claims are irrelevant since the minimum required claims of the filing creditors are satisfied by D's claim alone). Notice, though, that a joint filing by all 11 of the creditors other than D would still fail since their claims total only $9,800.

Chapter 13: Debt Adjustment Plan: Chapter 13 bankruptcy allows a debtor who is an individual with regular income to formulate and perform a plan for the repayment of creditors over an extended period. The benefit is that the debtor gets to retain nonexempt property. Chapter 13 is typically for individuals who have regular income and owe less than $465,275 of unsecured debts and less than $1,395,875 of secured debts.

Chapter 13 permits only voluntary petitions, and a trustee is appointed to supervise the debt restructuring of the consumer. The bankruptcy court must confirm or deny the plan. The approval of unsecured creditors is not needed for the plan to be confirmed.

The debtor submits a repayment plan that must involve repayment of at least as much of the debts as would have been repaid under Chapter 7 liquidation and may or may not involve discharge of some of the unpaid debts. The trustee may approve extensions of the due dates for loan payments for up to three years without court permission or five years with it. The benefit of Chapter 13 is that it allows the debtor to retain their property, even that which is nonexempt.

Chapter 9: Municipalities: Chapter 9 provides a procedure so that a municipality that has encountered financial difficulty and is insolvent may work with its creditors to adjust its debts. This provision is reserved for municipalities only.

Chapter 12: Family Farmers and Fishermen: Family farmers and fishermen may qualify for a specialized form of bankruptcy. Family farmers can take advantage of this simplified reorganization. Modeled after Chapter 13, Chapter 12 allows the debtor to retain all property and pay creditors out of future income.

Requirements for Discharge and Denial of Discharge

In general, unpaid claims are discharged by the bankruptcy court at the end of the case. There are certain cases in which a general discharge is denied:

- The debtor has inadequate books and records or intentionally destroys records
- The debtor refuses to explain a loss of assets (why assets are missing)
- The debtor has committed a bankruptcy offense
- The debtor has withheld records
- The debtor has refused to obey a court order

There are also certain procedural grounds for denying a discharge:

- There has not been a period of eight years since the time the debtor's last discharge from bankruptcy was granted
- The debtor has been involved in concealing property (such as a fraudulent transfer of property) within one year of filing the bankruptcy petition, with the intent to hinder, delay, or defraud creditors
- The debtor must be an individual. Corporations and partnerships do not receive a discharge under Chapter 7; these entities are dissolved

Once a discharge has occurred, a debt generally cannot be reinstated. The discharge on a debt may be revoked within one year of discharge, however, if a creditor can prove that the debtor committed fraud to conceal assets or otherwise reduce payments in the bankruptcy case.

A debtor's attempt to reaffirm a discharged debt after it has been discharged will not be valid. A debtor may reaffirm a debt prior to discharge, but:

- Reaffirmation must take place before the discharge is granted and be approved by the bankruptcy court
- The debtor must be informed by the court of the consequences of reaffirming the debt
- The debtor has 60 days to rescind the reaffirmation

Exceptions to a Full Discharge of Debts

The following types of debts are not included in the discharge:

- Alimony or child support (maintenance)
- Credit card purchases for luxury goods of $800 or more within 90 days of filing and cash advances of $1,100 or more within 70 days of filing
- Loans obtained by fraud or false representations
- Unscheduled/unlisted debt (any debts that the debtor failed to list on the schedule of debts required by the court will not be discharged)
- Student loans (with very limited hardship exceptions)
- Tax claims with the three year / two year requirements discussed in debtor-creditor section
- Any debt from a securities law violation under the Sarbanes-Oxley Act
- DUI injuries or wrongful death judgments
- Debts that result from intentional and malicious conduct that injures others

Compliance Issues with Federal Laws and Regulations

Representative Task (Application): Identify compliance issues with various federal laws and regulations (employment tax, qualified health plans, bankruptcy, worker classifications and anti-bribery) given a specific scenario.

Compliance Issues in Employment Taxes and Worker Classification

The first critical compliance issue in employment taxes is to be certain that the employer is correctly classifying workers as employees or independent contractors. Misclassification means that the employer will not have paid the correct amount of employment taxes for FICA and FUTA and could face penalties for failure to do so.

Compliance in this situation would require employers to do the following:

- Verify employee versus independent contractor status for current employees
- Review classifications of workers as employees versus independent contractors when they have been hired
- Ensure that all proper documentation is obtained for independent contractors and employees, including documentation that the independent contractors understand their responsibility for paying their quarterly estimated tax payments
- Use the availability of pre-certification processes for classification

In reviewing Granhold Laundry Service's list of employees, the auditors discover the following issues:

1. Granhold has four drivers who pick up and deliver laundry from 24 hotels that do business with Granhold. Granhold has not been withholding income tax for the drivers. The drivers follow a Monday through Friday schedule, working from 7:00 AM to 4:00 PM each day. They are given their routes each morning based on the size of hotel drop-offs and pickups as well as geographic efficiencies.
2. Granhold has two bookkeeping clerks who process invoices for Granhold from their homes. They are paid a flat fee monthly and have been treated as independent contractors. They are expected to be online Monday through Friday from 8:00 AM until 6:00 PM. They are using their own computers, and Granhold reimburses them for the cost of printer paper they use. Granhold has furnished each of them with a Pitney Bowes postage meter for mailing invoices to clients who do not use electronic invoicing and payment.
3. Granhold has two salespeople who make calls on hotels and restaurants to sell Granhold's linen service to them. The two salespeople set their own schedules and are rarely in Granhold's offices. They are paid on commission.
4. Granhold has hired a productivity expert from a consulting firm to review Granhold's processes and to make suggestions for improvements that will reduce production time and increase output. The expert is there every day, Monday through Saturday, from 8:00 AM until, often, 8:00 PM. The expert uses a computer owned by the consulting firm, is paid by the consulting firm, and has been at Granhold for six months.

Statement	Yes	No	Explanation
Granhold should be withholding income taxes for the four delivery drivers.		X	Delivery drivers fall under a special classification, and withholding income taxes is not required for delivery drivers who fit into a special category of workers who look like employees but have special status.
Granhold must pay FICA and FUTA on the delivery drivers.	X		These employee taxes must still be paid for the drivers who look like employees but have special status.
The two bookkeepers are independent contractors because they do not work on-site.		X	This one is a close call because they are working exclusively for Granhold. They keep regular hours, and their equipment is split between their ownership and Granhold's. Granhold should seek a ruling on their status.
The salespeople are independent contractors, and Granhold does not need to pay any payroll taxes on them.		X	Salespeople who work for the same company full-time must pay FICA and FUTA, but Granhold does not need to withhold federal income taxes.
Granhold need not pay payroll taxes on the productivity expert.	X		Although the productivity expert is there regularly, the work performed is that of an independent contractor.

Raphael, an attorney working in Granhold's legal department, earns $180,000 per year.

Statement	Yes	No	Explanation
Because Raphael is an attorney, Raphael is an independent contractor, and no payroll taxes are required.		X	An attorney working in-house for an employer is an employee, not an independent contractor.
Raphael does not owe Medicare taxes on any of the salary paid by Granhold.		X	There is **no** limit on the amount of wages subject to Medicare taxes. Therefore, Raphael **owes Medicare tax** on the **full salary**. Granhold is required to withhold the taxes and remit them to the IRS. In addition, the employer is responsible for remitting a matching amount.
Raphael owes Social Security taxes on the $180,000 wages.		X	For 2024, Social Security taxes are paid only on the **first $168,600 of wages earned**. Raphael does **not** owe Social Security for wages greater than $168,600. As with Medicare taxes, the Social Security taxes are withheld and remitted by Granhold, and the employer is responsible for remitting a matching amount.

Compliance Issues with PPACA and Qualified Health Plans

The critical issues in compliance with the PPACA provisions relate to the determination of whether the employer is an ALE and, if so, whether the employer plan meets the minimal essential coverage (MEC) required under the law.

Employers in compliance should be checking on their firm's status as an ALE and also reviewing their health insurance plan to determine if it meets the requirements for an MEC policy.

Martin Manufacturing, Inc., employs 40 full-time employees and 30 employees who work 20 hours per week. All employees work every workday except for personal time-off days (total PTO for each employee is 21 days). Martin has not provided health insurance for its employees because it believes that it has fewer than 50 employees and is not required to do so.

Statement	Yes	No	Explanation
Martin Manufacturing is correct that the PPACA does not require it to offer health insurance.		X	Martin is under the number 50 in full-time employees, but it is also required to take into account part-time employees.
Applying the PPACA computation methods, Martin actually has 60 FTEs.	X		There are the 40 full-time employees, but Martin must also take into account part-time employees who work less than 30 hours but more than 120 days per year. The number is calculated by dividing the total number of hours the part-time employees work in one week by 30. The number of hours the part-time employees work in a week is 600, which divided by 30 = 20 FTEs. 40 full-time plus 20 FTEs = 60 employees.
Martin must pay a fine for not offering health insurance.	X		The formula for calculating is number of employees (60 – 30) × $2,970 = $89,100

In reviewing a potential policy for adoption, one of Marvin's auditors obtained a list of the policy's features to determine if they are permitted under PPACA. Those features are listed in the left-hand column.

Statement	Yes	No	Explanation
The policy charges higher rates for women than men.		X	Gender discrimination is prohibited under PPACA.
The policy charges more for employees who use tobacco.	X		Insurers can charge more for tobacco users because of higher health costs.
Abortion is not covered under the policy.	X		Abortion is a nonessential health benefit under the PPACA.
The policy has a copay on medical care.	X		The copay cannot exceed certain maximums, but a copay is permitted under the PPACA.
The policy does not cover dental care.	X		Dental care is not required under the PPACA.

Compliance Issues in Bankruptcy

In bankruptcy, there are two critical areas for compliance. The first would be checking for voidable preferences that may be offered by customers teetering on bankruptcy. Unusual and/or large payments by customers could indicate a payment in advance of bankruptcy in order to give the creditor full payment before bankruptcy declaration. Those payments are set aside and would have to be returned to the bankruptcy trustee.

The second area for compliance issues would be in the discharge of customer debts. Once a customer has been through the bankruptcy process and received a discharge of debts, the pursuit of collection efforts could result in litigation against the company for the failure to honor a court order as well as harassment claims by the discharged debtor.

Blaine Architects is given a loan by First Thrift in Year 1, with First Thrift taking a mortgage on Blaine Architects' office building at the same time. Regular payments by Blaine on the loan are not preferential transfers, even if the regular payment is made on the monthly due date, which happens to be one day before the voluntary petition into bankruptcy is made. If, however, Blaine is given the loan in Year 1, but Blaine does not give First Thrift a mortgage on the Blaine office building until Year 3, the granting of the mortgage within 90 days before Blaine declares bankruptcy would be considered a preferential transfer. In the first situation, the exchange of value, the security interest, and the financing statement occurred at the same time. In the latter case, the debtor is providing the creditor with security for a loan, which moves First Thrift from a category of unsecured creditors to the top priority of secured creditor. The secured interest would have to be set aside as a preferential transfer of property.

Compliance Issues and Anti-Bribery Laws and Regulations

Compliance with the FCPA is a major focus in all companies that do business internationally. There is a list of areas that companies must focus on in order to prevent illegal payments under the FCPA. In fact, the U.S. Department of Justice offers reduced fines and sanctions to companies that have compliance tools in place when illegal payments under the FCPA occur despite the companies' efforts.

ABB was seeking contracts from the government of South Africa for work related to the expansion and operation of that country's energy resources. ABB was seeking contract work at Kusile Power Station, a plant owned by South Africa's state-owned energy company, Eskom. The Eskom official agreed to award ABB a $160 million contract for work at Eskom's Kusile Power Station if Eskom would hire a particular engineering firm. That engineering firm was run by a close friend of the Eskom executive. ABB agreed and hired the engineering firm at a price of $7.2 million. The Eskom executive then demanded a $720,000 brokerage fee for getting ABB the engineering firm. ABB executives passed on paying the "finder's fee," and the Eskom official awarded the contract to another engineering firm for $137 million and labeled ABB as "unqualified." That decision was ultimately revised, and ABB was awarded the contract with the money then flowing to Eskom. Much of the money on that contract was paid to the Eskom official, who was later indicted on money-laundering and corruption charges.

The money may have flowed indirectly, but the money did flow. The end result was that ABB paid a $351 million penalty and entered into a deferred prosecution agreement. The Justice Department mentioned the lack of adequate internal controls, the use of foreign agents without sufficient background information, and the failure to have higher-ranking executives sign off on payments.

REG 9
Business Structure

REG 9: Business Structure

9.01 Selection and Formation of Business Entity and Related Operation and Termination

Selection of a Business Entity

Businesses may be structured in numerous ways to attain various benefits. Ranging from a simple sole proprietorship (one-owner business) to large multinational corporations, firms are structured to gain various operational efficiencies and competitive advantages. The type of structure that a business owner chooses that will be best for its needs depends on, for example, plans for financing, liability issues, management and control desires, and ease of transfer.

Representative Task (Remembering & Understanding): Summarize the legal characteristics of various business entities.

Types of Business Organizations

Sole Proprietorship: A sole proprietorship is a single-owner business. The liabilities and assets in this form of doing business belong solely to its owner. Its profits and losses belong to the sole owner. The sole proprietorship is not a separate legal or taxable entity. Unlimited personal liability means that the sole proprietor's personal assets are subject to attachment and judgment by creditors of the sole proprietorship. This form of business is very informal.

If Matt starts a cupcake catering business out of his home and takes no formal legal action to organize in another form, Matt's business is a sole proprietorship.

General Partnership: A general partnership is defined as an association of two or more persons to carry on as co-owners of a business for profit. If the business makes a profit, that profit will "pass through" to the partners for income tax purposes. Whether distributed or not, profits are allocated and taxable directly to the partners.

If Matt's cupcakes often show up at catered dinners along with Adelita's salads, Matt may ask Adelita to join together in a catering service with a full menu and split the profits. Even if Matt and Adelita take no formal legal action to organize in another form, their new business will be a general partnership. If the partnership suffers financial reverses, Matt and Adelita will both be responsible to partnership creditors for the debts of the partnership.

Under the Revised Uniform Partnership Act (RUPA), which is the uniform law adopted in most states for governing partnerships, both the partnership assets and the assets of the general partners are subject to creditor attachment to satisfy liabilities of the partnership.

Limited Partnership: A limited partnership consists of at least one general partner and at least one limited partner. Limited partners give up their general management rights that partners in a general partnership have in exchange for limited liability that is the same as shareholders of a corporation. Only the general partner has personal liability.

If Matt and Adelita need financing for their new catering business, they might ask their wealthy friend, Jess, to become an investor. Jess does not intend to be active in the business and certainly does not wish to become generally liable for the debts of the catering business. If Matt and Adelita properly form a limited partnership, Jess will be protected from liability. However, Jess could lose limited liability status by taking an active role in managing the firm.

Limited Liability Partnership: Limited liability partnerships (LLPs) were created in most states to provide professionals who form general partnerships (eg, accountants, architects, physicians, dentists, veterinarians, and attorneys) with limited liability for malpractice/negligence claims. Becoming an LLP does not require a change in structure and retains all the other features of a general partnership.

In LLPs, partners are generally liable for (a) their own malpractice and (b) the malpractice of those they directly supervise. In exchange for providing this extensive liability protection, many states require LLPs to carry minimum levels of malpractice insurance to help ensure that clients harmed by malpractice will have a viable remedy.

Tad and Todd are CPAs who are general partners in T&T, a registered LLP. Following a comprehensive audit, Tad certified the financial statements of Wausau Bank. Within two weeks of Tad's certification, the federal government took over the bank after the bank could not provide customers with the funds they sought to withdraw from their accounts. Bank customers and shareholders filed suit against T&T. A judgment against T&T as a general partnership would mean that the partnership's assets could be seized to satisfy the judgment and that both Tad's and Todd's personal assets could also be seized for that judgment. However, as a registered LLP, only Tad's assets could be seized for the Wausau judgment (due to Tad's own malpractice). Todd's personal assets would be protected.

Limited Liability Limited Partnerships: Limited liability limited partnerships (LLLPs) are a relatively new form of business organization that allows the general partner(s) of a limited partnership to have the same limited liability as the limited partners. The general partners in an LLLP are not jointly and severally liable for the partnership debts.

Brooke is the general partner in EW, an LLLP that does excavation work. On one project, EW disposed of materials from a site in a manner that contaminated the water of a nearby town. The town filed suit against the LLLP. All of EW's assets would be subject to a judgment in a suit. In an ordinary limited partnership, if EW's assets were insufficient to pay the damages, the judgment creditors would turn to Brooke's personal assets as a general partner in an LP; however, in an LLLP, Brooke, as a general partner, would have no personal liability for EW's obligations.

Limited Liability Company: A limited liability company (LLC) is one of the newer forms of business organization. It allows owners to enjoy limited liability but to still have the pass-through tax benefits of the partnership form of business. In some cases, LLCs may also elect to be taxed as if they were S corporations. The LLC owners can have management rights, or they can designate one of the owners as a manager for the LLC.

William McGee owns a parcel of land and needs financing for the development of a hotel on that land. McGee has the expertise in the construction and operation of hotels. Bryce Hollister and Brooke Knight are investors looking for a real estate development opportunity. The three can form an LLC with all three as owners and William acting as the LLC's manager.

Corporation: A corporation is a separate legal entity owned by shareholders who will have limited liability. The use of an artificial legal entity encourages people to invest in others' business ideas.

Kay may buy XYZ Corporation stock because she feels secure that, even if XYZ Corporation goes bankrupt, she will not be liable to its creditors. Her potential loss is limited to the amount she invested when she bought XYZ stock. Typically, corporations are theoretically burdened by double taxation, meaning they pay corporate income tax on their profits. However, if the corporation then distributes some of its profits to shareholders in the form of dividends, the shareholders pay individual income tax on that dividend income. There are ways to minimize the impact of double taxation.

Subcategories and Combining Forms of Doing Business

There are some subcategories and issues related to the basic types of business structures.

Joint Venture: A general partnership for a specific activity or a one-time transaction.

Fox Oil Corporation is working with Renlund Oil Corporation for the purpose of developing a shale oil property. Their efforts of working together on a single project would be an example of a joint venture, which would be labeled a general partnership.

Subchapter C Corporation: A corporation with the usual double taxation of corporations is called a Subchapter C corporation.

Subchapter S Corporation: A C corporation can make an election under Subchapter S of the Internal Revenue Code and after meeting those requirements—such as having no more than 100 shareholders who unanimously agree to choose Subchapter S status, all of whom are legally in the United States—enjoy a single level of taxation. Double taxation is eliminated through a Subchapter S election. A Subchapter S corporation can flow through its income to its shareholders.

Regardless of income tax election, Subchapter S and Subchapter C corporations are formed the same way under state laws and have the same requirements for corporate governance and state annual filings and notifications.

Professional Corporation: A professional corporation (PC) allows accountants, doctors, lawyers, and some other professionals to gain the benefits of the corporate form, particularly that of offering benefits to employees. The shareholders in PCs enjoy limited liability (except for their own malpractice). With the newer forms of LLPs and LLCs for doing business, the PC entity is not used as often now. A PC can also choose Subchapter S status.

The Key Differences between the Business Structures for Purposes of the CPA Exam

- Ease of formation: formal requirements and informal creation
- Personal liability and limited liability
- Type of taxation: owner reporting and entity reporting; flow-through or pass-through and double taxation
- Level of control

The following chart provides a summary of these factors in each of the forms for doing business.

	Ease of Formation	Personal Liability	Taxation	Level of Control
Sole Proprietorship	No formal requirements	Yes	Owner is the business, reported on Schedule C, Form 1040	Owner has complete and independent control
General Partnership	Can be informal; formal requirements in some states	Yes	Flow-through	Partnership votes; unanimous votes in some circumstances
LP	Formal requirements	Personal liability for general partners only	Flow-through	General partner makes most decisions
LLP	Formal requirements; insurance mandates; special general partnership for professionals	Yes, except for professional negligence	Flow-through	Can operate as a general partnership, with all partners having a say in management
LLLP	Formal requirements; limited states allow	Limited liability, even for general partner	Flow-through	General partner has management authority
LLC	Formal requirements	No	Flow-through	Managing member runs day-to-day operations; can be given complete authority

	Ease of Formation	Personal Liability	Taxation	Level of Control
C Corporation	Formal requirements	No	Double taxation	Executives and board control corporation; shareholders vote for board members
S Corporation	Formal requirements, "S" election required	No	Flow-through	Executives and board control corporation; shareholders vote for board members
PC	Formal requirements	Yes, except for malpractice liability	Double taxation unless Subchapter S election	General corporation law applies

The Laws Governing Forms of Doing Business

States are not always in agreement about the laws that apply to the various types of business structures. There is a patchwork of laws across the states. As a result, the exam tests on the uniform laws (when they exist) governing the forms for doing business:

- Partnerships are governed by the Revised Uniform Partnership Act (RUPA)
- Limited partnerships are governed by the Revised Uniform Limited Partnership Act (RULPA)
- Corporations are governed by the Revised Model Business Corporation Act (RMBCA)

When there is no uniform law, the exam tests on concepts on which there would be agreement across the states or, in some areas, on a majority view of the states adopted through statute or case decisions in particular areas of business structures.

Formation of a Business Entity

Representative Task (Remembering & Understanding): Summarize the processes for formation and termination of various business entities.

The key to proper formal formation of a business entity is filing all the necessary paperwork and, where mandated, making a public disclosure of the creation of the entity. The failure to comply with these statutory requirements means that there is no entity and the owner is a sole proprietorship or, if there are multiple owners, there is a general partnership. Without proper formation, there is full personal liability in running a business.

Formation of Sole Proprietorships

No formal filing with the state is required for the creation of sole proprietorships. However, to do business as a sole proprietorship, the owner of a sole proprietorship may need to acquire a tax number and applicable licenses, such as those required for operating a restaurant or serving as a contractor. Businesses selling merchandise will need a sales tax license.

Formation of a General Partnership

Informal Formation of a General Partnership

Under the RUPA, the definition of a partnership is a voluntary association of two or more persons as co-owners in a business for profit. Under this definition, a partnership can be formed simply by the conduct of the parties. A written partnership agreement is not required for the formation of a partnership.

Janice and Maya are talented interior designers. They have been working together for builders in furnishing and decorating model homes. They both purchase furniture and window coverings for the model homes, as well as artwork, kitchen utensils and dishes, and tabletop decorations. The builders pay Maya and Janice a lump sum. Janice then subtracts the costs of all the items used in the home and turns one-half of what is left over to Maya. Janice and Maya have formed a partnership that will be governed by the RUPA.

For informally created partnerships, the RUPA is functionally a form contract that provides default rules for governing the partnership.

Formal Creation of a General Partnership

While a partnership can be formed informally, there are formal steps that offer partners more protection. A written partnership agreement is a means for governing the partners' relationships.

- When the parties have signed a written partnership agreement, the partnership is created
- The partnership will be governed by the provisions of the agreement
- If issues arise that have not been addressed in the partnership agreement, the RUPA provisions will apply to fill that void

Some states require partnerships to be registered or require a filing of a Statement of Partnership Authority. This statement discloses the partners' authority to contract for the partnership. Third parties can verify partners' authority by checking with the state.

Formation of a Limited Partnership (LP)

A limited partnership is a statutory creature. If those claiming to be limited partners have not properly filed the documents required for creating an LP, then they have only a general partnership, with full personal liability for all partners.

Nearly one-half of the states have adopted the Revised Uniform Limited Partnership Act (RULPA). The remaining half of the states have adopted the Uniform Limited Partnership Act, which has significant differences from the RULPA. The AICPA's blueprint for the exam does not list the 2001 Uniform Limited Partnership Act as a reference, so this section focuses on the RULPA.

Documents Required to Be Filed in Creating a Limited Partnership

- Articles of limited partnership or the partnership agreement
- Some states and some types of businesses will require background information on pending litigation, criminal records, regulatory sanctions, and/or bankruptcies
- Annual updates of information about the LP may be required

Formation of a Limited Liability Partnership (LLP)

An LLP is created under either the general partnership Uniform Partnership Act or the RUPA. There is no specific uniform law for LLPs.

Beyond the creation of a general partnership to establish an LLP, there are some additional steps for proper LLP formation:

- Those forming the LLP must be licensed as professionals (generally lawyers, architects, physicians, dentists, veterinarians, and accountants are eligible to create an LLP)
- Those forming the LLP should have a formal written agreement establishing the LLP. However, not all states require that the LLP agreement be filed
- There is also some type of registration or application that must be completed, usually called an Application to Register a Limited Liability Partnership
- LLPs may also have to register with the state bar or other licensing agents for their professions
- The LLP must establish that it carries sufficient malpractice insurance to cover litigation and damages in the event of a lawsuit by clients, patients, or shareholders of companies harmed through the negligent work of the professionals

Effects of Proper Formation of an LLP

- Those forming the LLP have turned a general partnership into a partnership that limits personal liability for certain liabilities of the LLP
- The partners in an LLP have limited personal liability for the LLP's obligations, except for the partner who has committed professional negligence and the negligence of those under the partner's direct control
- All assets of the LLP are still subject to seizure if a plaintiff obtains a judgment against an LLP
- The LLP does not pay state or federal income tax but may be required to file an annual report and pay an annual registration fee
- The LLP does not make any estimated tax payments. Individual partners would be required to make such payments based on their compensation from the LLP or the sharing of LLP profits

Effect of Improper Formation

If those creating the LLP did not comply with all the requirements for the formation of an LLP, then there is a general partnership with full personal liability; there is no LLP. Without proper formation, there is personal liability of the partners for the negligence of all partners.

Formation of an LLLP

An LLLP is another statutory creature that provides limited liability for even the general partners of a limited partnership by allowing the general partners to eliminate their joint and several liability for limited partnership debts. In an LLLP, the general partner's personal assets cannot be seized to satisfy partnership debts.

In real estate, many developers create a limited partnership with an LLC as the general partner. This layered structure adds complications and additional bookkeeping responsibilities. However, instead, in states where it is available, creating an LLLP is a way for the general partner to have limited liability without another layer of structure. CNN (Cable News Network) is an LLLP. CNN's owners are insulated from personal liability.

The formation requirements for LLLPs are found in the states' version of the Uniform Limited Partnership Act or the RULPA:

- The organizers must form a limited partnership
- Those forming the business will usually make an election to be an LLLP in their filing of a certificate of limited partnership with the state. Other states require more information and filings, but all states require public documents of some type to reflect LLLP status. The purpose of the public disclosure is to alert third parties to the limitations on collection of liabilities that would ordinarily be available from general partners in limited partnerships
- Most states require that LLLPs have "LLLP" in their names as another form of public notice of their status and the general partner's limited liability

With proper formation, the general partner in an LLLP does not have personal liability for partnership debts. If, however, the LLLP is not formed properly, the general partner is considered a general partner and is jointly and severally liable for the limited partnership's debts and liabilities once the partnership assets are exhausted.

Formation of an LLC

The Revised Uniform Limited Liability Companies Act (RULLCA) has not been adopted in every state. As a result, exam questions involve general issues in the formation and operation of LLCs.

An LLC is a legal entity that must be properly formed to create a legal entity and to provide the limited liability the organizers need. To properly form an LLC, there must be a public filing with the state. Some states require articles of organization to be filed. The articles of organization filing information is usually limited to:

- The name and address of the LLC
- The principal officers(s) of the LLC
- Background information on the LLC members
- Manager (if the LLC will have one)
- A statutory agent (the person who will receive service of process if the LLC is sued)

However, other states permit the filing of an operating agreement for formation *if* it includes all of the above articles of organization information. Most LLCs are created using just an operating agreement. Operating agreements generally include the following:

- Percentage of interest held by each owner
- Allocation of profits and losses
- Rights and duties of members
- Transfer rights

The Basics of Corporation Formation

Many states have adopted some version of the Revised Model Business Corporation Act (RMBCA), and the exam tests the provisions of the RMBCA.

The RMBCA requires filing of articles of incorporation that must include the following:

- Corporate name (indicating corporate status by use of "Corp.," "Inc.," etc.);
- Number of authorized shares;
- Address of the initial registered office of the corporation and the first registered agent at that address; and
- Names and addresses of the incorporators.

The general process for forming a corporation includes:

- Filing articles of incorporation with the secretary of state; and
- Publication of the articles of incorporation.

After the formal filing of the articles, the corporation must:

- Hold an organizational meeting in which a board of directors is elected and the contracts entered into by promoters are adopted or rejected;
- Draft and adopt bylaws for governance of the corporation; *and*
- Obtain certificates of authority to do business in other jurisdictions.
  - Corporations are viewed as "domestic" corporations in the state in which they are formed
  - They are "foreign" corporations in other states where they may wish to do business

LTD, Inc., is a corporation formed in Arizona. LTD, Inc., is opening offices in California, Oregon, and Utah. LTD is a domestic corporation in Arizona but must register as a foreign corporation in California, Oregon, and Utah.

What If a Corporation Is Not Formed Properly?

- The failure to comply with the filing requirements means that a valid corporation has not been formed
- Those who are running the unincorporated structure would have full personal liability for the corporation
- Some states do recognize *de facto* corporations when there has been a public filing but there was a signature missing or other clerical error in the filings made. Those running the entity would be protected as a corporate entity as long as they are in the process of correcting the filing errors

Pre-Formation of a Corporation: The Promoters of Corporations

Promoters: These are the individuals who form the corporation. Promoters are those who undertake to supply what the corporation needs before the corporation is formed. Promoters are entitled to have their pre-incorporation contracts covered when the corporation is formed if they meet certain requirements.

Promoter Duties: Because of their unique position, promoters may take advantage of others and therefore have been held to owe a fiduciary duty of loyalty to:

- The proposed corporation;
- Other promoters; *and*
- Contemplated investors.

Promoters are usually forbidden from profiting from pre-incorporation contracts (even if the contract is fair to the corporation) unless they:

- Make full disclosure to an independent board of directors and gain their approval; *or*
- Make full disclosure to all original shareholders and gain their approval.

Promoter Liability on Promoter Pre-Incorporation Contracts: The promoter is an agent acting for a corporation. However, to have a valid agency relationship, there must be both a principal and an agent. However, a promoter cannot contract as an agent for an entity that does not exist yet. The promoter is entering into contracts that are signed only by the promoter. There is no principal because the corporation does not yet exist, legally. The following rules apply to promoter contracts:

- Promoters are liable on the contracts they negotiate on the prospective corporation's behalf unless the contract with the third party clearly and explicitly indicates that the third party is looking only to the corporation for performance
- Even if the corporation is formed and adopts the contract, the promoter remains liable
- The promoter and corporation can seek a novation. A novation is a three-party contract between and among the promoter, the newly formed corporation, and the third party. The corporation is, in effect, ratifying the promoter's contract with a third party, and the third party is substituting the corporation (now formed) for the promoter

Jess is a promoter who will be forming Abco, Inc. Jess needs office space and signs a lease with Dexter Towers for a suite in one of its buildings. After Abco is formed, Jess, Dexter, and Abco could enter into a novation in which Jess is released from liability and Abco agrees to take over the lease.

Corporate Liability on Promoters' Contracts: A corporation is liable on contracts negotiated by its promoters if it comes into existence and ratifies the contract. The corporation can ratify the promoter's contracts in the following ways:

- Expressly (via the board of directors' resolution); *or*
- Impliedly (via knowing and voluntary acceptance following full disclosure of the benefits and costs of the contract).

This part of promoter liability is simply an example of ratification under the laws of agency.

Jess is a promoter who will be forming Abco, Inc. Jess needs office space and signs a lease with Dexter Towers for a suite in one of its buildings. If Abco moves into the Dexter building and begins paying rent, it has impliedly created its liability for the contract.

Once the corporation adopts the promoter's contracts, it has the right to enforce those contracts against third parties.

Summary of Formation Issues in Business Entities

	Document for Formation?	Formal Filing?	Other Filings?	Liability with Proper Creation	Liability without Proper Creation
Sole Proprietorship	No	No	Business licenses	Full personal liability	Penalties for failure to have license
Partnership (Informal)	No	No	Registration and licenses	All partners have full personal liability	Liability for failure to register or obtain license
Partnership (Formal)	Articles of partnership or partnership agreement	No	Registration; annual disclosures; licenses	All partners have full personal liability	All partners have full personal liability
Limited Partnership	Articles of limited partnership or limited partnership agreement	Yes	Annual disclosures; licenses	Full personal liability of general partner; limited liability for limited partners	All partners (general and limited) are treated as general partners with full personal liability
LLP (Professionals Only)	Articles of partnership or partnership agreement; plus registration requirements; plus malpractice insurance proof	Yes	Filing with state bar or other professional organizations	Partner who commits malpractice (negligence) is liable, but other partners are not liable unless they supervised the work	Full liability of all partnership assets for all malpractice
LLLP	Creation of a limited partnership plus disclosure of limited liability of general partner	Yes	Use of LLLP in name; annual updates	General partner has limited liability the same as limited partners	Full personal liability of the general partner—joint and several liability
LLC	Formal public filing required	Yes	Operating agreement; annual filing required	Limited liability for owners	No personal liability except for improper formation
Corporations	Yes—articles of incorporation must be filed with the state	Yes	Selection of Subchapter C or Subchapter S status for tax purposes; licenses; foreign corporation registrations	Shareholders have limited liability—will lose only their investment (if proper formation)	No personal liability unless issues with promoter; also, "watered shares" or corporate veil pierced

Jane and Francene have been running a business that provides technical support for small businesses and have been splitting the profits equally. Jane and Francene signed an operating agreement for the JF Tech Support, LLC. They assumed that they had created an LLC. Shortly after they signed the operating agreement, Jane missed a compliance issue on the website of one of their clients (Cherished Books, LLC), and Cherished Books is facing six-figure fines from both the EU and the FCC for the site's failure to provide warning notices about the site's use of cookies.

Statement	True	False	Explanation
Jane and Francene began as a general partnership.	X		They were co-owners in a business for profit.
Jane and Francene had full personal liability as general partners when they were operating as a general partnership.	X		General partners, in the absence of an agreement, are personally liable for debts and obligations of the partnership.
Jane and Francene did not have a partnership because there was no agreement.		X	A general partnership can be formed informally without an agreement or without filing.
Jane and Francene formed an LLC with their operating agreement.		X	An LLC requires some type of public filing. Without that, the LLC does not exist.
Jane and Francene will have no personal liability for the claim filed by the customer on the privacy violation.		X	They still have liability as general partners, and both are exposed to personal liability because no entity other than the general partnership existed.
Jane and Francene are protected because they would be considered an LLLP as a hybrid between partnership and LLC.		X	They both have liability as general partners. They did not inform the client of the EU and FCC requirements, and that is professional negligence. They did not create an LLC properly, so their general partnership status remains.

Termination of a Business Entity

Just as there are formal processes for creating business entities, there are also legal processes for terminating a business entity.

Sole Proprietorships

A sole proprietorship naturally terminates when the sole owner dies or otherwise departs the business. Owners may also terminate the business at any time they choose to do so.

The process of termination in a sole proprietorship is one of disposing and/or selling inventory and taking an inventory of all the assets, canceling accounts, and notifying governmental agencies about license terminations.

General Partnerships

The process to end a partnership may be governed by the partnership agreement, which outlines the grounds for dissolution and/or termination. If there is no partnership agreement, then the RUPA provides the grounds and process for termination.

There are three events that can lead to the termination of a general partnership: dissociation, dissolution, and winding up (also known as liquidation or termination). Under RUPA, the fact that partners are added to or removed from the partnership does not automatically lead to the dissolution of the partnership.

Dissociation: The causes of dissociation of a partner from the partnership include:

- Notice of a partner's express will to dissolve the partnership
- Death of a partner
- Bankruptcy of a partner
- Expulsion of a partner under the terms of the partnership agreement
- Occurrence of an event stipulated in the partnership agreement as causing dissociation

Alexa, Garrett, and James had been operating the AGJ general partnership. Following a long illness, Garrett has died. Their partnership agreement provides that the remaining partners can continue operating AGJ. AGJ need not be dissolved.

The Right to Continue: Under the RUPA, a partnership can continue after there has been dissociation, but the partnership must buy out the disassociated partner or the partner's estate. The buyout must pay the dissociating partner the value of the dissociating partner's interest.

Alexa, Garrett, and James had been operating the AGJ general partnership. Following a long illness, Garrett has died. They have no partnership agreement. AGJ can continue operating as a partnership, but it must pay Garrett's estate the value of Garrett's interest.

Liquidation and Termination: If the partnership is to be liquidated and terminated, there are priorities in the distribution of assets:

- Creditors (including partners) must be paid first. If there are insufficient assets to pay off creditors, then the partners (including the estates of deceased partners) will have to contribute to the partnership to satisfy the obligations
- If funds are left over after paying creditors, then the partnership distributes to partners the amounts equal to any excess of credits over charges in the partners' accounts

Alexa, Garrett, and James had been operating the AGJ general partnership. Following a long illness, Garrett has died. They have no partnership agreement. Alexa and James have decided to dissolve the partnership. They have been able to sell the partnership assets for $750,000, and the partnership had $50,000 in cash on hand. AGJ creditors are owed $848,000. The creditors will receive the $848,000, and Alexa, James, and Garrett's estate will each owe $16,000 from their personal assets to the creditors.

Termination of LPs, LLPs, and LLLPs

The process of dissociation, winding up, and liquidation (termination) for the various forms of limited partnerships (including LLPs and LLLPs) is sufficiently similar to that of general partnerships that it need not be separately treated. However, the departure of a limited partner will not result in the dissolution of a limited partnership.

The departure of a general partner in any of these forms of limited partnerships need not result in termination with proper planning (ie, there is a provision in the partnership agreement for handling the departure of a general partner). Still, to validly exist, there must be at least one general partner.

Corporations

Corporations may be voluntarily and involuntarily dissolved. Voluntary termination is by shareholder vote. Involuntary termination can be obtained by third parties in different ways. Both means have detailed procedural steps.

Involuntary Termination: Corporations may be involuntarily dissolved by the secretary of state (administratively) for such reasons as:

- Failure to pay franchise taxes;
- Failure to file annual reports; *or*
- Failure to properly establish and maintain a registered agent or office.

Corporations may be involuntarily dissolved by the courts (judicially).

Corporations may be involuntarily dissolved through action by the state attorney general if:

- The corporation has failed to file its annual reports;
- The corporation fraudulently obtained approval for its articles of incorporation; *or*
- The corporation has abused its legal authority.

Corporations may be involuntarily dissolved in an action by shareholders:

- If management is deadlocked;
- If those controlling the corporation are acting in an illegal or oppressive way, such as by looting the corporation or wasting its assets; *or*
- If the shareholders are deadlocked and cannot elect directors.

Corporations may be involuntarily dissolved in an action by creditors if:

- The creditor's claim has been reduced to judgment, the judgment remains unsatisfied, and the corporation is insolvent; *or*
- The corporation has admitted in writing that the creditor's claim is due and owing and the corporation is insolvent.

Liquidation: After dissolution, the corporate business and affairs must be wound up and liquidated. Directors will not be personally liable to claimants for claims barred or satisfied if they have complied with the RMBCA's statutory procedures of:

- Giving notice to known claimants;
- Publishing notice of dissolution;
- Requesting that other claimants present their claims; *and*
- Obtaining appropriate judicial determinations (eg, of the amount of collateral needed for payment of contingent claims, claims reasonably expected to arise after dissolution, or claims not yet made).

Once the corporate claims are paid, the order of distribution that follows is quite simple: remaining funds are distributed to the shareholders.

LLCs

For LLCs, the processes for termination commonly follow the dissociation–winding up–termination approach of RUPA for general partnerships. There is dissociation followed by dissolution or continued success.

LLC Dissociation: Events that cause a person to be dissociated as a member from an LLC, under the RULLCA, are the following:

- The person gives notice of express will to withdraw
- An event causes dissolution based on the operating agreement
- The person is expelled pursuant to the operating agreement
- The person dies
- The person is a corporation, partnership, or other organization that has been dissolved

LLC Dissolution Causes: Among the events that cause the LLC to dissolve, according to RULLCA:

- An event causes dissolution based on the operating agreement
- Consent of all members
- Passage of 90 consecutive days with no members
- Court order, upon application of a member, dissolving the LLC on grounds that the conduct of its activities is unlawful or "reasonably practicable" or violates the operating agreement
- Court order, upon application of a member, dissolving the LLC on grounds that those in control of the company are acting illegally or fraudulently or are oppressing members

LLC Dissolution Processes: The RULLCA contains detailed provisions on winding up of an LLC's business, including gathering assets and paying obligation to creditors (including members who are creditors). If any surplus remains, it is distributed:

- To each member whose contributions have not been repaid
- If any money remains, to members and dissociated members in equal shares

Financial Structure

The financing of a business entity controls ownership and voting rights. Understanding how entities are financed and the rights associated with those various means is critical in understanding legal rights, obligations, and duties of the owners and managers.

Partnerships: Financial Structure

Capital Accounts: Under the RUPA, each partner is deemed to have an account that is:

- Credited with an amount equal to the money plus the value of any other property, net of the amount of any liabilities, the partner contributes to the partnership and the partner's share of the partnership profits; and
- Charged with an amount equal to the money plus the value of any other property, net of the amount of any liabilities, distributed by the partnership to the partner and the partner's share of partnership losses.

Partners are to be reimbursed for payments made and indemnified for liabilities incurred in the ordinary course of the partnership business. Partners are to be reimbursed for advances to the partnership made beyond agreed capital contributions. These are loans, and the partners are creditors who generally enjoy equal footing to outside creditors.

An emergency arises, and partner Sandy personally pays $10,000 in order to preserve partnership property worth many times that amount. Sandy is entitled to be reimbursed for the emergency loan from partnership funds.

Right to Profits: The partnership agreements can provide for any distribution of profits the partners agree to follow. If there is no partnership agreement, then profits and losses are split equally. If there is an agreement to split profits 75/25 between two partners but no agreement on losses, then losses are also split 75/25.

On forming the ABC Partnership, the partners made the following capital contributions:

A. $100,000
B. $ 20,000
C. $200,000

There is no agreement on how profits or losses are split. Profits and losses will be split equally because capital contributions do not control profit distributions under the RUPA.

Distributions in Kind: Partners have no right to receive, and may not be required to accept, a distribution in kind (rather than in cash).

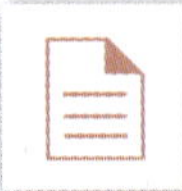

Sam dissociates from a partnership, and the remaining partners wish to continue the partnership and buy out Sam's interest. Calculations indicate that Sam is owed $50,000. The partners would like to give him a partnership tractor that is worth $50,000. Sam would prefer cash. Sam is entitled to insist on cash, even though it might inconvenience the partnership.

LPs, LLPs, and LLLPs: Financial Structure

These three forms are covered together because they are all created under the RULPA. The distribution of profits in limited partnerships, absent any agreement, is very different from the general partnership formulas. Each partner's profits and losses are determined by the value or percentage of the capital contributions that the partner has made.

Skye, Dobson, and Griffeths formed an LLLP. Their partnership agreement is silent on the sharing of profits and losses. Their capital contributions were $100,000, $200,000, and $300,000, respectively. Following the first year of operations, their LLLP has losses of $150,000. How are the losses distributed? Absent an agreement, the losses are split according to the partners' percentage of capital contribution. Skye would be liable for 1/6, Dobson would be liable for 1/3, and Griffeths would be liable for 1/2, or $25,000, $50,000, and $75,000, respectively, of the loss.

Corporate Financial Structure and Shareholder Distributions

Types of Corporate Securities

There are equity securities and debt securities in corporate finance.

Equity Securities: The basic types of equity securities are common stock, preferred stock, and treasury stock.

Common Stock: The owners of common stock are the true owners of a corporation. They bear the most risk and have the most to gain. Common shareholders have the following rights:

- To vote for directors
- To share pro rata in the profits of the corporation when paid out as dividends
- To share in the surplus of assets over liabilities, if any, when the corporation dissolves

Preferred Stock: Preferred shareholders may have economic rights that are superior to those of common shareholders in terms of either dividend rights or assets upon dissolution.

Treasury Stock: Treasury stock is common stock that was once issued to shareholders but has now been repurchased by the corporation. Such stock is often distributed to shareholders pro rata as a **share dividend**.

Paying for Equity Securities

Consideration: Shares must be issued in exchange for consideration that meets both quality and quantity tests.

Quality Test

The **quality test** requires that consideration be paid in a proper form: money, services performed, or property received. However, there is a trend to recognize broader forms of consideration as valid:

- "Any tangible or intangible benefit to the corporation, including cash, promissory notes, services performed, contracts for services to be performed, or other securities of the corporation"
- The board of directors is responsible for valuation of consideration offered. Absent a showing of bad faith, the board's valuation of consideration received in exchange for stock is presumed valid

The board of directors of ABC Corporation wishes to purchase a tract of land from X so that it can build a factory thereon. X likes ABC's prospects and wants 10,000 ABC shares as the sale price for the land rather than cash. The board authorizes the transaction. Disgruntled shareholder Z challenges the transaction on the grounds that the shares issued to X were worth more than the land received from X. To prevail, Z must prove not only that the land was worth less than the shares but also that the directors acted in bad faith.

Quantity Tests for Consideration

Par Value: Par value is **face value**. The consideration paid should be worth, at a minimum, the par value of the shares. The RMBCA has abolished the concept of par value, but it still exists in many states. Under the RMBCA, the board establishes a value for the shares, and the shareholder must pay that amount.

If shares are issued for less than par value (in states where that concept is still recognized) or less than the RMBCA authorized (by the board of directors) purchase price, then they are called **watered shares**. All the following have personal liability to creditors and other stockholders for the water:

- The board that allowed the sale;
- The buyer who paid too little; *and*
- Transferees of the original buyer who know that too little was paid for the shares initially and they have paid too little themselves.

The board of directors authorized the issuance of 10,000 shares of $1 par value stock for $20/share. The board allowed 1,000 shares to be sold to Sue for $10/share. Sue sold 500 of the shares to Sam for $10/share. Sue sold the other 500 shares to Ace for $10/share. Sam knew that Sue did not pay the authorized sale price; Ace does not have the information. If creditors of the corporation go unpaid, they may sue the board and Sue for $10,000 and Sam for $5,000 (the total recovery cannot exceed $10,000). Ace, however, is not liable because he did not know that Sue did not pay the authorized price.

Debt Securities

Those who buy debt securities are really loaning money to the corporation. Those who hold debt securities are not shareholders and do not have any of the rights that belong to shareholders. However, they do have the right to be repaid and to be paid specified interest whether the corporation is prospering or not.

There are three main types of debt securities:

- **Notes:** Short-term unsecured debt instruments
- **Debentures:** Long-term unsecured debt instruments
- **Bonds:** Debt instruments secured by corporate property. These are secured creditors of the corporation

Distributions to Shareholders from Corporations

Types of Dividends: Corporations can issue cash, stock, and property dividends.

Stock Dividend: This is a dividend issued by a corporation that has no readily available funds for cash dividends. Such a dividend does not reduce the corporate assets or transfer anything but paper to shareholders.

Stock Split: Shareholders are issued two or three shares for each one that they already hold. A stock split has no effect on the net worth of the corporation. Only paper has been transferred to the shareholders.

In a stock split, a division of the shares of stock, not of the earnings or profits of the corporation, takes place without any change in the earned surplus and capital accounts. In a stock dividend, some of the earnings or profits of the corporation is affected, with an irreversible allocation of corporate funds from the earned surplus to the capital account.

Property dividends take different forms. For example, one company in England that operates a crematorium occasionally delivers a certificate for a free cremation as a dividend to its shareholders. More typically, property dividends are in the form of shares of stock of other corporations that the distributing corporation has acquired.

Proper Payment of Dividends

When Dividends Can Be Paid

- Dividends can be paid only out of legally available funds and must be paid according to the rules on the company's various classes of shares
- A dividend may not be paid if it would render the corporation insolvent
- The insolvency test is the same test as the one applied for bankruptcy: Can the corporation meet its debt obligations as they come due?
- The dividend paid cannot exceed the corporation's surplus, defined as the "excess of the net assets of a corporation over its stated capital" (equity solvency)

The board of directors' decision to pay or not pay dividends and the choice of amounts are presumed to be valid. Shareholders who wish to challenge the board's declaration to pay dividends must prove that:

- The board acted in bad faith; and
- Funds to pay dividends did not exist in a legally available source.

Effect of Declaring Dividends: Once dividends are declared, the receiving shareholders are unsecured creditors of the corporation for that amount until they are actually paid.

Preferred Shareholders versus Common Stock Shareholder Dividend Rights: Preferred shares are usually cumulative. If the board chooses not to declare any preferred dividends in a given year, the right to receive them accumulates. When dividends are declared in a subsequent year, the board must pay both that year's preferred dividends and those that have cumulated unpaid **before any dividends are paid on common shares**.

- If the preferred shares are noncumulative, no arrearages arise from one year's nondeclaration and nonpayment
- If there is *some* money for dividends, holding preferred shares is beneficial because they are in line ahead of the common shareholders if insolvency threatens

LLCs: Financial Structure

Member Contributions: The key LLC financial provisions tend to reflect comparable corporate (or partnership, occasionally) provisions. Contributions to an LLC, as with a corporation or partnership, may be made in cash, property, or services. Obligations to contribute to an LLC are not excused by death, disability, or inability to perform and are enforceable by the creditors of the LLC who have relied upon them.

If member A agrees to contribute $50,000 to an LLC but dies before doing so, A's estate is liable to pay the amount.

If an LLC operating agreement describes member A's contribution of $50,000 to the LLC and A does not actually contribute that amount, creditor X of the LLC who loaned it money based on the belief that amount had been contributed by A could force A to make the contribution.

Member Distributions

- Like corporations, LLCs may not make distributions to members that would render the firm insolvent (either in the sense that it cannot pay its bills as they come due or in the sense that its total liabilities exceed its total assets)
- If a distribution is improperly made, the member or nonmember managers who approved it are personally liable to creditors, as are members who receive distributions they know to have been improperly made. Liability is limited to the amount above what could have been properly distributed
- If an LLC commits to make a distribution to members but does not make the distribution, the members become general, unsecured creditors of the LLC for purposes of that amount

Profits are shared as agreed in the operating agreement. If the operating agreement does not address profits, they are shared in accordance with members' capital accounts.

Organization	How Are Profits Shared?
Sole proprietorship	100% to owner
General partnership	As agreed in partnership agreement; if not addressed, then share profits equally. Losses shared in same manner as profits unless otherwise agreed in partnership agreement
Limited partnership	As agreed in partnership agreement; if not addressed, share according to capital contributions made and not returned
C corporation	100% to corporation
S corporation	To shareholders in accordance with percentage of stock ownership (per share, per day method)
LLC	As agreed in the operating agreement; if not addressed, then in accordance with capital account

9.02 Rights, Duties, Legal Obligations, and Authority of Owners and Management

Rights, Duties, Legal Obligations, and Authority of Owners and Management

Representative Task (Remembering & Understanding): Summarize the rights, duties, legal obligations, and authority of owners and management.

Representative Task (Application): Identify the rights, duties, legal obligations, and authority of owners and management given a specific scenario.

Who has what authority, and how much authority are they given? Under various business structures, there can be great sole discretion to act, as in a sole proprietorship. Partners are subject to the statutory limitations on their authority, as well as the limitations from the general principles of agency law. In a corporation, although a CEO may seem to hold a great deal of authority, that authority is limited by the corporation's bylaws, the board of directors, and any policy changes put into place by shareholder vote.

Sole Proprietorships

Voting and Control: The sole owner of a sole proprietorship makes all important decisions or delegates these decisions to others hired to work in the business.

Transfer and Dissolution: Major decisions, such as selling the business, dissolving the business, transferring the business, and settling litigation, are all decisions made by the sole proprietor.

Authority to Contract: The sole proprietor possesses all authority to contract and can even delegate contracting authority to employees.

Partnerships

Authority of Partners

Agency Law: In partnerships, agency law governs the authority of partners to bind the partnership. Partners have the following types of authority under agency law:

- Actual authority (expressed or implied)
- Apparent authority, which cannot exist where the third party is told of limitations on a partner's authority

Partnership Ratification: An act lacking both actual and apparent authority may still bind a partnership that ratifies the action expressly or by knowingly accepting the benefits of the agreement.

A partner agrees to admit a third party as a partner. No partner would have that authority acting alone. The third party could not rely on apparent authority because the law spells out admission of a partner as something that requires approval of all partners. If the partners met after the partner had negotiated with the third party and decided admitting a new partner was a good idea, the partnership could ratify the otherwise invalid admission.

Limitations on Partner Authority

Voting and Control: Under the RUPA, all partners have equal rights in the management and conduct of business affairs. Capital contributions do not set voting rights. Majority vote governs all ordinary course-of-business matters.

A and B each contributed $50,000 to form ABC Partnership, and C contributed $200,000. Under the RUPA, each partner will have an equal vote notwithstanding the differences in their financial contributions. If partners want voting rights proportionate to their capital contributions, those rights must be in a partnership agreement.

A, B, and C are partners. A and B vote to borrow money from the bank. C votes against. A and B prevail. The loan is valid, and C has the same liability as A and B on this partnership loan, even though C voted against the transaction.

Unanimous Consent Required: Under the RUPA, certain types of actions partners take require unanimity. Examples of "extraordinary matters" under the RUPA include:

- Admitting a new partner to the partnership
- Assigning partnership property
- Disposing of goodwill
- Submitting the partnership to arbitration or admitting liability (confession of judgment)
- Doing any other act that would make it impossible to carry on the ordinary business of the partnership

Creditor X is owed money by ABC Partnership. X wishes to have the partnership assign its trucks to X so that X can sell them to raise money to pay ABC's debt. Partners A, B, and C must all agree to the transfer.

A, B, and C own an ice cream store with the name ABC Creamery. X wishes to buy the store and to operate it under the name ABC Creamery. All partners must agree to the sale.

Duties of Partners

Fiduciary Duty: Partners owe each other a fiduciary duty—partners are principals and agents of each other. Partners must act in the best interests of the partnership. It is a breach of fiduciary duty for a partner to compete with the partnership, to make secret profits, or to be disloyal to the business by giving others the partnership's proprietary information.

Partner A is convincing customers of his ABC Financial Planning Partnership to use A's individual firm that A is just starting instead of continuing with ABC. B and C are not aware of A's new firm or the client poaching. A has committed a breach of fiduciary duty.

A, a member of the ABC Partnership, has negotiated a side deal with a competitor to furnish ABC Partnership's client information lists. This breach of loyalty is a breach of fiduciary duty by A.

Duty of Care: Each partner has a duty to not act in a grossly negligent or intentionally harmful manner in carrying out the business of the partnership. The standard for the breach of the duty of care is a high bar because there can be mistakes in doing business. This standard is one of reckless decisions and actions.

Partner A was responsible for applying for the firm's professional license. Because of his failure to tag the renewal date, the state agency assessed a $500 fine for late filing. Such a mistake does not meet the standard of gross negligence for establishing a breach of the duty of care.

Partner A has the responsibility for client collections. One client was almost 120 days behind in paying. Partner A learned that the client was in the hospital. Partner A went to the hospital to talk to the client about paying the ABC bill. The client was so upset after Partner A's dunning visit that the client had a heart attack immediately following the visit. Collection during a debtor's hospital stay is grossly negligent and perhaps reaches an intentional wrong. Such action would be a grossly negligent one.

Duty of Disclosure and Accounting: Partners have a duty to disclose information that affects the business of the partnership and, as a result, the partners.

An official from the EPA came to the ABC Partnership three months ago to inform them that ABC's building was located on a site that the EPA discovered had significant toxic waste. The EPA left a notice that required the submission of a plan for cleaning up the waste within three months. Partner A was the only one present at the time but did not disclose the visit or the order from the EPA to the other partners. When the months expired, the EPA came in with its own cleanup plan that it billed to ABC Partnership. A has breached the duty to disclose material information to other partners.

Partners have a duty to account—to provide any partner at any time with full and complete financial information.

A partner could ask to see the partnership bank statements, canceled checks, financial statements, contracts, and any other information that anyone managing a business would need access to.

Partner Liability

Tort Liability: Consistent with agency law, partnerships are generally liable for the torts committed by their partners or other agents within the scope of their employment or authority.

Joint and Several Liability: Under the RUPA, contract and tort liability are typically joint and several. Under joint and several liability, partnership creditors have the right to pursue remedies against any general partner and hold that partner completely liable without suing all general partners.

The RUPA provides that the assets of the partnership must be exhausted before the partnership creditor proceeds against the individual assets of the general partners.

Xeon Corporation is a creditor of ABC Partnership. Xeon is owed $350,000 and has a judgment against ABC Partnership, as well as A, B, and C individually. ABC has $50,000 in assets. ABC has been operating without a partnership agreement. Xeon will receive the $50,000 in assets and $100,000 each from A, B, and C.

Suppose that C is bankrupt. Xeon will receive the $50,000 in assets and $150,000 each from A and B.

Suppose that B and C are bankrupt. Xeon will receive the $50,000 in assets and $300,000 from A. A would have a right of contribution from B and C if they ever recover from their bankruptcies.

Late-Arriving Partners: When a new general partner joins an existing partnership, the new general partner is personally liable for all partnership debts incurred after the partner's acceptance into the partnership. However, a late-arriving partner is liable for preexisting debts only to the extent of the general partner's capital contribution.

LPs, LLPs, and LLLPs

These three forms are covered together because they are all created under the same RULPA. Their differing liability status is controlled by specific registrations under state law.

LPs

Typically, the financial risk (liability) of a limited partner who does not participate in management and control of the business is limited to the partner's investment in the partnership. However, a limited partner may incur personal liability for the firm's debts if:

- No limited partnership certificate was filed; *or*
- The certificate contained a false statement.

Limited partners are passive investors and must remain so to enjoy limited liability.

- If limited partners in limited partnerships become actively involved in the control of the limited partnership, they may forfeit their limited liability as to creditors who rely on their apparent role as general partners
- Limited partners who become involved in management create an apparent agency relationship with third parties (including creditors) who can assume from their management role that they have general partner (full liability) status
- Limited partners can do the following without losing their limited liability:
  - Vote on any matter as authorized by the partnership agreement
  - Inspect and copy the partnership records
  - Obtain financial information, tax returns, and other partnership information if just and reasonable
  - Assign their partnership interest
  - Receive the fair value of the partnership interest upon withdrawal

Limited partners' rights to profits:

- The distribution of profits in limited partnerships, absent any agreement, is very different from the general partnership formulas
- Each partner's profits and losses are determined by the value or percentage of any capital contributions that the partner has made

LLPs

Partners in an LLP have roughly the same rights and duties as partners in a general partnership.

The significant difference between an LLP and a general partnership is that partners in an LLP are not liable for the torts of other partners—only for their own and those of the people they supervise.

In many states, partners in an LLP are also sheltered from personal liability for partnership contractual obligations.

LLLPs

Partners in an LLLP have roughly the same rights and duties as partners in a limited partnership.

The key difference between an LLLP and a limited partnership is that even general partners may enjoy limited liability in an LLLP, whereas in a limited partnership, there must be at least one person or entity that bears general liability.

	Liability	Management	Duties
Sole Proprietorship	Full personal liability	100% control by sole proprietor	No conflicts
General Partnership	Full personal joint and several liability for all partners for partnership obligations	General partners all have a vote; material items require vote; day-to-day operations covered under agency law	Fiduciary duty
LP	Limited liability for limited partners, with exceptions for management involvement and failure to properly create LP	Only general partner manages with limitations on material actions; limited partners have votes on material actions by general partner	Fiduciary duty
LLP	Tort liability of limited partners is limited to partner who was negligent and any other partners involved in supervision	Like a general partnership—all have a say	Fiduciary duty
LLLP	Same as LP, with general partner also having limited liability	Same as in general partnership	Fiduciary duty

LLCs

The Operating Agreement: The operating agreement should indicate whether the LLC will be member managed or manager managed. Absent such a provision in the operating agreement, an LLC is assumed to be member managed.

Member Managed (or Owner Managed): LLC members may choose to run the business themselves. Under this model, the members of the LLC have the authority of general partners. Each member has equal rights in management. Ordinary business issues are decided by majority vote. Acts outside the ordinary course of business require unanimous approval. The operating agreement may be amended only with the consent of all members.

The nature of a member-managed LLC is most like a general partnership. However, unlike general partners, member managers in an LLC do not lose their limited liability by acting as member managers.

Manager Managed: In this model, the LLC behaves more like a limited partnership with a general partner. An LLC can choose in its operating agreement to delegate managerial powers to one or more members or can hire an outsider (professional manager). There is a designated manager given the authority to manage as a general partner. The manager of a manager-managed LLC must be disclosed in the articles of organization. Any change in managers in a manager-managed LLC must be filed with the state so that the authority of the manager is clear to third parties.

Modern Designs LLC has five members who are architects. So that the five members can focus on their work with clients, Modern Designs has hired a business manager, who can be designated as the manager for the LLC. A nonmember manager is permitted in an LLC.

Authority of LLC Managers: The authority of a manager in a manager-managed LLC should be outlined in the operating agreement.

- Some states require a filing that outlines the authority of members to contract
- The RULLCA provides that "a member is not an agent of the limited liability company solely by reason of being a member." However, an LLC that is manager managed is different, and the RULLCA removes "statutory apparent authority." Some states, however, still recognize statutory apparent authority for LLC members
- Limitations on the manager's authority can be put in the operating agreement
- Most operating agreements limit manager authority to day-to-day operations
- Operating agreements outline what actions require approval of the members and include the types of actions outlined in the RUPA and the RULPA, such as:
    - Admitting a new member
    - Transfer of a member's interest
    - Sale of the goodwill
    - Settlement of a suit or submitting the LLC to arbitration
- Some states require that the operating agreement be filed with the state so that the issues related to authority of members is clear to third parties

Removal of LLC Managers: A manager may be removed at any time (with or without cause) by a majority vote of the members. One of the difficulties with LLCs is that, often, the manager is a member of the LLC and holds a majority interest. Relieving a member manager with a majority interest can present challenges for the LLC.

Duties of LLC Members and Managers: Whether an LLC is managed by members or by nonmember managers, they owe duties of care and loyalty to the (other) members. The RULLCA prohibits an operating agreement from totally eliminating the duty of loyalty, the duty of care, or any other fiduciary duty. However, the RULLCA also provides that the operating agreement may identify specific types of activities that do not violate the duty of loyalty.

The business judgment rule will generally apply when managers' good-faith business decisions are challenged.

Corporations

The Corporate Pyramid: The corporation is typically viewed as a pyramid. Shareholders are passive investors whose input into corporate management is voting for directors. Directors then set overall corporate policy and select officers. Officers are at the top of the pyramid, making the day-to-day decisions that bind the firm.

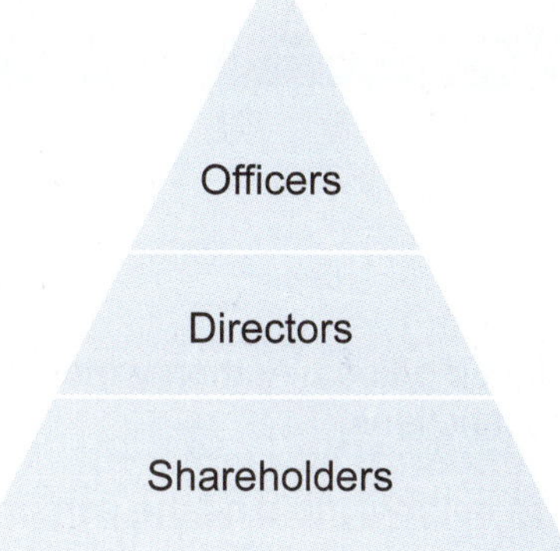

Directors

Election of Directors: Directors are elected by shareholders. The number of directors and how they are elected are usually specified in the articles of incorporation.

Some corporations have directors elected by a majority vote of the shareholders, with each shareholder having one vote per share. Some corporations have directors elected according to which candidates get the most votes, a majority not being necessary. Other corporations use cumulative voting, which gives a shareholder a total number of votes computed as follows: number of shares owned × number of directors to be elected.

If a shareholder owns 500 shares, then under one vote per share, the shareholder has 500 votes to cast. Under cumulative voting, that shareholder would have 500 shares times the number of directors to be elected. If there are four directors to be elected, then the shareholder has 2,000 votes. With cumulative voting, minority shareholders are better able to pool their votes to get a certain director elected.

Directors Have Broad Authority:

- Borrow money
- Sell corporate property
- Hire and fire officers and other employees
- Declare or refuse to declare dividends
- Make or refuse to make other distributions to shareholders
- Set the salaries of employees, officers, and even themselves
- Propose for shareholder approval:
  - Sale of major corporate assets
  - Mergers or consolidations with other firms
  - Dissolution
  - Amendments to the articles of incorporation

Officers

Corporate officers run the firm's day-to-day operations and typically have various types of authority to bind the firm, including:

Express Authority: Express authority may be derived from the following:

- Articles of incorporation
- Bylaws
- Directors' resolutions
- Statutes

Implied Authority: Derived by virtue of their offices: Authority most executives hold in running corporations—customary daily business functions.

Ratification: Top officers would not have authority to bind the corporation in extraordinary transactions, such as mergers or sales of major corporate assets. However, if an officer acted without either express or implied authority, the board of directors could ratify the actions of the executives.

Shareholders

Shareholder Rights:

- Voting rights (discussed above under directors)
- Dividend rights (dividends must be declared by board of directors)
- Access to books and records
- Freedom from personal liability for corporate debts and liabilities
- Ability to make shareholder proposals for management directives and bylaws changes

Piercing the Corporate Veil: Corporations are distinct legal entities; shareholders are not usually personally liable. The most shareholders can lose when investing in a corporation is the amount they spent to purchase the shares unless the corporate entity is not honored. However, if the corporate structural operation is not honored, courts can pierce the corporate veil and impose personal liability.

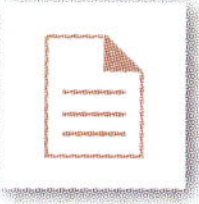

If XYZ Company went bankrupt tomorrow, its shareholders might lose their investment, but unlike general partners in a general partnership, they would not be personally liable for any outstanding obligations of XYZ Company.

The following considerations (usually in combination) may induce a court to pierce the corporate veil:

- Commingling of funds and other assets of the corporation with those of individual shareholders
- Diversion of the corporation's funds or assets for the personal use of shareholders
- Failure to maintain the necessary corporate formalities
- Failure to adequately capitalize the corporation for the reasonably foreseeable risks of the enterprise
- Use of the corporation as a mere shell or conduit to operate a single venture or some particular aspect of the business of an individual shareholder
- Absence of separately held corporate assets
- Formation and use of the corporation to assume the existing liabilities of another person or entity

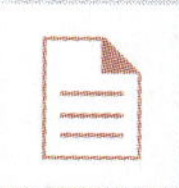

Rainbow Investments, Inc., is a general partner in the River Creek Shopping Center LP. Although River Creek had $10 million in cash at its formation, Rainbow Investments had only $1,000 as its capital. Brad Wilkinson is also the sole shareholder, director, and CEO of Rainbow Investments. The River Creek Shopping Center went bankrupt and could not complete construction of the shopping center. Contractors who worked on the shopping center were not paid. River Creek has no assets remaining. Brad told creditors that Rainbow Investments is not liable because of its limited corporate liability.

The contractors have filed suit against both Rainbow Investments and Brad. Rainbow never had adequate funding, records of meetings, or financial statements. The contractors will be able to pierce the corporate veil and attach Brad's assets because corporate formalities were not followed and the corporation was undercapitalized.

REG

Area III: Federal Taxation o Property Transactions

REG 10
Basis of Assets

REG 10: Basis of Assets

10.01 Basis of Assets

Overview

An asset is any *resource with an economic value*. Assets may be acquired for personal or business use and are either tangible (eg, car, house, equipment, building) or intangible (eg, patent, trademark). An intangible asset lacks physical substance but provides economic benefits through the rights and privileges associated with its possession. Generally, the basis of an intangible asset is usually the cost to buy or create it.

Assets may be considered personal (sometimes referred to as personalty) property or real property. Do not confuse personal property or personalty property with *personal-use* property. Personal property is tangible property that can be used by a business or an individual. Examples of personalty include machinery, computers, furniture, and automobiles. Real property is also tangible property and is commonly referred to as real estate. Examples include buildings (including permanent fixtures), land, land improvements, and mines. Property that is not realty is considered to be personalty.

For tax purposes, the basis of an asset is important because it is used to determine the tax consequences of certain transactions (eg, sales, exchanges, depreciation, amortization). The basis of assets for tax depends on (1) the way an asset is used by the taxpayer (eg, personal use, business use) and (2) how the taxpayer acquired the asset (eg, purchased, exchanged, inherited).

In addition, the tax basis of an asset may change over time due to capital improvements that have been made and depreciation or amortization deductions taken.

This section discusses basis determination for tangible assets:

- Purchased for business use
- Converted from personal use to business use
- Received as a gift or inherited
- Acquired through a wash sale

It also covers computing the basis of intangible assets for a business, such as organization and start-up costs, as well as loan costs.

Assets Purchased for Business Use

Representative Task (Application): Calculate the tax basis of an asset purchased for use in a trade or business.

Generally, when an asset is **purchased** for use in a trade or business, the cost includes *all ordinary and necessary* costs to **acquire** the property, **make** the property **ready** for its intended use, and **place** the property **into service**. This includes the amount paid in cash and any debt assumed. The sum of these costs is the property's depreciable tax basis or *amortizable tax basis*, which the business recovers through cost recovery deductions such as depreciation, amortization, or depletion. Fines and penalties incurred related to the asset (eg, violating pollution standards, building codes) are not included in basis because these are nondeductible costs.

The cost of real property (ie, buildings, land) includes all ordinary and necessary acquisition or construction costs and costs incurred to make the property ready for its intended use. Additional costs related to real estate purchases, such as recording fees, certain settlement costs, and real estate taxes assumed for the seller, are also part of the purchase price.

Shipping costs can be paid by either the buyer or the seller depending on the shipping terms.

- If shipped via **FOB shipping point**, title passes to the buyer when shipped, and the costs are *capitalized by the buyer* as part of the asset's basis
- If shipped via **FOB destination point**, legal title passes when the buyer receives the goods. Therefore, the shipping costs are paid by the seller and treated as a *selling cost* (does *not* impact the cost of the asset to the buyer)

Trade discounts reduce the regular cost or list price of an asset that is offered by the seller as an incentive to buy the asset. It is treated as a reduction from the actual purchase price.

Remember, the cost of a purchased asset includes the costs incurred to make it ready for its intended use. In addition, any cash received from the sale of salvaged materials is a *reduction* to the asset's basis.

- For example, land was purchased for $100,000 with its intended use to be a parking lot. The company paid $20,000 to have timber removed. Some of the timber was sold for $8,000. The basis of the land is $112,000 ($100,000 cost + $20,000 expense − $8,000 cash proceeds from timber)

Tax Basis for a Purchased Asset
Purchase price (less trade discounts)
+ Sales tax
+ Shipping (FOB shipping point)
+ Insurance while in transit
+ Installation costs
+ Cost to make ready for intended use (less cash received for salvaged materials)
+ Testing fees
Total tax basis for asset

Do not confuse a *trade discount* with a *purchase discount*. A purchase discount is a *reduction* in the amount due resulting from early payment of the amount due. A trade discount is an amount a supplier reduces its market price when selling to a reseller.

Once a business asset has been placed in service, routine maintenance and upkeep are expensed, not capitalized as part of the asset's cost. However, subsequent expenditures made that result in a betterment, restoration, or new or different use of the property must be capitalized (ie, added to cost of the asset).

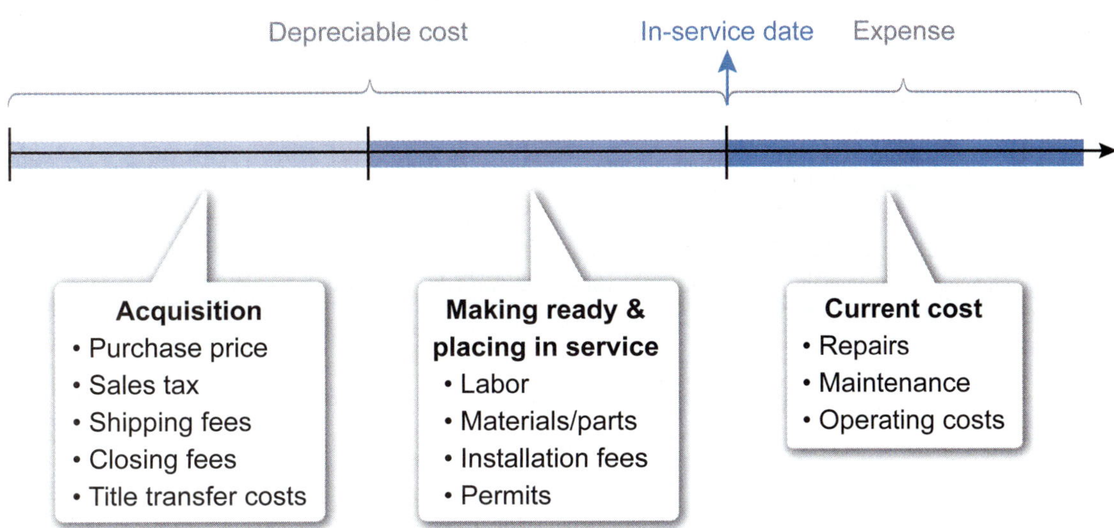

A business purchased a piece of equipment for use in the business. The costs associated with the acquisition of the equipment were:

List price	$55,000
Delivery charges, FOB destination	725
Installation fees	300
Sales tax	3,400

The company offers a 10% trade discount to the business. The EPA fined the business $1,000 for not adhering to antipollution regulations during the installation. What is the tax basis of the equipment for the business?

In this scenario, the business includes all the necessary costs incurred to acquire and place the equipment into service. Because the equipment is subject to a 10% trade discount, the purchase price of the equipment is $49,500 ($55,000 × 90%), not $55,000.

The equipment is shipped FOB destination, meaning that the seller pays the shipping costs, not the buyer; the delivery charges are not included in the tax basis.

Therefore, the tax basis of the equipment is **$53,200** ($49,500 purchase price less the trade discount + $300 installation fees + $3,400 sales tax). The $1,000 fine is a *nondeductible cost* and has no impact on the basis for the equipment.

UniQue Concrete runs a paving business. UniQue incurs the following expenses for its dump truck: replacement tires, oil changes, and a transmission overhaul. Which of the expenses should be capitalized?

An expense that results in a restoration or new or different use of the property must be capitalized as a new asset. Expenses that constitute routine maintenance or meet other safe harbor rules should be expensed immediately. The engine overhaul is likely to be required to be capitalized, while the oil change and replacement tires would be expensed currently.

Lump-Sum Assets Purchase

If a business purchases a group of assets for a lump sum (eg, land and building), the purchase price must be allocated among all of the assets acquired. This is required so that each asset has a basis to be used for depreciation, if applicable, and for determining the gain or loss on disposal.

The most common allocation method used for lump-sum purchases is based on the relative FMV (or appraised value) of the assets.

Allocation of Asset Values with Lump-Sum Purchase

$$\text{Individual asset allocated value} = \frac{\text{Individual asset appraised value}}{\text{Total assets appraised value}} \times \text{Lump sum (total cost)}$$

A company purchased three machines for a lump sum of $25,000. On the date of the purchase, the machines had the following FMVs:

Machine 1	$ 9,000
Machine 2	15,000
Machine 3	6,000
	$30,000

What is the basis for each machine?

The total purchase price of $25,000 is allocated based on the FMV of the machines.

Machine 1	($9,000 / $30,000) × $25,000 =	$ 7,500
Machine 2	($15,000 / $30,000) × $25,000 =	12,500
Machine 3	($6,000 / $30,000) × $25,000 =	5,000
		$25,000

Adjusted Tax Basis

Certain business assets are subject to depreciation or amortization. The initial basis of a business asset is reduced by the amount of recovery deductions to determine the *adjusted tax basis* (sometimes referred to as carrying value). The adjusted tax basis of an asset is used to calculate any realized gain or loss when the asset is disposed of.

Total capital cost of asset
\+ Capital improvements
− Depreciation or amortization expense taken

Adjusted tax basis

On the exam, pay careful attention to the wording regarding basis. The exam may use "basis" rather than "tax basis." If "adjusted tax basis" or "adjusted basis" is used, it is referring to the asset's cost less accumulated depreciation or amortization. For some problems involving adjusted book basis and adjusted tax basis, these two amounts are probably different due to the method of depreciation used.

Safe Harbor Rules

Businesses generally capitalize assets (except land and inventory) with useful lives over one year, but this can get cumbersome for relatively low-cost items. As an administrative convenience for taxpayers, regulations provide a **safe harbor** tax provision for certain tangible property (real or personal) that permits a taxpayer to deduct qualifying **de minimis costs** instead of capitalizing and depreciating those costs over the property's useful life.

- The taxpayer must treat the amount paid for the property as an expense for financial accounting purposes and adhere to the company's written accounting capitalization procedures
- Maximum Amount: Up to $5,000 of the cost of qualified property if the business has an applicable financial statement (F/S) and up to $2,500 for a business without an applicable F/S
- De minimis threshold is applied at the invoice level or at the item level if multiple items are listed on an invoice

De Minimis Safe Harbor for Expensing (Section 263)

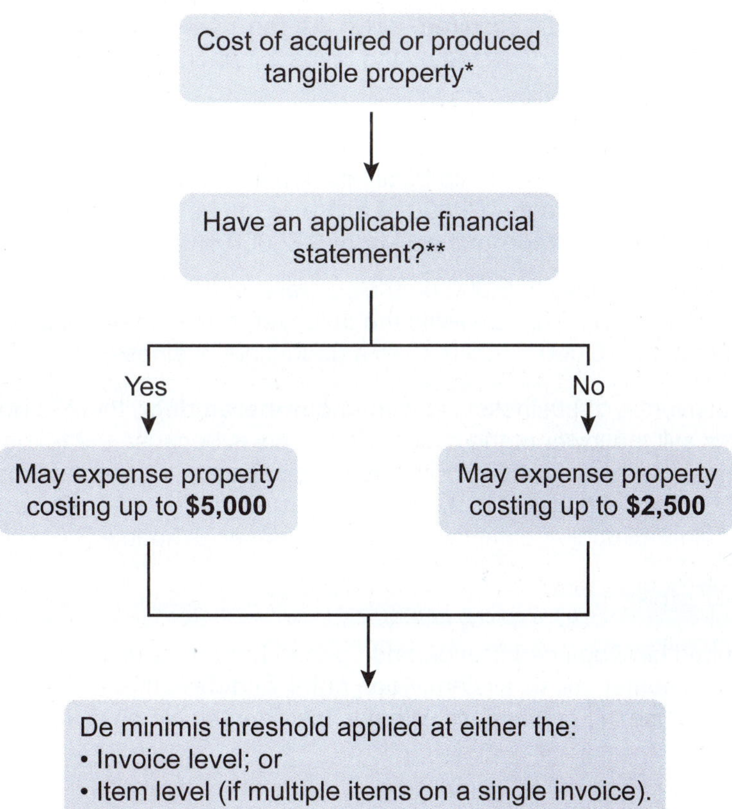

**Includes real and personal property except land and inventory.*
***Applicable financial statement is a financial statement (F/S) filed with SEC, audited F/S, or F/S provided to federal or state government.*

A corporation purchased 12 office conference chairs. Each chair cost $2,100, and the company received one invoice, which listed each chair separately. The chairs' useful life is estimated to be seven years. The corporation prepares *audited financial statements* and has a capitalization policy in place for financial reporting purposes that allows the chairs to be expensed. How much can the corporation elect to expense for the chairs in the year of purchase under the de minimis safe harbor for capital expenditures?

Here, the corporation may elect to expense the cost of the chairs at the **item level** since multiple items are listed on the invoice. Because the corporation has an applicable F/S and each chair is less than $5,000, a total of **$25,200** ($2,100 × 12 chairs) may be expensed.

Assets Converted from Personal to Business Use

Representative Task (Application): Calculate the tax basis of an asset converted from personal use to business use.

Personal assets are often converted to business use when an individual taxpayer pursues a business activity (eg, sole proprietorship, rental activity, farming). Generally, the **tax basis for the business-use asset** is the *lesser* of (1) the taxpayer's **adjusted basis** of the asset (ie, usually cost or carryover basis depending on how the asset was acquired) or (2) the **fair market value** (FMV) of the asset on the conversion date. No gain or loss is recognized by the taxpayer when converting a personal-use asset to a business-use asset.

- For example, a taxpayer purchased an asset for $20,000 several years ago for personal use but later decided to use it in his sole proprietorship business. On the date of conversion, the FMV was $22,000. The taxpayer does not recognize the $2,000 of appreciation as gain. Additionally, the basis of the business asset is $20,000, the lower of the FMV of $22,000 or the adjusted basis of $20,000
- If the FMV of the asset was only $15,000 on the conversion date, the FMV (ie, the smaller amount) is used as the business basis. This prevents the taxpayer from converting a potential *nondeductible* personal loss of $5,000 ($15,000 − $20,000) to a deductible business loss

If a personal asset is converted to business use with **encumbered debt**, there is **no impact** on the asset's business-use basis; it is still the lower of the cost or FMV. This is because the taxpayer is still liable for the debt, not the business (ie, a sole proprietorship is *not* a separate legal entity from the individual). However, any interest on the debt related to the business use is deducted on Schedule C (Profit or Loss from Business), Schedule E (Supplemental Income and Loss), or Schedule F (Profit or Loss from Farming).

Lindsay acquired her yoga certification and opened her own studio as a sole proprietor. She owned a computer, music system, yoga mats, and desk that she purchased several years ago and plans to use in her business. What is the depreciable basis that Lindsay should use for each asset?

Asset	Purchase Price	FMV at Time of Conversion
Computer	$4,000	$2,800
Music system	800	600
Yoga mats	960	500
Desk	2,870	3,000

Initial basis is the *lesser* of cost or FMV at date of conversion. Accordingly, the computer's basis is $2,800, the music system is $600, the yoga mats are $500, and the desk is $2,870.

Gifted or Inherited Property

Representative Task (Application): Calculate the tax basis of property received as a gift or as an inheritance from a decedent.

Overview

While an asset's basis is usually determined based on the amount paid for an asset, there are exceptions to this rule for property received as a gift or an inheritance. According to the IRS, "*a gift occurs when there is a transfer of property by one individual to another while receiving nothing, or less than full value, in return.*"

A gift may be real or personal property, whether tangible or intangible, that a taxpayer makes directly or indirectly (ie, through a trust) to another. Inherited property is bequeathed to a beneficiary from a decedent's estate. Both gifts and inheritances are considered transfers of wealth; the only difference is that one is made during a donor's lifetime (ie, gift), and the other occurs after the donor's death (ie, inheritance).

There are two parties when a gift is made. The donor is the person making the gift, and the donee is the recipient of the gift. A donor may gift up to $18,000 per donee a year (ie, statutory annual exclusion for 2024) without any gift tax consequences. If any gift tax is due on a taxable gift, the donor is responsible for the tax.

Basis of Property Acquired by Gift

A taxpayer's basis in property acquired by gift depends on both the *donor's adjusted basis* for the property and the property's *FMV* on the date of the gift and whether *any gift tax was paid by the donor*. Because most gifts are capital assets, a **capital gain or loss** is recognized when the donee sells the property. The donee's **holding period** dictates whether the capital gain or loss is *short term or long term* (ie, subject to preferential tax rates).

Appreciated Gifted Property

If the gift is *appreciated* property (ie, FMV when gifted > Donor's adjusted basis), the **donee's basis** and **holding period** are the **same** as the **donor's** (ie, gain basis, donee steps into the shoes of the donor). Therefore, when the donee sells the property, any *gain* or loss recognized is based on the **carryover** adjusted basis and holding period.

On May 1, Year 7, a taxpayer gave his nephew stock as a gift. The taxpayer had originally acquired the stock for $30,000 on November 1, Year 6. On the date of the gift, the stock had a FMV of $42,000. No gift tax was paid on the transaction. On August 31, Year 7, the nephew sold the stock for $45,000 to an unrelated party. What are the amount and character of the nephew's gain or loss on the sale in Year 7?

Because the stock was appreciated on the date of the gift (ie, $42,000 FMV > $30,000 donor's adjusted basis), the nephew assumed the donor's basis ($30,000) and holding period (begins on November 1, Year 6).

When the stock (a capital asset) was sold for $45,000, the nephew reports a $15,000 capital gain ($45,000 sales price − $30,000 basis). Since the holding period for the stock began on November 1, Year 6, and the stock was sold on August 31, Year 7, the capital gain is short term (ie, not greater than one year).

Depreciated Gifted Property

If the gift's FMV is **less** than the donor's **adjusted basis on the date of the gift** (ie, property has *declined* in value), the donee must keep track of **dual basis** (ie, both donor's adjusted basis, or gain basis, and FMV on date of the gift, or loss basis). The following rules apply when gifted *depreciated* property is sold, in order to *minimize* the gain or loss realized by the donee and so that the donee is *not* taxed on subsequent appreciation up to the donor's adjusted basis.

- If the gifted property is later sold for *more* than the donor's adjusted basis (ie, gain basis), the **donor's adjusted basis** and holding period are used to calculate the **gain**
- If sold for **less** than the FMV *when the property was gifted*, the **FMV** (ie, loss basis) is used to calculate the **loss**, and the donee's holding period begins on the date of the gift
- If the gifted property is sold for an amount *between* the donor's adjusted basis and the FMV when gifted, **no gain/loss** is recognized

On November 1, Year 3, a taxpayer gifted land with a FMV of $15,000 to his niece. The taxpayer had purchased the land on February 1, Year 3, for $17,000. No gift tax was paid on the gift. The niece sold the land to an unrelated party on October 1, Year 4, for $17,700. What is the amount and character of the niece's gain (loss) from the sale?

Because the value of the land had depreciated (ie, declined in value) on the date of the gift (ie, $17,000 donor's adjusted basis > $15,000 FMV), the niece had dual basis for the property (ie, $17,000 gain basis and $15,000 loss basis).

When the land (a capital asset) was sold for $17,700, the sales price was greater than the donor's $17,000 gain basis. Therefore, the niece received a $17,000 carryover basis and has a $700 ($17,700 sales price − $17,000 basis) capital gain. The gain is long term since the holding period began on February 1, Year 3, and the land was sold October 1, Year 4 (ie, greater than one year). By using the donor's basis, the niece is taxed only on appreciation over the donor's basis (ie, $700).

Assume the land was sold for $13,500. What is the amount and character of the niece's gain (loss) from the sale?

Since the land sold for less than the loss basis, the $15,000 FMV at the time of the gift is used as the basis to calculate the loss. The niece has a $1,500 capital loss ($13,500 sales price − $15,000 loss basis). The holding period began on November 1, Year 3 (the day of the gift), resulting in a short-term capital loss.

Assume the land was sold for $16,000. What are the amount and character of the niece's gain (loss) from the sale?

Here, the land is subsequently sold for an amount between $15,000 FMV when gifted and the $17,000 donor's adjusted basis. Accordingly, no gain or loss is recognized.

Basis of Gifted Property

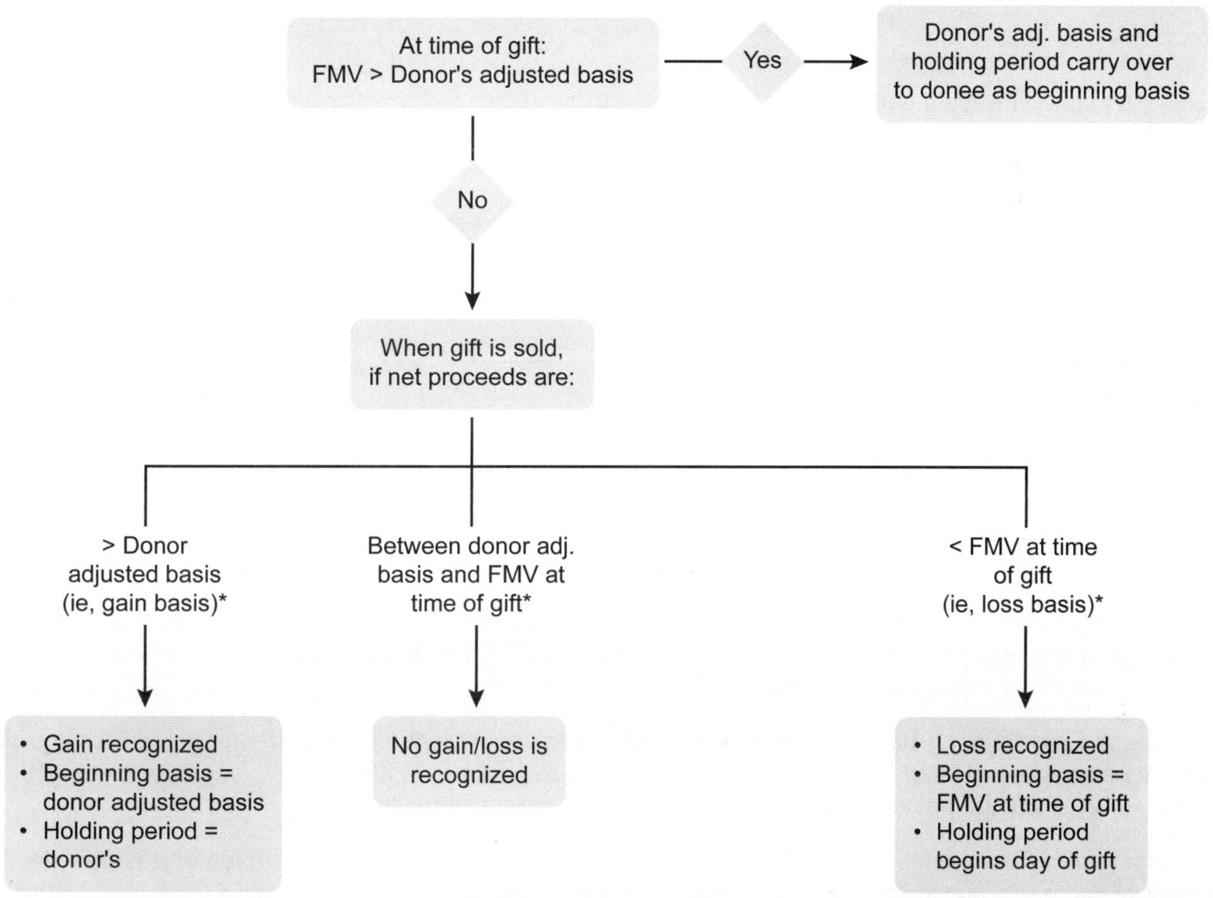

At time of gift: FMV > Donor's adjusted basis

Yes → Donor's adj. basis and holding period carry over to donee as beginning basis

No → When gift is sold, if net proceeds are:

- > Donor adjusted basis (ie, gain basis)* →
  - Gain recognized
  - Beginning basis = donor adjusted basis
  - Holding period = donor's
- Between donor adj. basis and FMV at time of gift* → No gain/loss is recognized
- < FMV at time of gift (ie, loss basis)* →
  - Loss recognized
  - Beginning basis = FMV at time of gift
  - Holding period begins day of gift

**Plus or minus adjustments incurred while held by the taxpayer (if applicable)*

When Gift Tax Is Paid by Donor

If the donor pays a gift tax on the gift, the portion of the tax paid attributable to the property's appreciation (ie, increase in value) at the date of the gift is added to the donee's basis (ie, considered an additional cost of the property). The formula used to determine this amount is shown below.

Donee's Basis When Gift Tax Is Paid

	Donor's adjusted basis
+	Portion of the gift tax paid due to appreciation
	Donee's basis

$$\frac{\text{FMV of gift} - \text{Donor's adjusted basis}}{\text{FMV of gift} - \text{Annual donor exclusion}} \times \text{Gift tax paid}$$

A taxpayer gave a gift of land worth $90,000 to a cousin. The land's original cost to the taxpayer was $30,000. As a result of the transfer, the taxpayer paid a gift tax of $12,000. Assuming an annual gift tax exclusion of $18,000, what is the cousin's tax basis in the land?

Because the gift was appreciated property (ie, $90,000 FMV when gifted > $30,000 adjusted basis), the cousin assumed the taxpayer's carryover basis (ie, $30,000) plus a portion of the gift tax paid by the taxpayer. The portion of the gift tax is calculated as:

$$\frac{\$90{,}000 \text{ FMV of gift} - \$30{,}000 \text{ donor's adjusted basis}}{\$90{,}000 \text{ FMV} - \$18{,}000 \text{ gift tax exclusion}} \times \$12{,}000 \text{ gift tax} = \$10{,}000$$

Therefore, the cousin's basis in the land is **$40,000** ($30,000 carryover basis + $10,000 part of gift tax)

Basis of Property Received through Inheritance

An individual's estate is subject to the estate tax, which is imposed on the *FMV* of the estate's assets. Inherited property is generally excludable from the recipient's (ie, heir's) gross income upon receipt, avoiding double taxation on the property's FMV.

Therefore, a **beneficiary's basis for inherited property** is generally the **FMV** of the property. This is often the FMV on the date of death; however, subject to certain requirements, the estate's executor can elect to use the FMV on an *alternative valuation date*, which is six months after the date of death.

- As a result of using FMV for the basis, the beneficiary is taxed on only the increase or decrease in value of the property during the beneficiary's period of ownership

The holding period for inherited assets is **deemed to be long term regardless of how long the beneficiary** held **the asset**. The original cost and acquisition date by the decedent are *ignored* in all determinations.

Note: The FMV basis rule is not applicable to **appreciated property** acquired by the decedent by gift within one year before death if such property then passes to the original donor or donor's spouse. Basis will equal the *decedent's adjusted basis* (generally donor's carryover basis) in the property immediately before death.

- For example, a son gives property with a FMV of $40,000 (basis of $5,000) to his terminally ill father within one year before his father's death. The property is included in his father's estate at $40,000; however, if the property passes to his son or his son's wife, the basis will remain at $5,000. If the property passes to any other heir, the heir's basis in the property will be $40,000

Determining Beneficiary's Basis for Inherited Property

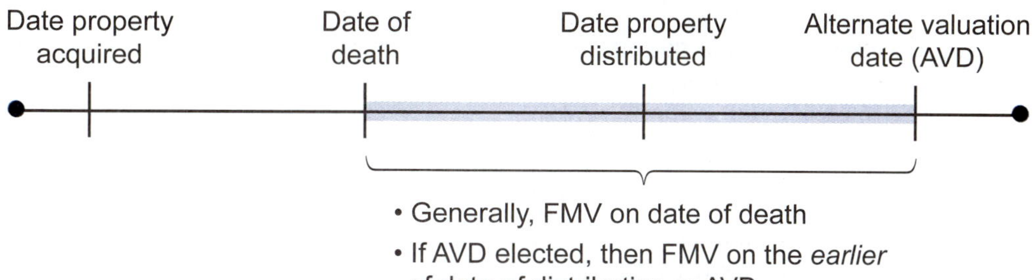

Ann received 100 shares of stock as an inheritance from her uncle Henry, who died January 20, Year 2. The stock had a FMV of $40,000 on the date of death. Her uncle acquired the stock for $12,000 on June 1, Year 1. The stock is distributed to Ann on May 1, Year 2. Assume the alternative valuation date is not elected. What is Ann's basis in the stock?

Ann's basis for the stock is its **FMV of $40,000** on the date of Henry's death. The inherited stock automatically has a long-term holding period even though her uncle owned the stock for less than one year.

Assume the stock was distributed to Ann on June 15, Year 2, when its FMV was $34,000. The alternative valuation date is elected (ie, July 20, Year 2), and the stock's FMV on that date was $30,000. What is Ann's basis in the stock?

If the alternative valuation date is elected, then Ann's basis for the stock is the stock's FMV on the *earlier* of the date of distribution or the alternative valuation date. Here, Ann's basis will be the stock's **$34,000 FMV** on June 15 (the date of distribution) since the stock was distributed to Ann within six months after the decedent's death.

Stock Acquired through a Wash Sale

Representative Task (Application): Calculate the tax basis of stock acquired through a wash sale.

Wash Sales

To prevent taxpayers from recognizing losses if they sell securities and buy them back shortly before or after the sale date, the wash sale rule was enacted. Tax law prevents a taxpayer from capturing the tax benefits of stock losses in the current year while their economic position has not changed.

A wash sale occurs when securities are sold at a **loss** and the taxpayer acquires the same or substantially identical securities within **30 days before** or **after** the sale. The repurchase period is 61 days: the day of sale plus 30 days before and after this date.

Losses from a **wash sale** are **not deductible**. The nondeductible loss is **added** to the basis of the acquired securities. Because wash sales apply **only** to losses, these rules do not apply to gains.

If the number of shares acquired is less than the number originally purchased, the disallowed loss must be **prorated** (ie, based on the shares acquired).

Wash Sales

**Disallowed loss is added to the basis of the replacement security*

A taxpayer engaged in the following transactions of Classy Corporation stock:

Date	Transaction	Amount
10/10/Year 1	Purchased 100 shares	$500
12/20/Year 2	Purchased 100 shares	$400
12/27/Year 2	Sold 100 shares from 10/10/Year 1	$410

What is the taxpayer's basis in the shares acquired on December 20, Year 2?

The shares sold on 12/27/Year 2 were sold at a $90 loss ($410 sales price − $500 cost). Because the taxpayer purchased an additional 100 shares of the *same stock seven days before* the sale, a wash sale occurred.

Losses from **wash sales** are **not deductible** because the taxpayer's economic position does not change. The nondeductible **loss** is **added** to the **basis** of the **acquired** security.

If the number of shares acquired is *less* than the number originally purchased, the disallowed loss must be **prorated** (ie, based on the shares acquired).

Therefore, the basis of the stock purchased on December 20, Year 2, is **$490** ($400 purchase price + $90 disallowed loss).

Basis of Intangible Assets

Representative Task (Application): Calculate the basis of intangible assets, including organization costs, start-up costs, and loan costs.

Overview

In contrast to physical assets, businesses also receive long-term value from assets that have no physical properties. **Intangible assets**, such as patents, trademarks, and goodwill, can comprise a significant portion of a business's overall value. Intangible assets included in an acquisition of a business are known as §197 assets and are amortized over 180 months (15 years) *regardless of their useful lives*. Other intangibles include organization costs, start-up costs, and loan costs. Intangible assets that are not §197 assets are amortizable only if they have a determinable life.

The basis of most **intangible assets** is usually the cost to buy or create the asset. Purchased intangibles include the purchase price, including sales taxes and similar charges paid to acquire the property. Amounts paid for performing services under an agreement do not create a separate and distinct intangible asset. Also, the value of an inventor's time spent on an invention or the value of an author's time spent authoring isn't included in the basis of a patent or copyright. For example:

- The basis of a patent that is created includes development costs such as costs for drawings, working models, and attorneys' and governmental fees
- The basis of copyright for the creator or author includes the costs incurred to acquire the copyright (eg, copyright fees, attorneys' fees, clerical assistance)

If a business purchases the assets of another business for a single purchase price, the purchaser must determine the initial basis of each of the assets it acquired in the transaction.

- To determine the basis, the purchaser allocates a portion of the purchase price to each tangible asset acquired (eg, cash, machinery, real property), then to each intangible asset, according to its fair market value
- The purchase price exceeding the FMV of each asset acquired is considered goodwill
- These acquired intangible assets are referred to as §197 intangibles and are amortized over 180 months

Examples of Section 197 Intangible Assets

Intangible assets:
- Copyrights
- Goodwill
- Intellectual licenses
- Noncompete covenants
- Patents
- Trademarks

Haywood, Inc., acquired a competitor's assets for $350,000. Of the $350,000 purchase price, $160,000 is allocated to tangible assets, and $65,000 is allocated to §197 intangible assets (patent, $25,000; customer list, $40,000). What is the basis of the purchased intangible assets including goodwill?

Haywood would allocate $350,000 as follows:

Amount to be allocated	$350,000
Tangible assets	(160,000)
Patent	(25,000)
Customer list	(40,000)
Remaining balance	$125,000
Allocated to goodwill	(125,000)
Balance	$ 0

Customer list: N corporation, a retailer, sells its products through its catalog and mail order system. N purchases a customer list from R corporation. N pays R $100,000 in exchange for the customer list. The $100,000 paid to R constitutes an amount paid to acquire an intangible asset from R and must be capitalized.

*Note in this example that if N internally created its own customer list, the expenditures would be **expensed** and not capitalized.*

Defense of title: R corporation claims to own an exclusive patent on a particular technology. U corporation brings a lawsuit against R, claiming that U is the true owner of the patent and that R stole the technology from U. The sole issue in the suit involves the validity of R's patent. R chooses to settle the suit by paying U $100,000 in exchange for U's release of all future claim to the patent. R's payment to U is an amount paid to defend or perfect title to intangible property and must be **capitalized**.

Compensation and overhead: P corporation, a commercial bank, maintains a loan acquisition department whose sole function is to acquire loans from other financial institutions. P is **not** required to **capitalize** (ie, can **expense** as ordinary and necessary business expenses) any portion of the compensation paid to the employees in its loan acquisition department or any portion of its overhead allocable to the loan acquisition department. Per the Treasury Regulations, employee compensation, overhead, and de minimis costs are treated as amounts that **do not** facilitate a transaction.

Organization Costs

Organization costs are costs incurred for forming a partnership or corporation (not applicable for a sole proprietorship since it is not a separate legal entity). Expenditures considered organization costs include:

- Legal fees incidental to the organization of the business, such as negotiating and drafting of the partnership agreement or corporate charter and bylaws
- Accounting services in forming the entity
- Filing fees
- Costs of organizational meetings of stockholders and directors

These costs are generally incurred prior to the starting of the business or shortly thereafter. Ordinarily, a partnership or corporation begins business when it starts the business operation for which it was organized (ie, starts earning revenue). The mere signing of a partnership agreement is not alone sufficient to show the beginning of business.

The **costs of selling or marketing** the ownership interest in a business (ie, stock or partnership interest) is a syndication cost, rather than an organization cost or start-up cost. Syndication costs cannot be deducted or amortized.

Osha, a cash-basis calendar-year partnership, began business on April 1, Year 5. Osha incurred and paid the following during Year 5:

Legal services associated with formation of the partnership	$15,260
Accounting fees associated with promoting and selling partnership interests	10,000

What amount of expenditures that Osha paid are organization costs?

The legal services of **$15,260** qualify as organizational expenses. However, the $10,000 of fees for promoting and selling partnership interests (ie, syndication costs) do not.

Start-Up Costs

Businesses incur **start-up costs** when a **new entity** is formed and when **new products** and **markets** are pursued. Start-up costs include those incurred in:

1. Creating an active trade or business;
2. Acquiring an active trade or business; and
3. Anticipation of an activity becoming an active trade or business.

Pre-opening costs that could be deducted as a business expense if incurred by an existing active business are start-up costs. However, because they are incurred prior to the time that business starts, the tax law requires that they be capitalized and not immediately deducted. For example, expenditures to advertise a new business and payments to employees before the business opens are start-up costs.

In addition, all costs associated with *investigating, creating, or deciding to acquire a trade or business* are classified as start-up costs. For example, consulting fees and amounts to analyze the potential for a new business are start-up costs if the new business begins. If the potential new business is not started, the costs are considered personal and not deductible.

Once a taxpayer decides to acquire a business, the costs to acquire it are not start-up costs and must be capitalized. That is, when deciding to acquire a new business, investigatory and other costs incurred by the acquirer prior to acquiring the target are start-up costs. Once the acquisition decision is made, acquisition costs are capitalized.

Start-up costs do not include costs for interest, taxes, and research and experimentation because these are governed by different rules. Interest and taxes may be deductible when they are incurred. Research and experimentation costs are amortized over five years when conducted inside the U.S.

A taxpayer formed a corporation that began business on April 1, Year 1. The following expenditures were incurred in getting the corporation started:

Expenditures	Date	Amount
Attorney fee to draft articles of incorporation and bylaws	February 10	$30,000
Accounting fees to obtain taxpayer identification number	February 15	500
March 1–March 31 wages	March 31	4,500
March 1–March 31 rent	March 31	2,000
Stock issuance costs	April 1	20,000
April 1–April 30 wages	April 30	12,000

What amounts of expenditures were start-up costs and organization costs for the corporation?

$30,500 ($30,000 + $500) organization costs for the attorney fees and accounting fees to form the corporation.

$6,500 ($4,500 + $2,000) start-up costs for the wages and rent before the business began.

The stock issuance costs do not qualify as organization costs or start-up costs and are not eligible for an immediate deduction or amortization; instead, they must be capitalized as a syndication cost. The April wages will be deductible as a regular business expense in April.

Election to Expense Organization and Start-Up Costs

For tax purposes, generally no *immediate* deduction is allowed for costs incurred to organize a business or for start-up costs. However, regulations provide that a business has **deemed to make an election to deduct** start-up and/or organizational expenses in the tax year in which the business began (ie, not required to attach election to tax return).

The deemed election allows the partnership or corporation to immediately *deduct* up to **$5,000** of **organization costs** as well as **$5,000** of **start-up costs** in the first year of business.

1. The remaining costs are amortized ratably, using the straight-line method, over 180 months beginning in the month the entity's business starts
2. The $5,000 immediate deduction for both organization costs and start-up costs must be reduced by the amount by which each set of costs exceeds $50,000
3. A business may choose to forgo the deemed deduction election by filing an election to capitalize start-up and/or organizational expenses

Election to Expense Organization and Start-Up Costs		
Total Costs	**Immediate Election**	**Amortization**
≤ $5,000	Total costs up to $5,000	None
> $5,000 ≤ $50,000	$5,000	Remaining costs* are amortized (straight-line method) over 180 months, starting in the month the entity's operations begin
> $50,000 < $55,000	$5,000 − (Total costs − $50,000)	
> $55,000	$0	

Election to Expense Organization and Start-Up Costs

**Remaining amount = Total costs − Immediate deduction*

A partnership began business on September 1, Year 4. It incurred and paid the following in Year 4:

Legal fees to prepare the partnership agreement	$25,000
Accounting fees to prepare the representations in offering materials	14,000

The $14,000 is a *nondeductible* syndication cost. Therefore, only the $25,000 is a qualified organizational expense. The partnership may deduct organization costs of **$5,444** for Year 4.

Immediate deduction	$5,000
Amortization [($25,000 − $5,000) × (4/180)]*	444
Total	$5,444

**Operations began September 1, so four months of amortization*

Loan Costs

Certain costs incurred in getting a loan, such as discount points, loan origination fees, mortgage insurance premiums, loan assumption fees, cost of a credit report, fees for an appraisal required by a lender, and refinancing fees, are **not** part of the encumbered property's basis. However, if the costs are associated with *business-use property*, these costs are *capitalized as loan costs* and can be amortized over the period of the loan.

Regulations provide that debt issuance costs (ie, loan costs) incurred by an issuer of debt (ie, a borrower) to "facilitate" a borrowing are required to be *capitalized*. A borrowing is any debt issuance (eg, bond, debenture, note, certificate, other indebtedness), including an acquisition of a trade or business or a change in the capital structure of a business entity.

Examples of costs that facilitate a borrowing include payments for:

- An investment bank to market a debt instrument;
- Attorneys to prepare offering documents;
- Underwriting fees;
- Financial advisory fees; and
- Any other costs related to the issuance of a debt instrument.

If the costs are deductible, they are amortized over the term of the debt instrument in the same manner as an **original issue discount** (OID). The amount of the debt issuance costs reduces the loan amount and is amortized over the life of the loan. Regulations do permit a current deduction for certain de minimis debt issuance costs that do not exceed $5,000.

REG 11
Cost Recovery

REG 11: Cost Recovery

11.01 Cost Recovery

Overview

Cost recovery for certain assets (eg, Section 1231 assets used in trade or business, depreciable assets used for income-producing activities) is permitted for tax purposes through depreciation. However, the tax code has its own methods and rules for determining the allowable expense. Although the *annual amount* deductible for tax depreciation expense may be *different* from what is allowed for financial accounting reporting, the same **total depreciable cost** of an asset is **eventually deducted** for both **books** and **tax**.

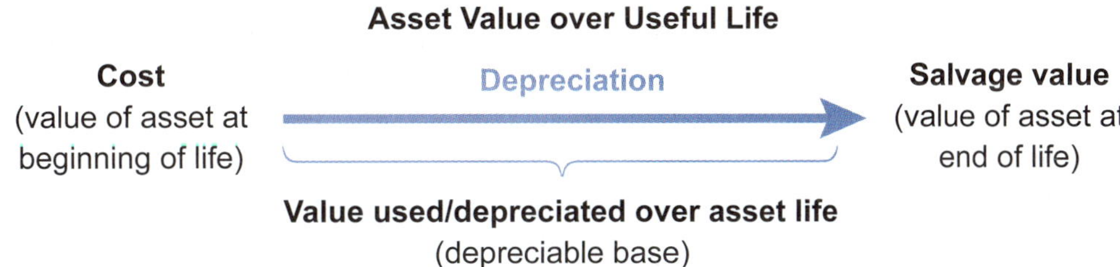

For tax purposes, cost recovery for depreciable assets is computed under a uniform method using class life periods (eg, 5, 7,10, 27.5 years) and conventions (eg, half-year, mid-month, mid-quarter) referred to as the **Modified Accelerated Cost Recovery System** (MACRS). This system generally allows for a shorter asset life than the one used for financial accounting purposes. In addition, MACRS uses **accelerated depreciation methods** for personal property, such as the **200%** and **150%** declining balance methods, and straight-line depreciation for realty.

When computing tax depreciation, first determine if the asset is **personalty** (eg, vehicles, furniture, equipment) or **realty** (buildings) because the **rules** for each **differ**. Buildings are the only type of depreciable realty. All other depreciable property is classified as personalty (ie, **personal property**).

The IRS provides MACRS tables that show the percentage of the asset's cost basis that can be depreciated each year based on the asset's classification. These tables are included at the end of the section for reference. Depreciation can also be computed using the appropriate depreciation formula (eg, double-declining balance, straight-line), rather than using the tables.

Review of the Cost Recovery Formulas	
Straight-line method	Annual depreciation = Cost / MACRS life
150% declining balance method	Annual depreciation = Carrying value* × (1.5 / MACRS life)
200% declining balance method	Annual depreciation = Carrying value* × (2 / MACRS life)

**Carrying value = Cost − Accumulated depreciation*

Note: Double-declining balance is used interchangeably with 200% declining balance.

In certain circumstances, a taxpayer may elect an alternative to MACRS: the straight-line method, half-year convention or the alternative depreciation system (ADS). In addition to the regular depreciation computed under MACRS, other special rules apply, including listed property, immediate expensing (Section 179), and additional first-year depreciation (bonus depreciation). Therefore, a taxpayer's **total cost recovery deduction** may be *more* than the regular depreciation amount.

Total Cost Recovery Deduction

= Section 179 expense + Bonus depreciation + Regular depreciation

Section 179 expense	Bonus depreciation	Regular depreciation
Limited to maximum amount and subject to phaseout	Statutory % of adjusted basis (after Section 179)	Figured using depreciable basis (after Section 179 and bonus depreciation)

For **certain intangible assets**, called Section 197 assets (eg, purchased patent), taxpayers are allowed straight-line **amortization** over a **15-year period**. Self-created intangible assets are not amortized.

On the exam, excerpts from the MACRS tables are generally provided only for task-based simulation type questions. For multiple-choice questions, candidates may be given percentages to select from (not complete tables) or be expected to compute the MACRS deduction using the depreciation formulas for the 200% declining balance, 150% declining balance, and straight-line method. In addition, the appropriate MACRS convention (eg, half-year, mid-month, mid-quarter) must be applied.

MACRS Depreciation

Representative Task (Application): Calculate tax depreciation for tangible business property using MACRS, including identification of the applicable recovery period and convention.

Federal tax law uses a method of depreciation called Modified Accelerated Cost Recovery System **(MACRS)** for property placed in service after 1986. This system **differs** from GAAP depreciation in three significant ways:

- The cost of the asset is deducted over a stated recovery period that is often **shorter** than the estimated useful life of the asset
- The recovery period for **new and used** property is identical
- Salvage values are **ignored**

What assets are depreciable? Only property used in business activities and income-producing activities (eg, rental real estate) is depreciable. Land is not depreciable whether used in a business or not. Property used for personal purposes (eg, personal computer and residence) and investment assets such as stocks and bonds are **not** depreciable.

TP invests in a large stock portfolio. She has a computer that is used solely for managing her stock portfolio. While the stocks she owns are not depreciable since they are investment assets, the computer can be depreciated because it is used in an income-producing activity. Note that if property is used for both personal and business/income-producing activities, depreciation is only allowed on the business or income/producing portion.

Computing MACRS Depreciation

To depreciate an asset, MACRS requires taxpayers to use the established:

- Depreciation method
- Recovery period (life)
- Depreciation convention

The *three depreciation methods* under MACRS are 200% (double) declining balance, 150% declining balance, and straight-line.

The recovery period is predetermined by the IRS. Each asset is categorized based upon its description. For example, office furniture (eg, desks and files) has a 10-year **class life** (ie, IRS deemed number of years and recovery period for most types of similar property) and a 7-year **asset recovery period** (ie, used to calculate depreciation).

Depreciation Conventions

Because all property is not acquired at the beginning of the year, **depreciation conventions** (eg, mid-year, mid-quarter, mid-month) are used to determine the *first and last years'* depreciation. Real property (eg, buildings) is subject to a **mid-month convention**, which allows a half month of depreciation in the month *acquired and disposed* plus a full month for all other months owned during the year.

Most **depreciable personalty** (eg, equipment) is treated as if it had been placed into service in the middle of the year (ie, **mid-year convention**), allowing six months of depreciation in the first year. However, to deter taxpayers from purchasing large amounts of property at year end simply to receive a half year of depreciation, MACRS includes a **mid-quarter convention** for personal property.

- The mid-quarter convention applies when > **40%** of the total cost of depreciable personalty is acquired during the last three months of the tax year (eg, October, November, December for a calendar year end)
- As a result, *all personal property* acquired during the year is treated as if it had been placed in service in the middle of the quarter in which it was acquired when the mid-quarter convention applies

Stryker LLC purchased two assets during the current year. On March 11, Stryker placed in service furniture (7-year property) with a tax basis of \$10,000, and on November 21, Stryker placed in service equipment (5-year property) with a tax basis of \$18,000. What convention applies to the property placed in service during the current year?

The **mid-quarter convention** applies.

In this scenario, more than 40% (ie, 64%) of the **total cost of the property** placed in service during the year was acquired during the last three months (eg, October, November, December). Therefore, the mid-quarter convention applies to all of the purchases during the year.

$$\frac{\text{Property acquired during last quarter of the year}}{\text{Total cost of property acquired during the year}} = \frac{\$18{,}000}{(\$18{,}000 + \$10{,}000)} = 64\%\text{ (rounded)}$$

On the exam, taxpayers have a calendar year end unless otherwise stated in the question. If the taxpayer has a fiscal year end, such as June 30, the 4th quarter for testing the mid-quarter convention consists of the months of April, May, and June.

The IRS provides MACRS tables to make it simpler to compute tax depreciation. The examples provided show how to compute depreciation using the depreciation formulas and also by using the MACRS tables. Note that there are four tables for mid-quarter, one for each quarter.

The MACRS tables always include the appropriate convention (half-year, mid-month, mid-quarter) for the **period the asset is purchased** but **not** for the **period the asset is sold**. However, when computing depreciation manually, be sure to apply the appropriate convention. The MACRS deduction is always computed using the **asset's original cost** (ie, salvage value is ignored).

Tangible Realty

This section provides the rules for the depreciation of tangible realty, which is classified as residential or nonresidential buildings. The recovery period is:

- **27.5 years** – for residential rental property (eg, apartment building)
- **39 years** – for nonresidential real property (eg, office building)

Depreciation rules:

- Land is *not* depreciable (if a building and land are purchased together, only the cost of the building is depreciable)
- *Straight-line* method is used
- Salvage (ie, residual) value of the building is *ignored*
- *Mid-month convention* is *required*. For example, if acquired on June 8, Year 3, the annual depreciation would be based on 6.5/12 months (half month for June and six months for July through December)

MACRS: Real Property			
Type	**Recovery Period**	**Depreciation Method**	**Depreciation Convention**
Nonresidential	39 years	Straight-line	Mid-month
Residential	27.5 years	Straight-line	Mid-month

Land is nondepreciable.

A taxpayer purchases an office building on 11/1/Year 1 for $500,000, which includes land with a value of $32,000. The residual value of the building is expected to be $80,000. What is the depreciation expense for Year 1 and Year 2?

Because the property is an office building, it is nonresidential realty. Therefore, the straight-line method, 39-year life, and mid-month convention are used

The cost of the building is $468,000 ($500,000 purchase price − $32,000 land). The residual value is ignored

For Year 1, the asset is depreciated for a half month for November and a full month for December (ie, 1.5 months). Year 1 depreciation is computed as: $468,000 / 39 years × (1.5 months / 12 months) = $1,500

For Year 2, a full year of depreciation expense (ie, $12,000) is permitted ($468,000 / 39 years = $12,000)

For the MACRS tables, use MACRS Table A-7a because this is *nonresidential* property. The asset was bought in November, so move across to Column 11. Column 11 is used for this asset's entire life.

Table A-7a. Nonresidential Real Property Mid-Month Convention Straight Line—39 Years

	Month Property Placed in Service											
Year	**1**	**2**	**3**	**4**	**5**	**6**	**7**	**8**	**9**	**10**	**11**	**12**
1	2.461%	2.247%	2.033%	1.819%	1.605%	1.391%	1.117%	0.963%	0.749%	0.535%	0.321%	0.107%
2-39	2.564	2.564	2.564	2.564	2.564	2.564	2.564	2.564	2.564	2.564	2.564	2.564
40	0.107	0.321	0.535	0.749	0.963	1.177	1.391	1.605	1.819	2.033	2.247	2.461

The depreciation for Year 1 is computed as: $468,000 × .321% = $1,502 (rounded)

For Year 2, use the second row listed as "2-39". This row would be used for depreciation for the next 38 years if the asset was kept in service, and the intersection of Row 2 and Column 11 is 2.564. $468,000 × 2.564% = $12,000 (rounded)

Note that there can be small rounding differences between using the MACRS tables and the depreciation formulas.

Assume the office building purchased above is sold on May 3, Year 12. What is the depreciation expense in Year 12 and accumulated depreciation on the date of the sale?

During the year of sale, the taxpayer can depreciate the asset for a half month for **May** and four months for January through April. Year 12 depreciation is computed as:

$468,000 / 39 years × (4.5 months / 12 months) = **$4,500**

Using MACRS Table A-7a, use the same intersection of Row 2 and Column 11, which is 2.564%. In the year of sale, the computation must be adjusted for the number of months owned, as follows:

$468,000 × 2.564% × (4.5 months / 12 months) = $4,500 (rounded)

Depreciation for Year 1	$ 1,500
Depreciation for Years 2 through 11 ($12,000 × 10)	120,000
Depreciation for Year 12	4,500
Total accumulated depreciation	$126,000

Tangible Personal Property (Nonrealty)

Tangible personalty used in a trade, business, or income-producing activity and held longer than one year (eg, equipment, furniture, computers) is assigned an asset class that establishes the specified depreciation period as shown in the table below.

MACRS: Personal Property			
Recovery Period	**Examples**	**Depreciation Method**	**Depreciation Convention**
3-year	• Small tools	Double-declining balance	Half-year
5-year	• Automobiles • Technology equipment, hardware (eg, computers, copiers, calculators) • Most farm equipment		
7-year	• Agricultural machinery and equipment • Furniture and fixtures		

The mid-quarter convention applies if more than 40% of personal property is purchased in the last three months of the tax year.

The MACRS depreciation method for personal property is:

- *Double-declining balance* (DDB/200% DB: 3-, 5-, 7-, 10-year property)
- *150% declining balance* (15-, 20-year property—rarely tested)
  - Declining balance switches to straight-line (S/L) when it results in a greater deduction

The **half-year convention** is used for personalty (unless the criteria for the mid-quarter convention are met). Under the half-year convention, the asset is depreciated for six months in the year of purchase and six months in the year of sale, regardless of the dates of purchase or sale.

The MACRS tables automatically reflect the half year in the year of the purchase (ie, Year 1); however, in the year of disposal, the percentage from the tables must be multiplied by 6/12 (or 1/2).

A client purchased office furniture for $490 on 2/1/Year 1. What is the depreciation expense for Year 1 and Year 2?

Furniture has a 7-year recovery period. Compute depreciation using the double-declining balance method: Annual depreciation = Carrying value × (2 / MACRS life)

Step 1: The depreciation rate is 2/7 (200% × 1/7 year life)

Step 2: The carrying value is $490 ($490 cost − $0 accumulated depreciation)

Step 3: In the year of acquisition, the half-year convention is applied, so the MACRS deduction is $490 × 2/7 × 1/2 = $70

In Year 2, the carrying value of $420 ($490 − $70) is used, and the MACRS deduction is $420 × 2/7 = **$120**

Use MACRS Table A-1 because the office furniture is personalty and the half-year convention applies.

Table A-1. 3-, 5-, 7-, 10-, 15-, and 20-Year Property Half-Year Convention

	Depreciation Rate for Recovery Period					
Year	**3-year**	**5-year**	**7-year**	**10-year**	**15-year**	**20-year**
1	33.33%	20.00%	14.29%	10.00%	5.00%	3.750%
2	44.45	32.00	24.49	18.00	9.50	7.219

- Use the column for 7-year property, which for Year 1 is 14.29%. Year 1 depreciation is computed as: $490 × 14.29% = **$70**
- For Year 2, multiply the percentage in Table 1 for Year 2 (24.49%) by the original cost of the asset: $490 × 24.49% = **$120**

A manufacturer of neoprene gaskets and aquatic clothing purchased $300,000 of special tools (3-year property) in Year 1 as follows:

Asset	Date Placed into Service	Cost
Molds	May 22	$ 55,000
Patterns	August 15	35,000
Rings	November 2	20,000
Molds	November 21	190,000
Total		$300,000

What is the depreciation for Year 1?

Special tools usually have a **3-year recovery period**, and the MACRS depreciation method using **double-declining balance** and the **half-year convention** is generally used. However, the **mid-quarter convention** (ie, 40% placed into service during the last quarter) **may apply**.

In this scenario, the **$20,000 purchase of rings and $190,000 purchase of molds** in the **last quarter** comprise **70% [($190,000 + $20,000) / $300,000]** of the total personal property assets placed in service during the year. Therefore, the mid-quarter convention applies (70% > 40%). The double-declining rate is **2/3**.

Under mid-quarter, depreciation that can be deducted for the first year depends on the **quarter each asset was placed in service**. Assets are treated as being placed in service in the middle of the quarter.

Asset	Quarter Placed in Service	Months Allowed	Depreciation
Molds	2nd qtr (May)	1/2 for May + 7 (June–Dec.) = 7.5	$55,000 × 2/3 × (7.5 / 12) = $22,917
Patterns	3rd qtr (August)	1/2 for Aug. + 4 (Sept.–Dec.) = 4.5	$35,000 × 2/3 × (4.5 / 12) = $8,750
Rings	4th qtr (November)	1/2 for Nov. + 1 for Dec. = 1.5	$20,000 × 2/3 × (1.5 / 12) = $1,667
Molds	4th qtr (November)	1/2 for Nov. + 1 for Dec. = 1.5	$190,000 × 2/3 × (1.5 / 12) = $15,833

Total depreciation in Year 1 is **$49,167** ($22,917 + $8,750 + $1,667 + $15,833)

Different MACRS tables are used for the mid-quarter convention. There are four tables, one for each quarter. For this problem, the tables for the 2nd, 3rd, and 4th quarters are used (A-3, A-4, A-5). Use the table that corresponds to the quarter the **asset was placed in service** for its entire life under the column for a 3-year recovery period.

Table A-3. 3-, 5-, 7-, 10-, 15-, and 20-Year Property Mid-Quarter Convention Placed in Service in Second Quarter

	Depreciation Rate for Recovery Period					
Year	**3-year**	**5-year**	**7-year**	**10-year**	**15-year**	**20-year**
1	41.67%	25.00%	17.85%	12.50%	6.25%	4.688%
2	38.89	30.00	23.47	17.50	9.38	7.148

Table A-4. 3-, 5-, 7-, 10-, 15-, and 20-Year Property Mid-Quarter Convention Placed in Service in Third Quarter

	Depreciation Rate for Recovery Period					
Year	**3-year**	**5-year**	**7-year**	**10-year**	**15-year**	**20-year**
1	25.00%	15.00%	10.71%	7.50%	3.75%	2.813%
2	50.00	34.00	25.51	18.50	9.63	7.289

Table A-5. 3-, 5-, 7-, 10-, 15-, and 20-Year Property Mid-Quarter Convention Placed in Service in Fourth Quarter

	Depreciation Rate for Recovery Period					
Year	**3-year**	**5-year**	**7-year**	**10-year**	**15-year**	**20-year**
1	8.33%	5.00%	3.57%	2.50%	1.25%	0.938%
2	61.11	38.00	27.55	19.50	9.88	7.430
3	20.37	22.80	19.68	15.60	8.89	6.872

Asset	Quarter Placed in Service	Rate from Applicable Table	Depreciation
Molds	2nd qtr (May)	41.67%	$55,000 × 41.67% = $22,919
Patterns	3rd qtr (August)	25%	$35,000 × 25% = $8,750
Rings	4th qtr (November)	8.33%	$20,000 × 8.33% = $1,666
Molds	4th qtr (November)	8.33%	$190,000 × 8.33% = $15,827

Total depreciation using the MACRS mid-quarter tables for Year 1 is **$49,162**. The $5 difference is due to rounding.

Compute the depreciation if the rings were sold on May 5, Year 3.

- Because the asset was originally purchased in the 4th quarter, Table A-5 is used. For Year 3, the asset was owned for the 1st quarter (three months) and was sold during the 2nd quarter
- The mid-quarter convention dictates that the asset is sold in the middle of the quarter, or 1.5 months. The total months of allowable depreciation for Year 3 is 4.5 months (3 + 1.5)

The depreciation is computed as:

$20,000 × **20.37%** (from MACRS table) × **4.5** months / 12 months = **$1,528**

Special Rules for Certain Personalty

- The cost of **leasehold improvements** made by a lessee generally must be recovered over the MACRS recovery period of the underlying property without regard to the lease term. Upon the expiration of the lease, any unrecovered adjusted basis in abandoned leasehold improvements is treated as a loss
- **Qualified improvement property** (ie, an improvement to the interior portion of nonresidential real property after the building has been placed in service) is recovered over a 15-year recovery period using the straight-line method and half-year convention (unless the mid-quarter convention applies)
- Special rules limit the amount of depreciation that can be claimed on *passenger automobiles*, which are vehicles that weigh 6,000 pounds or less. However, these limits are adjusted annually for inflation, so the exact dollar limits **do not** need to be memorized for the exam

Alternatives to MACRS

The taxpayer can elect **two alternatives** to MACRS.

- **Straight-line** can be used for **personalty** over the MACRS life of the asset. The same MACRS lives and conventions are retained for this method
- The **alternative depreciation system** (ADS) provides for **straight-line** over an *extended life*. ADS uses the same conventions as MACRS. The taxpayer must elect it for the entire class of property (eg, all 7-year property). ADS straight-line must be used for computing earnings and profits and for listed property used ≤ 50% for business purposes
- Taxpayers must use ADS for certain types of property (eg, tangible property used predominantly outside the U.S.)
- Off-the-shelf software is depreciated straight-line over 36 months

A taxpayer usually prefers to deduct the cost of an asset as quickly as possible to reduce their tax liability. However, if the taxpayer expects to have a higher tax rate in the future, they may prefer to delay more of the depreciation deduction. In that case, the taxpayer may want to elect the straight-line method or the ADS method.

A client purchased office furniture for $490 on 2/1/Year 1. The taxpayer elected to depreciate the asset using *MACRS with the straight-line method, half-year convention*. What is the depreciation expense for Year 1 and Year 2?

Furniture has a 7-year recovery period. The asset is depreciated over seven years using the half-year convention, so six months of depreciation is allowed in Year 1, as follows:

Year 1: **$35** ($490 / 7 years × 6/12 months)

Year 2: **$70** ($490 / 7 years)

Section 179 Deduction and Other Rules

Representative Task (Application): Determine property eligible for a Section 179 deduction.

The IRC permits business taxpayers to make a **Section 179 election** to immediately expense certain *new and used* depreciable business property (ie, *Section 179 Property*) instead of capitalizing and depreciating the asset using MACRS.

This is done as a way to stimulate investment in small businesses (and, in turn, the economy), simplify tax compliance, and reduce the burden of recordkeeping for depreciation purposes. Whether Section 179 is elected or MACRS depreciation is used, **the total depreciation expense** is the same; the difference is the timing of the depreciation expense.

Section 179 vs. Depreciation: Equal over Time

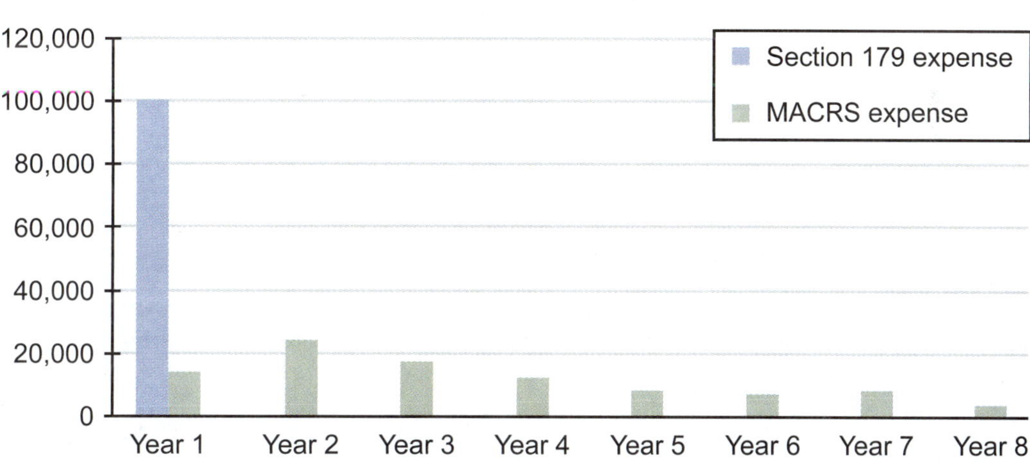

The maximum expense amount is **$1,220,000 for 2024**. Phaseout of the maximum amount of Section 179 expense begins at **$3,050,000** of **purchases of qualifying Section 179 property**; that is, the $1,220,000 limit is reduced $1 for every $1 spent over $3,050,000 on Section 179 property.

Thus, the election is not available if eligible asset purchases of qualifying Section 179 property exceed $4,270,000 (ie, the deduction would be completely phased out) for the year. Note that any amount disallowed for Section 179 is not carried back or forward. Instead the remaining basis of the asset would be depreciated using MACRS.

The asset's basis is **reduced** by the Section 179 deduction (but not below zero). The **remaining asset's balance** is **depreciated** using the applicable MACRS method and convention.

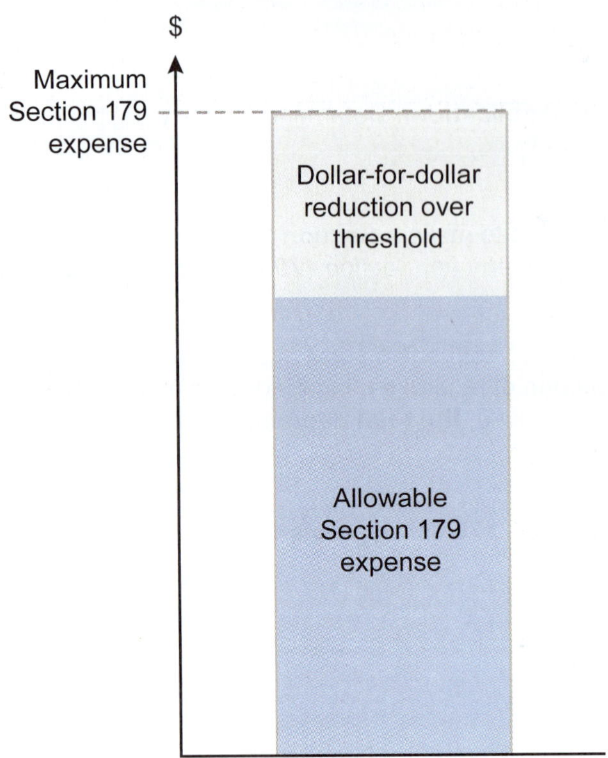

Section 179 Property

Property eligible for the Section 179 deduction must be acquired by purchase from an *unrelated party for use* in an *active trade or business* or property predominantly used for business (> 50%) and must be *one* of the following:

- Tangible personalty
- Off-the-shelf computer software
- Qualified improvement property
  - Any improvement to an interior portion of nonresidential real property after the building was first placed in service (eg, remodeling the dining area of a restaurant when it has become outdated)
  - Repairs and upgrades to roofs, heating and air conditioning, fire protection, and security systems added to nonresidential real property if done after the building was first placed in service

With respect to S corporations and partnerships, Section 179 limitations are applied at both the entity and owner level.

Property **not** qualifying for Section 179 election:

- Intangible property
- Realty (other than those listed above that qualify)
- Property acquired by purchase from a *related party*

Special Rules and Limitations for Section 179

The Section 179 deduction **cannot exceed** the net income from the business **without** regard to the **Section 179 deduction** (MACRS and bonus depreciation *are* included in net income). Any election to expense in excess of the *business income limit* is **carried forward indefinitely** and used in a year when income is sufficient.

A self-employed taxpayer had net business income of $260,000 in Year 2 before the deductions for $65,000 bonus depreciation, $29,500 MACRS depreciation, and $200,000 Section 179. What is the total Section 179 that is currently deductible?

- A taxpayer's Section 179 deduction is limited to the business income *without* the deduction for Section 179
- In this scenario, the Section 179 deduction is limited to **$165,500** ($260,000 net income − $65,000 bonus depreciation − $29,500 MACRS)
- The remaining **$34,500** ($200,000 − $165,500) can be **carried forward** indefinitely and expensed in future years when there is sufficient business income

Assume the maximum Section 179 election permitted is $1,220,000 and the phaseout threshold is $3,050,000 of qualifying assets purchased. Determine the maximum amount of Section 179 deduction allowed for the following independent scenarios.

	Example 1	**Example 2**	**Example 3***	**Example 4****
Qualified purchases	$30,000	$1,240,000	$3,350,000	$4,300,000
Solution				
Qualified purchases	$30,000	$1,240,000	$3,350,000	$4,300,000
Maximum election	(30,000)	1,220,000	920,000	0
Remaining depreciable basis	$ 0	$ 20,000	$2,430,000	$4,300,000

**In this example, qualified purchases of $3,350,000 exceed the threshold of $3,050,000 by $300,000. The election is reduced from $1,220,000 to $920,000 ($1,220,000 − $300,000).*

***For this example, no Section 179 is allowed since the qualifying purchases exceed the threshold by $1,250,000 ($4,300,000 − $3,050,000 threshold). The maximum deduction is $0 because the $1,250,000 reduction is greater than the maximum $1,220,000 deduction.*

In each example, the remaining basis (if any) is depreciated using the regular MACRS rules.

When electing Section 179, consideration should be given to which class of assets is used in order to maximize the taxpayer's deductions. Immediately expensing assets with the lowest first-year recovery percentage will maximize the current tax benefit of the depreciation expense.

On the exam, tax threshold amounts indexed for inflation will always be provided within the related problems.

Additional First-Year Depreciation (Bonus Depreciation)

Bonus depreciation is an additional allowance of depreciation in the first year when qualifying property is placed in service. Like the Section 179 deduction, this is yet another tool the government uses to stimulate business investments, simplify tax compliance, and reduce the burden of recordkeeping.

As such, it is frequently adjusted by Congress to suit the needs of the current economic environment. Unlike the 179 deduction, this provision is **not capped** at a certain dollar amount. For 2024, the bonus depreciation **percentage is 60% of depreciable cost**.

Bonus depreciation applies to qualified *new or used* assets (ie, tangible personalty with a MACRS life of 20 years or less) in the year placed in service, software, and qualified improvement property. Bonus depreciation applies unless the taxpayer elects out. The election to *not* use bonus depreciation is made for an **entire class of property**, such as 5-year property.

- The **order** of depreciation is Section 179 deduction, bonus depreciation, and then the regular MACRS depreciation expense deduction
- No AMT depreciation adjustment is required for any property that uses bonus depreciation

During August of Year 1, a taxpayer purchases used 5-year MACRS property for $2,000. Section 179 is *not* elected. What is the bonus depreciation for this asset assuming the percentage allowed in Year 1 is 60%? What is the total depreciation expense for Year 1?

- **Bonus** depreciation would be **$2,000** × 60% = $1,200
- The remaining cost of $800 ($2,000 − $1,200) is recovered using regular MACRS depreciation for 5-year property
- Double-declining balance factor is 2/5
- For the current year, *MACRS depreciation* is $160 [$800 × 2/5 × (6 months / 12 months)]. Mid-year (not mid-quarter) convention applies because the property was purchased in *August*
- **Total depreciation expense is $1,360** ($1,200 + $160)

Using the tables: MACRS depreciation in Year 1 is $160 ($800 × 20%). Total depreciation expense is $1,360 ($1,200 + $160).

Table A-1. 3-, 5-, 7-, 10-, 15-, and 20-Year Property Half-Year Convention

	Depreciation Rate for Recovery Period					
Year	**3-year**	**5-year**	**7-year**	**10-year**	**15-year**	**20-year**
1	33.33%	20.00%	14.29%	10.00%	5.00%	3.750%

On April 2, Year 4, a taxpayer purchased $2,000,000 of qualifying 5-year equipment for his business. The taxpayer used the 60% bonus depreciation and elected Section 179. The maximum Section 179 election permitted is $1,220,000. Compute the taxpayer's maximum depreciation deduction.

Cost of equipment	$2,000,000
Section 179 limitation	(1,220,000)
Balance	$ 780,000
Bonus depreciation ($780,000 × 60%)	(468,000)
Depreciable basis before MACRS	$ 312,000
MACRS (5-year, half-year convention)*	(62,400)
Remaining basis	$ 249,600

**$312,000 × (2/5) × (6/12) = $62,400*

The total depreciation expense is $1,750,400 ($1,220,000 + $468,000 + $62,400).

Note: The Section 179 deduction is not subject to a phaseout since the property acquired does not exceed $3,050,000.

Listed Property

Listed property is depreciable property that is used for both personal and business use. The most testable type of listed property is passenger automobiles (6,000 pounds or less). Other types of listed property include:

- Other property used for transportation, such as trucks, buses, boats, airplanes, and motorcycles, and
- Property generally used for entertainment, recreation, or amusement (including photographic, phonographic, communication, and video recording equipment).

Cell phones and computers are **not** considered listed property, even if used for both personal and business use.

To use regular MACRS rules, the business use of listed assets must be **greater than 50%** of total use (ie, predominantly used for business). Business use is limited to use in a trade or business. Investment use is **not** considered for meeting the 50% test, although investment use is considered when computing cost recovery.

Failure to meet the business-use test means cost recovery is **limited** to the amount computed using **ADS** (ie, straight-line without regard to salvage value, half-year convention). ADS depreciation must be used for the entire depreciable life of the asset, even if the 50% test is met in future years. In addition, the property is **not** eligible for Section 179 or bonus depreciation.

If the 50% test is *failed* in the current year but *accelerated depreciation* had been taken in previous years, the excess depreciation from prior years must be *recaptured*.

- For example, in Year 1 and Year 2, an automobile is used 60% for business use. The 200% declining balance method is used for Years 1 and 2. In Year 3, the business-use percentage is 45%, and the investment use is 12%
  - For Year 3, ADS straight-line depreciation must be used because the 50% test has been failed, but 57% of the asset's basis can be depreciated (45% + 12%)
  - Excess depreciation over straight-line from Years 1 and 2 must be *recaptured* in Year 3; additionally, the asset must be depreciated using ADS for the remainder of its depreciable life

Rhys purchased a truck for $30,000 in Year 1 that he uses 40% for business purposes and 60% for personal purposes. How much depreciation can he deduct in Year 1? Assume that trucks are 5-year property for the ADS.

Rhys fails the business-use test since his business use does not exceed 50% of total use. Therefore, he must use the ADS, which is straight-line depreciation over five years with a mid-year convention, as follows:

($30,000 / 5 years) × 6/12 months × 40% use = **$1,200**

Limitations on Passenger Vehicles

The IRC places limits on the amounts a taxpayer can write off for certain passenger automobiles (eg, bonus depreciation, MACRS). These limits are also known as the luxury automobile limits.

A passenger automobile is defined as "a four-wheel vehicle with a gross vehicle weight (GVW) rating of 6,000 pounds or less." Specifically excluded are special-use vehicles (eg, ambulances) and vehicles directly used in business (eg, taxis, rideshare cars like Uber, delivery trucks).

Below are the MACRS depreciation limits for passenger vehicles that are placed into service during 2024. These cost recovery limits are indexed annually, so they do not need to be memorized. These amounts are the maximum deduction if the vehicle is used 100% for business. For example, if the vehicle was used 60% for business in its first year, depreciation would be limited to $7,440 ($12,400 × 60%).

First Year	Second Year	Third Year	Each Remaining Year
$12,400	$19,800	$11,900	$7,160

If bonus depreciation is elected, the **maximum** amount is **$8,000**. Therefore, the first-year depreciation including bonus depreciation is increased to **$20,400** ($8,000 + $12,400). This limitation includes any amount expensed under Section 179.

The depreciation expense is limited to the **lesser** of the MACRS cost recovery or the limitations above adjusted for business use.

- For example, a taxpayer places a passenger vehicle costing $65,000 into service in Year 1. It is used 75% for business. The regular MACRS depreciation is $9,750 ($65,000 × 2/5 × 6/12 × 75%). The maximum limitation for the vehicle is $15,300 ($20,400 x 75%). The taxpayer may only deduct $9,750

On May 1, Year 6, a taxpayer purchased and placed into service a new automobile that cost $70,000. The vehicle is used 70% for business and 25% for the production of income, with the remainder being personal use. No bonus or Section 179 depreciation was elected. Compute the maximum depreciation expense for Year 6.

- The *business use* is 70%; therefore, the > 50% **business-use test is met, and ADS does not have to be used**
- Although the 25% production of income is ignored for determining whether the > 50% business-use test is met, it is **included** when *computing* the cost recovery. The percentage for cost recovery is **95%** (70% for business and 25% for production of income)
- The maximum depreciation is **$11,780**, which is the luxury automobile limitation amount for Year 1 adjusted for business use. The lower of the MACRS depreciation or the limited depreciation for listed property is used

Regular MACRS	$70,000 × 2/5 × 6/12 = $14,000 × 95% = $13,300*
Luxury automobile limitation	$12,400 × 95% = **$11,780**

**Using the tables: $70,000 × 20% × 95% = $13,300*

Table A-1. 3-, 5-, 7-, 10-, 15-, and 20-Year Property Half-Year Convention

	Depreciation Rate for Recovery Period					
Year	**3-year**	**5-year**	**7-year**	**10-year**	**15-year**	**20-year**
1	33.33%	20.00%	14.29%	10.00%	5.00%	3.750%

Amortization of Intangible Assets

Representative Task (Application): Calculate tax amortization for intangible assets.

The amortization rules for intangible assets are very different than the depreciation rules for tangible assets. Most acquired intangible assets, also known as Section 197 assets, are amortized straight-line over a 15-year period (ie, 180 months), beginning with the month in which the intangible is acquired. The **full-month convention** applies, allowing taxpayers to deduct amortization for the whole month no matter when acquired in the month of acquisition and in the month of disposal or sale. Self-created intangible assets are **not** amortized.

Examples of Section 197 Intangible Assets

Intangible assets:
- Copyrights
- Goodwill
- Intellectual licenses
- Noncompete covenants
- Patents
- Trademarks

An amortizable Section 197 intangible asset is any qualifying intangible asset which is **acquired by the taxpayer** and which is held in connection with the conduct of a trade or business.

- Qualifying intangibles include goodwill, going concern value, workforce, information base, know-how, customer-based intangibles, government licenses and permits, franchises, trademarks, and trade names
- Certain assets qualify as Section 197 intangibles only if acquired in connection with the acquisition of a trade or business; these include noncompete covenants, computer software, film, sound recordings, videotape, patents, and copyrights
- Certain intangible assets are expressly excluded from the definition of Section 197 intangibles (eg, types of financial interests in a corporation, partnership, trust, or estate, interests in land, computer software which is readily available for purchase by the general public)

No loss can be recognized on the disposition of a Section 197 intangible if the taxpayer retains other Section 197 intangibles acquired in the same transaction or in a series of transactions. Any disallowed loss is added to the basis of remaining Section 197 intangibles and recovered through amortization.

On April 10 of the current tax year, Juliet purchased a local consulting firm and began managing its operations. She paid $1,300,000 for the firm and allocated $80,000 of this price to goodwill and $25,000 to a copyright. What amount may Juliet deduct as amortization under Section 197?

Juliet may begin the amortization of the goodwill and copyright on April 1 (ie, nine months for the current year). The Section 197 deduction for amortization of these assets is calculated as follows:

Goodwill: $80,000 / 15 years × 9/12 **months** =	$4,000
Copyright: $25,000 / 15 years × 9/12 **months** =	1,250
Total amortization	**$5,250**

Juliet sells the copyright in a later year for $20,000. At the time of sale, the adjusted basis for the copyright was $21,500. What is her realized and recognized gain or loss?

Juliet's **realized loss** from the sale of the copyright is calculated as follows:

Amount realized	$ 20,000
Adjusted basis	(21,500)
Realized loss	**$ (1,500)**

Because Juliet still owns the goodwill from the same initial transaction, she **cannot recognize the loss**, and the **$1,500 disallowed loss** is added to the remaining basis of the goodwill.

Comprehensive Depreciation Example

A business purchased the following assets in Year 5:

Asset	Cost	Date Purchased
New truck – 5-year	$ 35,000	1/8/Year 5
New equipment – 7-year	233,000	6/5/Year 5
Used computer – 5-year	2,500	7/29/Year 5
New machinery – 7-year	970,000	8/10/Year 5
Trademark	25,000	3/9/Year 5

The available Section 179 expense for Year 5 is $1,220,000, and the threshold amount for phaseout is $3,050,000. Assume bonus depreciation is 60%. For rounding purposes, calculate depreciation using the exact percentages provided in the MACRS tables.

- For example, the midyear percentage of a 7-year asset from the MACRS table is 14.29% in the first year. Use this amount to calculate tax depreciation instead of:

$$2/7 \text{ years} \times 6/12 \text{ months} = 14.285714\%$$

Assume each question part is independent of the others.

Part 1: Compute the MACRS depreciation and amortization expense, assuming no Section 179 election and the taxpayer elects out of bonus depreciation.

Asset	Cost	Date Purchased	% from MACRS Table	MACRS Depreciation	Amortization
Truck – 5-year	$ 35,000	1/8/Year 5			N/A
Equipment – 7-year	233,000	6/5/Year 5			N/A
Computer – 5-year	2,500	7/29/Year 5			N/A
Machinery – 7-year	970,000	8/10/Year 5			N/A
Trademark	25,000	3/9/Year 5		N/A	
Total	$1,265,500				

Solution

Using the MACRS half-year convention table and appropriate recovery period, the total MACRS depreciation expense is **$179,409**. The table already accounts for the half-year convention in the first year for calculating cost recovery.

Amortization is cost recovery on intangible assets. A business can amortize the basis of these assets over a 15-year period, using straight-line amortization beginning with the month the intangible is acquired. The months the asset is purchased and is sold both qualify for a full month of amortization. The amortization of the trademark is **$1,389** ($25,000 / 15 years × 10/12 months).

Table A-1. 3-, 5-, 7-, 10-, 15-, and 20-Year Property Half-Year Convention

	Depreciation Rate for Recovery Period					
Year	**3-year**	**5-year**	**7-year**	**10-year**	**15-year**	**20-year**
1	33.33%	20.00%	14.29%	10.00%	5.00%	3.750%

Asset	Cost	Date Purchased	% from MACRS Table	MACRS Depreciation	Amortization
Truck – 5-year	$ 35,000	1/8/Year 5	20%	$ 7,000	N/A
Equipment – 7-year	233,000	6/5/Year 5	14.29%	33,296	N/A
Computer – 5-year	2,500	7/29/Year 5	20%	500	N/A
Machinery – 7-year	970,000	8/10/Year 5	14.29%	138,613	N/A
Trademark	25,000	3/9/Year 5		N/A	$1,389
Total	$1,265,500			**$179,409**	**$1,389**

Part 2: Assume the machinery was purchased on December 10 instead of August 10; compute the MACRS depreciation expense assuming Section 179 is not elected and the taxpayer elects out of bonus depreciation.

Asset	Cost	Date Purchased	% from MACRS Table	MACRS Depreciation	Amortization
Truck – 5-year	$ 35,000	1/8/Year 5			N/A
Equipment – 7-year	233,000	6/5/Year 5			N/A
Computer – 5-year	2,500	7/29/Year 5			N/A
Machinery – 7-year	970,000	12/10/Year 5			N/A
Trademark	25,000	3/9/Year 5		N/A	
Total	$1,265,500				

Solution

The half-year convention is subject to an important exception. If **> 40%** of the personalty is purchased and placed in service in the **4th quarter**, then the **mid-quarter convention** applies with respect to all personalty acquired during the taxable year.

For the business, 78.19% ($970,000 / $1,240,500) of the assets are placed in service in the 4th quarter. Note that the trademark is excluded from the denominator since it is not a qualifying asset for Section 179.

Therefore, the mid-quarter convention applies, and the assets are assumed to be placed in service midway through the quarter purchased. The mid-quarter convention tables must be used for all four assets purchased. The total depreciation is $88,845, and amortization of the trademark is $1,389.

Table A-2. 3-, 5-, 7-, 10-, 15-, and 20-Year Property Mid-Quarter Convention Placed in Service in First Quarter

	Depreciation Rate for Recovery Period					
Year	3-year	5-year	7-year	10-year	15-year	20-year
1	58.33%	35.00%	25.00%	17.50%	8.75%	6.563%

Table A-3. 3-, 5-, 7-, 10-, 15-, and 20-Year Property Mid-Quarter Convention Placed in Service in Second Quarter

	Depreciation Rate for Recovery Period					
Year	3-year	5-year	7-year	10-year	15-year	20-year
1	41.67%	25.00%	17.85%	12.50%	6.25%	4.688%

Table A-4. 3-, 5-, 7-, 10-, 15-, and 20-Year Property Mid-Quarter Convention Placed in Service in Third Quarter

	Depreciation Rate for Recovery Period					
Year	3-year	5-year	7-year	10-year	15-year	20-year
1	25.00%	15.00%	10.71%	7.50%	3.75%	2.813%

Table A-5. 3-, 5-, 7-, 10-, 15-, and 20-Year Property Mid-Quarter Convention Placed in Service in Fourth Quarter

	Depreciation Rate for Recovery Period					
Year	3-year	5-year	7-year	10-year	15-year	20-year
1	8.33%	5.00%	3.57%	2.50%	1.25%	0.938%

Asset	Cost	Date Purchased	% from MACRS Table	MACRS Depreciation	Amortization
Truck – 5-year	$ 35,000	1/8/Year 5	1st quarter table, 35%	$12,250	N/A
Equipment – 7-year	233,000	6/5/Year 5	2nd quarter table, 17.85%	41,591	N/A
Computer – 5-year	2,500	7/29/Year 5	3rd quarter table, 15%	375	N/A
Machinery – 7-year	970,000	12/10/Year 5	4th quarter table, 3.57%	34,629	N/A
Trademark	25,000	3/9/Year 5	N/A	N/A	$1,389
Total	$1,265,500			$88,845	$1,389

Part 3: Compute the total cost recovery deduction assuming the business elects Section 179 for the 7-year property first and then for the 5-year property, starting with the truck. In addition, bonus depreciation is used.

Asset	Cost	Section 179	Remaining Basis	Bonus (60%)	Remaining Basis	% from Table	MACRS	Total
Truck – 5-year	$ 35,000							
Equipment – 7-year	233,000							
Computer – 5-year	2,500							
Machinery – 7-year	970,000							
Total	$1,240,500							

Solution

Section 179 allows a business to **expense** rather than **capitalize** a limited dollar amount of property purchased in a year. The maximum deduction for the current year is $1,220,000. To minimize taxes, Section 179 should first be elected for 7-year property and then for 5-year property. The total property acquired does not exceed the threshold, so no phaseout of the Section 179 is required.

After expensing the cost of the 7-year property, only $17,000 of Section 179 ($1,220,000 – $233,000 – $970,000) remains for the 5-year property (ie, truck).

After Section 179, the bonus depreciation is applied using the current rate of 60%. The business is then allowed MACRS depreciation on the remaining basis using the MACRS half-year convention table (Table A-1) and appropriate recovery period. The business is allowed a total cost recovery deduction of **$1,233,940** (Section 179 of $1,220,000; bonus depreciation of $12,300; MACRS depreciation of $1,640).

Asset	Cost	Section 179	Remaining Basis	Bonus (60%)	Remaining Basis	% from Table	MACRS	Total
Truck – 5-year	$ 35,000	$ 17,000	$18,000	$10,800	$7,200	20%	$1,440	$ 29,240
Equipment – 7-year	233,000	233,000	0	0	0	14.29%	0	233,000
Computer – 5-year	2,500	0	2,500	1,500	1,000	20%	200	1,700
Machinery – 7-year	970,000	970,000	0	0	0	14.29%	0	970,000
Total	$1,240,500	$1,220,000	$20,500	$12,300	$8,200		$1,640	$1,233,940

Part 4: Assume the business made the same elections as in Part 3 above. If the business had a net income of $250,000 before any deduction for cost recovery, what is the taxable income assuming Section 179 is elected and bonus depreciation is used?

Solution

Section 179 is limited to taxable business income computed without regard to the deduction. However, deductions for bonus depreciation and MACRS are permitted.

Profit before any Section 179 or bonus	$250,000
Less: Bonus and MACRS depreciation ($12,300 + $1,640)	(13,940)
Available profit	$236,060
Section 179 deduction	(236,060)
Taxable income	$ 0

The remaining $983,940 ($1,220,000 limit − $236,060 amount used) of Section 179 is carried forward to future years.

Because bonus depreciation is 60% for the current year, a strategy for the taxpayer to decrease taxable income further would be to not elect Section 179. Then, 60% of the assets would be expensed using bonus depreciation plus allowable MACRS depreciation, and the taxable income limitation would not apply. In other words, bonus and MACRS depreciation can reduce taxable income to less than $0 and create a net loss.

Depreciation and Amortization Schedule

Representative Task (Analysis): Review a tax depreciation and amortization schedule for the current year and supporting documentation, including any source data used to create the schedule, to determine the completeness and accuracy of the expense amounts deducted for tax purposes.

Accounting firms use automated software to prepare tax returns for their clients. During this process, the software generates diagnostics for the tax preparer to check and clear before the tax return can be filed electronically to the IRS. This helps with the accuracy of the tax return being filed. Diagnostics can be informational, computational (validation), or critical. A critical diagnostic indicates that the tax return will not be electronically accepted by the IRS.

Businesses create depreciation and amortization schedules to calculate and keep track of how business or income-producing properties' costs are allocated to expense over time. Due to the different tax rules for depreciating and amortizing long-lived assets, businesses generally must maintain separate schedules for books and tax tracking depreciation, amortization, and net book (or tax) value.

Considerations When Determining the Completeness and Accuracy of Depreciation Deductions on a Depreciation and Amortization Schedule	
What property can be depreciated?	What property cannot be depreciated?
When was the asset placed in service?	What is the proper basis for depreciation?
Is the property used 100% for business?	What method is appropriate (DDB, 150DDB, or S/L)?
Is the property personalty or real property?	Is any property intangible and subject to amortization?
Does the property qualify for Section 179 or bonus depreciation?	Do any limits come into play?
Is the recovery period appropriate?	Which convention applies (HY, MQ, full-month)?
Were any assets sold during the year?	Any listed property or unusual items (qualified improvement property, large SUVs)?

Practice Analysis Scenario

Schools R Us (SRU) manufactures school supplies for the Midwest and has been very profitable in recent years. SRU has acquired several assets since the company was formed in Year 1. SRU has always prepared its own financials and tax returns, but this year (Year 3), its tax software has identified possible errors since this is the first time the bookkeeper has done a diagnostic review (Exhibit 5). SRU wants to have an accountant review the depreciation and amortization schedule that was prepared by its bookkeeper.

Additional Information:

- In Year 1, the maximum Section 179 was $60,000 due to the business income limitation, and no bonus depreciation was elected
- In Year 2, no Section 179 or bonus depreciation was taken
- Automobile #1 is used 40% for business, and Automobile #2 is used 100% for business; both are considered luxury automobiles
- The client list was purchased from an unrelated party
- In Year 3, the Section 179 amount is $1,220,000, and the threshold is $3,050,000. Bonus depreciation is 60%. The company has decided to use Section 179 for the 7-year property. In addition, bonus depreciation is elected for the $10,000 security system
- Note that errors may exist prior to Year 3

Requirement: Review the depreciation and amortization schedule, purchased acquisitions, and exhibits for accuracy and completeness. Use the diagnostics to pinpoint possible errors for assets placed in service during the current year. Provide a corrected schedule.

Asset Description	Date in Service	Cost	Business Use %	Section 179	Bonus Depreciation	Depreciable Basis	Life	Method/ Convention	Prior Depreciation	Current Depreciation
Furniture	1/28/YR1	30,000	100	10,000		20,000	5	DDB/HY	10,400	3,840
Equipment	2/13/YR1	82,000	100	50,000		82,000	7	DDB/HY	31,800	14,342
Automobile #1	6/27/YR1	38,000	40			38,000	5	DDB/HY	11,400	7,600
Computer System	10/7/YR2	35,000	100			35,000	3	DDB/HY	11,666	15,558
Automobile #2	3/8/YR3	70,000	100			70,000	5	DDB/HY		23,800
Security System	8/30/YR3	10,000	100		10,000	0	10	DDB/HY		0
Storage Building	7/13/YR3	700,000	100	700,000		0	39	SL/MM		0
Machinery	8/2/YR3	1,900,000	100	1,900,000		0	7	DDB/HY		0
Totals		2,865,000		2,660,000	10,000	245,000			65,266	65,140
Intangibles										**Amortization**
Customer List	1/15/YR3	25,000				25,000	15	SL/HY		833
Legend										
DDB=	**200% declining balance**									
150DDB=	**150% declining balance**									
SL=	**Straight-line method**									
HY=	**Half-year convention**									
MM=	**Mid-month convention**									
MQ=	**Mid-quarter convention**									
FM=	**Full-month convention**									

Enter in the corrected amounts.

Asset Description	Date in Service	Cost	Business Use %	Section 179	Bonus Depreciation	Depreciable Basis	Life	Method/ Convention	Prior Depreciation	Current Depreciation
Furniture	1/28/YR1	30,000	100	10,000						
Equipment	2/13/YR1	82,000	100	50,000						
Automobile #1	6/27/YR1	38,000	40							
Computer System	10/7/YR2	35,000	100							
Automobile #2	3/8/YR3	70,000	100							
Security System	8/30/YR3	10,000	100							
Storage Building	7/13/YR3	700,000	100							
Machinery	8/2/YR3	1,900,000	100							
Totals		2,865,000								
Intangibles										**Amortization**
Customer List	1/15/YR3	25,000								
Legend										
DDB=	**200% declining balance**									
150DDB=	**150% declining balance**									
SL=	**Straight-line method**									
HY=	**Half-year convention**									
MM=	**Mid-month convention**									
MQ=	**Mid-quarter convention**									
FM=	**Full-month convention**									

Exhibit 1: MACRS Asset Classification and Recovery Periods and Luxury Automobiles

MACRS Class Lives and Recovery Periods

Description	Class Life	Recovery Periods MACRS	Recovery Periods ADS
Automobiles	3	5	5
Information systems, including computers	6	5	5
Office furniture and equipment	10	7	10
Buses	9	5	9
Light-purpose trucks	4	5	5
Heavy-purpose trucks	6	5	6
Machinery	12	7	12
Qualified improvement property	20	15	20
Residential rental property		27.5	30
Nonresidential rental property		39	40

Maximum Depreciation for Luxury Automobiles

Year Placed into Service	First Year	Second Year	Third Year	Fourth Year
YR 3	$12,400	$19,800	$11,900	$7,160
YR 2	12,200	19,500	11,700	6,960
YR 1	11,200	18,000	10,800	6,460

Exhibit 2: MACRS Tables

Table A-1. 3-, 5-, 7-, 10-, 15-, and 20-Year Property Half-Year Convention

	Depreciation Rate for Recovery Period					
Year	**3-year**	**5-year**	**7-year**	**10-year**	**15-year**	**20-year**
1	33.33%	20.00%	14.29%	10.00%	5.00%	3.750%
2	44.45	32.00	24.49	18.00	9.50	7.219
3	14.81	19.20	17.49	14.40	8.55	6.677
4	7.41	11.52	12.49	11.52	7.70	6.177
5		11.52	8.93	9.22	6.93	5.713
6		5.76	8.92	7.37	6.23	5.285

Table A-2. 3-, 5-, 7-, 10-, 15-, and 20-Year Property Mid-Quarter Convention Placed in Service in First Quarter

	Depreciation Rate for Recovery Period					
Year	**3-year**	**5-year**	**7-year**	**10-year**	**15-year**	**20-year**
1	58.33%	35.00%	25.00%	17.50%	8.75%	6.563%
2	27.78	26.00	21.43	16.50	9.13	7.000
3	12.35	15.60	15.31	13.20	8.21	6.482
4	1.54	11.01	10.93	10.56	7.39	5.996

Table A-3. 3-, 5-, 7-, 10-, 15-, and 20-Year Property Mid-Quarter Convention Placed in Service in Second Quarter

	Depreciation Rate for Recovery Period					
Year	**3-year**	**5-year**	**7-year**	**10-year**	**15-year**	**20-year**
1	41.67%	25.00%	17.85%	12.50%	6.25%	4.688%
2	38.89	30.00	23.47	17.50	9.38	7.148
3	14.14	18.00	16.76	14.00	8.44	6.612
4	5.30	11.37	11.97	11.20	7.59	6.116

Table A-4. 3-, 5-, 7-, 10-, 15-, and 20-Year Property Mid-Quarter Convention Placed in Service in Third Quarter

	Depreciation Rate for Recovery Period					
Year	**3-year**	**5-year**	**7-year**	**10-year**	**15-year**	**20-year**
1	25.00%	15.00%	10.71%	7.50%	3.75%	2.813%
2	50.00	34.00	25.51	18.50	9.63	7.289
3	16.67	20.40	18.22	14.80	8.66	6.742
4	8.33	12.24	13.02	11.84	7.80	6.237

Table A-5. 3-, 5-, 7-, 10-, 15-, and 20-Year Property Mid-Quarter Convention Placed in Service in Fourth Quarter

	Depreciation Rate for Recovery Period					
Year	**3-year**	**5-year**	**7-year**	**10-year**	**15-year**	**20-year**
1	8.33%	5.00%	3.57%	2.50%	1.25%	0.938%
2	61.11	38.00	27.55	19.50	9.88	7.430
3	20.37	22.80	19.68	15.60	8.89	6.872
4	10.19	13.68	14.06	12.48	8.00	6.357

Table A-6. Residential Rental Property Mid-Month Convention Straight Line—27.5 Years

	Month Property Placed in Service											
Year	**1**	**2**	**3**	**4**	**5**	**6**	**7**	**8**	**9**	**10**	**11**	**12**
1	3.485%	3.182%	2.879%	2.576%	2.273%	1.970%	1.667%	1.364%	1.061%	0.758%	0.455%	0.152%
2-9	3.636	3.636	3.636	3.636	3.636	3.636	3.636	3.636	3.636	3.636	3.636	3.636

Table A-7a. Nonresidential Real Property Mid-Month Convention Straight Line—39 years

	Month Property Placed in Service											
Year	**1**	**2**	**3**	**4**	**5**	**6**	**7**	**8**	**9**	**10**	**11**	**12**
1	2.461%	2.247%	2.033%	1.819%	1.605%	1.391%	1.117%	0.963%	0.749%	0.535%	0.321%	0.107%
2-39	2.564	2.564	2.564	2.564	2.564	2.564	2.564	2.564	2.564	2.564	2.564	2.564
40	0.107	0.321	0.535	0.749	0.963	1.177	1.391	1.605	1.819	2.033	2.247	2.461

Table A-8. Straight Line Method Half-Year Convention

	Recovery Period in Years												
Year	**2.5**	**3**	**3.5**	**4**	**5**	**6**	**6.5**	**7**	**7.5**	**8**	**8.5**	**9**	**9.5**
1	20.0%	16.67%	14.29%	12.5%	10.0%	8.33%	7.69%	7.14%	6.67%	6.25%	5.88%	5.56%	5.26%
2	40.0	33.33	28.57	25.0	20.0	16.67	15.39	14.29	13.33	12.50	11.77	11.11	10.53
Year	**10**	**10.5**	**11**	**11.5**	**12**	**12.5**	**13**	**13.5**	**14**	**15**	**16**	**16.5**	**17**
1	5.0%	4.76%	4.55%	4.35%	4.17%	4.0%	3.85%	3.70%	3.57%	3.33%	3.13%	3.03%	2.94%
2	10.0	9.52	9.09	8.70	8.33	8.0	7.69	7.41	7.14	6.67	6.25	6.06	5.88

Exhibit 3: Real Estate Purchase Agreement

REAL ESTATE PURCHASE AGREEMENT

1) **THE PARTIES**. This Real Estate Purchase Agreement (the "Agreement") made on 7/13/Year 3 (the "Agreement Date"), between:

Schools R Us (the "Buyer") with a mailing address of 123 Elementary Drive, Milwaukee, WI, who agrees to buy, and

T & S Development, LLC (the "Seller") with a mailing address of 4592 Tall Tree Lane, Milwaukee, WI, who agrees to sell and convey real property as described in Section 2 & 3. The Buyer and the Seller shall be collectively known as the "Parties".

2) **LEGAL DESCRIPTION**. The real property along with improvements and fixtures thereon and with all appurtenant rights, privileges, and easements is best described as:

○ - Industrial Property
○ - Land (only)
○ - Office Building
○ - Retail Property
● - Mixed Use Property - Storage Building and Land

Tax Parcel ID: Lot 42 according to map or plat thereof as recorded in Plat Book 54, Page 6, of the Public Records of Milwaukee, Wisconsin.

3) **PURCHASE PRICE**. The buyer agrees to purchase the Property by payment of $700,000 (Seven Hundred Thousand Dollars)

The Property consists of a Storage Building valued at $600,000 and Land valued at $100,000.

All Cash Offer. No load or financing of any kind is required to purchase the Property.

Schools R Us — 7/13/Year 3
Buyer — Date

T & S Development LLC — 7/13/Year 3
Seller — Date

Exhibit 4: Invoice from Powell Machines

8/2/Year 3

Invoice No. 1234

To
Schools R Us
123 Elementary Drive
Milwaukee, WI 53201

Ship To
Same as receipt

Instructions
Deliver to back freight door

Quantity	Description	Unit Price	Total
4	CNC Machines	48,499.00	193,998.00
12	Mold Injection Machine	65,799.00	789,588.00
6	Paper Cutting Machines	42,199.00	253,194.00
2	Generators	1,599.00	3,198.00
3	Fourdrinier Machine	50,199.00	150,597.00
6	Binding Machine	12,399.00	74,394.00
5	Packing Equipment	68,599.00	342,995.00
	Subtotal		1,807,962.00
	Sales Tax	5%	90,398.10
	Shipping & Handling		1,639.90
	Total Due		1,900,000.00

Due upon receipt
Thank you for your business!

Powell Machines

tel 989-000-0000
Fax
Website: powellmachines@gmail.com
Email: purch@powell.com

Exhibit 5: Diagnostics

Type	Description
Informational	Section 179 immediate expensing has been entered on your asset input form. Verify that the property placed in service is qualified property and that limitations are properly applied.
Critical	Section 179 is limited to $1,220,000 for Year 3. Amounts entered do not comply with current limits.
Informational	Additional first-year depreciation (bonus depreciation) has been entered on your asset input form. Verify that the property placed in service is qualified property and that the current-year percentage is applied.

Steps for Completing the Task

- Look at the exhibits provided and compare amounts in source documents with corresponding cost basis on the depreciation schedule to determine if amounts reported are correct
- Determine if the life, method, and convention are correct for each asset listed
- Based on the dates placed in service, does any year appear to require use of the mid-quarter convention?
- Study the assets for which Section 179 or bonus depreciation has been claimed. Are these entries appropriate based on the type of asset placed in service?
- Recompute the depreciation, if required, based on observations and corrections made, paying particular attention to business use, limitations, and use of the correct tables

Using the cost recovery tables, remember that half-year, mid-quarter, and mid-month conventions are built into the appropriate tables. For mid-quarter, select the correct table and years applicable.

- When using the tables, for property acquired in Year 1, use the *first row* to compute the first year of depreciation, and for Year 2, use the second row, and for the current-year depreciation for Year 3, use row 3
- For **property acquired in Year 2**, use row 1 for the Year 2 depreciation and row 2 for the current-year depreciation for Year 3
- For **property acquired in the current year** (ie, Year 3), use row 1 to compute the depreciation

Year 1 Acquisitions

Furniture: The furniture placed in service in Year 1 is qualifying property, and Section 179 expense was appropriately taken, with the $10,000 amount reducing the depreciable basis. The class life of furniture is 10 years with a recovery period of seven years. However, the schedule *incorrectly* shows a recovery period of *five years* instead of **seven years**, which resulted in more depreciation expense than is allowed.

Table A-1. 3-, 5-, 7-, 10-, 15-, and 20-Year Property Half-Year Convention

	Depreciation Rate for Recovery Period					
Year	**3-year**	**5-year**	**7-year**	**10-year**	**15-year**	**20-year**
1	33.33%	20.00%	14.29%	10.00%	5.00%	3.750%
2	44.45	32.00	24.49	18.00	9.50	7.219
3	14.81	19.20	17.49	14.40	8.55	6.677
4	7.41	11.52	12.49	11.52	7.70	6.177

Year	Basis	Rate from Table A-1	Depreciation
1	$20,000	14.29%	$2,858
2	20,000	24.49%	4,898
			$7,756 → Prior depreciation
3	20,000	17.49%	**$3,498**

Asset Description	Date in Service	Cost	Business Use %	Section 179	Bonus Depreciation	Depreciable Basis	Life	Method/ Convention	Prior Depreciation	Current Depreciation
Furniture	1/28/YR1	30,000	100	10,000		20,000	7	DDB/HY	7,756	3,498

Equipment: The equipment placed in service in Year 1 is qualifying property, and Section 179 expense was appropriately taken. An error occurred when the $50,000 of Section 179 expense was **not** used to *reduce* depreciable basis and regular MACRS depreciation was computed using $82,000 instead of $32,000, resulting in *more* depreciation than is allowed.

Table A-1. 3-, 5-, 7-, 10-, 15-, and 20-Year Property Half-Year Convention

	Depreciation Rate for Recovery Period					
Year	**3-year**	**5-year**	**7-year**	**10-year**	**15-year**	**20-year**
1	33.33%	20.00%	14.29%	10.00%	5.00%	3.750%
2	44.45	32.00	24.49	18.00	9.50	7.219
3	14.81	19.20	17.49	14.40	8.55	6.677
4	7.41	11.52	12.49	11.52	7.70	6.177

Year	Basis	Rate from Table A-1	Depreciation
1	$32,000	14.29%	$ 4,573
2	32,000	24.49%	7,837
			$12,410 → Prior depreciation
3	32,000	17.49%	**$ 5,597**

Asset Description	Date in Service	Cost	Business Use %	Section 179	Bonus Depreciation	Depreciable Basis	Life	Method/ Convention	Prior Depreciation	Current Depreciation
Equipment	2/13/YR1	82,000	100	50,000		32,000	7	DDB/HY	12,410	5,597

Automobile #1: Luxury automobiles used for both business and personal use are considered listed property. In order to use the MACRS double-declining balance method, the business use must be greater than 50%. Here, the **business use is only 40%**. When property is not used predominantly for business use, depreciation must be figured using the **straight-line method** over the **ADS recovery period**. Depreciation expense must be multiplied by the business-use percentage to determine the allowable deduction. The **half-year convention** applies, so only six months of depreciation can be taken in Year 1.

Year	Basis	Table A-8	Depreciation	Adjusted for 40% Business Use
1	$38,000	$38,000 × 10% =	$3,800	$3,800 × 40% = $1,520
2	38,000	$38,000 × 20% =	7,600	7,600 × 40% = 3,040
				$4,560 → Prior depreciation
3	38,000	$38,000 × 20% =	**$5,597**	7,600 × 40% = **$3,040**

Asset Description	Date in Service	Cost	Business Use %	Section 179	Bonus Depreciation	Depreciable Basis	Life	Method/ Convention	Prior Depreciation	Current Depreciation
Automobile #1	6/27/YR1	38,000	40			15,200	5	SL/HY	4,560	3,040

Year 2 Acquisitions

Computer System: The computer system is 5-year property acquired in November, Year 2, and was the only asset placed in service in Year 2. When **more than 40%** of the total depreciable basis of all MACRS property is placed in service in the **last quarter** of the year (ie, October, November, December), the mid-quarter convention applies. Under this convention, property is treated as placed in service or disposed of at the midpoint of the quarter placed in service. Table A-5 has the mid-quarter convention built in for assets purchased during the last quarter of the year.

Table A-5. 3-, 5-, 7-, 10-, 15-, and 20-Year Property Mid-Quarter Convention Placed in Service in Fourth Quarter

	Depreciation Rate for Recovery Period					
Year	**3-year**	**5-year**	**7-year**	**10-year**	**15-year**	**20-year**
1	8.33%	5.00%	3.57%	2.50%	1.25%	0.938%
2	61.11	38.00	27.55	19.50	9.88	7.430
3	20.37	22.80	19.68	15.60	8.89	6.872
4	10.19	13.68	14.06	12.48	8.00	6.357

Year	Basis	Rate from Table A-5	Depreciation
2	$35,000	5%	**$ 1,750**
3	$35,000	38%	**$13,300**

Asset Description	Date in Service	Cost	Business Use %	Section 179	Bonus Depreciation	Depreciable Basis	Life	Method/ Convention	Prior Depreciation	Current Depreciation
Computer System	10/7/YR2	35,000	100			35,000	5	DDB/MQ4	1,750	13,300

Year 3 Acquisitions

Section 179 property includes tangible personalty, off-the-shelf computer software, and certain improvements to nonresidential buildings. Real property does not qualify. The cost of the Year 3 acquisitions that qualify for Section 179 equals $1,980,000 ($70,000 automobile + $1,900,000 machinery + $10,000 security system). Because the total cost of the property acquired is *below* the threshold of $3,050,000, the taxpayer may take the *maximum* Section 179 deduction of **$1,220,000**. Bonus depreciation is limited to 60% of the asset's cost. The business decided to elect Section 179 for the 7-year property and bonus depreciation for the security system.

Automobile #2: The luxury automobile is listed property used predominantly (ie, 100%) for business purposes, so use of the double-declining balance method is correct. However, the automobile is considered a luxury auto, and the depreciation deduction, including the Section 179 deduction and bonus depreciation allowance, is limited each year. For Year 3, the maximum allowed without claiming any special depreciation is $12,400.

Table A-1. 3-, 5-, 7-, 10-, 15-, and 20-Year Property Half-Year Convention

	Depreciation Rate for Recovery Period					
Year	**3-year**	**5-year**	**7-year**	**10-year**	**15-year**	**20-year**
1	33.33%	20.00%	14.29%	10.00%	5.00%	3.750%

Basis	Rate from Table A-1, Row 1	Depreciation
$70,000	20%	$14,000 but limited to **$12,400**

Asset Description	Date in Service	Cost	Business Use %	Section 179	Bonus Depreciation	Depreciable Basis	Life	Method/ Convention	Prior Depreciation	Current Depreciation
Automobile #2	3/8/YR3	70,000	100			70,000	5	DDB/HY		12,400

Storage Building: Certain property, such as land, cannot be depreciated. In this scenario, the bookkeeper mistakenly used the $700,000 total purchase price (land and building) from the *Real Estate Purchase Agreement* as the basis. Only the $600,000 cost of the building is depreciable. In addition, real property does not qualify for Section 179. The building is nonresidential real property, so Table A-7a, Row 1, Column 7 (since purchased in July), is used to compute depreciation using the straight-line method and mid-month convention over 39 years.

Table A-7a. Nonresidential Real Property Mid-Month Convention Straight Line—39 Years

	Month Property Placed in Service											
Year	**1**	**2**	**3**	**4**	**5**	**6**	**7**	**8**	**9**	**10**	**11**	**12**
1	2.461%	2.247%	2.033%	1.819%	1.605%	1.391%	1.117%	0.963%	0.749%	0.535%	0.321%	0.107%
2-39	2.564	2.564	2.564	2.564	2.564	2.564	2.564	2.564	2.564	2.564	2.564	2.564
40	0.107	0.321	0.535	0.749	0.963	1.177	1.391	1.605	1.819	2.033	2.247	2.461

Basis	Rate from Table A-7a, Row 1	Depreciation
$600,000	1.117%	$6,702

Asset Description	Date in Service	Cost	Business Use %	Section 179	Bonus Depreciation	Depreciable Basis	Life	Method/ Convention	Prior Depreciation	Current Depreciation
Storage Building	7/13/YR3	600,000	100			600,000	39	SL/MM		6,702

Machinery: The business elected Section 179 for 7-year property. Machinery is the only 7-year property acquired in Year 3. The maximum Section 179 expense is limited to $1,220,000. The remaining $680,000 basis ($1,900,000 − $1,220,000) is depreciated using MACRS.

Table A-1. 3-, 5-, 7-, 10-, 15-, and 20-Year Property Half-Year Convention

	Depreciation Rate for Recovery Period					
Year	**3-year**	**5-year**	**7-year**	**10-year**	**15-year**	**20-year**
1	33.33%	20.00%	14.29%	10.00%	5.00%	3.750%

Basis	Rate from Table A-1, Row 1	Depreciation
$680,000	14.29%	$ 97,172
Section 179		1,220,000
Total		$1,317,172

Asset Description	Date in Service	Cost	Business Use %	Section 179	Bonus Depreciation	Depreciable Basis	Life	Method/ Convention	Prior Depreciation	Current Depreciation
Machinery	8/2/YR3	1,900,000	100	1,220,000		680,000	7	DDB/HY		97,172

Security System: A security system is qualified improvement property that is eligible for Section 179 and bonus depreciation. The business used bonus depreciation for this property, which is 60% of the cost. Qualified improvement property has a 15-year cost recovery period and uses the straight-line method. For Year 3, the business erroneously took 100% (not 60%) of the cost as bonus depreciation. After the correct $6,000 bonus depreciation, the remaining $4,000 basis ($10,000 − $6,000) is depreciated using a 15-year life, straight-line depreciation, and the half-year convention.

Table A-8. Straight Line Method Half-Year Convention

	Month Property Placed in Service												
Year	**10**	**10.5**	**11**	**11.5**	**12**	**12.5**	**13**	**13.5**	**14**	**15**	**16**	**16.5**	**17**
1	5.0%	4.76%	4.55%	4.35%	4.17%	4.0%	3.85%	3.70%	3.57%	3.33%	3.13%	3.03%	2.94%

Basis	Rate from Table A-8, Row 1	Depreciation
Bonus depreciation 60%		$6,000
$4,000	3.33%	133
Total		$6,133

Asset Description	Date in Service	Cost	Business Use %	Section 179	Bonus Depreciation	Depreciable Basis	Life	Method/ Convention	Prior Depreciation	Current Depreciation
Security System	8/30/YR3	10,000	100		6,000	4,000	15	SL/HY		133

Customer List: Generally, Section 197 intangible assets are those *acquired* (*not* self-created) through the acquisition of a trade/business or investment. Using the straight-line method, the cost basis is **amortized** (ie, written off) **over 180 months (15 years) regardless** of the intangible asset's **useful life**. Amortization begins the month the intangible is acquired or the month the intangible is placed in service, whichever is later. In this scenario, the business erroneously used the half-month convention instead of a full month. The correct annual amount of amortization is **$1,667** ($25,000 / 15 × 12/12 months).

Intangibles										Amortization
Customer List	1/15/YR3	25,000				25,000	15	SL/FM		1,667

The completed correct **depreciation** and **amortization schedule is provided** below. Errors are presented in blue.

Asset Description	Date in Service	Cost	Business Use %	Section 179	Bonus Depreciation	Depreciable Basis	Life	Method/ Convention	Prior Depreciation	Current Depreciation
Furniture	1/28/YR1	30,000	100	10,000		20,000	7	DDB/HY	7,756	3,498
Equipment	2/13/YR1	82,000	100	50,000		32,000	7	DDB/HY	12,410	5,597
Automobile #1	6/27/YR1	38,000	40			15,200	5	SL/HY	4,560	3,040
Computer System	10/7/YR2	35,000	100			35,000	5	DDB/MQ4	1,750	13,300
Automobile #2	3/8/YR3	70,000	100			70,000	5	DDB/HY		12,400
Security System	8/30/YR3	10,000	100		6,000	4,000	15	SL/HY		133
Storage Building	7/13/YR3	600,000	100	0		600,000	39	SL/MM		6,702
Machinery	8/2/YR3	1,900,000	100	1,220,000		680,000	7	DDB/HY		97,142
Totals		$2,765,000		1,280,000	6,000	1,456,200			26,476	$141,812
Intangibles										**Amortization**
Customer List	1/15/YR3	25,000				25,000	15	SL/FM		1,667
Legend										
DDB=	**200% declining balance**									
150DDB=	**150% declining balance**									
SL=	**Straight-line method**									
HY=	**Half-year convention**									
MM=	**Mid-month convention**									
MQ=	**Mid-quarter convention**									
FM=	**Full-month convention**									

Discrepancies Identified by Automated Diagnostic and Validation Checks

Representative Task (Analysis): Review and resolve discrepancies identified by automated diagnostic and validation checks to ensure the completeness and accuracy of the depreciation and amortization expense reported on a tax return based on the source data used to prepare the return.

Automated Diagnostics and Validation Checks

Accounting firms use automated software to prepare tax returns for their clients. During this process, the software generates diagnostics for the tax preparer to check and clear before the tax return can be filed electronically with the IRS. This helps with the accuracy of the tax return being filed. Diagnostics can be informational, computational, or critical.

Some software packages label each diagnostic according to severity, such as:

- Red to indicate incomplete or inconsistent information that disqualifies a tax return from e-filing (so these are the most serious diagnostics),
- Yellow or gold to indicate a warning of a potential mistake, and
- Green to indicate a tax planning/tax savings opportunity (if applicable).

Responding to Diagnostics and Validation Checks

When a tax preparer sees diagnostics and validation checks, there are numerous actions that may be needed to correct them, such as:

- Correcting simple miskeyed information
- Contacting a superior or the client to clarify the purpose and particulars of a source document that is unfamiliar to the preparer and was erroneously entered on the tax return
- Obtaining additional information from the client
- Researching requirements for forms suggested in the diagnostics (eg, when is a Report of Foreign Bank and Financial Accounts (FBAR) needed on an individual tax return)

When completing a diagnostic and accuracy-based questions on the exam, remember that additional information may be required in order to address the diagnostic flagged. So, expect to occasionally see a choice such as "The tax preparer must request information from the client in order to resolve the issue." Do not assume that all the relevant information is provided.

Practice Scenario

Waterfly, Inc., manufactures high-end boats, personal watercraft, and kayaks. In the current year (Year 3), Waterfly made several purchases, which are included in the exhibits provided. Waterfly would like to maximize its deduction for its more expensive purchases by electing Section 179 on all eligible property. The maximum Section 179 deduction for Year 3 is $1,220,000, and the phaseout threshold is $3,050,000. Waterfly has elected out of bonus depreciation.

Additional Information:

- The luxury automobile had 4,000 business miles and 10,000 total miles for Year 3
- Business income before the deduction for Section 179 was $2,000,000 for Year 3
- Waterfly's in-house accountant has completed Form 4562, and the software generated automated diagnostics indicating errors

Check Form 4562 for accuracy, and review the exhibits and the diagnostic and validation checks below. Then ensure that the entries in Column A in the table below are correct, and if not, provide the correct response in Column B.

Diagnostic Check Report

Form 4562, Part I

Task 1: Diagnostic check – The software has identified that an asset ineligible for the Section 179 deduction has been entered on Line 6. Verify that the entries on Lines 2 and 6 are correct.

Task 2: Validation check – Lines 4 and 5 do not equal the maximum limitation for the Section 179 deduction.

Task 3: Validation check – On line 11, the business income limitation is the same as the Section 179 deduction. Verify that this is correct.

Form 4562, Part III

Task 4: Diagnostic check – The software has identified that an asset with the wrong MACRS recovery period has been entered on Line 19b. Verify that only 5-year property has been entered on line 5b.

Form 4562, Part IV

Task 5: Validation check – Verify that carry-through entries are correct on Lines 21 and 22.

Form 4562, Part V

Task 6: Diagnostic check – The software has identified a potentially incorrect entry on Line 26. Compute the correct entries for Part V.

Form 4562: Depreciation and Amortization

Part I: Election to Expense Certain Property under Section 179

	Original Entry	Correct Entry
Line 1, Maximum amount	1,220,000	
Line 2, Total cost of section 179 property placed in service	3,252,000	
Line 3, Threshold cost of section 179 property before reduction in limitation	3,050,000	
Line 4, Reduction in limitation	202,000	
Line 5, Dollar limitation for tax year	1,018,000	
Line 6, Total	3,252,000	
Line 7, Listed property	0	
Line 8, Total elected cost of section 179 property	3,252,000	
Line 9, Tentative deduction	1,018,000	
Line 10, Carryover of disallowed deduction	0	
Line 11, Business income limitation	1,018,000	
Line 12, Section 179 expense deduction	1,018,000	
Line 13, Carryover of disallowed deduction	0	

Part III: MACRS Depreciation

	Original Entry	Correct Entry
Line 19b(g), 5-year property depreciation deduction	2,851	
Line 19c(g), 7-year property depreciation deduction	0	

Part IV: Summary

	Original Entry	Correct Entry
Line 21, Listed property	6,400	
Line 22, Total	1,027,251	

Part V: Listed Property

	Original Entry	Correct Entry
Line 26(h), Depreciation deduction for property used more than 50% in a qualified business use	6,400	
Line 27(h), Depreciation deduction for property used 50% or less in a qualified business use	0	
Line 28(h), Total	6,400	

Exhibit 1: Email to Accounting Director from Property, Plant, and Equipment Clerk

To: Ksmith@bluecorp.com

From: Bfranklin@bluecorp.com

Subject: Cost for Land Purchased

Kerry,

Per your request I am providing the information regarding the cost of the undeveloped land located at 1234 Park Industrial Parkway:

Purchased: April 10, Year 3 for $126,000

No improvements have been made to the land this year. Please let me know if you have any questions.

Blake

Property, Plant, Equipment Accounting Clerk

Exhibit 2: Vehicle Sale Agreement

For and in consideration of the sum $32,000, inclusive with all sales tax, paid by cash, the receipt and sufficiency of which is hereby acknowledged, Cars R Us, Inc. (hereinafter, the "Seller"), does hereby, sell, assign, and transfer, to WATERFLY, INC. (hereinafter the "Buyer"), on February 25, Year 3, the following described motor vehicle:

- Vehicle Identification Number: 417VV418HH419SS
- Make and Model: Honda Accord
- Body Type: 2 door (under 6000 pounds)
- Color: White Odometer reading: 36,000 miles

Seller hereby notifies Buyer, and Buyer hereby acknowledges and agrees, that the asset is being sold as is without a warranty of any kind.

The motor vehicle will be delivered by the Seller to the Buyer on March 1, Year 3.

Arnold Pressman	*Jasmine Keeler*
Waterfly, Inc., Buyer	Cars R Us, Inc., Seller

Exhibit 3: Schedule of Asset Acquisition for Year 3 (7-Year Property)

	Acquisition Date	Date Placed into Service	Cost
Heavy machinery	2/15/YR3	3/2/YR3	$2,100,000
Manufacturing equipment	4/1/YR3	4/25/YR3	1,026,000
Boat lifts	5/1/YR3	5/27/YR3	14,256
			$3,140,256

Exhibit 4: Depreciation Table

Table A-1. 3-, 5-, 7-, 10-, 15-, and 20-Year Property Half-Year Convention

	Depreciation Rate for Recovery Period					
Year	**3-year**	**5-year**	**7-year**	**10-year**	**15-year**	**20-year**
1	33.33%	20.00%	14.29%	10.00%	5.00%	3.750%
2	44.45	32.00	24.49	18.00	9.50	7.219
3	14.81	19.20	17.49	14.40	8.55	6.677
4	7.41	11.52	12.49	11.52	7.70	6.177

Solution

Form 4562: Part I

Tasks 1–3

Line 2: Correct entry is **$3,140,256** (per Exhibit 3). The land purchased for $126,000 is not a depreciable asset and should not be included on Line 2 to calculate Section 179 expense. The automobile is not eligible for Section 179 since the business-use percentage is less than 50% (ie, 4,000 miles / 10,000 miles = 40%).

Line 4: Correct entry is **$90,256**. Because the total purchases of personalty eligible for Section 179 deduction are in excess of the threshold, the Section 179 amount available begins to phase out. The Section 179 phaseout is $90,256 ($3,140,256 − $3,050,000).

Line 5: Correct entry is **$1,129,744** ($1,220,000 available Section 179 − $90,256 phaseout).

Lines 6 and 8: Correct entry is **$3,140,256**. See explanation for line 2 above; only the machinery, equipment, and boat lifts are eligible for the Section 179 deduction.

Line 9: Correct entry is **$1,129,744**. The tentative deduction is $1,129,744 (lesser of line 5 or line 8).

Line 11: Correct entry is **$1,129,744**. Section 179 is the lesser of available Section 179 ($1,129,744) or the business income ($2,000,000).

Line 12: Correct entry is **$1,129,744**, the Section 179 deduction.

Form 4562: Part III

Line 19b(g): Correct entry is **$0**. The boat lifts are 7-year assets, not 5-year assets. However, Section 179 was elected, and the lifts ended up in total cost of property placed in service.

Line 19c(g): Correct entry is $287,302, computed as follows:

Heavy machinery	$2,100,000
Manufacturing equipment	1,026,000
Boat lifts	14,256
Subtotal	$3,140,256
Less: Section 179 (limited)	(1,129,744)
Remaining basis	**$2,010,512**
MACRS 7-year rate	× 14.29%
MACRS	**$ 287,302**

Form 4562: Part IV

Line 21: Correct entry is **$1,280**. It is a carryover from Line 27 in Part V (see below).

Line 22: Correct entry is **$1,418,326** ($1,129,744 Section 179 + $287,302 MACRS on 7-year property + $1,280 depreciation on automobile), which represents **total cost recovery**.

Form 4562: Part V

Line 26(h): Correct entry is **$0**. The automobile was not used more than 50%

Line 27(h): Correct entry is **$1,280**. Because business use is less than 50% (ie, 40%), the straight-line, half-year convention should be used and then adjusted for 40% business use ($32,000 / 5 years × 6/12 months × 40% = $1,280).

Form 4562: Depreciation and Amortization

Part I: Election to Expense Certain Property under Section 179

	Original Entry	Correct Entry	Task
Line 1, Maximum amount	1,220,000		
Line 2, Total cost of section 179 property placed in service	3,252,000	3,140,256	Task 1
Line 3, Threshold cost of section 179 property before reduction in limitation	3,050,000		
Line 4, Reduction in limitation	202,000	90,256	Task 2
Line 5, Dollar limitation for tax year	1,018,000	1,129,744	Task 2
Line 6, Total	3,252,000	3,140,256	Task 1
Line 7, Listed property	0		
Line 8, Total elected cost of section 179 property	3,252,000	3,140,256	Task 3
Line 9, Tentative deduction	1,018,000	1,129,744	Task 3
Line 10, Carryover of disallowed deduction	0		
Line 11, Business income limitation	1,018,000	1,129,744	Task 3
Line 12, Section 179 expense deduction	1,018,000	1,129,744	Task 3
Line 13, Carryover of disallowed deduction	0		

Part III: MACRS Depreciation

	Original Entry	Correct Entry	Task
Line 19b(g), 5-year property depreciation deduction	2,851	0	Task 4
Line 19c(g), 7-year property depreciation deduction	0	287,302	Task 4

Part IV: Summary

	Original Entry	Correct Entry	Task
Line 21, Listed property	6,400	1,280	Task 5
Line 22, Total	1,027,251	1,418,326	Task 5

Part V: Listed Property

	Original Entry	Correct Entry	Task
Line 26(h), Depreciation deduction for property used more than 50% in a qualified business use	6,400	0	Task 6
Line 27(h), Depreciation deduction for property used 50% or less in a qualified business use	0	1,280	Task 6
Line 28(h), Total	6,400	1,280	Task 6

REG

Area IV: Federal Taxation of Individuals

REG 12
Gross Income

REG 12: Gross Income

12.01 Gross Income (Inclusions and Exclusions)

Gross Income (Inclusions and Exclusions)

Representative Task (Application): Calculate the amounts that should be included in an individual's gross income as reported on Form 1040 – *U.S. Individual Income Tax Return*, including wages, interest and dividends, guaranteed payments received from a partnership, fringe benefits, income from a qualified retirement plan, and punitive damages.

Overview

The determination of **gross income** is an important concept in the U.S. individual income tax system because it serves as the **starting point** for **calculating** an **individual's tax liability**. The accurate calculation of gross income is essential to ensure that all taxable income is accounted for and the correct amount of tax is paid. U.S. tax law specifies that gross income includes **realized income** from *whatever source derived* unless exempted by statute. **Income** is **realized** when:

- A taxpayer engages in a transaction (including exchange of services) with another party, and
- The transaction results in a measurable change in property rights between parties.

Essentially, this all-inclusive approach means that all types of income an individual earns throughout the tax year, including active income (eg, wages, tips, bonuses, fringe benefits), portfolio income (eg, interest, dividends, capital gains), passive income (eg, rental properties, limited partnerships), and any other income, are included in gross income unless there is a specific exemption provided by the tax law.

Certain realized income is **exempted** (excluded) and never subject to tax, while realized income that will be taxed in a subsequent year is **deferred income**. Therefore, **gross income** for a taxpayer in any particular year can be defined as *realized income minus excluded and deferred income*.

Mock operates a retail business selling illegal narcotic substances. Mock had income from the sale of drugs of $250,000, cost of merchandise of $120,000, rent expense of $12,000, and salaries expense of $8,000. Is Mock required to report his income or allowed to deduct his expenses?

The IRC is influenced by social considerations regarding activities that are considered contrary to the public's well-being. For example, the all-inclusive approach for gross income includes income and gains from illegal and criminal activities (eg, sale of illegal drugs). In general, all ordinary and necessary expenses incurred in operating a business are deductible.

However, the IRC under Section 280E specifically disallows deductions for the trade or business expenses associated with illegal drug activity. Because the cost of merchandise is fundamental in calculating the gross profit on the sale of goods, it is the only expense allowed for illegal drug activities in determining net taxable income.

Mock is required to report $250,000 of income but only allowed to deduct the $120,000 cost of drugs sold. His net taxable income is **$130,000** ($250,000 − $120,000). To encourage proper tax compliance, the IRS cannot share information regarding the illicit income with law enforcement or other federal agencies without a court order.

Generally Income	Not Income
Compensation for services including: • Wages and salaries (W-2) • Tips • Fees for jury duty service • Bonuses and commissions • Unemployment compensation • Most fringe benefits, such as the rental value of using a company car on weekends for personal purposes • Bargain purchases of employer merchandise/services	• Health insurance coverage • Group term life insurance coverage, up to a $50,000 policy • Fringe benefits that primarily are incurred for the employer's benefit, such as free housing given to an on-site hotel manager • Immaterial fringe benefits, such as free photocopies made on the company machine • Employer-provided educational assistance • Up to $5,000 of benefits under an employer dependent care assistance plan • Employee discounts up to employer's gross profit percentage of regular merchandise price or up to 20% of FMV of employer services obtained at discount • Proceeds from qualified long-term care insurance policy • Distribution from a FSA or HSA for qualified expenses
• Prizes and awards • Gambling winnings • Illegal drug income (net of COGS) • Treasure trove (ie, if you find money or something of value and you keep it, it's taxable)	A prize or award that is both: • Tangible personal property up to certain dollar values • Received by an employee for their years of company employment or safety achievement OR a prize or award where: • No services required of recipient • Selected without action on recipient's part *and* • Payment assigned by recipient to a governmental unit or charitable organization

Generally Income	Not Income
• Interest accrued each year on a zero-coupon bond or bond purchased at a discount • Interest on U.S. Treasury obligation • Interest on Series HH U.S. savings bonds (paid semiannually)	• Interest on state or municipal bonds • Interest earned on qualified higher education bonds • Interest on a Series EE U.S. savings bond is not reported as income until the time that the bond is redeemed
• Cash dividends	• Stock dividends • Dividends received from an S corporation • Dividends received on a life insurance policy • Dividends received from a mutual fund that invests in tax-exempt bonds
Rent and royalties, including: • Rent collected in advance by a landlord • Nonrefundable deposits collected from tenants	Refundable security deposits
The **bargain discount** from exercising a stock option to buy an employer's stock for a price below market value	A special type of stock option, called an incentive stock option (ISO)
Proceeds withdrawn from a traditional IRA or pension plan if the original contributions to the plan were excluded or deducted from income	The portion, if any, of a traditional IRA pension withdrawal that represents the recovery of prior nondeductible contributions and all Roth IRA qualified withdrawals
Injury awards, if they are for: • Punitive damages • Lost business profits • Nonphysical injuries, such as age or race discrimination • Emotional distress (in excess of associated medical bills)	• Damages for bodily injury, pain and suffering, and lost wages • Emotional distress attributable to physical injury or sickness • Workers' compensation benefits
Up to 85% of Social Security benefits if the taxpayer has substantial income in addition to the benefits	Up to 100% of Social Security benefits if the taxpayer does not have much income in addition to benefits
• The interest component of an annuity. For example, assume that a person spends \$400 to buy an annuity of \$100 for each of five years, or \$500 proceeds in total. Since a \$100 interest profit is part of the \$500 proceeds, the portion of each payment that is reported as income is: Profit / Total proceeds = \$100 / \$500 = 20% • Income generated by gifts and inheritances (eg, rent received on inherited rental property)	• Gifts • Inheritances • Life insurance proceeds paid upon the death of the insured • Child support • Property settlement • Alimony (no longer considered income for divorces/separations executed *after* 2018).

Wages

Taxable **wages** are a **broad term** used in the determination of gross income. **Compensation items** that employers report and taxpayers must include in gross income include:

Taxable Wages

- Salaries and wages, including overtime and premium pay
- Vacation, sick, and holiday pay and PTO
- Bonuses, commissions, prizes, and awards
- Tips reported by the employee to the employer
- Business expense reimbursements made under a nonaccountable plan
- Taxable amounts paid to a nonqualified deferred compensation plan
- Nonqualified moving expenses and reimbursements
- Taxable educational assistance payments
- Noncash payments, such as taxable fringe benefits (see discussion below)
- Accident and health insurance premiums for 2%-or-more shareholder employees of an S corporation
- Taxable benefits from §125 plan if taxpayer chooses cash option
- Taxable cost of group term life insurance that exceeds $50,000
- Proceeds from employer-provided disability insurance
- Taxable portion of scholarships and grants (amounts other than tuition, books, and course supplies)

John worked at a factory and received an hourly wage of $20. Assume he worked 40 hours a week, 50 weeks a year. He worked 10 hours of overtime throughout the year at a rate of $30 per hour, and he also received premium pay of $5 per hour for working the night shift for his regular (ie, nonovertime) hours worked. Throughout the year, John took two weeks of vacation and was paid $1,600 for those weeks. Additionally, John received a bonus of $1,500 and holiday pay of $200. What are John's W-2 wages includable in gross income?

Hourly wage	$40,000	($20 × 40 hours) × 50 weeks
Overtime pay	300	($30 × 10 hours)
Premium pay	10,000	($5 × 40 hours) × 50 weeks
Vacation pay	1,600	
Bonus	1,500	
Holiday pay	200	
Total wages	**$53,600**	

Every type of income John received must be included in his gross income for tax purposes.

Manish is a student who began working part-time as a restaurant server in October of Year 4. He earned the following tips in Year 4, with each month's tips reported in a schedule submitted to the restaurant's management by the 10th of the following month:

October	$400
November	$215
December	$150

In addition, Manish received a scholarship in Year 4 which provided $5,000 for tuition, $5,000 for room and board, $1,000 for travel to study abroad, and $1,000 for books.

What total amount from the above should be included in Manish's Year 4 gross income?

When tips are reported in a schedule submitted to the employer's management, they are taxable in the period in which they are reported. Since Manish's tips are reported in the month following that in which they were received, only the tips received in October and November ($400 + $215 = $615) would be taxable.

Scholarships, to the extent they pay for tuition, books, or class supplies, are nontaxable. If a taxpayer receives educational assistance benefits from their employer under an educational assistance program, they can exclude up to $5,250 of those benefits each year (N/A in this scenario). The $5,000 received for room and board and the $1,000 received to study abroad are both taxable, resulting in gross income of **$6,615** ($615 + $5,000 + $1,000).

Sarah works for a company that has a nonaccountable plan (a nonaccountable plan does not require the employee to account for the expenditures and/or return excess reimbursements) for business expenses. Sarah spends $200 on a business trip for the company, and the company reimburses her with $300. Since the reimbursement is made under a nonaccountable plan, Sarah must include the entire $300 in her gross income.

However, if Sarah's business had an accountable plan, which requires that **all business expenses must be substantiated** to be reimbursed and **excess reimbursements returned to the employer**, Sarah would not have to include any of the reimbursement in her gross income, provided she turned in the receipts for her expenses and returned the additional $100 above her expenditures.

Fringe Benefits

A **fringe benefit** is **nonmonetary compensation** *for services performed* (eg, employee or contract labor). Unless *excluded by law*, employees recognize compensation or ordinary income on all benefits received. Taxable fringe benefits include items such as the following:

- Gym memberships (unless operated by and located on premises of employer)
- Automobile allowance on a personal car
- Use of a corporate jet
- Moving expense reimbursements
- Personal expenses paid by the employer
- Anything else not specifically excluded by law
- Parking reimbursements in excess of the exclusion amount ($315 per month in 2024)
- Employee discounts on sales > the average gross profit percentage for the employer's goods
- Employee discounts > 20% of the retail price offered to customers
- Proceeds from an employer-paid disability insurance policy
- Group term life insurance on coverage exceeding $50,000

Cafeteria plans allow employees to choose from a menu of certain fringe benefits (eg, accident insurance, life insurance, disability insurance, legal services) or to choose cash. Most of the menu choices are nontaxable fringe benefits. Any receipt of cash option that is elected is treated as taxable compensation.

Daryl's employer offers a benefit plan that allows employees to choose among a number of benefits. Each employee is allowed $9,000 in benefits. For Year 1, Daryl selected $4,200 in dependent care benefits, $600 in a business course that improves Daryl's job skills, $3,840 of parking ($320 per month), and $360 of cash. Assume the parking exclusion amount is $315 per month. How much must Daryl include in taxable income?

Daryl must include **$420 of the benefits received** in gross income, which equals $60 of parking benefits and $360 of cash.

Employees can exclude up to $5,000 ($2,500 if MFS) for child and dependent care services. The business course qualifies as a working condition benefit. Only $315 per month in parking can be excluded, with the difference of $60 ($5 per month × 12 months) includable in income in addition to the cash payment of $360.

In lieu of additional salary, an employer makes a $450 car payment for an employee. What is the tax consequence?

The **$450** is taxable income to the employee.

A taxpayer is the general manager of Summit Place Kia. The dealership allows employees to purchase up to two vehicles per year at a discount. Summit Place's average gross profit percentage is 15%. This year, the taxpayer purchased a Niro EV and an EV6.

Model	Employee Price	Dealer Cost	Fair Market Value
EV6	$48,700	$50,000	$61,000
NIRO EV	$43,500	$41,500	$50,000

What amount must the taxpayer include in gross income?

Employees may exclude ***qualified employee discounts*** for *property* received from income as long as the ***goods*** are not received at a discount greater than the average gross profit percentage for the employer's goods. Employees may also exclude ***qualified employee discounts*** for *services* received as long as the discount is ***not more than 20%*** off the retail price offered to customers.

The taxpayer must include **$3,150** ($12,300 − $9,150) in their **gross income**. The $12,300 ($61,000 FMV − $48,700 employee cost) discount on the EV6 model is *larger* than the allowable qualified employee discount of $9,150 ($61,000 sales price × 15%).

There is **no includable income** from the purchase of the Niro EV model. The discount of $6,500 ($50,000 FMV − $43,500 employee cost) is *less* than the average profit margin on that model of vehicle sold, or $7,500 ($50,000 sales price × 15%).

Ken was hired by Vance Company as a corporate executive and board of director member. This year, he received the following payments or benefits paid on his behalf.

Salary	$90,000
Contributions to qualified pension plan	6,500
Qualified health insurance premiums	9,500
Year-end bonus	15,000
Annual director's fee	5,000
Group term life insurance	200,000
Company car used exclusively by Ken's wife	8,000

Assume the annual IRS established uniform cost of insurance is $2.76 per $1,000 of coverage.

What amount must Ken include in gross income?

The salary, bonus, director's fee, and company car are taxable. The first $50,000 of group term life insurance provided by an employer is a nontaxable fringe benefit. The remaining $150,000 ($200,000 − $50,000) of life insurance is taxable at $2.76 per $1,000 of coverage [$2.76 × ($150,000 / $1,000) = $414]. The pension contributions and health insurance are excluded from Ken's income. Therefore, Ken must include **$118,414** in gross income.

Salary	$ 90,000
Bonus	15,000
Director's fee	5,000
Car benefits	8,000
Group term life	414
Total	$118,414

Discrimination Rules

Most fringe benefits **cannot discriminate** against **nonhighly compensated employees**. That is, the benefit cannot be extended to only those who are highly compensated. Highly compensated employees include officers, shareholders who own more than 5% of the company's voting stock, a highly compensated employee based on the facts and circumstances, and the spouses of anyone described in the previous categories.

If a benefit is discriminatory, then the highly compensated employees are taxed at the fair market value of the benefit received. Nonhighly compensated employees are not taxed on the value if it is otherwise excludable. The discrimination rules do not apply to the following fringe benefits (ie, highly compensated employees would **not** have to include in income):

- Health insurance premiums (as long as plan is not self-insured)
- Working condition fringe benefits
- Transportation and parking fringe benefits
- Lodging on the employer's premises

Interest (Schedule B)

Interest income is **investment income** on **financial instruments** that accrues over time. In general, all interest income is taxable unless a specific exception exists. Taxpayers report interest as income either when they receive it (cash basis) or when they earn it (accrual basis). Taxpayers must recognize prepaid interest as income when received, even if the taxpayer reports on the accrual basis.

- Series EE and I savings bonds are nonmarketable bonds issued by the U.S. Treasury that pay interest at time of redemption or maturity. As a U.S. Treasury bond, the interest is taxable at the federal level and *exempt from state taxation*
- A cash-basis taxpayer can choose either of the following methods for reporting interest income on Series EE or Series I bonds:
  - Report all interest when bonds are redeemed or sold
  - Report interest as the increase in the redemption value of the bond each year

Dividends (Schedule B)

The **distribution** of **cash** or **property** from a **corporation** is **taxable** to the extent the corporation has earnings and profits. The dividend income is categorized as ordinary or qualified dividend income and is taxed under different rate structures. Qualified dividends are taxed at special 0%, 15%, or 20%, rates *similar to long-term capital gains* (LTCGs). For 2018–2025, the applicable rate is determined based on income levels (adjusted for inflation after 2018). The rates for 2024 are as follows:

Tax Bracket/Rate	Single	Married Filing Jointly	Head of Household
0%	$0 – $47,025	$0 – $94,050	$0 – $63,000
15%	$47,026 – $518,900	$94,051 – $583,750	$63,001 – $551,350
20%	$518,901 +	$583,751 +	$551,351 +

Qualified dividends are from a domestic corporation and certain qualified foreign corporations. The taxpayer must hold the stock for 60+ days during the 121-day period beginning 60 days prior to ex-dividend date (ie, the date on which the dividend payee is determined, usually two days prior to the record date).

The following are **not** taxed as dividend income:

- Life insurance dividend if dividend is a return of premium
  - However, interest on the dividend is taxable
- Dividends received from an S corporation
- Stock dividends or stock splits on common stock
  - Stock dividends from preferred stock are taxable at FMV
- Liquidating dividend if dividend is a return of capital

A single taxpayer has income for the year consisting of $50,000 salary, $8,000 in dividend income from stocks, $7,000 in interest income from corporate bonds, $5,000 in municipal bond interest, $5,000 in short-term capital gains, and $5,000 in qualified distributions from their Roth IRA. What total amount from the above should be included in gross income on the taxpayer's tax return?

The taxpayer's gross income consists of their **$50,000** salary plus **$20,000** taxable portfolio income ($8,000 in dividends, $7,000 in corporate interest, and $5,000 in short-term capital gains). The $5,000 of municipal bond interest and the qualified distributions from a Roth IRA are specifically excluded from income by the tax code.

Guaranteed Payments Received from a Partnership

A taxpayer's gross income also includes their share of income or losses from **pass-through entities**, like partnerships, S corporations, and LLCs. **Guaranteed payments** are based on a separate *contractual relationship* between a partner and a partnership **without regard** to the **partnership's income**. They are usually made in exchange for services or for the use of capital and are **taxable** as *ordinary income* to the recipient partner. The payments are reported on a partner's Schedule K-1 based on the partnership tax year.

Guaranteed payments made to general partners for services and/or for the use of capital from a partnership are considered *self-employment income subject to self-employment tax*. For limited partners, only guaranteed payments for services are subject to self-employment tax.

Alberta files her tax return using a calendar year and is a partner in Angel Partnership, which has a tax year ending September 30. Angel Partnership made guaranteed payments to Alberta for services rendered of $3,000 per month in Calendar Year 3. The payments were increased to $3,500 per month for Calendar Year 4. Angel issued Alberta a Schedule K-1 for its fiscal years ending September 30, Year 3 and Year 4. What amount of guaranteed payments will Alberta report on her Year 4 tax return?

Oct. 1 – Dec. 31, Year 3	$ 9,000	($3,000 × 3 months)
Jan. 1 – Sept. 30, Year 4	31,500	($3,500 × 9 months)
Total	$40,500	

Alberta will report income of **$40,500** from guaranteed payments on her Year 4 tax return.

When the tax year of the P/S (eg, fiscal year of October 1 to September 30) does not coincide with the partner's tax year (eg, calendar year), the payments are reported based on the tax year of the P/S so that the IRS can match income on the taxpayer's return to the partner's Schedule K-1 received from the partnership.

The partner's distributive share and guaranteed payment flow to the partner on the last day of the P/S tax year. If the P/S is accrual and for some reason the guaranteed payment was not paid, it still flows down to the partner because the deduction is taken on the P/S return. This ensures the income reported on the partner's Schedule K-1 is in the same accounting period that the P/S takes the deduction for the payment.

Income Received from a Qualified Retirement Plan

Qualified retirement plans are employer-sponsored plans that meet the requirements of the Internal Revenue Code and ERISA to receive **tax-favored status**. Both the employer and employees benefit from these types of plans.

- For *employers*, the contributions are tax deductible, the plan can be a way to attract and retain good employees, and the business may receive tax credits to help offset the costs
- For *employees*, any contributions personally made to employer-sponsored traditional plans use pretax dollars. The taxation on the contributions and investment gains are deferred until withdrawn. Contributions made to a designated Roth plan sponsored by an employer are includable currently as income and grow tax-free. Both types of plans provide an effective way to accumulate retirement income

When withdrawals are made from these types of accounts, depending on the type of plan it is, the amount distributed may be includable in gross income. Distributions from traditional IRAs are taxed as ordinary income, and early distributions (before age 59.5) are generally subject to a 10% penalty. Qualified distributions from Roth plans are not taxable.

Qualified Distributions

Pension benefits and **annuities**, including distributions from IRAs (other than Roth IRA accounts), *may be taxable*. The amount considered a **return of capital** will ***not*** be taxable. If the taxpayer did not pay any portion of the cost of the pension plan, such as one in which all costs were incurred by an employer, **all** benefits are taxable.

Lump-sum distributions from qualified pension, profit-sharing, stock bonus, and Keogh plans (but not IRAs) may be eligible for special tax treatment. Certain distributions may be rolled over tax-free (within 60 days) to a traditional IRA account.

Annuities

An **annuity** is a contract between an individual and an insurance or investment company in which the individual pays a lump sum of money today to receive **regular**, **fixed payments** in the **future**. Earnings (usually interest) from an annuity accumulate on a tax-deferred (postponed) basis. How the annuity is funded (with pretax or posttax dollars) determines the tax treatment of the distributions.

Annuities are generally purchased by individuals with posttax dollars (after taxes have been paid). The individual recovers the cost of the original investment tax-free, but all accumulated earnings are taxable. To determine the nontaxable portion of the payments received each year, an exclusion ratio is used (investment in the annuity / expected return).

$$\frac{\textbf{Cost of annuity}}{\textbf{Expected total annuity payment}} = \textbf{Percentage of each payment excluded from income taxes}$$

Tax Treatment of Distributions from Annuities

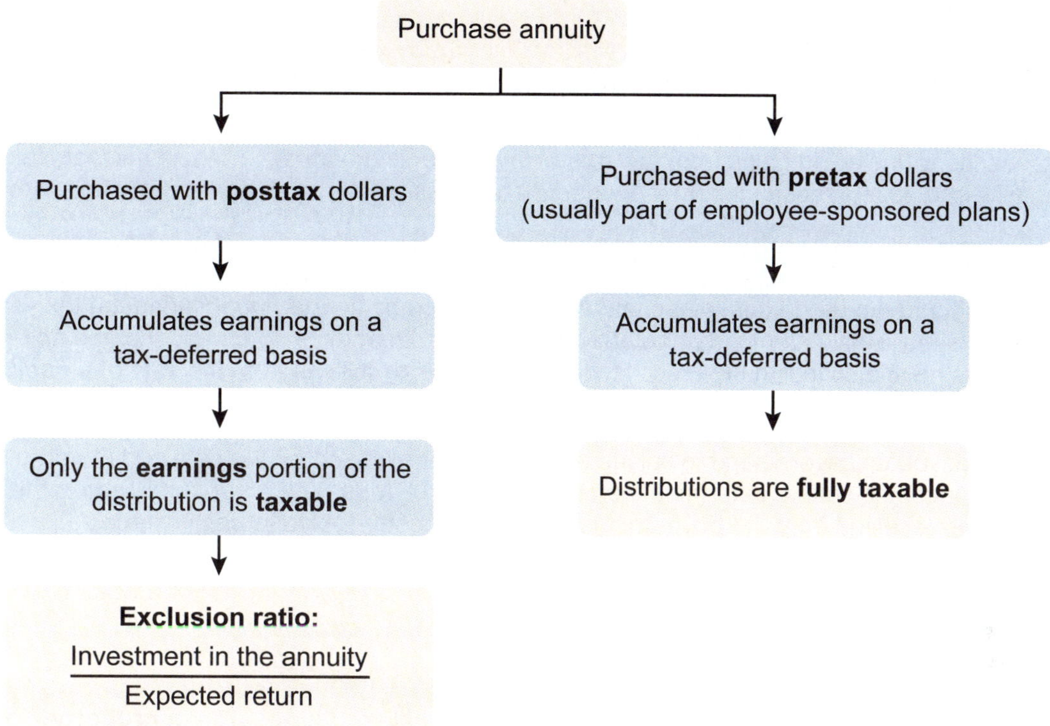

Exclusion ratio:

$$\frac{\text{Investment in the annuity}}{\text{Expected return}}$$

Injury Awards

Compensation for **physical injuries** is any payment that compensates for **damages** due to a physical injury or illness.

- If the action generating a payment is due to a physical injury or illness and the reimbursement of medical expenses paid was not itemized on Schedule A, then all damages received, including pain and suffering and workers' compensation, are *excludable from income*
- Punitive damages that a court might award to punish the defendant are always includable in income even if they are related to a physical injury or sickness

With **nonphysical injuries** such as age or race discrimination, slander, or libel, punitive damages and lost business profits are taxable and **included** in **gross income**.

- Attorneys' fees and costs recovered as part of a judgment must be included in income if the underlying recovery is included in gross income
- Payment to a wrongly incarcerated individual for loss of liberty, lost income, pain and suffering, and other physical and emotional injuries is excluded from income

Social Security Benefits

Taxpayers may be required to **include** up to **85%** of their **benefits** in gross income unless their modified AGI is under a certain threshold.

- Single taxpayers: If modified AGI + 50% of Social Security benefits ≤ $25,000, Social Security benefits are not taxable
- Married taxpayers filing separately: Taxable Social Security benefits are the lesser of (a) 85% of the Social Security benefits or (b) 85% of the taxpayer's modified AGI + 50% of Social Security benefits
- Married taxpayers filing jointly: If modified AGI + 50% of Social Security benefits ≤ $32,000, Social Security benefits are not taxable

Capital Gains and Gross Income

Representative Task (Application): Calculate the capital gain that should be included in an individual's gross income as reported on Form 1040 – U.S. Individual Income Tax Return from transactions, including gains from the sale of investments or virtual currencies, assets received as gifts and assets received from a decedent and classify them as long-term or short-term.

Gross income refers to the broad total of income sources earned by an individual during the tax year, less amounts that are specifically exempted or deferred by tax code. In addition to earned income and passive income, taxpayers must also include in gross income any **gains or losses** from the sale of a **capital asset** (eg, stocks, bonds, business interests, artwork, virtual currencies).

When selling an asset, taxpayers need to calculate the **amount realized** on the sale and the **adjusted basis** of each asset being sold to determine the **realized gain or loss**. The *amount realized* is the total value of everything received from the buyer minus any selling costs. Typically, cash is received when assets are sold, but sellers may also accept notes receivable, cryptocurrency, another asset, or debt relief as a means of payment.

Realized Gain and Loss

A **realized gain or loss** must be computed any time there is a sale or **disposition** of **property**. The term sale or disposition includes sales, exchanges, trade-ins, casualties, condemnations, thefts, and retirements. Realized gain or loss is computed as follows:

Realized gain or loss = Amount realized − Adjusted basis

Generally, realized gains during a year must be **recognized** by the taxpayer. To **recognize** a **gain simply** means to **include** it in **gross income**. To recognize a loss means the amount is deducted from income.

On June 1, Year 1, Clara sold 1,000 shares of stock of a publicly traded corporation for $28,000. Clara had purchased 500 shares of this stock on January 3, Year 1, for $52 per share. On April 1, Year 1, the stock had a 2-for-1 split. What is Clara's realized gain on the sale of stock?

Amount realized	$28,000
Adjusted basis (1,000 × $26 per share)	(26,000)
Gain realized	$ 2,000

The sale results in a ***gain***. Although the 2-for-1 stock split increased the number of shares from 500 to 1,000 and decreased the cost per share from $52 to $26, the total cost of the stock remains at **$26,000** (ie, 1,000 shares × $26 per share).

Not all realized gains will be recognized. If not recognized, they are either excluded or deferred to subsequent periods. The recognized gain will never exceed the realized gain. Assume that all realized gains are recognized unless a tax law provides otherwise.

Marilyn sold an asset to Xavier. Marilyn received $50,000 and a pickup truck worth $26,000. Marilyn also paid $6,000 in selling expenses. What amount did Marilyn realize on the sale?

Marilyn realized:
$70,000 (Cash $50,000 + Truck FMV $26,000 − $6,000 Selling expenses).

Marilyn then sold a piece of property to Xavier. Marilyn received $600,000 in cash, a note receivable for $120,000, and debt relief of $100,000. She also paid commissions of $30,000. In addition, Marilyn agreed to improve the property by building a garage at a cost of $20,000 before the sale. What amount did Marilyn realize on the sale?

Anything received by the seller during a sale or exchange is included in the amount realized. Most dispositions result in cash paid to the seller. However, the amount realized **includes, but is not limited to**, cash, the fair market value of any other property received (eg, marketable securities or a similar asset), or relief of debt. In addition, selling expenses reduce the amount realized.

Anything the seller gives up in the transaction is **added** to the basis of the property given up and is not considered part of the amount realized. Therefore, the garage improvement is ***not*** considered part of Marilyn's amount realized. Note, however, that making these capital improvements *increases* Marilyn's *adjusted basis* in the property, decreasing her *capital gain* once the property is sold.

Marilyn realized:
$790,000 ($600,000 Cash + $120,000 Note receivable + $100,000 Debt relief − $30,000 Commissions)

The *adjusted basis* of an asset is determined based upon how the asset was acquired by the taxpayer:

Asset Acquisition	Adjusted Basis Determination
Purchase	Cost + Capital improvements − Cost recovery deductions
Converted from personal to business use	If FMV > Basis; Basis = Adjusted basis If FMV < Basis; Basis = Lower of adjusted basis or FMV at date of conversion
Wash sales	Adjusted basis of new securities = Cost + Deferred loss from the wash sale
Inheritance	FMV at date of death or alternate valuation date, if elected
Gift	If FMV > Basis; Basis = Adjusted basis of donor If FMV < Basis; Basis = Lower of adjusted basis or FMV at date of gift, depending on the subsequent sales price

Special Basis and Holding Period Rules for Inheritances and Gifts

Inheritances

The receipt of an inheritance is nontaxable. The basis for *inherited property* is the basis used to determine *estate taxes for the decedent*. Usually, this is **FMV** on the date of **death**. If, however, an election is properly made in the filing of the estate tax return to use the **alternate valuation date (AVD)**, then the basis will be the earlier of:

- The date the property was **transferred** to the beneficiary
- **Six months** after the date of death

Inherited Property

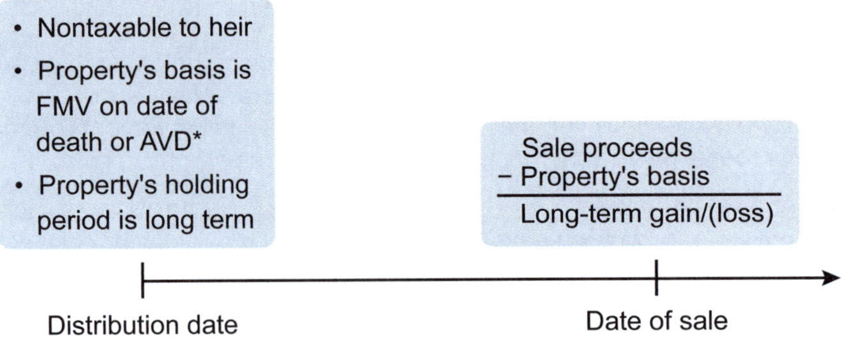

**If the alternate valuation date (AVD) is elected, the heir's basis is the FMV on the earlier of:*
1) the date the property was transferred to the heir, or
2) six months after death.

Assume that the decedent died on 2/1/Year 1 and that two different assets were distributed to the beneficiary: one on 4/24/Year 1 and the other on 10/25/Year 1. The basis of both assets would normally be the fair market value on 2/1/Year 1, the date of death. If, however, the executor of the estate properly elected the alternate valuation date, then the first asset's basis to the beneficiary is the value on 4/24/Year 1, and the second asset's basis to the beneficiary is the value on 8/1/Year 1, determined as follows:

Date	First Asset	Second Asset
Date of death	2/1/Year 1	2/1/Year 1
Date of distribution	4/24/Year 1	10/25/Year 1
Six months after death	8/1/Year 1	8/1/Year 1
Earlier of last two dates	4/24/Year 1	8/1/Year 1

On a subsequent sale, the gain or loss is **always** reported as **long term**, regardless of the actual holding period. The original cost and acquisition date by the decedent are ignored in all determinations, in part because there may be no practical way to determine these items and in part because the government wants to assess estate taxes on current values instead of original purchase costs.

Gifts

Gifts are **excluded** from **gross income**. Although the donor of a gift may have to report and pay gift taxes in some cases, the recipient (donee) of the gift generally does not report any taxable income on the receipt of the gift. When the recipient of the gifted property sells or disposes of the property, determining the correct adjusted basis and holding period is important to determine the *character* of the *gain or loss recognized*.

If the FMV of the asset is greater than the donor's basis on the date of the gift (ie, **appreciated property**), the basis and holding period *carry over* to the recipient.

When the value of the property on the date of the gift is lower than the donor basis (**decrease in value**), the donee must keep track of both the donor's basis and FMV (ie, dual basis rules). When the dual basis rules apply:

- The *donor's basis* (higher amount) is used to calculate a *subsequent gain* on sale, and the holding period includes that of the donor
- The *FMV* (lower amount) is used to calculate a *subsequent loss* on sale, and the holding period begins the day *after* the gift is made
- If the selling price is between the donor's basis and FMV, no gain or loss is recognized; therefore, the holding period is irrelevant

These rules minimize the gain or loss realized by the donee and do not tax the donee on subsequent appreciation up to the donor's adjusted basis.

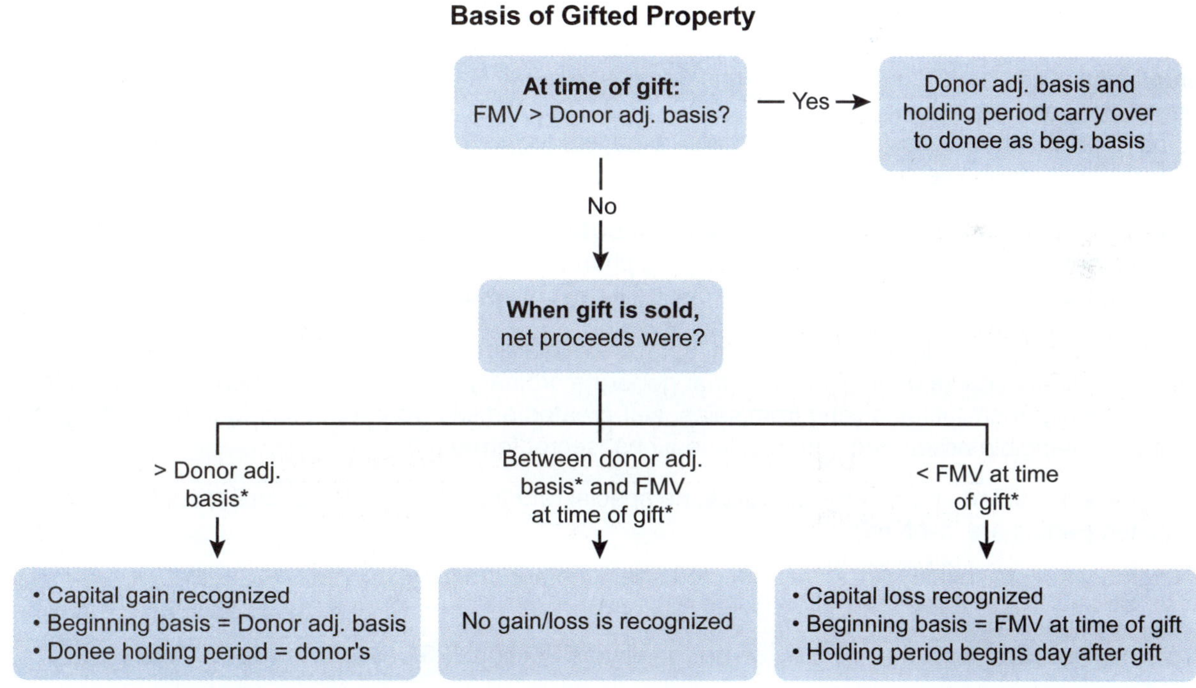

Greta purchased stock in Year 1 for $30,000, and she gave it to Ron in Year 8 after it had declined in value to $10,000. The following examples assume Ron resold the stock later in Year 8 for (a) $9,000, (b) $20,000, (c) $29,000, and (d) $39,000:

Because the stock has declined in value, the dual basis rules apply.

If the selling price is $9,000 (ie, less than FMV), the holding period begins the day after the gift, and Ron has a $1,000 **short-term realized loss** ($9,000 - $10,000).

If the selling price is $20,000 (ie, between donor's $30,000 basis and $10,000 FMV), Ron has **no gain or loss** (holding period is irrelevant).

If the selling price is $29,000 (ie, between donor's $30,000 basis and $10,000 FMV), Ron has **no gain or loss** (holding period is irrelevant).

If the selling price is $39,000 (ie, greater than donor's basis), the holding period carries over from the donor (ie, donor's purchase date), and Ron has a **$9,000 long-term realized gain** ($39,000 - $30,000).

Character of Assets

An asset's **character** is important because it **determines** the **tax treatment** of any **gain or loss recognized** when the asset is sold or disposed of. The three asset categories are **ordinary**, **capital**, and **Section 1231** assets. Ultimately, every gain or loss from these three categories is characterized as either ordinary or capital.

Differentiation is key because ordinary income (loss) is generally taxed at ordinary rates regardless of the holding period, and the losses are fully deductible against ordinary income. Capital assets, on the other hand, have **preferential rates** for noncorporate taxpayers (eg, 0%, 15%, 20%) if held for more than a year, while those held for one year or less do not.

Section 1231 gains and **losses** receive the **best** of **both worlds**: a net gain becomes a long-term capital gain, and a net loss becomes an ordinary loss. The character of assets **always** depends on the purpose or use of the asset and for how long a taxpayer owned it (ie, the holding period).

Ordinary Assets: Generally, refers to assets that were acquired or produced with the intention of being sold in the ordinary course of business and that generate ordinary income or loss when sold. Examples include inventory, receivables arising from sales, self-created artistic work (eg, copyrighted material), and self-created intangible assets (eg, patents, inventions, secret formulas).

- All gains are taxed at **ordinary tax rates**; no special rate/treatment or limitations apply (assuming no related parties are involved)
- Ordinary assets sold at a loss are deducted against other ordinary income
- Depreciable personal property and realty used in a business for *one year or less* also generate ordinary gains or losses since they do **not** qualify as Section 1231 assets or capital assets

Section 1231 Assets (*noncurrent business assets*): Assets used in the trade or business and held *longer* than one year, whose eventual sale or disposal is only incidental to the business. This category includes depreciable and amortizable property, land used in a business, and property, plant, and equipment.

- Holding period of property must be over one year
- If there is a net Section 1231 gain, the net gain is treated as a long-term capital gain (LTCG). The amount is included in the netting process of capital gains and losses (reported on Schedule D). Because of this special treatment, a net Section 1231 gain can be used to offset net capital losses that otherwise might not have been deductible in the current year
- If the net result is Section 1231 loss, the loss is treated as an ordinary loss (reported on Form 4797)

Depreciation recapture changes the character of the gain on the sale of a Section 1231 asset from Section 1231 gain to ordinary income. Remember that recapture changes only the character but not the amount of the gain. Recapture does not apply to losses.

Capital Assets (*nonbusiness assets*): Assets that do **not** qualify as ordinary income or Section 1231 assets. The most common type of capital assets are investment assets or personal-use assets.

- A net capital loss is limited to $3,000 per year. Any unused losses are carried forward indefinitely

Individual taxpayers generally prefer capital gains to ordinary income because certain capital gains are taxed at preferential rates and can be used to offset capital losses.

Examples of Capital Assets

- Primary residence
- Stocks, bonds, and other securities
- Mutual funds and retirement accounts
- Business interests (interests in partnerships, S corps)
- Vehicles
- Rental properties
- Artwork and collectibles
- Jewelry and precious stones
- Personal property
- Cryptocurrency
- Goodwill*

**Although goodwill is amortizable, it is not actually used by a business in a meaningful sense, since it doesn't diminish in value from usage; therefore, it is also treated as a capital asset.*

Capital Asset Use

Notice that the **tax character** of the asset **depends** on the **handling** by the **taxpayer**. A *personal computer* would be an ordinary income asset to the manufacturer of the computer, a Section 1231 asset to an accounting firm that acquired the computer for use by its employees and held long term, and a capital asset to a person who bought it to run educational software for their children at home.

Ramona is an artist who creates large mosaic tile installations. Determine the asset category under the following independent assumptions:

Ramona created an art installation that was purchased by the local hospital to display in its cardiac wing.

Ordinary asset: The art installation is an ordinary asset because it was produced with the intention of being sold in the ordinary course of business.

Ramona operates a small shop and gallery where she features her own work and that of local artists. She purchased a piece of sculpture, which is not for sale, many years ago from one of the local artists for the display window in her gallery.

Section 1231 asset: The sculpture is a Section 1231 asset since the asset is used in a trade or business and held for more than a year.

Ramona fell in love with a painting in her gallery that was created by one of the local artists. She purchased it to hang over the mantelpiece in her home.

Capital asset: The painting is a capital asset because it doesn't qualify as ordinary or Section 1231 property.

Capital Asset Holding Period

In general, short-term (S/T) capital transactions refer to sales that take place within a year of the acquisition date, and long-term (L/T) transactions are those held for longer than one year. There are two exceptions:

- **Inherited assets:** Sales are always classified as long term
- **Nonbusiness bad debts:** Write-offs are always classified as short-term capital losses

When a **security** becomes **worthless**, the holding period is calculated by treating the property as if it had been sold on the last day of the tax year in which it becomes worthless. *Worthless securities* generally receive capital loss treatment; however, if the loss is incurred by a corporation on an investment in an affiliated corporation (80% or more ownership), the loss is treated as an ordinary loss item.

Netting Process and Tax Treatment

As mentioned previously, **all assets** are ultimately **categorized** as either **ordinary** or **capital**, **long term** or **short term**. Gains and losses from capital assets are netted against one another to determine an overall net capital gain or loss. A similar netting process applies to Section 1231 assets.

Section 1231 assets (ie, used in a trade or business and held > 1 year) are classified as either *Section 1245* or *Section 1250*, with the *exception* of land. Although land can be a Section 1231 asset (eg, farmland used for agricultural purposes, rental property), it does **not** fall into either category because land is *not* depreciable.

Gains and losses from all Section 1231 assets (ie, both Section 1245 and Section 1250) are **netted**. Gains are subject to special treatment due to depreciation recapture (Section 1245 property) and unrecaptured depreciation (Section 1250 property). After netting, a **net Section 1231 gain** is treated as a **LTCG and netted with other capital gains and losses**. When there is a net Section 1231 loss, it is treated as an ordinary loss.

	Section 1245	**Section 1250**
Type of Asset	Depreciable personal property (tangible and intangible)	Depreciable real property*
Examples	Machinery, equipment, furniture	Buildings and their structural components, warehouses, rental property

Excludes land

Unrecaptured Section 1250 Gain for Individuals

When there is a **net Section 1231 gain**, **real property** sold at a gain by individuals has **unrecaptured 1250 gain**. The **lesser** of the gain or the amount attributable by depreciation deductions is taxed at a maximum rate of 25% (taxed at ordinary rate if lower than 25%) and not the preferential capital gains rates of 0%/15%/20% applicable to other types of LTCGs. The remainder of the gain is taxed at the 0%/15%/20% tax rates.

In Year 1, Lola bought a rental property for $450,000 and has claimed $100,000 of depreciation deductions against the asset. Lola has a marginal tax rate of 32%. In Year 4, Lola sold the property for $500,000. What is the amount and character of Lola's gain, and what effect does the sale have on Lola's tax liability, assuming this was the only asset she sold?

Description	Amount	Explanation
(1) Amount realized	$500,000	Given
(2) Original basis	450,000	Given
(3) Accumulated depreciation	100,000	Given
(4) Adjusted basis	$350,000	(2) − (3)
(5) Gain recognized	$150,000	(1) − (4)
(6) **Unrecaptured Section 1250 gain**	100,000	Lesser of (5) or (3)
(7) Remaining Section 1231 gain	$ 50,000	(5) − (6)

Unrecaptured Section 1250 gain: $100,000 × 25% 1250 rate = $25,000 tax

1231 gain (LTCG): $50,000 × 15% capital gain rate = $7,500 tax

Tax liability = $25,000 + $7,500 = $32,500

Netting Process

LTCG and LTCL are combined to determine the *net long-term capital gain or loss* for the year. Short-term capital gains (STCG) and losses (STCL) are combined to determine the net short-term capital gain or loss for the year. In addition, the netting determines which gains are subject to preferential tax rates.

An exception to the preferential rates on LTCG is those attributable to collectibles. Collectibles are defined as tangible personal property such as coins, art, stamps, alcoholic beverages, and antiques for investment purposes. Gold and silver are also classified as collectibles. Net capital gain from a "collectible" is taxed at a maximum rate of 28%.

If the netting of long-term and short-term combinations are **both gains**, stop; they are **reported separately**.

- **STCG:** Ordinary tax rates apply
- **LTCG:** Special tax rates apply (0%, 15%, and 20%) for individuals (but not corporations)

If **both** are **losses**, stop; they are **reported separately**.

- Loss treatment for individuals:
  - Net capital loss limit of $3,000 ($1,500 MFS) is deductible against ordinary income; short-term losses are claimed first
  - No carryback is allowed, but unused losses can be carried forward indefinitely; carryforwards retain their character as short term or long term
  - A net loss in any rate group is applied to reduce the net gain in the highest rate group first (see ordering rules below)

If there is a net gain and a net loss, they are combined to produce a single net capital gain or loss for the year, which will be treated as having the character of the larger of the two numbers being combined.

Ordering Procedure

Some **LTCGs** may be subject to special tax rates (eg, 15%, 25%, 28%), depending on the nature of each gain. To ensure that the LTCGs are taxed at the lowest preferential rate possible and provide the greatest benefit to taxpayers, an **ordering procedure** is followed:

When netting losses against long-term gains, the loss is offset in the following order:

1. LTCGs on collectibles (eg, stamps, coins) are taxed at 28%
2. Unrecaptured Section 1250 gains are taxed at 25%
3. Any remaining LTCGs are generally taxed at 15%

Ordering Procedure for Netting Capital Loss against Capital Gains

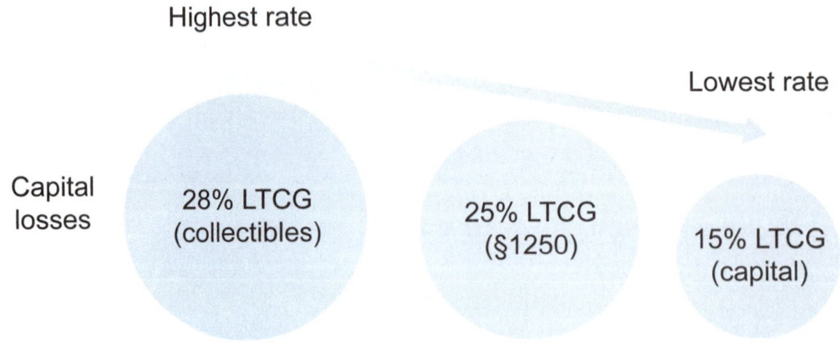

LTCG = long-term capital gains

Remember that sales of personal, family, or household assets at a loss are **not** allowed as capital losses and are not reported or considered in the netting process. They are presumed to represent consumption. For example, if a refrigerator is purchased for $1,000 and then sold 15 years later for $100, the drop in value is not a loss but the result of the use of the refrigerator for all those years (ie, **consumption loss**). **Gains** on the **sale** of **personal assets**, however, are **taxed**.

In Year 4, a taxpayer had the following transactions:

- Sold business equipment owned for three years for $10,000. The adjusted basis at the time of sale was $15,000
- Was informed that a friend who still owed the taxpayer $4,000 on a $12,000 nonbusiness loan made two years ago declared bankruptcy
- Sold stock for $3,000 gain that was inherited during the year

What are the amount and character of the taxpayer's capital transactions for Year 4?

The business equipment is a Section 1231 asset since it was used in a trade or business and held longer than one year. The sale results in a loss of $5,000 ($10,000 proceeds − $15,000 basis). Losses on 1231 assets are *ordinary*.

The $4,000 nonbusiness bad debt is *always* a *short-term capital loss*. The $3,000 gain on inherited stock is a LTCG because inherited property has a statutory holding period of long term in every case. There is only one STCL ($4,000) and one LTCG ($3,000). These are netted, with the character being determined by the larger number. In this case, **$1,000 ($3,000 − $4,000) net short-term capital loss**.

Other Capital Assets, Cryptocurrency

Digital assets are any digital representations of value that are recorded on a cryptographically secured distributed ledger or any similar technology. Digital assets include nonfungible tokens (NFTs) and virtual currencies (eg, cryptocurrencies and stablecoins).

Cryptocurrencies, such as Bitcoin and Ethereum, have become increasingly popular in recent years. While many view it as an investment opportunity, it is important to understand the tax implications of cryptocurrency.

- First, it's important to note that the IRS doesn't consider cryptocurrency as currency at all. The IRS treats cryptocurrency as **property** for **federal income tax purposes**. This means that cryptocurrency is taxed as a capital gain or loss when sold or exchanged for other property or services
- When crypto is sold, traded, or used as a form of payment, it is a disposition of digital assets; that disposal could result in gain or loss depending on the cost basis in the units disposed of and the value of the digital assets at the time of disposal. In other words, if the value of the good or real currency a taxpayer received is greater than their cost basis, a short-term or long-term capital gain will be realized

Not every transaction with **cryptocurrency** is **taxable**; exclusions include the following:

- Transferring digital assets between wallets the taxpayer controls
- Gifting or donating cryptocurrency
- *Buying* cryptocurrency with cash

A taxpayer bought a car in Year 1 for $56,000 using 2 Bitcoins that he purchased six months earlier for $36,400. Because the IRS treats cryptocurrency as a capital asset and not equivalent to cash, **$19,600 of gain** would be recognized for tax purposes ($56,000 − $36,400).

Since the Bitcoins were held **less than a year**, the gain would be a **short-term capital gain** subject to the taxpayer's marginal tax rate (assume 37% is the marginal rate in this example). The tax on the gain at a rate of 37% would be **$7,252**. The taxpayer is responsible for paying this amount on top of the purchase price of the car.

Like other capital assets, sales and dispositions of digital assets are reported and aggregated on Form 8949: Sales and Other Dispositions of Capital Assets.

Matthew, a married taxpayer, sold the following assets this year:

Asset	Sales Price	Cost	Details
2014 Ford Shelby Mustang GT500	$45,000	$62,000	Matthew drove the car on weekends with friends from the local Mustang Club of Mid-Michigan.
Warehouse	$600,000	$608,000	The warehouse was used in Matthew's business and held longer than one year. Depreciation deductions of $50,000 have been taken on the warehouse.
Bourbon collection	$16,000	$5,000	Matthew's rare Blanton bourbon collection was acquired by inheritance one month ago.
Ethereum cryptocurrency	$10,000	$70,000	After the collapse of FTX, Matthew sold his entire stake in cryptocurrency that he held for investment after only owning it for five months.
Cat forklift truck	$30,000	$30,000	The forklift was used in Matthew's warehouse and held exactly one year; depreciation deductions totaled $3,000.

In addition, Matthew sold stock in Alphabet for $11,000 to an unrelated party. The Alphabet stock was gifted to Matthew from his uncle three years earlier. At the time of the gift, Alphabet was worth $10,000, and the uncle's basis in the stock was $15,000.

Matthew also received a Schedule K-1 as the beneficiary of his great-aunt's estate. Box 4a showed an amount for net LTCG of $15,000.

What is the amount and character of each asset Matthew sold?

Apply the netting process to Matthew's capital gains (losses) and determine the effect on Matthew's tax liability assuming his marginal tax rate is 32% and his preferential tax rate is 15%.

Asset	Gain (Loss)	Character
Ford Shelby	$(17,000)	Personal capital asset; "consumption" loss disallowed
Warehouse	$42,000	Section 1231 subject to Section 1250 unrecaptured gain rate of 25%
Bourbon	$11,000	Long-term capital asset since acquired by inheritance; collectible subject to 28% rate
Crypto	$(60,000)	Short-term capital asset
Forklift	$3,000	Ordinary gain since business asset not held greater than one year; not subject to depreciation recapture
Alphabet stock	$0	Since the stock was received as a gift and sold for an amount between the FMV and basis on the date of the gift, no gain or loss is recognized
K-1 as beneficiary	$15,000	Net LTCG

When netting losses against long-term gains, the losses offset in the following order:

1. LTCGs on collectibles (28% rate)
2. Unrecaptured Section 1250 gains (25% rate)
3. Any remaining LTCGs at the preferential rate of the taxpayer

In this case, the loss of $60,000 offset all of the gain of $11,000 from the collectibles first, followed by all of the unrecaptured Section 1250 gain of $42,000 and $7,000 of the long-term gain from the K-1, leaving $8,000 of gain taxable at 15%.

Matthew will report an $8,000 LTCG taxed at 15% (ie, $1,200) and a $3,000 ordinary gain from the forklift taxed at 32% (ie, $960). His total tax liability is **$2,160** ($1,200 + $960).

Short-term capital loss	$(60,000)
Less: LTCG on collectibles (at 28%)	11,000
Less: LTCG (unrecaptured Section 1250 at 25%)	42,000
Less: LTCG (at 15%)	15,000
Net LTCG	$ 8,000

Gross Income Exclusions

Representative Task (Application): Calculate the amounts that should be excluded from an individual's gross income as reported on Form 1040 – U.S. Individual Income Tax Return, including tax-exempt interest, gifts received, and life insurance proceeds.

Gross income exclusions are a set of tax laws that allow certain types of **income** to be **excluded** from an individual's gross income for **tax purposes**. Congress has implemented these exclusions to promote certain policy objectives, encourage specific behaviors, or mitigate the effects of double taxation.

Determination of Gross Income

Gross income	–	Statutory exclusions	=	Gross income for tax return
§61(a): "All income from whatever source derived."		Examples: • Compensation for injuries • Workers' compensation • Gifts, inheritances • Employee fringe benefits		

Tax-Exempt Interest

State or Municipal Bonds

Interest earned on **state** and **local bonds** (municipal bonds) is **tax-exempt**. Governmental bonds are typically issued for public purposes, and their exclusion from income is seen to encourage state and local governments to invest in infrastructure and other projects that benefit the public. In contrast, U.S. government obligations (such as Treasury bills) are *taxable* for federal tax purposes.

U.S. Series Savings Bonds

Interest on Series I and Series EE savings bonds can be excluded at maturity or when redeemed if the taxpayer uses the proceeds to pay qualifying higher education expenses (tuition and fees; room and board do not qualify) in the year of redemption.

- The exclusion is available if the owner of the bond is at least 24 years old (the bond must not be held in a child's name)
- The interest is excluded in proportion to the educational expenses (tuition and fees) of the taxpayer, spouse, or dependent that are not reimbursed by nontaxable scholarships and Section 529 plan distributions
- The exclusion is phased out when modified AGI exceeds certain limits based on filing status

Tax Treatment of Earned Interest	
Included in Gross Income	Interest on: • State tax refunds • Zero-coupon bonds (accrued each year) • U.S. Treasury obligations • Series EE savings bonds
Excluded from Gross Income	Interest on: • State or municipal bonds • Qualified higher education bonds • Series EE savings bonds used for qualified higher education expenses

A married taxpayer redeems Series EE bonds, receiving $6,000 of principal and $4,000 of accrued interest. Assuming qualified higher education expenses total $9,000, accrued interest of **$3,600** [($9,000 / $10,000) × $4,000] can be **excluded** from **gross income**.

Assume the joint return of the married taxpayer has a modified AGI of $153,450 for Year 1, and the exclusion phases out beginning at $145,200 over a range of $30,000.

Excess AGI is $8,250 ($153,450 − $145,200). The reduction would be ($8,250 / $30,000) × $3,600 = $990. Thus, of the $4,000 of interest received, a total of **$2,610** ($3,600 − $990) can be **excluded** from **gross income**.

Exclusions That Mitigate Double Taxation

Congress has established specific exclusions to eliminate the double taxation for gifts, inheritances, life insurance payouts, and foreign earned income.

Gifts and Inheritances

Gifts and **inheritances** are taxed under federal estate and gift tax law. To avoid the double taxation of these transfers, their value is **excluded** from the income of the recipient. However, any subsequent earnings derived from the inherited or gifted assets, unless they come from a tax-free source, are generally taxable. Gifts may involve:

- Transfers of cash or property
- Sales of property at a bargain price to another family member
- Loans to family members on which a fair rate of interest is not charged (ie, imputed interest)
- Irrevocable trusts established for others in which income and/or corpus will eventually go to someone other than the taxpayer

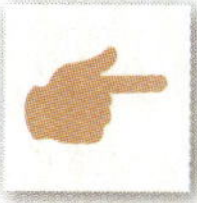

Whether an item is a gift depends on the intent of the donor, not the intent of the donee. For example, Sara rakes the leaves in Tina's yard as a gesture of kindness, but Tina decides to pay her $50 for her work. Even though Sara did not expect to be paid, Sara has $50 of income because Tina's intent was to pay her for the services she rendered.

Life Insurance Proceeds

Taxpayers receiving **life insurance proceeds**, paid for reason of death, are generally allowed to **exclude** the proceeds from gross income (interest received is taxable, however). If the insurance proceeds are paid over time, instead of in a lump sum, a portion of the payments represents interest and must be included in gross income.

If an estate subject to the estate tax (value of the estate exceeds the exemption amount) is named the beneficiary of a life insurance policy, the proceeds must be included in the decedent's gross estate.

In addition, the sale of an insurance policy is a taxable event. The seller has ordinary income for proceeds in excess of basis (ie, premiums paid) up to the amount of the cash surrender value. Any remaining proceeds are taxed as a capital gain. An exception exists if the policy is surrendered or sold by a terminally ill taxpayer.

- Accelerated death benefits from a life insurance policy can be excluded from income if the insured taxpayer is **terminally** ill. Terminally ill means that a physician has certified that death is likely to occur in 24 months or less
- If the taxpayer is chronically ill, accelerated death benefits are not taxable if used to pay for the taxpayer's long-term care. Chronically ill means that the individual cannot perform some common daily activities (eg, eating, bathing)

Tax consequences to purchaser: When the insurance proceeds are paid at the death of the insured, the **excess** of the **purchase price** of the policy plus any **subsequent premiums paid** is taxable as income to the purchaser.

Ansel owned a life insurance policy on his spouse but was short of cash. He sold the policy for $100,000 to Bridgett, an unrelated individual. Upon the death of Ansel's spouse, Bridgett received $500,000 from the life insurance company. What is the tax consequence to Bridgett?

Bridgett will be **taxed on $400,000** of income ($100,000 is return of capital). If Ansel had not sold the policy, then Ansel would have received $500,000 tax-free.

A taxpayer was the owner and beneficiary of a $200,000 life insurance policy on a parent. The taxpayer sold the policy to a friend for $25,000. The friend paid a total of $40,000 in premiums. Upon the death of the parent, the friend will receive $200,000 of proceeds and had paid a total of $65,000 ($25,000 for the policy plus $40,000 in subsequent premiums). What is the tax consequence to the friend?

The **$65,000 is treated as a tax-free** return of capital. The **$135,000** excess proceeds over the amounts paid are taxable.

Foreign Earned Income Exclusion

U.S. citizens are subject to tax on their **worldwide income**. To provide relief from potential double taxation, an individual meeting either a *bona fide residence test or a physical presence test* may elect to exclude an amount of income earned in a foreign country, as prescribed by the IRS, that is adjusted annually for inflation. Qualifying taxpayers also may elect to exclude additional amounts based on foreign housing costs.

To qualify, an individual must be (1) a U.S. citizen who is a foreign resident for an uninterrupted period that includes an entire taxable year (**bona fide residence test**) or (2) a U.S. citizen or resident present in a foreign country for at least 330 full days in any 12-month period (**physical presence test**).

Roth-Type Retirement Plans

Roth-type plans are funded with contributions made with **after-tax dollars**. To ensure these funds are not taxed twice, qualified distributions are excluded from income. The income accrues tax-free in these accounts, and withdrawals are excluded from taxable income provided that they are a qualified distribution, the account is held for at least five years, and they are made:

- Because the taxpayer is permanently disabled,
- After the death of the taxpayer, to a beneficiary of the taxpayer's estate,
- To the taxpayer once age 59.5, or
- To the taxpayer for a first-time home purchase (up to $10,000)

Any nonqualified early distributions may be subject to a 10% penalty tax.

Education-Related Exclusions

Certain types of income are **excluded** from taxation if the funds are used for **higher education**. These exclusions aid individuals in pursuing their studies and make obtaining academic degrees more affordable.

Scholarships and Grants

Scholarships and **grants** are a form of gift award and do not need to be repaid. They are tax-free if the following **criteria** are met:

- The taxpayer is a degree-seeking student at an accredited college or university
- The award doesn't exceed the qualified education expenses (tuition, fees, books, and required supplies and equipment)
- The award isn't used for other expenses, such as living expenses (room and board), travel, or optional equipment
- The scholarship or grant isn't paid in return for teaching, researching, or other tasks

Chase is an accomplished student and athlete. He receives a combined $25,000 in scholarships during the current tax year, consisting of $20,000 from his university and $5,000 from his local Chamber of Commerce. Chase's expenses during the current tax year are as follows:

- Tuition and fees $14,000
- Required textbooks $1,100
- Lab fees $200
- Rent $6,000
- Other expenses $3,700

How much of the scholarships amount must Chase report as income?

Chase can **exclude** the scholarships from income to the extent of $14,000 for tuition and fees, $1,100 for textbooks, and $200 lab fee, for a total of **$15,300**.

He must **include** the remaining **$9,700** in income. Rent expense and other expenses are not included as tuition, fees, and other required expenses for his courses.

Education Savings Accounts

Education savings account (ESA) plans incentivize people to save and then spend the savings on education.

Qualified Tuition Programs (QTP—529 Plans)

Taxpayers make **nondeductible contributions**, earnings accumulate tax-free, and withdrawals are also tax-free if the money goes toward paying qualified education expenses. Qualified education expenses include tuition, room and board, books, supplies, fees, computer hardware, software, peripherals, and internet access for **higher education** only.

- Part of the annual plan distribution may be used to pay for *tuition* only of *elementary and secondary* schools
- Contributions up to the annual gift tax exclusion can be made

Coverdell ESA

Coverdell ESAs provide the same incentive as QTP plans but include additional rules, such as an **annual contribution limit** of $2,000 per beneficiary and income phaseout.

- One difference is that Coverdell ESAs can be used for *qualified elementary and secondary* tuition and expenses
- Another difference is that an account can be set up for anyone (even someone unrelated to contributor) if the beneficiary is under the age of 18 or is a special-needs beneficiary
- Funds in the account must be distributed within 30 days of the beneficiary's 30th birthday (subject to tax and a 10% penalty) or transferred to the ESA of another family member of the same generation without triggering tax or penalty

Employer-Provided Exclusions

Employer-provided **nontaxable fringe benefits** are attractive to employees. These no-cost benefits are **excluded** from an employee's gross income, meaning they are not subject to federal income tax or Social Security and Medicare taxes (with some exceptions). This can result in significant savings for employees and may make certain benefits more affordable and accessible. Some common examples include:

Fringe Benefit	Description
Group term life insurance	Employer-paid premiums on up to $50,000 **group term** life insurance policies are excludable
Health benefits	Employer-paid premiums covering medical, dental, and long-term care
Food and lodging for the convenience of the employer	Meals provided on employer's premises and lodging provided as a condition of employment
Working condition fringe benefits	Benefits that would be deductible by the employee if the employee paid the expense rather than the employer
De minimis fringe benefits	Relatively small and infrequently provided benefits
No additional cost services	Benefits that don't cost the employer a material amount to provide

Fringe Benefit	Description
Qualified employee discounts	Reduced prices on employer's products or services; discount for merchandise limit is average gross profit percentage; services limited to 20% discount of value of services
Nominal gifts	Noncash gifts excluded if value is < $25
Safety and achievement awards	Awards for safety or length of service of up to $400 if not a qualified plan and $1,600 if part of a qualified plan
Transportation and parking	Mass-transit passes or qualified parking up to $315 per month or use of the company-owned carpool vehicles
Child and dependent care benefits	Up to $5,000 exclusion ($2,500 MFS) for cost of providing care for dependent under 13 years old or a disabled dependent regardless of age so that taxpayer can work
Education assistance	Up to $5,250 exclusion for tuition, books, and fees or eligible student loan repayments for the education of the employee
Adoption expenses	Employer-provided adoption assistance up to annually adjusted amounts and subject to phaseout based on AGI
Athletic facilities	Use of athletic facilities provided at location owned or leased by the employer

Nontaxable fringe benefits, with few exceptions, cannot be provided on a discriminatory basis (ie, they must be given to all employees and not just some).

Mickey was disabled last year. Mickey's employer-provided health insurance plan paid his medical expenses of $50,000, and his employer-provided disability insurance paid Mickey $40,000 for lost wages while he was disabled. Mickey may exclude the $50,000 but is taxed on the disability proceeds of $40,000 because the **employer** paid the insurance premiums.

Health and disability **insurance proceeds** are *excluded* if the **taxpayer paid the premiums**. Benefits under a policy purchased by the taxpayer are excluded even if payments are a substitute for lost wages. An exception to this rule is when the employee pays the premium with pretax dollars, such as through a cafeteria plan, in which case the insurance proceeds are taxable.

If the **employer paid the premium** for *disability insurance*, then proceeds from the disability policy are *taxed* to the recipient.

Health insurance reimbursements may be *excluded* even if the taxpayer's **employer paid the premiums**. In this case, medical expense reimbursements are excluded as long as the expenses reimbursed are for qualified medical expenses or if payment is received for loss of (or loss of the use of) a body part or permanent disfigurement. These exclusions apply for the employee and the employee's spouse and dependents included on the plan. Any excluded reimbursed expenses may not be deducted as an itemized medical expense on Schedule A.

Carole is a flight attendant. Carole and all other employees receive free flight benefits as part of their employee benefits package. If Carole uses 30 flights with a value of $15,320 this year, what amount, if any, is excluded from her gross income?

The flight benefits qualify as a no additional cost service and may be completely excluded from gross income. All **$15,320** is **excluded** because the airline would be operating the flights Carol took even if Carol wasn't flying on them.

EE employs Tom as a manager of a motel. EE provides lodging worth $2,000 to Tom in order to keep Tom on call in case of complaints. What amount, if any, is excluded from his gross income?

Tom may exclude the **$2,000** value of the lodging if EE requires that Tom accept the lodging as a condition of employment.

Dave is an attorney, and his law firm reimburses him for his dues to the American Bar Association and his subscription to the *National Law Review*. What amount, if any, is excluded from his gross income?

These **reimbursements** are **excluded** from **income** as working condition fringe benefits.

Terry is employed at an office supply store and is allowed to buy a computer for $1,000. The computer cost the store $900 and is offered for sale at $1,300. The store's gross profit is $400 ($1,300 − $900 store cost). Because Terry is paying $1,000 for the computer, his discount is $300 ($1,300 − $1,000). What amount, if any, is excluded from Terry's gross income?

Because Terry is paying at least the store's cost, the **$300** discount does not exceed the $400 gross profit and is **excluded** from **income**.

If the store also provides shipping services for customers, and Terry is allowed to ship items at a 20% discount or less, the discount will also be excluded from income. The tax law limits the discount to 20% of the value of services.

Exclusions Related to Sickness and Injuries

Taxpayers who are **sick** or **injured** may *exclude* **certain payments** from income.

- Reimbursements for medical expenses from health plans
- Disability benefits if the premiums were paid by the taxpayer
- Benefits for medical expenses whose premiums were paid by an employer are also excluded if the benefits do not exceed the actual qualified expenses

Employer-paid compensatory damages for **physical injuries or sickness** are *not* included in income because they are designed to compensate a person for a loss (ie, make the taxpayer "whole") and return the taxpayer to their original financial position.

- Nontaxable damages include workers' compensation and damages for emotional distress related to a physical injury

Damages for emotional distress *not related* to a physical injury are taxable. **Punitive damages are always taxable** because they enrich the taxpayer and are intended to punish the wrongdoer rather than compensate the victim.

- Damage awards that are taxable are reported by a taxpayer as **other income** on Schedule 1 of Form 1040

Nontaxable Compensatory Damage Awards Make Taxpayer Whole

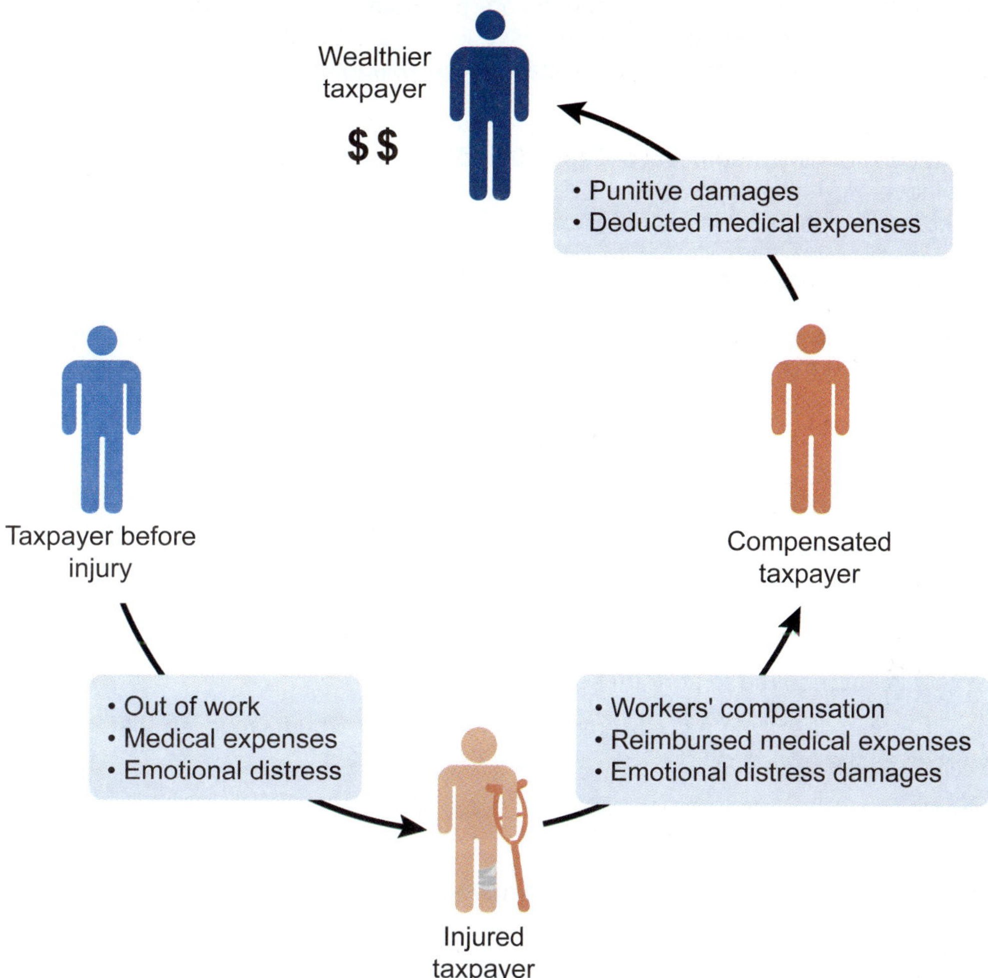

In Year 1, a taxpayer suffered bodily injury while at work. The taxpayer deducted related medical expenses of $10,000 in Year 1 and $5,000 in Year 2. In Year 3, the taxpayer won a workers' compensation claim and prevailed in a personal injury lawsuit, both in connection with the Year 1 injury. The taxpayer received the following damage award in Year 3 as settlement:

Punitive damages	$150,000
Workers' compensation	50,000
Reimbursement for medical expenses	25,000
Compensation for emotional distress caused by the injury	15,000

What amount of the settlement proceeds should be excluded from the taxpayer's income in Year 3?

The punitive damages are *taxable* because they enrich the taxpayer. The workers' compensation is nontaxable because the taxpayer is unable to work because of the work-related injury. Note that this treatment is *opposite* that of *unemployment compensation*, which is *fully taxable*.

In general, reimbursements for medical expenses are **not taxable** because they are compensating a taxpayer for an expense the taxpayer would not have incurred without the injury. However, amounts received as reimbursements for medical expenses are *taxable* to the extent the taxpayer took an itemized deduction for those expenses.

The taxpayer received reimbursements of $25,000 and must offset that amount by the $10,000 and $5,000 the taxpayer deducted in Year 1 and Year 2, respectively. Therefore, the taxpayer includes *$15,000* in income and can *exclude $10,000* of the medical expense reimbursements.

The compensation received for emotional distress is nontaxable because it related to a **physical injury.**

In total, the taxpayer can **exclude $75,000** of injury awards, which includes $50,000 in workers' compensation, $10,000 of medical reimbursements, and $15,000 for emotional distress compensation.

Exclusions for Prizes and Awards

Prizes or **awards** are generally taxable but can be excluded if they are for civic, artistic, educational, scientific, or literary achievements if:

- The recipient is selected without any action on recipient's part;
- The recipient is not required to perform services; and
- The amount is paid directly to a tax-exempt or governmental organization, so that the recipient never actually receives the award.

Forgiveness of Debt

In general, when a debtor's **debts** are **canceled**, **forgiven**, or **discharged**, such as through relief in bankruptcy, the amount forgiven is **taxable** to the debtor. However, there are certain debts that are not taxable when forgiven:

- When the debt is forgiven out of generosity as a gift or as a bequest or inheritance
- Certain student loans in qualifying forgiveness programs or due to student's death or total and permanent disability
- Debt that is canceled in a Title 11 bankruptcy case
- Debt that is canceled when the debtor is insolvent
- Qualified real property business indebtedness
- Qualified principal residence indebtedness (through 2025)
    - To qualify, the discharged loan must be secured by the principal residence and must have been incurred to purchase, build, or substantially improve the residence
    - The exclusion limit is $750,000 ($375,000 MFS)
- Forgiveness of debt for certain paycheck protection program (PPP) loans
    - To be eligible for loan forgiveness, the loan must have been used for eligible costs (ie, payroll, rent, utilities, personal protective equipment)

A client has assets consisting of cash and marketable securities with a basis of $250,000 and a fair market value of $155,000. The client has liabilities of $175,000, which include $130,000 of nondischargeable liabilities under the Bankruptcy Code.

For federal tax purposes, a debtor is insolvent if, immediately prior to discharge, the amount of the debtor's liabilities exceeds the FMV of the debtor's assets. All the debtor's assets and liabilities are included in the determination, even if they are not included in other legal situations (eg, bankruptcy). In contrast, a debtor is solvent if the FMV of assets held exceeds liabilities.

In this scenario, the client (ie, debtor) owes $175,000 of liabilities and holds assets with FMVs totaling $155,000. Because the client's liabilities exceed the FMV of assets, the client is insolvent by **$20,000** ($175,000 − $155,000).

The **amount allowed to be excluded** by an insolvent taxpayer is **limited to the amount of the insolvency.**

Child Support and Property Settlements

Payments for **child support** are **not taxable** to the one receiving the payments and are **not deductible** by the one making the payments. Property settlements to a former spouse under a divorce decree are not a taxable event. The basis in the property transfers to the transferee (carryover basis and holding period).

TCJA repealed the deduction of alimony (and the corresponding inclusion in income for the payee) for divorces/separations executed after 2018.

Jack and Diane divorced in the current year, and the court awarded Jack custody of their two children. The divorce decree requires Diane to give the following to Jack:

- Alimony of $1,800 per month until the earlier of 15 years, Jack's remarriage, or Jack's death
- Child support of $1,200 per month for each child until the earlier of the child's 18th birthday or the child's death
- Title to their residence, which has a fair market value of $360,000 and adjusted basis of $240,000

What are the tax consequences of these transactions for Jack and for Diane?

Jack has no income from receiving these items, and Diane does not receive a deduction. Because the divorce occurred *after 2018*, the alimony does not qualify as income for Jack or a deduction for Diane. The child support also has no tax consequences to either Diane or Jack. Jack's basis in the residence will be $240,000 (ie, carryover basis).

Gains on Sale of Principal Residence

Tax laws favor home ownership. One provision that encourages taxpayers to purchase a home as a primary residence is the provision that allows for the exclusion of gain when the house is sold. Taxpayers meeting certain ownership and use requirements may permanently exclude up to $250,000 ($500,000 MFJ) of the realized gain on the sale of their principal residence if the following requirements are met.

1. Homeowners have owned and used the residence for at least two of the last five years from the date of sale (the time need not be continuous; each test must total at least 730 days during the previous five years), and
2. Have not used the exclusion within the last two years.

Requirements for Exclusion of Gain on Sale of Residence

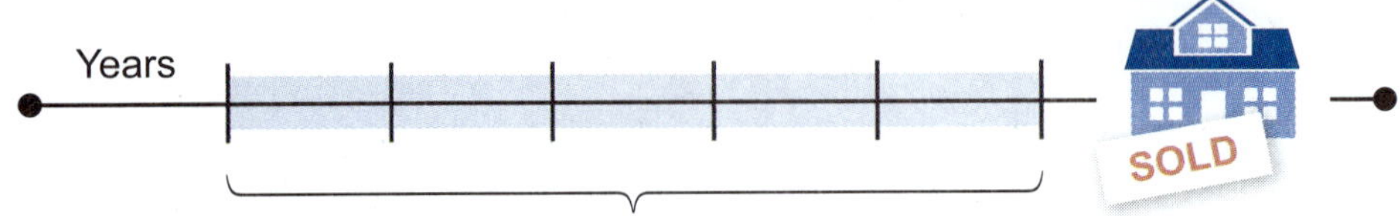

Owned and **used** property as residence for at least any **two years** during **five-year** period ending with date of sale*

**Exclusion cannot have been used within two years of the sale.*

Exceptions: If a taxpayer does not meet the two-year requirement because the taxpayer is forced to sell due to special circumstances, a **pro rata amount of the exclusion applies** based on the two-year requirement (ie, 24 months). The special circumstances include:

- Changes in place of employment (distance to new job must be > 50 miles from old residence)
- Health issues to obtain specialized care (not general well-being recommended by a physician)
- Other unforeseen circumstances (eg, involuntary conversion, war, casualty loss of residence, divorce, legal separation, death, birth of another child)

Partial Exclusion of Gain on Sale of Residence

$$\text{Excluded gain} = \$250{,}000 \times \frac{\text{\# of qualifying months}}{\text{24 months}}$$

$500,000 if married filing jointly

The computation for determining the amount, if any, of the recognized gain from the sale of personal residence is shown below:

Reported Gain from Sale of Personal Residence Eligible for Exclusion	
Sales price (less selling expenses)	$ XXX
Less adjusted basis (purchase price + capital improvements)	(XXX)
Realized gain	$ XXX
Less statutory exclusion ($500,000 if filing jointly)	(250,000)
Recognized gain reported on tax return but not below $0	$ XXX

Nonqualified Use of Personal Residence: The exclusion of gain does *not* apply to periods of **nonqualified use**. Nonqualified use generally includes any use other than as a principal residence (eg, rental).

- When this occurs, a pro rata amount of the *realized* gain is *recognized* (ie, taxable). The recognized amount is based on the ratio of the length of nonqualified use to the total time of ownership. Any **remaining** realized gain is *eligible* for the exclusion
- For example, if the remaining balance of realized gain is less than or equal to the exclusion, none of the remaining gain is recognized
- If a personal residence was used as rental property, the depreciation taken (or that could have been taken) affects the amount and characterization of part of the gain

Recognized Gain on Sale of Residence Allocated to Nonqualified Use

Net sales price	
Less adjusted basis (purchase price)	
Realized gain	
× Nonqualified use %	Number of nonqualifying years / Total years owned
Recognized gain	

A taxpayer purchased a house for $300,000 to be used as a personal residence. After living in the house for three years, the taxpayer rented the house for two years. At the end of the rental period, the taxpayer moved back in and lived in the house for an additional one year. The house then sold for $525,000. What amount of gain, if any, will the taxpayer recognize for federal tax purposes? What amount is excluded?

The taxpayer qualifies for the exclusion because they used the property as a residence for two of the last five years. However, during the six-year ownership period, two years were nonqualified use (rental). Therefore, **1/3 (two years out of six years)** of the realized gain is **recognized** before the application of the exclusion.

Sales price	$ 525,000
Less purchase price	(300,000)
Realized gain	$ 225,000
Nonqualified use allocation	× 1/3
Recognized gain	**$ 75,000**
Balance of realized gain ($225,000 − $75,000)	$ 150,000
Less **exclusion** (not to exceed $250,000)	**(150,000)**
Balance of gain recognized	$ 0

The taxpayer must **recognize** a gain of **$75,000** as a result of the nonqualified use of the residence. However, the remaining realized gain of $150,000 is less than the exclusion. Therefore, the balance of **$150,000** is **not** recognized.

Federal and State Tax Refunds

Federal income tax refunds are **not taxable**. **State income tax refunds** are **only taxable** in excess of the amount deducted as an **itemized deduction** in an earlier year, assuming the itemized deductions included a deduction for state and local income taxes. If the taxpayer chose to deduct sales tax instead of the state and local income taxes, no part of the refund is taxable. If a taxpayer used the standard deduction and did not itemize, state income tax refunds are not includable in income (tax benefit rule). In other words, if no benefit was derived from deducting the expenditure, no income needs to be included.

Tax Benefit Rule for State Tax Refunds

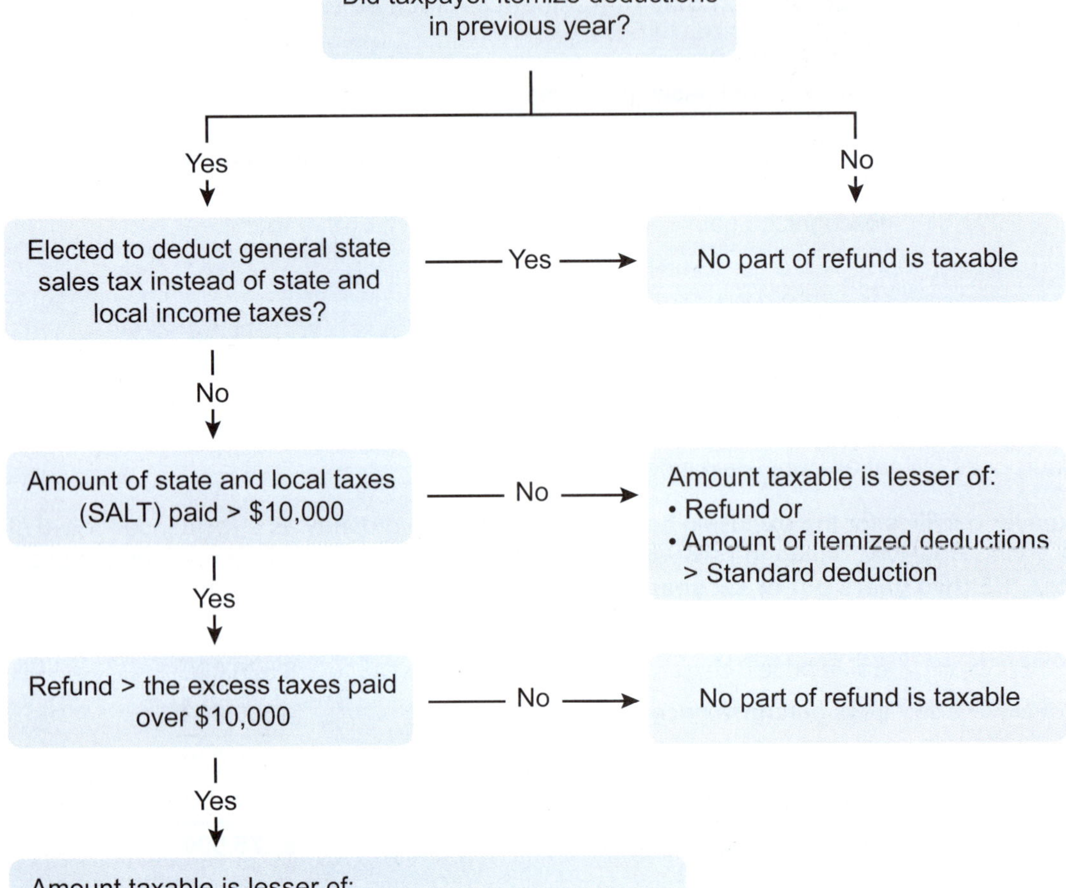

Baxter was able to itemize his deductions on last year's tax return. He deducted $2,300 in state income taxes paid. This year, Baxter received a refund for a state tax overpayment of $250. Does Baxter have to include the $250 in income this year?

Yes, Baxter must recognize the $250 in income, provided that the itemized deductions are at least $250 more than the standard deduction for Baxter's prior-year tax return. Under the tax benefit rule, if a taxpayer receives the benefit of a deduction in a previous year and then is reimbursed in a later year for all or a portion of that expense, it must be reported as income, but not to exceed the amount of the original deduction.

Gross Income Reported for a Decedent

Representative Task (Application): Calculate the income reported in the year of death for a decedent on Form 1040 – *U.S. Individual Income Tax Return.*

When a taxpayer dies, it is the responsibility of their **personal representative** or **surviving spouse** to file a **final income tax return** (Form 1040 or 1040-SR) on behalf of the deceased. In general, the final return is prepared and filed for a deceased person the same way it would be if the person were still alive. Certain unique filing and reporting rules must be followed, but generally, the final return includes all income, deductions, and eligible credits **up to the date of death**.

A **personal representative** of an estate is an executor, administrator, or anyone who is in charge of the decedent's property.

- Generally, an *executor* is named in a decedent's will to administer the estate and distribute properties as the decedent has directed
- An *administrator* is usually appointed by the court if no will exists, if no executor was named in the will, or if the named executor can't or won't serve

In general, an executor and an administrator perform the same duties and have the same responsibilities. One of the duties is to file the final income tax return in the year of death, if required, and any returns not filed for preceding years.

Filing Requirements

A decedent's **tax year ends** on the **date of death**; however, the due date of the final Form 1040 remains the same (typically April 15 of the following year). A final return is required if:

- Gross income from the beginning of the year through the date of death exceeds the filing thresholds for the decedent's filing status and age determined on the date of death
- The decedent meets any other filing requirements for individuals (such as having SE income)

If tax was withheld or if estimated tax was paid, even if a return isn't otherwise required to be filed, a return can be filed to claim a refund. The decedent may also be entitled to other credits that result in a refund.

Form 1310: Statement of Person Claiming Refund Due a Deceased Taxpayer must be filed to claim the refund unless:

- The surviving spouse is filing an original or amended joint return with the decedent
- The representative is filing the decedent's original return, and a copy of the court certificate showing the appointment is attached to the return

Filing a Final Return for a Deceased Spouse

When a spouse dies during the year, the **remaining spouse** is **considered married** for the **entire year** for federal income tax purposes, provided the remaining spouse doesn't remarry that year. A joint return can be filed for the year the spouse died but is not required. The return would show the decedent spouse's income before death and would show the remaining spouse's income for the entire year.

The qualifying surviving spouse filing status lets surviving spouses with dependents use the income tax brackets and standard deductions for joint filers for two years after a spouse's death when certain requirements are met.

Decedent's Method of Accounting

The method of accounting regularly used by the decedent before death also determines the includable income on the final return. **Cash-method** taxpayers only include items actually or constructively received through the date of death. If the decedent used an **accrual method**, only income items normally accrued before death are included on the final return.

Income in Respect of a Decedent

When reporting **income** of someone who has died, generally income is taxed in one of **three ways**:

- On the taxpayer's final 1040
- On the return of the beneficiary who receives the income
- On the estate's or trust's income tax return, if the estate or trust receives $600 of income or more

Income in respect of a decedent (IRD) refers to income the decedent had **earned** or had a **right to receive** during their **lifetime** that wasn't properly includable in their final income tax return (eg, rent, wages, dividends). IRD is excluded from the decedent's final income tax return and taxed to the taxpayer, typically the estate or the beneficiary, who actually or constructively collects the IRD. If taxed to an individual beneficiary, the income is reported as other income on Schedule 1 of Form 1040.

Johnson owned and operated an apple orchard and used the cash method of accounting. Johnson sold and delivered 1,000 bushels of apples to a canning factory for $2,000 but didn't receive payment before he died. The proceeds from the sale are *IRD*. Payment had not been made when the estate was settled, and the estate transferred the right to payment to Johnson's surviving spouse. When the surviving spouse collects the $2,000, that amount must be included in the surviving spouse's return. It isn't reported on Johnson's final return or the estate's return.

Assume the same facts as above, except that Johnson used the accrual method of accounting. The amount accrued from the sale of the apples would be included in Johnson's final return. Neither the estate nor the surviving spouse would realize IRD when the money is later paid.

Rashad, a cash-basis taxpayer, died during the current tax year on September 10. At the time of his death, he had earned but not received the following income:

- $3,800 of wages. His estate received the wages after his death
- $2,900 of rent that was due to him on rental property he owned. He bequeathed the rental property to his daughter, and she later received the $2,900
- $750 for dividends for which the record date was September 1. His son later received the dividends

How are these items taxed and to whom?

These items are all IRD. Rashad's estate will recognize the $3,800 in wages as ordinary income and pay taxes on it when filing the income tax return. The $2,900 is taxed as rental income to his daughter, who owned the property at the time the payment was made. The $750 is taxed as dividend income to his son because the record date was before the date of death.

Income Inclusions

Interest and Dividend Income

The final 1040 return reports **dividends** and **interest** earned by the decedent prior to their death. Any interest and dividends earned after the date of the decedent's death and paid to the estate or other recipient must be included on their returns.

Interest from U.S. savings bonds can be treated by the personal representative in three ways:

- Report all interest earned before death on the final Form 1040. If not reported, the interest is IRD and is not included in the final return
- Report interest earned prior to death on the estate's income tax return (Form 1041)
- If the personal representative does nothing, the taxpayer who cashes in the savings bonds must report the interest income (the estate, a beneficiary, or an assignee)

Partnership Income

The death of a partner closes the partnership's tax year for that partner, but it generally does not close the partnership's tax year for the remaining partners. The decedent's **distributive share** of **partnership items** must be figured as if the **partnership's tax year ended** on the **date** the **partner died**. To avoid an interim closing of the partnership books, the partners can agree to estimate the decedent's distributive share by prorating the amounts the partner would have included for the entire partnership tax year.

On the decedent's final return, include the decedent's distributive share of partnership items for the following periods:

- The partnership's tax year that ended within or with the decedent's final tax year (the year ending on the date of death)
- The period, if any, from the end of the partnership's tax year above to the decedent's date of death

Smith was a partner in XYZ partnership and reported their income on a tax year ending December 31. The partnership uses a tax year ending June 30. Smith died August 31, Year 2, and the estate established its tax year through August 31.

The distributive share of partnership items based on the decedent's partnership interest is reported as follows:

- **Final 1040 Return for the Decedent:** January 1 through August 31, Year 2, includes XYZ partnership items from the partnership tax year ending June 30, Year 2; and the partnership tax year beginning July 1, Year 2, and ending August 31, Year 2 (the date of death)
- **Income Tax Return of the Estate:** September 1, Year 2, through August 31, Year 3, includes XYZ partnership items for the period September 1, Year 2, through June 30, Year 3

S Corporation Income

If the decedent was a shareholder in an S corporation, the decedent's share of the S corporation's items of income, loss, deduction, and credits is included on the returns for the following periods:

- The corporation's tax year that ended within or with the decedent's final tax year (the year ending on the date of death)
- The period, if any, from the end of the corporation's tax year above through the decedent's date of death

Pass-through items are generally **allocated** to shareholders on a **per-share**, **per-day basis**. This general rule applies to the year a shareholder dies. However, the corporation can elect to close its books and use specific accounting to allocate income to the period through the date of death. If the election is made, shareholders affected by the stock transfer must consent. The executor or administrator of the decedent shareholder's estate consents to the election on behalf of a deceased shareholder.

Self-Employment Income

The decedent's final Form 1040 will include self-employment (SE) income actually or constructively received through the date of death. If the decedent was a general partner, then the decedent's SE income includes their share of the partnership's net business income or loss through the end of the month in which the death occurred. In this scenario, the partnership's income or loss is determined to be earned ratably over the partnership's tax year.

Deductions

Generally, the rules for deductions allowed to an individual also apply to the decedent's final income tax return. The final return will show deductible items the decedent paid (or accrued if an accrual-method decedent) before death.

Standard Deduction

If the taxpayer does not itemize deductions and takes the standard deduction, the **full amount** of the appropriate **standard deduction** is allowed regardless of when the death occurred.

Medical Expenses

Medical expenses paid before death by the decedent are deductible, subject to limits, on the final income tax return if deductions are itemized. This includes expenses for the decedent, as well as for the decedent's spouse and dependents. Medical expenses not paid before death are liabilities of the estate and are shown on the federal estate tax return.

- An **exception** exists for medical costs paid by the decedent's estate within one year of the day following death, which can be deducted either on Schedule A of the decedent's final Form 1040 or on the estate tax return Form 706 but not both

Deductions for Losses

Net operating losses from a prior year and any **capital losses** (including capital loss carryovers) **allocable** to the decedent cannot be carried over and used by the decedent's estate, nor can they be carried over and used in future tax years by a surviving spouse. These losses can only be deducted on the decedent's final income tax return. Any unused losses are forfeited.

A decedent's suspended **passive activity losses** are allowed on the final income tax return, subject to certain limitations. The amount of suspended loss is reduced by the step-up in the basis for the related asset to fair market value.

Danny owns a rental property. The building has a FMV of $650,000, an adjusted basis of $600,000, and suspended passive losses of $80,000. Danny does not have any other passive income.

If Danny dies during the year, the deductible suspended passive loss is limited to $30,000 [$80,000 suspended loss – ($650,000 FMV – $600,000 basis)]. Danny's representative can deduct the $30,000 on the final 1040 return.

The remaining $50,000 of passive loss is permanently lost as a deduction, but the beneficiary who received the building has a stepped-up basis of $650,000.

Credits

On the final income tax return, most tax credits that applied to the decedent before death can be claimed. Some of these credits are:

- Earned income credit
- Credit for the elderly or the disabled
- Child tax credit
- Adoption credit
- General business tax credit

Joe and Maria Pavone are 58-year-old, cash-basis taxpayers who file jointly. Joe is a factory foreman, and Maria is a part-time seamstress in a bridal shop. On October 1 of Year 1, Joe died in an auto accident. Virginia was named as the executrix in the will, and she agreed to file a joint return for Joe and Maria for Year 1.

The Pavones received the following in Year 1:

Item	Joe (Prior to Death)	Maria
Earned income	$90,000	$30,000
Savings account interest		300
Interest earned on municipal bonds	150	
Jury duty pay	200	
Life insurance proceeds		50,000
Share of net business income from Rose Partnership	5,000	

- Maria was the beneficiary of the life insurance policy on her husband's life. She received a lump-sum distribution. The Pavones had paid $5,000 in premiums
- Joe was a minority partner in Rose Partnership
- Maria received Joe's accrued vacation pay of $500 in Year 2

Determine the amount, if any, that is taxable and should be included in *Gross Income* on the Year 1 joint federal income tax return filed by Maria Pavone.

The decedent's income includable on the final return is generally determined as if the person were still alive but only includes income up to the date of death. The total of both Joe's and Maria's combined earned income of **$120,000** ($90,000 + $30,000) is reported on the final return.

The **$300 interest earned** on the **savings account** is fully **taxable**. Municipal bond interest is specifically **excluded** by law.

The **$200 jury duty pay** is considered earned income and is fully **taxable**.

Life insurance proceeds paid in a lump sum are generally **excluded** from gross income, unless purchased from a person other than the insurance company (eg, as an investment).

The **$5,000** reported from the **partnership's K-1** attributable to Joe is fully **taxable**. All income the decedent would have received had death not occurred that was not properly includable on the final return is IRD. Since Maria ultimately received the vacation pay, she is required to *report* the *income* in the year she receives it (ie, Year 2).

Earned income	$120,000
Savings account interest	300
Jury duty pay	200
Income from Rose Partnership	5,000
Total	**$125,500**

Analysis of Reportable Gross Income

Representative Task (Analysis): Review Form 1040 – U.S. Individual Income Tax Return and supporting documentation, including any source data used to create the return, to determine the completeness and accuracy of the gross income reported.

Considerations When Determining Gross Income	
Read through the Narrative	• Is taxpayer single or married? • Does taxpayer have dependents? • Can filing status be determined? • Are ages given for relevant players? • What tax year is pertinent? • What income items are presented? • What income exclusions are presented? • Is there any information that is unnecessary?
Examine the Source Documents	• What source documents are included? • Do the source documents support what is already known or help to clarify what is already known from the narrative? • Can the dollar amounts be traced to the information given to confirm no consistency errors exist? • Do amounts appear to be on the correct lines if tax forms are included?
Determine Sequence for Completing the Problem	• Develop an order for how to solve the problem ○ Top of the narrative to bottom ○ Top of the tax form to bottom ○ Review each source document and trace relevant info to tax return

Practice Analysis Scenario

Bailey Cream, age 32, is a widow who lives at 2811 Berry Street, in Loveland, CO, 80528. Her Social Security number is 123-45-6789. Bailey works for Crazy 8 Pilates as the club manager.

Crazy 8 offers several fringe benefits to its employees, such as being able to participate in group classes if space is available. Regular members pay $120 a month, and Bailey loves that she's able to attend two classes every week for free. Bailey also receives discounts on merchandise and gym equipment sold in the club's retail outlet.

This year, Bailey purchased a Pilates reformer machine for her home gym for $1,800. Bailey saved $300 since the machine retails for $2,100 (cost of $1,700 to Crazy 8). Crazy 8 Pilates' average gross profit percentage is 15%. Bailey also participates in Crazy 8's traditional 401(k) plan. A form W-2 reporting her Year 3 earnings and withholdings is provided.

Late in Year 2, Bailey and her husband, Frank, were in an auto accident. Bailey broke her left arm and hip, and the injuries to her husband were fatal. She was unable to work for a month and collected $3,000 from her disability insurance in Year 2. Bailey sued the driver and this year finally received a settlement. An email from her attorney is included detailing the lawsuit.

As the beneficiary of Frank's life insurance policy, Bailey received a $150,000 lump-sum distribution in Year 3. She also received a check for $1,500 from Frank's employer for vacation pay that he had accrued prior to his death but was not included on their tax return the year Frank died.

Unfortunately, Bailey struggled to pay bills because her medical insurance did not cover her physical therapy and Frank's funeral costs were expensive. Bailey has been able to work out a payment plan, which includes Loveland Rehab canceling $800 of the amount she owed it. As a result, Bailey has received a Form 1099-C from the rehab center.

The grocery store where Bailey shops also sells lottery tickets. Bailey likes to occasionally take a risk and will sometimes buy a ticket. In January of Year 3, she purchased a lottery ticket and won $5,000. She's kept a shoe box of other lottery tickets that were losers, totaling $400.

Bailey decided to invest the life insurance proceeds and windfall from the lottery ticket in several different investments. She received the following additional income:

- Interest of $260 from a mutual fund that invests in tax-free government obligations
- Interest income of $785 on U.S. Treasury bonds
- Interest of $50 associated with an amended federal income tax refund of $1,300 from Year 1
- Form K-1 for her investment as a 10% shareholder in Clean Air Corporation, a Subchapter S corporation

Bailey partially completed her own Form 1040, page 1, and Schedule 1 for Year 3. Review her tax forms for accuracy and completeness and provide corrected Excel spreadsheets for Schedule 1 and Form 1040, page 1. Bailey always takes the standard deduction.

Part 1: Bailey Cream—Form 1040, Schedule 1

The following is an abbreviated list of line items from **Form 1040, Schedule 1**. Based upon your analysis and computations of the narrative and exhibits given, enter the appropriate amounts as would appear on Form 1040, Schedule 1. Enter all values as positive whole numbers, except losses (if any), which should be entered using a minus sign. If no value is required, enter a zero (0) in lieu of leaving a cell blank.

Line Item	Description	Amount
Line 1	Taxable refunds, credits, or offsets of state and local income taxes	
Line 5	Rental real estate, royalties, partnerships, S corporations, trust, etc.	
Line 8b	Gambling income	
Line 8c	Cancellation of debt	
Line 8i	Prizes and awards	
Line 8z	Other income: type	
Line 8z	Other income: type	
Line 9	Other income, Add lines 8a through 8z	
Line 10	Additional Income, Add lines 1 through 9	

Part 2: Bailey Cream—Form 1040, Page 1

Shown below is an abbreviated list of line items from **Form 1040, page 1**. Based upon your analysis and computations of the narrative and exhibits given, enter the appropriate amounts as would appear on Form 1040, page 1. Enter all values as positive whole numbers, except losses (if any), which should be entered using a minus sign. If no value is required, enter a zero (0) in lieu of leaving a cell blank.

Line Item	Description	Amount
Line 1a	Total amount from Form(s) W-2	
Line 1h	Other earned income	
Line 2a	Tax-exempt interest	
Line 2b	Taxable interest	
Line 8	Other income from Schedule 1, line 10	
Line 9	Total income (Add lines 1a, 1h, 2b, and 8)	

Exhibits

Exhibit: Schedule 1 Additional Income and Adjustments Entries

Line 1: Taxable refunds, credits, or offsets of state and local income taxes		1,300
Line 5: Rental real estate, royalties, partnerships, trusts, etc.		4,040
Line 8b: Gambling	4,600	
Line 8c: Cancellation of debt	800	
Line 8z: Other income, court settlement for damages from accident	60,000	
Line 9: Total other income		65,400
Line 10: Combine lines 1 through 7 and 9 (total additional income)		70,740

Exhibit: Form 1040, Page 1, Entries

Line 1: Total amount from Form(s) W-2, box 1	58,000
Lina 2a: Tax-exempt interest	0
Line 2b: Taxable interest	835
Line 3a: Qualified dividends	0
Line 3b: Ordinary dividends	260
Line 7: Capital gain or (loss)	0
Line 8: Other income from Schedule 1, line 10	70,740
Line 9: Total income	129,835

22222	a Employee's social security number 123-45-6789	OMB No. 1545-0008	
b Employer identification number (EIN) 36-1652478		1 Wages, tips, other compensation 52,200	2 Federal income tax withheld 6,264
c Employer's name, address, and ZIP code Crazy 8 Pilates 100 Stretch Drive Loveland CO 80528		3 Social security wages 58,000	4 Social security tax withheld 3,596
		5 Medicare wages and tips 58,000	6 Medicare tax withheld 841
		7 Social security tips	8 Allocated tips
d Control number		9	10 Dependent care benefits
e Employee's first name and initial / Last name / Suff. Bailey Cream 2811 Berry Street Loveland CO 80528		11 Nonqualified plans	12a D 5,800
		13 Statutory employee ☐ Retirement plan ☑ Third-party sick pay ☐	12b
		14 Other	12c
f Employee's address and ZIP code			12d

15 State Employer's state ID number	16 State wages, tips, etc.	17 State income tax	18 Local wages, tips, etc.	19 Local income tax	20 Locality name
CO 19731421	52,200	2,610			

Form **W-2** **Wage and Tax Statement** Year 3 Department of Treasury—Internal Revenue Service

Email to Bailey Cream

To: BCream496@gmail.com

From: TTaltalker@Edmonds-law.com

Subject: Settlement of lawsuit

Mrs. Cream,

The Court has given notice that the final settlement of your legal action has been completed. A judgment was entered in your favor for the following:

$5,000 for medical expenses

$5,000 for emotional pain and suffering related to injuries sustained in the auto accident

$50,000 in punitive damages

Enclosed is a check in the amount of $60,000 as full and complete compensation for all damages suffered. Feel free to call me should you wish to discuss this matter further.

Sincerely,

Tom Taltaker, Esquire

Exhibit: K-1 from S Corp, Clean Air Corporation

Shareholder's Share of Current-Year Income Deductions, Credits, and Other Items	
Line 1: Ordinary business income (loss)	4,400

Information about shareholder	
Current-year allocation percentage	10%
Shareholder's number of shares: beginning of year	100
Shareholder's number of shares: end of year	100
Loans from shareholder: beginning of year	0
Loans from shareholder: end of year	0

☐ CORRECTED (if checked)

CREDITOR'S name, street address, city or town, state or province, country, ZIP or foreign postal code, and telephone no. Loveland Rehab 100 Care Lane Loveland, CO 80528	1 Date of identifiable event 11/9/Yr 3 2 Amount of debt discharged $ 800 3 Interest, if included in box 2 $	OMB No. 1545-1424 Form 1099-C For calendar Year Year 3	**Cancellation of Debt**
CREDITOR'S TIN 64-5552233 / DEBTOR'S TIN 123-45-6789 DEBTOR'S name Bailey Cream Street address (including apt. no.) 2811 Berry Street City or town, state or province, country, and ZIP or foreign postal code Loveland, CO 80528	4 Debt description 5 If checked, the debtor was personally liable for repayment of the debt . . . . ☐		**Copy B For Debtor** This is important tax information and is being furnished to the IRS. If you are required to file a return, a negligence penalty or other sanction may be imposed on you if taxable income results from this transaction and the IRS determines that it has not been reported.
Account number (see instructions)	6 Identifiable event code	7 Fair market value of property $	

Form 1099-C (keep for your records) www.irs.gov/Form1099C Department of the Treasury—Internal Revenue Service

Steps for Completing the Task

- Categorize the data given into income that is either included or excluded from gross income; remember the all-inclusive approach (unless specifically excluded) to determine what income items are taxable and what items are excludable
- Look for items that require a computation to determine the amounts that are either includable or excludable based on tax law
- Remember that source documents and supporting information usually "flow" to supporting tax return schedules and ultimately pages 1 and 2 of the Form 1040
- Complete the spreadsheets for Form 1040 and Form 1040, Schedule 1

Gross Income Inclusions	Amount	Explanation
W-2 wages	$52,200	Although $58,000 was earned, $5,800 of pretax dollars was used to fund the taxpayer's 401(k) plan. Therefore, taxable wages are reduced by the contributions and reported at $52,200.
Punitive damages from accident	50,000	Damages meant to punish the wrongdoer are taxable.
Income in respect of a decedent—accrued vacation pay	1,500	IRD is taxable to the beneficiary who inherits the income. IRD is untaxed income that a decedent earned or had a right to receive during their lifetime.
Cancellation of debt	800	The debt forgiveness was part of a payment plan. It was not made out of generosity, bankruptcy, or insolvency. Therefore, the exclusion exceptions do not apply, and the amount is taxable.
Gambling winnings	5,000	Gambling income is taxable, and gambling losses and expenses, if deductible, do not reduce gambling income but may be deductible on Schedule A.
Interest income	785	Interest on U.S. Treasury bonds is taxable.
Interest from federal tax refund	50	Interest is taxable in year received.
K-1 income from Clean Air Corporation	4,400	Income from a K-1 from an S corporation flows through and is taxed to the shareholder.
Total	**$114,735**	

Gross Income Exclusions	Amount	Explanation
401(k) deferrals	$5,800	Contributions (from W-2) deferred for income tax purposes until withdrawn.
Pilates club membership	1,440	No additional cost fringe benefit because it is at the employer's place of business and not another gym location.
Employee discount	300*	Discount does not exceed gross profit percentage.
Disability insurance	3,000	Paid in prior year, not in Year 3; in addition, assuming the taxpayer paid the policy premiums, the proceeds would not be taxable.
Compensatory damages from accident	10,000	Damages on account of a physical injury are nontaxable (eg, $5,000 for medical expenses and $5,000 for emotional pain and suffering related to injuries).
Life insurance proceeds	150,000	Lump-sum distributions are excluded from income.
Interest	260	Interest from mutual funds retains the character of the income to the fund; tax-free government obligations are nontaxable.
Federal income tax refund from prior years	1,300	Federal income taxes are not deductible, and refunds are not taxable.
Total	**$172,100**	

**Computation of employee discount*: *Bailey's discount on the Pilates reformer is $300 ($2,100 retail price − $1,800 Bailey paid). Her discount percentage of 14.29% ($300/$2,100) is less than Crazy 8 Pilates' gross profit percentage of 15%. Thus, the discounted purchase from Bailey's employer does not result in taxable income.*

Solution

The tables from Part 1 and Part 2 are provided below.

Line Item	Description	Amount
Line 1	Taxable refunds, credits, or offsets of state and local income taxes	0
Line 5	Rental real estate, royalties, partnerships, S corporations, trust, etc.	4,400
Line 8b	Gambling income	5,000
Line 8c	Cancellation of debt	800
Line 8z	Other income, punitive damages and IRD	51,500
Line 9	Total other income, Add Lines 8a Through 8z	57,300
Line 10	Combine lines 1 through 9 (total additional income)	61,700

Part 1: Schedule 1

- **Schedule 1, line 1:** The refund was from a prior federal income tax return and is therefore not taxable. However, the interest received is reportable by Bailey. The IRS generally pays interest on refunds delayed by more than 45 days after the filing deadline, all of which is taxable
- **Schedule 1, line 5:** Two numerals in this number were transposed on the Schedule 1 (ie, $4,040 instead of $4,400) prepared by Bailey. The correct amount from the K-1 source document is $4,400
- **Schedule 1, line 8b:** Gambling income is taxable and is not netted against gambling losses on Schedule 1. The entire $5,000 is included in income, while the $400 of gambling losses can be deducted on Schedule A if Bailey itemizes her deductions
- **Schedule 1, line 8c:** The cancellation of debt was correctly reported as $800
- **Schedule 1, line 8z:** Bailey had two types of income reportable as other income. Bailey incorrectly included the entire amount of her settlement from her accident as income. Of the damages, only $50,000 of punitive damages is taxable compared to the $60,000 that she reported. In addition, the accrued vacation pay that Bailey received this year of $1,500 is taxable IRD. This amount is also shown as other income, for a total of $51,500
- **Schedule 1, line 9:** After adjusting for errors and omissions, the total other income amount for line 8 items is $57,300
- **Schedule 1, line 10:** The total amount of additional income reported on Schedule 1 and carried over to Form 1040 is $61,700

Part 2: Form 1040

Line Item	Description	Amount
Line 1a	Total amount from Form(s) W-2, box 1	52,200
Line 1h	Other earned income	0
Line 2a	Tax-exempt interest	260
Line 2b	Taxable interest	835
Line 8	Other income from Schedule 1, line 10	61,700
Line 9	Total income (Add lines 1a, 1h, 2b, and 8)	114,735

- **Form 1040, line 1a:** Contributions to a traditional 401(k) plan are made pretax, meaning they reduce taxable income currently and are taxed when withdrawn. Bailey reported her wages at the $58,000 gross amount, not taking into consideration the $5,800 deferred (see W-2 form)
- **Form 1040, line 2a:** Interest from mutual funds retains the character of the income to the fund; tax-free government obligations are nontaxable, and Bailey erroneously reported the $260 dividends as ordinary
- **Form 1040, line 2b:** Bailey correctly reported taxable interest of $835, which consists of $785 interest from the Treasury bond and $50 income tax refund
- **Form 1040, line 8:** The corrected amount of other income of $61,700 from Schedule 1 flows forward to the 1040
- **Form 1040, line 9:** Adding the amounts from line 1z through 8 totals the correct total income of $114,735

Discrepancies Identified by Automated Diagnostic and Validation Checks

Representative Task (Analysis): Review and resolve discrepancies identified by automated diagnostic and validation checks to ensure the completeness and accuracy of the gross income reported on Form 1040 – U.S. Individual Income Tax Return based on the source data used to prepare the form.

Automated Diagnostics and Validation Checks

Accounting firms use various types of **automated software** to prepare tax returns for their clients. While each type of software is different and nuanced, the general setup involves a back-end data entry and **informational center**, frequently called the **organizer**. The organizer can be used to find relevant forms that are needed to complete the tax return, record estimated tax payments, import source documents for income, and complete tax reconciliations, among other tasks.

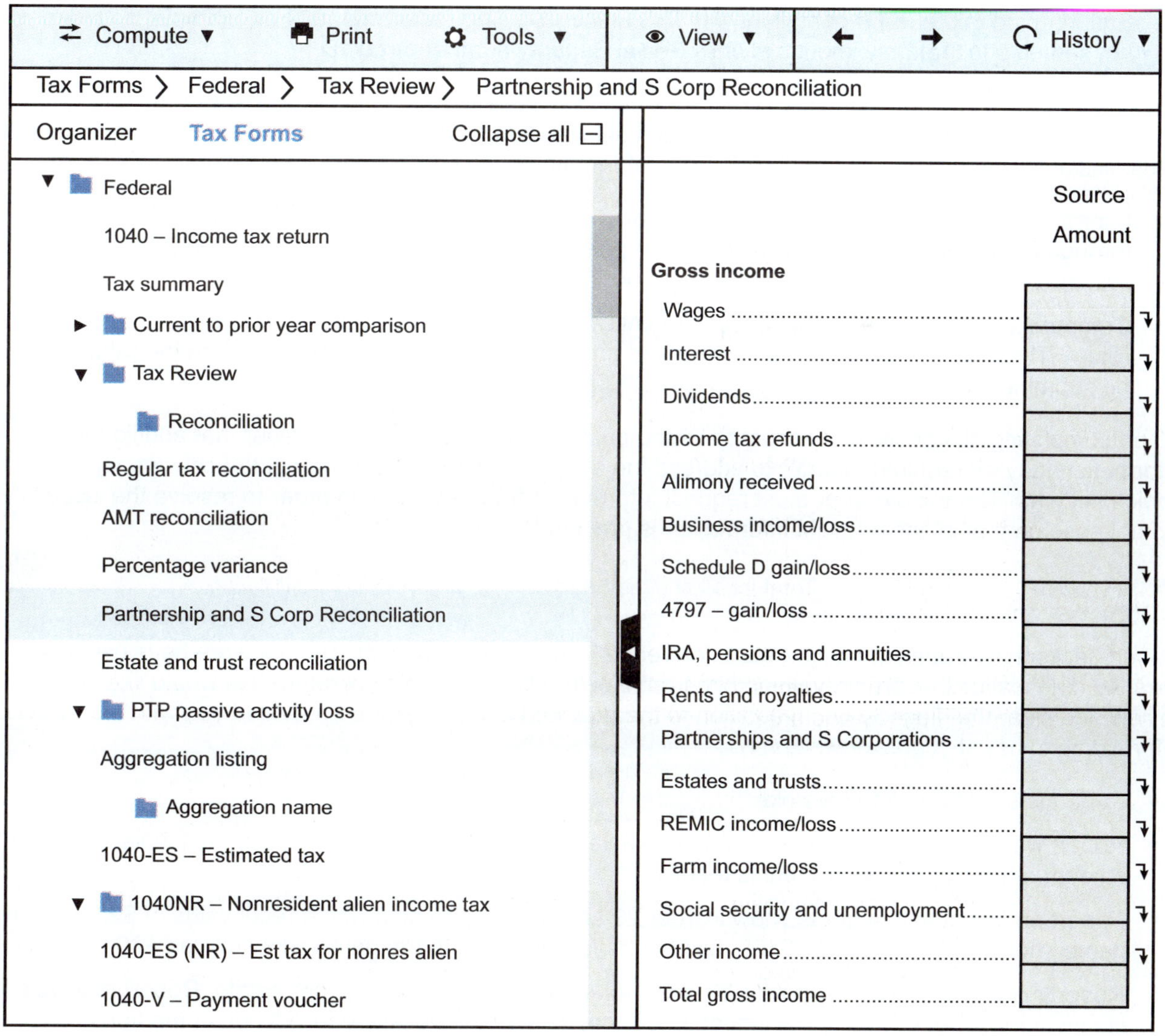

Compute ▼ Print Tools ▼ | View ▼ | ← → History ▼

Tax Forms > Federal > Tax Review > Partnership and S Corp Reconciliation

Organizer **Tax Forms** Collapse all ⊟

- ▼ Federal
  - 1040 – Income tax return
  - Tax summary
  - ► Current to prior year comparison
  - ▼ Tax Review
    - Reconciliation
  - Regular tax reconciliation
  - AMT reconciliation
  - Percentage variance
  - Partnership and S Corp Reconciliation
  - Estate and trust reconciliation
  - ▼ PTP passive activity loss
  - Aggregation listing
    - Aggregation name
  - 1040-ES – Estimated tax
  - ▼ 1040NR – Nonresident alien income tax
  - 1040-ES (NR) – Est tax for nonres alien
  - 1040-V – Payment voucher

Gross income	Source Amount
Wages	
Interest	
Dividends	
Income tax refunds	
Alimony received	
Business income/loss	
Schedule D gain/loss	
4797 – gain/loss	
IRA, pensions and annuities	
Rents and royalties	
Partnerships and S Corporations	
Estates and trusts	
REMIC income/loss	
Farm income/loss	
Social security and unemployment	
Other income	
Total gross income	

For example, assume a tax preparer receives three 1099-INTs from different bank accounts from their client. The preparer can input or import the 1099s into the software, and a schedule showing all three with a total of taxable interest is presented in the organizer. When the preparer prints the return itself, only the total taxable interest will be displayed on page 1 of Form 1040.

A benefit of utilizing tax return software is that it can reduce the time preparers spend doing tasks (eg, manual data entry, phaseout calculations) that can be completed more efficiently using technology.

- For example, most tax software has the ability to import source documents like W-2s, 1099s, etc. that can be aggregated in the organizer before flowing to the applicable line item on the tax return
- This process is a lot faster than manually typing each line item from a source document. Although most effective tax software completes these types of tasks efficiently and accurately, preparers should still have checks in place that verify the amounts on the source document match what's being reported in the software

During the tax return preparation process, the software generates **diagnostics** for the tax preparer to check and clear before the tax return can be **filed electronically** to the IRS. These diagnostic checks are useful for several reasons, including:

- Improving the accuracy of the tax return being filed. For example, software can catch errors preparers might have missed, like business income not tying between Schedule 1 and Schedule C
- Ensuring the tax return is compliant with IRS electronic filing requirements. For example, software will not submit a tax return without a client's Social Security number or tax ID

Not all of the tax software diagnostics are the same. The actual names of the diagnostics themselves are different depending on the software used. In addition, the **diagnostics** can **vary** in type (eg, related to e-file transmission or the return itself) or severity (eg, informational, computational, or severe).

- Informational diagnostics provide helpful reminders and data points that the preparer will want to read through during the review process. While the preparer will want to consider these diagnostics, they can still technically submit the tax return without addressing each one
- Computational and severe diagnostics are critical to successfully completing and transmitting the tax return. These diagnostics must be addressed and *cleared* by the tax preparer before the return can be submitted

When completing diagnostic and accuracy-based questions on the exam, remember that additional information may be required in order to address the diagnostic flagged. So, expect to occasionally see a choice such as "The tax preparer must request information from the client in order to resolve the issue." Do not assume that all the relevant information is provided.

Practice Scenario

Robert Jackson is preparing his tax return for Year 23, the current tax year. The software he is using is creating diagnostics that are preventing him from electronically filing his tax return. He would like you to review and clear the diagnostics. In addition to the attached exhibits, Robert provided you with the following information to assist your review.

- Robert is single and 24 years old
- Robert works part-time for Leland's Market while attending Northwest University on scholarship as a student-athlete on the men's tennis team
- Robert participated in a game show in Year 23 and won a television with a retail value of $2,200; his game show entrance fee was $100, and his travel expenses to the game show totaled $75
- Robert's aunt passed away in Year 23, and Robert was a beneficiary of her estate; Robert received life insurance proceeds and a diamond necklace; he sold the necklace for $3,000 immediately after receiving it

- Robert received confirmation from his credit card company of cancellation of debt on his credit card; his credit limit on the card was $5,000
- Last year, Robert filed a lawsuit for sexual discrimination; the case was settled in Year 23

The focus in this task-based simulation is on the calculation of gross income. The task is to determine which items are:

- Fully included in gross income
- Partially included in gross income (ie, limited amount)
- Excluded from gross income

Review the various exhibits, which consist of source documents and draft tax forms prepared by Robert. Then, address the software diagnostics by selecting the appropriate answer below from the drop-down menu provided. Select "no action required" if the return is already correct and the diagnostic can be ignored.

Considerations When Determining Gross Income	
Read through the Narrative	• Is the taxpayer single or married? • Does the taxpayer have dependents? • Can filing status be determined? • Are ages given for relevant players? • What tax year is pertinent? • What income items are presented? • What income exclusions are presented? • Is there any information that is unnecessary?
Examine the Source Documents	• What source documents are included? • Do the source documents support what is already known or help to clarify what is known from the narrative? • Can the dollar amounts be traced to the information given to confirm no consistency errors exist? • Do amounts appear to be on the correct lines if tax forms are included?
Determine Sequence for Completing the Problem	• Develop an order for how to solve the problem ○ Top of the narrative to bottom ○ Top of the tax form to bottom ○ Review each source document and trace relevant info to tax return

	Diagnostic/Validation Check	Options to Clear Diagnostic
1	*Severe:* Alimony received was entered on Schedule 1, page 1, but the year of divorce and payer's Social Security number are not provided. Check to determine if alimony received is includable in income.	Alimony income for this taxpayer is $0 Alimony income for this taxpayer is $300 Alimony income for this taxpayer is $3,600 No action required
2	*Severe:* Total unemployment compensation amount imported from Form 1099-G does not match amount reported on Form 1040, Schedule 1, line 7.	The correct amount of unemployment compensation is $300 The correct amount of unemployment compensation is $2,700 The correct amount of unemployment compensation is $3,000 No action required
3	*Informational:* An amount was entered in the previous year for qualified dividend income from John Deere, Inc.; no qualified dividends from this payer reported on the current-year tax return.	The correct amount of qualified dividend income is $0 The correct amount of qualified dividend income is $1,500 The correct amount of qualified dividend income is $3,300 No action required
4	*Severe:* Total wages amount imported from Form W-2 does not match amount reported on Form 1040, page 1, line 1.	The correct amount of wages is $0 The correct amount of wages is $29,975 The correct amount of wages is $36,400 No action required
5	*Informational:* Jury duty pay of $2,200 reported on Form 1040, Schedule 1, line 8h. Confirm Form 1099 or other verification received by taxpayer from applicable jurisdiction.	The correct amount of jury pay is $0 The correct amount of jury pay is $1,000 The correct amount of jury pay is $3,000 No action required
6	*Informational:* Verify the amount of scholarship income received by taxpayer that is includable in gross income. Amounts received in excess of qualified education expenses must be included.	The correct amount of includable scholarship income is $0 The correct amount of includable scholarship income is $16,800 The correct amount of includable scholarship income is $12,800 No action required

	Diagnostic/Validation Check	Options to Clear Diagnostic
7	*Informational:* Interest income reported on previous year's tax return for 1099-INT from Nashville State Bank; no interest from this payer reported on the current-year tax return.	The correct amount of includable interest income is $1,800 The correct amount of includable interest income is $2,200 The correct amount of includable interest income is $3,100 No action required
8	*Informational:* Other income of $52,800 reported on Form 1040, Schedule 1, line 8z. Confirm Form 1099 or other verification received by taxpayer to verify amount reported.	Other income equals $130,000, capital gain income equals $200 Other income equals $55,000, capital gain income equals $2,800 Other income equals $25,000, capital gain income equals $52,800 No action required
9	*Severe:* Form 1099-C imported but no cancellation of debt income reported on Schedule 1, page 1, line 8c.	The correct amount to include in income is $1,000 The correct amount to include in income is $3,100 The correct amount to include in income is $5,000 No action required

Exhibits: Draft Tax Return Entries

Exhibit: Form 1040, Page 1, Draft Tax Return Entries	
Line 1: Total amount from Form(s) W-2, box 1	32,760
Lina 2a: Tax-exempt interest	0
Line 2b: Taxable interest	0
Line 3a: Qualified dividends	0
Line 3b: Ordinary dividends	1,800
Line 7: Capital gain or (loss)	0
Line 8: Other income from Schedule 1, line 10	67,300
Line 9: Total income	101,860
Line 10: Adjustments to income	0
Line 11: Adjusted gross income	101,860

Exhibit: Schedule 1 Additional Income and Adjustments Entries

Line 2: Alimony received		4,800
Line 7: Unemployment compensation		2,700
Line 8h: Jury duty pay	2,200	
Line 8r: Scholarship and fellowship grants not on W-2	4,800	
Line 8z: Other income, life insurance proceeds, inherited necklace	52,800	
Line 9: Total other income		59,800
Line 10: Combine lines 1 through 7 and 9 (total additional income)		67,300

Exhibits: Source Documents

IN THE CIRCUIT COURT OF THE SEVENTH JUDICIAL CIRCUIT,
IN AND FOR KANE COUNTY, ILLINOIS

MARRIAGE SETTLEMENT AGREEMENT

Robert Jackson of 182 Golfview Drive, St. Charles, IL, born April 15, 1999, and Sarah Jackson of 330 Rex Road, Geneva, IL, born June 12, 2000, being sworn, do hereby verify that the following statements are true and correct and that except as otherwise specifically stated this Agreement serves as a full and final settlement of all matters arising from the dissolution of their marriage, including division of all property rights, debts, spousal support, child custody, and child support. The parties affirm that this Agreement contains a fair, just, and equitable division of property and, subject to Court approval, agree as follows:

1) MARRIAGE DATE: The parties were married to each other on May 05, 2018. The parties share one (1) minor child, Bobby Jackson, born on December 28, 2018. The parties are not currently expecting any children.

2) SEPARATION DATE: The parties' date of physical separation is August 17, 2021.

3) CAUSE OF DISSOLUTION: The parties acknowledge that the marriage has been irretrievably broken due to irreconcilable differences, and they are beyond reconciliation.

4) CHILD SUPPORT: The parties acknowledge that the issue of child support has been determined by the Kane County Judicial Court of Geneva, IL, under docket/case number 12345. Under this court order, Sarah Jackson is responsible for child support in the amount of $400 monthly. The court maintains continuing and exclusive jurisdiction over issues relating to the minor children of the marriage.

5) SPOUSAL SUPPORT/ALIMONY: Robert Jackson has a gross monthly income of $5,000 from all sources and total monthly expenses of $3,500. Sarah Jackson has a total monthly income of $10,000 per month from all sources and has the ability to pay spousal support. Sarah Jackson agrees to pay Robert Jackson spousal support of $300 per month until the ex-spouse remarries or dies.

22222	a Employee's social security number 123-45-6789	OMB No. 1545-0008	
b Employer identification number (EIN) 48-1236789		1 Wages, tips, other compensation 36,400	2 Federal income tax withheld 3,640
c Employer's name, address, and ZIP code Leland's Market 500 North Avenue St. Charles, IL 60174		3 Social security wages 36,400	4 Social security tax withheld 2,257
		5 Medicare wages and tips 36,400	6 Medicare tax withheld 528
		7 Social security tips	8 Allocated tips
d Control number		9	10 Dependent care benefits
e Employee's first name and initial / Last name / Suff. Robert Jackson 182 Golfview Drive St. Charles, IL 60174		11 Nonqualified plans	12a
		13 Statutory employee ☐ Retirement plan ☐ Third-party sick pay ☐	12b
		14 Other	12c
f Employee's address and ZIP code			12d

15 State	Employer's state ID number	16 State wages, tips, etc.	17 State income tax	18 Local wages, tips, etc.	19 Local income tax	20 Locality name
IL	12-456798	36,400	1,802			

Form **W-2** **Wage and Tax Statement** Year 23 Department of Treasury—Internal Revenue Service

Exhibit: Other Tax Forms Information

Form	Line	Payer	Amount
Form 1099-G Certain Government Payments	Line 1 Unemployment Compensation	Social Security Administration	3,000
Form 1099-G Certain Government Payments	Line 4 Federal Income Tax Withheld	Social Security Administration	300
Form 1099-DIV Dividends and Distributions	Lina 1a Total Ordinary Dividends	John Deere, Inc.	1,800
Form 1099-DIV Dividends and Distributions	Line 1b Qualified Dividends	John Deere, Inc.	1,500
Form 1099-MISC Miscellaneous Information	Line 3 Other Income	The Prize Is Right	2,200
Form 1098-T Tuition Statement	Line 1 Payments received for qualified tuition	Northwest University	12,000
Form 1098-T Tuition Statement	Line 5 Scholarships or grants	Northwest University	16,800
Form 1099-C Cancellation of Debt	Line 1 Date of identifiable event	ABC Credit Card Company	2/1/Year 23
Form 1099-C Cancellation of Debt	Line 2 Amount of debt discharged	ABC Credit Card Company	3,100

Davis and Associates
123 Lawyer Lane
Madison, WI 53707
608-447-4747
davisassoc@gmail.com

October 15, Yr 23

Mr. Robert Jackson
182 Golfview Drive
St. Charles, IL 60174

Dear Robert,

I am the attorney for you aunt, Mrs. Ethyl Jackson, who passed away on June 10, Yr 23. I am so sorry for your loss. Ethyl has named you in her will as a beneficiary of the following items:

1) Life insurance proceeds of $50,000
2) Diamond necklace (fair market value $2,800, basis $2,500)

Please consult your tax accountant regarding these items and how they might affect your Yr 23 tax return. If you have any questions regarding this matter, please do not hesitate to contact me.

Sincerely,

Jerome Davis

Davis and Associates
123 Lawyer Lane
Madison, WI 53707
608-447-4747
davisassoc@gmail.com

Mr. Robert Jackson
182 Golfview Drive
St. Charles, IL 60174

March 23, Yr 23

RE: Settlement of lawsuit

Dear Robert,

The court has given final notice that the final settlement of your legal action has been completed. A judgment has been entered in your favor for the following:

1) $75,000 award for sexual discrimination
2) $25,000 punitive damages
3) $30,000 for emotional distress

Enclosed is a check for $130,000 as full and complete consideration for all damages suffered.

Please consult your tax accountant regarding these items and how they might affect your Yr 23 tax return. If you have any questions regarding this matter, please do not hesitate to contact me.

Sincerely,

Jerome Davis

Solution

	Diagnostic/Validation Check	Options to Clear Diagnostic
1	*Severe:* Alimony received was entered on Schedule 1, page 1, but the year of divorce and payer's Social Security number are not provided. Check to determine if alimony received is includable in income.	**Alimony income for this taxpayer is $0** Alimony income for this taxpayer is $300 Alimony income for this taxpayer is $3,600 No action required

Alimony payments for divorces finalized before 2019 are deductible for the payer and includable in income for the recipient. For divorces finalized after 2018, the opposite is true. Child support payments are never includable in income by the recipient and never deductible by the payer.

This diagnostic is alerting the tax preparer that the $3,600 ($300 per month for 12 months) of alimony received from Robert's ex-spouse requires additional information, specifically the divorce year and spouse's Social Security number. Because Robert's divorce was finalized in Year 21 (ie, after 2018), he does not include his alimony received as income. The divorce year and amount of alimony received come from the *Marriage Settlement Agreement* exhibit.

The software will know whether the income must be included but only if the divorce year is provided. Additionally, the IRS requires the recipient spouse's Social Security number to be provided. Entering this information in the organizer would clear this diagnostic.

	Diagnostic/Validation Check	Options to Clear Diagnostic
2	*Severe:* Total unemployment compensation amount imported from form 1099-G does not match amount reported on Form 1040, Schedule 1, line 7.	The correct amount of unemployment compensation is $300 The correct amount of unemployment compensation is $2,700 **The correct amount of unemployment compensation is $3,000** No action required

This diagnostic is alerting the tax preparer that an amount reported on a tax form does not tie to a source document; in this case, Schedule 1 does not tie to the *1099-G Certain Government Payments* exhibit. Unemployment compensation is taxable income that must be reported on Schedule 1, page 1. The federal income tax withheld does not reduce reportable income but is shown as a reduction of the taxpayer's income tax liability (similar to W-2 tax withholdings) on Form 1040, page 2.

To clear the diagnostic, the tax preparer should report total unemployment compensation of $3,000 on Schedule 1.

	Diagnostic/Validation Check	Options to Clear Diagnostic
3	*Informational:* An amount was entered in the previous year for qualified dividend income from John Deere, Inc.; no qualified dividends from this payer reported on the current-year tax return.	The correct amount of qualified dividend income is $0 **The correct amount of qualified dividend income is $1,500** The correct amount of qualified dividend income is $3,300 No action required

	Diagnostic/Validation Check	Options to Clear Diagnostic
3	When income is reported in a previous year and not in the current year, informational diagnostics are frequently generated alerting the tax preparer of the change. The diagnostic is informational because there are legitimate reasons why income would be reported in one year and not the following year. For example, it's plausible that Robert no longer has the John Deere investment or that the company simply didn't distribute qualified dividends to shareholders. In this scenario, Robert received $1,800 of total ordinary dividends, of which $1,500 are taxed as qualified dividends (taxed at preferential rates), as reported on the *1099-DIV Dividends and Distributions* exhibit. While Robert correctly reported the ordinary dividends on his draft return, he erroneously excluded the qualified dividends. Both amounts must be reported on Form 1040, page 1, lines 3a and 3b. Once the tax preparer inputs $1,500 of qualified dividends from John Deere in the organizer, this informational diagnostic will be cleared.	
4	*Severe:* Total wages amount imported from form W-2 does not match amount reported on Form 1040, page 1, line 1.	The correct amount of wages is $0 The correct amount of wages is $29,975 **The correct amount of wages is $36,400** No action required
	This diagnostic is alerting the taxpayer that an amount reported on a tax form does not tie to a source document; in this case, Form 1040, page 1, does not tie to the *W-2 Wage and Tax Statement* exhibit. The full amount of wages from line 1 of Form W-2 is taxable income that must be reported on Form 1040, page 1. The federal income tax withheld does not reduce reportable income but is shown as a reduction of the taxpayer's income tax liability on Form 1040, page 2. Because Robert erroneously reduced gross income by the amount of federal income tax withheld, the tax preparer should report total wages of $36,400 on Form 1040, page 1, line 1, to clear the diagnostic.	
5	*Informational:* Jury duty pay of $2,200 reported on Form 1040, Schedule 1, line 8h. Confirm Form 1099 or other verification received by taxpayer from applicable jurisdiction.	**The correct amount of jury pay is $0** The correct amount of jury pay is $1,000 The correct amount of jury pay is $3,000 No action required
	This diagnostic is asking the tax preparer to verify that there is a source document for jury pay of $2,200 reported, presumably because no such document was imported. Upon reviewing the return, the tax preparer should also notice (even if not alerted via a tax software diagnostic) that nothing was reported under Prizes and Awards on Schedule 1, even though Robert reported winning a TV from a game show. Based on this information, the tax preparer can conclude that Robert erroneously reported $2,200 of his prizes awarded from the game show from the *1099-MISC Miscellaneous Income* exhibit on the wrong line on Schedule 1 (ie, as jury duty pay). To fix the return and clear the diagnostic, the tax preparer should remove the $2,200 amount from line 8h (jury duty pay) and move it to line 8i (prizes and awards).	

	Diagnostic/Validation Check	Options to Clear Diagnostic
6	*Informational:* Verify the amount of scholarship income received by taxpayer that is includable in gross income. Amounts received in excess of qualified education expenses must be included.	The correct amount of includable scholarship income is $0 The correct amount of includable scholarship income is $16,800 The correct amount of includable scholarship income is $12,800 **No action required**

As a student-athlete, Robert received *Form 1098-T: Tuition Statement*, which reports the amount of scholarships he was awarded and the amounts received by the university to pay for tuition and related expenses. This diagnostic is reminding the tax preparer to confirm whether any of the scholarship received by Robert must be included in income.

Line 1 of the 1098-T reports that $12,000 of the $16,800 received was used to pay for tuition and other qualified education expenses. The remainder of $4,800 ($16,800 − $12,000) that was used for other, nonqualified purposes (eg, room and board) must be reported on Schedule 1, page 1, line 8r. Robert correctly reported this $4,800 amount on the draft tax return; therefore, no further action is required by the tax preparer.

	Diagnostic/Validation Check	Options to Clear Diagnostic
7	*Informational:* Interest income reported on previous year's tax return for 1099-INT from Nashville State Bank; no interest from this payer reported on the current-year tax return.	The correct amount of includable interest income is $1,800 The correct amount of includable interest income is $2,200 The correct amount of includable interest income is $3,100 **No action required**

When income is reported in a previous year and not in the current year, informational diagnostics are frequently generated alerting the tax preparer of the change. The diagnostic is informational because there are legitimate reasons why income would be reported in one year and not the following year. For example, in this scenario, it's plausible that Robert could have closed the bank account, or the bank could be paying variable interest and therefore paying little to no interest in the current year.

Because there is no source document from this bank or any relevant information about this source of income in the exhibits or the scenario, Robert correctly did not report interest income on the draft tax return. Therefore, no further action is required by the tax preparer.

	Diagnostic/Validation Check	Options to Clear Diagnostic
8	*Informational:* Other income of $52,800 reported on Form 1040, Schedule 1, line 8z. Confirm Form 1099 or other verification received by taxpayer to verify amount reported.	**Other income equals $130,000, capital gain income equals $200** Other income equals $55,000, capital gain income equals $2,800 Other income equals $25,000, capital gain income equals $52,800 No action required

	Diagnostic/Validation Check	Options to Clear Diagnostic
8	This diagnostic is alerting the tax preparer to verify the amount of other income reported on Schedule 1. This line on the return can be heavily scrutinized because there frequently is not a matching document (eg, Form 1099) received by the IRS to verify. In this scenario, the inheritance information comes from the *Davis and Associates letter* exhibit (which would not be reported to the IRS). As a beneficiary/recipient of an inheritance, Robert does not include the life insurance proceeds or the receipt of property. However, Robert immediately sold the property he inherited and therefore must report the gain on the difference between the proceeds and his basis in the property. His basis in the inherited property is the FMV on the date of death (no alternate valuation date information provided), and the holding period is always long term for inherited property. Therefore, Robert must report \$200 of income (\$3,000 proceeds − \$2,800 basis) from the sale of the necklace. Although Schedule D Capital Gains and Losses is not provided as an exhibit, Robert should report the gain from the sale of physical goods on Schedule D and attach it to his return. With Schedule D completed, this amount would actually flow to line 7 of Form 1040, page 1, instead of other income on Schedule 1. The other *Davis and Associates letter* exhibit reports the details of the damage awards Robert received from his lawsuit settlement. Damage awards received because of physical injury, physical sickness, and workers' compensation are excludable from income. However, all other types of damage awards are included in gross income, including sexual discrimination. Additionally, punitive damages are always included in gross income. Therefore, the total of these items, or \$130,000, must be reported on Schedule 1, page 1, as other income.	
9	*Severe:* Form 1099-C imported but no cancellation of debt income reported on Schedule 1, page 1, line 8c.	The correct amount to include in income is \$1,000 **The correct amount to include in income is \$3,100** The correct amount to include in income is \$5,000 No action required
	This diagnostic is alerting the tax preparer that a source document imported has no corresponding amount reported on the tax return. The *1099-C: Cancellation of Debt* exhibit reports that \$3,100 of Robert's credit card debt was forgiven. Cancellation of debt is typically included in gross income on Schedule 1, page 1. Cancellation of credit card debt is **not an exception** and must be included. The taxpayer should report the entire \$3,100 on Schedule 1, page 1, line 8c, to clear the diagnostic. Note that Robert's credit card limit provided in this question is irrelevant.	

Correct Tax Form Entries

Correct Form 1040, Page 1, Tax Return Entries	
Line 1: Total amount from Form(s) W-2, box 1	36,400
Lina 2a: Tax-exempt interest	0
Line 2b: Taxable interest	0
Line 3a: Qualified dividends	0
Line 3b: Ordinary dividends	1,800
Line 7: Capital gain or (loss)	200
Line 8: Other income from Schedule 1, line 10	143,100
Line 9: Total income	181,500
Line 10: Adjustments to income	0
Line 11: Adjusted gross income	181,500

Correct Schedule 1 Additional Income and Adjustments Entries		
Line 2: Alimony received		0
Line 7: Unemployment compensation		3,000
Line 8c: Cancellation of debt	3,100	
Line 8i: Prizes and awards	2,200	
Line 8r: Scholarship and fellowship grants not on W-2	4,800	
Line 8z: Sexual discrimination lawsuit awards	130,000	
Line 9: Total other income		140,100
Line 10: Combine lines 1 through 7 and 9 (total additional income)		143,100

REG 13
Reporting of Items from Pass-Through Entities

REG 13: Reporting of Items from Pass-Through Entities

13.01 Reporting of Items from Pass-Through Entities

Treatment of Pass-Through Items for Disregarded Entities

Representative Task (Application): Use information provided from disregarded and pass-through entities in which an individual has an ownership interest to report an owner's share of ordinary business income (loss) and separately stated items on an individual's tax return.

Business Entity Tax Classification

When forming a new business entity, considerations for how an entity should be established must be determined. The choice of business entity type is crucial, as it affects how the business will be taxed, the rules under which it must operate, and the rights and responsibilities of its owners.

Two classifications that establish the criteria under which a business entity operates are legal and tax. The entity can be **legally classified** as a corporation, a limited liability company (LLC), a general partnership (GP), a limited partnership (LP), or a sole proprietorship.

- Corporations, LLCs, general partnerships, and limited partnerships are considered legal entities separate from their owners (eg, shareholders, members, or partners, respectively), which means generally that the owners are not personally responsible for the corporation's debts or legal obligations
- This is because the entity exists as a separate legal operation with its own assets and liabilities. Sole proprietorships, on the other hand, are **not** treated as separate from their owners unless formed as a single-member LLC. The business and the owner are considered one and the same, meaning that the owner is personally liable for the business's debts and obligations

A limited liability company (LLC) is a business structure allowed by state statute. Depending on the elections made by the LLC and the number of members, the IRS will treat an LLC as a corporation, as a partnership, or as part of the LLC owner's tax return (a "disregarded entity").

Specifically, a domestic LLC with at least two members is classified as a partnership for federal income tax purposes unless it files Form 8832 and affirmatively elects to be treated as a corporation. For income tax purposes, an LLC with only one member is treated as an entity disregarded as separate from its owner, unless it files Form 8832 and elects to be treated as a corporation.

Entities are also classified by their **tax classification**. The business entity is either a separate taxpaying entity on the income it makes or a **pass-through entity** (eg, partnerships, S corporations). Pass-through entities are called such because the net business income (loss) and other tax items from these entities "pass" through to their owners, who are responsible for paying the income taxes.

- The *default* tax classification for a corporation is a C corporation. C corporations are separate taxpaying entities and use Form 1120 to report income, gains, losses, deductions, and credits and to determine taxable income (TI) and income tax liability
- A corporation may elect to be treated as an S corporation (a pass-through entity) if certain requirements are met

Tax Classification of a Business Entity

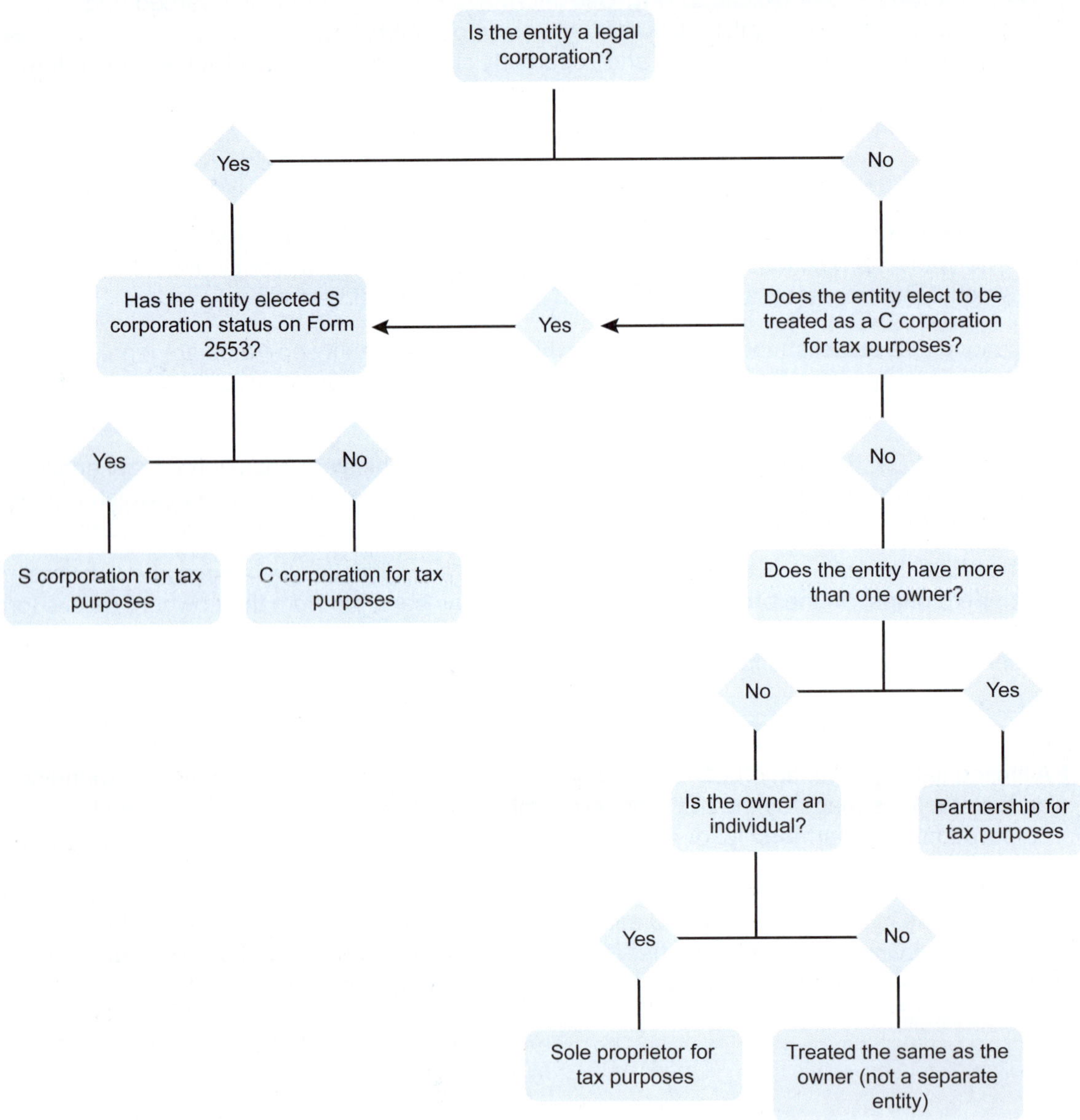

A taxpayer owned 40% of the outstanding stock of a C corporation. During the tax year, the corporation reported $400,000 in taxable income and distributed a total of $70,000 in cash dividends to its shareholders. The corporate income tax rate is 21%.

As a separate taxpaying entity, the C corporation will pay income tax of $84,000 computed as ($400,000 × 21%). The taxpayer will report $28,000 ($70,000 × 40%) of dividend income on their personal tax return and pay either regular rates or preferential rates if the dividends are qualified.

A taxpayer owned 40% of the outstanding stock of an S corporation. During the tax year, the S corporation reported $400,000 in taxable income and distributed a total of $70,000 in cash to its shareholders.

As a *pass-through entity*, the S corporation will *pay no income tax* on its taxable income. The taxpayer would report their *share of the income*, $160,000 ($400,000 S corporation income × 40% ownership). The $28,000 distribution is a nontaxable return of capital and will reduce the taxpayer's stock basis.

Disregarded Entity: Sole Proprietorship

A sole proprietorship is an unincorporated business structure owned by one individual taxpayer. For tax purposes, there is **no distinction between a sole proprietorship and its owner** (ie, a disregarded entity). Therefore, the owner directly receives the business income, deductions, gains, losses, and credits rather than receiving them indirectly through a pass-through entity and reports them on Schedule C.

- A break given by the Tax Cuts and Jobs Act for Schedule C filers and other pass-through businesses is a 20% qualified business income (QBI) deduction

Business gross income includes "all income from whatever source derived" and expenses according to IRC Section 162, which states, "There shall be allowed as a deduction all the ordinary and necessary expenses paid or incurred during the taxable year in carrying on any trade or business."

- Therefore, the activity must have the objective of making a profit and not just the pursuit of a hobby or personal goals. Income from a disregarded entity is entered directly on Part I of **Schedule C**, while expenses are entered on Part II

Examples of typical ordinary and necessary business expenses include advertising, car and truck expenses, depreciation, insurance, legal fees, interest, office expenses, rent, repairs, supplies, travel, and employee wages.

Disregarded entities report other expenditures on their Form 1040 as appropriate.

- For example, charitable contributions and the personal portion of property taxes and mortgage interest expense from a home office are reported on Schedule A along with the taxpayer's other itemized deductions
- Health insurance premiums, including premiums for long-term care, are also not reported on Schedule C but on Schedule 1 of Form 1040 along with retirement contributions for the self-employed

In July of this year, Renee, a pet groomer, started a sole proprietorship called Grooming with Love (GWL). GWL uses the cash method of accounting, and Renee produced the following financial information for this year:

GWL collected $22,000 in cash for grooming completed during the year and an additional $500 in cash for grooming for next year.

Customers owe GWL $1,300 for grooming completed this year, which Renee expects to collect in January of next year.

GWL made the following expenditures:

Shop rent	$6,000
Utilities	800
Advertising	300
Supplies (shampoo, bows, etc.)	2,100
Insurance	800
Interest	400

The shop rent, utilities, and advertising covered the six months that GWL operated. $1,600 of supplies was used this year, and the remaining $500 should be used up by February of next year. The insurance policy is a 12-month policy covering six months this year and six months next year. The interest paid relates to interest accrued on a $10,000 loan made to Renee in July of this year. Renee used half of the loan to pay the rent on the shop and the other half to buy municipal bonds.

The income and expenses flow directly to Renee's Schedule C and Form 1040. Net profit from the business equals $12,300 ($22,500 − $10,200).

Income: Under the cash method, revenues are recorded when received whether earned or not. Revenues are not, however, recorded for accounts receivable. GWL will recognize $22,500 of revenue for the first six months of the year ($22,000 + $500).

Expenses: GWL will be allowed to deduct only one-half of the interest expense ($200, the portion of loan proceeds that relates to the business). The amount paid to purchase tax-exempt bonds is not deductible. The full amount of supplies ($2,100), rent ($6,000), utilities ($800), and advertising ($300) is deductible. The insurance ($800) is allowed to be deducted in full under the 12-month rule. Total expenses are $10,200.

Pass-Through Entities

A **pass-through** entity, such as a partnership or S corporation, is an entity **distinct from** its **owners** for tax purposes and is generally not subject to income tax at the entity level. Instead, entity ordinary business income (loss), tax credits, and other separately stated items (eg, capital gains, interest, dividends, charitable contributions) pass through to the owners. The owners then include their share of the income on their personal tax returns and pay tax on the income, even if it is not distributed.

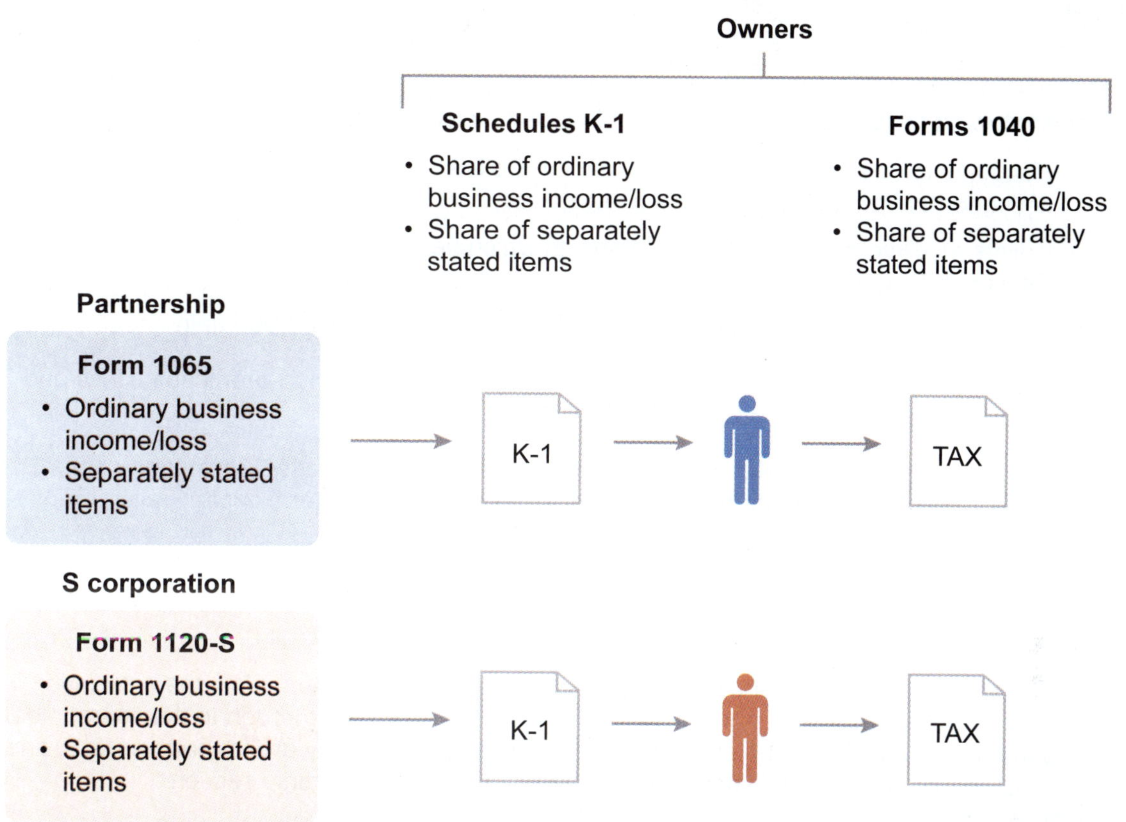

An **LLC** is strictly a *legal structure* and does **not** refer to an entity's taxability. Instead, a multiple-member LLC chooses how to be treated for tax purposes; its options include being treated as a partnership, C corporation, or S corporation (if certain requirements are met). If no election is made, the LLC is treated as a partnership for tax purposes. Since an LLC can be a partnership or an S corporation for tax purposes, LLCs can be pass-through entities.

- A single-member LLC can elect to be treated as a corporation (C corp or S corp) or a disregarded entity. If no election is made, the LLC is treated as a disregarded entity, and its activities are reported on Schedule C if the member is an individual or on the single-member corporation return if the member is a corporate owner

Treatment of Pass-Through Items for Partnerships (Form 1065 & Schedule K-1)

A P/S files an annual information return (Form 1065) to report its **ordinary business income (loss)** and **separately stated items**.

- Form 1065 includes the allocation of those amounts to **each partner on a Schedule K-1** based on **ownership interest** (eg, 55%)
- A P/S ordinary net business income (loss) focuses on the income (loss) generated by the operations of the business itself. It excludes the separately stated items
- **Separately stated items** (eg, tax-exempt interest, dividends, capital gains, Section 1231 gains) are **not** part of the P/S ordinary net business income (loss) because they are subject to statutory limitations or special rules when reported on the individual partners' Form 1040 tax returns
- Each partner must report these income and loss items even if they don't receive cash distributions from the partnership during the year
- Distributions from a P/S are considered a return of capital and do not affect the net business income

The following example demonstrates the importance of separately stated items being passed through to a partner.

The following facts apply to Collins, an individual taxpayer, during the current year:

- Hodge, who owed a $2,000 personal debt to Collins for the past three years, declared bankruptcy
- Collins received a K-1 from a partnership in which he is a general partner showing a net Section 1231 gain of $10,000
- Collins sold stock he inherited in June of the current year for a $3,000 gain

In this scenario, Collins treats the worthless personal debt as a $2,000 short-term capital loss and the $3,000 sale of the inherited stock as a long-term capital gain.

The $10,000 gain reported on his K-1 (a Section 1231 asset) would be netted against any other Section 1231 assets sold. Because there are none, the gain is treated as a long-term capital gain. Collins reports a net long-term capital gain of $11,000 ($3,000 + $10,000 − $2,000).

Items that are reported separately are frequently tested on the exam. Also, the calculation of income and identification of special items that need to be passed through to the shareholders separately are handled in the same way for S corporations as they are for partnerships, and such concepts are normally addressed on the exam in the partnership section.

Guaranteed Payments to Partners

Payments based on a separate *contractual relationship* between a partner and P/S for **services rendered** by the partner or **use of the partner's capital** are known as **guaranteed payments**. Salaries are not paid to partners; instead, a P/S pays guaranteed payments. For tax purposes, guaranteed payments, determined without regard to the income of the P/S that is engaged in a trade or business, that are paid to any partner for *services* are treated as self-employment income. The payments are:

- Deductible as an expense on the *P/S tax return* to determine ordinary business income (loss)
- Taxable as ordinary *income* to the partner receiving the payment (reported on K-1)
- Subject to self-employment tax by the partner
- Subject to the net investment income tax by the partner if for interest
- Not included in the calculation of the QBI deduction

RZNY L.P. is a calendar-year, cash-basis limited partnership. Marc Liu, an individual, owns a 55% interest in RZNY as a general partner. During Year 4, RZNY had the following results. The table below displays RZNY's ordinary business income, separately stated items, and amounts reported to Mr. Liu on his K-1.

Description	RZNY L.P.	Liu K-1 (55% Interest)	Reportable on 1040
Sales	$10,000,000		
Cost of goods sold	7,000,000		
General and administrative costs	1,500,000		
Guaranteed payment to Marc Liu	112,000	$112,000*	Schedule E Supplemental Income and Loss
Ordinary business income	1,388,000	763,400	Schedule E Supplemental Income and Loss
Ordinary dividends	100,000**	55,000	Schedule B
Qualified dividends	30,000	16,500	Form 1040, pg 1
Taxable interest income	180,000	99,000	Schedule B
Municipal bond interest	20,000	11,000	Form 1040, pg 1
Distributions to Marc Liu	70,000	70,000	

**The guaranteed payment is deductible by the partnership in determining ordinary business income and also reportable on the K-1 and subject to self-employment (SE) tax. Because Mr. Liu is a general partner, the ordinary business income is also subject to S/E tax.*

***Ordinary dividends include the amount of qualified dividends, and the amount of qualified dividends are also required to be reported separately. Both taxable and tax-exempt interest are reported separately on the K-1.*

In general, partners do not recognize gain or loss from operating distributions. Mr. Liu's distribution is a return of his capital interest and will reduce his outside basis by the amount (but not below zero). However, when the partnership distributes money that exceeds a partner's basis in his P/S interest, he will recognize a gain equal to the excess.

Allocating Partners' Shares of Income (Loss)

The allocation of a P/S net business income generally is based on percentages established in the P/S agreement. However, P/S have flexibility in allocating profit and loss as long as the partners agree, and the special allocations have substantial economic effect. The method for dividing net income may take into account partners' time devoted to the partnership (ie, a salary allowance) and/or reward partners for their capital investment (ie, an interest allowance).

- These allowances (which do not represent amounts paid and are not treated as expenses) are used to equitably distribute net income/loss. When the net income is allocated, the allowances are considered first to ensure the partners are compensated for their time and/or investment
- The allowances reduce the net income available to be divided among the partners. Any remaining net income is allocated according to the **profit** ratios. However, if the allowances **exceed** the net income, the remainder is a **loss** that is divided according to the **loss** ratios

Allocation of Partnership Net Income/Loss to Partners

Partnership net income/loss to be allocated	–	Special allocations (eg, bonuses) and allowances (eg, salary and interest) granted to individual partners	=	Remaining net income/loss to be allocated to partners*

****Allocated using established partner percentages***

Thomas and George formed a partnership in Year 4. The partnership agreement provides for annual salary allowances of $70,000 for Thomas and $30,000 for George. The partners share profits equally and losses in a 60/40 ratio. The partnership had net business earnings of $90,000 for Year 5 before any allowance to partners. What amount of these earnings should be credited to each partner's capital account?

The salary allowance for each partner is considered before the allocation of the net business earnings. If the allowance exceeds the net earnings, a temporary "loss" is created that must be allocated to the partners according to their loss ratios (ie, 60/40).

In this scenario, a $10,000 loss is created after the allocation of the allowances. The loss is allocated $6,000 to Thomas ($10,000 × 60%) and $4,000 to George ($10,00 × 40%). This results in Thomas reporting $64,000 of the $90,000 income and George reporting $26,000, as shown below.

	Thomas	George	Total
Net business earnings			$ 90,000
Salary allowance	$70,000	$30,000	(100,000)
Remainder (excess allowances over income)			$(10,000)
Allocated according to loss ratio	(6,000)	(4,000)	10,000
Net income allocated	$64,000	$26,000	$ 0

Loss Limitations for Partners

Operating losses reported to partners can generate current tax benefits if a partner is allowed to deduct them against other sources of income. They are deductible only if a taxpayer can clear three separate hurdles. A partner's deductible loss is limited to the lesser of:

- The partner's tax **basis** in the partnership interest;
- The partner's amount **at risk**; or
- The **passive activity loss limitations**, if applicable

A partner's basis in a P/S at year end is adjusted for the partner's share of income and losses, liability changes, additional contributions, and distributions.

- Basis may **never fall below zero**. If allocated losses exceed the *year-end* basis, any *excess loss is disallowed* as a current deduction and is carried forward to future years until there is sufficient basis to absorb the loss
- In addition, a partner may not deduct more than the amount at risk. Generally, a partner's amount at risk equals basis. However, if the partner is not personally liable to repay any liability used to determine the partner's basis, the partner's at-risk amount equals the basis *reduced* by such liability

- Losses limited by the at-risk rules are carried forward indefinitely until a partner can utilize them by generating additional at-risk amounts or until the partner sells their partnership interest
- Passive activity loss limitations (PAL) prevent partners (in rental real estate P/S and passive activities) from using losses generated by these flow-through entities to offset other types of income

Self-Employment Tax

Self-employed taxpayers (ie, sole proprietors, independent contractors, general partners in a partnership) are required to pay 15.3% in self-employment (SE) tax (ie, FICA taxes) on net earnings of $400 or more. The individual taxpayer (not the business entity) is responsible for self-employment tax, and it is computed on Form SE (self-employment tax). Examples of self-employment income include:

- Net earnings from a sole proprietorship
- General partners' distributive share of net P/S business income
- Guaranteed payments made to any partner for services from a partnership that is engaged in a trade or business

The 15.3% FICA taxes comprises 12.4% for Social Security on net earnings up to $168,600 (for 2024) and 2.9% Medicare taxes on all net earnings (no limit).

To help offset having to pay the additional amount of FICA taxes, self-employed individuals are allowed a deduction for AGI of one-half (50%) of the self-employment taxes (ie, what an employer would normally pay).

- For example, if the self-employment taxes are $6,400, the taxpayer takes a deduction for AGI of $3,200

When determining the **net earnings** for self-employment, *no deduction* for 7.65% of the matching "employer" FICA taxes is permitted (eg, not deducted on Schedule C). Therefore, when computing the self-employment tax on Form SE, only **92.35%** (100% − 7.65%) of the net earnings is subject to the tax. Generally on the exam, the net earnings subject to SE tax are provided. However, a Form SE may be used as an exhibit in a task-based simulation that shows the 92.35% of net earnings used as the base computation for self-employment tax.

A taxpayer's net earnings subject to self-employment tax are $80,000. Compute the self-employment tax.

$$\$80,000 \times 15.3\% = \$12,240$$

In addition, the taxpayer would be able to deduct one-half of the self-employment taxes as a deduction for AGI ($12,240 × 1/2 = $6,120).

Treatment of Pass-Through Items for S-Corporations (Form 1120-S and Schedule K-1)

As a flow-through entity, an S corporation does not pay tax and shares many tax similarities with P/S. The S corporation must file an information return (Form 1120-S).

Like a P/S, the S corporation determines the net business income or loss as well as separately stated items (the same items listed for a P/S), which are reported to each shareholder on a Schedule K-1. Shareholders report their pro rata share (ie, proportionate) of the S corporation's net business income as well as the separately stated items.

Distributions generally are not taxed if there is sufficient stock basis. All shareholders then report their share of the income on their personal tax returns and pay tax on that income even if they do not receive distributions during the year.

Unlike partners, S corporation shareholders are not subject to self-employment tax on their distributive share of the net business income. Shareholders do **not** receive guaranteed payments like partners can. If a shareholder performs services that are considered wages, a W-2 is issued. If the services performed are professional in nature (eg, accounting or legal fees), a Form 1099 is issued.

Allocating Shareholders' Shares of Income (Loss)

Unlike partnerships, S corporations do **not** have flexibility in allocating profit and loss. S corporations generally allocate income and loss items to shareholders **pro ratably** according to the number of shares owned and the number of days they owned the stock.

- If there is no change in ownership during the year, then the percentage of stock owned is used to determine the amount passed through
- If a change in ownership occurred, then each shareholder's percentage is weighted for the number of days the stock was held. When computing the days owned, the seller is considered as owning the stock on the day it was sold

Assume an S corporation with 100 shares outstanding reported $365,000 of net business income in Year 1 (a 365-day year). One shareholder purchased five shares on 11/30/Year 1 and held them through the end of the year. What amount of net business income does the shareholder report in Year 1?

The shareholder reports **$1,550** as computed below.

Compute per-day income	$365,000 / 365 days = $1,000 per day
Compute per-day, per-share income	$1,000 / 100 shares = $10
Allocate income to shareholder based on the number of days the shares were owned	$10 × 5 shares × 31 days* = $1,550

**31 days of December*

Loss Limitations

S corporations have loss limitations similar to those for partnerships. Three hurdles must be cleared in addition to the excess business losses limitation described above under P/S.

- Basis Limitation: Losses are limited to amount invested (ie, stock basis) + amount loaned to company (ie, debt basis). Remember that S corporation shareholders are not allowed to include debt in their basis unless the loan was made directly to the S corporation. Basis cannot go below zero; losses are suspended until the shareholder has sufficient basis to absorb the loss
- At-Risk Rules: Losses are further limited by the investor's amount "at risk" under IRC Sec. 465 (similar to basis rules but amounts at-risk do not include amounts for which the investor bears no economic risk of loss). Note: For S corporations, basis is often equal to the amount "at risk"
- Passive Activity Rules: If the S corporation activity is considered passive to the shareholder, then the passive activity rules apply. Passive losses generally can only offset passive income

Below is an example of items reported on Schedule K and flowing through to a 10% S corporation shareholder's Form 1040. Then, at the shareholder level, in addition to the ordinary business income, salary, and charitable contributions, the $1,000 capital loss is aggregated with the shareholder's other capital losses of $2,490 and limited to the maximum annual capital loss deduction of $3,000.

Schedule K of an S Corporation

Ordinary Net Business Income	Corporation	10% Shareholder	
Sales	$200,000		
Cost of goods sold	(60,000)		
Rent expense	(25,000)		
General and admin. expenses	(5,000)		
Salary to shareholder	(8,000)	$ 8,000 →	100% of the salary is reported by the shareholder
Ordinary net business income	$102,000	$10,200	
Separately Stated Items			
Charitable contributions	$ 30,000	$ 3,000	
Capital loss	$ 10,000	$ 1,000 →	

Shareholder's other capital loss	$(2,490)
Capital loss from S corporation	(1,000)
Total capital losses	$(3,490)
Annual limitation	3,000
Carryforward to next tax year	$ (490)

Qualified Business Income

The TCJA established a deduction for individuals, trusts, and estates that have qualified business income (QBI) from a qualified business and meet certain requirements. QBI is generated by S corporations, partnerships, sole proprietorships, trusts, estates, and even some Schedule E businesses.

Qualified Business Income (QBI)	
Includes*	**Does Not Include**
• Income • Deductions • Gains • Losses	• C corporation income • Reasonable compensation • Guaranteed or other payments to a partner for services • Investment income • Capital gains/losses • Deductions allocable to investment income or capital gains/losses

**Items related to conducting ordinary business operations*

Section 199A defines a qualified business by exception (ie, defined by what it is not). A qualified business is any business (or trade) that is not:

- A specified service trade or business (SSTB); or
- A service performed as an employee (eg, guaranteed payments for services, compensation paid to the shareholder).

The deduction can be up to **20% of QBI** received. The **pass-through entity** that creates QBI does **not** claim the deduction; instead, the deduction is claimed on the *tax return* of an eligible *individual*, trust, or estate. For an individual, the **deduction is from AGI** to arrive at taxable income.

- To assist a taxpayer with the calculation of the 20% deduction, pass-through entities (eg, partnerships, S corporations) must disclose each taxpayer's share of QBI and any other information required to calculate their QBI deduction
- The computation of the QBI deduction threshold can be complex since it is subject to numerous limitations and AGI thresholds. As such, the computation is addressed by a separate representative task in another chapter. However, the simplest computation is as follows: A taxpayer has $23,000 of QBI from a P/S. The QBI deduction is $4,600 ($23,000 × 20%)

REG 14
AGI and Taxable Income Adjustments

REG 14: AGI and Taxable Income Adjustments

14.01 Adjustments and Deductions to Arrive at Adjusted Gross Income and Taxable Income

Overview

Taxpayers are concerned with reporting the correct amount of **includible income**, but they should also be aware of all of the potential **deductible expenses** as well. An individual taxpayer may have the opportunity to **deduct certain expenses** (eg, student loan interest) when calculating **adjusted gross income** (AGI) or when calculating **taxable income** (ie, itemized deductions or the qualified business income [QBI] deduction).

It is crucial to understand the differences in expenses, where they are deductible (if at all), and what the tax benefit would be. Individuals who deduct expenses in calculating AGI (referred to as above the line or for AGI) will always receive a benefit because a taxpayer's AGI is used as a threshold in determining eligibility for certain tax deductions and credits.

- The reduction of the taxpayer's AGI can help in other areas of the tax law, such as the deductibility of medical expenses or the ability to use the child tax credit
- If an individual has available expenses identified as itemized deductions, the total of itemized deductions must exceed their standard deduction to receive a benefit from those expenses

The following illustration shows an individual taxpayer's tax formula in calculating AGI and taxable income as well as how to arrive at the taxpayer's tax due or refund.

Individual Tax Calculation (Form 1040)

- Wages, taxable retirement distributions
- Other income and adjustments (Sch. 1)
- Interest and dividends (Sch. B)
- Sole proprietorship income/loss (Sch. C)
- Capital gain/losses (Sch. D)
- Rental and income/loss from flow-through entities (Sch. E)
- Farming income/loss (Sch. F)

Gross income

− *For* AGI deductions (above the line)

= Adjusted gross income (AGI)

− *From* AGI deductions (below the line)

= Taxable income

× Tax rates

= Income tax liability

+ Other taxes

− Credits

− Withholdings

− Prepayments

= Tax due (refund)

Deductions for:

- Traditional IRA contributions
- Student loan interest
- Educator expenses
- Health savings plan
- 1/2 of SE tax
- Alimony paid*
- Moving expenses for military

From AGI deductions:

- *Greater* of standard deduction or itemized deductions on Schedule A (COMITT)
- Deduction for qualified business income

Other taxes:

- Self-employment
- AMT
- Net investment income
- Additional Medicare tax

Credits:

- Child tax credit
- Credit for other dependents
- Child and dependent care
- Foreign tax credit
- Educational credits
- Credit for elderly or disabled

**Divorce agreement prior to 2019*

The term *modified adjusted gross income* (MAGI) refers to AGI adjusted for certain income and deductions (eg, tax-exempt income, foreign earned income deduction). It is used to determine a taxpayer's eligibility for certain deductions, tax credits, and retirement plan contributions. On the exam, if needed, modified AGI is provided.

Adjustments to Arrive at Adjusted Gross Income (AGI)

Representative Task (Application): Identify adjustments allowed in the calculation of adjusted gross income given a specific scenario, including a contribution to a qualified retirement plan, contribution to a health savings plan, and self-employment expenses.

Deductions for AGI: Overview

Deductions **for** AGI are useful in several ways:

1. Lower AGI results in greater deductions in other areas on the tax return
2. Greater credits are allowed
3. They are always deductible, so lower taxable income

The following section will break down various items used to compute AGI using the mnemonic I-EMBRACED, Health, and Farmers. Note, technically income or loss from rental activities (Schedule E), a sole proprietorship (Schedule C), and farming (Schedule F) are considered part of gross income, which is used to determine AGI and not explicitly deductions for AGI. However, these items are explained in this section to aid in the overall understanding and computation of AGI.

I-EMBRACED, Health, and Farmers
I - **I**nterest in student loans
E - Self-**e**mployment deductions
M - **M**oving expenses (for military taxpayers)
B - **B**usiness expenses (Schedule C)
R - **R**ental, royalty, and flow-through entities (Schedule E)
A - **A**limony paid (prior to 2019)
C - **C**ontributions to certain retirement plans
E - Contributions to **e**ducation savings accounts
D - Jury **d**uty
Health - Contribution to health savings plans
Farm - Farming income (Schedule F)

Interest on Student Loans for Higher Education

The lesser of *qualified* student loan interest paid or $2,500 is allowed as a deduction for AGI. However, the deduction is subject to a *phaseout* based on modified AGI. For 2024, the phaseout range is $30,000 for taxpayers filing jointly (starting at $165,000 MAGI), and the phaseout for single, HOH, and QSS taxpayers is $15,000 (starting at $80,000 MAGI). A student loan exists when a taxpayer uses the loan proceeds to pay for qualified higher educational expenses of the taxpayer, their spouse, or dependents. **No deduction** is allowed if the taxpayer is *married filing separately* or if the taxpayer can be *claimed as a dependent* on another person's tax return.

A taxpayer is 27 and files as single on their individual income tax return. They paid $4,800 of student interest expense in the current year. If their MAGI is $82,000, how much can the taxpayer deduct for student loan interest expense? Assume that the student loan deduction phaseout for single taxpayers starts at $80,000 MAGI and ends at $95,000.

The taxpayer can deduct **$2,167**, calculated as follows:

$333 phased-out amount = $2,500 × ($82,000 MAGI − $80,000 phaseout starting point) / $15,000 phaseout range

$2,167 taxpayer deduction = $2,500 statutory allowable deduction − $333 phased-out amount

Self-Employment Deductions

Self-Employment Tax: Self-employed taxpayers (ie, sole proprietors, independent contractors, general partners in a partnership) are required to pay **15.3% in self-employment tax** (ie, FICA taxes) **on net earnings of $400 or more**. The 15.3% FICA taxes comprise 12.4% for Social Security on net earnings up to $168,600 (for 2024) and 2.9% Medicare taxes on all net earnings (no limit).

- To help offset the additional amount of FICA taxes, self-employed individuals are allowed a **deduction** *for* AGI of **one-half** (50%) of the **self-employment taxes** (ie, what an employer would normally pay)
- For example, if the total self-employment taxes paid are $6,400, the taxpayer takes a *for* AGI deduction of $3,200

When determining the net earnings for self-employment, no deduction for 7.65% of the FICA taxes is permitted. Therefore, when computing the self-employment tax on Form SE, only 92.35% (100% – 7.65%) of the net earnings is subject to the tax. Although this is probably not tested on the exam, a Form SE (self-employment) may be used as an exhibit.

Medical Insurance Premiums: Self-employed taxpayers may take a *for* AGI deduction for **100%** of medical insurance premiums paid for the taxpayer, the taxpayer's spouse, dependents, and children under the age of 27 if two requirements are met:

- No member of the family may have coverage through an employer
- The amount of the deduction cannot exceed the taxpayer's self-employment income (eg, from Schedule C or Schedule F)

Partners: A partner with net earnings from self-employment may deduct the cost of medical insurance.

S Corporation Shareholder: A 2% or more shareholder in an S corporation may deduct the cost of health insurance when the insurance premiums are paid or reimbursed by the corporation and included in the shareholder's wages.

Moving Expenses for Military

The deduction for moving expenses has been suspended for 2018–2025 for most individuals. There is an exception for members of the U.S. armed forces on active duty, but this exception is less likely to be tested.

Business Expenses (Schedule C—Sole Proprietorship and 1099 Income)

If an individual participates in a trade or business activity that is engaged in for profit (ie, not a hobby activity), then the expenses will be deductible if incurred in operating that trade or business and are ordinary, necessary, and reasonable. Examples include:

- All costs of running a business
- All taxes paid by the business
- Bad debts recognized under direct write-off method
- The Uniform Capitalization Rules (UNICAP – Section 263A), if applicable, require that certain costs be capitalized to inventory produced or held for sale ($30 million gross-receipts test applies)
- Interest paid in advance is not deductible when paid, even by a cash-basis taxpayer
- Prepaid expenses (eg, prepaid rent, insurance) generally are not deductible when paid, even by a cash-basis taxpayer
    - Only the amount that applies to use of rented property during the tax year can be deducted; the rest can be deducted over the period to which it applies
    - Exception: Prepaid amounts are deductible if such amounts do not extend a right or benefit to the taxpayer beyond the earlier of:
        - 12 months after date the taxpayer first realizes the right or benefit, or
        - The end of the following tax year after the payment was made.
- Gifts to customers up to $25 per recipient per year
- $4 per promotional item
- 50% business meals (entertainment expenses no longer deductible after 2017)
- 100% travel
- Hobby losses
    - Expenses (other than cost of goods sold) are not currently deductible, as miscellaneous 2% deductions have been suspended until 2026

On December 1, Year 10, an individual taxpayer pays a $12,000 insurance premium for trucks used in their business. The premium is for a one-year term that begins on February 1, Year 11. Can the taxpayer deduct the entire $12,000 premium in Year 10 under the 12-month rule if they are a cash-basis taxpayer?

As a cash-basis taxpayer, the taxpayer must first determine the earlier of:

- 12 months after benefits first begin (February 1,Year 12), or
- The end of the year after the year in which the taxpayer made the payment (December 31, Year 11).

The *earlier* date is December 31, Year 11. Because the benefit from the premium extends to January 31, Year 12 (ie, *after* 12/31/Year 11), the taxpayer does not meet the 12-month rule. They must therefore capitalize the $12,000 in Year 10, and the premium will be deductible over the period to which it relates. The taxpayer can deduct $11,000 [$12,000 × (11 months / 12 months)] in Year 11 and $1,000 [$12,000 × (1 month / 12 months)] in Year 12.

Rental, Royalty, and Flow-Through Entities (Schedule E)

Generally, income is taxable *when earned* by an **accrual-basis taxpayer** and *when received* by a **cash-basis taxpayer**. When rents or royalties are received in advance, however, even an accrual-basis taxpayer will include them in taxable income in the period received.

Passive Activities and Passive Losses

- A **passive activity** is any business venture in which the taxpayer *does not materially participate*
  - Includes but is not limited to:
    - All limited partnership interests
    - All rental activities (unless taxpayer is a *real estate professional*)
  - There are **seven tests** for **material participation**
    - A material participant is generally involved in the operations of the business on a regular and continuous basis
    - The most common of the seven tests is that the taxpayer participates in the activity more than 500 hours in a year
- **Passive activity losses (PALs)** are *generally* deductible only to the extent of passive gains
  - Unused losses carried forward until disposal of activity
  - **Real estate professional exception:** If a taxpayer is considered a *real estate professional*, then losses from real estate rental activities may be treated as ordinary business losses and, thus, deducted against ordinary income
  - A taxpayer is a real estate professional if:
    - More than half of the taxpayer's personal services performed in trades/businesses during the year were performed in *real property trades/businesses*, and
    - The taxpayer *materially participated* in such activities for more than *750 hours* during the year.
  - **Active participation exception:** If a taxpayer only actively participates in the rental activity and owns at least a 10% interest in the activity, they may deduct up to $25,000 of losses against ordinary income each year
    - Deduction is reduced by 50% of MAGI over $100,000
    - No deduction if MAGI exceeds $150,000
    - The formula for the phaseout is: $25,000 − [(MAGI − $100,000) × 50%]

These rules apply to individuals, estates, trusts (other than grantor trusts), closely held or non-publicly-traded C corporations, and personal service corporations. There is no limit on PALs that may be deducted by grantor trusts, partnerships, and S corporations since they are flow-through entities, and these items are passed through to the individual shareholders and partners.

Passive Activity Loss Rules

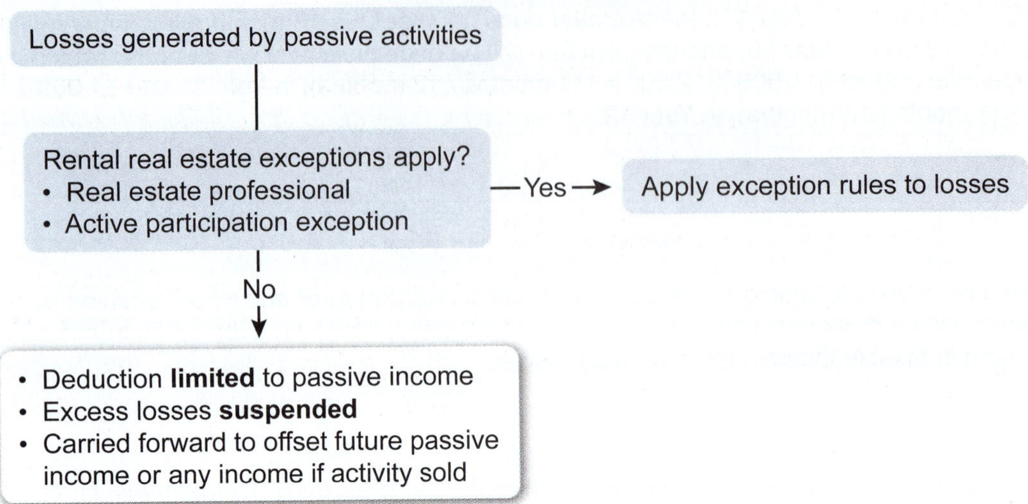

A taxpayer with a rental property meets the active participation requirements and has modified AGI of $110,000. The maximum amount of net losses from rental activities the taxpayer can deduct is $20,000 = $25,000 – [($110,000 MAGI – $100,000 threshold) × 50%].

Assume, instead, the taxpayer has MAGI of $133,000 and is an active manager in rental realty. They own a 12-unit apartment building that generated a loss of $24,000 this year. How much of this loss can reduce their ordinary income?

The taxpayer's current-year deduction is $8,500 = $25,000 − [($133,000 − $100,000) × 50%]). The remaining loss of $15,500 ($24,000 − $8,500) is suspended and carried forward.

- Allocation is required when various passive activities involve both gains and losses
  - Excess loss allocated among activities involving losses
  - Allocation in proportion of activity's loss to total of losses

Assume an entity has three passive activities with losses totaling $100,000 and one passive activity with a gain of $25,000.

Activity 1: $20,000 loss
Activity 2: $30,000 loss
Activity 3: $50,000 loss
Activity 4: $25,000 gain

The excess loss of $75,000 ($100,000 – $25,000) will be *allocated* as follows:

Activity 1: $20,000 / $100,000 × $75,000 = $15,000
Activity 2: $30,000 / $100,000 × $75,000 = $22,500
Activity 3: $50,000 / $100,000 × $75,000 = $37,500

Rental of Personal-Use Property

The treatment of rental income and expenses for a dwelling unit that is also used for personal purposes (eg, **vacation home**) depends on whether the taxpayer uses it as a home. A dwelling unit is used as a home if **personal use exceeds** the greater of **14 days** or **10%** of the number of **days rented**.

- If a dwelling unit is used as a home and is rented for less than 15 days during the tax year, rental income is excluded from gross income, and expenses are not deductible as rental expenses (mortgage interest expense and real estate taxes can be deducted on Schedule A)
- If it is rented for more than 14 days:
  - And personal use is more than the greater of 14 days or 10% of the number of days rented (considered a home), rental income is included, and deductions are limited to gross rental income
    - The expenses must be prorated between rental use and personal use; unused deductions may be carried forward to future years
  - And personal use is not more than the greater of 14 days or 10% of the number of days rented (considered a real rental), rental income is included, and all expenses allocated to the rental portion are allowed
    - Expenses in excess of income are subject to passive activity loss limits
- Depreciation is discussed in detail in another section
- Income from flow-through entities (eg, partnerships, S corporations) is taxable to the individual in the period in which it is reported (Schedule K-1) by the flow-through entity

	Residence with Minimal Use	Nonresidence	Residence with Significant Rental Use
Rental Use	Rental use ≤ 14 days	Rental use > 14 days and *not* personally used for > of 14 days or 10% of rental days	Rental use > 14 days and personally used for > of 14 days or 10% of rental days
Rental Income	Excluded from income	Included as income	Included as income
Mortgage Interest and Property Taxes	Deductible as itemized deductions	*Personal-use* mortgage interest is not deductible; personal-use property taxes are deductible as itemized deductions	*Personal-use* mortgage interest and property taxes are deductible as itemized deductions
Other Rental Expenses	Not deductible	Deductions allowed but must be *allocated* between rental and personal days Rental loss allowed but subject to passive activity loss and at-risk rules	Deductions allowed but must be *allocated* between rental and personal days Ordering rules apply for deductions for expenses No rental loss allowed; disallowed rental expenses are carried forward

A taxpayer rented their vacation home for 10 days during the year. Rental income was $2,500, and rental expenses (excluding mortgage interest and property taxes) were $1,000. Here, because the rental use was < 15 days, none of the rental income or rental expenses are reported.

Assume that the taxpayer used their vacation home for five days and rented it for 70 days. Because the rental use was > 14 days and *not* personally used for > 14 days or 10% of rental days (10% × 70 days = 7 days), it is considered a rental property and not a residence.

Assume the same facts as the previous example except the personal-use days were 20. The rental-use days (70) are > 14 days and personal-use days (20) are > 14 days *or* 10% of rental days (7 days). Accordingly, the expenses are allocated between personal and rental use using a 22.2% (20 days / 90 days) and 77.8% (70 days / 90 days) allocation. However, no rental loss is permitted, as deductible allocated expenses are limited to rental income.

Alimony Paid

TCJA has repealed the deduction of alimony paid (and the corresponding inclusion in income for the payee) for divorces/separations executed after 2018. Alimony payments attributable to divorce/separation agreements finalized prior to 2019 will remain deductible by the payer and includible in the recipient's income. To be considered alimony, payment must satisfy all the following conditions:

- Cash only or its equivalent (not property)
- Apart when payments made (do not live together)
- Not child support (payments are applied to child support first)
- Not designated as property settlement (not taxable and not deductible)
- Own tax return for payer and payee
- Terminates on death of recipient

Tax Treatment of Alimony Payments	
Divorce Decree Is Issued or Modified:	
In 2018 or earlier • Income to payee • Deductible by payer	In 2019 or later • Not income to payee • Not deductible by payer

Payments for child support and property settlements are exempt from taxation and are thus not deductible by the payer. Because divorce settlements are not taxable, the recipient spouse assumes the payer spouse's carryover basis and holding period for the property.

Contributions to Retirement Plans

Any taxpayer with earned income is generally entitled to establish and make contributions to an **Individual Retirement Account (IRA)**. They can do so even if they are actively participating in other pension or profit-sharing plans. For purposes of eligibility for the IRA, earned income includes:

- Salaries and wages
- Net self-employment income

Contributions are limited for 2024 to the lower of earned income or $7,000 ($14,000 MFJ) per year, per individual (+$1,000 for individuals 50+). A married couple filing a joint return can establish and contribute $7,000 ($8,000 50+) each to separate IRAs as long as the earned income of the couple is at least $14,000 ($16,000 if both 50+). IRAs come in two basic varieties:

- Traditional
- Roth

Traditional IRAs

Contributions to a traditional IRA are deductible in arriving at AGI unless both of the following conditions apply:

- The individual is actively participating in another pension or profit-sharing plan
- The individual's MAGI exceeds a threshold amount; 2024 amounts are:
  - Single filers: phaseout range starts at $77,000, ends at $87,000
  - MFJ filers: phaseout range starts at $123,000, ends at $143,000

For a married couple, if the individual is not actively participating in another plan but the individual's spouse is a participant, contributions for the nonparticipating spouse cannot be deducted if the joint MAGI exceeds $240,000 for 2024.

The phaseout is computed as:

$$\frac{\text{MAGI} - \text{Phaseout range starting point}}{\text{Phaseout range (ie, \$10,000 or \$20,000)}} \times \text{IRA contribution limit}$$

In 2024, a single taxpayer's employer included them in a qualified pension plan. In addition, the taxpayer made a $7,000 contribution to an IRA. How much can the taxpayer deduct for the IRA contribution if their MAGI is $79,000?

Because the taxpayer is an active participant in another plan, their MAGI must be verified to determine if their IRA contribution deduction is limited. Because the taxpayer's MAGI is greater than $77,000, *some* of the deduction is phased out, as follows:

Phaseout amount:

($79,000 − $77,000) / $10,000 × $7,000 = $1,400 phaseout amount

Therefore, the taxpayer's IRA contribution is $7,000 and deduction is $5,600 ($7,000 − $1,400).

Withdrawals from a **traditional IRA** are **fully taxable** (except to recover nondeductible contributions made earlier) and are taxed at the individual's ordinary income tax rate. Contributions in excess of the permitted amount are subject to a 6% excise tax each year until withdrawn.

Roth IRAs

Contributions to a **Roth IRA** are **not deductible**. The limit on contributions to a Roth IRA is the same as those to a traditional IRA: lower of earned income or $7,000 ($8,000 for those 50+). The benefit of a Roth IRA is that all withdrawals after the age of 59 1/2 are exempt from taxation (as long as the Roth IRA has been in effect for at least five years), including both contributions and earnings. Withdrawals of contributions are exempt from taxation in all cases.

The full contribution limit for Roth IRAs applies to taxpayers with MAGI below $146,000 ($230,000 MFJ) for 2024. The allowed contribution amount is reduced above these thresholds. Roth IRAs are not available if the taxpayer's MAGI exceeds, for 2024, $161,000 ($240,000 MFJ).

Early Withdrawal Penalties

Withdrawals from either type of IRA prior to the age of 59 1/2 may result in a tax penalty of 10% of the amount withdrawn (in addition to the inclusion in gross income). The penalty does not apply (but amounts withdrawn from a traditional IRA are still included in gross income) when the withdrawal is the result of:

- Payment of deductible medical expenses
- Payment of qualified higher education costs
- Death or disability of the participant
- First-time purchase of a home (up to $10,000 withdrawal)
- The birth or adoption of a child (up to $5,000 withdrawal per child for each parent)

	Traditional IRA	Roth IRA
Contribution Limit?	$7,000 (+$1,000 catch-up contribution for ≥ age 50) Limited to taxable compensation	
Contributions Deductible?	Yes	No
Contribution Deadline?	Filing deadline without extensions (most likely April 15)	
Contribution Income Limit?	No	< $161,000 ($240,000 MFJ) for 2024
Withdrawals Generally Taxable?	Yes 10% penalty for distributions prior to age 59 1/2*	No
Required Minimum Distributions (RMDs)?	Yes, at age 73	No

**For Roth IRAs, only the earnings portion would be subject to the penalty.*

Self-Employed Taxpayers

Self-employed taxpayers may establish retirement plans. Contributions on behalf of the owner are deducted from gross income in arriving at AGI.

Other retirement contributions that may be deducted from gross income include:

- **Keogh plans** (ie, qualified retirement plans)
- **Simplified employee pensions** (SEPs)
- **SIMPLE plans**

These plans are established by business owners. On an individual return, contributions on behalf of the owner are deducted from gross income in arriving at AGI, while contributions on behalf of employees of the owner are claimed as ordinary business deductions in the computation of net business profit or loss.

Due to their low contribution limits, individually managed retirement accounts (eg, IRAs) are not attractive options for self-employed taxpayers.

Keogh plans are qualified retirement plans for self-employed taxpayers and include defined-benefit and defined-contribution plans (eg, profit-sharing, money purchase plans). These plans were created to allow those taxpayers to make significantly higher tax-deferred contributions from their self-employment income to a retirement plan. However, the law no longer distinguishes between corporate and other types of plan sponsors. Therefore, the term Keogh is not frequently used.

Plan	Suited For	Contribution Limits
Simplified employee pension (SEP IRA)	Self-employed individuals or small business owners with no or few employees	Lesser of: • 25% of net self-employment income after the deduction for the contribution* or • $69,000 for 2024
SIMPLE IRA Plan (Savings incentive match plan for employees)	Larger businesses, with up to 100 employees	Lesser of: • 100% of earnings from self-employment or • $16,000 ($19,500 for age ≥ 50) for 2024
Simple 401(k) plans	Self-employed individual with no employees (exception for a spouse)	As employee: • 100% of compensation or • $23,000 for 2024 As employer: • 25% of net self-employment income after the deduction for the contribution* or • $69,000 for 2024

**Net self-employment (SE) income = SE income less deduction 1/2 of SE tax. A shortcut for the 25% computation is 20% net self-employment income before the deduction.*

A self-employed single taxpayer is 33 years old and contributed to a simplified employee pension (SEP IRA) for nine years. If the taxpayer reports net self-employment income of $100,000, what is the maximum contribution that the taxpayer can make to the SEP IRA in 2024?

The taxpayer may contribute the lesser of:

1. 25% of net self-employment income; or
2. $69,000.

Therefore, the maximum contribution is $25,000 ($100,000 × 25%).

Contributions to Education Savings Accounts

Contributions of up to **$2,000 per year** can be made on behalf of any beneficiary (even someone unrelated to the contributor) under the age of 18 to **Coverdell Education Savings Accounts (ESA)**. Contributions are not deductible, but amounts may be withdrawn free of taxation to pay elementary, middle, high school, and college expenses (including tuition, fees, books, and room and board) of the beneficiary.

- Amounts not spent by the time the beneficiary reaches the age of 30 are distributed to the beneficiary and subject to taxation and penalties
- However, unspent amounts may be transferred to the ESA of another family member of the same generation without taxation or penalties

Qualified Tuition Programs (QTP—529 plans) were set up to allow a taxpayer to make nondeductible contributions to be used for qualified higher education (undergraduate and graduate level). Earnings accumulate tax-free as long as the money stays in the plan and is used for educational purposes (eg, tuition, room and board, books).

- There is a federal penalty of 10% if the funds are withdrawn for noneducational purposes
- Can contribute up to annual gift tax exclusion (18,000 for 2024) or file an election that allows contributions larger than the exclusion amount to be taken into account ratably over five years ($90,000 total)
- Up to $10,000 of distributions from a 529 plan may be used, per student, for elementary or secondary school tuition expenses

Other Contributions

An **ABLE account** is a tax-advantaged savings account available to the disabled. Similar to a 529 plan, *nondeductible contributions* may be made to an ABLE account on behalf of a disabled beneficiary, and the earnings in the account accumulate tax-free as long as the money is spent on qualifying expenses for the beneficiary.

- Qualifying expenses include education, housing, transportation, and assistive technology
- Contributions are limited to the annual gift tax exclusion ($18,000 for 2024)
- Through 2025, rollovers from 529 plans may be made to ABLE accounts (within annual contribution limits) for the same designated beneficiary or a family member of the designated beneficiary

Early Withdrawal Penalty

A premature interest withdrawal penalty (eg, from a certificate of deposit) is deductible.

Jury Duty

The fee received for jury duty is always included in gross income, but the amount is *deductible for AGI* if the payment is remitted to the taxpayer's employer. However, any amounts received for mileage and meals are not considered income.

Health Savings Accounts (HSAs)

Contributions to **Health Savings Account (HSA)** may be deducted by a self-employed taxpayer or employee. To participate, the taxpayer must have a high-deductible health plan (HDHP) that meets the following requirements:

- Deductible must be at least $1,600 (2024) for self-only coverage and $3,200 (2024) for family coverage
- Contribution is limited to *lesser* of deductible or limit of $4,150 in 2024 for self-only and $8,300 in 2024 for family. Taxpayers 55 or older may increase the limit by $1,000

Contributions: Amounts contributed by employer are *excluded* from W-2 gross income and reduce the amount that the employee can contribute. If the individual directs their employer to allocate a portion of their earnings to HSA, the employer does not include this amount as wages on the employee's W-2.

Distributions: Distributions from an HSA are **tax-free** if used for qualified medical expenses.

- Schedule A deduction cannot be claimed for expenses paid from the HSA
- Distributions that are not used for medical expenses are subject to taxation and 20% penalty
- No penalty if distributions are made after the account beneficiary dies, becomes disabled, or turns age 65

At the beginning of the year, a married taxpayer had $900 in their health savings account. They contributed $4,000 of their $50,000 salary to their HSA. Their employer contributed $2,500 to the taxpayer's HSA also. During the current year, the taxpayer paid $3,200 of qualified medical expenses for their family from the HSA. The HSA has investment earnings of $62 this year. What are the tax effects of these transactions in 2024?

- $4,000 of wages contributed to HSA: not taxable
- $2,500 contributed to HSA by employer: not taxable
- $3,200 distribution to pay qualified medical expenses: not taxable, no penalty applies
- $62 of investment earnings: not taxable

The taxpayer cannot deduct the $3,200 spent on medical expenses as an itemized deduction. The taxpayer's total contributions of $6,500 ($4,000 + $2,500) are less than the 2024 annual contribution limit for family plans.

Farm Income

Schedule F is used to report farming activities (similar to Schedule C). Expenses include car and truck expense, chemicals and pesticides, depreciation and Section 179 deductions, feed purchased, fertilizers, mortgage interest, seeds, and plants. The net earnings from raised livestock, produce, and grains held for sale and livestock and other items bought for resale are subject to self-employment income.

- Accounting methods include cash, accrual, crop method (cost of producing the crop deducted in the year the crop income realized), or the hybrid/combination method if used consistently
- Farmers may elect to average farm income over three years
- Form 479S, Sale of Business Property, is used to report gains and losses from the sale of animals not held primarily for sale (ie, not inventory); livestock held for draft, breeding, dairy, or sporting purposes; and farmland or depreciable farm equipment

Other Adjustments for AGI

Educator Expenses: A teacher can deduct up to $300 (2024) of unreimbursed expenses related to books, equipment, and supplies used in their classroom if the teacher is educating students in grades K–12. If MFJ and both spouses are teachers, the deduction is $600.

Personal Legal Fees:

- *Discrimination lawsuits:* An individual who has filed a claim for **unlawful discrimination** can deduct attorney fees and other court costs
- *Whistleblower claims:* Attorney fees and court costs related to awards to **whistleblowers** are deductible
- In both cases, the deduction is limited to the amount included in the taxpayer's gross income due to the judgment or settlement resulting from the claim

Itemized Deductions

Representative Task (Application): Identify itemized deductions allowed in the calculation of taxable income given a specific scenario, including medical expenses, qualified residence interest expense, casualty losses, taxes, and charitable contributions.

Itemized Deductions Overview

An individual taxpayer must determine what their total deductible itemized deductions are and whether they exceed their standard deduction. Itemized deductions are reported on **Schedule A** and include the following (**COMITT**):

- Charitable contributions
- Other deductions
- Medical expenses
- Interest expense
- Taxes
- Theft and casualty losses

Standard Deduction

A taxpayer may claim a standard deduction, and the amount depends on the taxpayer's filing status. This is an *alternative* to claiming itemized deductions. The IRS provides every taxpayer a standard deduction based on filing status ($14,600 single / $29,200 MFJ / $21,900 HOH in 2024).

- The amount of the standard deduction is increased if the taxpayer (and/or spouse if MFJ) reached their 65th birthday during the tax year or if the taxpayer (and/or spouse) is legally blind. If 65 or older or blind, the additional deduction is $1,550 or $1,950 (2024) depending on filing status. If a taxpayer is both 65 or older and blind, the additional deduction amount is double (ie, $3,100 or $3,900)
- If being claimed as a *dependent* of another, the standard deduction is the greater of $1,300 (2024) or earned income plus $450, never to exceed the regular standard deduction

The dollar amounts of the standard deductions are indexed for inflation and change on an annual basis. The CPA exam consistently avoids testing amounts that change each year.

Charitable Contributions

Charitable contributions to qualified organizations are generally deductible to the extent the taxpayer has provided cash or property that exceeds any value received from the charity. For example, if the taxpayer makes a contribution to their local public television station for $240 and receives books and videos worth $60 in return, the actual charitable contribution is only $180.

- If donations of $250 or more are given, written substantiation from the donee organization is required
- Donations are deductible in the year the charity receives the funds. Contributions made by credit card are deductible when they are charged
- Ordinary payments to charitable organizations for services rendered (eg, school tuition paid to a parochial school) are **not** contributions
- Only donations to *qualified organizations* are deductible; donations to needy individuals are **not** deductible
- Volunteer services to a charitable organization may **not** be deducted except for out-of-pocket costs incurred in the performance of the volunteer work. Examples include transportation expenses between home and the site of the work, like mileage, parking, and tolls
- Overall contributions are generally limited to 50% of AGI
- Contributions exceeding any of the AGI limitations may be carried forward up to five years

Amounts paid in exchange for the rights to purchase seats at a college athletic event are no longer deductible.

Contributions of property are normally subject to **two rules**:

Ordinary Income Rule: Property is ordinary income property if its sale at FMV on the date it was contributed would have resulted in ordinary income or in short-term capital gain. This includes inventory, self-created works of art, and capital assets held for less than one year.

- The amount deductible is the property's FMV minus the amount that would be ordinary income or short-term capital gain if the property was sold for its FMV
- Generally, this rule limits the deduction to the lower of the tax basis in the property or the FMV on the date of the contribution
- The deduction of such property is limited to 50% of AGI in a tax year

Long-Term Capital Gain Rule: Property is capital gain property if its sale at FMV on the date of the contribution would have resulted in a long-term capital gain. Long-term capital gain property includes nonbusiness capital assets held more than one year and inherited assets (considered long term regardless of holding period) that have increased in value, such as stocks, bonds, and personal items (eg, furniture).

- This allows the taxpayer to claim the higher FMV of long-term capital gain property
- The deduction of such property is limited to 30% of AGI in a tax year
- If the property contributed is tangible personal property and the charitable organization does not use the property in a manner that is related to its tax-exempt purpose, the donor can deduct only the adjusted basis of the property (rule only applies if deduction is more than $5,000)

TCJA increased the limitation for cash contributions donated to public charities to 60% of AGI through 2025.

Contribution Limitations*		
Type of Contribution	**Type of Organization**	**% of AGI**
Cash	50% limitation organization	60%
	30% limitation organization	30%
Property • Declined in value; or • Ordinary income	50% limitation organization	50%
	30% limitation organization	30%
Property (long-term capital gain)	50% limitation organization	30%
	30% limitation organization	20%

**Noncomprehensive list*

A taxpayer purchased stock for $5,000 and after owning it for six months donated the stock to a local museum. At the time of the donation, the stock's FMV was $8,000. Because the stock is a capital asset owned for less than one year, it is ordinary income-producing property. Therefore, the taxpayer's **contribution is $5,000** ($8,000 FMV – $3,000 appreciation).

If the taxpayer decided to donate the stock after one year, the contribution would have been the **$8,000 FMV**.

A taxpayer donated an organ to a local church to be used during its worship services. The organ was purchased five years ago for $80,000 and has a FMV of $100,000 at the time of the contribution. Because the church is using the organ in the capacity of its function, the taxpayer has a **$100,000 charitable donation** (ie, appreciated long-term capital gain property, so use FMV) subject to AGI limitations.

Assume that the church sold the organ instead of using it. Now the taxpayer's contribution is limited to **$80,000 (basis)** because the church did not use the gift to carry out its function.

A taxpayer with AGI of $100,000 donates stock to a 50% qualified charity. The stock was purchased 10 years ago for $10,000 and was worth $40,000 on the date of the contribution. Since it qualifies as appreciated long-term capital gain property, the taxpayer may claim the FMV of $40,000, except that this exceeds 30% of AGI, so the deduction in the tax year is limited to $30,000 (ie, $100,000 AGI × 30% limitation). The remaining $10,000 ($40,000 – $30,000) can be carried forward.

An individual taxpayer has AGI of $100,000 and makes the following contributions:

- Cash of $10,000 to Habitat for Humanity
- Cash of $500 to a man experiencing homelessness
- Clothing with a FMV of $400 and a cost of $1,600 to the Salvation Army
- Services provided to his church as a handyman valued at $800
- Credit card charge of $400 to the local university for basketball tickets
- Stock held for three years with a FMV of $2,200 and adjusted basis of $1,300 to their church

How much can the taxpayer deduct as a charitable contribution?

The taxpayer can deduct **$12,600** ($10,000 cash + $400 FMV of clothing + $2,200 FMV of stock). The amount is below the 50% and 30% limitations.

The cash given to the man experiencing homelessness is not deductible because the man is not a qualified charitable organization. Neither the FMV of *services* provided to the church nor the credit card charge for university basketball tickets are permitted charitable deductions.

Charitable Contributions Deduction for Individual Taxpayers

Overriding rules:

- Must be made to a qualified organization
- Deduction is less any value received from the organization for the contribution

Type of Contribution	Examples	Allowable Deduction
Cash	• Cash, check, credit cards	Amount of cash, check, or charge
Ordinary income property	• Inventory	Generally, the lesser of the property's adjusted tax basis or the FMV on date contributed*
Short-term capital gain or loss property (ie, held for ≤ 1 year)	• Stocks, bonds, land, buildings • Personal items	
Section 1231 assets	• Trade or business assets	
Long-term capital gain or loss property	• Stocks, bonds, land, buildings • Personal items	FMV of property on date of contribution
Certain long-term capital gain property not used for related purpose	• Tangible personal property • Artwork	Adjusted tax basis on date of contribution

**This is a shortcut to the FMV: Short-term capital gain or ordinary income if property had been sold.*

Note: Depreciable property is subject to special rules when determining the amount of the charitable deduction and is beyond the scope of REG.

Other Deductions

Gambling losses are deductible as an itemized deduction to the extent of winnings. Therefore, if a taxpayer does not itemize their deduction, no deduction is allowed for gambling losses. Gambling winnings are reported in *income* separately on Form 1040. Excess losses may not be carried over to another tax year.

Professional gamblers can deduct nonwagering business expenses on Schedule C to the extent of gambling winnings.

- For 2018–2025, gambling losses include any expense incurred in connection with a gambling activity for any individual taxpayer (not just professionals) if such expense would otherwise be allowed as a deduction
- This means other related expenses incurred (eg, travel expense to and from a casino), in addition to the cost of wagers, are deductible up to gambling winnings

Estate taxes on income in respect of a decedent (IRD) are deductible.

Miscellaneous itemized deductions subject to 2% of AGI limitation have been suspended for 2018–2025 (ie, they will not be deductible again until 2026).

Nina works as a waitress but also enjoys betting on baseball games. Nina won $12,000 from gambling and lost $14,500. What are the tax consequences to Nina?

Nina must report the **gambling winnings of $12,000** on Form 1040, Schedule 1, and can deduct a **$12,000 gambling deduction** on Schedule A. Gambling losses are deductible only to the extent of gambling winnings.

What if Nina was a professional gambler?

Nina must report the gambling winnings of $12,000 on Form 1040, Schedule C (self-employment income), and can deduct a $12,000 wagering deduction on Schedule C. Again, gambling losses are deductible only to the extent of gambling winnings for professional gamblers.

Medical Expenses, Paid and Not Reimbursed

A taxpayer may incur substantial medical expenses in a given year but not be allowed a deduction due to the 7.5% of AGI limitation that applies. Also, if a taxpayer has health insurance, the insurance reimbursement must be deducted from the medical expenditure to determine the allowable medical expense. Note: if the taxpayer does not itemize their deductions, then no deduction for medical expenses is permitted.

Deductible **Medical Expenses**	***Nondeductible*** **Medical Expenses**
Most medical services and devices (eg, hospitals, doctors, dentists, nurses, labs, eye exams, x-rays, hearing aids and batteries, prescription glasses and contacts, crutches, wheelchairs, etc.)	Costs for general health improvement that are not treatments for specific medical conditions
Prescription drugs and insulin (less any insurance reimbursements)	Nonprescription drugs and medicines, medical marijuana
Long-term care insurance premiums on qualified policies	Premiums on life insurance and disability insurance
Transportation costs for medical and dental care (actual expenses for cab, bus, ambulance, or personal vehicle expenses like mileage, tolls, and parking)	Plastic surgery (except to cure disfiguring illnesses, injuries, or birth defects)
Costs to install medically prescribed facilities in a home to the extent the costs exceed the increase in the value of the home (eg, elevator, swimming pool for physical therapy)	Medicare portion of Social Security and self-employment taxes
Health insurance premiums (except to the extent they've already been claimed for self-employed taxpayers in arriving at AGI or were paid out of HSAs with tax-free funds)	Funeral, burial, and cremation expenses

Other Medical Costs: Medical costs must be paid by the taxpayer (or spouse) during the tax year. However, the medical costs may be on behalf of the taxpayer, spouse, a dependent, or other people for whom the taxpayer provides over 50% of support, even if they do not qualify as dependents because the income or joint return tests are not satisfied.

- Medical expenses paid for a deceased spouse or dependent are deductible as medical expenses in the year paid, regardless of whether they were paid before or after the decedent's death
- Payments made by credit card are deductible when charged (ie, not when credit card balance is paid)

Fred and Betty, both age 35, have an AGI of $55,000 and paid the following out-of-pocket medical expenses during the tax year.

Hospital and doctor bills	$3,200
Prescription medications	1,350
Health insurance premiums	4,400
Prescription eyeglasses	500
Nonprescription sunglasses	300
Membership to fitness center to lose weight	400
Nutrisystem membership fee	250
12-week program to stop smoking (prescribed by doctor)	1,200
Teeth cleaning and root canal	650
Cosmetic surgery for a nonmedical facelift	6,000

Neither Fred nor Betty is self-employed. What is their deduction for medical expenses this year?

Nonprescription sunglasses are not deductible because they are not medically necessary. The fitness center membership and the Nutrisystem fee are not deductible because these are not part of a treatment plan provided by a medical professional. The surgery for a facelift is not deductible because this occurred solely for cosmetic purposes. Fred and Betty's medical expense deduction of **$7,175** is calculated as follows:

Hospital and doctor bills	$ 3,200
Prescription medications	1,350
Health insurance premiums	4,400
Prescription eyeglasses	500
Stop smoking program	1,200
Dental services	650
Total	$11,300
Less: 7.5% of $55,000 AGI	(4,125)
Medical expense deduction	$ 7,175

Interest Paid

There are two types of interest that taxpayers can deduct as an itemized deduction, investment interest and home mortgage interest. Interest related to a business activity or production of income activity is deductible on Schedules C, E, or F. Personal interest expense is **not** deductible (eg, credit card interest).

Type	Deductible?	Explanation
Mortgage interest expense (acquisition debt)	*Yes*	Limited to $750,000 indebtedness for 2018 to 2025, limitation only applies to debt incurred after 12/15/2017 Interest prorated if in excess of limit Acquisition indebtedness means debt used to buy, build, or substantially improve the home that secures the loan Includes loans that replace previous acquisition indebtedness May be claimed on both a primary and secondary residence Includes points paid to acquire (deduct immediately) and to refinance (amortize)
Mortgage interest expense (home equity debt)	*No*	Generally not deductible unless loan proceeds used for capital improvements to the home
Investment interest expense (excludes interest from passive activities)	*Yes*	Refers to interest paid on borrowings used to make personal investments, such as margin loans in the purchase of stock Limited to net investment income* for the year Unused amount carried forward indefinitely Interest paid in advance is not deductible in the period paid, even by a cash-basis taxpayer Required to be allocated over the tax years to which it applies
Personal interest expense	*No*	Any interest that is not mortgage, investment, student loan, or business interest Examples include interest on personal auto loans and credit cards

**Interest income, dividend income, capital gains, and passive investment income less certain investment expenses (eg, commissions)*

A single taxpayer has the following items of income and expense for the current year:

Interest income	$12,000
Net short-term capital gain	16,000
Investment interest expense	32,000
Investment advisor fee	4,500

How much of the investment interest expense can the taxpayer deduct as an itemized deduction?

The taxpayer's net investment income is $28,000 ($12,000 + $16,000). The investment advisor fee is not deductible and cannot reduce net investment income. The taxpayer's deduction for **investment interest expense is $28,000**; the remaining $4,000 ($32,000 – $28,000) can be carried forward indefinitely.

In January of Year 1, a taxpayer takes out a $500,000 mortgage to purchase a primary home with a FMV of $800,000. In February of Year 1, the taxpayer takes out a $200,000 home equity loan to put an addition on the main home.

Both loans are secured by the main home, and the total does not exceed the cost of the home; so all the interest is deductible since the total of both loans, **$700,000** ($500,000 + $200,000), does **not** exceed the $750,000 limitation.

Assume that the taxpayer uses the $200,000 home equity loan to purchase a vacation home instead. Since the loan is secured by the main home and not the vacation home, the interest on the home equity loan would **not** be deductible. However, if the taxpayer takes out a separate loan that is secured by the vacation home, then the interest on that loan would be deductible as acquisition indebtedness.

Marco owns a principal residence and has acquisition debt of $590,000. He also owns a vacation home with acquisition debt of $370,000. He paid interest expense of $18,990 on his principal home and paid interest expense of $14,100 on the vacation home. Both homes were purchased in 2020. In the current year, Marco took out a home equity credit line of $25,000 to pay off credit card debt and buy an automobile and paid $2,700 of interest expense.

How much of mortgage interest expense is deductible?

Interest is deductible on only $750,000 of acquisition debt because the debts were taken out after December 15, 2017. Interest on home equity debt is not deductible unless the loan was used to substantially improve the residence (in this case it was not). The debt from both residences totaled $960,000 ($590,000 + $370,000), and the total interest expense paid on both residences is $33,090 ($18,990 + $14,100).

The interest must be **prorated** because only the interest on *$750,000 of debt* is deductible:

$$\frac{\$750,000}{\$960,000} \times \$33,090 = \textbf{\$25,852 deductible interest}$$

Taxes Paid

If a taxpayer **itemizes**, **certain taxes** may be **deducted** on Schedule A (subject to limits for 2018–2025). The total deduction for state and local taxes is limited to $10,000 for MFJ and single taxpayers ($5,000 MFS) for 2018 through 2025. There is no carryover or carryback of taxes exceeding the limitation. Examples of state and local taxes are real estate, property, income tax, and sales tax, which are discussed below.

- State and local **personal property taxes** (eg, with registration on a car, a tax based on the value of the vehicle would be deductible but not standard fees)
- State and local **real estate property taxes** (must be the owner of the property, joint tenancy is okay). Taxes due in a year in which the property is sold are apportioned between the buyer and seller on a daily basis within the real property tax year
    - Assessments for improvements (eg, streets, sewers) are **not** deductible but are added to the basis of the property
    - Deductions for foreign real property taxes are **not** currently allowed
- Individuals can deduct the *greater* of personal **state and local income paid** or **sales taxes paid** (based on actual amount paid or an IRS table)
- **Other taxes** include foreign income taxes paid and the generation-skipping tax imposed on certain income distributions from trusts. A taxpayer may claim a credit or deduction for foreign taxes but not both. Other taxes are not part of the $10,000 SALT limitation
- Fees, fines, federal, and FICA are **not** deductible
    - There is no deduction for taxes paid to the federal government or for gas or excise taxes
    - Fees charged by state and local governments may not be deducted unless they are based specifically on income or property values

A single taxpayer paid the following taxes during the current year:

Real estate taxes on personal residence	$ 4,800
Real estate taxes on land held for investment	1,700
State income tax	5,200
State sales tax	5,800
Fishing license	75
Real estate taxes on vacation home in Spain	3,000
Federal income tax	16,000
Ad valorem tax on personal-use automobile	500

How much can they deduct as an itemized deduction?

All the taxes are deductible except for the foreign property tax paid and federal income tax. The fishing license is not deductible because it is not a tax. The sales tax is deducted instead of the state income tax because it is the larger of the two. Their total available deduction is $12,800, but the current tax law limits the deduction to $10,000.

Theft and Casualty Losses

Eligible personal **casualty losses** that **exceed 10%** of **AGI** and $100 per event may be deducted on Schedule A. A casualty loss is a sudden event (eg, theft or destruction) that causes the taxpayer to lose an asset or for its value to seriously drop over the course of a period not exceeding 30 days. Accidental breakage of items in the home by family members is not considered a casualty event. Progressive deterioration is also not included (eg, termite, moth, or drought damage).

The loss is measured by the drop in FMV caused by the event but is limited to the tax basis of the asset. Costs incurred by the taxpayer to repair damaged property increase the tax basis of the property but do not affect the drop in FMV loss measurement.

The deduction for personal casualty losses is now generally limited to losses attributable to federally declared disasters for 2018 through 2025. This limitation does not apply to the extent the taxpayer has personal casualty gains; that is, any personal casualty loss may be deducted to the extent of the personal casualty gain.

Assume a taxpayer purchased their home for $100,000. The home was worth $200,000 prior to a fire caused by a federally declared disaster, and the fire reduced the property's value to $120,000. The taxpayer spent $50,000 to repair the damage resulting from the fire.

The drop in FMV from the event was $200,000 − $120,000 = $80,000. The tax basis of the property is $100,000 + $50,000 = $150,000. The loss that may be claimed is $80,000, the lower of the loss in FMV ($80,000) or tax basis ($150,000).

Assume all the same facts, except that the taxpayer bought the home for $10,000 in an auction. In this case, the taxpayer's basis in the property is $10,000 + $50,000 = $60,000. Thus, even though the loss in FMV is still $80,000, the loss that may be claimed is limited to the taxpayer's $60,000 basis.

Once the loss is determined, it must be reduced by all of the following:

- Insurance and government reimbursements that the taxpayer is entitled to receive (if reimbursements exceed the loss, an involuntary conversion gain has occurred)
- $100 per event
- 10% of AGI per year

A taxpayer lives in Missouri, and their town was devastated by a tornado. The area was declared a federal disaster area. They paid $195,000 for their home and belongings eight years ago. The fair market value of their home and belongings was $255,000 before the tornado and $0 afterward. Their insurance company reimbursed them $160,000. The taxpayer has AGI of $65,000 in the current year. The taxpayer's deductible casualty loss is calculated as follows:

Lesser of decline in FMV ($255,000) or AB of property ($195,000)	$195,000
Less: Insurance reimbursements	(160,000)
Less: $100 per casualty	(100)
Less: 10% × $65,000 of AGI	(6,500)
Casualty loss deduction	**$ 28,400**

Carryover Rules for Individuals

	Carryback	Carryforward
Charitable Contributions	No	5 years
Net Operating Losses (NOL) (Including Excess Business Losses)	No	Indefinitely
Net Capital Losses (in Excess of $3,000 Annual Limitation)	No	Indefinitely
Investment Interest	No	Indefinitely
Net Passive Losses	No	Indefinitely, or may be claimed when the investment is sold
Net Gambling Losses	No	No

Practice Scenario

Maverick Hill files as a single taxpayer and has an AGI of $54,000. In the current year, Maverick purchased a new home. Maverick has provided the following information to their accounting firm, JJX LLP:

Doctor bill for annual checkup	$ 220
Surgeon bill for broken arm	1,400
Hospital bill	2,300
Dentist bill for root canal	700
Eye exam and glasses	450
Gym membership	750
Advil	110
Prescription medication	550
State income tax	2,900
Local sales tax	3,100
Real estate taxes	6,300
Personal property tax	1,200
Mortgage interest expense	6,500
Groceries	2,200
Uniforms as a nurse	750
Cash charitable contributions	4,400
Clothing given to Salvation Army (FMV $450, basis $2,250)	
Tax preparation fees	350
Personal cell phone	1,200
Substantiated gambling losses (gambling income is $2,450)	4,200

Based on this information provided by the client, the staff accountant at JJX prepared the following Schedule A Itemized Deductions schedule. Review the schedule and make corrections, if necessary, based on the list of Maverick Hill's expenditures provided.

Item	Correction to Draft Schedule A Required?	Corrected Amount
Medical		
Taxes		
Interest		
Charitable contributions		
Other		
Total		

Exhibit

Draft Schedule A prepared by JJX staff accountant (see next page)

SCHEDULE A (Form 1040)

Department of the Treasury
Internal Revenue Service

Itemized Deductions

Attach to Form 1040 or 1040-SR

Go to *www.irs.gov/ScheduleA* for instructions and the latest information

Caution: If you are claiming a net qualified disaster loss on Form 4684, see the instructions for line 16

OMB No. 1545-0074

Year 1

Name(s) shown on Form 1040 or 1040-SR: Maverick Hill

Your social security number: 123-45-6789

Section	Line	Description	Box	Amount	Box	Amount
Medical and Dental Expenses		**Caution:** Do not include expenses reimbursed or paid by others.				
	1	Medical and dental expenses (see instructions)	1	6,480		
	2	Enter amount from Form 1040 or 1040-SR, line 11 [2] 54,000				
	3	Multiply line 2 by 7.5% (0.075)	3	4,050		
	4	Subtract line 3 from line 1. If line 3 is more than line 1, enter -0-			4	2,430
Taxes You Paid	5	State and local taxes.				
	a	State and local income taxes or general sales taxes. You may include either income taxes or general sales taxes on line 5a, but not both. If you elect to include general sales taxes instead of income taxes, check this box ☐	5a	2,900		
	b	State and local real estate taxes (see instructions)	5b	6,300		
	c	State and local personal property taxes	5c	1,200		
	d	Add lines 5a through 5c	5d	10,400		
	e	Enter the smaller of line 5d or $10,000 ($5,000 if married filing separately)	5e	5,000		
	6	Other taxes. List type and amount:	6			
	7	Add lines 5e and 6			7	5,000
Interest You Paid Caution: Your mortgage interest deduction may be limited. See instructions.	8	Home mortgage interest and points. If you didn't use all of your home mortgage loan(s) to buy, build, or improve your home, see instructions, and check this box ☐				
	a	Home mortgage interest and points reported to you on Form 1098. See instructions if limited	8a	6,500		
	b	Home mortgage interest not reported on you on Form 1098. See instructions if limited. If paid to the person from whom you bought the home, see instructions and show that person's name, identifying no., and address	8b			
	c	Points not reported to you on Form 1098. See instructions for special rules	8c			
	d	Reserved for future use	8d			
	e	Add lines 8a through 8c	8e			
	9	Investment interest. Attach form 4952 if required. See instructions	9			
	10	Add lines 8e and 9			10	6,500
Gifts to Charity Caution: If you made a gift and got a benefit for it, see instructions.	11	Gifts by cash or check. If you made any gift of $250 or more, see instructions	11	4,400		
	12	Other than by cash or check. If you made any gift of $250 or more, see instructions. You must attach Form 8283 if over $500	12	2,250		
	13	Carryover from prior year	13			
	14	Add lines 11 through 13			14	6,650
Casualty and Theft Losses	15	Casualty and theft loss(es) from a federally declared disaster (other than net qualified disaster losses). Attach form 4684 and enter the amount from line 18 of that form. See instructions			15	
Other Itemized Deductions	16	Other—from list in instructions. List type and amount: Gambling losses			16	2,450
Total Itemized Deductions	17	Add the amounts in the far right column for lines 4 through 16. Also, enter this amount on Form 1040 or 1040-SR, line 12			17	23,030
	18	If you elect to itemize deductions even though they are less than your standard deduction, check this box ☐				

For Paperwork Reduction Act Notice, see separate instructions. Schedule A (Form 1040)

Solution

Medical

Doctor bill for annual checkup	$ 220
Surgeon bill for broken arm	1,400
Hospital bill	2,300
Dentist bill for root canal	700
Eye exam and glasses	450
Prescription medication	550
Total allowable medical expenses	$5,620
Less: 7.5% AGI threshold	(4,050)
Net medical deduction	$1,570

The staff accountant *incorrectly* calculated total allowable medical and dental expenses of $6,480 by including the over-the-counter drugs ($110) and the gym membership ($750). These are not deductible medical expenses, and Schedule A must be corrected accordingly.

Taxes

Local sales tax	$3,100
State and local real estate taxes	6,300
State and local personal property taxes	1,200
Total state and local taxes	$10,600
Deductible state and local taxes ($10,000 limit)	$10,000

The staff accountant made two errors when calculating Maverick Hill's deductible state and local taxes.

First, total state and local taxes of $10,400 are *incorrectly* calculated by including Maverick's state and local *income* tax ($2,900) instead of their local *sales* tax ($3,100). Taxpayers can deduct the *greater of* the two.

Second, the staff accountant *incorrectly* limited Maverick's SALT deduction to $5,000. This is the limit for *MFS* taxpayers; *single* taxpayers may take a $10,000 deduction.

Interest

The staff accountant *correctly* determined that the $6,500 of home mortgage interest expense is deductible on Schedule A.

Charitable Contributions

Cash charitable contributions:	$4,400
FMV of clothing	450
Total charitable contributions	$4,850

The staff accountant *incorrectly* calculated total gifts to charity of $6,650 by taking the basis of the donated clothes ($2,250) as a deduction rather than the clothes' FMV ($450). The FMV of the clothing is the deductible amount to Maverick because that is a better proxy of the value received by the Salvation Army at the time the clothes were received. Total charitable contributions must be adjusted accordingly.

Note: the total charitable contributions are less than any applicable AGI limit.

Other Itemized Deductions

Deductible gambling losses	$2,450
Total other itemized deductions	$2,450

The staff accountant *correctly* calculated other itemized deductions, which includes only a portion of the gambling losses. Maverick can deduct gambling losses to the extent of gambling winnings and, therefore, may take a gambling loss of $2,450 as another itemized deduction.

All other expenses provided by Maverick are nondeductible expenses:

- Uniforms as a nurse (employee business expenses are generally not deductible)
- Groceries and cell phone (personal in nature, not deductible)
- Tax prep fees (previously a miscellaneous 2% floor deduction, not currently applicable due to TCJA)

Item	Correction to Draft Schedule A Required?	Corrected Amount
Medical	Yes	$ 1,570
Taxes	Yes	10,000
Interest	No	6,500
Charitable contributions	Yes	4,850
Other	No	2,450
Total	Yes	**$25,370**

Qualifying Business Income (QBI) Deduction

Representative Task (Application): Calculate the qualifying business income (QBI) deduction for federal income tax purposes.

QBI: Overview

Individual taxpayers are allowed a 20% deduction for qualified business income from pass-through entities (partnerships, limited liability companies, and S corporations) and sole proprietorships.

- The availability of the deduction depends on the type of business (eg, service/nonservice) and the taxpayer's taxable income (TI) before the deduction
- The QBI deduction is deducted from AGI, but it is not considered an itemized deduction

Congress created the QBI deduction for tax years after 2017 to level the playing field for taxpayers engaged in flow-through entities. In 2017, when the corporate tax rate was lowered to 21%, the highest individual tax rate was 37%. This differential of 37% versus 21% seemed inequitable, so Congress created the QBI deduction.

Level of TI	2024 MFJ Amounts	Eligibility for QBI Deductions
Below threshold	$0–$383,900	Full deduction allowed for any business
Between threshold and upper limit	$383,901–$483,900	Wage/property limitation partially applies If nonqualified business, another reduction applies
Above upper limit	Over $483,900	Full wage/property limitation applies Must be qualified business

Qualified Business

Qualified business means **any business other than** a **Specified Service Trade** or **Business** (SSTB). An SSTB is any business involving the performance of services in the fields of health, law, accounting, actuarial science, performing arts, consulting, athletics, financial services[1], brokerage services[1], or any business where the principal asset of such business is the reputation or skill of one or more of its employees/owners.

- Notice that this specifically *does not include* engineering and architecture since they are a part of building something
  - Contrast that to accountants, lawyers, etc., who only provide services
  - Thus, Congress decided payment for services generally should be taxed the same as wages (ie, *without* a 20% deduction)

Qualified Business Income

QBI means the net amount of qualified items of income, gain, deduction, and loss from a qualified business within the U.S. QBI does *not* include:

- Reasonable compensation paid to the taxpayer
- Guaranteed payments or other payments paid to a partner for services rendered
- Capital gains/losses
- Dividends (or the equivalent)
- Interest income (eg, investment interest income) other than business interest income

1 *Financial and brokerage services that consist of investing and investment management, trading, or dealing in securities, partnership interests, or commodities.*

The QBI deduction is determined at the partner/shareholder level, so each partner/shareholder takes into account their allocable share of each qualified item of income, gain, deduction, and loss and is treated as having W-2 wages and unadjusted basis of qualified property equal to their allocable share of such items. To compute the QBI, first reduce the activity's taxable income by each of the following:

- 50% of the self-employment tax
- The self-employed health insurance deduction
- Any retirement plan contributions based on this income

Deductible QBI per Business

Wage/Property Limitation: The deductible amount per business is equal to 20% of the business's QBI but is generally limited to the greater of:

- 50% of W-2 wages, or
- 25% of W-2 wages + 2.5% of unadjusted basis of qualified property (ie, entity's depreciable tangible assets used in the production of QBI).

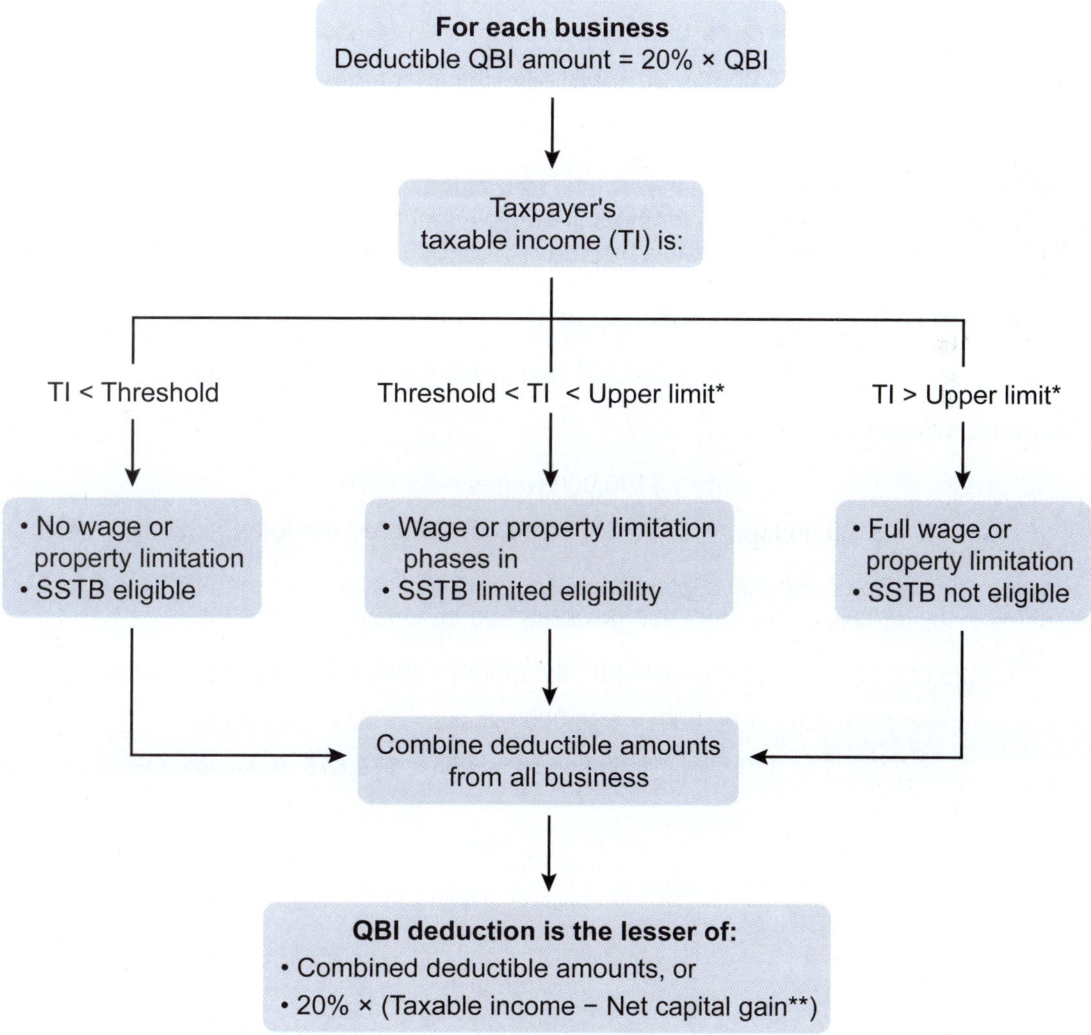

Lower Income Level 1—Below Threshold

If the taxpayer's modified taxable income does not exceed the threshold ($383,900 MFJ / $191,950 others for 2024), the wage/property limitation above does **not** apply.

Sara, a sole proprietor, is married and will file a joint return in Year 1. Sara has $300,000 of net business income after the reduction for the self-employment tax from a T-shirt business and modified taxable income of $325,000. W-2 wages were $100,000, and the unadjusted basis of qualified property is $60,000. What is the deductible QBI for the T-shirt business?

20% × $300,000 = **$60,000** deductible QBI

The wage/property limitation does not apply because the modified taxable income is under the threshold.

Middle Income Level 2—Between Threshold and Upper Limit

For taxpayers with modified taxable income up to $100,000 MFJ ($50,000 for others) over the threshold, the limitation will *partially* apply depending on where the taxpayer's income is in that $100,000/$50,000 phase-in range above the threshold. That is, the deduction is reduced by the amount equal to:

- [(TI – threshold) / $100,000] × (20% QBI – limitation) for MFJ taxpayers
- [(TI – 1/2 MFJ threshold) / $50,000] × (20% QBI – limitation) for other taxpayers

Assume the same facts as the last example, except that in Year 2 Sara increases their net business income after reduction for the self-employment tax from the T-shirt business to $425,000, and their modified taxable income is $425,000. W-2 wages are $100,000, and the unadjusted basis of qualified property is $60,000. What is the deductible QBI for the T-shirt business when the threshold is $383,900 for joint returns?

20% × $425,000 = $85,000 deductible QBI before limitation

Wage/property limitation, greater of:

50% × $100,000 wages = $50,000

(25% × $100,000 wages) + (2.5% × $60,000 qualified property) = $26,500

Here, the wage limitation of $50,000 applies because modified TI is greater than $383,900, but only *partially* since modified TI is below $483,900 (ie, $383,900 threshold + $100,000).

[($425,000 TI − $383,900 threshold) / $100,000] × ($85,000 − $50,000 limitation)

($41,100 / $100,000) × $35,000 excess = $14,385 *reduction*

$85,000 − $14,385 partial limitation/reduction = **$70,615** *deductible* QBI

Highest Income Level 3—Above Upper Limit

Assume the same facts as the last example, except that Sara increases their net business income from the T-shirt business to $485,000 and modified taxable income to $485,000 in Year 3. W-2 wages are $100,000, and the unadjusted basis of qualified property is $60,000. What is the deductible QBI for the T-shirt business?

20% × $485,000 = $97,000

Wage/property limitation, greater of:

50% × $100,000 wages = $50,000

(25% × $100,000 wages) + (2.5% × $60,000 qualified property) = $26,500

Here the wage limitation of $50,000 would apply in full because Sara's TI is above the upper limit, so *deductible* QBI is **$50,000**.

Exception for Specified Service Trade or Businesses (SSTB)

When the taxable income of a taxpayer is less than the upper limit (ie, the sum of the threshold amount plus $100,000 MFJ or $50,000 other filers), then any specified service business of the taxpayer (ie, a nonqualified business) will be treated as a qualified business. However, only the applicable percentage of qualified income/deduction items, W-2 wages, and the unadjusted basis of qualified property is used in the calculations when TI exceeds the threshold.

- *Applicable percentage* means:
  - 100% – [(TI – threshold) / $100,000] for MFJ taxpayers
  - 100% – [(TI – 1/2 MFJ threshold) / $50,000] for all others
- In other words, the deduction:
  - Is allowed in full for nonqualified businesses if the taxpayer's TI falls below the threshold amount
  - Is phased out for every dollar over the threshold, up to the $100,000 MFJ (or $50,000) limit

Randy is single and is the sole owner of an S corporation that provides home health care. In Year 1, the business produces $195,000 of net business income and modified taxable income. W-2 wages were $500,000, and the unadjusted basis of qualified property is $25,000. What is Randy's deductible QBI for the home health care business when the threshold is $191,950 for single individuals?

Randy's business is a SSTB because home health care is a service business.

First, the applicable percentage is determined: 100% – [($195,000 TI – $191,950) / $50,000] = 93.9%

Then the percentage is applied to the QBI calculation: 20% × ($195,000 TI × 93.9%) = $36,621

Wage/property limitation: greater of:

50% × ($500,000 wages × 93.9%) = $234,750

[25% × ($500,000 wages × 93.9%)] + [2.5% × ($25,000 property × 93.9%)] = $117,962

Here, the wage/property limitation does not apply; therefore, the *deductible* QBI is **$36,621**.

Note: If the wage/property limitation had been low enough to apply, the same partial application calculation that applies in the middle income category above would have to be applied on top of this applicable percentage reduction.

Overall QBI Deduction Limit per Taxpayer

There is yet another limitation; the overall QBI deduction per taxpayer is generally limited to the lesser of:

- Combined deductible QBI for all businesses owned, or
- 20% × (TI – NCG)
  - TI = Taxable income computed without QBI deduction
  - NCG = Net capital gain (includes qualified dividends)

Roger, who is married to Louisa, has taxable income* of $310,000 that includes $20,000 of Louisa's income from a part-time job, a net capital gain of $10,000, and $280,000 ordinary business income from Roger's CPA Review S corp. Since this is his only business, his $56,000 deductible QBI (ie, $280,000 × 20%) is considered his combined QBI amount. Thus, Roger's QBI deduction is limited to the *lesser of*:

Combined QBI amount of $56,000, or
20% × ($310,000 − $10,000 NCG) = $60,000

**Taxable income = AGI – standard/itemized deductions (ie, TI before QBI deduction).*

QBI Deduction Summary

<table>
<tr><th>TI* < Threshold
(Level 1)</th><th>TI > Upper limit**
(Level 3)</th><th>Threshold < TI < Upper limit
(Level 2)</th></tr>
<tr><td colspan="3">1. Determine deductible QBI per business</td></tr>
<tr><td colspan="3">Deductible QBI before limitations = 20% × QBI</td></tr>
<tr><td></td><td colspan="2">Wage/property limitation, greater of:
• 50% of wages, or
• 25% of wages + 2.5% of unadjusted basis of qualified property</td></tr>
<tr><td></td><td></td><td>Phase-in reduction of wage/property limitation
[(TI – threshold) / Phase-in range] × (Deductible QBI – limitation)</td></tr>
<tr><td>SSTBs allowed</td><td>No SSTBs</td><td>Applicable % for SSTBs =
100% – [(TI – threshold) / Phase-in range]</td></tr>
<tr><td colspan="3">2. Determine QBI deduction
Overall taxpayer limitation—Lesser of:
• Combined deductible QBI for all businesses, or
• 20% × (TI – NCG***)</td></tr>
</table>

**Taxable income before QBI deduction.*

***Upper limit = threshold + phase-in range (ie, $100,000 MFJ or $50,000 others).*

****Net capital gain also includes qualified dividends.*

Accuracy of AGI and Taxable Income

Representative Task (Analysis): Review Form 1040 – U.S. Individual Income Tax Return and supporting documentation, including any source data used to create the return, to determine the accuracy of the adjusted gross income and taxable income reported.

Overview

Being able to determine whether a deduction is reported for AGI or from AGI is important to ensure accuracy of both AGI and taxable income. Remember that some deductions are limited or may not be permitted. Carefully review the provided information and supporting documents to confirm that each item receives the appropriate tax treatment.

Practice Scenario

Bailey Cream, age 32, is a widow who lives at 2811 Berry Street, in Loveland, CO, 80528. Her Social Security number is 123-45-6789. Bailey works for one employer and has received a form W-2 reporting her Year 29 earnings and withholdings. Assume the current-year standard deduction for Bailey's filing status is $14,600.

In Year 25, after a protracted battle with cancer, Bailey's husband, Frank, passed away. Unfortunately, their medical insurance did not cover the entire hospital stay, so Bailey has struggled to pay the medical bills over the past several years. Thankfully, she's been able to work out a payment plan, which includes Loveland Community Hospital canceling $11,000 of the amount she owed them. As a result, Bailey has received a Form 1099-C from the hospital.

The grocery store where Bailey shops, the Go Green Supermarket, also sells lottery tickets. Bailey likes to occasionally take a risk and will sometimes buy a ticket. In January of Year 29, she purchased a $5 ticket and won $5,000. As a result, she received a Form W-2G from the Colorado Lottery. Also, during February of Year 29, Bailey's Aunt Kitty kindly sent her a birthday gift of $2,500.

Enjoying her recent windfall from her lottery winnings and her birthday gift, Bailey decided to invest the money by purchasing stock. Bailey received a Form 1099-DIV for this investment. In addition, Bailey decided to invest in a certificate of deposit with State Exchange Bank. She received a Form 1099-INT.

Bailey is also a 10% shareholder in Clean Air Corporation and received a K-1.

Bailey has the following expenses:

State income tax withheld	$ 665
Sales tax	1,050
Property taxes on investment land	3,300
Groceries	3,600
Rent paid	24,000
Charitable contributions	5,000
Utilities paid	2,400

Bailey has completed her Form 1040 page 1 and Schedule 1. Review the forms for accuracy and completeness based on the exhibits provided. Some additional items to consider for the review:

- Which income items should be included, and which items should be excluded?
- Which expense items should be included as adjustments for AGI and from AGI?
- Should Bailey itemize deductions or take the standard deduction?
- Are all of the source documents and information provided by Bailey necessary to prepare and review the tax return?

After reviewing the exhibits and partial tax return, indicate if the provided items were correctly calculated and confirm the correct amount in the tables provided.

Schedule 1

Line Item	Description	Adjustment Required?	Correct Amount
Line 3	Business income (loss) Schedule C		
Line 5	Rental real estate, royalties, partnerships, S corporations		
Line 8b	Gambling income		
Line 8c	Cancellation of debt		
Line 9	Other income, Add lines 8a–8z		
Line 10	Additional income, Add lines 1–9		

Form 1040, Page 1

Line Item	Description	Adjustment Required?	Correct Amount
Line 1	Wages		
Line 2a	Tax-exempt interest income		
Line 2b	Taxable interest income		
Line 3a	Qualified dividend income		
Line 3b	Ordinary dividend income		
Line 8	Other income from Schedule 1, line 10		
Line 9	Total income (Add lines 1, 2b, 3b, & 8)		
Line 10	Adjustments to income from Sch. 1, line 26		
Line 11	Adjusted gross income		
Line 12	Standard deduction or itemized deductions		
Line 13	QBI deduction		
Line 14	Add lines 12 & 13		
Line 15	Taxable income		

Exhibits: Source Documents

22222	a Employee's social security number 123-45-6789	OMB No. 1545-0008	
b Employer identification number (EIN) 93-1571892		1 Wages, tips, other compensation 45,000	2 Federal income tax withheld 6,750
c Employer's name, address, and ZIP code Wag Your Tail 100 Pooch Drive Loveland CO 80528		3 Social security wages 45,000	4 Social security tax withheld 2,790
		5 Medicare wages and tips 45,000	6 Medicare tax withheld 653
		7 Social security tips	8 Allocated tips
d Control number		9	10 Dependent care benefits
e Employee's first name and initial Last name Suff. Bailey Cream 2811 Berry Street Loveland CO 80528		11 Nonqualified plans	12a
		13 Statutory employee ☐ Retirement plan ☐ Third-party sick pay ☐	12b
		14 Other	12c
f Employee's address and ZIP code			12d

15 State	Employer's state ID number	16 State wages, tips, etc.	17 State income tax	18 Local wages, tips, etc.	19 Local income tax	20 Locality name
CO	19731421	45,000	665			

Form **W-2** Wage and Tax Statement Year 29 Department of Treasury—Internal Revenue Service

Other Tax Forms Information

Form	Line	Payer	Amount
Form 1099-C Cancellation of Debt	Line 1 Date of identifiable event	Loveland Community Hospital	11/9/Year 29
Form 1099-C Cancellation of Debt	Line 2 Amount of debt discharged	Loveland Community Hospital	11,000
Form W-2G Certain Gambling Winnings	Line 1 Reportable winnings	Colorado Lottery	5,000
Form W-2G Certain Gambling Winnings	Line 2 Date won	Colorado Lottery	2/14/Year 29
Form W-2G Certain Gambling Winnings	Line 3 Type of wager	Colorado Lottery	Lotto
Form 1099-DIV Dividends and Distributions	Lina 1a Total ordinary dividends	Consolidated Edison	1,800
Form 1099-DIV Dividends and Distributions	Line 1b Qualified dividends	Consolidated Edison	1,500
Form 1099-INT Interest Income	Line 1 Interest income	State Exchange Bank	800
Form 1099-INT Interest Income	Line 8 Tax-exempt interest	State Exchange Bank	1,200

K-1 from S Corp, Clean Air Corporation

Shareholder's Share of Current-Year Income, Deductions, Credits, and Other Items	
Line 1: Ordinary business income (loss)	4,400

Information about Shareholder	
Current-year allocation percentage	10%
Shareholder's number of shares: beginning of year	100
Shareholder's number of shares: end of year	100
Loans from shareholder: beginning of year	0
Loans from shareholder: end of year	0

Exhibits: Draft Tax Return Schedules

Draft Tax Return: Schedule 1 Additional Income and Adjustments Entries		
Line 5: Rental real estate, royalties, partnerships, trusts, etc.		4,400
Line 8b: Gambling	4,995	
Line 8c: Cancellation of debt	0	
Line 9: Total other income		4,995
Line 10: Combine lines 1 through 7 and 9 (total additional income)		9,395

Draft Tax Return: Form 1040 Page 1 Entries	
Line 1: Total amount from Form(s) W-2, box 1	45,000
Lina 2a: Tax-exempt interest	0
Line 2b: Taxable interest	2,000
Line 3a: Qualified dividends	1,500
Line 3b: Ordinary dividends	1,800
Line 7: Capital gain or (loss)	0
Line 8: Other income from Schedule 1, line 10	9,395
Line 9: Total income	58,195
Line 10: Adjustments to income	0
Line 11: Adjusted gross income	58,195
Line 12: Standard deduction or itemized deductions	9,355
Line 13: QBI deduction	0
Line 15: Taxable income	48,840

Solution

Bailey's Form W-2 Wage and Tax Statement indicates $45,000 of taxable wages reported in box 1. Bailey *correctly* reported this amount on Form 1040, page 1, line 1.

Bailey received a Form 1099-C Cancellation of Debt from Loveland Community Hospital. The hospital canceled $11,000 of medical debt for Bailey as part of her payment plan.

- Cancellation of debt is generally taxable unless certain exceptions apply. These exceptions include debt forgiven in cases of bankruptcy or insolvency, discharge of qualified student loans, debt forgiven as gift, bequest, or inheritance, etc.
- None of the debt cancellation exceptions apply in this scenario; therefore, the $11,000 of income from box 2 on Form 1099-C is includible on Bailey's Schedule 1, line 8c. Since Bailey *did not report* this income on Schedule 1, it must be corrected accordingly

Bailey received a Form W-2G Certain Gambling Winnings from the Colorado Lottery. The *gross amount* of reportable winnings in box 1 ($5,000) must be reported on Schedule 1, line 8b.

- Since gambling losses are deductible to the extent of gambling winnings, the cost of the lottery ticket ($5) is a wagering expense that can be deducted on Schedule A
- Bailey *incorrectly netted* these amounts on Schedule 1, line 8b; therefore, the schedule must be adjusted accordingly

Bailey received Form 1099-DIV Dividends and Distributions from Consolidated Edison. Box 1a provides $1,500 of *ordinary dividend income*, which must be reported on Form 1040, line 3a.

- Qualified dividend income in box 1b should still be reported on Form 1040, page 1, but is not included in AGI
- Bailey prepared line 3 on Form 1040 *correctly*, so no adjustment is required

Bailey received Form 1099-INT Interest Income from State Exchange Bank. Box 1 provides $800 of *interest income*, which must be reported on Form 1040, line 2b.

- *Tax-exempt interest* income in box 8 should still be reported on Form 1040, page 1, box 2a, but is not included in AGI
- An adjustment to the draft page 1 of the 1040 is required because Bailey prepared line 2 *incorrectly* by adding these amounts together and reporting the total on line 2b

Bailey received a Schedule K-1 Shareholder's Share of Income, Deductions, Credits from Clean Air Corporation, an S corp.

- The only item on the K-1 is ordinary business income, which Bailey *correctly* reported on her draft Schedule 1, line 5. As such, no adjustment is required
- The earnings reported from the S corporation qualify for the QBI deduction. Therefore, the taxpayer is entitled to an $880 QBI deduction ($4,400 × 20%) reported on line 13, Form 1040

Bailey's itemized deductions total $9,355 ($1,050 sales tax + $3,300 property tax + $5,000 charitable contributions + $5 gambling expense).

- The *higher* of state and local income tax or sales tax (higher in this scenario) can be deducted as itemized deductions (but not both)
- None of the expenses provided by Bailey are for AGI (ie, above the line) deductions
- The groceries, rent paid, and utilities are not deductible
- Although Bailey correctly calculated her itemized deductions, she failed to consider that the higher standard amount is the amount that should flow to page 1 of her Form 1040. As such, an adjustment to page 1 is required
- The birthday gift of $2,500 received from Aunt Kitty is not includible in taxable income to Bailey (the recipient)

Schedule 1

Line Item	Description	Adjustment Required?	Correct Amount
Line 3	Business income (loss) Schedule C	No	0
Line 5	Rental real estate, royalties, partnerships, S corporations	No	4,400
Line 8b	Gambling income	Yes	5,000
Line 8c	Cancellation of debt	Yes	11,000
Line 9	Other income, Add lines 8a–8z	Yes	16,000
Line 10	Additional income, Add lines 1–9	Yes	20,400

Form 1040 Page 1

Line Item	Description	Adjustment Required?	Correct Amount
Line 1	Wages	No	45,000
Line 2a	Tax-exempt interest income	Yes	1,200
Line 2b	Taxable interest income	Yes	800
Line 3a	Qualified dividend income	No	1,500
Line 3b	Ordinary dividend income	No	1,800
Line 8	Other income from Schedule 1, line 10	Yes	20,400
Line 9	Total income (Add lines 1, 2b, 3b, & 8)	Yes	68,000
Line 10	Adjustments to income from Sch. 1, line 26	No	0
Line 11	Adjusted gross income	Yes	68,000
Line 12	Standard deduction or itemized deductions	Yes	14,600
Line 13	QBI deduction	Yes	880
Line 14	Add lines 12 & 13	Yes	15,480
Line 15	Taxable income	Yes	52,520

Automated Diagnostic and Validation Checks

Representative Task (Analysis): Review and resolve discrepancies identified by automated diagnostic and validation checks to ensure the completeness and accuracy of the adjusted gross income and taxable income reported on Form 1040 – U.S. Individual Income Tax Return based on the source data used to prepare the form.

Practice Scenario

Fynn and Fiona Stabler are married and file a joint tax return in Year 32. Fynn was divorced from his first spouse on June 22, Year 18, and pays her $12,000 per year as part of a court-ordered alimony settlement (assume the pre-2019 alimony rules apply here). The Stablers' standard deduction is $29,200. They have a dependent child and are eligible for the $2,000 child tax credit. Neither Fynn nor Fiona is a tax accountant, and they use Universal Tax software to prepare their return themselves. The software has generated the following diagnostics that need to be resolved before the return can be e-filed.

Fynn and Fiona have hired you to resolve the diagnostics so that they can e-file their return. Review the various exhibits, which consist of source documents and draft tax forms prepared by the Stablers. Then, address the Universal Tax software diagnostics below by selecting the appropriate answer from the drop-down menu provided. Select "no action required" if the return is already correct and the diagnostic can be ignored.

	Diagnostic Received	Choose Correct Answer to Clear Diagnostic
1	*Severe:* Social Security tax paid of $9,280 entered in organizer does not match W-2. Verify correct Social Security withheld.	$8,280 $8,556 $9,280 No action required
2	*Informational:* Interest income reported on previous year's tax return for 1099-INT from Nashville State Bank; no interest from this payer reported on the current-year tax return.	Correct interest income from this payer: $200 Correct interest income from this payer: $680 Correct interest income from this payer: $880 No action required
3	*Informational:* Dividend income reported on previous year's tax return for 1099-DIV from John Deere, Inc.; no dividend from this payer reported on the current-year tax return.	Correct dividend income from this payer: $0 Correct dividend income from this payer: $3,300 Correct dividend income from this payer: $3,420 No action required
4	*Informational:* Verify that debt forgiveness from 1099-C Music Mortgage Co. was for principal residence; verify if debt forgiveness from 1099-C Music Mortgage Co. is includible in income.	Debt forgiveness was for principal residence; cancellation of debt income of $52,000 must be reported Debt forgiveness was not for principal residence; cancellation of debt income of $52,000 must be reported Debt forgiveness was for principal residence; no cancellation of debt income needs to be reported No action required

	Diagnostic Received	Choose Correct Answer to Clear Diagnostic
5	*Severe:* K-1 from Windy LLC reports distribution in excess of taxpayer's basis; capital gain not reported on Schedule D or Form 1040, page 1.	Taxpayer must report \$2,500 capital gain Taxpayer must report \$3,500 capital gain Taxpayer must report \$42,000 capital gain No action required
6	*Severe:* Alimony paid was entered on Schedule 1, page 2, but the year of divorce and recipient's Social Security number are not provided. Check to determine if alimony is deductible.	Alimony deduction is \$0 for alimony paid after 2019 Alimony deduction limited to \$10,000 for alimony paid after 2019 Correct alimony deduction is \$12,000; divorce enacted before 2019 No action required

Exhibits: Source Documents

22222	a Employee's social security number 123-45-6789	OMB No. 1545-0008	
b Employer identification number (EIN) 36-1002245		1 Wages, tips, other compensation 138,000	2 Federal income tax withheld 27,600
c Employer's name, address, and ZIP code Jared Consulting Co. 111 Main Street Nashville, TN 37011		3 Social security wages 138,000	4 Social security tax withheld 8,556
		5 Medicare wages and tips 138,000	6 Medicare tax withheld 2,001
		7 Social security tips	8 Allocated tips
d Control number		9	10 Dependent care benefits
e Employee's first name and initial / Last name / Suff. Fynn Stabler 202 Garden Road Nashville, TN 37011		11 Nonqualified plans	12a
		13 Statutory employee ☐ Retirement plan ☐ Third-party sick pay ☐	12b
		14 Other	12c
f Employee's address and ZIP code			12d

15 State	Employer's state ID number	16 State wages, tips, etc.	17 State income tax	18 Local wages, tips, etc.	19 Local income tax	20 Locality name
TN	36-1002245	138,000	0			

Form **W-2** **Wage and Tax Statement** Year 32 Department of Treasury—Internal Revenue Service

Other Tax Forms Information

Form	Line	Payer	Amount
Form 1099-INT Interest Income	Line 1 Interest income	Nashville State Bank	680
Form 1099-DIV Dividends and Distributions	Lina 1a Total ordinary dividends	John Deere Inc.	3,420
Form 1099-DIV Dividends and Distributions	Line 1b Qualified dividends	John Deere Inc.	3,420
Form 1099-C Cancellation of Debt	Line 1 Date of identifiable event	Music Mortgage Company	4/2/Year 32
Form 1099-C Cancellation of Debt	Line 2 Amount of debt discharged	Music Mortgage Company	52,000
Form 1099-C Cancellation of Debt	Line 4 Debt description	Music Mortgage Company	Cancellation of debt on principal residence

K-1 from Partnership, Windy LLC

Partner's Share of Current-Year Income, Deductions, Credits, and Other Items	
Line 1: Ordinary business income (loss)	3,300
Line 5: Interest income	200

Partner's Capital Account Analysis	
Beginning capital account	36,000
Current-year net income (loss)	3,500
Withdrawals and distributions	(42,000)
Ending capital account	(2,500)

Exhibits: Tax Forms Completed by the Stablers

Draft Tax Return: Form 1040, Page 1	
Line 1a: Total amount from Form(s) W-2, box 1	138,000
Lina 2a: Tax-exempt interest	0
Line 2b: Taxable interest	200
Line 3a: Qualified dividends	0
Line 3b: Ordinary dividends	0
Line 7: Capital gain or (loss)	0
Line 8: Other income from Schedule 1, line 10	3,300
Line 9: Total income	141,500
Line 10: Adjustments to income	(12,000)
Line 11: Adjusted gross income	129,500
Line 12: Standard deduction or itemized deductions	(29,200)
Line 13: QBI deduction	0
Line 15: Taxable income	100,300

Draft Schedule 1 Additional Income and Adjustments to Income Entries	
Line 19a: Alimony paid	12,000
Line 24z: Other adjustments	0
Line 26: Total adjustments to income	12,000

Solution

	Diagnostic Received	Choose Correct Answer to Clear Diagnostic
1	*Severe:* Social Security tax paid of $9,280 entered in organizer does not match W-2. Verify correct Social Security withheld.	$8,280 **$8,556** $9,280 No action required
	Form W-2 shows the amount of Social Security tax withheld from Fynn's paycheck equals $8,556. This software diagnostic has alerted the taxpayer that the amount of tax withheld reported in the organizer equals $9,280. To clear this diagnostic, either the amount on Fynn's W-2 or the amount in the organizer must change, so that both numbers match. Since there is no way to change Fynn's W-2 (or any reason to believe the amount on the W-2 is incorrect), the preparer should update the amount withheld in the organizer to $8,556.	
2	*Informational:* Interest income reported on previous year's tax return for 1099-INT from Nashville State Bank; no interest from this payer reported on the current-year tax return.	Correct interest income from this payer: $200 **Correct interest income from this payer: $680** Correct interest income from this payer: $880 No action required
	When income is reported in a previous year and not in the current year, informational diagnostics are frequently generated alerting the tax preparer of the change. The diagnostic is informational because there are legitimate reasons why income would be reported in one year and not the following year. For example, in this scenario, it's plausible that Fynn could have closed the bank account, or the bank account could be variable interest and paying little to no interest in the current year. However, Form 1099-INT from Nashville State Bank does report taxable interest income of $680. It's possible the Stablers forgot to import this source document. Regardless of the reason, the diagnostic correctly alerted the tax preparer of the missing entry. The tax return could still be filed even if this diagnostic was not cleared, but the Stablers would likely receive a matching notice from the IRS later. Therefore, the tax preparer should enter $680 received from Nashville State Bank to clear the diagnostic.	
3	*Informational:* Dividend income reported on previous year's tax return for 1099-DIV from John Deere, Inc.; no dividend from this payer reported on the current-year tax return.	Correct dividend income from this payer: $0 Correct dividend income from this payer: $3,300 **Correct dividend income from this payer: $3,420** No action required
	When income is reported in a previous year and not in the current year, informational diagnostics are frequently generated alerting the tax preparer of the change. The diagnostic is informational because there are legitimate reasons why income would be reported in one year and not the following year. For example, in this scenario, it's plausible that Fynn could have sold his stock investment or the company he invested in isn't paying dividends to shareholders in the current year. Form 1099-DIV from John Deere, Inc., does report taxable dividend income of $3,420, which means the tax software did correctly identify a missing income item. The tax return could still be filed even if this diagnostic was not cleared, but the Stablers would likely receive a matching notice from the IRS later. Therefore, the tax preparer should enter $3,420 received from John Deere to both correct the return and clear the diagnostic.	

	Diagnostic Received	Choose Correct Answer to Clear Diagnostic
4	*Informational:* Verify that debt forgiveness from 1099-C Music Mortgage Co. was for principal residence; verify if debt forgiveness from 1099-C Music Mortgage Co. is includible in income.	Debt forgiveness was for principal residence; cancellation of debt income of $52,000 must be reported Debt forgiveness was not for principal residence; cancellation of debt income of $52,000 must be reported **Debt forgiveness was for principal residence; no cancellation of debt income needs to be reported** No action required

This diagnostic is alerting the tax preparer that Form 1099-C received from Music Mortgage Co. shows a cancellation of debt of $52,000 and to verify if the debt relief relates to the taxpayers' principal residence. This is because forgiveness of debt on a *principal residence* is not taxable under current law (limited to $750,000).

The preparer can verify the address on the 1099-C with other tax documents provided by the Stablers (eg, Fynn's W-2) and confirm that the mortgage forgiveness does relate to the taxpayers' principal residence. Because the amount of mortgage debt forgiven is less than $750,000, there is no income to include from the 1099-C on the tax return. To clear the diagnostic, the software likely has a checkbox in the organizer or other way to confirm that this debt relief relates to the taxpayer's principal residence.

	Diagnostic Received	Choose Correct Answer to Clear Diagnostic
5	*Severe:* K-1 from Windy LLC reports distribution in excess of taxpayer's basis; capital gain not reported on Schedule D or Form 1040, page 1.	**Taxpayer must report $2,500 capital gain** Taxpayer must report $3,500 capital gain Taxpayer must report $42,000 capital gain No action required

This diagnostic alerted the tax preparer that the Schedule K-1 from Windy LLC shows a distribution ($42,000) in excess of the taxpayer's basis ($39,500 = $36,000 beginning basis + $3,500 partner's share of income) within the partner's capital account analysis. The portion of the distribution that is in excess of Fynn's basis must be reported as a capital gain because Fynn's basis in the partnership cannot be less than zero.

In this scenario, the software diagnostic correctly alerted the taxpayer of the potential capital gain. To clear the diagnostic and correct the tax return, the correct capital gain to report is $2,500 ($42,000 – $39,500) on Schedule D and page 1 of the tax return.

	Diagnostic Received	Choose Correct Answer to Clear Diagnostic
6	*Severe:* Alimony paid was entered on Schedule 1, page 2, but the year of divorce and recipient's Social Security number are not provided. Check to determine if alimony is deductible.	Alimony deduction is $0 for alimony paid after 2019 Alimony deduction limited to $10,000 for alimony paid after 2019 **Alimony deduction is $12,000; divorce enacted before 2019** No action required

This diagnostic is alerting the tax preparer that the $12,000 for AGI deduction for alimony paid that the Stablers took requires additional information. Fynn has paid alimony of $12,000 each year to his ex-wife from a divorce in Year 18. The alimony in this scenario is deductible because the divorce was finalized prior to January 1, 2019.

The software will know whether or not the deduction is permitted but only if the divorce year is provided. In addition, the IRS requires the recipient spouse's Social Security number to be provided. Entering this information in the organizer and on Schedule 1, page 2, would clear this diagnostic.

REG 15
Loss Limitations

REG 15: Loss Limitations

15.01 Loss Limitations

Overview

The IRC has established several loss limitations to deter individual taxpayers from generating losses with the sole purpose of reducing their income tax liability. These limitations prevent taxpayers from benefiting from certain loss deductions from transactions that are entered into to create a tax loss.

- Examples include losses from wash sales, losses between related parties, hobby activities, capital losses, passive activity losses, losses from the sale of personal assets, losses limited by the at-risk amount, and an overall excess business loss limitation
- The at-risk and passive loss rules are aimed at curtailing the use of tax shelters
- A loss is reduced by reimbursement from insurance, if applicable

Deductible losses by individual taxpayers are generally limited to the following:

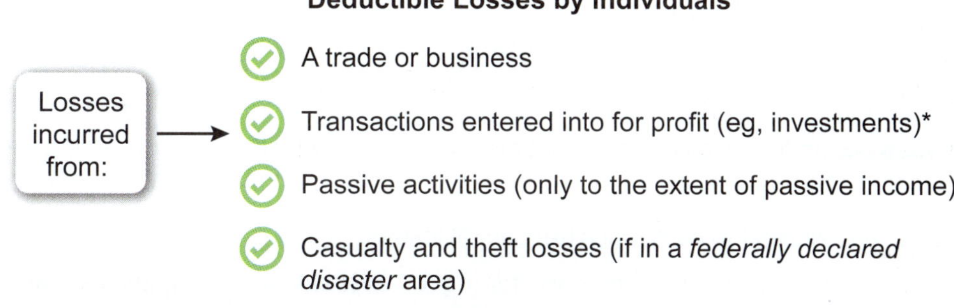

**Net capital losses are limited to $3,000 ($1,500 if married filing separately) per year.*

Realized Gains and Losses

The starting point for determining any gain or loss on a sale is to determine the *amount realized from the sale* (eg, sales price plus or minus adjustments) and the asset's adjusted basis at the time of sale.

- If the asset is depreciable, depreciation must be computed up to the day of sale or disposal in order to determine an accurate adjusted basis for the asset
- Not all realized gains are necessarily recognized (ie, taxable and reportable to the IRS), and losses may be subject to deductible limitations

Realized Gain or Loss on Sale or Disposal

Realized gain or loss = Amount realized − Adjusted basis of asset

Amount realized:
Cash received
+ FMV of property and/or services received
+ Debt relief (buyer assumes debt)
− Selling expenses

Adjusted basis of asset:
Original cost
+ Improvements
− Accumulated depreciation

Net Loss Allowed on Sale of Capital Assets

Representative Task (Application): Calculate the net tax loss allowed on the sale of capital property, including netting of capital gains and losses and capital loss carryforwards.

Note: In this chapter, short-term capital gain = STCG; short-term capital loss = STCL; long-term capital gain = LTCG; and long-term capital loss = LTCL.

Tax Treatment of a Net Capital Loss

If a **net capital loss** (ie, netting of all capital asset dispositions) is incurred for the year, individuals are allowed to deduct up to **$3,000** ($1,500 if married filing separately) of the loss against *ordinary income*.

- Individuals are **not** allowed to carry back net capital losses
- However, remaining losses retain their character (eg, LT capital loss, ST capital loss) and are carried forward indefinitely. Short-term losses are claimed first

Capital Assets

Capital assets are generally *nonbusiness* tangible assets (ie, do *not* qualify as ordinary income or Section 1231 assets used in a trade or business).

- Examples include personal investment assets (eg, land, real estate, securities), nonbusiness bad debts, interest in a partnership, other personal-use assets (eg, personal residence, vehicles, furniture, appliances, boats), and purchased (not self-created) literary, musical, or article compositions
- Although gains from personal-use assets are taxable, **losses are not deductible**

Capital Asset Holding Period

A capital asset is classified as either **short term** or **long term based** on the holding period. When a capital asset is sold that was owned for:

- **≤ 1 year**, then it is short term
- **> 1 year**, then long term

To compute the holding period, include the day *after* the property was acquired through the day disposed.

There are *exceptions* to the holding period classification, which are frequently tested on the exam:

- The sale of an **inherited asset** is always classified as *long term*. The basis used for the sale is the FMV at date of death or six months after death, depending on whether the executor makes the alternate valuation date election
- The write-off of **nonbusiness bad debts** is always classified as *short-term capital losses*, regardless of the actual holding period. The basis of the debt is the unrecovered amount
- When a **security becomes worthless**, the holding period is calculated by treating the stock as if it had been sold on the *last day* of the tax year in which it becomes worthless

On the exam, pay special attention to the acquisition and sales dates to ensure the proper determination of short-term or long-term holding period.

Netting Process and Tax Treatment

When a taxpayer disposes of a capital asset, the gain (loss) will be classified as either long term or short term. The combination of all capital assets transactions:

- Will produce an overall **net capital gain or loss**, or
- If only long-term and short-term capital gains, there is **no** netting, or
- If only long-term and short-term capital losses, there is **no** netting.

Note: If a taxpayer has an overall *net Section 1231 gain* (ie, from trade or business assets), it is included in the netting process of capital gains and losses. However, a net Section 1231 loss is treated as an ordinary loss (excluded from the netting process).

Netting of Capital Gains and Losses for Individuals

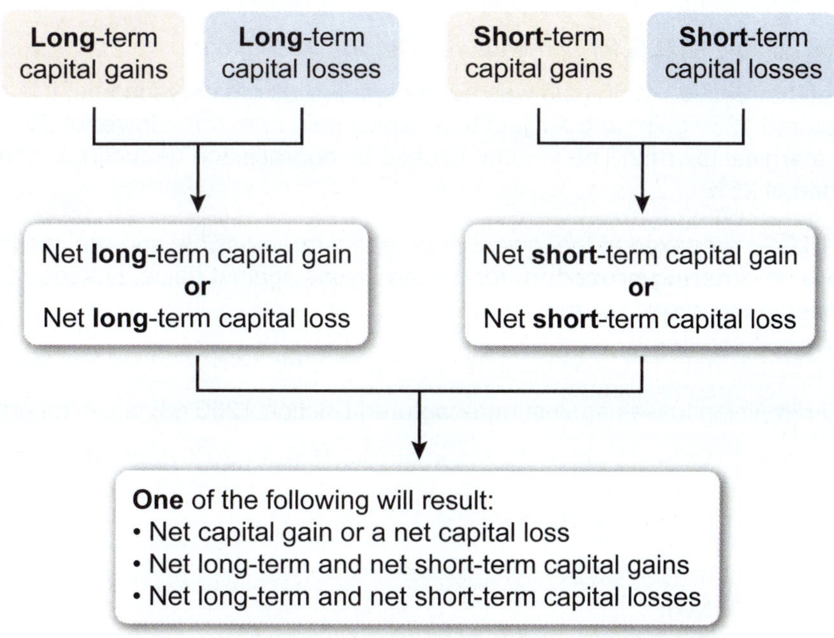

For individual taxpayers, net capital losses are limited to $3,000 per year.

An individual taxpayer has the following capital gains and losses during the current tax year. Determine the overall net capital gain or loss. Treat each scenario independently.

1. LTCG of $100 and STCG of $80
2. LTCL of $100 and STCL of $80
3. LTCG of $100 and STCL of $80
4. LTCL of $80 and STCG of $100
5. LTCL of $100 and STCG of $80
6. LTCG of $80 and STCL of $100

Transactions 1 and 2 **cannot** be netted since there are only gains or only losses. However, transactions 3 through 6 are *netted*.

Transactions	Netting Result
3. LTCG of $100 and STCL of $80	Net LTCG of $20
4. LTCL of $80 and STCG of $100	Net STCG of $20
5. LTCL of $100 and STCG of $80	Net LTCL of $20
6. LTCG of $80 and STCL of $100	Net STCL of $20

Ordering Procedure Used When Netting Capital Gains and Losses

A net LTCG is taxed at **special rates** (0%,15%, and 20%) for individuals, and a net STCG is taxed at the taxpayer's **ordinary** tax rate.

- A special LT tax rate of **28%** applies to all gains and losses on *collectibles* reported on Schedule D. Collectibles include works of art, rugs, antiques, metals (gold), gems, stamps, coins, alcoholic beverages, and other certain tangible property
- Another special tax rate is **25%** for *unrecaptured Section 1250 gains*
    - To the extent that Section 1250 gain was not recaptured as ordinary income, it is characterized as "unrecaptured 1250 gain" and subject to a capital gain rate of the lower of 25% or the individual's marginal tax rate. The amount caused by depreciation deductions is taxed at a maximum rate of 25%

To ensure that the LTCGs are taxed at the *lowest preferential rate possible* and provide the greatest benefit to taxpayers, there is an **ordering procedure** for netting losses against gains. Losses offset the gains in order from the highest to the lowest tax rate as follows:

- First, apply losses against LTCGs on collectibles (eg, stamps, coins), which are taxed at 28%
- Second, apply remaining losses against unrecaptured Section 1250 gains, which are taxed at 25%
- Third, any remaining LTCGs are generally taxed at 0%, 15%, or 20% depending on the taxpayer's income level

An individual taxpayer, whose marginal tax rate is 32%, had the following gains and losses during the year:

Long-term capital gain (15% rate)	$3,500
Collectibles gain (28% rate)	6,000
Long-term capital gain (unrecaptured Section 1250 at 25%)	9,000
Short-term capital loss	(13,000)

To ensure that the LTCGs are taxed at the lowest preferential rate possible, an ordering procedure is followed. Losses offset the gains in order from the highest to the lowest tax rate.

Here, the $13,000 losses offset the gains in the following order: collectibles gain and then unrecaptured Section 1250, resulting in a $2,000 unrecaptured Section 1250 gain taxed at 25% and a $3,500 long-term capital gain taxed at 15%.

	LT Gain	Offsetting Loss	Remaining LT Gain
Collectibles gain (28%)	$ 6,000	$ (6,000)	$ 0
Unrecaptured Section 1250 (25%)	9,000	(7,000)	2,000
LT capital gain (15%)	3,500	0	3,500
Totals	$18,500	$(13,000)	$5,500

A single taxpayer has a $6,200 capital loss carryover from last year. The loss comprises a $5,000 STCL and a $1,200 LTCL. During the current tax year, the taxpayer incurred the following capital gains and losses:

STCG	$4,000
STCL	(7,000)
LTCG	3,000
LTCL	(500)

What amount is the taxpayer's net capital gain or loss for the current year?

The STCGs and STCLs are netted, and the LTCGs and LTCLs (including the carryover loss) are netted.

Short Term		Long Term	
STCG	$ 4,000	LTCG	$3,000
STCL	(7,000)	LTCL	(500)
ST CL carryover	(5,000)	LTCL carryover	(1,200)
Net STCL	$(8,000)	Net LTCG	$1,300

Net capital loss ($8,000 − $1,300)	$(6,700)
Current-year deductible amount	**3,000**
STCL carryover	**$(3,700)**

At-Risk Loss Limitations

Representative Task (Application): Calculate the amount of ordinary business loss allowed for an individual materially participating in the operations of a pass-through entity with sufficient basis in the entity.

Flow-through entities (ie, partnerships and S corporations) cannot claim a net operating loss (NOL). Therefore, when a pass-through entity incurs a business operating loss, it is distributed to the owners (ie, partners, shareholders). However, an owner's share of the loss is only deductible to the extent of the following: basis, at-risk, and passive activity limitations. Remember, since basis may **never fall below zero**, a deductible loss is first limited by basis.

These rules prevent taxpayers from deducting a loss *greater* than the amount they have at risk in that activity (ie, the amount the taxpayer could lose in the activity if the activity became worthless).

For the at-risk rule, a **loss** is **defined** as the *excess of allowable deductions from the activity (including depreciation or amortization) over the income received from the activity.* A **deductible loss may not exceed the taxpayer's at-risk amount**. Note that the tax basis and at-risk amount could be the same amount. If the activity is a passive activity, the loss deduction is further limited to passive income from other passive activities.

Deductible Loss from Flow-Through

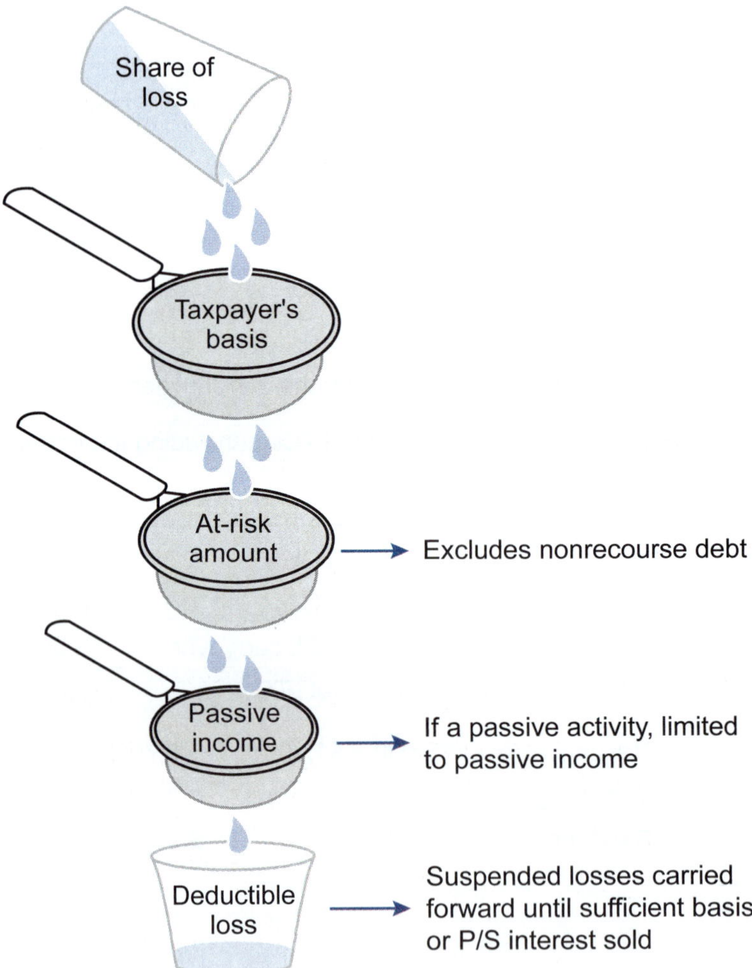

Calculation of Partner's Basis

Partner's initial contribution (or amount paid, if purchased)

Increased by:
- Additional contributions
- Share of increase in partnership liabilities
- Share of partnership income/other income

Decreased by:
- Cash and property distributions
- Share of reduction in partnership liabilities
- Share of partnership losses/other deductions

Partner's ending basis (not below zero)

To calculate at-risk amount, *exclude* nonrecourse debt

If there is an insufficient at-risk amount, any disallowed loss is *suspended* and carried forward indefinitely until there is sufficient basis and/or at-risk amount.

- A taxpayer's current-year at-risk amount is *reduced* by any disallowed losses carried over from the previous year(s)
- If the activity is *disposed*, the suspended at-risk losses may be used to reduce any gain from the sale; however, any excess suspended at-risk losses are lost (ie, forfeited)

Treatment of Suspended At-Risk Losses

Carried forward indefinitely to future years until the partner has sufficient basis and at-risk amount

↓

Is activity sold or disposed?

↓ Yes

Suspended losses offset the gain on sale with any remaining balance forfeited

Determining the Amount at Risk

A taxpayer's at-risk amount is generally the same as their *basis* in the activity, including their share of *recourse* debt (ie, personally liable), amounts personally pledged as security for property not used in the activity, and *qualified* nonrecourse debt financing.

- Taxpayers are generally not liable (ie, at risk) for *nonrecourse* debt or if the lender is not a creditor (ie, partner)
- An exception exists for *qualified nonrecourse debt*, which is any nonrecourse debt that is collateralized by real property used in the activity of holding real property

- Generally, borrowed amounts from related parties are *excluded* from the at-risk amount
- The at-risk amount is determined at the end of each tax year
- The at-risk amount also includes direct bona fide loans from the taxpayer to the pass-through entity (for P/S, the loan increases the partner's basis; for S corporations, direct loans do not affect the shareholder basis but rather create a debt basis)

Partners and At-Risk Amount

Each partner has an **outside tax basis** for their interest in a partnership (P/S) that is used to determine the deductibility of P/S losses and the treatment of distributions. Because the **general partners** may ultimately be **responsible** for **P/S debt**, their basis is **increased** by their **pro rata** share of **all** P/S debt, recourse and nonrecourse.

The amount of debt included in the at-risk amount depends on whether the partner is a general or limited partner. A *limited partner's* basis is increased for *nonrecourse* debt only. In addition, there is **qualified nonrecourse debt** (ie, debt is secured by real property used in the business activity). It is treated the same as recourse debt regarding its effect on basis and at-risk amount.

Types of Partnership (P/S) Liabilities

Type	Partner Liability	Applies To	Included in Outside Basis	Included in At-Risk Amount
Recourse Debt	• Liable for proportionate share (eg, A/P, loans, notes)	General partners	✔	✔
Nonrecourse Debt	• *Not* personally liable • Secured by collateral (eg, inventory)	General and limited partners	✔	✘
Qualified Nonrecourse Debt	• *Not* personally liable • Secured by real property used in the activity of holding real property (eg, rental)	General and limited partners	✔	✔

Note: Limited partners are not personally liable for P/S debt, except for a deficit restoration of capital.

At-risk rules prevent partners from *deducting losses greater* than the amount of their *personal liability* (ie, economic risk of loss from recourse debt) in the P/S.

- Nonrecourse liabilities (eg, liabilities secured by collateral) provide basis for distributions but generally do not provide basis for deducting losses because the partners do not bear the risk for the loss
- Therefore, a partner's at-risk amount generally is equal to the taxpayer's basis less any P/S nonrecourse debt (ie, not personally liable, such as a note payable secured by collateral) included in basis
- Any losses suspended (ie, not currently deductible) based on these limitations are carried forward indefinitely to future years until the partner has sufficient basis or at-risk amount

Kale and Jessie are equal partners in K&J Associates, a general partnership. K&J has the following liabilities at the end of the current year:

Accounts payable	$18,000
Unsecured bank loan	50,000
Note payable secured by collateral	25,000

What amount of the *debt* is included in Kale's at-risk amount in the partnership?

- When determining Kale's basis in the P/S, $46,500 [($18,000 + $50,000 + $25,000) × 50%] (ie, 50% of **all** of P/S debt) is included
- However, the P/S **recourse** debt consists of the $18,000 accounts payable and the $50,000 unsecured loan. Kale's **at-risk amount only includes the recourse debt** of **$34,000** [($18,000 + $50,000) × 50%]
- The note payable, which is secured by collateral, is *nonrecourse debt* and therefore is **excluded** from determining the at-risk amount

On September 30, Year 5, Melba contributed $40,000 cash and equipment with an adjusted tax basis of $10,000 and a fair market value of $15,000 in exchange for a 25% general partner interest. The partnership had existing $60,000 recourse debt and $8,000 nonrecourse debt on September 30. What is the tax basis and at-risk amount for Melba's partner interest on September 30, Year 5?

Contributions of property increase the partner's basis in the P/S by the property's adjusted tax basis (not FMV) at the time of the contribution. Because Melba is a general partner, she is responsible for her share of any recourse and nonrecourse debt.

Her **tax basis** is increased for her **25% share** of **all of the P/S liabilities** (eg, recourse, nonrecourse). However, the **at-risk** amount **excludes** her share of **nonrecourse** debt.

Cash contribution	$40,000
Adjusted basis of equipment contributed	10,000
25% of all P/S debt [($60,000 + $8,000) × 25%]	17,000
Melba's tax basis	**$67,000**
Less: 25% of nonrecourse debt ($8,000 × 25%)	(2,000)
Melba's at-risk amount	**$65,000**

On December 31, Year 5, the following occurred:

- Melba received a $30,000 distribution
- The P/S recourse debt decreased by $10,000, and the nonrecourse debt increased by $4,000
- Melba's share of the P/S loss for Year 5 is $34,000

How much of the loss can Melba deduct?

Starting with Melba's tax basis on September 30, her basis is adjusted for the cash distribution as well as her 25% share of the decrease in recourse debt and 25% of the increase in nonrecourse debt.

Note that because her beginning basis includes her 25% of the debt, only 25% of the increase and decrease are needed as an adjustment.

Melba's tax basis on September 30, Year 5	$67,000
Less: 25% *decrease* in recourse debt ($10,000 × 25%)	(2,500)
25% *increase* in nonrecourse debt ($4,000 × 25%)	1,000
Less: cash distribution	(30,000)
Melba's tax basis	**$35,500**
Less: 25% of nonrecourse debt ($2,000 + $1,000)	(3,000)
Melba's at-risk amount	**$32,500**

Although Melba has a tax basis sufficient to deduct the $34,000 loss, she is **limited to the amount at risk**, which is only **$32,500**. The $1,500 ($34,000 − $32,500) excess loss is suspended and may be carried forward and taken when she has a sufficient at-risk amount.

S Corporation Shareholders and At-Risk Amount

S corporations, like partnerships, are pass-through entities. Each shareholder reports their pro rata amount of the corporation's ordinary business income (loss) and separately stated items. Unlike partners, shareholders are **not** liable for the S corporation's debt; therefore, **no** adjustment is required to their basis for corporation debt.

However, direct loans from a shareholder of the corporation represent a separate "debt basis." A shareholder may increase their at-risk amount for these loans. Therefore, an S corporation shareholder's at-risk amount is equal to the taxpayer's basis plus any loans the shareholder directly made to the S corporation (ie, debt basis).

Calculation of Shareholder's Basis in an S Corporation
Shareholder's beginning basis in corporation
+ Additional contributions
+ Percentage share of corporation's ordinary income and separately stated income, gains
− Distributions from corporation (ie, cash and property)
− Percentage share of corporation's operating loss and separately stated deductions, losses
Ending shareholder basis*

**Shareholder basis cannot fall below zero.*

In Year 1, a taxpayer purchased, for $35,000, an interest in an S corporation in which the taxpayer materially participates. The taxpayer's share of the business's net loss in Year 1 is $22,000, and they received a $25,000 cash distribution on December 31, Year 1. What amount of the loss can the taxpayer deduct under the at-risk rules?

- Under the at-risk rules, the deductible loss is limited to the shareholder's basis in the S corporation plus any debt basis. Here, there is no debt basis (ie, no direct loans to the corporation)
- Therefore, at-risk rules *limit the amount of loss* that can be currently deducted to the shareholder's basis of **$10,000** ($35,000 beginning balance − $25,000 distribution). The $12,000 excess loss ($22,000 − $10,000) is suspended and carried forward until there is sufficient outside basis and at-risk amount

Assume the taxpayer directly loaned the S corporation $15,000 during Year 1. None of the debt has been repaid. What amount of the loss can the taxpayer deduct under the at-risk rules?

- Since direct loans from a shareholder increase the at-risk amount, the taxpayer's **at-risk amount is now $25,000** ($35,000 beginning balance − $25,000 distribution + $15,000 debt basis)
- The taxpayer uses $10,000 of the $22,000 loss to reduce basis in the S corporation to zero. Then, the taxpayer uses the remaining $12,000 loss ($22,000 − $10,000) to reduce debt basis. All of the $22,000 loss is currently deductible. There is no suspended loss
- The debt basis is reduced to $3,000 ($15,000 debt basis − $12,000 loss). Debt basis must be reinstated before the shareholder's basis in the corporation

Excess Business Loss

Individual taxpayers are also subject to the **excess business loss** limitation, which is designed to limit the amount of loss deducted annually on an individual's tax return. Losses exceeding a statutory threshold amount (for 2024, $610,000 for MFJ, $305,000 for all other taxpayers) are **disallowed losses** in the current year and carried forward as a net operating loss (NOL).

- For taxpayers with losses from pass-through entities (eg, partnerships, S corporations), the limitation is applied *after* the outside basis, at-risk, and passive activity loss limitations
- For example, a single taxpayer had a $310,000 loss from an S corporation in which the taxpayer actively participates. After applying basis and at-risk limitations, the loss is limited to $306,000. Now, the excess business loss limitation is applied. Accordingly, the taxpayer may only deduct $305,000. The remaining $1,000 ($306,000 − $305,000) is carried forward as an NOL

Disallowed Losses

Representative Task (Application): Calculate losses disallowed for tax purposes, such as from a hobby, wash sale, or sale of a personal-use asset.

Taxpayers are **not** permitted to deduct losses associated with personal-use assets or personal activities that are **not** entered into for profit, such as hobbies, or wash sales that do not alter the taxpayer's economic position. In addition, gambling losses are generally only deductible to the extent of winnings.

Hobby Losses

It is not uncommon for taxpayers to pursue activities that may have both personal and profit intentions. Common examples include dog breeding, photography, artistic endeavors, fishing, craft making, and horse racing. Depending on whether the primary incentive behind the activity is personal enjoyment or to make a profit, the IRS may consider the activity a hobby.

- If the activity is deemed to be entered into to make a profit, then the income and expenses are reported on Schedule C, and a loss, if incurred, is allowed
- However, if the activity is treated as a hobby, the activity may **not** create a deductible loss. Instead, gross profit (ie, *gross income less cost of goods sold*) generated by the activity is taxable and reported as other income on Schedule 1 of the taxpayer's tax return; expenses other than cost of goods sold are reported on Schedule A, if the taxpayer itemizes deductions and if permitted

The reported hobby income (Gross receipts − Cost of goods sold) is subject to *income tax* but **not** subject to the 15.3% self-employment tax. However, if deemed a business, the expenses are deductible, but the net income is subject to self-employment taxes.

SCHEDULE 1 (Form 1040)
Department of the Treasury Internal Revenue Service

Additional income and adjustments to income
▶Attach to Form 1040, 1040-SR, or 1040-NR.
▶Go to www.irs.gov/Form 1040 for instructions and the latest information.

OMB No. 1545-0074
Attachment Sequence No. **01**

Name(s) shown on Form 1040, 1040-SR, or 1040-NR | **Your social security number**

Part I Additional income

1	Taxable refunds, credits, or offsets of state and local income taxes	1	
2a	Alimony received	2a	
b	Date of original divorce or separation agreement (see instructions) ▶		

h	Prizes and awards	8h	
i	Activity not engaged in for profit income	8i	
j	Stock Options	8j	
k	Income from the rental of personal property if you engaged in the rental for profit but were not in the business of renting such property	8k	

Deductions for hobby expenses are limited to the amount of gross profit (ie, cannot create a loss) and are subject to an *ordering procedure* based on the nature of the expense.

- Expenses that are normally deductible, such as property taxes and mortgage interest expenses, are considered first. Note these expenses are only deductible if the taxpayer itemizes deductions
- Next, other expenses that would be normally deductible as ordinary and necessary business expenses (eg, utilities, repairs) for a for-profit activity are deducted[1]
- Finally, any amount for depreciation or amortization is deducted[1]

1 *These expenses are treated as miscellaneous itemized deductions on Schedule A; however, the deduction for miscellaneous itemized deductions has been suspended from 2018 to 2025.*

But what is a hobby? Regulations have established **nine factors** that are considered when determining if an activity is a hobby or a for-profit business. There is no minimum number of factors that must be met; instead the evaluation of an activity is subjective in nature.

1. Is the activity conducted in a business manner?
2. Does the taxpayer (or their advisors) have required expertise?
3. How much time and effort is spent on the activity?
4. Does the taxpayer expect that the assets will appreciate in value?
5. Has there been any previous success by taxpayers in similar activities?
6. What is the history of income or losses from the activity?
7. What is the relationship of profits earned to losses incurred?
8. What is the financial status of the taxpayer? Are there other substantial sources of income?
9. Are there elements of personal pleasure or recreation in the activity?

Because the evaluation of an activity is subjective, Section 183 provides a **general rule** that is often used. If the activity produces a profit in **at least three out of the previous five tax years**, it is presumed the activity was entered into to make a profit (ie, not a hobby).

- Even if an activity is a for-profit one year, circumstances may change, and it could be considered a hobby the next year
- If the intention is to be a for-profit activity and not a hobby, the taxpayer should act like a business, for example, have a business name, business bank account, business website, email address, and/or telephone number, advertise as a business, etc.

If the activity involves horses, the presumptive rule is changed to producing a profit in at least two of the previous seven tax years.

A taxpayer conducts a service activity that is classified as a hobby. In the current year, the activity had the following items:

Gross receipts	$14,500
Insurance	(1,000)
Advertising	(2,100)
Property taxes	(800)
Website costs	(1,100)

How are the income and expenses reported on the taxpayer's return?

The taxpayer must report the **$14,500 gross receipts as other income**. The **$800** of taxes is **deductible** on **Schedule A** if the taxpayer itemizes deductions. The other costs are miscellaneous itemized deductions and not deductible from 2018 through 2025.

A taxpayer who is employed full-time as a teacher has recently taken up wood carving as a side business. He takes custom orders as well as selling his wood creations at local fairs. The taxpayer uses 15% of his home's square footage to make the wood carvings. During the current tax year, the following income and expenses were incurred related to this activity.

Gross receipts	$7,500
Cost of the wood	(4,800)
Cost of carving supplies	(250)
Annual mortgage interest expense on house	(8,500)
Annual property taxes on house	(4,200)
Annual utilities for house	(3,000)

In addition, depreciation based on 15% of his house is $2,700. Assume the taxpayer itemizes his deductions. If his activity is deemed to be a *hobby*, what amount is reported on his tax return?

If it is a hobby, then no loss is permitted. Gross profit is reported as other income, and the expenses are deducted following the ordering procedure.

Gross receipts	$7,500
Less: cost of goods sold ($4,800 wood + $250 supplies)	(5,050)
Gross profit	$2,450
Less: 15% of mortgage interest (15% × $8,500)	(1,275)
Less: 15% of property taxes (15% × $4,200)	(630)
Net profit before other expenses	$ 545
Less: 15% of utilities (15% × $3,000)	(450)
Net profit before depreciation	95
Less: depreciation ($2,700 limited to $95)	(95)
Net income	$ 0

The taxpayer reports gross profit of $2,450 **as other income** on his tax return. Because the taxpayer itemizes his deductions, the amounts for mortgage interest and property taxes are deducted on Schedule A. However, the $450 for utilities and $95 of depreciation are nondeductible since miscellaneous itemized deductions have been suspended from 2018 to 2025.

What if the activity is deemed to be a for-profit business?

The income and expenses are reported on Schedule C, and a loss of $2,605 ($95 income before depreciation − $2,700 depreciation) is recognized.

Wash Sales

To prevent taxpayers from recognizing losses if they sell securities and buy them back shortly before or after the sale date, the wash sale rule was enacted. A **wash sale** occurs when securities are sold at a loss and the taxpayer acquires the same or substantially identical securities within **30 days** before or after the sale.

- Losses from wash sales are *not* deductible because the taxpayer's economic position does not change
- The nondeductible loss is added to the basis of the acquired stock. If the number of shares acquired is less than the number originally purchased, the disallowed loss must be prorated (ie, based on the shares acquired)

A taxpayer purchased 100 shares of stock in XYZ Corporation for $300 in Year 1. On December 20, Year 2, an additional 100 shares in the company were purchased for $200. On December 27, Year 2, the 100 shares acquired in Year 1 were sold for $210.

Since a purchase of substantially identical securities occurred only seven days earlier, the loss of $90 ($210 − $300) on December 27, Year 2, *cannot* be deducted. Instead, the basis of the shares acquired on December 20, Year 2, is increased by $90 to $290 ($200 + $90).

A taxpayer purchased 200 shares of ABC stock for $24,000 on May 1, Year 1. On March 31, Year 2, 100 shares were sold for $7,000. Twenty days later, the taxpayer purchased 50 shares of ABC stock for $5,000.

A wash sale has occurred since the taxpayer repurchased 50 shares of the same stock within 30 days of the March 31, Year 2, sale. Because the taxpayer only reacquired 50 (ie, half) of the 100 shares, half of the $5,000 loss is disallowed and added to the basis of the 50 shares reacquired. Therefore, the taxpayer's recognized loss is $2,500, as shown below.

Loss from March 31:	$7,000 sales price − ($24,000 × 100 shares / 200 shares) $7,000 − $12,000 = $(5,000)
Less disallowed loss:	$(5,000) loss × (50 shares reacquired / 100 shares sold) = $(2,500)
Recognized loss:	$5,000 − $2,500 = $2,500

Basis for the 50 reacquired shares is $7,500 ($5,000 purchase price + $2,500 disallowed loss).

Sale of Personal Assets

Losses on the sale of assets held for personal use or household use at prices less than original cost are **not reported**, as they are presumed to represent consumption. For example, if a refrigerator is purchased for $1,000 and then sold 15 years later for $100, the decrease in value is **not** a deductible loss but the result of the use of the refrigerator for all those years (**consumption loss**).

- The only exception regarding a deduction for loss from a personal-use asset is for *casualty losses* attributable to federally declared disasters (2018–2025)
- Under the broad interpretation of Section 61 (*income from whatever source derived is taxable unless explicitly excluded in the IRC*), **gains** on the **sale of personal-use assets** are **taxable**, although there are limited exclusions
- Generally, all personal-use assets are capital assets

A single taxpayer had the following sales during the current tax year:

Sale	Holding Period	Gain (Loss)
Personal jet ski	Long-term	$(1,200)
Personal pickup truck	Short-term	2,200
Household washer and dryer	Long-term	(900)
20 shares of ABC stock	Long-term	(4,000)
Land held for investment	Short-term	1,600

What is the taxpayer's net gain or loss reported on the tax return?

Gains from personal-use assets are taxable (personal pickup truck); however, losses are *not* deductible. Therefore, the losses on the *jet ski* and *washer and dryer* are **not** deductible and not included in the netting process.

Short-term capital gains (losses)		
Personal pickup truck	$2,200	
Land held for investment	1,600	
Total STCG		$3,800
Long-term capital gains (losses)		
20 shares of ABC stock		(4,000)
Net capital loss		**$ (200)**

Gambling Losses

Taxpayers are required to report **all** of their gambling winnings on *Schedule 1, Additional Income and Adjustments to Income*. Gambling losses are tax deductible, but only to the *extent of gambling winnings*. However, the deduction is claimed on Schedule A, Itemized Deductions. So, if a taxpayer uses the standard deduction, **none** of the gambling losses are deductible. Special rules apply to professional gamblers.

Accuracy of the Losses Reported on Form 1040

Representative Task (Analysis): Review Form 1040 – U.S. Individual Income Tax Return and supporting documentation, including any source data used to create the return, to determine the accuracy of the losses reported.

Overview

Being able to determine the amount of loss allowable resulting from asset dispositions and losses from other activities is critical to ensuring the appropriate tax treatment. Typically, a taxpayer will have several dispositions of assets during a tax year and may have losses from various activities (eg, hobbies, wash sales, partnerships, S corporations).

Each disposition must be evaluated to confirm that the correct amount of gain or loss has been calculated and the nature of gain or loss is classified in accordance with the tax regulations. In addition, the netting of capital assets should be reviewed for accuracy, and finally, confirm that the tax treatment of the net capital loss is appropriate (ie, net capital loss limited to $3,000).

Ordinary business losses allowed for an individual materially participating in the operations of a pass-through entity are limited by basis and at-risk rules. Therefore, the taxpayer's basis and at-risk amount must be determined to confirm that the correct amount of loss is deducted. In addition, a passive loss may be limited by passive income.

Amounts on Form 1040 generally originate from other forms. A good strategy is to look at the supporting schedules and forms before evaluating Form 1040.

Typical Items to Look for When Examining Loss Documents

- Determine the holding period for property (LT or ST); pay special attention to acquisition and disposal dates
- Check for the proper netting process of capital gains and losses
- Treatment of capital losses: net capital loss limitation for individuals, $3,000 per year ($1,500 for MFS)
- A Section 1231 *net* gain is included in the netting process of other capital gains and losses; a Section 1231 *net* loss is treated as ordinary loss (no limitation)
- No tax deduction for hobby losses, losses from the sale of personal-use assets, and wash sales involving stock
- Check for any direct loans from an S corporation shareholder to the corporation that can be considered debt basis for the purpose of determining at-risk amounts
- Check for sufficient basis and at-risk amounts for an individual materially participating in the operations of a pass-through entity
- Suspended losses due to at-risk amounts are carried forward and can be used when basis and at-risk amounts are restored

Practice Scenario

Nora Nebali, single and age 33, is a general partner in Coastal Associates. Nora spends her free time creating holistic soaps as a hobby. She prepared her tax return for Year 4 and has asked you to review the return for accuracy.

Additional information:

- Her basis in the partnership *before* considering the items listed on her Schedule K-1 is $33,000. Nora has a 50% interest in the partnership. The distribution listed was cash
- She also worked as a part-time employee for a consulting firm. Her W-2 statement of wages reported gross wages of $40,000
- Nora received $15,000 in qualified dividends
- Nora has itemized deductions of $16,000
- Assume the total from Form 8949, Sales and Other Dispositions of Capital Assets, is transferred to Schedule D and then to Form 1040, line 7

Review the exhibits and the provided tax schedules, Form 1040, page 1, Schedule 1, page 1, and Form 8949. Then, complete the table below. Nora's reported amounts are located in column C. If required, enter the correct amounts in column D. Do *not* leave any row in column D blank. If an amount is zero, enter "0."

A	B	C	D
Form 8949			
Part I		**Nora's Entry**	**Correct Entry**
Line 1a, Col H	Green stock gain (loss)	700	
Line 1b, Col. H	Purple stock gain (loss)	(2,000)	
Line 2, Col. H	Total	(1,300)	
Form 8949			
Part II			
Line 1a, Col. H	Yellow stock gain (loss)	(4,500)	
Line 1b, Col. H	Fishing boat gain (loss)	(5,000)	
Line 2, Col. H	Total	(9,500)	
Schedule 1			
Line 5	Partnership loss	(22,000)	
Line 8j	Hobby	(1,800)	
Line 9	Total of 8a–8z	(1,800)	
Line 10	Total	(23,800)	
Form 1040, page 1			
Line 1a	Wages	40,000	
Line 3b	Dividend income	15,000	
Line 7	Capital gain/loss	(10,800)	
Line 8	Other income, Sch. 1	(23,800)	
Line 11	AGI	20,400	
Line 12	Itemized deductions	(16,000)	
Line 15	Taxable income	4,400	

Exhibit 1: K-1 from Partnership, Coastal Associates

Partner's Share of Current-Year Income, Deductions, Credits, and Other Items	
Line 1: Ordinary business income (loss)	(22,000)

Partner's Share of Liabilities	Beginning	Ending
Nonrecourse	10,000	15,000
Qualified nonrecourse		
Recourse	26,000	18,000

Partner's Capital Account Analysis	
Beginning capital account	55,000
Current-year net income (loss)	(22,000)
Withdrawals and distributions	(10,000)
Ending capital account	23,000

Exhibit 2: Hobby Income and Expenses

Gross receipts	$3,300
Cost of goods sold	2,100
Utilities expense	800
Advertising expense	1,600
Supplies	600

Exhibit 3: Capital Asset Transactions

Asset Type	Date Acquired	Date Sold	Purchase Price	Sales Price
Green stock (500 shares)	2/1/YR4	6/1/YR4	$ 3,300	$ 4,000
Purple stock (1,000 shares)	6/5/YR4	7/3/YR4	$10,000	$ 8,000
Yellow stock (400 shares)	9/30/YR1	12/20/YR4	$ 7,200	$ 2,700
Fishing boat (personal use)	4/15/YR1	11/30/YR4	$20,000	$15,000

In addition, Nora purchased 1,000 shares of Purple, Inc., stock on July 31, Year 4, for $4,500.

Exhibit 4: Form 1040, Page 1, Entries

Line 1a: Total amount from Form(s) W-2, box 1	40,000
Line 3a: Qualified dividends	15,000
Line 3b: Ordinary dividends	15,000
Line 7: Capital gain or (loss)	(10,800)
Line 8: Other income from Schedule 1, line 10	(23,800)
Line 9: Total income	20,400
Line 12: Standard deduction or itemized deductions	(16,000)
Line 15: Taxable income	4,400

Exhibit 5: Schedule 1 Additional Income and Adjustments Entries

Line 5: Rental real estate, royalties, partnerships, trusts, etc.	(22,000)
Line 8j: Activity not engaged in for profit income	(1,800)
Line 9: Total other income	(1,800)
Line 10: Combine lines 1 through 7 and 9 (total additional income)	(23,800)

Exhibit 6: Form 8949 Sales and Other Dispositions of Capital Assets

Short-Term Transactions

Description of Property	Date Acquired	Date Sold or Disposed	Proceeds	Cost or Other Basis	Gain or (Loss)
Green stock	02/01/YR 4	06/01/YR 4	4,000	3,300	700
Purple stock	06/05/YR 4	07/03/YR 4	8,000	10,000	(2,000)
Total			12,000	13,300	(1,300)

Long-Term Transactions

Description of Property	Date Acquired	Date Sold or Disposed	Proceeds	Cost or Other Basis	Gain or (Loss)
Yellow stock	09/30/YR 1	12/20/YR 4	2,700	7,200	(4,500)
Fishing boat	04/15/YR 1	11/30/YR 4	15,000	20,000	(5,000)
Total			17,700	27,200	(9,500)

Complete Table

A	B	C	D
Form 8949			
Part I		**Nora's Entry**	**Correct Entry**
Line 1a, Col. H	Green stock gain (loss)	700	700
Line 1b, Col. H	Purple stock gain (loss)	(2,000)	0
Line 2, Col. H	Total	(1,300)	700
Form 8949			
Part II			
Line 1a, Col. H	Yellow stock gain (loss)	(4,500)	(4,500)
Line 1b, Col. H	Fishing boat gain (loss)	(5,000)	0
Line 2, Col. H	Total	(9,500)	(4,500)
Schedule 1			
Line 5	Partnership loss	(22,000)	(5,000)
Line 8j	Hobby	(1,800)	1,200
Line 9	Total of 8a–8z	(1,800)	1,200
Line 10	Total	(23,800)	(3,800)
Form 1040, page 1			
Line 1a	Wages	40,000	40,000
Line 3b	Dividend income	15,000	15,000
Line 7	Capital gain/loss	(10,800)	(3,000)
Line 8	Other income, Sch. 1	(23,800)	(3,800)
Line 11	AGI	20,400	48,200
Line 12	Itemized deductions	(16,000)	(16,000)
Line 15	Taxable income	4,400	32,200

Hobby Loss

Gross receipts	$3,300	
Cost of goods sold	(2,100)	
Gross profit	**$1,200**	
Utilities expense	800	Nondeductible
Advertising expense	1,600	Nondeductible
Supplies	600	Nondeductible

Nora's soap-making activity is a hobby. A hobby is **not** considered a business and therefore is not reported on Schedule C. The hobby's gross profit of $1,200 is reported on Schedule 1, line 8j. The remaining hobby expenses are not deductible.

Partnership Loss

Nora received a K-1 reflecting an ordinary business loss of $22,000. Once her basis in the P/S is updated for the change in liabilities and the cash distribution, the loss is first **limited to basis** (ie, basis may not go below zero) and limited by the at-risk amount. Therefore, a $5,000 loss is reported on Schedule 1, line 5.

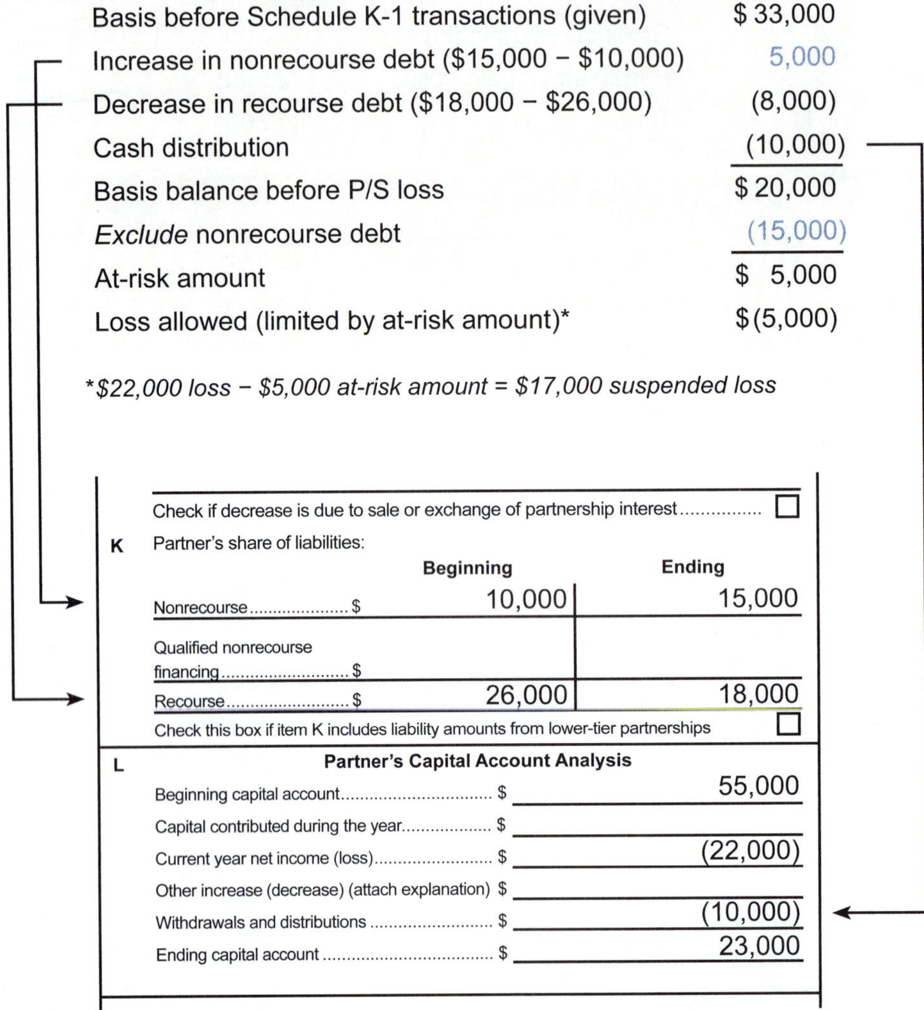

Basis before Schedule K-1 transactions (given)	$ 33,000
Increase in nonrecourse debt ($15,000 − $10,000)	5,000
Decrease in recourse debt ($18,000 − $26,000)	(8,000)
Cash distribution	(10,000)
Basis balance before P/S loss	$ 20,000
Exclude nonrecourse debt	(15,000)
At-risk amount	$ 5,000
Loss allowed (limited by at-risk amount)*	$ (5,000)

**$22,000 loss − $5,000 at-risk amount = $17,000 suspended loss*

Check if decrease is due to sale or exchange of partnership interest ☐

K Partner's share of liabilities:

	Beginning	Ending
Nonrecourse $	10,000	15,000
Qualified nonrecourse financing $		
Recourse $	26,000	18,000

Check this box if item K includes liability amounts from lower-tier partnerships ☐

L **Partner's Capital Account Analysis**

Beginning capital account $	55,000
Capital contributed during the year $	
Current year net income (loss) $	(22,000)
Other increase (decrease) (attach explanation) $	
Withdrawals and distributions $	(10,000)
Ending capital account $	23,000

Capital Transactions

- **Sale of Purple stock:** This transaction is a wash sale because Nora sold her shares at a loss and within 30 days repurchased identical shares of Purple, Inc., stock on July 31, Year 23, for $4,500

As a result, Nora's **recognized** loss is $0. The disallowed loss is an adjustment to the basis of the identical stock. The $2,000 disallowed loss is added to the basis of the Purple stock purchased on July 31, Year 4. The new basis is $6,500 ($4,500 + $2,000).

- **No loss is permitted from the sale of a personal-use asset**. Therefore, the $5,000 loss from the fishing boat is disallowed
- The remaining sales transactions are for the Green and Yellow stock. The correct net loss is $3,800. However, net capital losses are limited to $3,000 per year ($1,500 if MFS). Therefore, Nora's net capital loss is limited to $3,000 (deduction flow-through from Schedule D), reported on Form 1040, page 1, line 7. The $800 unused capital loss is carried forward indefinitely

Asset Type	Sales Price	Purchase Price	Gain (Loss)
Green stock	$4,000	$3,300	$ 700
Yellow stock	2,700	7,200	(4,500)
		Net capital loss	$(3,800)
		Annual limitation	(3,000)
		Carryover loss to next year	$ (800)

Resolve Discrepancies Identified by Automated Diagnostic and Validation Checks

Representative Task (Analysis): Review and resolve discrepancies identified by automated diagnostic and validation checks to ensure the completeness and accuracy of the loss limitations reported on Form 1040 – U.S. Individual Income Tax Return based on the source data used to prepare the form.

Automated Diagnostics and Validation Checks

Accounting firms use automated software to prepare tax returns for their clients. During this process, the software generates diagnostics for the tax preparer to check and clear before the tax return can be filed electronically with the IRS. This helps with the accuracy of the tax return being filed. Diagnostics can be informational, computational, or critical.

Some software packages label each diagnostic according to severity, such as:

- Red for incomplete or inconsistent information that disqualifies a tax return from e-filing (so these are the most serious of diagnostics),
- Yellow or gold for a warning of a potential mistake, and
- Green for a tax planning/tax savings opportunity (if applicable).

Below are examples of automated diagnostics and validation checks generated by tax software:

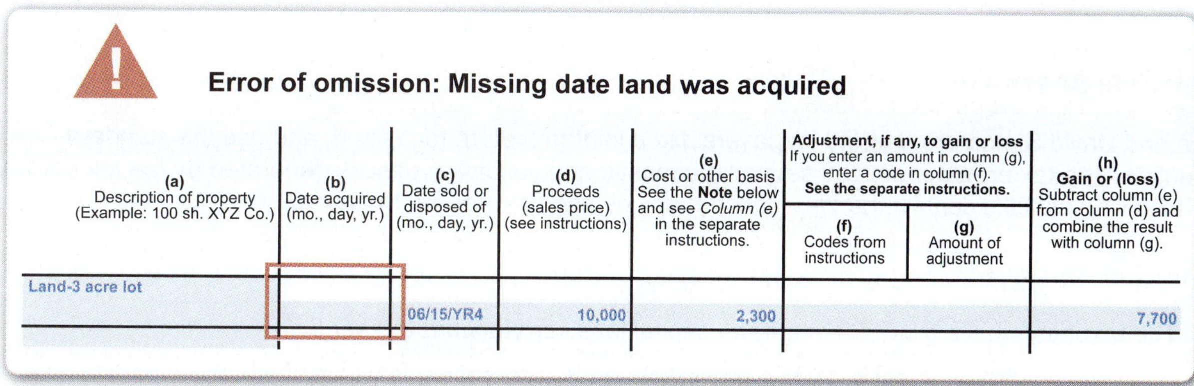

Error of omission: Missing date land was acquired

(a) Description of property (Example: 100 sh. XYZ Co.)	(b) Date acquired (mo., day, yr.)	(c) Date sold or disposed of (mo., day, yr.)	(d) Proceeds (sales price) (see instructions)	(e) Cost or other basis See the **Note** below and see *Column (e)* in the separate instructions.	Adjustment, if any, to gain or loss If you enter an amount in column (g), enter a code in column (f). **See the separate instructions.**		(h) **Gain or (loss)** Subtract column (e) from column (d) and combine the result with column (g).
					(f) Codes from instructions	(g) Amount of adjustment	
Land-3 acre lot		06/15/YR4	10,000	2,300			7,700

Warning: No deduction for SE tax reported

Self-Employment form SE has been filed. No corresponding deduction of one-half of the SE tax has been reported

15 Deductible part of self-employment tax. Attach Schedule SE **15**

Explanation: Let's try to reduce your tax liability

You may be able to contribute to a traditional IRA account before April 15th.

- Do you currently participate in an employer-sponsored retirement plan?
- Does your spouse participate in any employer-sponsored retirement plan?
- Are you 50 or older?

Responding to Diagnostics and Validation Checks

When a tax preparer sees diagnostics and validation checks, there are numerous actions that may be needed to correct them, such as:

- Correcting simple miskeyed information
- Contacting a superior or the client to clarify the purpose and particulars of a source document that is unfamiliar to the preparer that was erroneously entered on the tax return
- Obtaining additional information from the client
- Researching requirements for forms suggested in the diagnostics (eg, when is a Report of Foreign Bank and Financial Accounts [FBAR] needed on an individual tax return)

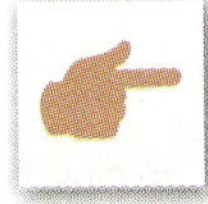

When completing diagnostic and accuracy-based questions on the exam, remember that additional information may be required in order to address the diagnostic flagged. So, expect to occasionally see a choice such as "The tax preparer must request information from the client in order to resolve the issue." Do not assume that all the relevant information is provided.

Practice Scenario

Nova and David Simon are married taxpayers, file a joint tax return for Year 6, and use the standard deduction. The tax preparer noticed several diagnostic and validation checks generated by the tax software. The following exhibits contain the information that was used to prepare the tax return.

Additional Information

- The taxpayers have a $4,000 long-term capital loss carryforward to Year 6
- Nova owns a 50% interest in Miles Corporation, an S corporation, in which she actively participates. She made a bona fide loan to the S corporation on June 1, Year 6, of $10,000. She received a repayment of $2,300 (which included $300 interest) on December 1, Year 6. Her stock basis prior to any items reported on the K-1 is $4,000. Nova's W-2 and Schedule K-1 information are provided in Exhibit 1

- Nova had $26,000 in gambling winnings and $8,000 in gambling losses for the current year
- The taxpayers sold numerous assets during the year (Exhibit 5)
- David has a hobby that generated income (Exhibit 6)

Initial Adjusted Gross Income Reported	
Wages per W-2	$80,000
Interest income (from loan)	300
Capital gain or loss from Schedule D	(2,500)
Other income (loss) from Schedule 1	(34,750)
Adjusted gross income	**$43,050**

Required: Review each diagnostic received and select the correct answer from the drop-down menu.

Diagnostic #1, Schedule 1	**Select the Correct Answers from the Drop-Down Menus**
Schedule 1: Line 5, Rental real estate, partnerships, S corporations, etc. Losses from S corporations should be reviewed to determine if deductible.	A. (8,000) B. (9,800) C. (10,200) D. (12,000)
Schedule 1: Line 8b, Gambling A loss is reported on Line 8b.	A. 0 B. (8,000) C. 18,000 D. 26,000
Schedule 1: Line 8j, Activity not engaged in for profit income Income is reported from an activity not engaged for profit.	A. 0 B. 4,750 C. 6,550 D. 9,800
Diagnostic #2, Form 8949	
Form 8949 has descriptions that appear to be personal-use assets. Check totals for Line 2, Column (d), (e), and (h).	A. 34,500, 37,000, (2,500) B. 23,000, 20,000, 3,000 C. 25,500, 22,000, 3,500 D. 18,000, 17,000, 1,000

Diagnostic #3	Select the Correct Answers from the Drop-Down Menus
Schedule D: Line 12, Net long-term gain or (loss) from partnerships, S corporations, from Schedule(s) K-1 Total does not agree with gains and/ or losses from Schedule K.	A. 1,800 B. (1,800) C. 2,200 D. (2,200)
Schedule D: Line 14, Long-term capital loss carryover Amount does not agree with carryover loss.	A. 0 B. 3,000 C. 4,000 D. 5,800
Schedule D: Line 16, Total of net short-term capital gain (loss) and net long-term capital gain (loss) including carryovers Total does not reflect carryovers.	A. (2,300) B. (2,500) C. (3,000) D. (4,300)
Enter the correct adjusted gross income for the taxpayers.	

Exhibit 1: W-2 Form, Schedule K-1

22222	a Employee's social security number 123-45-6789	OMB No. 1545-0008	
b Employer identification number (EIN) 34-1234567		1 Wages, tips, other compensation 80,000	2 Federal income tax withheld 16,800
c Employer's name, address, and ZIP code TST Inc. 101 Ace Road Jasper TN 38589		3 Social security wages 80,000	4 Social security tax withheld 4,960
		5 Medicare wages and tips 80,000	6 Medicare tax withheld 1,160
		7 Social security tips	8 Allocated tips
d Control number		9	10 Dependent care benefits
e Employee's first name and initial Nova	Last name Simon	Suff. 11 Nonqualified plans	12a
123 Garden Springs Drive Jasper TN 38589		13 Statutory employee ☐ Retirement plan ☐ Third-party sick pay ☐	12b
		14 Other	12c
f Employee's address and ZIP code			12d

15 State	Employer's state ID number	16 State wages, tips, etc.	17 State income tax	18 Local wages, tips, etc.	19 Local income tax	20 Locality name
TN	12-333333	80,000	4,000			

Form **W-2** **Wage and Tax Statement** Year 6 Department of Treasury—Internal Revenue Service

K-1 from S Corp, Miles Corporation

Shareholder's Share of Current-Year Income, Deductions, Credits, and Other Items	
Line 1: Ordinary business income (loss)	(12,000)
Line 8a: Net long-term capital gain (loss)	(1,800)

Information about Shareholder	
Current-year allocation percentage	50%
Shareholder's number of shares: beginning of year	10,000
Shareholder's number of shares: end of year	10,000
Loans from shareholder: beginning of year	0
Loans from shareholder: end of year	8,000

Exhibit 2: Schedule 1 Additional Income and Adjustments to Income Entries

Line 5: Rental real estate, royalties, partnerships, trusts, etc.	(12,000)
Line 8b: Gambling	(18,000)
Line 8j: Activity not engaged in for profit income	(4,750)
Line 9: Total other income	(22,750)
Line 10: Combine lines 1 through 7 and 9 (total additional income)	(34,750)

Exhibit 3: Form 8949 Sales and Other Dispositions of Capital Assets

Short-Term Transactions

Description of Property (a)	Date Acquired (b)	Date Sold or Disposed (c)	Proceeds (d)	Cost or Other Basis (e)	Gain or (Loss) (h)
Pool table	03/01/YR 5	02/15/YR 6	9,000	15,000	(6,000)
Painting	05/01/YR 5	04/15/YR 6	2,500	2,000	500
100 shares of ABC Corp stock	04/15/YR 6	08/01/YR 6	18,000	17,000	1,000
Two acres of land	12/31/YR 5	12/15/YR 6	5,000	3,000	2,000
Total (Line 2)			34,500	37,000	(2,500)

Exhibit 4: Schedule D Capital Gains and Losses

Line 3, Total short-term transactions from Form 8949 (Proceeds)	34,500
Line 3, Total short-term transactions from Form 8949 (Cost or Other Basis)	37,000
Line 3, Total short-term transactions from Form 8949 (Gain or (Loss))	(2,500)
Line 7, Net short-term capital gain (loss)	(2,500)
Line 12, Net long-term gain or (loss) from partnerships, S corporations	0
Line 14, Long-term capital loss carryover	0
Line 16, Combine lines 7, 12, and 14	(2,500)

Exhibit 5: Capital Asset Transactions

Asset Type	Date Acquired	Date Sold	Purchase Price	Sales Price
Pool table (personal use)	3/1/YR5	2/15/YR6	$15,000	$9,000
Painting (displayed in home)	5/1/YR5	4/15/YR6	2,000	2,500
100 shares of ABC Corp. stock	4/15/YR6	8/1/YR6	17,000	18,000
Two acres of land	12/31/YR5	12/15/YR6	3,000	5,000

In addition, Nora purchased 25 shares of ABC Corp. stock on 8/15/YR6 for $4,000.

Exhibit 6: Hobby Income and Expenses

Gross receipts	$15,000
Cost of goods sold	(5,200)
Gross profit	$ 9,800
Utilities	(950)
Advertising expense	(1,100)
Website expenses	(1,200)
Depreciation expense	(1,800)
Net income	$ 4,750

Solution

Diagnostic #1, Schedule 1	Select the Correct Answers from the Drop-Down Menus
Schedule 1: Line 5, Rental real estate, partnerships, S corporations, etc. Losses from S corporations should be reviewed to determine if deductible.	A. (8,000) B. (9,800) **C. (10,200)** D. (12,000)
Schedule 1: Line 8b, Gambling A loss is reported on Line 8b.	A. 0 B. (8,000) C. 18,000 **D. 26,000**
Schedule 1: Line 8j, Activity not engaged in for profit income Income is reported from an activity not engaged for profit.	A. 0 B. 4,750 C. 6,550 **D. 9,800**
Diagnostic #2, Form 8949	
Form 8949 has descriptions that appear to be personal-use assets. Check totals for Line 2, Column (d), (e), and (h).	A. 34,500, 37,000, (2,500) B. 23,000, 20,000, 3,000 **C. 25,500, 22,000, 3,500** D. 18,000, 17,000, 1,000
Diagnostic #3	
Schedule D: Line 12, Net long-term gain or (loss) from partnerships, S corporations, from Schedule(s) K-1 Total does not agree with gains and/or losses from Schedule K.	A. 1,800 **B. (1,800)** C. 2,200 D. (2,200)
Schedule D: Line 14, Long-term capital loss carryover Amount does not agree with carryover loss.	A. 0 B. 3,000 **C. 4,000** D. 5,800
Schedule D: Line 16, Total of net short-term capital gain (loss) and net long-term capital gain (loss) including carryovers Total does not reflect carryovers.	**A. (2,300)** B. (2,500) C. (3,000) D. (4,300)
Enter the correct adjusted gross income for the taxpayers.	**103,600**

Line 5, Schedule 1: Loss and Shareholder's Stock and Debt Basis

An S corporation shareholder's ability to deduct losses from the corporation is limited to their at-risk amount. For S corporation shareholders, the at-risk amount equals their *stock basis plus any debt basis*.

Here, during the year, the shareholder loaned the corporation $10,000 and received a repayment of $2,000. The $300 paid for interest does not affect the loan balance. At the end of Year 4, the debt basis is $8,000 ($10,000 − $2,000); this amount is also reported on the K-1.

Nova's stock basis before the K-1 (given)	$4,000	
Long-term capital loss	(1,800)	
Basis before loss	$2,200	
Loss limited by basis	(2,200)	**Total deductible loss: $10,200** ($2,200 + $8,000)
Ending basis	$ 0	
Debt basis	$8,000	**Suspended loss:** $12,000 − $10,200 = **$1,800**
Loss limited by at-risk rules	(8,000)	
Debt basis	$ 0	

Line 8a, Schedule 1: Gambling Activities

Gambling **winnings** are reported on Schedule 1. The losses **cannot** be *netted* against the winnings. Gambling losses are only deductible to the extent of gambling winnings. In this scenario, the error made was netting the winnings against the losses. Furthermore, when netting, the gambling winnings and losses were inverted, resulting in an erroneous net loss of $18,000 ($26,000 *losses* − $8,000 *winnings*).

However, because no netting is permitted, the losses are reported on Schedule A (ie, the taxpayer must itemize). Here, the gross winnings of **$26,000 are reported on Schedule 1**. *None* of $8,000 losses are deductible since the taxpayer uses the standard deduction.

Line 8j, Schedule 1: Hobby Activities

Hobby losses are not deductible. In this scenario, there is no loss; however, the expenses other than cost of goods sold are only deductible on Schedule A (ie, the taxpayer must itemize their deductions). Furthermore, the expenses listed are miscellaneous itemized deductions, which are not deductible from 2018 to 2025.

The correct amount reported on Schedule 1, line 8j, from the hobby is $9,800 (not a $4,750 loss).

Gross receipts	$15,000	
Cost of goods sold	5,200	
Gross profit	**$ 9,800**	
Utilities	(950)	Nondeductible expenses
Advertising expense	(1,100)	
Website expenses	(1,200)	
Depreciation expense	(1,800)	
Net loss	$ 4,750	

Form 8949, Line 2, Column (d), (e), and (h): Sale of Capital Assets

Gains, not losses (ie, pool table), from personal-use assets are taxable. Therefore, the amounts reported on Form 8949 are as follows:

Asset	Purchase Price	Sales Price
Painting (displayed in home)	$ 2,000	$ 2,500
100 shares of ABC Corp. stock	17,000	18,000
Two acres of land held for investment	3,000	5,000
Total	$22,000	$25,500

Short-term capital gain ($25,500 − $22,000) = $3,500

Line 2, Column (d), (e), and (h) values are $25,500, $22,000, and $3,500, respectively.

Note that it does **not** matter that Nova acquired 25 shares of ABC Corp. stock on 8/15/YR6 for $1,800. There was **not a wash sale** because **no loss** was incurred; there was a $1,000 gain. Wash sales are only for losses.

Schedule D, Line 12: Net Long-Term Capital Loss from an S Corporation

The $1,800 loss from box 8a of Schedule K-1 should be entered on line 12, so it can be netted with the current capital gains and losses.

Schedule D, Line 14: Capital Loss Carryover

Line 14 should be **$4,000**. The amount was provided in the narrative.

Schedule D, Line 16: Does Not Reflect the Carryover

Line 16 is a **net capital loss** of **$2,300,** as computed below. The $2,300 capital loss is carried from Schedule D to Form 1040, page 1.

Short-term capital gain from above	$ 3,500
Long-term capital loss carryforward	(4,000)
Long-term capital loss from Schedule K-1	(1,800)
Total capital losses deducted on Schedule D	**$(2,300)**

Adjusted Gross Income

Wages per W-2	$ 80,000
Interest income (from loan)	300
Capital gain or loss from Schedule D	(2,300)
Other income from Schedule 1: [($10,200) + $26,000 + 9,800]	25,600
Adjusted gross income	**$103,600**

REG 16
Filing Status

REG 16: Filing Status

16.01 Types of Filing Status

Filing Status

Representative Task (Remembering & Understanding): Recall taxpayer filing status for tax purposes.

Taxpayer(s) must select a filing status on their tax return, which is used to determine the tax rates on income and the value of various deductions, credits, thresholds, and limitations. An individual's filing status may change from year to year depending on personal circumstances. When a taxpayer is eligible for more than one filing status, they should select the status that minimizes their tax liability.

There are currently five filing statuses: single, married filing jointly (MFJ), married filing separately (MFS), head of household (HOH), and qualifying surviving spouse (QSS). The QSS was referred to as qualifying widow(er) prior to 2022. The statuses are primarily established by a taxpayer's marital status on the last day of the tax year. Generally, married taxpayers may file MFJ or MFS.

Unmarried taxpayers typically file as single or HOH; however, certain exceptions exist. In addition, the ability to claim an individual as a taxpayer's dependent (ie, either a qualifying child or qualifying relative) can affect filing status.

Married Filing Jointly (MFJ)

This filing status is used for taxpayers who are legally married, which is determined on the last day of the tax year (taxpayers must have the same tax year). If one spouse dies during a tax year, the IRS considers the taxpayers married for the entire year (ie, a taxpayer does not have to remarry in the year of death of the spouse to file MFJ). However, if the surviving spouse remarries before the end of the tax year, the decedent spouse must file married filing separately (MFS).

- Taxpayers living together in a common law marriage recognized in the state where they reside or where the common law marriage began may file MFJ
- MFJ includes same-sex married couples, not registered domestic partnerships or civil unions (*Obergefell v. Hodges*); thus, any rules that apply to MFJ/MFS also apply to same-sex married individuals
- Both spouses are jointly and severally liable for paying any and all federal income tax; this means either party can be held independently responsible for paying the full amount of the tax. Because of this potential liability, some spouses prefer to file MFS
- Married taxpayers generally cannot file a joint return if either one is a nonresident alien at any time during the tax year. However, if an election is made to treat a nonresident alien spouse as a U.S. resident for income tax and wage withholding purposes by both spouses, they may file MFJ. By making the election, their worldwide income is subject to U.S. income taxation
- Taxpayers are considered unmarried for the whole year if, on the last day of the year, they are divorced or are legally separated under a divorce or legal separate maintenance decree

Married Filing Separately (MFS)

Taxpayers who are legally married may choose for various reasons to file separately. Married filing separately requires that the spouses divide income and expenses (according to ownership).

Therefore, each spouse files their own return and is responsible for paying their own tax. In a community property state, income and expenses are split 50/50 between the spouses, regardless of which spouse earned the income or paid the expenses. A taxpayer may change their filing status from MFS to MFJ by filing an amended return within three years of the original due date of the tax return.

Special rules also apply to prevent taxpayers from receiving benefits from filing separately. For example:

- If one spouse itemizes, the other spouse must itemize deductions also, even if the other spouse has no itemized deductions
- Neither spouse can claim the earned income credit
- Neither spouse can claim the child and dependent care credit
- Neither spouse can claim an education credit
- An expense or credit is not allowed for adoption expenses
- The deduction for net capital losses is limited to $1,500 (rather than $3,000)

Qualifying Surviving Spouse (QSS)

Taxpayers who are **not married** may qualify to use the more advantageous tax rates of MFJ taxpayers if they meet the requirements of *qualifying surviving spouse*. This filing status was enacted to help alleviate the financial hardships a taxpayer with a dependent child, stepchild, or adopted child may face after the death of their spouse.

The filing status is available for only the **two years** *after* the year of the death of a spouse. After the two years, the taxpayer will file as either single or head of household. In addition, **all** of the following requirements must be met.

- In the year of the spouse's death, the taxpayers qualified to file a joint return
- The surviving spouse provides over 50% of the cost of maintaining a household
- The surviving spouse has a dependent child (or stepchild but *not* a foster child) live in the household for the **entire** year (temporary absences are allowed)
- Taxpayer has not remarried as of the end of the tax year

Head of Household (HOH)

Head of household status is used by taxpayers who are unmarried (or considered unmarried for tax purposes, such as an abandoned spouse) as of the last day of the tax year. Tax rates and the standard deduction amounts are less favorable than MFJ and QSS but more favorable than MFS or single.

To qualify, the taxpayer must meet **both** of the following:

- Taxpayer must have paid for **more than 50%** of the costs of maintaining a household; **and**
- Taxpayer must have a **qualifying person** who is claimed as a **dependent** living in the household for **more than 50%** of the year. Temporary absences are permitted (eg, vacations, school)
  - A qualifying person may be a **qualifying child** (child, stepchild, grandchild, adopted or fostered child) or a **qualifying** relative (parent, grandparent, aunt, uncle, niece, nephew, in-laws or step-in-laws)

- A dependent *parent* does not need to live in the household; however, the taxpayer must pay for maintaining more than 50% of the household in which the parent resides
- Note: A custodial parent who has released the right to claim the dependency exemption to the noncustodial parent by filing Form 8332 may still qualify for HOH status. Form 8332 does not qualify the noncustodial parent for HOH status

Costs of Maintaining a Home

Qualifying Costs	Nonqualifying Costs
• Rent	• Clothing
• Utilities	• Education costs
• Mortgage interest	• Medical costs
• Food (if eaten in the home)	• Transportation
• Repairs and maintenance	• Vacations
• Property insurance	• Life insurance
• Property taxes	

Exceptions When Married Taxpayers Can Claim HOH

Abandoned Spouse Exception

When a taxpayer is still *legally married* but has lived apart from their spouse for the **last six months of the year**, the IRS allows for the abandoned spouse provision. The taxpayer is considered *unmarried* for tax purposes and, therefore, is *not* restricted to file as MFJ or MFS.

This is permitted because in certain cases the taxpayer may not be able to locate their spouse and obtain information needed to file a joint return and obtain the spouse's signature. Also, it prevents the taxpayer from having to file MFS and be subject to a higher tax rate and denied certain tax benefits.

Instead, the taxpayer may **file as HOH** if the following requirements are met. To qualify, the married taxpayer must:

- Not file a joint tax return
- Pay more than 50% of the cost of maintaining a household
- Have a **qualifying child**, who can be claimed as the taxpayer's dependent, live in the household for more than 50% of the year
- Not have allowed the spouse to live in the household during the last six months of the year

Nonresident Alien Spouse Exception

When a married taxpayer's spouse is a nonresident alien at any time during the year and the election to treat the alien spouse as a resident alien is **not** made, the taxpayer is considered unmarried for the purpose of HOH.

Don't get confused. For qualifying surviving spouse, the taxpayer must maintain the residence for the dependent **child** for the entire year. For HOH, the taxpayer must provide the residence for the qualifying **person** (ie, qualifying child or relative) for more than half the year.

Single

If an unmarried taxpayer does not qualify for one of the other filing statuses, their filing status is single. Filing as single is the least advantageous filing status with regard to tax rates.

Filing Status Flowchart

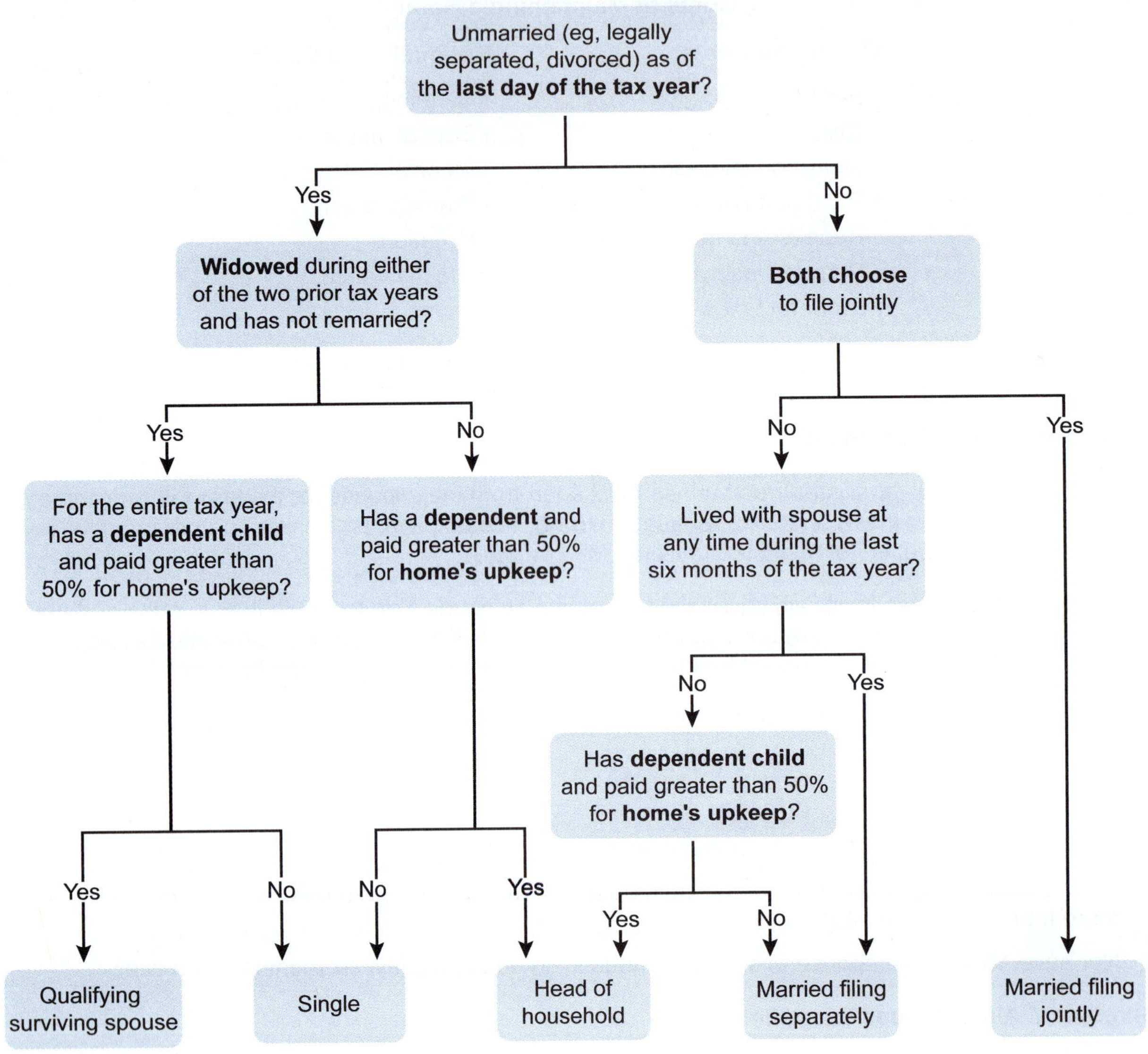

Unmarried (eg, legally separated, divorced) as of the **last day of the tax year**?

- Yes → **Widowed** during either of the two prior tax years and has not remarried?
  - Yes → For the entire tax year, has a **dependent child** and paid greater than 50% for home's upkeep?
    - Yes → Qualifying surviving spouse
    - No → Single
  - No → Has a **dependent** and paid greater than 50% for **home's upkeep**?
    - No → Single
    - Yes → Head of household
- No → **Both choose** to file jointly
  - No → Lived with spouse at any time during the last six months of the tax year?
    - No → Has **dependent child** and paid greater than 50% for **home's upkeep**?
      - Yes → Head of household
      - No → Married filing separately
    - Yes → Married filing separately
  - Yes → Married filing jointly

Filing Status Examples

Parker and Marie are married and have two dependent children. Marie died in October of Year 1. Parker has not remarried and continues to maintain a home for himself and his two children during Year 1, Year 2, Year 3, and Year 4. What are Parker's most advantageous filing statuses for Year 1, Year 2, Year 3, and Year 4?

Year 1 – **Married filing jointly:** A couple may file a joint return if they are married as of the end of the tax year or when one spouse has died during the tax year if they were married as of the date of death. As a result, Parker would qualify to file a joint return for Year 1.

Years 2 and 3 – **Qualifying surviving spouse:** A taxpayer may file a tax return as a qualifying widow or widower (ie, surviving spouse) for *two tax years after the year in which a spouse dies* provided:

- The couple qualified to file a joint return for the year of death;
- The taxpayer provided over 50% of the cost of maintaining the principal residence of a dependent child or stepchild; and
- The taxpayer had *not* remarried as of the end of the current year.

Year 4 – **Head of household:** In Year 4, Parker may no longer file as a qualified widower but may file as a head of household, which is an unmarried taxpayer who maintains a home that is the principal residence of a qualifying person, such as a child, for more than 50% of the year.

A spouse died on December 31, Year 1. The couple had no dependents. What should be the filing status of the remaining spouse in Year 1?

The taxpayers are considered married the entire year, regardless of when one of the spouses dies. Therefore, the remaining spouse will file as MFJ for Year 1.

What should be the filing status of the remaining spouse in Year 2?

The remaining spouse (ie, surviving spouse) does not have a *dependent child* living in the household; therefore, the qualifying surviving spouse filing status does not apply.

Because there is *no qualifying dependent*, the taxpayer is not eligible for the HOH status. **Single** is the only filing status available.

Types of Dependents

Representative Task (Remembering & Understanding): Recall relationships meeting the definition of dependent for purposes of determining taxpayer filing status.

Personal Exemptions

Prior to 2018, a taxpayer could claim a personal exemption for themselves, their spouse, and qualifying dependents. However, no deduction for personal exemptions (including dependency exemptions) is permitted from 2018 to 2025. Because the personal exemption dollar amount is used to determine other tax benefits, the amount is adjusted for inflation and published every year. For 2024, the amount is $5,050.

Dependents

Certain tax benefits claimed on behalf of another taxpayer (eg, medical deduction, earned income tax credit, educational credits) and filing status require either a qualifying child or a qualifying relative, also known as dependents. A person is a taxpayer's dependent if *all* requirements are met for a *qualifying child* or a *qualifying relative*.

In order to file as HOH, the taxpayer must have a *qualifying child* or *qualifying relative* as a *dependent*. In order to file as qualifying surviving spouse status, the taxpayer must have a *qualifying child* as a *dependent*. No other filing status requires the taxpayer to have a dependent.

Two tests that **all** dependents must meet (ie, a qualifying child or qualifying relative) are:

1. **Citizenship test: All dependents** must be a U.S. citizen or a resident of the U.S., Canada, or Mexico. There is an exception for an adopted child; in that case, the taxpayer must be a U.S. citizen or U.S. national, and the child must be a member of the taxpayer's household
2. **Joint return test:** A **married dependent** cannot file MFJ with their spouse unless they are filing only to receive a total refund of taxes withheld or estimated taxes paid and are not required to file (eg, income below filing requirement level)

On the exam, these two tests are assumed to have been met unless information is provided to indicate otherwise.

Tie-Breaker Rules: Only one taxpayer may claim a person as a dependent; if more than one taxpayer is eligible to claim a qualifying child as a dependent, tie-breaker rules apply as follows:

- A parent of the child takes precedence
- If both taxpayers are parents, the parent the child *lives with longest* during the tax year takes precedence. However, the parent who has custody can sign a waiver (Form 8332) on a yearly basis to grant the other parent the ability to claim the child as their dependent
- If the child lives equally with both parents, then the parent with the highest AGI takes precedence
- If no taxpayer is a parent, then the person with the highest AGI takes precedence

Other Rules: Neither death nor divorce will dissolve any of the relationships established by marriage (eg, once your mother-in-law, always your mother-in-law).

If a taxpayer can be claimed by another taxpayer, they may not claim anyone as a dependent (ie, a dependent cannot claim a dependent).

Qualifying Child vs. Qualifying Dependent

The main difference regarding the required tests between the *qualifying child* and *qualifying relative* are the additional **age** test for a qualifying child and **gross income test** for a qualifying relative.

<table>
<tr><th rowspan="2">Test or Requirement</th><th colspan="2">Must Be Met For:</th></tr>
<tr><th>Qualifying Child</th><th>Qualifying Relative</th></tr>
<tr><td>Citizenship</td><td>Yes</td><td>Yes</td></tr>
<tr><td>No joint return</td><td>Yes</td><td>Yes</td></tr>
<tr><td>Relationship</td><td>Yes</td><td rowspan="2">Yes*</td></tr>
<tr><td>Residence</td><td>Yes</td></tr>
<tr><td>Support</td><td>Yes</td><td>Yes</td></tr>
<tr><td>Age</td><td>Yes</td><td>No</td></tr>
<tr><td>Gross income</td><td>No</td><td>Yes</td></tr>
</table>

For qualifying relative, the person* ***either* *meets the relationship test (ie, a qualified relative) or meets a residence test by being a member of the household for the entire year.*

Qualifying Child: SARR

In addition to meeting *both* the citizenship and joint return tests discussed above, a qualifying child must meet the following four tests:

Support Test	• **Child** must **not** have provided > 50% of their own support (eg, food, clothing, shelter, medical care); however, the taxpayer does **not** have to provide more than 50% of support • Scholarships are *not* included in the support test for *children*
Age Test	• Must be *under* age 19, or 24 if a full-time student for at least any portion of five months of the year at the end of the tax year, and must be younger than the taxpayer or the taxpayer's spouse • If the child is disabled, there is *no* age limit
Residence Test	• Must live with the taxpayer *50%* of the year; temporary absences are permitted (eg, vacation, illness, education)
Relationship Test	• Must be taxpayer's child, adopted child, stepchild, foster child, sibling, stepsibling, or descendant or a descendant of any such individual* (eg, nephew or grandchild)

**Excludes grandparents, parents, aunts, uncles, in-laws, cousins*

Federal tax law determines who may claim a child as a dependent on a federal income tax return. Even if a state court order allocates the ability to claim the child to a noncustodial parent, the noncustodial parent must comply with the federal tax law to claim the dependent.

Qualifying Relative: IRRS

A qualifying relative is a person who is *not* a qualifying child. As with a qualifying child, a qualifying relative must meet *both* the citizen and joint return tests. In addition, the following tests must be met:

Income Test	• Dependent's gross income must be ≤ $5,050 for 2024. Gross income is defined as only the income that is taxable (eg, excludes nontaxable Social Security, tax-exempt interest, nontaxable part of scholarship)
Relationship / Residence Test	• **Relationship:** Must be a **qualifying relative**, which includes grandparents and parents, aunts, uncles, most in-laws (brother- or sister-in-law, mother- or father-in-law, son- or daughter-in-law), as well as children who do **not** meet the test for a qualifying child. These relatives do **not** have to live with the taxpayer all year **or** • **Residence:** A **member of the household** (eg, cousins, friends) who must live with the taxpayer for the **entire year** (temporary absences permitted)
Support Test	• Taxpayer must provide over 50% of total annual support of the dependent (eg, food, shelter, medical expenses, some capital purchases) • Unlike a child, scholarships are included as support from another source when determining whether the > 50% is met

Computation for the Support Test

When determining whether the taxpayer satisfies the > 50% support test for a qualifying relative, the computation is as follows:

$$\frac{\text{Amount the taxpayer contributed toward the dependent's support}}{\text{Total support paid for the dependent from all sources*}} = \text{Must be} > 50\%$$

**Includes amount paid by the dependent*

- Total support includes the amount paid for shelter, food, clothing, education, medical and dental costs, insurance premiums for medical coverage, and transportation, as well as other necessities
- When there is more than one member of a household, any costs not directly for a particular dependent must be allocated among all the dependents
- If a taxpayer supports more than one parent, the support must be computed for each parent

Remember that the support test for a qualifying child is slightly different than for a qualifying relative. A qualifying child must **not** have provided more than 50% of their own support (there is no requirement that the taxpayer must provide > 50%). However, for a qualifying relative, the taxpayer must provide over 50% of the dependent's total support.

Multiple Support Agreement for Qualifying Relatives and Members of the Household

What happens if no one person provides more than 50% of the dependent's support? When two or more taxpayers' contributions to the support of a dependent is > 50%, a **multiple support agreement** can be filed allowing one of the taxpayers to claim the person as dependent.

An individual can be claimed as a dependent by any taxpayer who paid **more than 10% of the support**. The other eligible taxpayers who agreed not to claim the person must sign the agreement.

Vince is 84 years old and lives by himself in Detroit. Vince's gross income for the year is $3,000. Vince's support is provided as follows: himself (5%), his daughters Regina (25%) and Rachel (30%), his son Mark (5%), his friend Don (15%), and his niece Sharon (20%). Absent a multiple support agreement, of the parties named above, who may claim Vince as a dependent?

Because no taxpayer provides over half of Vince's support individually, **no one is eligible** to claim Vince as a dependent qualifying relative. In addition, since Don (the friend) fails the relationship test, Vince would have to live with Don for the entire year to qualify as his dependent.

Under a multiple support agreement, who is eligible to claim Vince as a dependent qualifying relative?

No one outright meets the > 50% support test. Regina, Rachel, Sharon, and Mark combined provided more than half of Vince's support (80%). Because Vince is a qualifying relative to the four taxpayers, the relationship test is met. However, only **Regina, Rachel, and Sharon** are eligible to claim Vince under a multiple support agreement since they each contributed more than 10% of the support. Mark is **not** eligible because he did not provide over 10% support. Don still fails the relationship test.

Assume that Regina is allowed to claim Vince as a dependent under a multiple support agreement. Regina is single, and Vince is her only dependent. What is Regina's filing status?

Regina must file as **single**. Because she claims Vince as a dependent under a multiple support agreement, Vince is not a qualifying person for HOH status.

Additional Examples

A single taxpayer maintains a household and provides full support for his child, a 19-year-old daughter, who works full-time as a yoga instructor. The daughter earned $20,000 during the year and lives at home. In addition to his daughter, the taxpayer provides more than half of the support of his widowed sister, who lives out of state and has income of $2,500, as well as his father, who lives in the same town as the taxpayer. Because his father has only nontaxable Social Security benefits, the taxpayer maintains more than 50% of his father's household. What is the taxpayer's filing status?

The taxpayer has two filing options, **single or HOH**. To qualify as HOH, the taxpayer must have provided for more than *50% of the costs of maintaining a household* and have a qualifying person who is *claimed as a dependent* living in the household for more than *50% of the tax year*.

A qualifying person* may be a qualifying child (child, stepchild, grandchild, adopted or fostered child) or a qualifying relative (parent, grandparent, aunt, uncle, niece, nephew, in-laws or step-in-laws). A dependent parent does **not** need to live in the household; however, the taxpayer must pay for maintaining more than 50% of the household in which the parent resides.

In this scenario, the *daughter* is neither a qualifying child (fails age test) nor a qualifying relative (fails gross income test). Although the *sister* is a qualifying relative, she is not a member of the taxpayer's household for more than 50% of the year. The father is also a qualifying relative; however, the father is **not** required to live with the taxpayer, but the taxpayer must provide more than 50% of the cost of his father's household. Therefore, the **father** will qualify as the taxpayer's **dependent**, entitling the taxpayer to **file as HOH**.

Although the sister does **not** meet the requirements for a dependent for the purpose of filing HOH, she can be *claimed* by the taxpayer as a *dependent*. The taxpayer provided more than 50% of the sister's support, and she has gross income less than $5,050. A qualifying relative is **not** required to live with the taxpayer in order to be claimed as a *dependent*.

Note that a person who meets the requirements to be claimed as a dependent by being a member of the household for the entire year (eg, cousin, friend) is* ***excluded* *as a qualifying person for determining HOH filing status.*

A married couple furnishes more than 50% support for their three children, Jane, Lucy, and Sam. Jane, age 16, earned $6,000 from babysitting and lives at home. Lucy, age 20, is married (her spouse is 25 years old) and filed a joint tax return for the year with her spouse in order to receive a refund for all of the withheld taxes from his $4,000 in wages. Lucy and her spouse live with her parents. Sam, age 24, is a full-time graduate student and lives with his aunt. He has earned income of $3,000. Based on the information provided, determine the number of dependents that the taxpayers may claim.

The taxpayers may claim four dependents (Jane, Lucy, Lucy's spouse, and Sam).

- Because there is no gross income test for a qualifying child, Jane, age 16, **may be claimed** as a dependent
- Because Lucy and her spouse filed a joint return only to receive a full *refund* of withheld taxes, they meet the joint return test for both a qualifying child and qualifying relative. Since Lucy is age 20 and not a full-time student, she fails the age test for qualifying child. The spouse is not a qualifying child to the taxpayers. However, both Lucy and her spouse (ie, the taxpayer's son-in-law) are *qualifying relatives*. There is no age test for a qualifying relative, and Lucy and her spouse's income is less than $5,050. Therefore, the taxpayer **may claim Lucy and her spouse** as dependents
- Although Sam is a full-time student, he is **not** younger than 24; therefore, he is *not* a qualifying child. Sam is a qualifying relative and meets the gross income test. A qualifying relative does *not* have to live with the taxpayers to be a dependent. Accordingly, the taxpayers may claim Sam as a dependent
- The aunt **cannot** claim Sam as a dependent since she did **not** provide more than 50% of his support

Determining Filing Status

Representative Task (Application): Identify taxpayer filing status for tax purposes given a specific scenario.

Overview

A taxpayer's filing status may change from year to year. Therefore, each year, taxpayers should consider which of the five filing statuses is most advantageous based on their circumstances. For example, if a taxpayer can qualify to file as HOH instead of single, that would minimize their tax liability.

The beginning point when determining filing status for tax purposes is whether the taxpayer is *married* on the last day of the tax year. If yes, then generally **MFJ or MFS** are the only two filing statuses available for the taxpayers. There are *exceptions*:

- When one spouse dies during the year, the remaining spouse is still considered married that year and as such may file as **MFJ**. After the year of death, the remaining spouse *may* qualify to file as qualifying surviving spouse for the next two years
- Conversely, a married person can be considered **unmarried** (abandoned spouse) in certain situations and may be permitted to file as HOH

Once marital status is determined, the taxpayer should consider if they are supporting a person who would qualify as their **dependent**. Having a dependent may allow the taxpayer to be eligible to file as **HOH** (including abandoned spouse) or as a **qualifying surviving spouse**.

- The rules for a dependent to qualify a taxpayer to file as HOH are slightly *different* from the rules applied when determining if the person is a dependent for other purposes (eg, medical expenses, tax credits)
  - Always determine if the person qualifies as a dependent first and then apply the more stringent rules for HOH
- For the qualifying surviving spouse filing status, the *dependent child* must live in the household for the **entire** year. However, to claim the *child as dependent*, the child must live in the household for > 50% of the tax year

If the taxpayer has no qualifying dependent, then the taxpayer files as **single**.

A taxpayer provides more than 50% of the support for each of the following individuals. Considering each individual separately, which of the individuals qualify the taxpayer to file HOH?

- A taxpayer's sister who earned $4,000 in wages and does not live with the taxpayer
- A taxpayer's friend who lived with the taxpayer the entire year and received $5,500 of taxable income
- A taxpayer's disabled child, age 35, who lived with the taxpayer for the entire year. The child earned $8,000 from a part-time job
- A taxpayer's grandchild, age 25, who lived with the taxpayer for seven months and earned $500 in dividends

Do not get confused between what qualifies a dependent to allow a taxpayer to file as HOH and what is needed for a person to be considered a dependent. To qualify as HOH, the taxpayer must have provided *more than 50% of costs of maintaining a household* and have a *qualifying person* who is claimed as a *dependent* living in the household for more than **50% of the year**.

A qualifying person may be a qualifying child (child, stepchild, grandchild, adopted or fostered child) or a qualifying relative (parent, grandparent, aunt, uncle, niece, nephew, in-laws or step-in-laws).

- A **taxpayer's sister** is a *qualifying relative* and as such does **not** need to live with the taxpayer to be considered a dependent. In addition, the gross income does not exceed $5,050. Therefore, the taxpayer may *claim the sister* as a dependent. However, to allow the taxpayer to file HOH, the sister must live in the household for more than 50% of the time. Therefore, she can be claimed as a dependent, but that **does not qualify** the taxpayer to file **HOH**
- The taxpayer may **not** file HOH since a friend is **not** considered a qualifying person. In addition, the taxpayer may **not claim the friend** as a dependent. Although the friend meets the *member of household* test for a dependent, their gross income exceeds $5,050
- A **taxpayer's child** is a qualifying child even though the child is age 35; there is no age limit when a child is disabled. There is no gross income test for a qualifying child. The child is the taxpayer's *dependent*. Because the child lives with the taxpayer, the child will **qualify the taxpayer** to file as **HOH**
- The **taxpayer's grandchild** is too old to be a qualifying child; however, the grandchild can be a *qualifying relative*. Because the grandchild's income does not exceed $5,050, the taxpayer *may claim the grandchild* as a dependent. Since the qualifying person lives with the taxpayer for more than 50% of the year, the taxpayer **qualifies to file HOH**

Virginia is 28 years old and single. Virginia paid all the costs of maintaining her household for the entire year. Virginia's niece, Jessica, lived in Virginia's home from April 1 through the end of the year. Jessica is 15 years old and has gross income of $5,000. What is Virginia's filing status?

To qualify as HOH, the taxpayer must have provided more than 50% of costs of maintaining a household and have a qualifying person who is claimed as a dependent living in the household for more than 50% of the year.

Because Jessica is a qualifying child, Virginia may claim her as a dependent. Since a qualifying child is a qualifying person for HOH status, Virginia is **eligible to file as HOH**.

Assume Jessica is 20 years old, is not a full-time student, and had gross income of $7,000. What is Virginia's filing status?

Using SARR, Jessica does **not** meet the age requirements to be considered a qualifying child because she is not under age 19 and not under age 24 and a full-time student. Using IRRS, Jessica fails the income test. Virginia's only option is to file as a **single** taxpayer.

Assume Virginia and Jessica are cousins. Jessica is 18 years old, has gross income of $3,000, and is not a full-time student. Jessica lived in Virginia's home for the entire year.

Virginia is required to file as a **single** taxpayer. Jessica does **not** have a qualifying relationship with Virginia to be either a qualifying child or qualifying relative (cousins do *not* count) as required for HOH.

However, Jessica qualifies as Virginia's *dependent* because she was a *member of Virginia's household* for the *entire* year.

REG 17
Computation of Tax and Credits

REG 17: Computation of Tax and Credits

17.01 Computation of Tax and Credits

Refundable versus Nonrefundable Credits

Representative Task (Remembering & Understanding): Recall and define the difference between a refundable and nonrefundable tax credit.

Congress allows a considerable number of tax credits to advance social policies and encourage behavior deemed beneficial to society. Certain credits promote specific industries or groups of taxpayers by providing these taxpayers with incentives called tax credits.

Tax credits are a dollar-for-dollar reduction in a taxpayer's tax liability in the period to which the credit applies. When the amount of the credit exceeds the amount of applicable tax due, unused credits may be able to be carried back or forward, depending on the provisions of the credit, or refunded to the taxpayer.

Tax deductions, in contrast, reduce *taxable income*. The benefits of tax deductions are dependent on a taxpayer's marginal tax rate, but the benefits of tax credits are not.

Generally, tax credits fall under one of five groups as shown below:

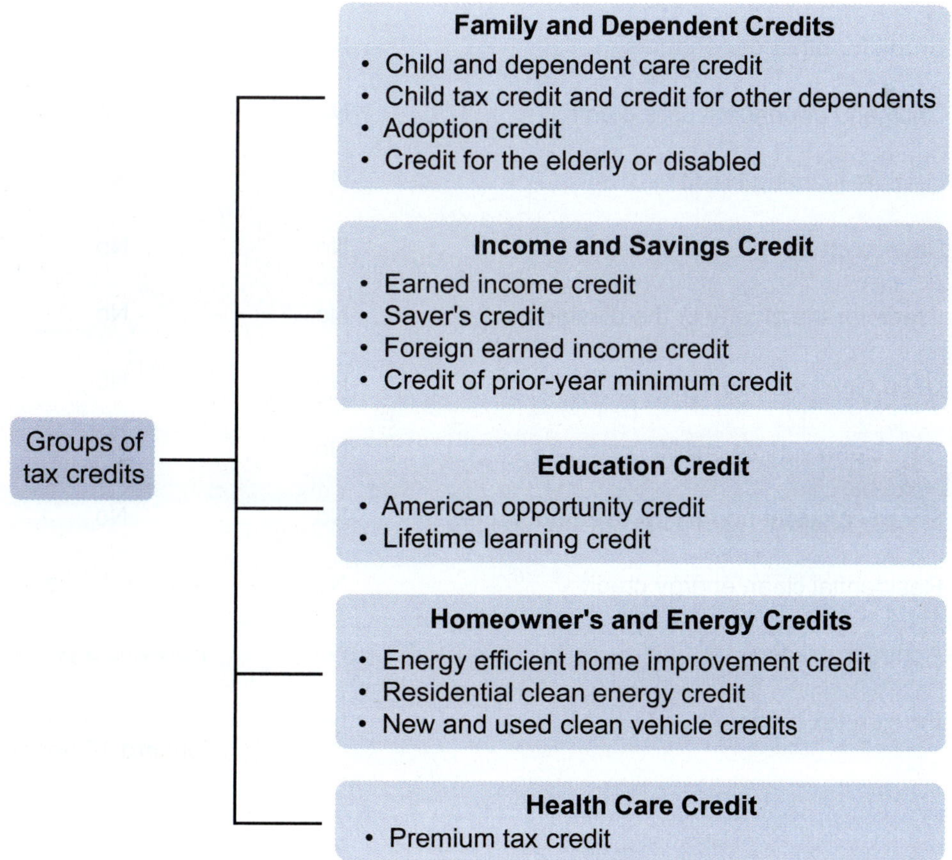

Tax credits are either nonrefundable, refundable, or partially refundable. A **nonrefundable credit** can reduce the tax liability to zero; any excess is not refunded to the taxpayer. It expires without providing tax benefits unless it can be carried over to a different year.

However, with a **refundable credit**, the excess is refunded to the taxpayer. Note that the credit may be fully or partially refundable.

- The credit is treated similarly to taxes that were paid by, or withheld from, the taxpayer. A refundable tax credit is applied against the tax liability and, if the credit exceeds the amount of the liability, will result in a refund to the taxpayer
- Low-income taxpayers may have little to no tax liability, so *nonrefundable* credits may not provide a significant benefit to them. When the goal of economic policy is to benefit these taxpayers, refundable credits are generally used
- In addition, some unused nonrefundable credits are permitted to be carried back and/or forward to offset an individual's tax liability

Characteristics of Common Tax Credits

Tax Credit	Refundable	Carryover
Earned income tax credit	Yes	No
Premium tax credit	Yes	No
Child tax credit	Partially	No
American opportunity tax credit	Partially	No
Credit for other dependents	No	No
Child and dependent care credit	No	No
Lifetime learning credit	No	No
Saver's credit	No	No
Credit for the elderly or the disabled	No	No
Used clean vehicle credit	No	No
New clean vehicle credit	No	No
Energy efficient home improvement credit	No	No
Residential clean energy credit	No	Forward 1 year
Adoption credit	No	Forward 5 years
Foreign tax credit	No	Back 1 year; forward 10 years

Which of the following are refundable credits?

- Adoption credit
- Child and dependent care credit
- Credit for the elderly or the disabled
- Earned income tax credit

Of the credits listed, the **earned income tax credit** is the only refundable credit. Therefore, if the amount of the credit exceeds a taxpayer's liability, the excess is refunded to the taxpayer.

Order of Credits

To ensure that taxpayers receive the greatest benefit possible from tax credits, credits are applied against the tax liability in a certain order.

- First, because personal nonrefundable credits are limited to the tax liability, they are first applied against the tax liability
- Second, refundable credits are applied because the excess (or a portion of the excess) is refundable
- Note that only a few credits permit the carryover of any unused credit

A single taxpayer has a tax liability of $4,000. The tax liability is eligible for $1,500 lifetime learning credit and $3,200 earned income tax credit. Without an order to follow when applying the tax credits, the taxpayer would lose some of the tax benefits.

For example, if the $3,200 earned income tax credit is applied first, the liability is reduced to $800. Then, only $800 of the lifetime learning credit could be used, with the balance lost forever.

However, if the nonrefundable lifetime learning credit is applied first against the tax liability, the remaining $2,500 of liability ($4,000 − $1,500) is offset by the earned income tax credit. The tax liability is still reduced to zero, but since the earned income credit is refundable, the taxpayer will receive a $700 refund ($2,500 − $3,200).

Refundable Credits

The are currently two fully refundable credits: the Premium tax credit and the Earned income tax credit (remember PE)

- **Premium tax credit** is a tax credit provided by the Affordable Care Act that is designed to make health insurance affordable to individuals with modest incomes who purchase their health insurance through the health insurance marketplace. People can choose to have the premium tax credit go directly to their insurance company to help pay part of their premiums or wait until they file taxes to claim the credit. The credit is 72.5% of the premiums paid
- **Earned income tax credit (EITC)** was enacted to encourage lower-income taxpayers to seek employment and to help mitigate employment taxes on that income. It is based on a taxpayer's earned income up to a certain threshold. Taxpayers must have some type of earned income for the year (eg, wages, salary, tips, self-employment income). The credit is based on IRS tables

Tax law related to the EITC generally defines a qualifying child like the dependency rules do (ie, age, residency, and relationship tests). However, the qualifying child *can* provide more than 50% of their own support and still qualify as a dependent for purposes of the EITC.

This year, Jane has calculated her taxable income at $8,150 and her gross tax liability at $850. She is entitled to a saver's credit of $132 and an earned income tax credit of $3,995.

Jane will be able to use the saver's credit to reduce her tax liability to $718. Because the earned income credit is refundable, Jane will use it to reduce her tax liability to zero and will receive an income tax refund of $3,277 ($850 − $132 − $3,995).

Partially Refundable Credits

Some credits have a maximum threshold for the amount that is refundable. Examples include the **C**hild tax credit and the **A**merican opportunity tax credit (remember **CA**).

- The child tax credit gives a tax break to taxpayers who provide a home for dependent children. TCJA set the child tax credit at $2,000 per qualifying child (same definition as the dependency rules) under age 17 for 2018–2025. For 2024, the amount that may be refundable is limited to $1,700
- The American opportunity tax credit is one way Congress encourages taxpayers and their dependents to seek higher education. This credit is for postsecondary (ie, post–high school) education. The maximum credit is $2,500, and 40% of the credit is refundable

Nonrefundable Credits

The rest of the tax credits fall under the category of nonrefundable credits. Several of the credits are presented below:

- The **credit for other dependents** is a $500 credit allowed for dependents who are not "qualifying children" for purposes of the $2,000 child tax credit (discussed above)
- The **child and dependent care credit** is available if the taxpayer requires care for a child under age 13 or a disabled dependent in order to be gainfully employed. The credit is based on the smallest of the dependent care expenses, earned income, or $3,000 (for care of one dependent) or $6,000 (for care of multiple dependents)
- The **credit for elderly or disabled** is available only to those age 65 and older or those who are retired on permanent and total disability. Such individuals must have AGI below a statutory threshold
- The **lifetime learning credit** encourages higher education. The credit applies to the cost of tuition and fees for any course of instruction to acquire or improve one's job skills. A comparison between the two education credits is provided below
- The **saver's credit** is available for low- or moderate-income workers to enable and encourage them to make voluntary contributions to IRAs and 401(k) plans. The amount of the credit is up to $1,000 ($2,000 MFJ) for making contributions to an IRA or an employer-sponsored retirement plan
- The **adoption credit** is available for costs incurred in adopting a child under the age of 18. The credit is limited for 2024 to the first $16,810 of costs. Credits exceeding the tax liability are not refundable but may be carried forward up to five years. The credit is allowed in the year the adoption is finalized

- The **foreign tax credit** provides relief to taxpayers who earn income in other countries. It reduces the amount of double tax that would result from paying U.S. tax on their worldwide income and also paying tax to the foreign country where they earned their income. The credit is not refundable but can be carried back one year and forward 10 years
- The **new clean vehicles credit** is a provision under the Inflation Reduction Act of 2022 that promotes investment of clean vehicles purchased in 2023 or after. To qualify, an individual must buy the qualifying vehicle for their own use, not for resale, and use it primarily in the U.S. New plug-in electric vehicles (EV) or fuel cell vehicles (FCV) may qualify. The vehicles must meet critical minerals and battery component requirements and undergo final assembly in North America. In addition, the vehicle's manufacturer suggested retail price cannot exceed $80,000 for vans, pickup trucks, or sport utility vehicles and $55,000 for other vehicles. The credit amount depends on when the vehicle was placed in service and results in a credit up to:
    - $3,750 if the vehicle meets the critical minerals requirement only
    - $3,750 if the vehicle meets the battery components requirement only
    - $7,500 if the vehicle meets both
    - In addition, modified adjusted gross income (AGI) in the year of delivery or the year before (whichever is less) may not exceed $300,000 for MFJ, $225,000 for HOH, and $150,000 for all other filers
- The **used clean vehicle credit** is available for individuals who buy a qualified EV or FCV in 2023 or after from a licensed dealer for $25,000 or less. The credit equals 30% of the sale price up to a maximum credit of $4,000. A qualified vehicle must have a battery capacity of at least seven kilowatt hours and have a model year at least two years earlier than the purchase date. To qualify, a taxpayer must:
    - Be an individual who bought the vehicle for use and not for resale
    - Not be the original owner
    - Not be claimed as a dependent on another person's tax return
    - Not have claimed another used clean vehicle credit in the three years before the purchase date
    - Not have modified AGI in excess of $150,00 for MFJ, $112,500 for HOH, and $75,000 for all other filers
- The **energy efficient home improvement credit** encourages homeowners to invest in energy improvements or clean energy in their existing homes. The amount of the credit is 30% for energy efficiency improvements, property expenditures, and home energy audits. Generally, the limit is $600 for any single property item and $1,200 for the entire credit for most taxpayers. Other limits also apply depending on the type of improvement. The credit *cannot* be carried back or forward
- The **residential clean energy credit** is a 30% credit for certain qualified expenditures made for residential energy efficient property for either an existing home or a newly constructed home. Examples include solar panels, solar water heaters, fuel cell property expenditures, wind turbines, and geothermal heat pumps. There is generally no overall dollar limit except in the case of fuel cell property. The credit can be *carried forward one year*

Estimated Tax Payments and Safe Harbor Requirements

Representative Task (Remembering & Understanding): Recall and define the safe harbor requirements for individual estimated tax payments to avoid penalties.

Estimated Tax Payments and Underpayment Penalties

The IRS requires all taxpayers to use a **pay-as-you-go tax system**. Taxpayers must pay their estimated federal tax liability as the income is earned or received during the year rather than when the tax return is due. The total federal tax liability includes income tax, any self-employment tax, and, if applicable, additional Medicare tax and/or net investment income tax.

When the tax return is filed, a taxpayer receives a refund if the amount paid exceeds their tax liability. If the tax liability is greater (ie, an underpayment has occurred), the taxpayer owes the additional tax. Failure to make or pay *sufficient* estimated payments in *any payment period* may subject the individual taxpayer to an *underpayment penalty*, which should be avoided.

The pay-as-you-go system uses **two** methods, withholding and estimated tax payments.

- **Withholding:** Taxpayers who are *employees* have their estimated federal taxes withheld from their payroll checks based on information they provide the employer on Form W-4. The employer remits the taxes on their behalf to the IRS. Individual taxpayers who have withholding on salaries and wages may not need to make estimated tax payments to the IRS during the year
- **Estimated tax payments:** Taxpayers may be self-employed, may be independent contractors, or may receive taxable income from other sources (eg, interest, dividends, retirement payments, commissions, income from pass-through entities). Because there is no employer to withhold the taxes on these types of income, these taxpayers are required to make quarterly estimated tax payments throughout the year
  - For some types of nonemployee income, the taxpayer may have the ability to request withholding by the payer. Examples include unemployment compensation, investment accounts, pensions, and retirement benefits
  - If a taxpayer has taxable income from any third-party payer that does *not* withhold federal income tax, the taxpayer should determine if estimated tax payments are required

For taxpayers who have both W-2 wages and nonwithholding income, a strategy to avoid making estimated tax payments and any penalty would be to request an increase in the withholding from their wages. This request may be made near year end. Because the withholding is deemed to be withheld throughout the year, the taxpayer avoids the underpayment penalty that might otherwise apply to earlier quarters.

Exceptions to the Underpayment Penalty

A **de minimis exception** to the underpayment penalty exists if the tax owed on the current tax return is less than **$1,000**. In addition, *no* estimated tax payments are required and *no* penalty is assessed for any taxpayer who meets **all** of the following three requirements:

- No tax liability (ie, taxes due) in the prior year
- The prior tax year covered the entire 12 months of the year
- The taxpayer is a U.S. citizen or resident alien for the entire current tax year

Because estimating an individual's taxes is not an exact science, the IRC allows several "safe harbor" *exceptions* to the *assessment* of the underpayment penalty when a taxpayer is required to make estimated tax payments.

Safe Harbor Exceptions

- **Prior-year tax liability:** No penalty is assessed if the withholdings and estimated payments totaled at least **100%** of the prior-year tax liability unless the taxpayer had *more than $150,000 of AGI* in the prior year. In the latter case, payments must exceed *110%* of the prior-year tax liability to utilize this exception in the current year
- **Current tax liability:** No penalty is assessed if the payments covered at least 90% of the current-year tax liability
- **Annualized income method:** No penalty is assessed if the cumulative payments for each quarter cover the tax on the income to date (assuming it continues at the same rate for the remainder of the year). This method can be beneficial if a taxpayer's income is not received evenly throughout the year and may be less than the amount calculated using the regular installment method

Do not confuse the penalty for underpayment of estimated taxes with the failure-to-pay penalty that is assessed for not paying the balance of the tax liability reported on the tax return by the due date or approved extension date.

A taxpayer's adjusted gross income for Year 6 was $163,500 with a corresponding tax liability of $32,700. In Year 7, the taxpayer estimates his adjusted gross income will be $198,000 with an expected tax liability of $43,000. None of the earnings are subject to withholding. What is the minimum amount of estimated tax payments for Year 7 that the taxpayer can make to avoid a penalty for underpayment of estimated tax?

Because the taxpayer's prior-year AGI is **greater** than $150,000 (ie, $163,500), the taxpayer must pay estimated taxes equal to the *lesser* of:

- 110% of the Year 6's (prior year) total tax liability ($32,700 × 110% = **$35,970**), or
- 90% of the Year 7's (current year) total tax liability ($43,000 × 90% = **$38,700**).

Therefore, the taxpayer must make estimated tax payments of least $35,970 in Year 7 to avoid the underpayment penalty.

A taxpayer had AGI of $80,000 and made no estimated tax payments for the current tax year. The total tax liability for the current year is $19,800, and the taxpayer had federal income taxes withheld from wages during the current year of $19,000. The taxpayer's prior-year tax liability was $16,000. What is the taxpayer's penalty for underpayment of taxes?

The **de minimis exception** (no payments required and no penalty) applies since the tax owed on the return is less than $1,000 (ie, $19,800 − $19,000 = $800). There is no penalty assessed.

Assume the same facts except the current-year withholdings were only $17,200. In addition, the prior-year AGI was $74,000. What is the taxpayer's penalty for underpayment of taxes?

The difference between the amount owed and withheld is *not* less than $1,000 (ie, $19,800 − $17,200); so the de minimis rule does **not** apply, and the taxpayer must look to the safe harbor provisions to determine if they are subject to a penalty.

Because the taxpayer's prior-year AGI is *less* than $150,000 (ie, $74,000), the taxpayer must pay estimated taxes and/or have withholding equal to the lesser of:

- 100% of the prior-year total tax liability, which is $16,000; or
- 90% of the current-year total tax liability, which is $17,820 ($19,800 × 90%).

Since the amount withheld in the current year is $17,200 (ie, greater than $16,000), there is **no** penalty.

Payment Due Dates and Underpayment Penalty

If estimated tax payments are required, they are due by the 15th day of the *4th*, *6th*, and *9th* months of the taxable year and by the *15th of January* the following year (1040-ES). Although estimated tax payments are often referred to as quarterly payments, the tax payments are divided into four periods (not quarters). Each period has a specific payment due date.

Generally, the amount of each estimated payment is the same for each period unless one of the special methods is used (eg, annualization of income). The amount should be adequate to cover the tax due on the income earned or received during that period. This aligns with the pay-as-you-go concept. Form 1040-ES is used to file the estimated tax payments.

Payment Period	Due Date
January 1–March 31	April 15
April 1–May 31	June 15
June 1–August 31	September 15
September 1–December 31	January 15 of the next year

Fiscal-year taxpayers, farmers, and fishermen have special rules regarding the payment periods.

Failure to make or pay *sufficient* estimated payments in *any payment period* may subject the individual taxpayer to an *underpayment penalty*. The amount of the underpayment is the *excess* of the *required payment* over the *amount paid* on or before the quarterly due date.

- The penalty is figured separately for each installment due date. Therefore, a taxpayer may owe the penalty for an earlier payment due date even if the taxpayer paid enough tax later to make up the underpayment
- For instance, if a taxpayer's income is earned entirely in the first quarter of the year, but the taxpayer makes four equal installments that add up to the correct estimated tax due, the taxpayer will be subject to an underpayment penalty for not paying the entire estimated tax in the first quarter. Likewise, if the taxpayer's income is earned in the 3rd and 4th quarters of the tax year, estimated payments would be due only for those two quarters

The IRS does allow taxpayers who earn income unevenly throughout the year to avoid underpayment penalties by *annualizing* their income.

A taxpayer's tax liability for the year, including federal income tax and self-employment taxes, is $7,000 based on wages earned as an employee and self-employment income earned teaching fitness classes as shown below:

First quarter	$1,000
Second quarter	$1,500
Third quarter	$2,000
Fourth quarter	$2,500

However, only $6,500 in taxes were withheld from the taxpayer's paycheck, and no estimated payments were made. Compute the taxpayer's over- or underpayments for each quarter.

Quarter	(1) Required Withholding	(2) Actual Withholding*	(1) – (2) Over or (Under) Withholding
First quarter	$1,000	$1,625	$ 625
Second quarter	1,500	1,625	125
Third quarter	2,000	1,625	(375)
Fourth quarter	2,500	1,625	(875)
Total	$7,000	$6,500	

**$6,500 / 4 = $1,625*

Calculating an Individual's Tax Liability

Representative Task (Application): Calculate the tax liability based on an individual's taxable income given a specific scenario, including consideration of the net investment income tax.

Individuals must determine and report to the government their taxable income and income tax liability each year based upon a formula. An individual's filing status, income, deductions, tax bracket, and credits go into this calculation. Once taxable income has been determined, the tentative income tax liability is computed using the tax table or tax rate schedules.

The tax liability is *increased* for additional taxes due by the taxpayer (eg, self-employment tax, net investment income tax) and *decreased* by any tax credits allowed (eg, child tax credit), but not below zero. Any tax withheld (eg, from wages, retirement) and estimated tax payments made are deducted to determine if additional tax is owed or a refund due.

Individual Tax Calculation (Form 1040)

Taxable income
× Tax rates
= Income tax liability
+ Other taxes
− Credits
Net tax liability
− Withholdings
− Prepayments
= **Tax due (refund)**

Other taxes:
- Self-employed
- AMT
- Net investment income tax
- Additional Medicare

Credits:
- Child tax credit
- Credit for other dependents
- Child and dependent care
- Foreign tax credit
- Educational credits
- Credit for elderly or disabled

Net Investment Income Tax (NIIT)

A surtax called the **Unearned Income Medicare Contribution Tax** (ie, net investment income tax [NIIT]) is imposed on the **unearned income** (eg, interest, dividends) of individuals, estates, and trusts. NIIT was enacted to have wealthier individuals whose income mostly comes from investments pay amounts into Medicare.

The tax is assessed only on U.S. citizens and resident aliens with net investment income exceeding certain thresholds. Although trusts generally are subject to the tax, trusts that are exempt from income tax (eg, charitable trusts, grantor trusts) are exempt from the NIIT.

The surtax is 3.8% of the **lesser of**:

- Net investment income (**NII**): Total investment income minus investment expenses (eg, advisory fees); **or**
- **Excess** modified AGI (**MAGI**) **over** the **threshold** amount.

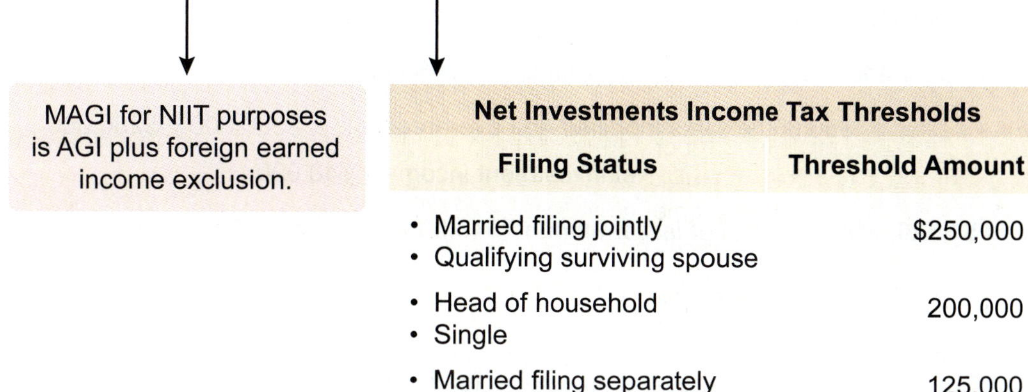

MAGI for NIIT purposes is AGI plus foreign earned income exclusion.

Net Investments Income Tax Thresholds	
Filing Status	**Threshold Amount**
• Married filing jointly • Qualifying surviving spouse	$250,000
• Head of household • Single	200,000
• Married filing separately	125,000

Net investment income, used to compute the NIIT, is the total amount of money received from assets such as stocks, bonds, and mutual funds, *reduced* by allowable investment expenses. Tax-exempt interest, veterans' benefits, excluded gain from the sale of a principal residence, retirement plan distributions, and any amounts subject to self-employment tax are *excluded*.

Computation of Net Investment Income (for the NIIT)

NII = Investment income − Deductible investment expenses

Investment Income	Taxable income from assets held for investment and not derived from ordinary trade or business (ie, income from business activities for which the taxpayer does not materially participate). Generally includes: • Interest, dividends, annuities, royalties • Investment income from partnerships, S corporations, estates, trusts • Short-term capital gains • Long-term capital gains (if election made)
Investment Expenses	Expenses directly associated with production of investment income. Examples include commissions, brokerage fees, investment interest (may be limited). Note: The deduction for most investment expenses (other than interest) on Schedule A is suspended through 2025 (considered miscellaneous itemized deductions subject to 2% AGI floor).

Roger and Louisa's AGI (and modified AGI) is $200,000, and they file jointly. Their investment income is $40,000. How much net investment income tax will Roger and Louisa owe?

Because modified AGI ($200,000) is less than the $250,000 threshold for MFJ, Roger and Louisa will **not** be subject to the NIIT.

What if Roger and Louisa's AGI (and modified AGI) is $300,000?

$50,000 excess modified AGI over threshold = $300,000 − $250,000

Net investment income = $40,000.

NIIT is **$1,520**, which is 3.8% of *lesser* amount ($40,000 × 3.8% = $1,520).

The NIIT effectively makes the tax rate on long-term capital gains and qualified dividends 23.8% (20% + 3.8%) for high-income taxpayers (over $583,750 MFJ and over $518,900 single for 2024). It still applies if income is under the high-income threshold of over $250,000, but the rate would be 15% + 3.8% = 18.8%.

Ray and Brooke Jacoby are married, filing jointly, and have AGI of $260,000. Their income consisted of wages of $280,000 (of which $120,000 is eligible for the foreign earned income exclusion), $5,000 of interest income from corporate bonds, $7,000 of municipal bond interest, $10,000 of dividend income, and a long-term capital gain (LTCG) of $85,000. Given a 3.8% net investment income tax rate, what is their liability related to this surtax?

Description	Amount	Explanation
(1) Net investment income	$100,000	$5,000 interest* + $10,000 dividends + $85,000 LTCG
(2) Modified AGI	380,000	$260,000 AGI + $120,000 foreign exclusion
(3) Modified AGI threshold	(250,000)	
(4) Modified AGI > threshold	$130,000	(2) − (3)
(5) NII tax base	$100,000	*Lesser* of (1) or (4)
NII tax	**$3,800**	(5) × 3.8%

**The tax-exempt interest of $7,000 is excludable.*

Additional Medicare Tax

- Another additional tax besides regular income tax that a taxpayer may be subject to is the **additional Medicare tax** of 0.9%. Both employees and employers have to pay FICA taxes on compensation paid to their employees
- Taxpayers who earn compensation in excess of $200,000 ($125,000 for MFS; $250,000 combined for MFJ) are subject to this additional tax for compensation above the threshold. Employers are **not** subject to the additional Medicare tax

Isabelle, a single taxpayer, received $465,000 in employee compensation consisting of wages, sales commission, and performance bonus. Isabelle would have an additional Medicare tax of $2,385 [($465,000 − $200,000) × .9%].

Patrick is a single taxpayer. In the current year, Patrick has $195,000 of taxable income, which includes $50,000 of long-term capital gain that is taxed at a 15% preferential rate. Assume his modified AGI is $210,000 and his marginal tax rate is 24%. Patrick has made federal income tax payments of $40,000 and qualifies for a residential clean energy credit of $600.

Compute Patrick's total tax, including net investment tax liability, and his net tax due or refund.

(1)	Taxable income	$195,000	
(2)	Preferentially taxed income	50,000	
(3)	Income taxed at ordinary rates	$145,000	(1) – (2)
(4)	Tax on income taxed at marginal tax rate	34,800	(3) × 24%
(5)	Tax on preferentially taxed income	7,500	(2) × 15%
(6)	Income tax	$ 42,300	(4) + (5)
(7)	Net investment income tax	380	3.8% × lesser of $50,000 of net investment income or ($210,000 modified AGI − $200,000) threshold = 3.8% × $10,000 = $380
(8)	Total tax	$ 42,680	(6) + (7)
(9)	Income tax payments	(40,000)	
(10)	Tax credit	(600)	
(11)	Tax due	**$ 2,080**	(8) – (9) – (10)

REG

Area V: Federal Taxation of Entities

REG 18
Differences between Book and Tax Income (Loss)

REG 18: Differences between Book and Tax Income (Loss)

18.01 Differences between Book and Tax Income (Loss)

Permanent vs. Temporary Differences Reported on Schedule M-3

Representative Task (Application): Identify permanent vs. temporary differences to be reported on Schedule M-3 in a given scenario.

Overview

Corporations must comply with different reporting rules for tax purposes and for GAAP (generally accepted accounting principles). Therefore, the corporation must prepare a reconciliation of book income to taxable income on line 28 of the tax form (before special deductions such as the dividends-received deduction and the net operating loss deduction) **on Schedule M-1**.

The purpose of this schedule is to identify to the IRS amounts that are reported differently for GAAP and tax purposes. The calculation begins with book income. It is then increased/decreased by items that cause taxable income to be higher/lower than book income.

Two important steps to remember about tax differences are determining the current amount of the difference and whether the difference increases (1st column of M-1) or decreases (2nd column of M-1) taxable income.

Schedule M-1 **Reconciliation of Income (Loss) per Books With Income per Return**
Note: The corporation may be required to file Schedule M-3 (see instructions).

1	Net income (loss) per books		7	Income recorded on books this year not included on this return (itemize):	
2	Federal income tax per books		a	Tax-exempt interest $	
3	Excess of capital losses over capital gains		b	Other (itemize):	
4	Income subject to tax not recorded on books this year (itemize):				
			8	Deductions on this return not charged against book income this year (itemize):	
5	Expenses recorded on books this year not deducted on this return (itemize):		a	Depreciation . . . $	
a	Depreciation . . . . . $		b	Charitable contributions $	
b	Charitable contributions $		c	Other (itemize):	
c	Travel and entertainment $				
d	Other (itemize):		9	Add lines 7 and 8	
6	Add lines 1 through 5		10	Income—line 6 less line 9	

Because the reconciliation of book income to taxable income uses the amount reported on line 28 of the corporate tax form (ie, taxable income *before* the dividends-received deduction and net operating loss deduction), *neither* of these two items are timing differences. The dividends received are the *same* for books and tax. After line 28, the company may take a dividends-received deduction on the tax return. If information regarding either item is provided in a problem regarding M-1 or M-3 adjustments, the information can be ignored.

For corporations with total assets of $10 million or more, Schedule M-3 is prepared in lieu of Schedule M-1 and is, in essence, simply a more detailed form than schedule M-1. Unlike Schedule M-1, the Schedule M-3 income and expense differences are separately reported as *temporary* or *permanent differences*. Schedule M-3 also reconciles worldwide consolidated net income (loss) per the income statement to the net income (loss) per income statement of includible corporations. Income/loss reconciliation items are shown as single line items.

Schedule M-3, Part I, asks certain questions about the corporation's financial statements and reconciles financial statement net income (loss) for the corporation (or consolidated financial statement group).

Schedule M-3, Parts II and III, reconcile financial statement net income (loss) for the U.S. corporation (or consolidated tax group, if applicable), as reported on Schedule M-3, Part I, line 11, to taxable income on Form 1120, page 1, line 28. Schedule M-3, Parts II and III, consist of four columns:

- Column (A): Income (Loss) per Income Statement
- Column (B): Temporary Difference (or Timing Difference): A temporary difference is any difference that will reverse in a future tax year. This can include income/expense recognized in financial statements before it is taxable/deductible or income/expense reported as taxable/deductible before it is recognized in financial statements
- Column (C): Permanent Difference: Permanent differences are transactions that won't reverse in a future tax year
- Column (D): Income (Loss) per Tax Return

Schedule M-1 vs. M-3 Reconciliations	
At the end of the tax year, if a corporation has:	
Total receipts and total assets < $250,000	No reconciliation required
Total assets > $250,000 but < $10 million	Schedule M-1 is required but may file M-3
Total assets ≥ $10 million	Schedule M-3 is required

Permanent vs. Temporary Differences

To determine taxable income each year, a corporation's accounting (ie, book) net income must be adjusted for income and expense items that are treated differently for tax purposes. A corporation reconciles book income to taxable income on Schedule M-1 or M-3 to account for these differences. There are two types of differences: temporary and permanent.

- **Temporary differences** result from the same items being calculated differently for accounting (eg, GAAP) than for tax purposes in any given reporting year. Over time, these differences eventually are recognized for both book and tax purposes; thus, the difference is only temporary. Examples include estimated bad debts, warranty expense, excess depreciation, excess capital losses, excess charitable deductions, and NOL carryovers

- **Permanent differences** are items that are income or deductions in the year for either book or taxable income but not both. These differences *do not reverse* over time. Examples include tax-exempt interest, officers' life insurance premiums where the company is the beneficiary, and nondeductible expenses (eg, fines, 50% of meals, entertainment expenses, country club dues)

Reconciliation of Book Income to Taxable Income

- Federal income tax expense, fines/penalties
- Nondeductible expenses
- Excess depreciation per the *books*, charitable contributions, and capital losses
- Tax gain on sale of assets in excess of book gain

Net income for the year per the books
\+ Expenses deducted on books but not on tax return
\+ Income currently taxable but not included in book income
− Income reported on books but not on tax return
− Deductions on tax return but not recorded on books
Taxable income

- Tax-exempt interest
- Officers' life insurance proceeds
- Excess *tax* depreciation
- Carryovers from charitable contributions, NOLs, and capital losses

Temporary and permanent differences are either added to or deducted from book income (depending on the circumstance) to determine taxable income.

- For example, premiums paid on a key-person life insurance policy are deducted as an expense for book income but *nondeductible* for taxable income. Accordingly, this is a permanent difference that should be **added back** to book income in the Schedule M-1 or M-3 reconciliation
- Another example of a permanent difference is municipal bond interest received. The interest is part of book income but *not taxable* income and therefore must be **subtracted** from book income to arrive at taxable income
- A temporary adjustment such as the *excess tax depreciation* (resulting from using MACRS tax depreciation) is a deduction for calculating *taxable income* but **not** an *expense for book income (books use GAAP depreciation methods)*. The excess must be **subtracted** from book income to reconcile to taxable income. Over time, the book depreciation will be greater than the tax depreciation. At that point, the excess book depreciation is **added back** to book income to arrive at taxable income

Item	Permanent or Temporary	Why
Life Insurance for Officers and Key Employees	Permanent	• For books, proceeds are includible, premiums are expensed and deducted • For tax, because life insurance proceeds received from policies on key employees (when the company is the owner and beneficiary) are nontaxable, the premiums paid on these policies are nondeductible
Fines and Penalties	Permanent	• For books, expensed and deducted • For tax, fines resulting from breaking a law; therefore, no deduction is permitted
Entertainment	Permanent	• For books, expensed and deducted • For tax, incurred mostly for personal pleasure; therefore, no deduction is allowed
Meals	Permanent	• For books, expensed and deducted • For tax, 50% is allowed; the rest is not deductible
Municipal Interest Income and Related Expenses	Permanent	• For books, included as income and expensed • For tax, tax-exempt interest is excluded and related expenses nondeductible
Federal Income Tax Expense*	Permanent	• For books, expensed • For tax, no deduction allowed
Unearned Income	Temporary	• For books, income deferred • For tax, recognized as income
Warranty Expense	Temporary	• For books, estimated and expensed each year • For tax, only warranty claims paid during the current year are deductible
Depreciation Expense	Temporary	• For books, GAAP depreciation methods used • For tax, MACRS used
Bad Debt Expense (Credit Losses)	Temporary	• For books, credit losses are estimated and expensed each year • For tax, only actual bad debts written off during the current year are deductible
Charitable Contribution Carryforward	Temporary	• For books, the contribution was deducted in full in the year incurred • For tax, amount exceeding the threshold is nondeductible; deductible in year contribution is below threshold

Item	Permanent or Temporary	Why
Net Operating Loss Carryforward	Temporary	• For books, created in year loss occurred • For tax, allowed to be used to offset income in carryforward year
Like-Kind Exchanges	Temporary	• For books, gains recognized • For tax, gains deferred
Capital Loss Carryovers	Temporary	• For books, recognized when incurred • For tax, limited to capital losses

**Pay careful attention to whether the book income provided is net income or income before federal income tax. If before federal income taxes, then no permanent difference.*

A calendar-year C corporation has total assets of $25 million. It reported net income per the books of $210,000. In addition, the following information is available:

Federal income taxes per books	$114,000
Tax depreciation in excess of book depreciation	$ 66,000
Charitable contributions per books	$ 46,000

On the M-3 reconciliation, what amount is reported as taxable income?

A corporation's deduction for charitable contributions is limited to a maximum of 10% of taxable income (calculated without deducting charitable contributions, capital loss carryovers, and the dividends-received deduction).

Any disallowed contributions are carried forward up to five tax years. The difference in book income and taxable income is due to the permanent difference of the federal income tax, the temporary difference for the excess tax depreciation, and limited deductions allowed for tax for the contributions.

Net income per books	$210,000
+ Nondeductible federal income taxes (permanent)	114,000
+ Charitable contribution deduction (temporary)	46,000
− Additional tax depreciation allowed (temporary)	(66,000)
Taxable income before contribution deduction	$304,000
− Contribution deduction allowed*	(30,400)
Taxable income	$273,600

**304,000 × 10% = $30,400*

ABC, Inc., is an accrual-basis, calendar-year C corporation that uses the allowance method for bad debts (credit losses). In the current year, it reported book income before federal income taxes of $300,000. In addition, ABC reported the following:

Corporate bond interest	$30,000
Tax-exempt interest income	45,000
Interest incurred on debt used to carry the municipal bonds	4,000
Excess book depreciation over tax depreciation	6,000
Actual account receivables written off	7,000

The beginning balance in the allowance for uncollectible accounts was $30,000, and the ending balance was $40,000. Total assets are $55 million. What is ABC's current-year taxable income as reconciled on its Schedule M-3?

Since $45,000 tax-exempt interest income is nontaxable, it is deducted from the book income. Any expense incurred to generate the nontaxable income is nondeductible for tax purposes. Therefore, the $4,000 interest expense is added back.

The $6,000 excess book depreciation over tax is also added back to book income.

In this scenario, ABC uses the allowance method for book purposes (ie, bad debts are estimated and expensed each year) (ie, matching principle). Reconstruction of the T-account shows that $17,000 was the amount of estimated bad debt expense (credit losses) for book purposes.

For tax purposes, only the direct write-off method is permitted, so the tax deduction should be $7,000 (the amount written off). As a result, the book expense is greater than the tax expense allowed by $10,000 ($17,000 − $7,000). To reconcile book income to taxable income, ABC must add back the $10,000 that is not deductible for taxable income.

Allowance for Uncollectible Accounts

Debit		Credit		
Write-offs	7,000	Beg. bal.	30,000	
		Accrued expense	?	→ $17,000
		End bal.	40,000	

Book income before federal taxes	$300,000
− Tax-exempt interest (permanent)	(45,000)
+ Expense related to tax-exempt income (permanent)	4,000
+ Excess book depreciation over tax depreciation (temporary)	6,000
+ Difference in bad debt expense (temporary)	10,000
Taxable income	$275,000

Book/Tax Differences to Be Reported on a Schedule M-1 or M-3

Representative Task (Application): Calculate the book/tax differences to be reported on a Schedule M-1 or M-3.

Schedule M-1

The starting point on Schedule M-1 is net book income (or loss) per books. Then determine if the income or expense item is treated differently for tax purposes than for book purposes. Differences between book income and taxable income fall into four distinct categories.

- Expenses *deducted* for book income that are not deductible for taxable income: Must *add* nondeductible expense back to book income
- Income *included* in book income that is not included in taxable income: Must *deduct* nontaxable income from book income
- Income *not included* in book income that is included in taxable income: Must *add* income to book income
- Expenses *not deducted* for book income that are deducted for taxable income: Must *deduct* expense from book income

Trigger, Inc.'s book income of $276,000 included municipal interest income of $1,600 and entertainment expense of $2,600. Charitable contributions of $3,800 were carried forward from a prior year into the current year. What is Trigger's taxable income based on this information?

Trigger's taxable income is $273,200. Municipal interest income is not included in income for tax purposes and must be subtracted from book income. Entertainment expenses are not deductible for tax purposes and must be added back to book income.

Charitable contribution carryforwards are allowed for tax purposes and must be subtracted from book income to arrive at taxable income. The charitable contribution carryforward does not exceed the 10% of income limitation, so the full amount can be deducted.

Book income	$276,000
Less: Municipal interest income	(1,600)
Plus: Entertainment expenses	2,600
Less: Charitable carryforward	(3,800)
Taxable income	$273,200

Rafter, Inc., has book income after federal income tax expense of $520,000. Rafter is an accrual-basis taxpayer for both book reporting and tax reporting. Compute Rafter's taxable income given the information below:

Federal income tax	$112,350
Book depreciation	56,000
Charitable contribution carryforward	11,000
Tax depreciation	68,000
Excess capital loss	2,000
Municipal interest income	1,300
Entertainment expenses	4,400

Solution

Book income	$520,000
Federal income tax expenses	112,350
Excess capital loss	2,000
Entertainment expenses	4,400
Municipal interest income	(1,300)
Charitable contribution carryforward	(11,000)
Tax depreciation > book depreciation ($68,000 − $56,000)	(12,000)
Taxable income	**$614,450**

Identify and Calculate Possible Book/Tax Differences

Representative Task (Analysis): Review an entity's adjusted book trial balance and supporting documentation to identify and calculate possible book/tax differences.

Overview

When reviewing the adjusted trial balance, review the items listed to see if anything stands out as an item that would be treated differently in calculating book income versus taxable income. Is anything listed that would indicate that it is an accrual, would result in a timing difference, or is not deductible in calculating taxable income?

Book to tax differences are treated as follows: Start with book income[1] and then:

- Add expenses deducted for book purposes but not deducted on the tax return
- Add income currently taxable but excluded from book income
- Subtract income reported for book purposes but not taxable on the tax return
- Subtract deductions reported on the tax return but not reported for book purposes

1 *Be sure to determine if book income is before or after the deduction for federal income taxes.*

Sample Scenario

Evergreen, Inc., was created in Year 12 to provide tables, chairs, and equipment for events in its surrounding community. It has net income from books of $32,900. The in-house accountant has created an adjusted trial balance. The company uses the accrual-basis accounting method.

What to look for:

- Is there any information or dollar amount from the source documents that contradicts what has been entered on the adjusted trial balance?
- What items are typically entered on Schedule M-1?
- Does anything stand out as possibly being a book to tax difference such as an accrual, timing difference, or nondeductible item in calculating taxable income?

Steps

- Review the exhibits including the adjusted trial balance
- Identify and calculate possible book/tax differences using the following table. If the item listed is not a book-tax difference, enter N/A in columns 4 and 5
- After considering the book-tax differences, determine taxable income reported on line 28, Form 1120 (before NOL and special deductions)

Column 1	Column 2	Column 3	Column 4	Column 5
Item	**Amount Reported on Tax Return**	**Difference between Book and Tax Amount**	**Temporary or Permanent Difference**	**Added to or Deducted from Book Income**
Wages Expense				
Federal Tax Paid				
Dividend Income				
Rent Revenue				
Depreciation Expense				
Entertainment Expense				
Municipal Interest Income				
Dividends-Received Deduction				
Service Revenue				
Charitable Contributions				

Evergreen's Taxable Income	

Exhibit 1: Adjusted Trial Balance

Evergreen, Inc.
Adjusted trial balance
12/31/Year 12

Account title	**Debit**	**Credit**
Cash	$101,800	
Accounts receivable	3,300	
Supplies	2,100	
Equipment	10,000	
Accum. depreciation		$2,000
Accounts payable		1,000
Utilities payable		500
Interest payable		600
Unearned rent revenue		1,800
Federal tax payable		8,500
Wages payable		2,900
Common stock		5,000
Retained earnings		62,000
Service revenue		50,200
Rent revenue		1,800
Interest income		600
Dividend income		3,000
Wages expense	2,900	
Supplies expense	800	
Rent expense	1,800	
Depreciation expense	2,000	
Insurance expense	400	
Entertainment expense	1,200	
Utility expense	500	
Charitable contribution expense	4,000	
Interest expense	600	
Federal income tax expense	8,500	
Total	$139,900	$139,900

Exhibit 2: Charitable Contribution Letter

To: Evergreen, Inc.
125 Main Street
Chicago, IL 60606

From: Habitat for Humanity
Atlanta, GA 30301

Thank you for your organization's contribution of $4,000 made on December 1, Year 12. We appreciate your continued support for Habitat for Humanity. Your contribution will help build homes for the underserved members of our community. We could not continue to provide these needed services without the support from dedicated organizations like yours.
Thanks,

Habitat for Humanity

Exhibit 3: Depreciation Information

Evergreen, Inc.
Depreciation worksheet
12/31/Year 12

Asset	Straight-line depreciation
Equipment	$2,000

From: kflowers@evergreen.com
Sent: December 31, Year 12
To: jsimmons@evergreen.com
Subject: Section 179 election

Joseph,

The tax department has decided to elect Section 179 for the equipment purchase this year for $10,000. Please let me know if you require any additional information.

Thank you,
Kim Flowers
Associate Manager, Tax Department, Evergreen, Inc.
P: +1.234.657.8910

Exhibit 4: Equipment Rental Agreement

Equipment Rental Agreement

Evergreen, Inc.
Customer: Cook County Building Services
Date: October 31, Year 12

Invoice 127

Asset	Rental period	Amount
Tables	11/1/Year 12–02/28/Year 13	$3,600

Exhibit 5: Form 1099-INT

☐ CORRECTED (if checked)

Field	Value
PAYER'S name, street address, city or town, state or province, country, ZIP or foreign postal code, and telephone no.	Cook County Savings Bank 10 State Street Chicago, IL 60606
Payer's RTN (optional)	
OMB No. 1545-0112	Form 1099-INT
For calendar Year	12
Interest Income	Copy B For Recipient
PAYER'S TIN	36-12345678
RECIPIENT'S TIN	45-98765432
RECIPIENT'S name	Evergreen, Inc.
Street address (including apt. no.)	55 North Avenue
City or town, state or province, country, and ZIP or foreign postal code	Chicago, IL 60606
FATCA filing requirement	☐
Account number (see instructions)	
1 Interest income	$
2 Early withdrawal penalty	$
3 Interest on U.S. Savings Bonds and Treasury obligations	$
4 Federal income tax withheld	**$**
5 Investment expenses	$
6 Foreign tax paid	$
7 Foreign country or U.S. territory	
8 Tax-exempt interest	$ 600
9 Specified private activity bond interest	$
10 Market discount	$
11 Bond premium	$
12 Bond premium on Treasury obligations	
13 Bond premium on tax-exempt bond	
14 Tax-exempt and tax credit bond CUSIP no.	
15 State	
16 State identification no.	
17 State tax withheld	$ $

This is important tax information and is being furnished to the IRS. If you are required to file a return, a negligence penalty or other sanction may be imposed on you if this income is taxable and the IRS determines that it has not been reported.

Form 1099-INT (keep for your records) www.irs.gov/Form1099INT Department of the Treasury—Internal Revenue Service

Exhibit 6: Dividends

From: kdonnelly@evergreen.com
Sent: December 31, Year 12
To: kflowers@evergreen.com
Subject: Dividends-received deduction

Kim,
Per your request regarding the dividend income, the dividends received this year were from ABC Corporation, a domestic company. Evergreen owns less than 20% of ABC Corporation and therefore is eligible for 50% dividends-received deduction.

Thank you,

Ken Donnelly
Accounting Clerk, Investments Department, Evergreen, Inc.
P: +1.234.657.8910

Solution

Column 1	Column 2	Column 3	Column 4	Column 5
Item	**Amount Reported on Tax Return**	**Difference between Book and Tax Amount**	**Temporary or Permanent Difference**	**Added to or Deducted from Book Income**
Wages Expense	$2,900	$0	N/A	N/A
Federal Tax Paid	0	8,500	Permanent	Added back
Dividend Income	3,000	0	N/A	N/A
Rent Revenue	3,600	1,800	Temporary	Added back
Depreciation Expense	10,000	8,000	Temporary	Deduct from
Entertainment Expense	0	1,200	Permanent	Added back
Municipal Interest Income	0	600	Permanent	Deduct from
Dividends-Received Deduction	1,500	1,500	N/A	N/A
Service Revenue	50,200	0	N/A	N/A
Charitable Contributions	3,980	20	Temporary	Added back

Evergreen's Taxable Income	**$35,820**

Explanations

Wages Expense

Wage expense is reported the same for book income and taxable income. It is not a timing difference.

Federal Income Tax per Books

Federal income tax paid of **$8,500** is a deduction in calculating book income, but it is not deductible in calculating taxable income. This **permanent** difference must be **added back to book income** to arrive at taxable income.

Dividend Income

There is **no difference** regarding the amount of dividends reported on the tax return. The dividends-received deduction is a deduction after line 28, taxable income before special deductions. The M-1 reconciles tax income to line 28.

Rent Revenue

Evergreen had a contract with Cook County and received a payment of $3,600 to provide equipment for four months from November 1, Year 12, to February 28, Year 13. For book income purposes, Evergreen reported $1,800 of rent income for the months of November and December (ie, matching principle) and the remaining $1,800 as unearned revenue (a liability). For tax purposes, Evergreen will report $3,600 for rent received in advance, creating a book to tax difference of $1,800 ($3,600 − $1,800). The **$1,800 temporary difference** must be **added to book income**.

Depreciation Expense

For book purposes, Evergreen used straight-line depreciation and reported $2,000 of depreciation expense for the $10,000 of equipment purchased. For tax purposes, Evergreen elected Section 179 and expensed the equipment purchase and reported depreciation expense of $10,000. The **$8,000** ($10,000 − $2,000) **temporary** difference must be **deducted from book income**.

Entertainment Expense

Evergreen reported $1,200 for entertainment expenses. For tax purposes, this is not deductible, creating a **permanent difference** of **$1,200**. It must be **added back to book income** to arrive at taxable income.

Municipal Interest Income

The $600 of nontaxable interest can be found on the 1099 form in box 8. The interest is included in income for book purposes, but it is not taxable for tax purposes. The **$600 permanent** difference must be **deducted from book income** to arrive at taxable income.

Dividends-Received Deduction

Reconcile book income to **taxable income** reported on **line 28**, **Form 1120** (ie, taxable income *before* tax special deductions). Therefore, the $1,500 ($3,000 × 50%) tax deduction is **not** a consideration in the reconciliation of book and tax income.

Service Revenue

The company uses the accrual basis of accounting and records its revenue accordingly. No information is provided that would indicate that any tax adjustment to this amount is required.

Charitable Contribution

For book purposes, the charitable contribution of $4,000 was deducted. For tax purposes, charitable contributions are deductible but limited to 10% of taxable income *before* the charitable contribution and before special deductions. The charitable contribution allowed for tax purposes is only $3,980, as computed below. The **$20** ($4,000 − $3,980) **temporary difference** must be **added back to book income** to arrive at taxable income.

Net income per books	$32,900
+ Nondeductible federal income taxes	8,500
+ Rent received in advanced	1,800
+ Charitable contribution deduction	4,000
+ Nondeductible entertainment expense	1,200
− Tax-exempt income	(600)
− Additional tax depreciation allowed	(8,000)
Taxable income *before* contribution deduction 10% limitation	$39,800
	× 10%
Charitable deduction permitted	$ 3,980

Taxable Income

Using the $39,800 taxable income from the above table and deducting the allowed charitable contribution of $3,980 results in **$35,820** ($39,800 − $3,980) **taxable income** reported on line 28 of the tax return.

Completeness and Accuracy of the Book/Tax Differences

Representative Task (Analysis): Review a C corporation's adjusted book trial balance and supporting documentation, including relevant source data used to create the trial balance, to determine the completeness and accuracy of the book/tax differences reported on Form 1120 – U.S. Corporation Income Tax Return.

Sample Scenario

ElderlyCare, Inc., was created in Year 16 to provide elder care services in its surrounding community. It also provides rental of wheelchairs, oxygen tanks, and walkers. The in-house accountant, Patty, has created an adjusted trial balance and Schedule M-1 for the current year. Review the Schedule M-1 below for accuracy.

Schedule M-1 **Reconciliation of Income (Loss) per Books With Income per Return**
Note: The corporation may be required to file Schedule M-3 (see instructions).

1	Net income (loss) per books	40,000	7	Income recorded on books this year not included on this return (itemize):	
2	Federal income tax per books	9,000	a	Tax-exempt interest $ 800	
3	Excess of capital losses over capital gains		b	Other (itemize):	
4	Income subject to tax not recorded on books this year (itemize):				800
5	Expenses recorded on books this year not deducted on this return (itemize):		8	Deductions on this return not charged against book income this year (itemize):	
a	Depreciation $		a	Depreciation $ 2,000	
b	Charitable contributions $ 5,000		b	Charitable contributions $	
c	Travel and entertainment $		c	Other (itemize):	
d	Other (itemize): Bad debt expense 500	5,500	9	Add lines 7 and 8	2,800
6	Add lines 1 through 5	54,500	10	Income—line 6 less line 9	51,700

Exhibit 1: Adjusted Trial Balance

Elderly Care, Inc.
Adjusted trial balance
12/31/Year 21

Account title	Debit	Credit
Cash	$120,000	
Accounts receivable	4,400	
Allowance for credit losses		$500
Supplies	2,200	
Equipment	10,000	
Accum. depreciation		2,000
Accounts payable		1,000
Utilities payable		700
Interest payable		400
Unearned rent revenue		2,400
Federal tax payable		9,000
Wages payable		2,600
Common stock		5,000
Retained earnings		81,000
Service revenue		52,800
Rent revenue		1,200
Interest income		800
Wages expense	2,600	
Travel expense	2,400	
Depreciation expense	2,000	
Insurance expense	300	
Bad debt expense	500	
Utility expense	600	
Charitable contribution expense	5,000	
Interest expense	400	
Income tax expense	9,000	
Total	$159,400	$159,400

Exhibit 2: Charitable Contribution Letter

Habitat for Humanity

December 27, Year 21

To: ElderlyCare, Inc.
120 Main Street
Fort Myers, FL 33901

From: Habitat for Humanity
Atlanta, GA 30301

Dear Patty,

Thank you for your organization's contribution of $5,000 made on December 1, Year 21. We appreciate your continued support for Habitat for Humanity. Your contribution will help build homes for the underserved members of our community. We could not continue to provide these needed services without the support from dedicated organizations like yours.
Thank you,

Habitat for Humanity

Exhibit 3: Equipment Rental

Equipment Rental Agreement

ElderlyCare, Inc.
Customer: Lee County Elder Services
Date: November 1, Year 21

Invoice 127

Asset	Lease period	Amount
Wheelchairs	12/1/Year 21–02/28/Year 22	$3,600

Exhibit 4: Depreciation Worksheet

ElderlyCare, Inc.
Depreciation worksheet
12/31/Year 21

Asset	Straight-line depreciation	Section 179 elected
Equipment	$2,000	$10,000

Exhibit 5: Letter Referencing Bad Debt

December 10, Year 21

From: Horatio Brummel
222 Heads Way
Fort Myers, FL 33901

To: ElderlyCare, Inc.
120 Main Street
Fort Myers, FL 33901

Dear Patty,

I am sorry, but I am unable to pay my invoice of $150 for last week's care. My daughter is coming to live with me as I am unable to care for myself and take care of my finances. I will not need your services going forward. Thank you for the care you have provided to date. I will recommend your services to my friends.
Thank you for understanding.

Horatio

Exhibit 6: Form 1099-INT

☐ CORRECTED (if checked)

PAYER'S name, street address, city or town, state or province, country, ZIP or foreign postal code, and telephone no.
Lee County Savings Bank
100 Fiddlesticks Drive
Fort Myers, FL 33901

Payer's RTN (optional)

OMB No. 1545-0112
Form **1099-INT**
For calendar Year 21

Interest Income

1 Interest income $

2 Early withdrawal penalty $

Copy B

For Recipient

PAYER'S TIN: 36-12345678

RECIPIENT'S TIN: 45-98765432

3 Interest on U.S. Savings Bonds and Treasury obligations $

RECIPIENT'S name
ElderlyCare, Inc.

Street address (including apt. no.)
120 Main Street

City or town, state or province, country, and ZIP or foreign postal code
Fort Myers, FL 33901

FATCA filing requirement ☐

Account number (see instructions)

4 Federal income tax withheld $

5 Investment expenses $

6 Foreign tax paid $

7 Foreign country or U.S. territory

8 Tax-exempt interest $ 800

9 Specified private activity bond interest $

10 Market discount $

11 Bond premium $

12 Bond premium on Treasury obligations

13 Bond premium on tax-exempt bond

14 Tax-exempt and tax credit bond CUSIP no.

15 State

16 State identification no.

17 State tax withheld $ $

This is important tax information and is being furnished to the IRS. If you are required to file a return, a negligence penalty or other sanction may be imposed on you if this income is taxable and the IRS determines that it has not been reported.

Form **1099-INT** (keep for your records) www.irs.gov/Form1099INT Department of the Treasury—Internal Revenue Service

Exhibit 7: Business Travel

ElderlyCare, Inc.
Year 21
Business travel

March 9, Yr 21 – Conference in Atlanta:

Airfare	$385
Hotel	500
Meals	121
Total	$1,006

July 29, Yr 21 – Conference in Dallas:

Airfare	$290
Hotel	929
Meals	175
Total	$1,394

Correct Schedule M-1

Schedule M-1 **Reconciliation of Income (Loss) per Books With Income per Return**
Note: The corporation may be required to file Schedule M-3 (see instructions).

1	Net income (loss) per books	32,000	7	Income recorded on books this year not included on this return (itemize):		
2	Federal income tax per books	9,000	a	Tax-exempt interest $	800	
3	Excess of capital losses over capital gains		b	Other (itemize):		
4	Income subject to tax not recorded on books this year (itemize): Unearned rent revenue	2,400				800
5	Expenses recorded on books this year not deducted on this return (itemize):		8	Deductions on this return not charged against book income this year (itemize):		
a	Depreciation $		a	Depreciation $	8,000	
b	Charitable contributions $ 990		b	Charitable contributions $		
c	Travel and entertainment $ 148		c	Other (itemize):		
d	Other (itemize): Bad debt expense 350	1,488				8,000
			9	Add lines 7 and 8		8,800
6	Add lines 1 through 5	44,888	10	Income—line 6 less line 9		36,088

Line 1: Net income per books – To compute the book income, deduct the expenses listed on the adjusted trial balance from the revenues listed. The correct **book income is $32,000** ($54,800 − $22,800).

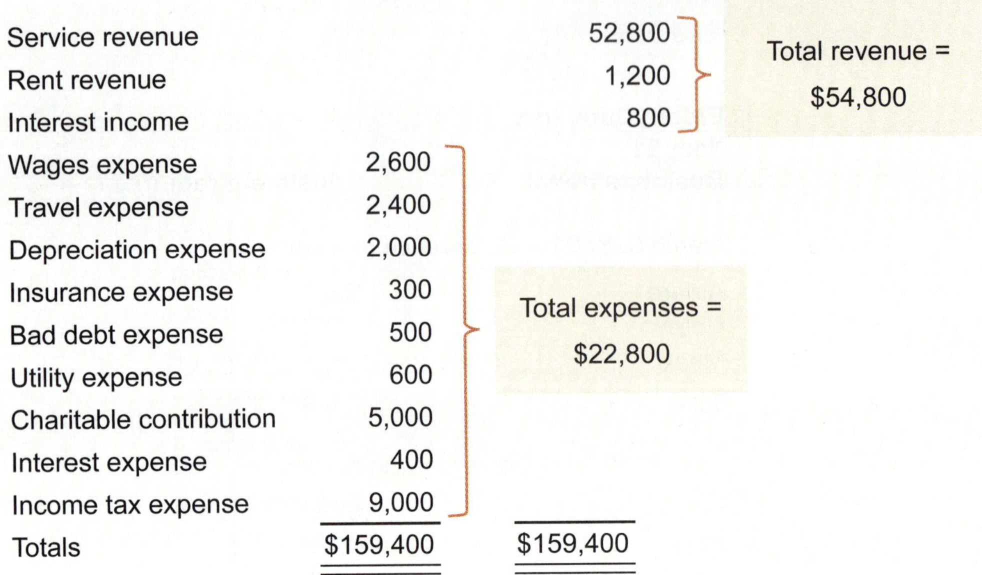

Service revenue		52,800
Rent revenue		1,200
Interest income		800
Wages expense	2,600	
Travel expense	2,400	
Depreciation expense	2,000	
Insurance expense	300	
Bad debt expense	500	
Utility expense	600	
Charitable contribution	5,000	
Interest expense	400	
Income tax expense	9,000	
Totals	$159,400	$159,400

Total revenue = $54,800

Total expenses = $22,800

Line 2: Federal income tax per books – The $9,000 federal income tax paid is a deduction in calculating book income, but it is not deductible in calculating taxable income. This permanent difference must be **added back to book income** to arrive at taxable income.

Line 3: Excess of capital losses over capital gains – Not applicable to this problem.

Line 4: Income subject to tax not recorded on books this year – ElderlyCare had a contract with Lee County and received a payment of $3,600 to provide equipment for three months from December 1, Year 21, to February 28, Year 22. For book income purposes, ElderlyCare reported $1,200 ($3,600/3) of rent income for the month of December and unearned revenue of $2,400. For tax purposes, ElderlyCare will report $3,600 as taxable revenue, creating a **book to tax difference of $2,400** ($3,600 − $1,200).

Line 5: Expenses recorded on books this year not deducted on this return

Line 5a: Depreciation – The $8,000 ($10,000 − $2,000) excess tax depreciation is reported on line 8(a) and *not* here. When **book** depreciation *exceeds* the tax depreciation, an amount would be entered here.

Line 5b: Charitable contribution – For book purposes, the charitable contribution of $5,000 was deducted. For tax purposes, charitable contributions are deductible but limited to 10% of taxable income before the charitable contribution and before special deductions. Therefore, only $4,010 of the $5,000 is deductible. This creates a **$990 temporary difference** ($5,000 − $4,010).

Book income	$32,000
Charitable contributions	5,000
Federal tax paid	9,000
Unearned rent revenue (taxable)	2,400
Nondeductible bad debts	350
Meals (50%)	148
Tax-exempt interest income	(800)
Excess tax depreciation	(8,000)
Taxable income before charitable contribution	$40,098
Limitation	× 10%
Charitable contribution allowed	$ 4,010

Line 5c: Travel and entertainment – For book purposes, $296 ($121 + $175) from Exhibit 7 was deducted for business meals. For tax purposes, only **$148** of business meals are deductible ($296 × 50%).

Line 5d: Other – For book purposes, ElderlyCare estimated its bad debt expense and deducted $500. For tax purposes, ElderlyCare must use the direct write-off method. Therefore, only the $150 confirmed uncollectible is deducted on the tax return (Exhibit 5). The **adjustment required is an add-back of $350** ($500 − $150).

Line 6: Sum of lines 1 through 5d – The net income per books plus the additions are $44,888 ($32,000 + $9,000 + $2,400 + $990 + $148 + $350).

Line 7: Income recorded on books this year not included on this return – The $800 municipal interest income (Exhibit 6) is included in income for book purposes, but it is not taxable.

Line 8: Deductions on this return not charged against book income this year

Line 8a: Depreciation – For book purposes, ElderlyCare used straight-line depreciation and reported $2,000 of depreciation expense for its equipment purchase of $10,000. For tax purposes, ElderlyCare elected Section 179 and expensed the equipment purchase and reported depreciation expense of $10,000. Therefore, the additional expense taken on the tax return is **$8,000** ($10,000 − $2,000).

Line 9: Sum of lines 7 through 8c – The M-1 subtractions are $8,800 ($800 + $8,000).

Line 10: Line 6 less line 9 equals **$36,088** ($44,888 − $8,800).

To double check: the $36,088 ($40,098 − $4,010) taxable income would be the $40,098 taxable income before the charitable deduction that was computed for line 5(b) less the allowable $4,010 charitable deduction.

REG 19
C Corporations

REG 19: C Corporations

19.01 Computations of Taxable Income, Tax Liability, and Allowable Credits

Overview

A C corporation as outlined in IRC Subchapter C is a separate taxable entity from the owners (ie, shareholders). A business entity that is taxed as a corporation must be incorporated under state law. An incorporated entity will be taxed as a C corporation unless it is has made an election to be taxed as an S corporation (must meet certain requirements). The word *corporation* in this chapter and the exam refers to a C corporation. If a corporation has elected "S" status, the term "S corporation" is used.

A corporation is subject to double taxation, meaning that income is taxed once when earned by the corporation and a second time when distributed to a shareholder. Corporations report taxable income on Form 1120, U.S. Corporation Income Tax Return. Amended corporate tax returns are filed on Form 1120X.

Corporate shareholders have limited liability, and shareholders often hire managers to run the day-to-day operations of the corporation.

Corporation Characteristics	
Limited liability	Shareholders are not responsible for corporation's debt
Independent life	Shareholder death does not dissolve the corporation (ie, it is perpetual)
Ease of transfer	Ownership is considered transferrable property
Taxation	Corporation files and pays income tax
Centralized management	Corporation is overseen by an internal group (ie, board of directors)

Return due dates and extensions are no longer tested on the exam.

Taxable Income for C Corporations

Representative Task (Application): Calculate taxable income for a C corporation.

Corporate Taxable Income Computation

The rules for the tax items that are included in income and allowed as deductions for corporations are very similar to the rules for individuals who have a sole proprietorship. Therefore, many of the income and expense rules for corporations will be familiar. However, there are distinctions regarding the computation of taxable income for a corporation as compared to other entities.

On the tax return, most expenses are reported as *ordinary deductions* to arrive at **income before** NOL (net operating loss) **and special deductions**. Some deductions (eg, **charitable contributions**) are subject to limitations.

NOL and a few special deductions (eg, dividends-received deduction) are not considered ordinary because they do not exist for accounting purposes but are allowed by tax statute. Accordingly, these items are deducted *after* calculating the *income before NOL and special deductions* to arrive at taxable income (TI). Once TI is determined, the gross tax liability is calculated. Tax credits (eg, foreign tax credit, general business credit) reduce the liability. Therefore, allowable tax credits are always *deducted* from the gross tax liability.

The basic tax formula for computing corporate taxable income is shown below. Corporate *expenses* must be deducted in the following order:

- All deductions (including NOL carryforwards) except for charitable contributions, dividends-received deduction, and capital loss carrybacks
- Charitable contributions
- Dividends-received deduction (DRD)
- Capital loss carrybacks

Corporate Income Tax Formula (Form 1120)
Gross income (worldwide)
− Ordinary deductions before special deductions*
Taxable income for charitable contribution deduction
− Charitable deduction
= Taxable income for dividends-received deduction**
− Dividends-received deduction (DRD)
= Taxable income before capital loss carrybacks
− Capital loss carrybacks
= Taxable income
× 21% tax rate
Gross tax liability
− Tax credits (foreign tax credit/general business credit)
= Net regular income tax liability
+ Alternative minimum tax (if applicable)
= Total corporate tax liability

**This line includes NOL carryforwards and capital loss carryforwards. It does not include special deductions, which are the charitable contribution deduction, dividends-received deduction, and capital loss carrybacks.*

***NOL carryforwards do not reduce taxable income for computing the DRD, but they do reduce taxable income for the charitable contribution limitation.*

Reconciliation of Corporate Book Income to Taxable Income

C corporations use Form 1120 for reporting income, gains, losses, deductions, and credits and to determine taxable income and income tax liability. To arrive at taxable income, a corporation adjusts its book net income for certain income and expense items (temporary and permanent) that are treated differently for tax purposes.

For example, on the tax return, MACRS cost recovery is used instead of book depreciation, municipal interest is nontaxable, and generally no estimated expenses are permitted (deductions are limited to the amount paid). Schedule M-1 or M-3 is filed to summarize these adjustments.

Reconciliation of Book Income to Taxable Income

- Federal income tax expense, fines/penalties
- Nondeductible expenses
- Excess depreciation per the *books*, charitable contributions, and capital losses
- Tax gain on sale of assets in excess of book gain

Net income for the year per the books
\+ Expenses deducted on books but not on tax return
\+ Income currently taxable but not included in book income
− Income reported on books but not on tax return
− Deductions on tax return but not recorded on books
Taxable income

- Tax-exempt interest
- Officers' life insurance proceeds
- Excess *tax* depreciation
- Carryovers from charitable contributions, NOLs, and capital losses

A corporation reports the following:

- Pretax book income of $543,000
- Depreciation on the tax return is $20,000 greater than depreciation on the financial statements
- Rent income reportable on the tax return is $36,000 greater than rent income per the financial statements
- Fines for pollution appear as a $10,000 expense in the financial statements
- Interest earned on municipal bonds is $25,000

What is the corporation's taxable income?

- Due to different depreciation methods and special tax provisions, $20,000 additional depreciation is allowed for taxes (deducted from book income)
- For taxes, revenue is recognized at the earlier of when it is earned or received. Therefore, advance rent is taxed when received (added to book income)
- Because fines result from breaking a law, no deduction is permitted for taxes (added back to book income)
- To encourage investment infrastructure at the state and local level, municipal bond interest is nontaxable (deducted from book income)

In this scenario, the additional depreciation and nontaxable interest are subtracted from book income. The nondeductible fines and additional taxable rent revenue are added to book income. Therefore, **taxable income is $544,000**, as shown below:

Book net income	$543,000
Add:	
Taxable rent revenue	36,000
Nondeductible fines	10,000
Deduct:	
Additional tax depreciation	(20,000)
Nontaxable municipal interest	(25,000)
Taxable income	**$544,000**

Corporate Alternative Minimum Tax

Similar to the federal income taxation of individuals, Congress had provided a corporate alternative minimum tax (AMT) beginning in 1987. The Tax Cuts and Jobs Act of 2017 repealed the corporate AMT, so it was not in effect from 2018 to 2022. The Inflation Reduction Act of 2022 has reinstated the corporate AMT, but it is a much different type of tax than in the past and applies to a very small number of corporations.

The new corporate AMT is effective for tax years beginning after 2022 and includes a 15% tax on the adjusted financial statement income of applicable corporations. The minimum tax applies only to the extent that it exceeds the regular income tax.

- An applicable corporation exists if the average annual adjusted financial statement income for a three-tax-year period that ends after 2021 exceeds $1 billion
- Adjusted financial statement income is the corporation's net income or loss reported on its audited financial statements. The Joint Committee on Taxation has estimated that the new corporate AMT will apply to no more than 150 of the Fortune 500 companies

Special Rules for Corporate Income Computation

There are **two** types of corporations that have special rules that apply in certain situations.

- **Personal Service Corporation:** A corporation whose principal activity is the performance of personal services performed by employees who own substantially all of the stock; for example, a medical corporation whose owners are also the doctors providing the medical services
- **Closely Held Corporation:** A corporation is a closely held corporation if at any time during the last half of the taxable year, more than 50% of the value of its outstanding stock is owned, directly or indirectly, by or for not more than five individuals

Passive loss limits do not apply to corporations, except personal service corporations and closely held corporations.

- Closely held corporations can use passive losses to offset active corporate income but not portfolio income
- Personal service corporations cannot offset passive losses against active corporate income or portfolio income

Accounting Methods and Periods: General

Accrual vs. Cash: In general, the following entities **cannot** use the cash method of accounting and must use the accrual method:

- C corporations
- Partnerships that have C corporations as partners
- Tax shelters, defined as an entity other than a C corporation for which ownership interests have been offered for sale in an offering required to be registered with federal or state security agencies

Notwithstanding the above, the following entities can use the **cash** method of accounting:

- Any corporation (or partnership with C corporation partners) whose annual gross receipts do not exceed $30 million (2024). The test is satisfied for a prior year if the average annual gross receipts for the previous three-year period do not exceed $30 million. Once the test is failed, the entity must use the accrual method for all future tax years. This exception does not apply to tax shelters
- Certain farming businesses
- Personal service corporations

Tax Year End: Corporations can choose a **fiscal year end** unless the corporation makes an "S" election or qualifies as a personal service corporation. Personal service corporations generally must use a calendar year end.

Accounting Methods and Periods: Income

For accrual-method corporations, revenue generally will be recognized at the **earlier** of when **earned or collected**. Income is *earned* when all events have occurred that fix the taxpayer's right to the income and the amount can be reasonably determined (ie, the all-events test has been met).

- The **all-events test** is considered to be met no later than when the income is included in revenue in the applicable financial statements (F/S) of the taxpayer

Advance payments for services (ie, unearned income or deferred revenue) generally must be recognized in the year received.

- However, if the deferral method is elected, the taxpayer has to include only the payments in gross income in the year of receipt if they are also included in the taxpayer's financial statements
- The remaining payments are taxed in the following year (even if not yet earned). The election does not apply to certain advance payments, such as rent and insurance premiums received

Taxpayers must recognize income no later than the year in which the income is included on an applicable financial statement. An *applicable financial statement* is a statement that conforms to GAAP and is reported in a 10-K, an audited financial statement used for a nontax purpose, *or* filed with a federal agency (but not for tax purposes). An *applicable financial statement* also includes a financial statement that conforms to IFRS.

Income Type	Cash Method	Accrual Method
General rule	Income when cash received	All-events test met and amount determined with reasonable accuracy
Advance payments received for interest income and rent revenue	Income when cash received	Income when cash received
Advance payments for services	Income when cash received	Income when received unless elect to defer income, for no more than one year, and also deferred for financial reporting

Accounting Methods and Periods: Deductions

In general, deductions on a corporate tax return are claimed in accordance with the same matching principle used for GAAP purposes. As a result, expenses can be deducted in the period that they are accrued for financial reporting purposes. An accrual-basis taxpayer can accrue an expense if the transaction meets *both* an **all-events test** *and* an **economic performance test.**

The **all-events test is met** when the existence of a liability is established and the amount of liability can be determined with reasonable accuracy.

Economic performance occurs when property and/or services have been provided. Certain accrued items that are expected to be paid within a short period of time after accrual may be deducted when accrued if they are paid within **2.5 months** of the tax year end. These items include the following payments to employees: wages, bonuses, and vacation pay.

There are *two major exceptions* to the economic performance rule:

- The taxpayer can deduct refunds, rebates, awards, prizes, provision of warranty work or service contracts, taxes, and insurance premiums when actually paid even if economic performance has **not** occurred
- If the expenditure is a recurring item, and economic performance occurs within 8.5 months after the close of the tax year (or when the return is filed, if earlier), then the expenditure generally can be deducted in the year incurred

For prepaid expenses related to a business under the cash method, an immediate deduction can be taken when paid as long as the benefits from the expenditure do not extend beyond the earlier of:

- 12 months after benefits first begin, or
- The end of the year after the year in which the payment was made.

If the 12-month rule is not met, the deduction must be spread over the period for which the expenses apply.

On December 1, Year 8, a calendar-year taxpayer pays a $10,000 property insurance premium with a one-year term that begins on February 1, Year 9. For the $10,000 to be deductible for Year 8, the benefits from the expenditure cannot extend beyond the *earlier* of:

- 12 months after benefits first begin (January 31, Year 10), *or*
- The end of the year after the year in which the payment was made (December 31, Year 9).

The earlier of these two dates is **December 31, Year 9**, and the benefits extend past this date to January 31, Year 10.

Therefore, the amount paid must be **capitalized and is not deductible for Year 8**. The premium will be deductible over the period to which it relates, which will be 11 months for Year 9 and one month for Year 10.

What if the policy has a term beginning on December 15, Year 8?

Now the benefits from the expenditure do not extend beyond the earlier of:

- 12 months after benefits first begin (December 14, Year 9), *or*
- The end of the year after the year in which the payment was made (December 31, Year 9).

The benefits end on **December 14, Year 9**, so they do **not** extend beyond December 14, Year 9. Thus, the taxpayer is not required to capitalize the payment and may **deduct** the **$10,000 payment in Year 8**.

Employee Compensation

Corporations can deduct the following items related to employee compensation: salaries, wages, bonuses, and vacation pay (if accrued during tax year and paid within **2.5 months** of year end), payroll taxes, and fringe benefits. In addition, up to $1 million of compensation expense for certain **covered employees** is permitted.

- Covered employees include the principal executive officer, the principal financial officer, and the three other highest paid executive officers of a public corporation
- Compensation expense for these purposes includes commissions and other performance-based compensation but excludes nontaxable fringe benefits
- Once an employee is considered a covered employee, their status as such never changes. Compensation to other employees can be fully deducted as long as it is reasonable

Premiums on life insurance to benefit an employee's family are deductible as a fringe benefit. However, if the corporation is the beneficiary of a life insurance policy on an employee, the premiums paid on such policies are not deductible since the proceeds are generally not taxable.

Deducting Accrued Compensation

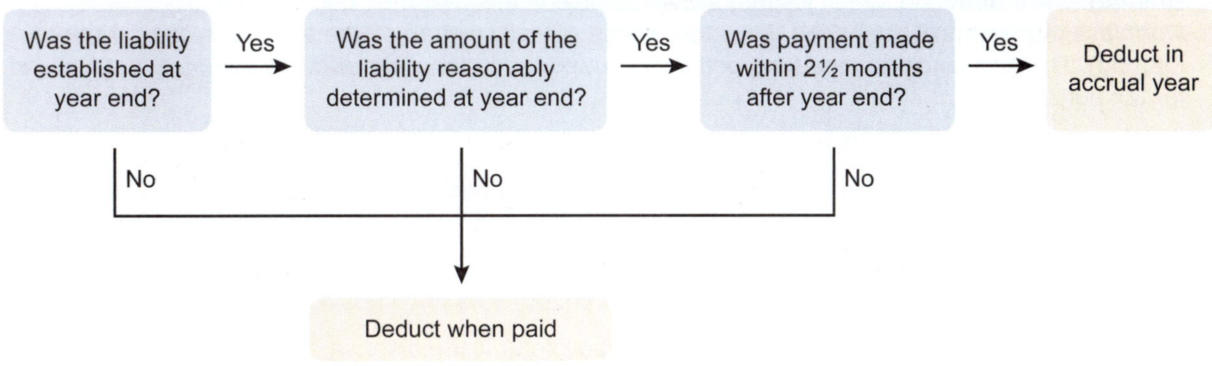

An accrual-method calendar-year corporation had $600,000 in compensation expense for book purposes in Year 2. Included in this amount was a $60,000 accrual for Year 2 nonshareholder bonuses. The corporation paid the Year 2 bonuses of $60,000 on March 1, Year 3. In its Year 2 tax return, what amount should be deducted as compensation expense?

- Generally, employers deduct compensation when it is paid to employees. Accrual-method employers also deduct compensation liabilities (eg, bonuses) in the year that the liabilities meet the all-events test, including economic performance
- For compensation liabilities, all-events are met as employees render services; therefore, all-events are met in Year 2 for compensation for Year 2 services rendered
- Compensation liability economic performance occurs to the extent that payments are made by the 15th day of the 3rd month following the employer's year end (eg, March 15 for calendar years). The deduction equals the amount timely paid even if a different amount was accrued for book purposes

In this scenario, the corporation's Year 2 $600,000 book compensation includes $540,000 of regular compensation paid for Year 2 services plus $60,000 of bonus liabilities. The $540,000 paid is deductible in Year 2. Because the $60,000 of bonuses were paid by March 15, Year 3, they are also deductible. **Therefore, $600,000 ($540,000 + $60,000) is deductible in Year 2**.

A corporation recently hired a new principal financial officer and provided the following compensation package during the current tax year:

- Annual salary of $1,900,000
- Nontaxable fringe benefits of $215,000
- Annual bonus tied to company performance of $500,000

What can the corporation deduct related to the principal financial officer's compensation?

Because the principal financial officer is considered a covered employee, the compensation (ie, salary and bonus) that can be deducted by the corporation is limited to $1,000,000. In addition, the company can deduct the nontaxable fringe benefits of $215,000. Therefore, **the total deduction for the corporation is $1,215,000**.

Bad Debt, Warranty Expense, and Other Estimated Losses

Estimated losses are accrued for book purposes but cannot be claimed for tax purposes until they are actual losses; thus, they will cause temporary book-tax differences to be reported on Schedule M-1 or M-3.

- **Business bad debts** (ie, credit losses) are deductible in the year they become *partially or wholly worthless*, but amounts cannot be deducted unless *actually written off the books* (ie, direct write-off method). The allowance method for credit losses used for financial reporting is generally not allowed for tax purposes
- **Warranty costs** cannot be claimed until *repairs are actually made* or a refund issued
- **Lawsuits** – Unlike GAAP, the tax code does *not* permit the deduction of losses just because they are probable and estimable. The loss is not deducted until the all-events test has been met
- **Marketable debt securities** – Changes in market value are *not* reported on the tax return. Gains and losses are only recognized for tax purposes at the time of sale or disposition
- **Inventory** – Declines in market value are not deductible until the disposal of the inventory occurs

A corporation reports $22,300 in warranty expense on its income statement for Year 7. During the year, $6,200 was spent on warranty claims to customers. What amount is deductible on the corporation tax return in Year 7?

For tax purposes only, the actual amount of warranty claims paid is deductible. Therefore, the corporation can deduct only **$6,200 as a warranty expense**.

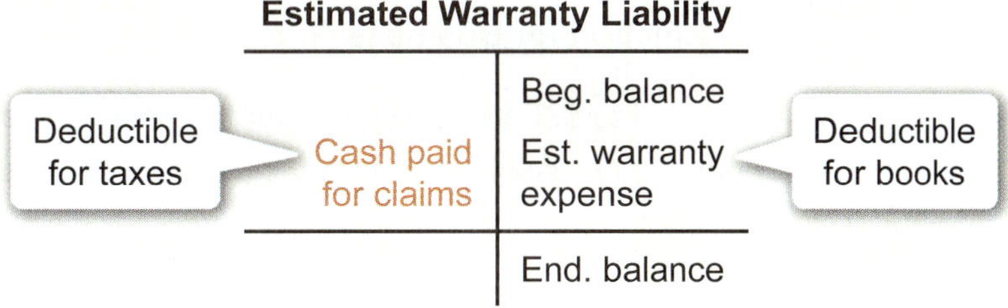

Interest Expense

Interest expense is *not* deductible if loan proceeds are used for *tax-exempt investments*. Note: The net investment income limitation on interest expense deductions does **not** apply to corporations.

Unless the taxpayer meets the $30 million gross receipts test (2024) or qualifies under another specific exemption for certain businesses, such as real property development, the **business interest deduction** is **limited** to the **sum** of the following, with any disallowed interest expense being *carried forward* to the next tax year:

- Business interest income (does not include investment interest/income),
- 30% of the taxpayer's adjusted taxable income, and
- The taxpayer's floor plan financing interest for the tax year. "Floor plan financing interest" means interest paid or accrued on debt that is used to finance motor vehicles held for sale or lease and that is secured by that same inventory.

Casualty Losses

For casualty losses related to business property, the deduction is the lesser of:

- *Adjusted basis* immediately before the casualty, or
- Decline in value if not completely destroyed.

Note that the limitations that apply to personal casualty losses (ie, the $100 floor, 10% of AGI limitation, and federally declared disaster requirement previously discussed) for individuals do **not** apply to business casualty losses.

Other General Costs

Taxes – Corporations can deduct various *state, local, and foreign taxes* on the federal return; however, **no** deduction for federal income tax is permitted. The $10,000 limit on state and local taxes applicable to individuals for itemized deductions does **not** apply to corporate deductions of taxes.

Research and experimental/development expenses – These are costs that are related to the development or improvement of a product in the experimental or laboratory sense. Research and development expenses incurred after 2021 must be amortized over 60 months. For the year that these expenses are incurred, they can be amortized for six months regardless of when incurred during the year.

Costs of issuing stock – These costs are treated as adjustments to the proceeds from sale rather than deductions.

Business gifts – A corporation can deduct the cost of business gifts given to individuals (ie, customers, clients, vendors). However, to discourage abuse, the IRS limits the deduction to $25 per person per tax year. For purposes of the $25 limit, gifts costing $4 or less that are considered promotional gifts (eg, pen, calendar, key chain) are excluded.

Deduction for Business Gifts

- Limited to $25 per individual per tax year*
- *Cannot* be considered entertainment
- Excludes promotional items costing $4 or less

**Incidental costs (eg, engraving, packing, shipping) are excluded from the $25 limit if they do not add substantial value to the gift.*

Nondeductible expenses – A corporation may not deduct fines, penalties, political contributions, entertainment expenses, and 50% of business meals. In addition, certain expenses must be capitalized and amortized or depreciated over time.

Dividends-Received Deduction

Corporations may purchase equity stock (ie, common or preferred) of other corporations. The dividends-received deduction (DRD) is unique to corporations and exists to mitigate or reduce triple taxation that could occur if a corporation owns stock in another corporation. The DRD does not completely avoid triple taxation because it does not always apply, and when it does apply, it often does not completely offset the dividend income received. The DRD is a percentage (%) of the dividends received from a domestic corporation. Domestic corporations include foreign-owned companies that are traded on a U.S. securities market exchange.

The DRD cannot be claimed by S corporations, personal service corporations, and personal holding companies.

The full amount of the dividends received are reported on the tax return, and if eligible, the DRD is taken based on taxable income before the NOL deduction and special deductions.

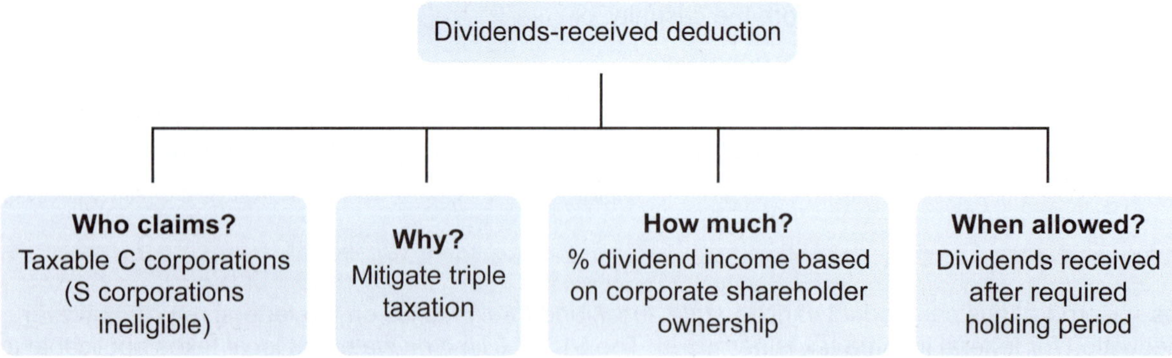

Eligible stock – To be eligible, the stock must be of a **domestic corporation**, and the taxpayer must hold the interest at least 46 days during the 91-day period beginning 45 days prior to ex-dividend date. The ex-dividend date is the day after the record date for the dividend.

46-Day DRD Holding Period Requirement

Amount of DRD – The DRD percentage depends on the level of stock owned by the corporation. Note that a 100% DRD is allowed for **foreign-source dividends** received from a foreign corporation if the U.S. corporate shareholder owns at least 10% of the voting power or value of the stock.

Dividends-Received Deduction (DRD)*	
Ownership in Investment	**Allowed DRD**
< 20%	50%
≥ 20% but < 80%	65%
≥ 80% (affiliated)	100%

**DRD is only available for C corporations.*

On the exam, if the stock ownership percentage is not provided, assume it is less than 20% and use 50% to determine the DRD.

DRD Limitation

The DRD is limited by a percentage of taxable income unless the DRD creates or adds to a net operating loss. Taxable income used to compute the DRD is computed as the corporation's taxable income before any net operating losses, any capital loss carrybacks, and the dividends-received deduction.

The following steps are used to compute the DRD:

Step 1. Compute the **full DRD** by multiplying dividends received by the deduction percentage (50%, 65%, or 100%).

Step 2. Multiply taxable income as defined above by the deduction percentage to produce the **limited DRD**.

Step 3. Subtract Step 1 from taxable income before dividends-received deduction.

Step 4. If Step 3 produces a loss, then the DRD limitation does not apply and the full DRD is the deduction.

Step 5. If Step 3 produces a positive amount, the dividends-received deduction is the lesser of Step 1 (**full DRD**) or Step 2 (**limited DRD**).

ABC Corporation received $100 in dividends from a domestic corporation (ABC owned less than 20% of the stock). If ABC has taxable income before the DRD of $200, then the DRD is computed as follows:

Step 1. Compute the **full DRD** by multiplying dividends received by the deduction percentage (50%, 65%, or 100%). **$100 × 50% = $50**

Step 2. Multiply taxable income as defined above by the deduction percentage to produce the **limited DRD**. **$200 × 50% = $100**

Step 3. Subtract Step 1 from taxable income before dividends-received deduction. **$200 − $50 = $150**

Step 4. N/A because Step 3 did not produce a loss. If Step 3 produces a loss, then the DRD limitation does not apply and the **full DRD** is the deduction.

Step 5. If Step 3 produces a positive amount, the dividends-received deduction is the lesser of Step 1 (**full DRD**) or Step 2 (**limited DRD**). **Lesser of $50 or $100 is $50**

If ABC has taxable income before the DRD of $90, then the DRD is reduced to $45.

Step 1. Compute the **full DRD** by multiplying dividends received by the deduction percentage (50%, 65%, or 100%). **$100 × 50% = $50**

Step 2. Multiply taxable income as defined above by the deduction percentage to produce the **limited DRD**. **$90 × 50% = $45**

Step 3. Subtract Step 1 from taxable income before dividends-received deduction. **$90 − $50 = $40**

Step 4. If Step 3 produces a loss, then the DRD limitation does not apply and the **full DRD** is the deduction.

Step 5. If Step 3 produces a positive amount, the dividends-received deduction is the lesser of Step 1 (**full DRD**) or Step 2 (**limited DRD**). **Lesser of $50 or $45 is $45**

ABC Corporation received $100 in dividends from a domestic corporation (ABC owned less than 20% of the stock). If ABC has taxable income before the DRD of $10, then the DRD is computed as follows:

Step 1. Compute the **full DRD** by multiplying dividends received by the deduction percentage (50%, 65%, or 100%). **$100 × 50% = $50**

Step 2. Multiply taxable income as defined above by the deduction percentage to produce the **limited DRD**. **$10 × 50% = $5**

Step 3. Subtract Step 1 from taxable income before dividends-received deduction. **$10 − $50 = $(40)**

Step 4. If Step 3 produces a loss, then the DRD limitation does not apply and the **full DRD** is the deduction. **$50**

DRD Comprehensive Problem

Assume a corporation's gross revenue consists of sales and $100 in dividend income, and deductions other than the DRD total $490. Also assume the dividend was received from another taxable domestic corporation in which the investor holds a 2% interest, so that the appropriate DRD percentage is 50%. Five examples are provided below in which sales are (a) $530, (b) $500, (c) $470, (d) $420, and (e) $410. The calculation of taxable income is as follows:

	(a)	(b)	(c)	(d)	(e)
Sales	530	500	470	420	410
Dividend income	100	100	100	100	100
Gross income	630	600	570	520	510
Ordinary deductions	(490)	(490)	(490)	(490)	(490)
TI before DRD	140	110	80	30	20
DRD (50%)	(50)	(50)	(40)	(50)	(50)
Taxable income	90	60	40	(20)	(30)

Notice that the DRD is based on the dividend income ($100 × 50% = $50) in most examples. Only in example (c), in which TI before DRD is lower than $100 but not lower than $50, is the exception applicable, and the DRD is limited to TI before DRD ($80 × 50% = $40). The limitation does not apply when there is an NOL after subtracting the full DRD amount—examples (d) and (e).

Charitable Contributions

The **initial amount** of a charitable contribution deduction is the same for corporations as for individuals:

- For long-term capital gain property, the deduction equals the FMV of the property
- For other property, the deduction is: FMV − Short-term capital gain or ordinary income if property had been sold. For example, short-term capital property with a FMV $8,000 and an adjusted basis of $6,000 results in a $6,000 contribution ($8,000 − $2,000 appreciation). A shortcut is the lesser of the property's adjusted tax basis or the FMV on date contributed (ie, $6,000)

Type of Contribution	Examples	Allowable Deduction
Cash	• Cash, check, credit cards	Amount of cash, check, or charge
Ordinary income property	• Inventory	Generally, the lesser of the property's adjusted tax basis or the FMV on date contributed*
Short-term capital gain or loss property (ie, held for ≤ 1 year)	• Stocks, bonds, land, buildings • Personal items	
Section 1231 assets	• Trade or business assets	
Long-term capital gain or loss property	• Stocks, bonds, land, buildings • Personal items	FMV of property on date of contribution
Certain long-term capital gain property not used for related purpose	• Tangible personal property • Artwork	Adjusted tax basis on date of contribution

** This is a shortcut to the FMV − Short-term capital gain or ordinary income if property had been sold.*

The **limit** on the **deduction** is **10% of adjusted taxable income** (before deduction for contributions, the DRD, NOL carryforwards, and capital loss carrybacks). Any excess charitable contribution carries forward for five years. There is no carryback.

Corporate Charitable Contribution Deduction is *Lesser* of:

Actual amount contributed **OR**	10% of corporate taxable income **before:**
	• Charitable contributions, • NOL or capital loss carrybacks, and • Dividends-received deduction

Corporations reporting taxable income on the *accrual method* can elect to treat as paid during the tax year any contributions paid by the due date for filing the corporation's tax return (not including extensions), if the contributions were authorized by the board of directors during the tax year.

Assume that Roger Corp. has $200 million in gross income, $50 million in ordinary deductions, $20 million in charitable contributions, a $35 million DRD, and no capital loss carryback. The limit on the charitable contribution deduction is computed (in millions) as follows:

Gross income	$200
Ordinary deductions	(50)
Adjusted taxable income	$150
Charitable contribution (limited)	**(15)***
DRD	(35)
Taxable income	$100

Roger Corp. has $20 million in charitable contributions, but the maximum deduction is* ***10%* *of its $150 million adjusted taxable income = $15 million, so $5 million ($20 million − $15 million) is carried forward up to five years.*

Exception: A corporation's contribution of inventory or depreciable property or land used in its trade or business to charities that use the property in a manner related to the exempt purpose and solely for the care of the ill, needy, or infants, or where the property is used for research purposes under specified conditions, is subject to special rules.

The deduction is the **lesser** of:

- Adjusted basis of property + 50% × (FMV − Adjusted basis), or
- 2 × Adjusted basis.

This rule applies for contributions of wholesome food inventory by corporations and other businesses to charities that use the food in an appropriate manner. These contributions can be deducted up to 15% of taxable income from the food operations.

The corporation can elect to deduct accrued contributions if the contributions are actually paid in the first 3.5 months following the year end. (For corporations with a June 30 year end, the deadline is 2.5 months following year end, which is September 15).

The books of a calendar-year, accrual-method corporation for Year 10 disclose net income of $350,000 after deducting a charitable contribution of $125,000. The contribution was authorized by the board of directors on December 24, Year 10, and was actually paid on January 31, Year 11.

The allowable charitable contribution deduction for Year 10, if the corporation elects to deduct it when accrued, is $47,500, calculated as follows:

($350,000 + $125,000) × 10% = $47,500

The remaining $77,500 ($125,000 − $47,500) is carried forward for up to five years.

Practice Scenario

When completing the problem, it is useful to review the corporate income *tax formula*.

	Gross income
Less:	Deductions (including NOL carryforwards)*
	Taxable income for charitable limitation
Less:	Charitable contributions (≤ 10% of above)
	Taxable income for DRD (excludes NOL carryforwards)
Less:	DRD
	Taxable income before carrybacks
Less:	Capital loss carryback
	Taxable income

**Excludes charitable contributions, DRD, capital loss carryback*

Required: Action, Inc., is a calendar-year-end, accrual-basis C corporation. For each independent situation below, calculate the taxable income (loss) reported on Form 1120, U.S. Corporation Income Tax Return. Column A lists preliminary taxable income excluding additional tax return items shown in column B. Enter the taxable income (loss) in the associated cells.

	A Preliminary Taxable Income (Loss)	B Additional Tax Return Item(s)	C Form 1120, Line 30 Taxable Income (Loss)
1	$100,000	$20,000 of charitable contributions	
2	$160,000	$15,000 of charitable contributions	
3	$200,000	$10,000 of charitable contributions and $20,000 of dividends from less-than-20%-owned domestic corporations	
4	$250,000	$40,000 of dividends received from a 45%-owned domestic corporation	
5	$80,000	$10,000 of dividends received from a 10%-owned domestic corporation and a $20,000 net operating loss carryover from 2019—no carryback election was made	
6	$(40,000)	$5,000 of charitable contributions and $10,000 of dividends received from a 15%-owned domestic corporation	
7	$(20,000)	$200,000 of dividends received from a 25%-owned domestic corporation	

Solution

Note: Any excess charitable contribution is carried forward for five years. There is no carryback.

Line 1: Charitable contribution deduction is limited to 10% of taxable income, before the deduction of the contributions, or $10,000 ($100,000 × 10%). Taxable income is **$90,000** ($100,000 − $10,000).

Line 2: Charitable contribution deduction is limited to 10% of taxable income, or $16,000 ($160,000 × 10%). Thus, all contributions ($15,000) are deductible. Taxable income is **$145,000** ($160,000 − $15,000).

Line 3: Charitable contribution deduction is limited to 10% of taxable income before special deductions, or $22,000 ($220,000 × 10%). Thus, all contributions ($10,000) are deductible. Taxable income after the charitable contribution deduction is $210,000 ($220,000 − $10,000).

Since Action owns less than 20% of the stock, the DRD percentage is 50%. The full DRD is $20,000 × 50%, or $10,000. The DRD is limited to 50% of taxable income after the charitable deduction ($210,000), which is $105,000. So, the full $10,000 DRD is deductible.

Taxable income before dividends	$200,000
Dividends	20,000
Taxable income before special deductions	$220,000
Charitable contributions	(10,000)
Taxable income after charitable deduction	$210,000
DRD	(10,000)
Taxable income	**$200,000**

Line 4: Since Action owns 45% of the stock, the DRD percentage is 65%. The full DRD is $40,000 × 65%, or $26,000.

The DRD is limited to 65% of taxable income ($290,000), which is $188,500. So, the full $26,000 DRD is deductible.

Taxable income before dividends	$250,000
Dividends	40,000
Taxable income before special deductions	$290,000
DRD	(26,000)
Taxable income	**$264,000**

Line 5: NOL carryforwards are not allowed for computing the DRD limit. The full DRD is $10,000 × 50%, or $5,000. The DRD is limited to 50% of taxable income ($90,000), which is $45,000.

So, the full $5,000 DRD is deductible. Note that 50% is used in these computations since Action owns less than 20% of the stock. The NOL is limited to 80% of taxable income from before the NOL, or $68,000 ($85,000 × 80%).

Taxable income before dividends and NOL carryforward	$80,000
Dividends	10,000
Taxable income before special deductions	$90,000
DRD	(5,000)
Taxable income before NOL	$85,000
NOL carryforward from 2019	(20,000)
Taxable income	**$65,000**

Line 6: Charitable contribution deduction is limited to 10% of taxable income, or $0 since there is no income. Thus, none of the contributions are deductible. The full DRD is $10,000 × 50%, or $5,000. The taxable income limitation does not apply for the DRD in this scenario since a loss would occur if the full DRD was deducted.

So, the full $5,000 DRD is deductible. Note that 50% is used in these computations since Action owns less than 20% of the stock.

Taxable loss before dividends	$(40,000)
Dividends	10,000
Taxable income before special deductions	$(30,000)
Charitable contributions	(0)
Taxable loss after charitable deduction	$(30,000)
DRD	(5,000)
Taxable loss	**$(35,000)**

Line 7: The full DRD is $200,000 × 65%, or $130,000. The DRD is limited to 65% of taxable income ($180,000), which is $117,000. Note that 65% is used in these computations since Action owns 20% or more of the stock but less than 80%.

Taxable loss before dividends	$ (20,000)
Dividends	200,000
Taxable income before special deductions	$180,000
DRD	(117,000)
Taxable income	**$ 63,000**

	A **Preliminary Taxable Income (Loss)**	**B** **Additional Tax Return Item(s)**	**C** **Form 1120, Line 30 Taxable Income (Loss)**
1	$100,000	$20,000 of charitable contributions	**$90,000**
2	$160,000	$15,000 of charitable contributions	**$145,000**
3	$200,000	$10,000 of charitable contributions and $20,000 of dividends from less-than-20%-owned domestic corporations	**$200,000**
4	$250,000	$40,000 of dividends received from a 45%-owned domestic corporation	**$264,000**
5	$80,000	$10,000 of dividends received from a 10%-owned domestic corporation and a $20,000 net operating loss carryover from 2019—no carryback election was made	**$65,000**
6	$(40,000)	$5,000 of charitable contributions and $10,000 of dividends received from a 15%-owned domestic corporation	**$(35,000)**
7	$(20,000)	$200,000 of dividends received from a 25%-owned domestic corporation	**$63,000**

Net Operating Loss and Capital Loss of a C Corporation

Representative Task (Application): Calculate the current year net operating or capital loss of a C corporation and the limitations on use in the current year contributions.

Capital Gains and Losses

A capital asset is property owned by a taxpayer that is not inventory, a receivable, Section 1231 property (depreciable property and real property used in a trade or business), self-created intangible property, or consumable supplies. In general, the disposition of a capital asset (eg, land, investments) results in a capital gain or loss. The amount of gain or loss is the difference between the asset's adjusted basis and the amount realized from the disposition.

Netting

It is common for corporations to dispose of numerous capital assets in one tax year. Capital gain or loss amounts from each individual asset (transaction) are aggregated and reported as one number on the corporate tax return (ie, a net capital gain or a net capital loss).

- If the C corporation has an overall net capital gain, that gain is reported as ordinary income
- If the C corporation has an overall net capital loss, no deduction is allowed against ordinary income. Instead, the corporation is required to carry back or carry forward the net capital loss to offset net capital gains in other tax years
- To simplify recordkeeping and because corporations do not receive a preferential tax rate for capital gains, all corporate net capital losses that are carried back or forward are considered short-term capital losses regardless of their actual nature

Section 1231 Property: If the corporation has Section 1231 assets (ie, assets used in a trade or business that are held longer than one year) that are disposed, the Section 1231 gains and losses are initially netted.

- A net Section 1231 gain is added to other long-term capital gains and included in the *capital gain/loss netting process*
- A net Section 1231 loss is treated as an ordinary loss, which offsets ordinary income and is never treated as a capital loss

Netting of Capital Gains and Losses for C Corporations

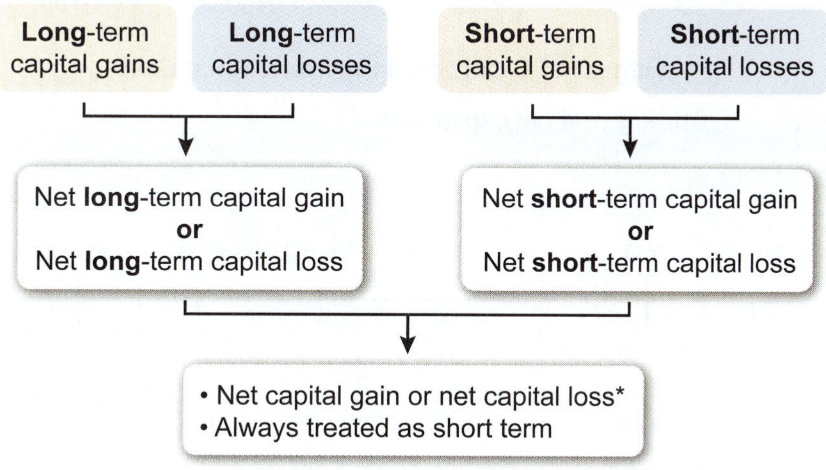

**Although net capital gains are taxable, no deduction is allowed for a net capital loss.*

A corporation had the following transactions for the current tax year:

Operating net income	$53,000
Short-term capital gain	5,000
Short-term capital loss	(19,000)
Long-term capital gain	6,000
Net Section 1231 gain	2,000

What is the corporation **taxable income**?

Short-term capital gain	$5,000	
Short-term capital loss	(19,000)	
Net short-term capital loss		$(14,000)
Long-term capital gain	$6,000	
Net Section 1231 gain	2,000	
Net long-term capital gain		8,000
Net capital loss		$ (6,000)

The $6,000 net capital loss **cannot** offset the $53,000 of net operating income because net capital losses are not deductible for corporations. Therefore, the **taxable income is $53,000**.

Carryover Rules

Capital loss carryovers must be applied in a particular order.

- First, the corporation is required to **carry back** the loss **three years** to offset (ie, reduce) any *prior* capital gains. Starting with the earliest of those years, the loss is applied chronologically until it is used up
- Second, the corporation will **carry forward** any remaining loss to offset *future* capital gains for up to **five years**; unused losses expire after the 5th year
- Capital losses carried over can only be used to offset **capital gains** (not ordinary income) and cannot generate (or increase) a net operating loss. These rules prevent corporations from significantly reducing taxable income in any single tax year by selling off capital assets to substantially lower their taxes. In such a case, the carryback would be **limited to taxable income**

Treatment of C Corporations' Net Capital Loss

Note: Carrybacks and carryforwards are always treated as a short-term capital loss.

A corporation incurred a $210,000 capital loss in Year 4 and has the following tax information:

	Year 4	Year 3	Year 2	Year 1
Capital gain (loss)	$(210,000)	$18,000	$43,000	$10,000
Taxable income	185,000	128,000	37,000	99,000

What amount of capital loss is available for carryover to future tax years?

Starting with the earliest of the three years, the loss is applied chronologically until it is used up. Any remaining loss is then carried forward to offset future capital gains for up to five years. A carried-back loss cannot create a net operating loss (NOL) in a prior year. In such a case, the carryback would be limited to taxable income.

Year 4 capital loss	$(210,000)
Less: Year 1 capital gains	10,000
Less: Year 2 capital gains*	37,000
Less: Year 3 capital gains	18,000
Capital loss carryforward to Year 5	$(145,000)

**In Year 2, the offset is limited by the taxable income.*

At the end of Year 8, Kappa Corp., a calendar-year C corporation, sold a tract of land for $10,000 it had originally purchased for $45,000 in Year 1. Kappa has reported taxable income of $20,000 every year from Year 4 to Year 10. Additionally, Kappa has reported a net capital gain of $5,000 every year from Year 4 to Year 7 and also in Year 9 and Year 10. In regards to Kappa's net capital loss from the land sale:

- First, Kappa carries back the loss to Year 5, Year 6, and Year 7 to offset the net capital gains in those years ($15,000 total)
- Second, Kappa carries forward the losses to Year 9 and Year 10 to offset the capital gains in those years ($10,000 total)
- With a net capital loss of $35,000 ($10,000 proceeds − $45,000 purchase price) generated in Year 8, $10,000 ($35,000 − $15,000 − $10,000) remains to be carried forward to Year 11
- Note: The capital gain generated in Year 4 cannot be offset because that period's gain occurred more than three years ago (ie, beyond the Year 8 carryback period)

Net Operating Loss

Many corporations are not profitable every year. If a corporation's allowable deductions exceed its gross income for tax purposes, a net operating loss (NOL) is generated. NOLs are useful because they can offset taxable income in other tax years. If an entity has multiple years' worth of NOLs to offset taxable income in a particular year, the oldest NOL is applied first. NOLs generally may be carried forward *indefinitely* and are **limited to 80% of taxable income** for the year to which they are carried.

However, due to NOL rules in the Tax Cuts and Jobs Act (TCJA) of 2017 and the CARES Act of 2020, NOL *carryover periods* and *deductibility* depend on the *specific tax year* in which the NOL was *generated*.

- **NOLs** generated in tax years **before 2018** can be carried forward 20 years and carried back two years. In either scenario, the NOLs can offset 100% of taxable income. This means the NOL carryover can reduce taxable income in the year carried over to $0. Note: The taxpayer may forgo the carryback
- **NOLs** generated **after 2020** can be carried forward indefinitely but **cannot** be carried back. These NOLs, when carried forward, can reduce taxable income by only 80%
  - For example, if an entity generates a $300 NOL in 2021 and has $200 of taxable income in 2022, the NOL can be carried forward but can reduce taxable income only to $40 [$200 − ($200 × 80%)]. The 80% limitation applies *after* deducting NOL carryforwards from NOLs generated prior to 2018 (ie, the 100% deductible NOLs)
- **NOLs** generated from **2018 to 2020** can be carried forward indefinitely and carried back five years. The usage of these NOLs is a hybrid between the two sets of rules above. Note: The taxpayer may forgo the carryback
  - If the NOLs will be used to offset taxable income in a tax year *prior to 2021*, 100% of taxable income can be offset (ie, reporting $0 of taxable income is permitted)
  - If the NOLs will be used to offset taxable income in tax year 2021 or later, 80% of taxable income can be offset (ie, taxable income cannot be reduced to $0). Once again, the 80% limitation applies after deducting NOL carryforwards from NOLs generated prior to 2018

Any current-year NOL (if applicable) is calculated prior to deducting charitable contributions or NOL carryovers from other years.

Year Generated	Carryforward	Carryback
Before 2018	20 years. Deduction = 100% of TI before NOL	2 years. Deduction = 100% of TI before NOL
2018 to 2020	Indefinite. Deduction = 100% (utilized in tax years before 2021) or 80% (utilized in 2021 and future tax years) of TI before NOL*	5 years. Deduction = 100% of TI before NOL
After 2020	Indefinite. Deduction = 80% of TI before NOL*	N/A

**80% deduction applies after deducting NOL carryforwards from NOLs generated prior to 2018 (if applicable).*

In 2023 and 2024, a corporation's business deductions exceeded its gross income by $50,000. In 2025, gross income exceeded business deductions by $20,000. Assume the post-2020 NOL rules apply (ie, NOL was generated and used after 2020).

- In 2025, the corporation can utilize $16,000 ($20,000 × 80%) of NOL and offset it against its taxable income. Because of the 80% limitation, the corporation reports taxable income of $4,000 ($20,000 − $16,000)
- After the NOL utilization in 2025, $34,000 ($50,000 − $16,000) of eligible NOL carryforward remains from the NOL generated in 2023 (ie, oldest NOL used first)
- The entire $50,000 NOL carryforward remains from 2024

Corporation Tax Credits

Representative Task (Application): Calculate the credits allowable as a reduction to tax for a C corporation.

There are many tax credits that corporations can use to offset their tax liability. Many of these focus on specific industries and are not testable on the exam. The most common credits are presented below.

Foreign Tax Credit

The U.S. taxes worldwide income, which is income from all sources, including income from foreign countries. The purpose of this credit is to prevent double taxation of foreign income that is subject to income tax in the foreign jurisdiction.

The credit is limited to the *foreign tax credit limitation*, which is computed as the *lower* of:

Foreign income tax paid, or

$$\text{U.S. tax on worldwide income} \times \frac{\text{Foreign-sourced taxable income}}{\text{Worldwide taxable income}}$$

Excess foreign tax credits carry back one year and forward 10 years. The excess amount is the foreign taxes paid or accrued for a tax year that exceeds the foreign tax credit limitation.

ABC Corporation has $320,000 of U.S.-source income and $70,000 of foreign-source income, and ABC paid foreign taxes of $14,000. The U.S. income tax liability before the foreign tax credit is $42,000. ABC's foreign tax credit is limited to the lower of the foreign tax paid of $14,000 or:

$$\text{U.S. tax on worldwide income} \times \frac{\text{Foreign-sourced taxable income}}{\text{Worldwide taxable income}}$$

$$\$42{,}000 \times \frac{\$70{,}000}{(\$320{,}000 + \$70{,}000)} = \$7{,}538$$

ABC's foreign tax credit is limited to $7,538. ABC has a foreign tax credit carryback/carryforward of $6,462 ($14,000 − $7,538).

A corporation may choose to take either a credit or a deduction for eligible foreign income taxes paid or accrued. The choice is made annually.

General Business Credit

The purpose of most business tax credits is to provide tax incentives for companies that engage in certain activities (eg, enhanced oil recovery, research) that help stimulate the economy or address societal concerns (eg, low-income housing, renewable energy). These credits are *nonrefundable*, but unused credits may be **carried back (one year)** and **carried forward (20 years)** to offset taxable income.

More than 30 such business tax credits are currently available. Although each credit is calculated separately, taxpayers are allowed to combine all their business credits into one *general business credit* each tax year (subject to limitations). Combining the credits simplifies reporting and recordkeeping under one uniform set of rules.

The general business credit is the sum of:

- The business credit carryforwards carried to the current taxable year,
- The amount of the current-year business credits, and
- The business credit carrybacks carried to the current taxable year.

While each credit is calculated independently, the combination of credits is subject to an overall limit.

- The general business credit is limited to the taxpayer's net income tax reduced by 25% of *the net income tax* that exceeds $25,000
- *Net income tax* is the regular tax liability, reduced by certain nonrefundable tax credits (eg, foreign tax credit)

General Business Credit

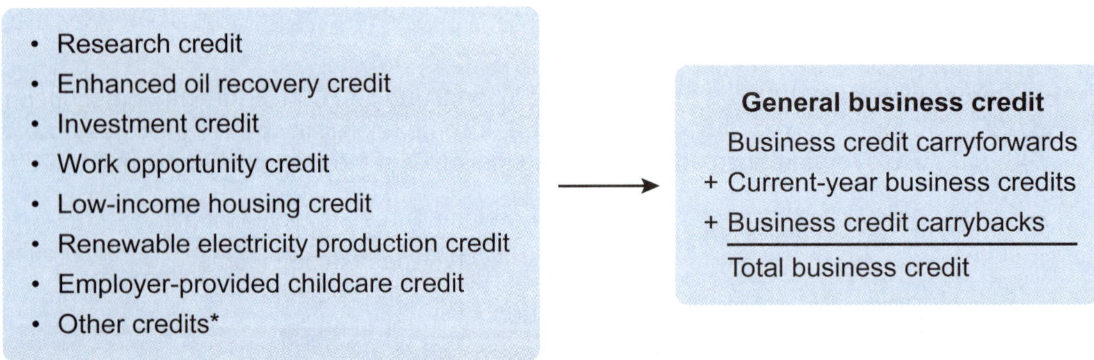

**More than 30 separate credits*

A corporation has net income tax of $125,000 this year and a general business tax credit of $70,000. The corporation has no other credits. What is the maximum general business credit allowed in the current year?

The maximum credit would be $100,000 [$125,000 net income tax − ($125,000 net income tax − $25,000 statutory threshold) × 25%]. Since the credit is only $70,000, the entire amount can be claimed in the current year.

Admiral Corporation's general business credit for the current year is $120,000. Admiral's net income tax is $130,000. Admiral has no other tax credits. The general business credit allowed for the tax year is computed as follows.

Net income tax	$130,000
Less: statutory threshold	(25,000)
Net amount	$105,000
Statutory percentage	× 25%
25% of net income tax > $25,000	$ 26,250

The maximum credit Admiral can claim is $103,750 ($130,000 net income tax − $26,250). Admiral has $16,250 ($120,000 business credit available − $103,750 currently used) of unused general business credits that may be carried back one year and then forward 20 years.

Rehabilitation Credit

A credit is allowed for the rehabilitation of certain buildings. The rehabilitation credit percentage depends upon the type of expenditure. Expenditures to rehabilitate certified historic structure are eligible for a 20% credit. The credit is claimed evenly over a five-year period.

- The adjusted basis of the property is reduced by the amount of credit
- To qualify for the credit, straight-line depreciation or ADS must be used for the building

Small Employer Health Insurance Credit

An eligible small employer (ESE) can claim a credit equal to 50% of its nonelective contributions for health insurance for its employees (25% for small tax-exempt employers). To be eligible for the credit, an ESE has to contribute at least 50% of the cost of the employee's insurance premiums under a contribution arrangement.

- The full amount of the credit is available only to an ESE that has 10 or fewer full-time equivalent employees and whose employees have average annual full-time equivalent wages of less than $32,400 (2024). The credit is fully phased out once the number of full-time employees reaches 25 and/or the average wages reach $64,800 (2024)

Work Opportunity Tax Credit (WOTC)

This **elective** credit is calculated on the amount of wages paid per eligible employee during the first year of employment. The credit is 40% of qualified wages, with a maximum credit of $2,400.

- The credit is targeted at certain employee groups, such as veterans and long-term unemployment recipients
- The WOTC reduces the deduction for wages

Research Credit

Incremental research expenditures are eligible for a 20% credit. The research must be conducted within the U.S. and does not apply to research for commercial production, surveys, or social science research. Taxpayers may elect to use an alternative simplified research credit. This is equal to 14% of the excess of qualified research expenses over 50% of the average research expenses for the last three years.

Employer-Paid Medical and Family Leave Credit

Businesses can claim a general business tax credit equal to 12.5% of wages paid to qualifying employees while on family and medical leave. The employee must receive at least 50% of the wages normally paid to an employee. All qualifying employees must receive at least two weeks of annual paid family and medical leave.

- The 12.5% is increased by 0.25 percentage points for each percentage point by which the wages paid exceed 50%
- Credit percentage can never exceed 25%

Business Energy Credits

Congress created the business energy credit as a tax incentive to implement the government policy to encourage the production and use of, or conversion to, business equipment using energy sources other than oil or gas as a primary source of industrial or agricultural energy. The energy credit comprises numerous credits with various percentages ranging generally from 10% to 30% for property such as:

- Qualified fuel cell property
- Solar energy equipment property
- Qualified small wind energy property
- Waste energy recovery property
- Geothermal property
- Qualified microturbine property
- Combined heat and power system property
- Geothermal heat systems property

The Inflation Reduction Act of 2022 added a new advanced manufacturing credit. The credit is 25% of the investment in tangible depreciable property that is either constructed, reconstructed, or erected by the taxpayer or is new property acquired by the taxpayer. The tangible property can include, in addition to equipment, buildings or building portions if they are not used for office space, administrative functions, or other functions not related to manufacturing. The investment has to be made in a facility whose primary purpose is the manufacture of semiconductors or semiconductor manufacturing equipment.

19.02 State and Local Tax Issues

Nexus with Respect to State and Local Taxation

Representative Task (Remembering & Understanding): Define the general concept and rationale of nexus with respect to state and local taxation.

Because many businesses conduct operations in more than one state, a significant issue is determining which states have the authority to levy a tax on a particular business. For example, a business that is incorporated in Tennessee may have a manufacturing plant in Arizona and its headquarters in South Carolina, and it sells a product to a company in Michigan. Which state(s) has the authority to tax the transaction? If a state has **nexus** for a transaction, that means it has the authority to tax the transaction.

Definitions

To determine nexus, there are some definitions that need to be known.

Domestic Corporations: Entities incorporated under the laws of a particular state.

Foreign Corporations: Corporations incorporated in another state.

In general, an entity is allowed to do business in states other than the one in which it was formed or is physically located. **Public Law 86-272**, referred to as the **Interstate Income Act of 1959**, allows a business to go, or send a representative, into a state to solicit orders for goods without being subject to a net *income tax*. The law applies exclusively to orders for tangible personal property and either:

- Orders solicited by employees that are approved, and shipped from, outside the state; or
- Orders solicited by independent contractors that are shipped from outside the state.

A state may impose an income tax on an entity that is doing business in that state if the entity establishes **nexus** in a state, indicating that it has a presence in that state.

Paint Corporation, a State A corporation, sends sales representatives to State B who maintain a show room for one week. As a result of these advertising efforts, State B residents order $100,000 of paint. The paint orders were approved in State A and shipped from State A to State B. Is Paint Corporation subject to State B income tax?

No, Paint Corporation is not subject to State B income tax. While Paint Corporation established nexus through its presence in State B, it is protected against State B income tax by Public Law 86-272 because its solicitation efforts were for the sale of tangible, personal property.

Using the same facts as above, assume Paint Corporation has $100,000 of paint sales to State B residents and, in addition, provides $50,000 of painting services to State B residents. Is Paint Corporation subject to State B income tax?

Yes, Paint Corporation is subject to State B income tax. Public Law 86-272 only protects out-of-state sellers against state income tax nexus for the sale of tangible, personal property. Here, Paint Corporation sold tangible, personal property and provided services in State B. Thus, Paint Corporation is not protected by Public Law 86-272.

Public Law 86-272 does not define the term "solicitation" as it applies to the protected solicitation of sales. However, the U.S. Supreme Court has provided guidance on whether specific activities constitute solicitation.

Public Law 86-272 Solicitation Protection

Activity	Protected	Nonprotected
Advertising	✔	
Providing free samples or promotional materials	✔	
Maintaining a sample room for two weeks or less ("trade show rule")	✔	
Owning personal property used in sales activities	✔	
Training non-sales-representative employees		✘
Making repairs		✘
Installing or supervising installation of property		✘
Checking customer inventory level for reorder	✔	
Communicating customer inquiries or feedback to home office	✔	
Recruiting, training, or evaluating sales representatives through use of homes or hotels	✔	
Maintaining an office (other than an in-home office)		✘
Securing deposits or approving/accepting orders		✘
Investigating creditworthiness		✘
Collecting outstanding accounts or repossessing property		✘

Note: Nonprotected activities are normally subject to a de minimis threshold. Immaterial, nonprotected activities may not give rise to an income tax obligation.

Blue Corporation, a State A corporation, engages in the following activities:

- Sends a sales representative to State B who provides free samples for the company's product
- Sends a sales representative to State C who communicates customer feedback to the State A home office
- Sends a sales representative to State D who advertises the company's services
- Sends a sales representative to State E who repairs company products
- Sends a sales representative to State F who accepts down payments for the sale of the company's product

With which states does Blue Corporation receive protection from Public Law 86-272?

State	PL 86-272 Protection	Explanation
State B	Yes	Advertising is a protected form of solicitation
State C	Yes	Communicating customer feedback is a protected form of solicitation
State D	No	Public Law 86-272 only protects the solicitation for the sale of goods, not services
State E	No	Making repairs is a nonprotected activity under Public Law 86-272
State F	No	Accepting down payments is a nonprotected activity under Public Law 86-272

Unless Blue Corporation wants to establish nexus in State D, State E, and State F, it should avoid engaging in these activities or, alternatively, take different actions that are considered protected forms of solicitation under Public Law 86-272.

Judicial Decisions

There are several judicial decisions that provide important guidance for determining nexus.

Complete Auto Transit v. Brady: The Supreme Court developed four tests to determine jurisdiction to tax:

1. Business activity must have substantial nexus with state
2. The tax must be fairly apportioned
3. The tax cannot discriminate against interstate commerce
4. The tax must be fairly related to services that the state provides

South Dakota v. Wayfair, Inc. and Quill Corp. v. North Dakota: In the *Wayfair* decision, the Supreme Court held that states could assert nexus for sales and use tax purposes *without requiring a seller's physical presence in the state.*

This overturned the Supreme Court's decision in *Quill Corp. v. North Dakota*. The Supreme Court found that the ruling in *Quill* banning sales tax collection when businesses lack physical presence in a state was incorrect. The Court reasoned that *Quill* was "a judicially created tax shelter for businesses that decide to limit their physical presence and still sell goods and services" to a state's residents.

The practical implication of *Wayfair* is that states can levy the sales and use tax on those who reside in their state and purchase items sold in other states via the internet. That is, the state can still levy a sales and use tax on the online transaction even if a resident purchases from a business that does not have a physical location in the resident's state.

Nexus

A state may only impose tax on an out-of-state corporation if there is **nexus**, a sufficient physical or economic connection, with the state. Although the requirements for nexus vary among states, nexus is generally created for income tax purposes when an entity meets *any* of the following:

- Is domiciled in the state
- Derives income from sources within the state other than from the sale of tangible personal property
- Has employees in the state performing duties other than soliciting sales
- Owns capital or property (eg, an office building) in the state

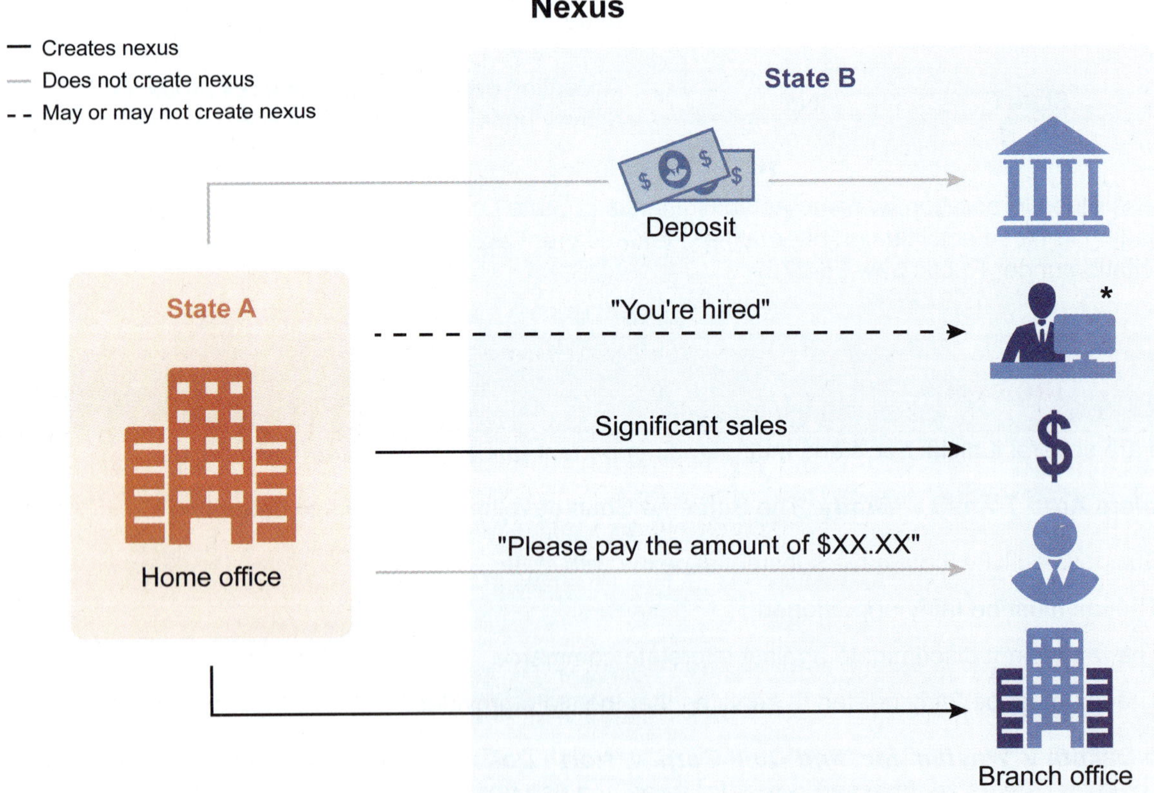

Nexus depends on where employees perform services, not where they reside.

Traditionally, states established nexus through *physical* presence (eg, having a branch office in a state). While this nexus standard still exists, many states have expanded the definition to include a form of *economic* nexus.

For example, the Multistate Tax Commission has adopted the **Factor Presence Nexus Standard**, namely, a model law that concludes "there is state income tax nexus" if any of the following economic criteria are *exceeded* in a given state:

- $50,000 of property;
- $50,000 of payroll;
- $500,000 of sales; or
- 25% of the entity's total property, payroll, or sales.

Remember that states, as sovereign entities, set their own tax standards. Thus, a state may adopt the model Factor Presence Nexus Standard as constructed or, alternatively, adopt greater or lesser standards/ thresholds to establish economic nexus.

Nexus is the key in tax planning for corporations engaging in activities in other states. In fact, most corporations conduct a nexus study to determine the states with which it has created nexus through physical, electronic, or other economic means. In this framework, corporations should strive to establish nexus with low-tax states and avoid nexus with high-tax states.

Red Corporation, a State A corporation, engages in the following activities:

- Sells $1 million of goods in State A
- Maintains a branch office in State B
- Deposits $1,000 into a State C bank account
- Hires a State D resident employee who works in State A

With which states does Red Corporation have income tax nexus?

State	Income Tax Nexus	Explanation
State A	Yes	Red Corporation creates nexus through commercial domicile and State A sales
State B	Yes	Red Corporation creates nexus through the State B branch office
State C	No	Generally, depositing money into an external bank account, by itself, does not create nexus
State D	No	Nexus is determined by employee performance of service location, not based on employee residence

Apportionment and Allocation with Respect to State and Local Taxation

Representative Task (Remembering & Understanding): Define the general concept and rationale of apportionment and allocation with respect to state and local taxation.

A corporation may have nexus with more than one state for state and local income tax purposes if it sells its products and/or services in more than one state. If that is the case, then the business income has to be apportioned to the states that have nexus. Business income is apportioned among the states in which it is earned based on apportionment factors such as sales, property, and payroll. Generally, each state establishes its own apportionment formula utilizing a combination of one or more of these factors.

Business Income and Nonbusiness Income

Corporations must divide the state tax base between **business income** (eg, sale of inventory) and **nonbusiness income** (eg, sale of an investment). Business income is generally generated:

- From business's regular operations (transactional test), or
- From the sale of property that is an integral part of the business (functional test).

Nonbusiness income is generally investment income and income from transactions **not** part of regular operations. If investment income is generated by regular business operations, it is business income.

Businesses must **apportion** *business income* (divide income among states) and **allocate** *nonbusiness income* (assign income to a particular state) in accordance with the Uniform Division of Income for Tax Purposes Act (UDITPA).

- UDITPA is a model act that was adopted by the National Conference of Commissioners on Uniform State Laws and the American Bar Association to promote uniformity in state allocation and apportionment rules. Not all states have adopted this act. The act provides that if income-producing activity occurs in more than one state, the receipts are assigned to the state where the greatest cost of performance was incurred
- Intangible assets are excluded from the property factor under the standard formula. If the allocation and apportionment provisions of UDITPA do not fairly represent the extent of the taxpayer's business activity in the state, the taxpayer may petition for, or the tax administrator may require, with respect to all or any part of the taxpayer's activity, if reasonable:
    - Separate accounting
    - The exclusion of any one or more of the factors
    - The inclusion of one or more additional factors that will fairly represent the taxpayer's business activity in this state
    - The employment of any other method to effectuate an equitable allocation and apportionment of the taxpayer's income

Apportionment vs. Allocation of Income (When Nexus Exists)

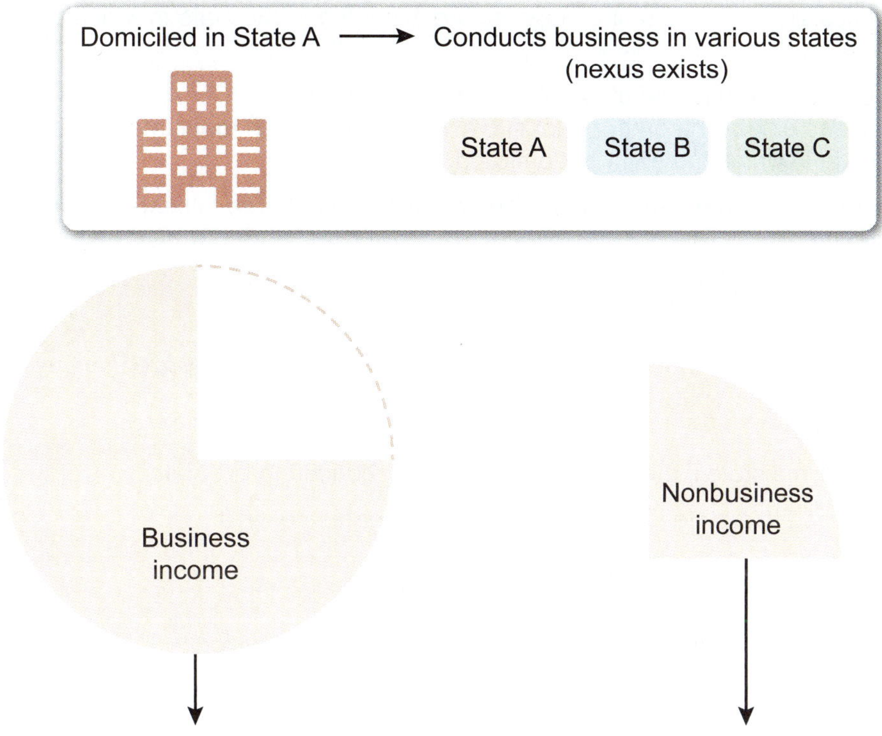

Apportioned (divided) among the states generally using a three-factor formula (sales, payroll, property)

Allocated (assigned) to a state generally based on nature of the property (ie, real property net rents allocated to the state where property is located)

Allocation of Nonbusiness Income

In general, states have discretion to apply different tax rules to different types of income. Since not all income generated by an entity is from its business operations, the allocation of nonbusiness income is based on the nature of the income or the nature of the property.

Net Rents and Royalties

- Net rents and royalties from real property are generally allocated to the state in which the property is *located*, while net rents or royalties from tangible personal property are generally allocated to the state in which the *property is used*
- If the entity is not subject to income tax in the state in which property is used, net rents and royalties are allocated to the state in which the entity is domiciled (headquartered)
- If the property is utilized in multiple jurisdictions, income will be allocated to each on the basis of the ratio of the number of days the property earned rents or royalties in that state to the total number of days on which rents or royalties were earned from use of the property

Capital Gains and Losses

- Capital gains and losses on the sale of real estate are allocated to the state in which the real estate is *located*
- Capital gains and losses on the sale of tangible personal property are allocated to the state in which the property is *located* unless the entity is not subject to income tax in that state, in which case it is allocated to the state in which the entity is domiciled
- Capital gains and losses on the sale of intangible personal property are allocated to the state in which the entity is *domiciled*

Royalties on Patents and Copyrights

- Royalties on patents and copyrights are allocated to the state in which they are *used* by the payer of the royalties, or, when the entity is not subject to income tax in that state, they are allocated to the entity's state of *domicile*
  - A patent is utilized in a state if the patented product is produced in the state
  - A copyright is utilized in a state if printing or publication originates in it

Interest and Dividends

Interest and dividends are allocated to the state in which the entity is domiciled.

Small Company is domiciled in Oregon. Small has invested some of its excess cash reserves with a financial firm in North Carolina. The investment income earned from these investments is allocated to and taxed in Oregon because it is nonbusiness income.

If the investment was part of Small's regular business operations, then the income would be business income and would be apportioned to North Carolina because it is business income.

Green Corporation, a State A corporation, has a State A tax base of $525,000. Of this amount, $200,000 derives from passive income (eg, interest, rent, and dividends), meaning Green Corporation has $325,000 of business income ($525,000 − $200,000). Thus, using state tax rules, Green Corporation will apportion the $325,000 of business income and allocate the $200,000 of nonbusiness income.

During the year, Red Corporation, a State A corporation, had $10,000,000 of taxable income, comprising $7,500,000 business income and $2,500,000 nonbusiness income. The $2,500,000 of nonbusiness income consisted of:

$2,000,000 rental income from real property located in State B

$300,000 dividend income

$200,000 interest income

What is Red Corporation's allocated nonbusiness income to State A and to State B?

- State A is allocated the $300,000 of dividend income and the $200,000 of interest income because Red Corporation is domiciled in State A
- State B is allocated the $2,000,000 of rental income because the real property generating the rental income is located in State B

State Taxable Income Using Apportionment Factors

Representative Task (Application): Calculate state taxable income using the applicable apportionment factors given a specific scenario.

Apportionment of Business Income

The U.S. Supreme Court has allowed states great flexibility to choose an apportioning formula and to tax income of an interstate business. For example, some states use only one apportionment factor. Others vary in how they weigh the factors. In apportioning business income, states generally set their apportionment formula based on some combination of three factors: **property, payroll, and sales**.

Property factor equals the value of the entity's real and tangible personal property in the state, divided by the value of all the entity's real and tangible property (**Average value of property in state / Value of all property**).

- Property is valued at its average for the year using historical cost or book value (Cost − Accumulated depreciation) depending on the state
- Property rented or leased *by* the business for operations is included and is valued at *eight times* net annual rent
- Property is included only if used in the production of business income
- Property the business rents (investment property) is excluded
- Property in transit (eg, inventory) is sourced to the state of destination

Payroll factor equals the total amount paid for compensation (payroll) in the state by the entity, divided by the total compensation paid everywhere by the entity (**Total payroll in state / Total payroll**).

- Payroll includes salaries, bonuses, commissions, and other compensation including fringe benefits, if taxable under federal law
- Payroll generally does *not* include payments to independent contractors
- Compensation is included only if related to the production of business income
- Payroll for each employee is apportioned to a single state based on where the employee performs the majority of services

Sales factor equals total sales by the entity in the state during the tax period, divided by the entity's total sales made everywhere (**Total sales in state / Total sales**).

- Sales of tangible, personal property are sourced to the state of destination; however, under the throwback rule, if the business does not have nexus with the state of destination, then the sale is "thrown back" to the state of shipment (eg, if shipped from State A to State B but no income tax nexus with State B, then source to State A)
- Sales of services are apportioned to the state of performance; however, a state may choose to apportion sales of services based on market-based sourcing (ie, where the client is located)
- Government sales are sourced to the state from which they were shipped

During the current year, Orange Corporation, a State A corporation, has the following historical cost for real and personal property:

State	Beginning Property	Ending Property	Net Annual Rents
State A	$100,000	$200,000	$50,000
State B	300,000	400,000	0
Total	$400,000	$600,000	$50,000

Assuming income tax nexus, what are the property factors for State A and State B?

State	Value of Property (Average)	+	Value of Rented Property	=	Total Property	Property Factor
State A	$150,000 = ($100,000 + $200,000) / 2		$400,000 = $50,000 × 8		$550,000 = $150,000 + $400,000	61.1% = $550,000 / $900,000
State B	$350,000 = ($300,000 + $400,000) / 2		$0		$350,000 = $350,000 + $0	38.9% = $350,000 / $900,000
Total	$500,000		$400,000		$900,000	100%

Weighted Factor Formulas

In application of the apportionment factors, some states use an **equally weighted three-factor formula**. Here, the three ratios are added together and divided by three. The result is multiplied by business income to determine the amount of business income apportioned to the state.

However, many states use a **double-weighted sales factor** or use only a **single sales factor** to apportion income. In these situations, the formula above would be adjusted, but the apportionment concept remains the same; each factor is calculated as the state's percentage over the total in all the states.

State Equally Weighted, Three-Factor Apportionment Formula

$$\text{Share of income apportioned to state} = \left[\frac{\dfrac{\text{Statewide property}}{\text{Total property}} + \dfrac{\text{Statewide payroll}}{\text{Total payroll}} + \dfrac{\text{Statewide sales}}{\text{Total sales}}}{3} \right] \times \text{Total income}$$

Assume Multistate Corp. conducts business in two states and has provided relevant information as follows:

Item	Total	State A	State B
Sales	$4,000,000	$1,000,000	$3,000,000
Average property	5,000,000	2,000,000	3,000,000
Compensation	1,000,000	200,000	800,000
Interest income (nonbusiness)	40,000		
Business taxable income before apportionment	500,000		

State A and State B use the UDITPA apportionment formula to compute state taxable income for Multistate Corp.'s business income. Multistate Corp. is headquartered in State B.

Apportionment of the **business income:**

State A

The sales factor is $1,000,000 / $4,000,000 = 25%.

The property factor is $2,000,000 / $5,000,000 = 40%.

The compensation factor is $200,000 / $1,000,000 = 20%.

The apportionment factor is (25% + 40% + 20%) / 3 = 28.33%. As a result, $500,000 × 28.33% = $141,667 of Multistate Corp.'s business income is taxed by State A.

State B

The sales factor is $3,000,000 / $4,000,000 = 75%.

The property factor is $3,000,000 / $5,000,000 = 60%.

The compensation factor is $800,000 / $1,000,000 = 80%.

The apportionment factor is (75% + 60% + 80%) / 3 = 71.67%. As a result, $500,000 business taxable income × 71.67% = $358,333 of Multistate Corp.'s business income would be taxed by State B.

The interest income is **nonbusiness income**, so it is all allocated to State B, where Multistate is headquartered.

What if State A gives double weight to the **sales** factor?

The apportionment factor would now be (25% + 25% + 40% + 20%) / 4 = 27.5%. State B's apportionment factor would be the same at 71.67%. Note that the total allocation now does not add up to 100% but to 99.17% (27.5% + 71.67%).

During the current year, Red Corporation, a State A corporation, had a $10,000,000 state tax base, comprising $7,500,000 of business income and $2,500,000 of nonbusiness income. Assume Red Corporation has income tax nexus and the associated property, payroll, and sales with the below states:

State	Property	Payroll	Sales
State A	$ 400,000	$1,350,000	$2,300,000
State B	100,000	150,000	200,000
State C	200,000	550,000	900,000
State D	300,000	950,000	1,600,000
Total	$1,000,000	$3,000,000	$5,000,000

With regard to State B, what is Red Corporation's sales, property, and payroll factors?

10% property factor ($100,000 State B property / $1,000,000 total property)

5% payroll factor ($150,000 State B payroll / $3,000,000 total payroll)

4% sales factor ($200,000 State B sales / $5,000,000 total sales)

What is State B's apportioned share of business income if Red Corporation uses an equally weighted three-factor, a double-weighted sales factor, and a single sales factor?

$475,000 equally weighted three-factor State B apportioned business income
(10% property + 5% payroll + 4% sales) / 3 × $7,500,000 business income

$431,250 double-weighted sales factor State B apportioned business income
(10% property + 5% payroll + 4% + 4% sales) / 4 × $7,500,000 business income

$300,000 single sales factor State B apportioned business income
4% sales × $7,500,000 business income

REG 20
S Corporations

REG 20: S Corporations

20.01 Eligibility and Election

Overview

Corporations are a type of legal entity recognized by the U.S. tax system as a separate taxpaying entity. A **C corporation** files a tax return (**Form 1120**) and pays income taxes on its taxable income. C corporations that desire to be treated for tax purposes in a manner like partnerships (ie, filing a tax return but not paying taxes directly) may elect **S corporation** status if eligible. An S corporation retains its legal corporate status and corporate characteristics. For example, shareholders:

- Enjoy limited liability, and
- Can be employees (separation of ownership and management).

However, unlike C corporations, S corporations act as conduits for taxable income (**flow-through or pass-through entities**). That is, an S corporation files an information return (**Form 1120-S**) reporting its income or loss. The income or loss is categorized (**Sch. K**) and allocated to the shareholders (**Sch. K-1**), who must report their allocations on their personal tax returns.

Designation as an S corporation is **solely a tax classification**. Corporations are formed under applicable state incorporation laws (ie, legally, there is no S versus C distinction). For tax purposes, a corporation defaults to C classification. If a corporation is eligible for and makes an election, C status is overridden, and S status supersedes. Other eligible entities (eg, LLCs) can also elect S corporation tax status.

C corporation rules are found in Internal Revenue Code **Subchapter C**. S corporation rules are found in Internal Revenue Code **Subchapter S**. For S corporations, if the C and S rules overlap, S rules take precedence. However, if S rules do not address a situation, C rules apply. For example, there are no S rules regarding the tax treatment of a shareholder's exchange of property for stock. Consequently, Code Section 351 applies just as it does for C corporations.

The S corporation rules were created to encourage the growth of small and family-owned businesses. Prior to the 1950s, when the S corporation rules were enacted, an entrepreneur had only two options: form a partnership and avoid double taxation but expose themselves to higher risk or form a C corporation, which would shield the entrepreneur from risk but impose more than one layer of taxation on profits.

The S corporation option allows for the best of both worlds. Companies retain legal corporate characteristics, are treated as flow-through entities for tax purposes, and have ownership restrictions designed to make S corporation status available to only small businesses.

Eligibility and Election

Representative Task (Remembering & Understanding): Recall eligible shareholders for an S corporation for tax purposes.

Shareholder Eligibility Requirements

Certain shareholder requirements must be satisfied for a business to meet S corporation eligibility **(simple and small)**

There can be no more than **100 shareholders** (family members and their estates, with a common ancestor no more than six generations above, and their spouses may be treated as a single shareholder for purposes of this rule).

- Co-owners of stock count as one shareholder
- Spouses count as one shareholder unless a divorce has been finalized
- Each beneficiary of a shareholding trust is counted as a separate shareholder

All shareholders must be **individuals**; no C corporations, partnerships, or other trusts are allowable as shareholders.

- **Exception:** Fiduciaries who own shares for the direct benefit of a person, including the following: estates (bankruptcy or testamentary) and testamentary trusts

All shareholders must be U.S. **residents or citizens**; nonresident aliens are *not* eligible.

An S corporation can own stock in a C corporation or an S corporation or be a partner in a partnership. In addition, an S corporation can be a parent corporation, but it cannot be a subsidiary of any corporation except another subchapter S corporation.

S Corporation: Family Members Who Count as a Single Shareholder

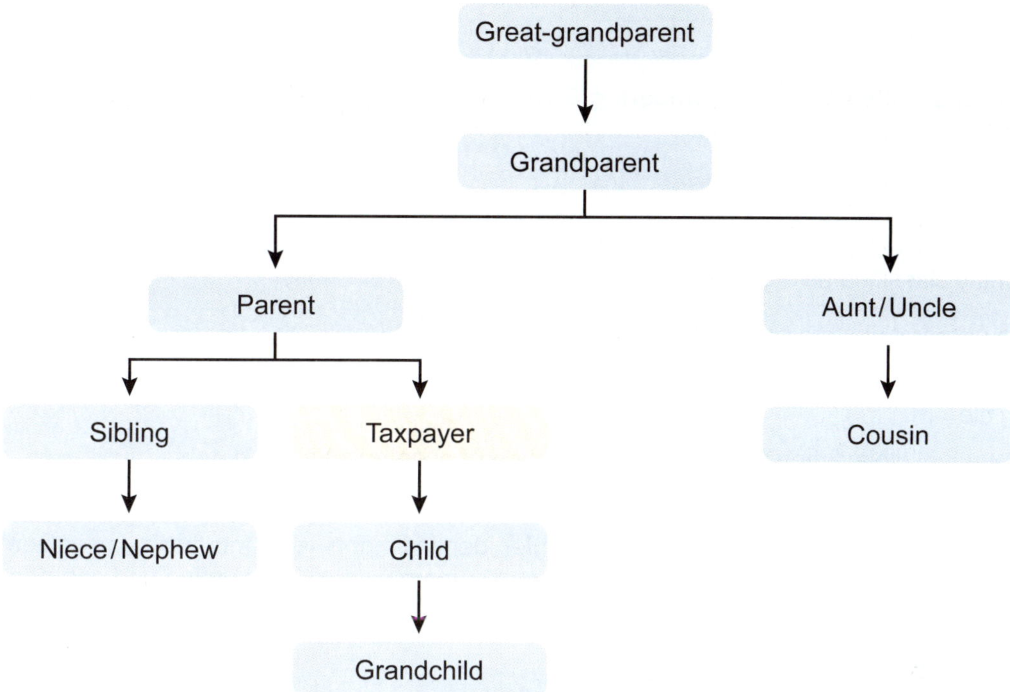

Note: Includes half, step, and adopted relations as well as spouses of any member in the tree.

A taxpayer gives one share of stock in Harold Corp., an S corporation, to each of the following individuals: a nephew, a son, an adopted stepdaughter, and a grandson.

After the distribution of the stock, **no new additional shareholders** will result from the distribution.

Shareholders who are directly related and no more than six generations removed are treated as a single shareholder, making it easier for family businesses to qualify for an S election. Each of the shareholders in this example meets the definition of family for S corporation ownership purposes, so they are counted as a single shareholder.

S Corporation Eligibility Requirements

Representative Task (Remembering & Understanding): Recall S corporation eligibility requirements for tax purposes.

To qualify for an S election, a corporation must meet eligibility requirements. The corporation must be a U.S. **domestic** entity classified as a corporation for tax purposes.

- Foreign corporations are not eligible
- Certain members of affiliated groups, parents of subsidiaries, financial institutions, and DISCs are not eligible
- Banks are ineligible if they use the reserve method of accounting for bad debts

There can be only **one class** of stock (eg, no preferred stock). This requirement must be fully understood. One class of stock means that each share must confer identical rights to distributions and liquidation proceeds. Voting rights may differ. Thus, two classes of common stock—one voting and one nonvoting—do **not** violate the one class of stock requirement.

A taxpayer wants to create an S corporation called MRP. Because the taxpayer wants all her shareholders to have an equal voice in future decisions made for the company, she gives them equal voting rights and decides that those who take on a more active role in the company will have priority in terms of distribution and liquidation rights.

Unfortunately, MRP is not eligible to make an S election. The one class of stock requirement mandates that distributions to owners must be made on a pro rata basis determined by stock ownership percentages (not how much a shareholder participates in business activities).

Requirements for S Corporation Election (Think Small & Simple)

- No more than 100 shareholders
- Shareholders must be individuals (or certain estates or trusts)
- Shareholders must be either U.S. residents or citizens
- Must be a domestic corporation
- Only one class of stock is allowed

S Election

The election to become an S corporation must be made **unanimously (100%)** by the shareholders (including those with nonvoting shares), since this decision means they agree to be personally liable for the income taxes resulting from the election. Both spouses must consent if the stock is jointly owned.

The election can be made at any time on **Form 2553**, but it must be made by the 15th day of the 3rd month of the tax year (March 15 for calendar corporations, **2.5 months**) for it to be effective for the current year. Any election made after that cannot become effective until the start of the following tax year.

If a timely election is made retroactive to the start of the current year, all S corporation requirements must be met in the entire preelection period, **including unanimous shareholder consent**. If the conditions are not met during the preelection period (ie, missing consent from a shareholder who owned shares during the preelection period), the election will be deferred to the start of the following year.

Effective Date of S Corporation Election

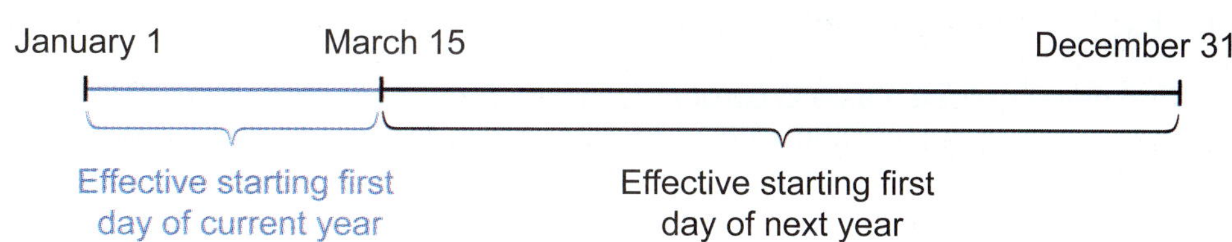

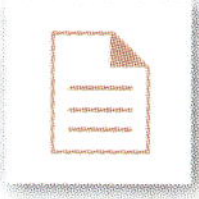

Village Corp., a June 30 fiscal-year-end corporation, began business in Year 1. Village makes a valid S Corporation election on September 5, Year 8, with the unanimous consent of its shareholders. The eligibility requirements for S status were met throughout Year 8. On what date did Village's S status become effective?

Village Corp. **made the election within the first 2.5 months** of its tax year (September 15 for a June 30 fiscal-year-end corporation), met all S corporation requirements for the period, and had unanimous consent. As a result, the election will be effective for the current year, on **July 1, Year 8**.

On February 10, Year 4, Ace Corp., a calendar-year corporation, elects S corporation status, and all shareholders owning shares as of that date consent to the election. Consent is not received from a shareholder who sold all their shares on January 15, Year 4. Ace meets all other eligibility requirements for S status during the preelection portion of the year.

If a timely election is made retroactive to the start of the current year, all S corporation requirements must be met in the entire preelection period, **including unanimous shareholder consent**. If the conditions are not met during the preelection period (ie, missing consent from a shareholder who owned shares during the preelection period), the election will be deferred to the start of the following year.

January 1, Year 5, is the earliest date Ace can be recognized as an S corporation.

S Corporations Converted from C Corporations

When C corporations elect S corporation status, special rules apply to ensure that any **accumulated earnings and profits (AEP)** from prior C corporation years are taxed as dividends when distributed. This prevents a C corporation from electing S corporation status merely to avoid tax on distributions that would have been taxable dividends had the S election not been made.

For S corporations with AEP at the time of conversion, a separate account, called an **accumulated adjustments account** (AAA), must be maintained. The AAA is an accumulation of income or losses from the time the entity has been an S corporation.

An S corporation that never operated as a C corporation or an S corporation without AEP is not subject to these special rules. In these cases, distributions are nontaxable to the extent of shareholder stock basis, and if the distributions exceed the shareholder stock basis, capital gain is realized equal to the excess distribution. This treatment is similar to that of partnerships.

S Corporation Status Termination

Representative Task (Application): Identify situations in which S corporation status would be revoked or terminated for tax purposes.

Termination of S corporation status can occur through three circumstances. The corporation can:

- *Voluntarily revoke* its election,
- *Involuntarily terminate* the election from **failure to meet requirements**, or
- *Involuntarily terminate* the election from **an excess of passive investment income**.

Voluntary Revocation

A **voluntary revocation** of the S election is made if shareholders holding **more than half** of the shares (including nonvoting shares) of the S corporation stock agree. The corporation files a statement with the IRS revoking the election and specifying the effective date. If a date is not specified, a *voluntary* revocation made:

- Within the first 2.5 months of the year is effective on the 1st day of that taxable year
- After the first 2.5 months of the year shall be effective on the 1st day of the following year

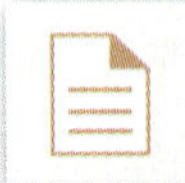

An S corporation has a December 31 year end. A revocation not specifying a revocation date that is made on or before March 15, Year 8, is effective as of January 1, Year 8.

A revocation not specifying a revocation date that is made after March 15, Year 8, is effective as of January 1, Year 9.

If a revocation is filed March 11, Year 8, and specifies a revocation date of July 1, Year 8, the corporation ceases to be an S corporation on July 1, Year 8.

For purposes of determining when a S corporation status is effective, as well as for determining when an S corporation is voluntarily terminated without specifying a revocation date, the 2.5-month rule applies.

That is, if election or revocation (without specifying a revocation date) happens within 2.5 months of the beginning of the tax year, then it is effective as of the beginning of that tax year. Otherwise, it is effective as of the beginning of next tax year.

Involuntary Termination

An S corporation's status will be revoked automatically (**involuntary termination**) if an event occurs that causes it to violate one of the small and simple requirements (eg, if shares are sold to a nonresident alien). The termination is effective on the date of the violation.

Per Sec. 1362, termination will ***involuntarily*** occur if the S corporation has passive investment income **(PII)** exceeding *25% of its gross receipts* for each of three consecutive years and if, during these three years, the corporation was a corporation with AEP attributable to **prior C corporation status**. If the S corporation never operated as a C corporation or does not have C corporation AEP, this provision *does not* apply.

- The termination for excess PII is effective on the 1st day of the tax year following the 3rd consecutive year of violation. PII includes receipts from rents, royalties, dividends, interest (including tax-exempt interest), and annuities. While net capital gain is included in gross receipts, it is not included in PII

Once an S corporation's status has been terminated or voluntarily revoked, it cannot reelect such status for **five years without IRS permission**. The waiting period is required to prevent corporations from alternating entity types based on their current tax situation. The entity may request IRS permission for earlier election if more than 50% of its shares are held by shareholders who were not owners at the time of termination or if the termination was not within the shareholders' or corporation's control.

S Corporation Termination

Type	Termination Event	Effective Date
Voluntary (Revocation)	Shareholders holding > 50% of shares (voting and nonvoting) consent to revocation	Specified date on or after election date OR: • First day of current tax year if within first 2 1/2 months of tax year • First day of following tax year if after first 2 1/2 months of tax year
Involuntary (Termination)	Fails to meet S corporation requirements (eg, ≤ 100 shareholders)	When termination event occurs
Excess Passive Earnings	Passive investment income > 25% of gross receipts for three consecutive years and accumulated E&P* from C corporation years	1st day of the 4th year

**E&P is earnings and profits, a measure of a company's economic earnings from which to pay dividends.*

An involuntary termination caused by a violation of eligibility requirements (as well as a voluntary termination specifying a revocation date at any time during the tax year) will generally create a short S corporation year and a short C corporation year, resulting in the need to allocate income between them. If no special election is made, the income must be allocated on a daily basis between the two based on a 365-day year.

Zinco Corp. was a calendar-year S corporation. Zinco's S status terminated on April 1, Year 3, when Case Corp. became a shareholder. During Year 3 (a 365-day calendar year), Zinco had nonseparately computed income of $310,250. If no election was made by Zinco, what amount of the income, if any, was allocated to the S corporation short year for Year 3?

An S election termination can be effective at any time during the tax year, which results in the need to **allocate income** between the short years for the **S corporation** and the **C corporation**. Absent an election, the income must be allocated on a **daily basis** between the two.

Step	Calculation	Amount
Calculate per-day income	Total income for the year / 365	$310,250 / 365 = $850 per day
Allocate income to S corporation short tax year	Number of S corporation days × per day income	90 days* × $850 = **$76,500**
Allocate remaining income to C corporation short tax year	Total income − S corporation allocation	$310,250 − $76,500 = $233,750

**In this scenario, Zinco Corp.'s S corporation short year was 90 days (31 days in January, 28 days in February, and 31 days in March). Thus, $76,500 was allocated to the S short year.*

20.02 Determination of Ordinary Business Income (Loss) and Separately Stated Items

Determination of Ordinary Business Income (Loss) and Separately Stated Items

Representative Task (Application): Calculate ordinary business income (loss) and separately stated items for an S corporation for tax purposes.

Operating Rules Overview

S corporations report income to shareholders on a year end consistent with that of the shareholders. Because S corporation shareholders are generally individuals, a **calendar year end is the default**. S corporations may elect a fiscal year end (with IRS permission) if there is a business purpose for the election.

- The most common business purpose is to elect a natural business year. A natural business year is a year in which 25% or more of the gross receipts occur in the last two months of the year for three consecutive years

S corporations make **most of their tax elections at the entity level** (eg, the election to amortize organization and start-up costs). They also choose which basis of accounting to use and **may choose the cash method** unless selling inventory is a material income-producing factor for them. In that case, the accrual or hybrid method must be used.

Under the Sec. 267 related party rules, an S corporation is considered related to its shareholders (regardless of their ownership percentages). Thus, an accrual-method S corporation may **deduct expenses** and interest **owed to cash-method shareholders only when paid**.

An accrual-method calendar-year S corporation accrued $2,000 of salary to a cash-method employee (a 1% shareholder) during Year 8 but does not make payment until February, Year 9. The $2,000 will be deductible by the corporation in Year 9 and reported by the shareholder-employee as income in Year 9.

Nonseparately and Separately Stated Items

Because S corporations are flow-through entities, they generally do **not** pay tax at the entity level. Instead, S corporation activities are divided between nonseparately calculated **net ordinary business income/ losses** and separately **stated items**, which are allocated pro rata to each shareholder based on the number of outstanding shares each shareholder owns on each day of the tax year (**"per share, per day"**).

These items are passed through according to their percentage of ownership based on the **daily allocation method** (ie, each shareholder calculates their share of income [loss] and separately stated items on a daily basis).

- If there is *no change* in ownership during the year, then simply use the **percentage of stock** owned to determine the amount passed through. If a change in ownership occurred, then each shareholder's percentage is **weighted** for the number of days the stock was held. The seller is deemed to own the shares on the day of the sale
- If all shareholders with changing ownership percentages agree, the S corporation can allocate income (loss) and separately stated items to the specific periods the income (losses) were realized (**specific identification method**)

S corporations must determine and report ordinary business income (loss) and separately stated items on a **Schedule K** each year. The total amounts reported on Schedule K are allocated to shareholders based on their ownership percentages (ie, 100% of all ordinary and separately stated items are reflected on the Schedule K, but a 10% shareholder receives a Schedule K-1 showing an allocation of 10% of each item). Unlike partnerships, S corporation shareholders are **not** allowed special allocations.

Pass-Through Items from S Corporation to Shareholders

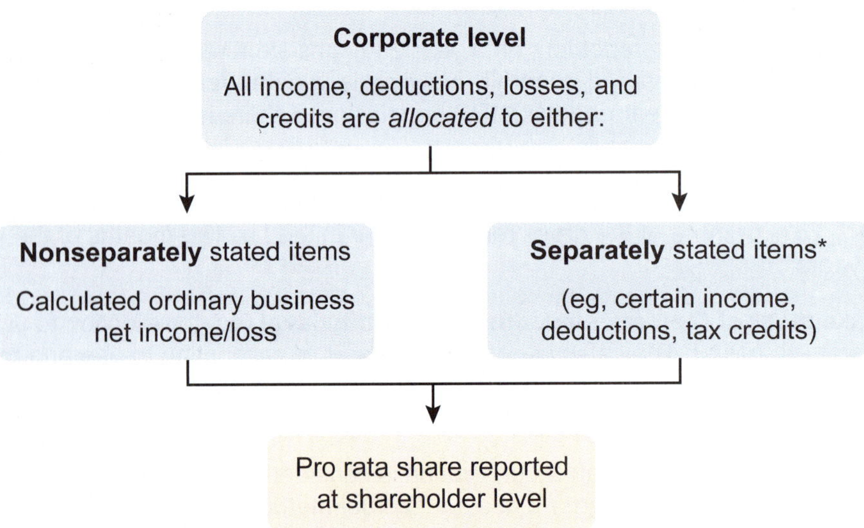

**Any items subject to statutory limitations or special rules when reported on the shareholder's tax return.*

Separately stated items can be income, losses, deductions, or credits that are reported separately from the S corporation's ordinary income/deductions to the shareholder because these items are subject to statutory limitations or special rules when reported on the shareholder's tax return (eg, capital gains, Section 179, tax-exempt interest income). The items retain their character to the owners when reported on the individual's tax return (ie, Form 1040).

Examples of common separately stated items:

Separately Stated Item	Reason Not Included in Ordinary Income
Capital gains and losses	Limit on deductibility of net capital losses
Section 1231 gains and losses	Classification of net gain as capital gain
Investment income (eg, dividends and interest)	Investment interest limitation

Separately Stated Item	Reason Not Included in Ordinary Income
Passive income (ie, rents/royalties)	Passive activity loss limitations
Charitable contributions	Must itemize to deduct, % of AGI limitations
Section 179 depreciation election	Dollar limit on use of election per year
Section 199A qualified business income, allocated wages, and unadjusted basis of qualified property (attached to K-1)	Used for qualified business (QBI) deduction
Tax credits	Limited to tax liability
Tax-exempt income	Affects shareholder basis but not taxable
Nondeductible expenses	Affects shareholder basis but not deductible

Health and accident insurance premiums and other fringe benefits paid by an S corporation on behalf of a more than 2% shareholder-employee are deductible by the S corporation as compensation and includible in the shareholder-employee's gross income on Form W-2. The same benefits provided to shareholder-employees with equal to or less than 2% ownership are still deductible by the corporation but are *excluded* from the shareholder-employee's gross income on Form W-2.

S corporations are **not entitled** to most special corporate deductions, such as the dividends-received deduction. However, they also generally **do not pay** special corporate taxes (ie, alternative minimum tax, personal holding company tax, or accumulated earnings tax).

Nonseparately stated ordinary income is ordinary income regardless of who earns, or is allocated, it. Gain from selling inventory is always ordinary. Similarly, Section 1245 recapture is always ordinary income and is not separately stated.

Compare to Section 1231 gains. These will be treated differently by different shareholders. One shareholder allocated Section 1231 gain may have no Section 1231 losses and will report the allocated gain as capital. But another shareholder with the same allocation may have Section 1231 losses and will reduce allocated gain by these losses.

As of January 1 of the current year, Taxpayer 1 owns all 100 shares of ABC, a calendar-year S corporation. On February 9 (the 40th day of the current year), Taxpayer 1 sells 25 shares to Taxpayer 2. For the current year (365 days), ABC reports $73,000 in nonseparately stated income and makes no distributions to shareholders. What amount of income should Taxpayer 1 report from ABC?

Taxpayer 1 should report income of $56,750, calculated using the daily income of $200 per day ($73,000 / 365 days) for the 40 days Taxpayer 1 owned 100% of the shares ($200 × 40 days = $8,000), plus 75% of the daily income for the 325 days after the sale ($200 × 325 days × .75 = $48,750). $48,750 + $8,000 = $56,750.

Alternatively, the calculation can be done by focusing on the ownership percentage:
$73,000 × [(100% × 40 / 365) + (75% × 325 / 365)] = $56,750.

Note that the seller is deemed to own the shares on the day of the sale.

An S corporation reported the following on its Year 8 income statement:

Sales revenue	$560,000
Interest income (from investments)	800
Municipal bond interest	1,060
Cost of goods sold	(295,000)
Salary to owners Jay and Bayley	(120,000)
Employee wages	(65,000)
Depreciation expense	(10,000)
Section 179 expense	(4,000)
Rent expense	(24,000)
Charitable contributions	(500)
Supplies expense	(360)
Short-term capital loss	(1,000)
Net income	$ 42,000

Jay and Bayley are owners of the corporation. Jay owns 40%, and Bayley owns 60%. What amount of net ordinary business income and separately stated items are allocated to them for Year 8?

First, the book income is adjusted to reverse separately stated items to determine net ordinary business income. Then, the nonseparately stated ordinary business income and the separately stated items are allocated to the shareholders.

Description	S Corporation	Jay (40%)	Bayley (60%)
Year 8 net income	$42,000		
– Investment interest income	(800)		
– Municipal bond interest	(1,060)		
+ Section 179 expense	4,000		
+ Charitable contributions	500		
+ Short-term capital loss	1,000		
Net ordinary business income	$45,640	**$18,256**	**$27,384**
Separately stated items:			
Interest income	800	**320**	**480**
Municipal bond interest	1,060	**424**	**636**
Section 179 expense	(4,000)	**(1,600)**	**(2,400)**
Charitable contributions	(500)	**(200)**	**(300)**
Short-term capital loss	(1,000)	**(400)**	**(600)**

Jay and Bayley will treat their shares of the corporation's net ordinary business income as ordinary income. The separately stated items will be "picked up" in each shareholder's Form 1040 and combined with the shareholder's income, losses, deductions, or credits from other sources to calculate the correct amount for reporting.

The important thing to know is that separately stated items may be reported differently for each shareholder that receives a K-1. For example, one shareholder may have their charitable contributions limited based on their adjusted gross income, while another may not.

Ordinary business income from an S-corporation may be eligible for the 20% QBI deduction.

Impact of Ordinary Business Income (Loss) and Separately Stated Items on the AAA

Representative Task (Application): Calculate the impact of current year operations on an S corporation's accumulated adjustments account.

The AAA is maintained at the corporate level (unlike stock basis, which is shareholder-specific) and is used to record activity from the time of an S corporation's qualifying election. The AAA may have a negative balance; however, distributions may **not** cause the AAA to go negative or increase a negative balance.

Note that tax-exempt income and related deductions do not affect the AAA. These items, along with tax-exempt life insurance proceeds and related nondeductible life insurance premiums paid, accumulate in the other adjustments account (OAA). The OAA is for nontaxable income and related deductions. The AAA is used to determine the *taxability* of certain distributions to shareholders. AAA is calculated as:

	Beginning-of-year AAA balance
+	Separately and nonseparately stated income/gain (excluding tax-exempt income)
−	Separately and nonseparately stated losses/deductions up to the income increase (including nondeductible expenses not related to tax-exempt income)
=	**AAA available for distributions**
−	Distributions (cannot cause AAA to go below $0 or increase a negative balance)
=	**AAA after distributions (cannot be below zero)**
−	Separately and nonseparately stated losses and deductions in excess of the income increase (including nondeductible expenses not related to tax-exempt income)
=	**End-of-year AAA balance**

S corporation AAA, unlike shareholder stock basis and debt basis, is one of the few tracked items permitted to have a negative balance. AAA can be negative from entity-level losses, but distributions to shareholders cannot cause AAA to become negative.

Distributions are **deemed paid from AAA first unless an election is made to bypass AAA**. The order of distributions for both S corporations with no AEP and S corporations with AEP (assuming no bypass election is made) are as follows:

	Order	Distribution Source	Shareholder Treatment	
Corp. *without* AEP	1	AAA (up to shareholder basis)	Tax-free	Corp. *with* AEP
Corp. *without* AEP	2	Remaining AAA (if any)	Capital gain	Corp. *with* AEP
	3	AEP	Taxable dividend	Corp. *with* AEP
	4	Remaining shareholder basis (if any)	Tax-free	Corp. *with* AEP
	5	Any remaining distribution	Capital gain	Corp. *with* AEP

Bypass Election: If a corporation with AEP makes the bypass election, AEP is deemed distributed first (resulting in dividend income to shareholders), making the order 3, 1, 2, 4, 5.

The S corporation AAA ordering rules allow S corporations to make distributions to the extent of the year's opening AAA balance tax-free, regardless of the operations of the company for the year.

TZD was originally formed as a C corporation and reported Year 2 taxable income (and earnings and profits) of $50,000. Effective at the beginning of Year 3, it made a valid S corporation election. In Year 3, TZD recording the following items:

Gross receipts	$95,000
Wages	35,000
Dividend income	300
Charitable contributions	1,000
Rent expense	15,000
Capital loss	5,000
Business meals expense (50% deductible)	600

What is the amount of TZD's year-end AAA for Year 3, assuming no distributions were made?

	Description	Amount	Explanation
	Beginning-of-year AAA balance	$ 0	
+	Separately and nonseparately stated income	95,300	$300 dividends + $95,000 gross receipts
−	Separately and nonseparately stated losses and deductions up to income	(56,600)	$35,000 wages + $15,000 rent + $300 deductible meals + $1,000 charitable + $5,000 capital loss + $300 nondeductible meals expense = $56,600
=	**AAA available for distributions**	**$38,700**	
−	Distributions (limited to available AAA)	0	
=	**End-of-year AAA balance**	**$38,700**	

Assume the same facts, except that TZD distributed $40,000 to its shareholders in Year 3. What is TZD's AAA at the end of Year 3?

	Description	Amount	Explanation
	Beginning-of-year AAA balance	$ 0	
+	Separately and nonseparately stated income	95,300	$300 dividends + $95,000 gross receipts
–	Separately and nonseparately stated losses and deductions up to income	(56,600)	$35,000 wages + $15,000 rent + $300 deductible meals + $1,000 charitable + $5,000 capital loss + $300 nondeductible meals expense = $56,600
=	**AAA available for distributions**	**$38,700**	
–	Distributions (limited to available AAA)	(38,700)	$1,300 of the $40,000 distribution is not from AAA.
=	**End-of-year AAA balance**	**$ 0**	

Classification of Items as Ordinary Business Income vs. Separately Stated Items

Representative Task (Analysis): Review federal Form 1120S – U.S. Income Tax Return for an S Corporation and supporting documentation, including any source data used to create the return, to determine the completeness and accuracy of the classification of items as ordinary business income (loss), separately stated or nondeductible.

With an S corporation, items of income and expense are classified as either separately stated items or nonseparately stated items. Nonseparately stated items are *included* in the calculation of ordinary income or loss in the operation of the business. Separately stated items are tax items that could potentially impact shareholders' tax liabilities in different ways.

What to Look for When Solving a Task-Based Simulation Question

- What type of income/expense is being generated?
- Identify separately stated items and nonseparately stated items
- In what year was the income received or expense paid?
- Are any nondeductible expenses identified?
- Are correct dollar amounts entered on Form 1120S, page 1?
- What is reported on Schedule K, page 3?
- Are the entries carried over from other tax forms correct?
- Check for transposition errors and computation errors for gains and losses

When completing diagnostic and accuracy-based questions on the exam, remember that additional information may be required in order to address the diagnostic flagged. So, expect to occasionally see a choice such as "The tax preparer must request information from the client in order to resolve the issue." Do not assume that all the relevant information is provided.

Practice Scenario

Snowflake, Inc., is a calendar-year S corporation incorporated in Year 5. The S election was made in Year 5. In Year 12, the in-house accountant prepared Form 1120S. You have been hired to review the accountant's entries.

Steps

1. Review the accountant's entries below
2. Review the exhibits
3. Enter your correct entries using the following table:

Line Item	Description	Accountant's Entry	Correct Entry
Page 1, Line 1a	Gross receipts or sales	1,250,000	
Page 1, Line 2	Cost of goods sold	650,000	
Page 1, Line 5	Other income	6,300	
Page 1, Line 11	Rent	24,000	
Page 1, Line 12	Taxes and licenses	300	
Page 1, Line 14	Depreciation expense	144,000	
Page 1, Line 20	Other deductions	7,200	
Page 1, Line 22	Ordinary business income	124,100	
Page 3, Line 4	Interest income	900	
Page 3, Line 5a	Ordinary dividends	1,800	
Page 3, Line 5b	Qualified dividends	2,200	
Page 3, Line 8a	Long-term capital gain	3,600	
Page 3, Line 10	Other income	6,300	
Page 3, Line 11	Section 179 deduction	0	
Page 3, Line 12a	Charitable contributions	5,100	
Page 3, Line 16c	Nondeductible expenses	1,600	

Accountant's Form 1120S: Other Income

Snowflake, Inc. Form 1120S Other Income, Page 1, Line 5	
Dividend income—Form 1099-DIV	$1,800
Interest income—Form 1099-INT	900
Long-term capital gain—Form 1099-B	3,600
Total	$6,300

Accountant's Form 1120S: Other Deductions

Snowflake, Inc. Form 1120S Other Deductions, Page 1, Line 20	
Office expenses	$1,600
Entertainment expenses	500
Charitable contribution—Letter from charitable organization	5,100
Total	$7,200

Green Peace Giving Statement

Snowflake Inc.
December 15, Year 12

Dear Snowflake, Inc.,

Thank you for your generous contribution of $1,500. The donation will be used to further our efforts to address climate change and to protect vital lands and waters. Thank you.

Jason Brunstetter, CFO
Green Peace
1000 Park Place, Washington DC 2001

No goods or services were provided in exchange for the contribution.

Accountant's Form 4562 (see next page)

Form **4562**
Department of the Treasury
Internal Revenue Service

Depreciation and Amortization

(Including Information on Listed Property)
Attach to your tax return.
Go to *www.irs.gov/Form4562* for instructions and the latest information.

OMB No. 1545-0172
Year 12

Name(s) shown on return	Business or activity to which this form relates	Identifying number
Snowflake, Inc.	Snowflake, Inc.	48-1002003

Part I Election to Expense Certain property Under Section 179
Note: If you have any listed property, complete Part V before you complete Part I.

1	Maximum amount (see instructions)	1	1,220,000
2	Total cost of section 179 property placed in service (see instructions)	2	100,000
3	Threshold cost of section 179 property before reduction in limitation (see instructions)	3	3,050,000
4	Reduction in limitation. Subtract line 3 from line 2. If zero or less, enter -0-	4	0
5	Dollar limitation for tax year. Subtract line 4 from line 1. If zero or less, enter -0-. If married filing separately, see instructions	5	1,220,000

6 (a) Description of property	(b) Cost (business use only)	(c) Elected cost
Machinery	100,000	100,000
7 Listed property. Enter the amount from line 29	7	

8	Total elected cost of section 179 property. Add amounts in column (c), lines 6 and 7	8	100,000
9	Tentative deduction. Enter the smaller of line 5 or line 8	9	100,000
10	Carryover of disallowed deduction from line 13 of prior year Form 4562	10	0
11	Business income limitation. Enter the smaller of business income (not less than zero) or line 5. See instructions	11	124,100
12	Section 179 expense deduction. Add lines 9 and 10, but don't enter more than line 11	12	100,000
13	Carryover of disallowed deduction to next year. Add lines 9 and 10, less line 12	13	

Note: Don't use part II or Part III below for listed property. Instead, Use Part V.

Part II Special Depreciation Allowance and Other Depreciation (**Don't** include listed property. See instructions)

14	Special depreciation allowances for qualified property (other than listed property) placed in service during the tax year. See instructions	14	
15	Property subject to section 168(f)(1) election	15	
16	Other depreciation (including ACRS)	16	

Part III MACRS Depreciation (**Don't** include listed property. See instructions.)

Section A

17	MACRS deductions for assets placed in service in tax years beginning before this year	17	44,000
18	If you are electing to group any assets placed in service during the tax year into one ore more general asset accounts, check here ☐		

Section B—Assets Placed in Service During Current Tax Year Using the General Depreciation System

(a) Classification of property	(b) Month and year placed in service	(c) Basis for depreciation (business/investment use only—see instructions	(d) Recovery period	(e) Convention	(f) Method	(g) Depreciation deduction
19a 3-year property						
b 5-year property						
c 7-year property						
d 10-year property						
e 15-year property						
f 20-year property						
g 25-year property			25 yrs.		S/L	
h Residential rental property			27.5 yrs.	MM	S/L	
			27.5 yrs.	MM	S/L	
i Nonresidential real property			39 yrs.	MM	S/L	
				MM	S/L	

Section C—Assets Placed in Service During Current Tax Year Using the Alternative Depreciation System

20a Class life					S/L	
b 12-year			12 yrs.		S/L	
c 30-year			30 yrs.	MM	S/L	
d 40-year			40 yrs.	MM	S/L	

Part IV Summary (See instructions.)

21	Listed property. Enter amount from line 28	21	
22	Total. Add mounts from line 12, lines 14 through 17, lines 19 and 20 in column (g), and line 21. Enter here and on the appropriate lines of your return. Partnerships and S corporations—see instructions	22	144,000
23	For assets shown above and placed in service during the current year, enter the portion of the basis attributable to section 263A costs.	23	

For Paperwork Reduction Act Notice, see separate instructions. Form **4562**

Other Exhibits

Information from Other Tax Forms		
Form 1099-B, Year 12	**Proceeds from Broker Exchange Transactions**	
Box 1a	Description of property	1,000 shares of Blizzard Corp.
Box 1b	Date acquired	02/26/Year 10
Box 1c	Date sold or disposed	05/17/Year 12
Box 1d	Proceeds	$6,600
Box 1e	Cost or other basis	$4,000
Form 1099-DIV, Year 12	**Dividends and Distributions**	
Box 1a	Total ordinary dividends	$2,200
Box 1b	Qualified dividends	$1,800
Form 1099-INT, Year 12	**Interest Income**	
Box 1	Interest income	$900

Solution

Items in bold represent corrections.

Line Item	Description	Accountant's Entry	Correct Entry
Page 1, Line 1a	Gross receipts or sales	1,250,000	1,250,000
Page 1, Line 2	Cost of goods sold	650,000	650,000
Page 1, Line 5	Other income	6,300	**0**
Page 1, Line 11	Rent	24,000	24,000
Page 1, Line 12	Taxes and licenses	300	300
Page 1, Line 14	Depreciation expense	144,000	**44,000**
Page 1, Line 20	Other deductions	7,200	**1,600**
Page 1, Line 22	Ordinary business income	124,100	**223,400**
Page 3, Line 4	Interest income	900	900
Page 3, Line 5a	Ordinary dividends	1,800	**2,200**
Page 3, Line 5b	Qualified dividends	2,200	**1,800**
Page 3, Line 8a	Long-term capital gain	3,600	**2,600**
Page 3, Line 10	Other income	6,300	**0**
Page 3, Line 11	Section 179 deduction	0	**100,000**
Page 3, Line 12a	Charitable contributions	5,100	**1,500**
Page 3, Line 16c	Nondeductible expenses	1,600	**500**

When preparing Form 1120S, income and deductions are divided between nonseparately stated items (ie, used to compute net ordinary business income) and separately stated items. Separately stated items can be income, losses, deductions, or credits that are reported separately from the S corporation's ordinary income/deductions to the shareholder because these items are subject to statutory limitations or special rules when reported on the shareholder's tax return (eg, capital gains, Section 179, charitable contributions).

In this scenario, several errors were made computing the net ordinary business income.

Page 1, Line 5: Other Income

Interest income, dividend income, and capital gains are all **separately** stated items and should be entered on **Schedule K**, not page 1 of Form 1120S. No amount should be entered on this line.

Page 1, Line 14: Depreciation Expense

Section 179 is a **separately stated item** and should be entered on **Schedule K**, not page 1 of Form 1120S. **MACRS depreciation of $44,000** ($144,000 − $100,000, Section 179) should be included on page 1, line 14, of Form 1120S.

Page 1, Line 20: Other Deductions

Other deductions incorrectly include the nondeductible entertainment expense and the charitable contribution. These two items are separately stated and are reported on Schedule K. In addition, the wrong amount is shown for the charitable contribution. The amount is $1,500, not $5,100. The correct amount for other deductions should be **$1,600 for the office supplies**.

Page 1, Line 22: Ordinary Business Income

Originally reported	$124,100
Add back:	
Section 179 depreciation	100,000
Entertainment expense and contribution included with other deductions	5,600
Less:	
Other income that is reported on Schedule K	(6,300)
Corrected net ordinary business income	**$223,400**

Page 3, Lines 5a and 5b: Ordinary and Qualified Dividends

Although these are separately stated items and should be recorded on Schedule K, the amounts for these two items were entered incorrectly. Per the 1099-DIV provided, the **qualifying dividends are $1,800**, and the **ordinary dividends are $2,200**.

Page 3, Line 8a: Long-Term Capital Gain

The gain on the sale is incorrectly computed. According to the 1099-B, the **gain on the sale** should be **$2,600** ($6,600 proceeds − $4,000 cost basis).

Page 3, Line 10: Other Income

This line should be blank. The income items of interest, dividends, and long-term capital gain are reported on separate lines on Schedule K so they can retain their nature and character when reported by the shareholders.

Page 3, Line 11: Section 179

Section 179 is a separately stated item. The **$100,000** from Form 4562, line 8, should be entered on Schedule K, line 11.

Page 3, Line 12a: Charitable Contributions

Charitable contributions are a separately stated item and should be reported on Schedule K, not page 1 of Form 1120S. Charitable contributions were entered incorrectly as $5,100. The correct entry is $1,500.

Page 3, Line 16c: Nondeductible Expenses

Entertainment expenses are not deductible and should be included on Schedule K, not page 1 of Form 1120S.

Discrepancies Identified by Automated Diagnostic and Validation Checks

Representative Task (Analysis): Review and resolve discrepancies identified by automated diagnostic and validation checks to ensure the completeness and accuracy of the ordinary business income (loss) and separately stated items reported on Form 1120S – U.S. Income Tax Return for an S Corporation based on the source data used to prepare the form.

Accounting firms use automated software to prepare tax returns for their clients. During this process, the software generates diagnostics for the tax preparer to check and clear before the tax return can be filed electronically with the IRS. These diagnostics help with the accuracy of the tax return being filed. Diagnostics can be informational, computational, or critical. A critical diagnostic indicates that the tax return will not be electronically accepted by the IRS.

When attempting to solve a task-based simulation question about S corporations, consider the following items:

- What are the different types of diagnostics presented?
- What type of income/expense is being generated?
- Identify separately stated items
- Identify nonseparately stated items
- In what year was the income received or expense paid?
- Any nondeductible expenses identified?
- Are correct dollar amounts entered on Form 1120S, page 1?
- What is included in Other Income on Form 1120S, page 1?
- What is included in Other Deductions on Form 1120S, page 1?
- Are the entries carried over correctly from Form 1120S, page 1, to Schedule K?
- Is the correct amount reported as W-2 wages versus what was reported on Schedule K allocated items?

Practice Scenario

Sleep City, Inc., is an S corporation that was formed on January 31, Year 7. The business uses the accrual method and has two shareholders; Jake owns 40%, and Lily owns 60%. Sleep City's in-house accountant prepared Form 1120S for the tax year ending December 31, Year 7.

- Sleep City paid Lily $75,000 in wages and issued a W-2
- The corporation made a cash distribution of $30,000 to Lily, and Jake received a distribution of $20,000
- Lily's stock basis at the beginning of the year was $25,000. During the year, she made an additional $3,000 contribution

Review the tax forms prepared by the accountant, the exhibits, and the diagnostic/validation checks below. Select a correct answer from the drop-down menu provided.

Diagnostic/Validation Check Received	Choose Correct Answer from Drop-Down Menu
1. Validation Check: Verify the accuracy of other income reported on Form 1120S, Page 1, Line 5.	The correct other income is $0. The correct other income is $800. The correct other income is $1,650. The correct other income is $2,450.
2. Validation Check: Verify the accuracy of ordinary business income (loss) reported on Form 1120S, Line 22.	The correct amount is $3,350. The correct amount is $2,850. The correct amount is $1,400. The correct amount is $900.
3. Validation Check: The amount entered on Page 1, Line 7 does not agree with the W-2 keyed in. Verify the accuracy of Form W-2, Boxes 1, 3, 5, and 16.	The correct amount of wages is $102,010. The correct amount of wages is $105,000. The correct amount of wages is $75,000. The correct amount of wages is $30,000.
4. Validation Check: Verify the accuracy of other deductions reported on Form 1120S, Page 1, Line 20.	The correct other deductions are $0. The correct other deductions are $500. The correct other deductions are $1,700. The correct other deductions are $2,200.
5. Validation Check: Verify the accuracy of interest income reported on Schedule K, Line 4.	The correct taxable interest income is $0, and the correct tax-exempt interest income is $0. The correct taxable interest income is $800, and the correct tax-exempt interest income is $0. The correct taxable interest income is $0, and the correct tax-exempt interest income is $800. The correct taxable interest income is $800, and the correct tax-exempt interest income is $800.
6. Validation Check: Verify the accuracy of ordinary and qualified dividends reported on Schedule K, Lines 5a and 5b.	The correct ordinary dividend income is $2,300, and the correct qualified dividend income is $2,300. The correct ordinary dividend income is $1,650, and the correct qualified dividend income is $1,650. The correct ordinary dividend income is $3,950, and the correct qualified dividend income is $3,950. The correct ordinary dividend income is $2,300, and the correct qualified dividend income is $1,650.

Accountant's Tax Forms

Accountant's Form 1120S, Page 1

Form **1120-S** — Department of the Treasury, Internal Revenue Service

U.S. Income Tax Return for an S Corporation

Do not file this form unless the corporation has filed or is attaching form 2553 to elect to be an S corporation.
Go to *www.irs.gov/Form1120S* for instructions and the latest information.

Year 7

A S election effective date: 02/14/YR 7	Name: Sleep City, Inc.	**D** Employer identification number: 48-1002003
B Business activity code number (see instructions)	Number, street, and room or suite no. If a P.O. box, see instructions.: 500 Drousy Lane	**E** Date incorporated: 01/31/YR 7
C Check if Sch. M-3 attached ☐	City or town, state or province, country, and ZIP or foreign postal code: Acton, MA 01720	**F** Total assets (see instructions) $

TYPE OR PRINT

G Is the corporation electing to the an S corporation beginning with this tax year? See instructions. ☐ Yes ☐ No

H Check if: **(1)** ☐ Final return **(2)** ☐ Name change **(3)** ☐ Address change **(4)** ☐ Amended return **(5)** ☐ S election termination

I Enter the number of shareholders who were shareholders during any part of the tax year 2

J Check if corporation: **(1)** ☐ Aggregated activities for section 465 at-risk purposes **(2)** ☐ Grouped activities for section 469 passive activity purposes

Caution: Include **only** trade or business income and expenses on lines 1a through 22. See the instructions for more information.

Income	1a	Gross receipts or sales 590,000 **b** Less returns and allowances ___ **c** Balance	1c	590,000
	2	Cost of goods sold (attach Form 1125-A)	2	345,000
	3	Gross profit. Subtract line 2 from line 1c	3	245,000
	4	Net gain (loss) from Form 4797, line 17 (attach Form 4797)	4	
	5	Other income (loss) (see instructions—attach statement)	5	2,450
	6	**Total income (loss).** Add lines 3 through 5	6	247,450
Deductions (see instructions for limitations)	7	Compensation of officers (see instructions—attach Form 1125-E)	7	75,000
	8	Salaries and wages (less employment credits)	8	100,000
	9	Repairs and maintenance	9	500
	10	Bad debts	10	
	11	Rents	11	24,000
	12	Taxes and licenses	12	600
	13	Interest (see instructions)	13	
	14	Depreciation from Form 4562 not claimed on Form 1125-A or elsewhere on return (attach Form 4562)	14	40,000
	15	Depletion **(Do not deduct oil and gas depletion.)**	15	
	16	Advertising	16	1,800
	17	Pension, profit-sharing, etc., plans	17	
	18	Employee benefit programs	18	
	19	Energy efficient commercial buildings deduction (attach Form 7205)	19	
	20	Other deductions (attach statement)	20	2,200
	21	**Total deductions.** Add lines 7 through 20	21	244,100
	22	**Ordinary business income (loss).** Subtract line 21 from line 65	22	3,350

Accountant's Form 1120S, Schedule K

Schedule B **Other Information** (see instructions) *(continued)*

		Yes	No
12	During the tax year, did the corporation have any non-shareholder debt that was canceled, was forgiven, or had the terms modified so as to reduce the principal amount of the debt? If "Yes," enter the amount of principal reduction $		
13	During the tax year, was a qualified subchapter S subsidiary election terminated or revoked? If "Yes," see instructions		
14a	Did the corporation make any payments that would require it to file Form(s) 1099?		
b	If "Yes," did or will the corporation file require Form(s) 1099?		
15	Is the corporation attaching Form 8996 to certify as the Qualified Opportunity Fund? If "Yes," enter the amount from Form 8996, line 15 $		
16	At any time during the tax year, did the corporation: (a) receive (as a reward, award, or payment for property or services); or (b) sell, exchange, or otherwise dispose of a digital asset (or a financial interest in a digital asset)? See instructions		

Schedule K **Shareholders' Pro Rata Share Items**

Section	Line	Item		Line	Total amount
Income (Loss)	1	Ordinary business income (loss) (page 1, line 22)		1	3,350
	2	Net rental real estate income (loss) (attach Form 8825)		2	
	3a	Other gross rental income (loss)	3a		
	b	Expenses from other rental activities (attach statement)	3b		
	c	Other net rental income (loss). Subtract line 3b from line 3a		3c	
	4	Interest income		4	800
	5	Dividends: a Ordinary dividends		5a	1,650
		b Qualified dividends	5b		
	6	Royalties		6	
	7	Net short-term capital gain (loss) (attach Schedule D (Form 1120-S))		7	
	8a	Net long-term capital gain (loss) (attach Schedule D (Form 1120-S))		8a	
	b	Collectibles (28%) gain (loss)	8b		
	c	Unrecaptured section 1250 gain (attach statement)	8c		
	9	Net section 1231 gain (loss) (attach Form 4797)		9	
	10	Other income (loss) (see instructions) Type:		10	
Deductions	11	Section 179 deduction (attach Form 4562)		11	
	12a	Charitable contributions		12a	
	b	Investment interest expense		12b	
	c	Section 59(e)(2) expenditures Type:		12c	
	d	Other deductions (see instructions) Type:		12d	
Credits	13a	Low-income housing credit (section 42(j)(5))		13a	
	b	Low-income housing credit (other)		13b	
	c	Qualified rehabilitation expenditures (rental real estate) (attach form 3468, if applicable)		13c	
	d	Other rental real estate credits (see instructions) Type:		13d	
	e	Other rental credits (see instructions) Type:		13e	
	f	Biofuel producer credit (attach Form 6478)		13f	
	g	Other credits (see instructions) Type:		13g	
International	14	Attach Schedule K-2 (Form 1120-S), Shareholders' Pro Rata Share Items—International, and check this box to indicate you are reporting items of international tax relevance ☐			
Alternative Minimum Tax (AMT) Items	15a	Post-1986 depreciation adjustment		15a	
	b	Adjusted gain or loss		15b	
	c	Depletion (other than oil and gas)		15c	
	d	Oil, gas, and geothermal properties—gross income		15d	
	e	Oil, gas and geothermal properties—deductions		15e	
	f	Other AMT items (attach statement)		15f	
Items Affecting Shareholder Basis	16a	Tax-exempt interest income		16a	
	b	Other tax-exempt income		16b	
	c	Nondeductible expenses		16c	
	d	Distribution (attach statement if required) (see instructions)		16d	50,000
	e	Repayment of loans from shareholders		16e	
	f	Foreign taxes paid or accrued		16f	

Accountant's Other Income Statement

Sleep City, Inc.
Form 1120S
Other income, Line 5

Interest income	$ 800
Dividend income	1,650
Total	$2,450

Accountant's Other Deductions Statement

Sleep City, Inc.
Form 1120S
Other deductions, Line 20

Office expense	$1,700
Entertainment expense	500
Total	$2,200

Accountant's Tax Forms, Prepared for Lily

Information from Other Tax Forms		
Form W-2, Year 7	**Wage and Tax Statement**	
Box 1	Wages, other compensation	$107,010
Box 2	Federal income tax withheld	$21,402
Box 3	Social Security wages	$107,010
Box 4	Social Security tax withheld	$6,635
Box 5	Medicare wages and tips	$107,010
Box 6	Medicare tax withheld	$1,552
Form 1099-DIV, Year 7	**Dividends and Distributions**	
Box 1a	Total ordinary dividends	$2,300
Box 1b	Qualified dividends	$1,650
Form 1099-INT, Year 7	**Interest Income**	
Box 8	Tax-exempt interest	$800

Solution

Diagnostic/Validation Check Received	Choose Correct Answer from Drop-Down Menu
1. Validation Check: Verify the accuracy of other income reported on Form 1120S, Page 1, Line 5.	The correct other income is $0. The correct other income is $800. The correct other income is $1,650. The correct other income is $2,450.
2. Validation Check: Verify the accuracy of ordinary business income (loss) reported on Form 1120S, Line 22.	The correct amount is $3,350. The correct amount is $2,850. The correct amount is $1,400. The correct amount is $900.
3. Validation Check: The amount entered on Page 1, Line 7 does not agree with the W-2 keyed in. Verify the accuracy of Form W-2, Boxes 1, 3, 5, and 16.	The correct amount of wages is $102,010. The correct amount of wages is $105,000. The correct amount of wages is $75,000. The correct amount of wages is $30,000.
4. Validation Check: Verify the accuracy of other deductions reported on Form 1120S, Page 1, Line 20.	The correct other deductions are $0. The correct other deductions are $500. The correct other deductions are $1,700. The correct other deductions are $2,200.
5. Validation Check: Verify the accuracy of interest income reported on Schedule K, Line 4.	The correct taxable interest income is $0, and the correct tax-exempt interest income is $0. The correct taxable interest income is $800, and the correct tax-exempt interest income is $0. The correct taxable interest income is $0, and the correct tax-exempt interest income is $800. The correct taxable interest income is $800, and the correct tax-exempt interest income is $800.
6. Validation Check: Verify the accuracy of ordinary and qualified dividends reported on Schedule K, Lines 5a and 5b.	The correct ordinary dividend income is $2,300, and the correct qualified dividend income is $2,300. The correct ordinary dividend income is $1,650, and the correct qualified dividend income is $1,650. The correct ordinary dividend income is $3,950, and the correct qualified dividend income is $3,950. The correct ordinary dividend income is $2,300, and the correct qualified dividend income is $1,650.

1. The correct **other income is $0**. Interest income and dividend income are reported on Schedule K as separately stated items and are **not** reported on Form 1120S as other income. Also, the interest income is tax-exempt according to Form 1099-INT, provided in the exhibits. The tax-exempt interest income should be reported on Schedule K, line 16a.
2. The net ordinary business income reported on Form 1120S, line 22, is incorrect due to the other reporting errors. The correct amount is $1,400.

Originally reported	$3,350
Deduct other income incorrectly reported on Form 1120S	(2,450)
Add back nondeductible entertainment expense included in other deductions	500
Correct net ordinary business income	$1,400

3. The correct amount of **wages is $75,000**. The corporation incorrectly included the distribution and Lily's share of net ordinary business income as wages on the W-2. The correct amount is reported on Form 1120S.
   - Only wages are reported on Form W-2
   - Distributions reduce Lily's basis and are not part of wages
   - Ordinary business income is not included in wages but is reported on Lily's K-1 and included on her Schedule E, page 2, of her individual income tax return
   - Because the wages were incorrectly reported, the amount withheld for Social Security tax and Medicare is incorrect. A corrected W-2 must be filed
4. The correct **other deductions are $1,700**. The office expense of $1,700 is deductible as an ordinary and necessary business expense. Entertainment expenses of $500 are not deductible and are treated as a separately stated item reported on Schedule K.
5. The correct **taxable interest income is $0**, and the correct **tax-exempt interest income is $800**. Form 1099-INT indicated that tax-exempt interest income of $800 was generated, not taxable interest income. These amounts are separately stated items reported on Schedule K.
6. The correct **ordinary dividend income is $2,300**, and the correct **qualified dividend income is $1,650**. Form 1099-DIV indicated that ordinary dividend income is $2,300 and qualified dividend income is $1,650. Ordinary dividend income represents the total amount of dividend income received. Qualified dividend income represents what amount will be taxed at a preferential rate. These items are separately stated on Schedule K.

Corrected Tax Forms

Form **1120-S**

Department of the Treasury
Internal Revenue Service

U.S. Income Tax Return for an S Corporation

Do not file this form unless the corporation has filed or is attaching form 2553 to elect to be an S corporation.
Go to *www.irs.gov/Form1120S* for instructions and the latest information.

Year 7

A S election effective date 02/14/YR 7	TYPE OR PRINT	Name Sleep City, Inc.	**D Employer identification number** 48-1002003
B Business activity code number (see instructions)		Number, street, and room or suite no. If a P.O. box, see instructions. 500 Drousy Lane	**E** Date incorporated 01/31/YR 7
C Check if Sch. M-3 attached ☐		City or town, state or province, country, and ZIP or foreign postal code Acton, MA 01720	**F** Total assets (see instructions) $

G Is the corporation electing to the an S corporation beginning with this tax year? See instructions. ☐ Yes ☐ No

H Check if: **(1)** ☐ Final return **(2)** ☐ Name change **(3)** ☐ Address change **(4)** ☐ Amended return **(5)** ☐ S election termination

I Enter the number of shareholders who were shareholders during any part of the tax year 2

J Check if corporation: **(1)** ☐ Aggregated activities for section 465 at-risk purposes **(2)** ☐ Grouped activities for section 469 passive activity purposes

Caution: Include **only** trade or business income and expenses on lines 1a through 22. See the instructions for more information.

Income	1a	Gross receipts or sales 590,000 **b** Less returns and allowances ___ **c** Balance	1c	590,000
	2	Cost of goods sold (attach Form 1125-A)	2	345,000
	3	Gross profit. Subtract line 2 from line 1c	3	245,000
	4	Net gain (loss) from Form 4797, line 17 (attach Form 4797)	4	
	5	Other income (loss) (see instructions—attach statement)	5	0
	6	**Total income (loss).** Add lines 3 through 5	6	245,000
Deductions (see instructions for limitations)	7	Compensation of officers (see instructions—attach Form 1125-E)	7	75,000
	8	Salaries and wages (less employment credits)	8	100,000
	9	Repairs and maintenance	9	500
	10	Bad debts	10	
	11	Rents	11	24,000
	12	Taxes and licenses	12	600
	13	Interest (see instructions)	13	
	14	Depreciation from Form 4562 not claimed on Form 1125-A or elsewhere on return (attach Form 4562)	14	40,000
	15	Depletion **(Do not deduct oil and gas depletion.)**	15	
	16	Advertising	16	1,800
	17	Pension, profit-sharing, etc., plans	17	
	18	Employee benefit programs	18	
	19	Energy efficient commercial buildings deduction (attach Form 7205)	19	
	20	Other deductions (attach statement)	20	1,700
	21	**Total deductions.** Add lines 7 through 20	21	243,600
	22	**Ordinary business income (loss).** Subtract line 21 from line 65	22	1,400

Form 1120-S Page 3

Schedule B **Other Information** (see instructions) *(continued)*

		Yes	No
12	During the tax year, did the corporation have any non-shareholder debt that was canceled, was forgiven, or had the terms modified so as to reduce the principal amount of the debt?		
	If "Yes," enter the amount of principal reduction . . . $		
13	During the tax year, was a qualified subchapter S subsidiary election terminated or revoked? If "Yes," see instructions		
14a	Did the corporation make any payments that would require it to file Form(s) 1099?		
b	If "Yes," did or will the corporation file require Form(s) 1099?		
15	Is the corporation attaching Form 8996 to certify as the Qualified Opportunity Fund?		
	If "Yes," enter the amount from Form 8996, line 15 . . . $		
16	At any time during the tax year, did the corporation: (a) receive (as a reward, award, or payment for property or services); or (b) sell, exchange, or otherwise dispose of a digital asset (or a financial interest in a digital asset)? See instructions		

Schedule K **Shareholders' Pro Rata Share Items**

Section	Line	Item			Line	Total amount
Income (Loss)	1	Ordinary business income (loss) (page 1, line 22)			1	1,400
	2	Net rental real estate income (loss) (attach Form 8825)			2	
	3a	Other gross rental income (loss)	3a			
	b	Expenses from other rental activities (attach statement)	3b			
	c	Other net rental income (loss). Subtract line 3b from line 3a			3c	
	4	Interest income			4	
	5	Dividends: a Ordinary dividends			5a	2,300
		b Qualified dividends	5b	1,650		
	6	Royalties			6	
	7	Net short-term capital gain (loss) (attach Schedule D (Form 1120-S))			7	
	8a	Net long-term capital gain (loss) (attach Schedule D (Form 1120-S))			8a	
	b	Collectibles (28%) gain (loss)	8b			
	c	Unrecaptured section 1250 gain (attach statement)	8c			
	9	Net section 1231 gain (loss) (attach Form 4797)			9	
	10	Other income (loss) (see instructions) . . . Type:			10	
Deductions	11	Section 179 deduction (attach Form 4562)			11	
	12a	Charitable contributions			12a	
	b	Investment interest expense			12b	
	c	Section 59(e)(2) expenditures . . . Type:			12c	
	d	Other deductions (see instructions) . . . Type:			12d	
Credits	13a	Low-income housing credit (section 42(j)(5))			13a	
	b	Low-income housing credit (other)			13b	
	c	Qualified rehabilitation expenditures (rental real estate) (attach form 3468, if applicable)			13c	
	d	Other rental real estate credits (see instructions) . . Type:			13d	
	e	Other rental credits (see instructions) . . . Type:			13e	
	f	Biofuel producer credit (attach Form 6478)			13f	
	g	Other credits (see instructions) . . . Type:			13g	
International	14	Attach Schedule K-2 (Form 1120-S), Shareholders' Pro Rata Share Items—International, and check this box to indicate you are reporting items of international tax relevance ☐				
Alternative Minimum Tax (AMT) Items	15a	Post-1986 depreciation adjustment			15a	
	b	Adjusted gain or loss			15b	
	c	Depletion (other than oil and gas)			15c	
	d	Oil, gas, and geothermal properties—gross income			15d	
	e	Oil, gas and geothermal properties—deductions			15e	
	f	Other AMT items (attach statement)			15f	
Items Affecting Shareholder Basis	16a	Tax-exempt interest income			16a	800
	b	Other tax-exempt income			16b	
	c	Nondeductible expenses			16c	500
	d	Distribution (attach statement if required) (see instructions)			16d	50,000
	e	Repayment of loans from shareholders			16e	
	f	Foreign taxes paid or accrued			16f	

Form **1120-S**

20.03 Basis of Shareholder's Interest

Stock Basis of Shareholder's Interest

Representative Task (Application): Calculate a shareholder's stock basis in an S corporation for tax purposes resulting from business operations, cash contributions by the shareholder, and cash distributions to the shareholder.

For S corporation shareholders to determine the gain or loss on the sale of their interests in an S corporation, the tax consequences of distributions, and the deductibility of losses, they must calculate their basis in the corporation's stock. A shareholder's basis in a corporation is called **"outside basis"** (versus a corporation's basis in its assets, which is called **"inside basis"**).

If a shareholder has purchased S corporation stock from another shareholder or from the corporation itself, the new shareholder's basis is simply the purchase price of the stock.

If a shareholder exchanges property for stock, the basis will depend upon whether the exchange is taxable or nontaxable. Generally, an exchange of property for property is taxable. Each transferor recognizes gain or loss on the difference between the FMV of the property received and the adjusted basis in the property transferred. However, an **exchange of property for stock** may qualify as **nontaxable** to the extent that:

- A transferor exchanges **property, including cash, solely for stock**, and
- The property transferor, or transferor group, **controls** the S corporation immediately after the exchange (ie, owns **at least 80%** of the transferee S corporation).

In a nontaxable exchange, a transferor's **basis** in the stock received is equal to the tax basis of the property transferred, less any liabilities assumed by the S corporation for the property contributed (*substituted basis*). Any gain recognized (ie, receipt of boot, excess liability relief) increases the stock's basis, and any property received other than stock reduces basis by the fair market value of the property received. This is similar to the process for calculating the initial basis for a C corporation shareholder.

The rules for nontaxable transfers of property in exchange for stock (Section 351) are the same rules that apply to C corporations.

Clark and Hunt organize Jet, an S corporation. Clark contributes cash, and both Clark and Hunt transfer other property in exchange for Jet stock as follows:

	Adjusted Basis	Fair Market Value	Percentage of Stock Acquired
Clark (cash)	$ 60,000	$ 60,000	
Clark (property)	50,000	100,000	
Clark (total)	$110,000	$160,000	40%
Hunt	$120,000	$240,000	60%

What is Clark's basis in Jet stock?

In a nontaxable exchange, a transferor's **basis** in the stock received **includes** the amount of **cash** and the transferor's **adjusted basis** (not FMV) **in the property** transferred. Stock basis reflects property basis because the transferor's investment in the property continues through stock ownership.

Clark's basis is **$110,000** ($60,000 cash, plus $50,000 *adjusted basis* in the property transferred).

Sheila receives S corporation stock in a tax-deferred exchange by contributing land with a tax basis of $30,000 and encumbered by a $10,000 mortgage. What is Sheila's initial basis in her S corporation stock?

Shareholder Stock Basis after Deferred Exchange	Sheila's Basis
Adjusted basis of property transferred	$30,000
+ Cash transferred	0
+ Recognized gain from receipt of boot	0
+ Recognized gain from excess liability relief	0
− Cash received	0
− FMV of property received	0
− Shareholder liabilities assumed by S corporation	(10,000)
= Shareholder stock basis (not below zero)	$20,000

Sheila's initial basis in the S corporation is **$20,000**, which is the $30,000 carryover tax basis of the land, minus the $10,000 mortgage assumed by the S corporation.

Shareholder's Stock Basis

Each shareholder in an S corporation has a tax stock basis for their interest that is used to determine the deductibility of pass-through losses, the treatment of distributions, and gain or loss on disposition. Basis is adjusted during each accounting period for the shareholder's pro rata share of the calculated ordinary income/loss, separately stated items, contributions, and distributions. The shareholder's basis may never fall below zero.

All items of income, regardless of character, will increase or decrease a shareholder's basis in an S corporation. This annual adjustment is required to prevent income or losses from being double counted (ie, double taxed or double deducted) by shareholders, either when they sell the stock or when they receive distributions.

- For example, tax-exempt income increases the shareholder's basis. If basis is not increased, the tax-exempt income will be "taxed" on the eventual disposition of the stock through a larger gain or smaller loss

Distributions from the corporation *reduce* basis as a nontaxable return of capital, but never below zero. However, if cash distributions *exceed* basis, then basis is reduced to zero, and any excess distribution is taxed as capital gain (ie, the stock is a capital asset).

To ensure that distributions receive the best tax treatment possible (ie, nontaxable return of capital), a shareholder's basis is always increased first for income items, then decreased for distributions, and finally decreased for losses and other deductions.

- This ordering allows the largest amount of basis to offset distributions against and perhaps avoid a taxable capital gain. If there is insufficient basis remaining after the distributions are deducted to absorb the losses and other deductions, a suspended loss is created that can be carried forward and used when basis is restored

Calculation of Shareholder's Basis in an S Corporation
Shareholder's beginning basis in corporation
+ Additional contributions
+ Percentage share of corporation's ordinary income and separately stated income, gains
− Distributions from corporation (ie, cash and property)
− Percentage share of corporation's operating loss and separately stated deductions, losses
Ending shareholder basis*

**Shareholder basis cannot fall below zero.*

Adjustments can never reduce a shareholder's outside basis in their S corporation stock below zero. Basis represents the shareholder's investment in the stock. Because it is not possible to have a negative investment, it is not possible to have a negative outside basis.

An S corporation has an ordinary loss from business activity of $6,000 and made a $7,000 cash distribution to its sole shareholder during calendar Year 7. The sole shareholder had a stock basis of $8,000 on January 1, Year 7.

The stock basis of $8,000 is first reduced by the $7,000 cash distribution, which would be nontaxable and would reduce stock basis to $1,000. Only $1,000 of the $6,000 ordinary loss would be allowable as a deduction to the shareholder for Year 7 due to the tax-basis limitation.

January 1, Year 7, balance	$8,000
Cash distribution	(7,000)
Remaining basis	$1,000
Amount of loss deductible (limited by basis)	(1,000)
December 31, Year 7, balance	$ 0

The unused $5,000 loss ($6,000 − $1,000) is suspended and carried forward until there is sufficient basis.

Notice that *without* the ordering rules, the $8,000 would be reduced by the $6,000 loss, resulting in only a $2,000 basis available for the distribution. This would trigger a $5,000 capital gain ($7,000 distribution − $2,000 basis). Instead, the ordering rules avoid any gain recognition and result in a carryforward loss of $5,000.

An S corporation has tax-exempt income of $5,000, a net ordinary business loss of $9,000, and a long-term capital gain of $2,000 for calendar Year 4. Its sole shareholder had an outside stock basis of $6,000 on January 1, Year 4. During Year 4, the shareholder made a $1,000 capital contribution and received a $3,000 cash distribution. What is the shareholder's outside stock basis at the end of Year 4?

Basis at beginning of Year 4	$ 6,000
Additional contributions to capital	1,000
Shareholder's share of long-term capital gain	2,000
Shareholder's share of tax-exempt income	5,000
Basis before distributions	$14,000
Distributions	(3,000)
Basis after distributions	$11,000
Shareholder's share of nondeductible expenses	(0)
Shareholder's share of ordinary business losses	(9,000)
Basis at end of Year 4	$ 2,000

Insufficient Stock Basis before Reduction for Losses and Deductions

Because a shareholder's stock basis may never be reduced below zero, there may be times when there is insufficient stock basis to absorb the pass-through losses and deductions after the deduction for distributions. When this occurs, the shareholder may *not* pick and choose which items to currently deduct to reduce basis to zero.

Instead, the loss and deduction items must be **prorated** to determine the amount of each item that is currently deductible.

- Allocation formula:
  (Individual loss or deduction / Total unused losses and deductions) × Remaining basis
- The unused amounts retain their character and are carried forward to be used when there is sufficient stock basis

Because both the taxability of a distribution and the deductibility of a loss for a shareholder are dependent on stock basis, there are ordering rules in computing the basis. Stock basis is adjusted annually, as of the last day of the S corporation year, in the following order:

1. Increased for income items and excess depletion;
2. Decreased for distributions;
3. Decreased for nondeductible items, noncapital expenses, and depletion; and
4. Decreased for items of loss and deductions.

Debt Basis in an S Corporation

Representative Task (Application): Calculate changes in a shareholder's debt basis in an S corporation resulting from current year repayment of debt.

Because S corporation shareholders have liability protection like a C corporation, debts of the corporation do **not** impact the shareholder's stock basis. However, **direct loans** made by the shareholder to the corporation will create **debt basis**, which may be used to deduct pass-through losses. Shareholder losses are limited in four ways:

- Tax basis
- At-risk amount
- Passive activity
- Excess business losses

To be considered a direct loan, the debt must meet the IRC definition of a "bona fide debt" (ie, an arm's-length debtor/creditor relationship). There must be an obligation to repay the debt and a willingness of the shareholder to enforce collection. Loan guarantees on behalf of an S corporation (ie, promise to pay if borrower defaults) are **not** considered direct loans for the purpose of debt basis.

Corporate losses (not distributions) allocated to a shareholder are first deductible to the extent of stock basis and then to the extent of debt basis.

- Distributions **never** affect debt basis
- Shareholders must track their stock basis and debt basis separately. Debt basis adjustments include lending money directly to an S corporation, losses, subsequent years' income, and debt repayment
- As with stock basis, debt basis may **never** be negative

If debt basis is reduced by losses, it must be restored (up to the original outstanding amount) by the shareholder's subsequent net increase in stock basis resulting from all positive and negative basis adjustments. The debt basis is adjusted before any increase is made in the stock basis. If there is a net *decrease* in future basis adjustments, there is no restoration of debt basis; all adjustments go to stock basis.

If repayments are received *before* the debt basis is restored, any repayments in *excess* of the debt basis amount are taxed as a *gain* to the shareholder.

- For example, a shareholder loaned an S corporation $10,000, and the shareholder's debt basis is currently $4,000 because of losses previously taken against the debt basis. If the S corporation repaid $6,000 of the loan, the debt basis would be reduced to $0 (cannot be negative), and $2,000 excess ($6,000 repayment − $4,000 debt basis) would be a taxable gain to the shareholder

A taxpayer owns 50% of an S corporation's stock and materially participates in the corporation's activities. At the beginning of the year, the taxpayer had a stock basis of $25,000 and made a $13,000 loan to the corporation. During the year, $3,000 of the loan was repaid, and the taxpayer's share of the corporation's *loss* for the year was $40,000.

Since $3,000 of the loan was repaid during the year, the debt basis is reduced to $10,000 ($13,000 − $3,000).

This leaves a total of $35,000 ($25,000 stock basis + $10,000 debt basis) of basis to absorb part of the loss for the year. The loss is deductible to the extent of the shareholder's combined bases as of the end of the year.

So, the taxpayer's bases will both be reduced to zero, allowing **$35,000 to be deducted** and leaving a **$5,000 loss suspended** until the shareholder's *basis* is increased enough to absorb the loss.

	Stock Basis	**Debt Basis**
Beginning basis	$25,000	$13,000
Repayment		(3,000)
Balance	$25,000	$10,000
Net ordinary business loss (limited by basis)	(25,000)	(10,000)
Ending basis	$ 0	$ 0

Mary owns 25% of an S corporation. At the beginning of the year, her stock basis is $28,000, and her debt basis is $8,000. At the end of the current year, Mary's share of net ordinary business income is $15,000, and her share of tax-exempt income is $1,500. In addition, she receives a cash distribution of $50,000. There is sufficient corporate AAA. What are the tax consequences to Mary?

Mary's stock basis of $28,000 is first increased due to her share of the ordinary income and tax-exempt income, then reduced by the distributions, but not below $0. She will recognize $5,500 as capital gain income (ie, excess cash distribution over stock basis). Note that the *excess distributions* may **not** reduce debt basis. The excess cash distributions trigger a $5,500 capital gain ($50,000 − $44,500) to Mary.

	Stock Basis	**Debt Basis**
Beginning balance	$28,000	$8,000
Net ordinary business income	15,000	
Tax-exempt income	1,500	
Balance before distribution	$44,500	
Distribution (limited by basis)	(44,500)	
Basis at end of year	$ 0	$8,000

Green has a stock basis of $20,000 in an S corporation. Green loans $12,000 *directly* to the S corporation. The S corporation allocates $30,000 of ordinary business loss to Green for the current year. What amount of loss is deductible by the shareholder?

First, $20,000 of the loss offsets Green's stock basis, reducing it to $0. Next, Green may use $10,000 of debt basis to deduct the remaining $10,000 ($30,000 loss − $20,000 stock basis) of loss. Therefore, Green deducts a $30,000 loss, has a $0 stock basis, and has a remaining debt basis of $2,000 ($12,000 − $10,000).

	Stock Basis	Debt Basis
Beginning balance	$20,000	$12,000
Net ordinary business loss	(20,000)	(10,000)
Basis at end of year	$ 0	$ 2,000

If the S corporation repaid $3,000 of the loan when Green's debt basis was still $2,000, the debt basis would be reduced to $0 (cannot be negative), and $1,000 ($3,000 repayment − $2,000 debt basis) would be a **taxable gain** to Green.

Assume the following year that the corporation still owes Green the $12,000 loan. Green's allocated share of income items is $19,000, and he received a $2,000 cash distribution. There is a net *increase* in basis adjustments of $17,000 ($19,000 − $2,000). Therefore, the first $10,000 restores **debt** *basis* back to $12,000 ($2,000 current debt basis + $10,000). The balance of adjustments is allocated to stock basis.

	Stock Basis	Debt Basis
Balance (from previous year)	$ 0	$ 2,000
Net ordinary business income	9,000	10,000
Distribution	(2,000)	
Basis at end of year	$7,000	$12,000

Assume Green's distribution was $20,000 instead of $2,000. How does this change the tax consequences?

Now there is a $1,000 **net decrease** in basis adjustments for the subsequent year ($19,000 − $20,000). **No adjustment is made to debt basis.** Instead, the stock basis is first increased to $19,000 for the positive adjustments, and then the stock basis is reduced by the cash distributions, but not below zero.

	Stock Basis	Debt Basis
Balance (from previous year)	$0	$2,000
Net ordinary business income	19,000	
Distribution (limited by basis)	(19,000)	
Basis at end of year	$0	$2,000

The $1,000 ($20,000 − $19,000) excess distribution over basis is taxable as a capital gain.

REG 21
Partnerships

REG 21: Partnerships

21.01 Ordinary Business Income (Loss) and Separately Stated Items

Ordinary Business Income (Loss) and Separately Stated Items for a Partnership

Representative Task (Application): Calculate ordinary business income (loss) and separately stated items for a partnership for tax purposes, including consideration of guaranteed payments disbursed.

Overview

A business operated as a partnership (P/S) is not recognized as a separate taxable entity under income tax laws. Instead, it is considered a **flow-through entity** (ie, pass-through). The partners report their **pro rata share** of the P/S's income, expenses, gains, losses, and tax credits on their individual tax returns.

- A P/S's tax items flow to the partners on the last day of the P/S tax year. Income is reported by the partners regardless of whether it is distributed. A P/S files an informational Form 1065 (ie, reports its ordinary net business income (loss) and separately stated items), and a Schedule K-1 is distributed to each partner, so they have the information to file their respective tax returns
- The character (eg, ordinary income, capital gain) of P/S tax items is determined at the P/S level. The character of the tax item stays the same when it flows to the partners. For example, a long-term capital gain (LTCG) recognized by the P/S is still a LTCG to the partners when it flows to them. A charitable contribution at the P/S level maintains its character as a charitable contribution when it flows to the partners

Every P/S must have at least **one general partner**. Additional partners may be general or limited partners. No matter what type of partner, each partner receives their distributive share of pass-through items. Differences exist regarding personal liability for P/S debt and which income items are subject to self-employment tax.

A partner's interest in a P/S may be a capital interest, a **profits interest**, or a combination of both. Profits and losses are allocated to each partner based on each partner's profit and loss sharing ratio. The P/S agreement should stipulate which type of interest a partner has acquired.

- One of the advantages of a P/S is that partners have tremendous flexibility in determining how profits and losses are shared. In addition, special pass-through items may be **allocated** to a particular partner (eg, Partner A is allocated 50% of the P/S's depreciation even though they are a 25% partner)
- For example, a partner could have a 50% **profit-sharing ratio** but a 20% **loss-sharing ratio**. Or the profit-sharing ratio could be 50% this year, 60% next year, and 35% the following year. The partners decide how they choose to share profits and losses

Generally, under Section 721, when a P/S is formed, there are no tax consequences to the contributing partner or the P/S. Cash distributions from the P/S to a partner are treated as a *return of capital* and are generally **not** taxed (unless the amount exceeds the partner's basis). Hence, the income is taxed only once. This distinction between a P/S and a corporation is important because corporate income is subject to double taxation.

Being able to **compute a partner's basis in the P/S** is one of the most important concepts in P/S taxation since it is used to **limit** the deductibility of P/S losses and the tax treatment of certain distributions.

- Basis initially equals cash and the adjusted basis of contributed property
- A partner's basis account fluctuates during the year for additional contributions, distributions from the P/S, increases and decreases in their share of P/S debt, and their pro rata share of P/S ordinary net business income (loss) as well as pass-through items from the P/S

Characteristics of a Partnership	
Minimum Number of Owners	• Two partners, of which at least one must be a general partner
Types of Owners	• No restrictions
Liability	• Unlimited for general partner(s) • Limited for limited partners
Contributions upon Formation	• Generally nontaxable
Federal Income Tax	• Entity not taxed • Taxed at partner level
Tax Returns	• Form 1065 • Schedule K-1 distributed to partners
Actively Participating Partners	• May be compensated with "guaranteed payments" • Not an employee (reported on Schedule K-1, not W-2)
Self-Employment Tax	• All guaranteed payments for services are self-employment income (general and limited partners) • General partner pays self-employment tax on their pro rata share of P/S's net ordinary business income
Distributions	• Not required to be proportionate

On the exam, partners are general partners unless otherwise indicated.

Separately Stated Items and Nonseparately Stated Items

Since a P/S is a flow-through entity, its tax items are divided into one of two categories: **nonseparately stated items** and **separately stated items**. The distinction is important due to the tax treatment of certain income and expenses for tax purposes.

Pass-Through Items from a Partnership

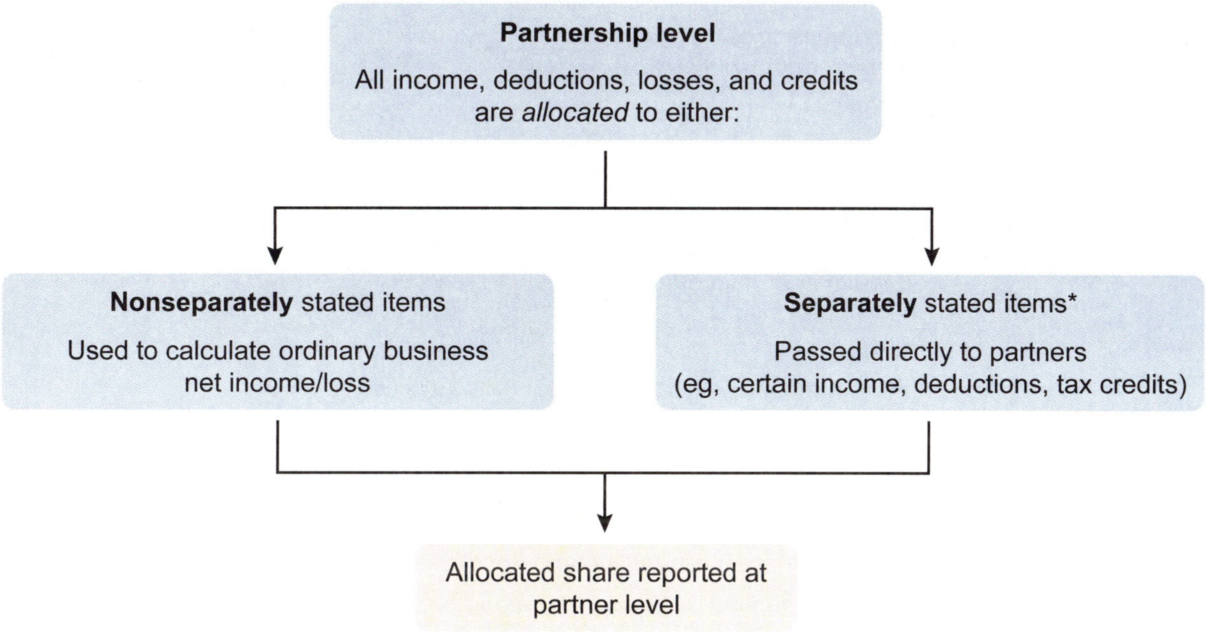

**Any items subject to statutory limitations or special rules when reported on the partner's tax return.*

Nonseparately stated items comprise the partnership's **net ordinary business income or loss** and are reported on Form 1065. Accordingly, each partner's pro rata share of the net ordinary business income (loss) is reported on the partner's Schedule K-1. This net business income is considered **self-employment income to general partners** whether or not it is *actually* distributed.

- For example, if a partner's pro rata share of a P/S's net ordinary business income is $55,000, that amount is subject to income tax. It does not matter if the partner received the $55,000 or not. Because a P/S is a pass-through entity, the income tax is paid at the *partner* level

Examples of **nonseparately stated items** that are used to compute the P/S's net ordinary income or loss include:

- Sales less cost of goods sold
- Business expenses such as employee salaries and wages*, utilities, rents, bad debts, supplies, and repairs
- Deduction for guaranteed payments to partners (discussed later)
- Depreciation (excludes Section 179 deduction)
- Amortization
- Section 1245 recapture and Section 1250 recapture

Note: Partners are not employees of the P/S and are ***not*** *paid a salary.*

Simplified Partnership Ordinary Business Income (Loss) Calculation

Gross income/receipts		xxxxx
Less cost of goods sold		(xxxxx)
Gross profit		xxxxx
Less deductions for		
Salary	xxxxx	
Guaranteed payments	xxxxx	
Repairs and maintenance	xxxxx	
Bad debts	xxxxx	
Rent	xxxxx	
Interest (business related)	xxxxx	
Depreciation	xxxxx	
Other expenses*	xxxxx	
Total deductions		(xxxxx)
Partnership ordinary business income (loss)		xxxxx

**Selling, administrative, and other operational costs (eg, supplies).*

Separately stated items are any tax items (deductions, income, gains, losses, tax credits, etc.) that might affect each partner's tax liabilities differently because these items are subject to *statutory limitations or special rules* when reported on the individual partners' Form 1040 tax returns.

- For example, long-term capital gains are taxed at a lower preferential tax rate depending on the taxpayer's rate bracket
- Also included in separately stated items is any item that is specifically allocated in a manner different from the regular profit and loss sharing ratios (eg, the depreciation expense allocated to a specific partner)
- These items are **excluded** from the computation of a P/S's net ordinary income or loss
- Separately stated items also include a partner's share of **nondeductible business expenses** such as 50% of meals or a fine

Separately Stated Item	Reason Not Included in Ordinary Income
Capital gains and losses	Netting of all capital gains and losses; limit on deductibility of net capital losses; special rates for LTCGs
Section 1231 gains and losses	Netting of all Section 1231 gains and losses; classification of net gain as capital gain and net loss as ordinary loss
Dividends and investment interest	Investment interest expense limitation; treated as portfolio income for passive loss rules
Passive activities	Passive activity loss limitations
Charitable contributions	Must itemize to deduct; several AGI limitations for individual partners

Separately Stated Item	Reason Not Included in Ordinary Income
Section 179 election	Dollar limit on use of election per year
Tax credits	Generally, limited to tax liability
Tax-exempt income	Reported on Form 1040; increases partner's basis
Nondeductible expenses	Reduces partner's basis
Special allocations	Any tax items that are allocated in a manner different from the regular profit and loss sharing ratios are separately stated

Partnership AB has two equal partners and made a charitable contribution of $25,000 this year. Partner A and Partner B itemize their deductions. Each partner's share of the contribution is $12,500.

- Because the charitable contribution has the potential to affect the partners' tax liabilities differently, the contribution must flow to the partners as a separately stated item
- If Partner A has other cash charitable contributions that already exceed 60% of AGI limitation for charitable contributions for the tax year, they must carry over the $12,500 contribution
- However, if Partner B has other contributions below the 60% limitation, they will be able to deduct all or some of the $12,500 contribution
- Even if both Partner A and Partner B could deduct the contribution in full, the contribution must still be separately stated. It is the *potential* for different treatment that requires a tax item to be separately stated

An individual taxpayer and Corporation C are equal partners in the IC Partnership. During the current year, IC sold a capital asset that it owned for four years and recognized a $12,000 long-term capital loss (LTCL). How is the $12,000 LTCL reported by each partner?

- C Corporations are only allowed to offset capital losses against capital gains. Any net capital loss is carried back three years, then carried forward five years to offset capital gains. Any remaining unused losses expire. Corporation C would therefore need $6,000 of capital gains to utilize the full benefit of its 50% share of the LTCL ($6,000) in the current year
- Individual taxpayers are limited to no more than $3,000 of net capital loss deductions in any one tax year. Excess amounts are carried forward indefinitely until used in a future tax year. The individual taxpayer partner would therefore need an additional $3,000 of capital gains to utilize the full benefit of their 50% share of the LTCL ($6,000) in the current year

Distributions from the P/S to a partner are not an expense of the P/S and therefore are excluded from the computation of net ordinary business income. Distributions are **not** a **separately stated item** either. Generally, each partner treats distributions as a **nontaxable return of capital**.

CDE Partnership had the following items of income and expense for Year 3. What is the amount reported as the partnership's net ordinary business income or loss?

Sales revenue	$300,000
Dividend income	12,000
Cost of goods sold	87,000
Wages	130,000
Depreciation expense	22,000
Cash distribution to Partner C	25,000
Short-term capital loss	(3,500)
Bad debt expense	1,000
Utilities expense	8,500
Advertising expense	2,000

- Nonseparately stated items are used to compute the P/S's net ordinary business income or loss. Any item that could affect each partner's tax liabilities differently due to various tax treatments and thresholds (ie, separately stated items) is *excluded* from the computation of the P/S's net ordinary business income
- Here the separately stated items are the *dividend income* and the *short-term capital loss*
- Cash *distributions* to partners are **not** an expense of the P/S

The **net ordinary business income is $49,500**:

Sales revenue	$300,000
Less: Cost of goods sold	(87,000)
Gross profit	$213,000
Less:	
Wages	(130,000)
Depreciation expense	(22,000)
Bad debt expense	(1,000)
Utilities expense	(8,500)
Advertising expense	(2,000)
P/S's net ordinary business income	**$ 49,500**

Guaranteed Payments

One item that is unusual and unique to partnerships is guaranteed payments to partners. These payments are based on separate contractual relationships between a partner and a partnership for services rendered by a partner (like wages) or for the use of a partner's capital (like interest). They may be a fixed dollar amount or a percentage of a partner's capital investment but can never be based on the amount of partnership income or loss.

Guaranteed payments are:

- Deductible as an expense when computing the P/S's net ordinary business income or loss
- Taxable as ordinary income to the partner receiving the payment (reported on partner's Schedule K-1)

Other things to know about guaranteed payments include:

- Although **guaranteed payments for services** are not subject to withholding requirements by the partnership, they are subject to self-employment tax on the partner's tax return
- Guaranteed payments received by general partners for the *use of capital* are subject to the self-employment tax; however, if received by limited partners, they are *not* subject to the self-employment tax
- Guaranteed payments for interest may be subject to the net investment income tax at the partner level
- Because these payments are made to partners, neither type of guaranteed payment is included in the calculation of the qualified business income deduction (QBI)
- Unlike separately stated partnership items (eg, capital gains, dividends), guaranteed payments do not directly affect a partner's outside basis

Guaranteed Payments

- Payment amount not based on partnership income or loss
- Can be for services or special use of partner's capital
- A deduction when computing partnership ordinary income
- Separately stated item on recipient partner's K-1
- Taxable to the recipient partner as ordinary income
- Does not directly affect partner's tax basis

During the year, a P/S reported net ordinary business income of $220,000. A 50% general partner received a cash distribution of $10,000 and guaranteed payments during the year totaling $25,000. What are the tax consequences of these transactions to the partner?

- The $25,000 of guaranteed payments was deducted by the P/S when determining the net business income. Accordingly, the payments are reported as income (subject to self-employment tax) to the partner
- The $10,000 cash distribution was **not** deducted by the P/S. It is treated as a nontaxable return of capital to the partner (assuming the partner has sufficient basis). The distribution reduces the partner's basis but not below zero
- In addition, the partner reports $110,000 (50% of $220,000) as income, whether or not it was received. Because the partner is a general partner, the $110,000 is also subject to self-employment tax

On the exam, questions may use the term "salary" paid to a partner. This refers to guaranteed payments. Partners are not employees of the partnership.

Reporting guaranteed payments: When the tax year of the P/S (eg, a fiscal year of October 1 to September 30) does not coincide with the partner's tax year (eg, calendar year), the payments are reported based on the tax year of the P/S. This ensures that the income is reported on the partner's Schedule K-1 during the same accounting period that the P/S takes the deduction for the payment.

Reporting Guaranteed Payments Based on P/S Tax Year

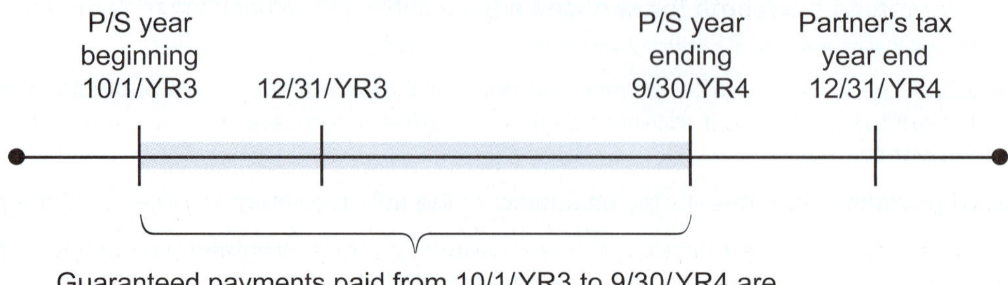

Guaranteed payments paid from 10/1/YR3 to 9/30/YR4 are reported on partner's Year 4 Schedule K-1

P/S = partnership

During calendar Year 1, ABC Partnership paid a $2,000 guaranteed monthly payment to one of its partners, Andy Anderson. The amount was increased to $3,000 monthly in calendar Year 2. Andy's individual tax return is filed using a calendar year, but ABC uses a September 30 fiscal year end. What amount does Andy report as income in Year 2?

- The guaranteed payments reported by Andy on his individual tax return for Year 2 are not the $36,000 ($3,000 per month × 12 months) that he received in Year 2
- The P/S only paid $33,000 during the 12 months that ended September 30, Year 2 ($2,000 per month × 3 months in Year 1, plus $3,000 per month for 9 months in Year 2)
- The **$33,000** for Year 2's guaranteed payments are **reported on Andy's Schedule K-1** for the year ended September 30, Year 2, from the P/S

Taxable Amounts to a Partner

- Partners report their share of a partnership's (P/S) business *net income or loss* on their individual tax returns. The amount reported may be based on a partner's *ownership* percentage (eg, 50%) or stipulated as a *percentage of profits and losses* (eg, 75%, 25%)
- Cash distributions received to the extent of the partner's outside basis are nontaxable (ie, return of capital)
- Payments that are based on a separate contractual relationship between a partner and P/S for services rendered by the partner are known as guaranteed payments. For tax purposes, guaranteed payments are *treated* as if they were made to a *nonpartner*. The payments are *deductible* as an expense on the *P/S tax return* to determine net income (loss) and are *taxable* as *income* to the partner performing the services

Taxable Amounts Reported from a Partnership (P/S)

Share of P/S business net income (loss) Share of separately reported P/S income and expense items Guaranteed payments received for services from P/S Cash distributions *in excess* of basis	→	Income reported by a partner on individual tax return

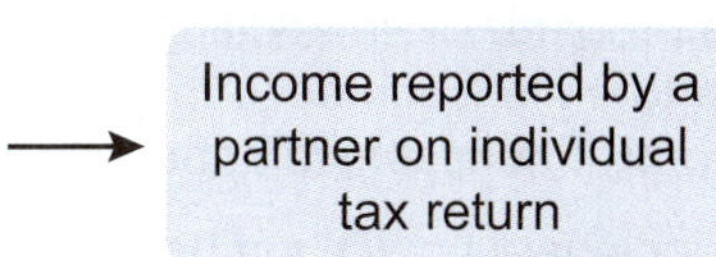

On January 2, Year 3, Arch and Bean contributed cash equally to form the JK Partnership. Arch and Bean share profits and losses in a ratio of 75% to 25%, respectively. For Year 3, the partnership's net income was $40,000. The partnership reported dividend income of $10,000. A distribution of $5,000 was made to Arch during Year 3. JK paid Arch and Bean each a guaranteed payment of $6,000 for services rendered to the partnership. What amount of income will Arch report from the partnership in Year 3?

- According to the profit and loss ratio in this scenario, Arch reports $30,000 (75% × $40,000) of P/S net income and $7,500 (75% × $10,000) as dividend income
- The guaranteed payment to each partner has already been deducted to determine JK Partnership's $40,000 net income; however, Arch reports ordinary income of $6,000 for his payment
- The $5,000 distribution is nontaxable because Arch has sufficient basis before the distribution, at least $37,500 ($30,000 + $7,500)
- Therefore, Arch reports income of $43,500 ($30,000 + $6,000 + $7,500)

Automated Diagnostic and Validation Checks

Representative Task (Analysis): Review and resolve discrepancies identified by automated diagnostic and validation checks to ensure the completeness and accuracy of ordinary business income (loss) and separately stated items reported on Form 1065 – U.S. Return of Partnership Income based on the source data used to prepare the form.

Automated Diagnostics and Validation Checks

Tax software packages use automated diagnostics and e-file validation checks (also referred to as "alerts" or "cautions") to warn the preparer of potential mistakes in a tax return they are preparing and to provide an additional layer of review, which mitigates the chance of errors.

These flagged items need to be reviewed for proper treatment and fall into these *two categories:*

- **Automated Diagnostics** alert a tax preparer of data entry that is inconsistent with other data entry, or that appears incorrect, and are generated by the tax software during and at the completion of tax return preparation. Automated diagnostics include such things as:
    - No general partners indicated in a limited partnership
    - Profit/loss sharing ratios do not sum to 100% across partners
    - Guaranteed payment listed on the partnership tax return but not allocated on a partner's K-1

- **E-file Validation Checks** warn a tax preparer of data entry that needs to be edited or added before the tax return can be e-filed with the IRS or state(s) and are generated just before or after e-filing has been unsuccessfully attempted. E-file validation checks include such things as:
  - Warning a preparer of an additional required form or schedule required on the tax return they are attempting to e-file, such as prompting the preparer to include Form 8283, Noncash Charitable Contributions, if noncash contributions exceed $500
  - Failure to include a tax ID number (eg, employer identification number, Social Security number) for a partner on a K-1

These warnings should *not* be ignored or deleted without careful consideration because they assist in ensuring tax return preparation accuracy. Some software packages label each diagnostic according to severity, such as:

- Red for incomplete or inconsistent information that *disqualifies a tax return from e-filing* (so these are the most serious of diagnostics);
- Yellow or gold for a warning of a potential mistake; and
- Green for a tax planning/tax savings opportunity.

Below are examples of automated diagnostics and validation checks generated by tax software:

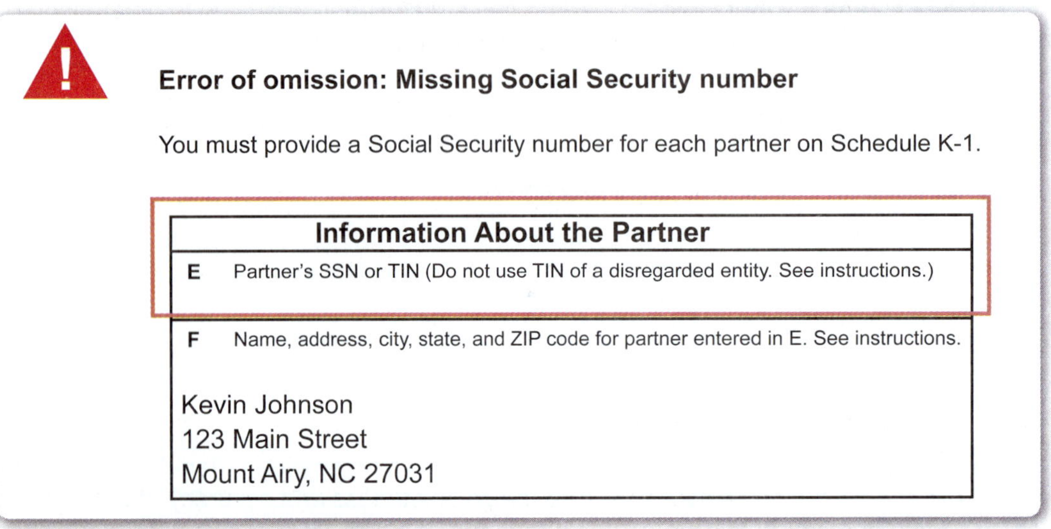

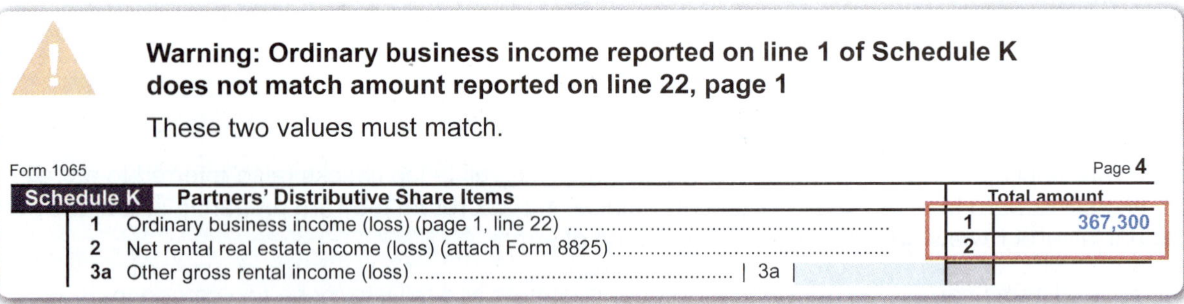

Although a P/S is a pass-through entity and does not pay tax, an example of a tax planning alert is provided for an individual taxpayer.

Explanation: Let's try to reduce your underpayment penalty by updating some information.

You may be able to reduce or eliminate any penalty for underpayment of estimated tax by entering the tax amount for last year's tax return.

$ [ ]

☐ Check here if your tax last year was zero.

If the adjusted gross income on your return last year was more than $150,000 ($75,000 if MFS) you must enter 110%

Examples of Diagnostics Related to Partnership Returns

A diagnostics report can be generated for any form or entry page on a tax return. Areas that should be reviewed for partnerships include the following:

- Determine what any missing amounts should be
- Do not assume that the other amounts entered are correct. Check the question data to ensure accuracy
- Ensure that tax items are classified properly as separately stated or nonseparately stated
- Ensure that any tax items that are specially allocated are reported on Schedule K
- Ensure that guaranteed payments are reported in three places: (1) as a nonseparately stated deduction on page 1 of Form 1065, (2) on Schedule K, Form 1065, and (3) on the appropriate partner's Schedule K-1

When completing diagnostic and/or accuracy-based questions on the exam, remember that additional information may be required in order to address the diagnostic flagged. So, expect to occasionally see a choice such as *The tax preparer must request information from the client in order to resolve the issue.*

Practice Scenario

The NIU General Partnership, a cash-basis taxpayer, has been in existence since July 4, Year 11. Ned, Irene, and Uriah are partners and have the following profit and loss sharing ratios.

Ned	60%
Irene	25%
Uriah	15%

For its tax year ended December 31, Year 12, NIU had the following items of income and loss:

Partnership Tax Item	Amount
Sales income	$100,000
Interest income	6,000
Municipal interest income	2,500
Long-term capital gain	32,000
Long-term capital loss	23,000
Section 1231 gain	8,000
Section 1245 recapture	3,000
Net rental real estate income	11,000
Cost of goods sold	52,000
Salaries	18,000
Guaranteed payment to Ned (services)	12,000
Advertising expense	4,000
Supplies expense	6,500
Depreciation expense*	13,000
Charitable contribution (cash)	6,000
Section 179 expense	18,000
State income taxes	5,000
Payroll taxes	1,500
Investment interest expense	2,000
Life insurance premium on partners' lives (owned by NIU)	3,000
Fines	1,000

**Depreciation expense of $13,000 is allocated 100% to Ned.*

Cash distributions were made to the partners on December 1, Year 12, as follows:

Ned	$10,000
Irene	$ 5,000
Uriah	$ 1,500

A staff accountant at your firm has completed the first draft of NIU's partnership tax return for Year 12. The following diagnostic and validation checks have been provided by the firm's tax return software. Based on the information provided above, review the diagnostics and validation checks and respond to the questions provided.

Diagnostic #1

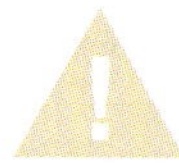

Warning: Schedule K guaranteed payment

You have entered a guaranteed payment for services on Schedule K, but a guaranteed payment is not entered for the partners. Please make sure that these amounts match.

4a	Guaranteed payments for services
4b	Guaranteed payments for capital
4c	Total guaranteed payments

Explanation

Guaranteed payments are reported on Schedule K in the income section to show that guaranteed payments were paid to the partners as a group, and the payments must be reported as income. The total of the guaranteed payments shown on Ned's, Irene's, and Uriah's Schedule K-1s must equal the amount shown on Schedule K, Form 1065.

Diagnostic #2

Warning: Page 1 guaranteed payment

You have entered a guaranteed payment for services on Schedule K, but there is not a deduction for guaranteed payments shown on page 1. Make sure that these amount match.

10	Guaranteed payments to partners	**10**	

Explanation

Guaranteed payments are reported in three places: (1) as a nonseparately stated deduction on page 1 of Form 1065, (2) on Schedule K, Form 1065, and (3) on the appropriate partner's Schedule K-1.

Diagnostic #3

Warning: Depreciation expense

You have not entered depreciation expense on Form 1065, page 1, but you did deduct depreciation expense on last year's tax return. Ensure that depreciation expense is computed and entered correctly.

16a	Depreciation (if required, attach Form 4562)	16a			
b	Less depreciation reported on Form 1125-A and elsewhere on return	16b		16c	

Explanation

Depreciation expense generally needs to be reported each year unless the adjusted basis of all depreciable assets is $0. Depreciation expense should be shown as a nonseparately stated item on Form 1065, page 1, unless the depreciation is specially allocated, in which case it is shown on Schedule K as a separately stated item. Note: Sometimes there is a reason an income or expense item is no longer being reported, such as the asset is no longer owned.

Diagnostic #4

Warning: Cost of goods sold

You have entered inventory on the balance sheet and sales on page 1, but you do not have an entry for cost of goods sold.

1a	Gross receipts or sales	1a	100,000		
b	Returns and allowances	1b			
c	Balance. Subtract line 1b from line 1a			1c	100,000
2	Cost of goods sold (attach Form 1125-A)			2	
3	Gross profit. Subtract line 2 from line 1c			3	100,000

Explanation

If the partnership sold inventory during the year, then it must have a deduction for the cost of the inventory items sold.

Diagnostic #5

Warning: Profit-sharing ratios

The profit-sharing ratios for the partners must add up to 100%. Ensure that the profit-sharing ratios are entered correctly and add up to 100%.

Ned **J** Partner's share of profit, loss, and capital (see instructions):

	Beginning	Ending
Profit	60 %	60 %
Loss	60 %	60 %
Capital	60 %	60 %

Irene **J** Partner's share of profit, loss, and capital (see instructions):

	Beginning	Ending
Profit	20 %	20 %
Loss	20 %	20 %
Capital	20 %	20 %

Uriah **J** Partner's share of profit, loss, and capital (see instructions):

	Beginning	Ending
Profit	15 %	15 %
Loss	15 %	15 %
Capital	15 %	15 %

Explanation

The partners' profit, loss, and capital sharing ratios must add up to 100%.

Questions Based on Diagnostics	Select the Correct Answers from the Drop-Down Menus
Diagnostic #1	
Line 4a, guaranteed payments for services, on Ned's Schedule K-1 should be:	A. \$0 B. \$4,000 C. \$7,200 **D. \$12,000**
Line 4a, guaranteed payments for services, on Irene's Schedule K-1 should be:	**A. \$0** B. \$4,000 C. \$7,200 D. \$12,000
Line 4a, guaranteed payments for services, on Uriah's Schedule K-1 should be:	**A. \$0** B. \$4,000 C. \$7,200 D. \$12,000

Questions Based on Diagnostics	Select the Correct Answers from the Drop-Down Menus
Diagnostic #2	
The guaranteed payment entered on line 10 of Form 1065, page 1, should be:	A. $0 B. $7,200 **C. $12,000** D. $36,000
Diagnostic #3	
The depreciation entered on line 16a of Form 1065, page 1, should be:	**A. $0** B. $3,000 C. $13,000 D. $16,000
The depreciation entered on Ned's Schedule K-1 should be:	A. $0 B. $3,000 **C. $13,000** D. $16,000
Diagnostic #4	
The cost of goods sold entered on line 2 of Form 1065, page 1, should be:	A. $0 B. $3,000 C. $48,000 **D. $52,000**
Diagnostic #5	
The profit-sharing ratio for Ned on his K-1 should be:	A. 0% B. 25% C. 33 1/3% **D. 60%**
The profit-sharing ratio for Irene on her K-1 should be:	A. 0% **B. 25%** C. 33 1/3% D. 50%
The profit-sharing ratio for Uriah on his K-1 should be:	A. 0% **B. 15%** C. 25% D. 33 1/3%

NIU should make the above corrections, then rerun the diagnostics to make sure that the corrections are properly made and that these diagnostics are resolved.

Diagnostic 1

Ned is the only partner who received a guaranteed payment, so he has an entry on Schedule K-1, line 4a, while Irene and Uriah do not.

Diagnostic 2

The guaranteed payment of $12,000 is deducted on page 1 of Form 1065 as a *nonseparately* stated item.

Diagnostic 3

Depreciation is usually deducted on page 1 of Form 1065 as a nonseparately stated item. However, any tax item that is specially allocated must be reported as a separately stated item on the partners' Schedule K-1s. The depreciation expense is allocated 100% to Ned this year, so his K-1 will show $13,000 of depreciation expense. None of the depreciation expense is allocated to Irene and Uriah.

Diagnostic 4

The $52,000 for cost of goods sold was inadvertently omitted from page 1 of Form 1065 as a nonseparately stated item. It should be reported on line 2 of Form 1065, and the gross profit will change to $48,000.

Diagnostic 5

The information provided with this diagnostic shows that Irene's profit-sharing ratio was entered incorrectly as 20% when it should be 25%. Ned's and Uriah's profit-sharing ratios were entered correctly.

Completeness and Accuracy of the Classification of Items on a Partnership Tax Return

Representative Task (Analysis): Review federal Form 1065 – U.S. Return of Partnership Income and supporting documentation, including any source data used to create the return, to determine the completeness and accuracy of the classification of items as ordinary business income (loss), separately stated or nondeductible.

Overview

Determining whether a tax item is classified as separately stated or nonseparately stated is essential to properly completing Form 1065.

Typical Items to Look For When Computing Partnership Income

- Identify all separately stated items that must be reported on Schedule K
- Nonseparately stated items are reported on Form 1065, page 1
- Are there any specially allocated items that must be reported on Schedule K?
- Ensure that specially allocated items are reported on the appropriate partners' Schedule K-1s
- Make sure guaranteed payments are reported in three places: (1) as a nonseparately stated deduction on page 1 of Form 1065, (2) on Schedule K, Form 1065, and (3) on the appropriate partner's Schedule K-1
- Make sure that a guaranteed payment is reported on the appropriate line depending on whether it is for services or capital
- Distributions are not deductible when computing partnership income
- Ensure that the proper profit and loss sharing ratios are used for allocating tax items to the partners

Practice Scenario

This scenario is based on the same facts used in the previous scenario for NIU General Partnership.

The NIU General Partnership, a cash-basis taxpayer, has been in existence since July 4, Year 11. Ned, Irene, and Uriah are partners and have the following profit and loss sharing ratios.

Ned	60%
Irene	25%
Uriah	15%

A staff accountant at your firm has completed the first draft of NIU's partnership tax return for Year 12. A copy of Form 1065 and related schedules are provided below.

- Review federal Form 1065, U.S. Return of Partnership Income, and supporting documentation, including any source data used to create the return, to determine the completeness and accuracy of the classification of items as ordinary business income (loss), separately stated or nondeductible
- Complete the schedule at the end of this practice scenario to correct any incorrect information on the tax return
- Assume that NIU attempted to correct all the diagnostics provided in the previous TBS. Part of your task is to determine if they were properly corrected

For its tax year ended December 31, Year 12, NIU had the following items of income and loss:

Partnership Tax Item	Amount
Sales income	$100,000
Interest income	6,000
Municipal interest income	2,500
Long-term capital gain	32,000
Long-term capital loss	23,000
Section 1231 gain	8,000
Section 1245 recapture	3,000
Net rental real estate income	11,000
Cost of goods sold	52,000
Salaries	18,000
Guaranteed payment to Ned (services)	12,000
Advertising expense	4,000
Supplies expense	6,500
Depreciation expense*	13,000
Charitable contribution (cash)	6,000
Section 179 expense	18,000
State income taxes	5,000
Payroll taxes	1,500
Investment interest expense	2,000
Life insurance premium on partners' lives (owned by NIU)	3,000
Fines	1,000

**Depreciation expense of $13,000 is allocated 100% to Ned.*

Cash distributions were made to the partners on December 1, Year 12, as follows:

Ned	$10,000
Irene	$ 5,000
Uriah	$ 1,500

Tax Item		As Shown on Original Return	Insert Corrected Number If Needed
Form 1065, page 1			
1a	Gross receipts or sales	$100,000	
2	Cost of goods sold	52,000	
6	Net gain (loss) from Form 4797 (recapture)	0	
8	Total income (loss)	48,000	
9	Salaries	18,000	
10	Guaranteed payments to partners	12,000	
14	Taxes and licenses	6,500	
16a	Depreciation	13,000	
20	Other deductions	20,500	
22	Ordinary business income (loss)	(22,000)	
Schedule K			
1	Ordinary business income (loss)	(22,000)	
2	Net rental real estate income	11,000	
4a	Guaranteed payments	12,000	
5	Interest income	6,000	
9a	Net long-term capital gain	9,000	
11	Other income (loss) – Section 1245 recapture	3,000	
12	Section 179	18,000	
13a	Contributions	6,000	
13b	Investment interest expense	2,000	
13d	Other deductions – supplies	6,500	
13d	Other deductions – depreciation	0	
18a	Tax-exempt interest income	0	
18c	Nondeductible expenses	0	
19	Distributions of cash and marketable securities	16,500	

Additional Information For Partnership Tax Return

Form 1065, Line 20, Other Deductions

Description	Amount
Advertising	$ 4,000
Supplies	16,500
Total	**$20,500**

Solution

Use the following steps to complete this TBS:

Step 1: Review the tax items provided and determine whether the item should be separately stated or nonseparately stated.

Step 2: Determine if separately stated items are correctly reported on Schedule K and nonseparately stated items are correctly reported on page 1 of Form 1065.

Step 3: Identify tax-exempt income and nondeductible expenses and make sure that they are reported correctly on Schedule K.

Step 4: Review other information on the draft Form 1065 to identify any other errors.

Step 5: Complete the table provided for the tax items shown that are reported incorrectly on the draft Form 1065.

Steps 1–3: The following table identifies whether each item is income, a deduction, tax-exempt income, or a nondeductible expense. The final column indicates that the item is reported on Schedule K if separately stated and on page 1 of Form 1065 if nonseparately stated.

Partnership Tax Item	Amount	Classification	Reported On
Sales income	$100,000	Income	Page 1
Interest income	6,000	Income	Schedule K
Municipal interest income	2,500	Tax-exempt income	Schedule K
Long-term capital gain	32,000	Income	Schedule K
Long-term capital loss	23,000	Loss	Schedule K
Section 1231 gain	8,000	Income	Schedule K
Section 1245 recapture	3,000	Income	Page 1
Net rental real estate income	11,000	Income	Schedule K
Cost of goods sold	52,000	Deduction	Page 1
Salaries	18,000	Deduction	Page 1
Guaranteed payment to Ned (services)	12,000	Deduction/income	Page 1 and Sch. K
Advertising expense	4,000	Deduction	Page 1
Supplies expense	6,500	Deduction	Page 1
Depreciation expense (allocated to Ned)	13,000	Deduction	Schedule K
Charitable contribution (cash)	6,000	Deduction	Schedule K
Section 179 expense	18,000	Deduction	Schedule K
State income taxes	5,000	Deduction	Page 1
Payroll taxes	1,500	Deduction	Page 1
Investment interest expense	2,000	Deduction	Schedule K
Life insurance premium on partners' lives (owned by NIU)	3,000	Nondeductible	Schedule K
Fines	1,000	Nondeductible	Schedule K

Steps 4–5: The following errors were identified when comparing the classifications shown above to the draft Form 1065.

Form 1065, Page 1, Line 16a: Depreciation

Depreciation is usually deducted on page 1 of Form 1065. However, NIU allocated all the depreciation to Ned this year, so it is a specially allocated tax item. Therefore, it must be reported on line 13d of Schedule K.

Form 1065, Page 1, Line 20: Other Deductions

The schedule for other deductions shows that the cash distributions of $16,500 to the partners were deducted. Distributions do not reduce the partnership's ordinary business income. Cash distributions should be reported on Schedule K, line 19a.

Schedule K, Line 11: Other Income – Section 1245 Recapture

Section 1245 recapture is ordinary income that is reported on page 1 of Form 1065. It is not a separately stated item and is not reported on Schedule K. It is reported on line 6 of page 1.

Schedule K, Line 13d: Other Deductions – Supplies

Supplies expense is an ordinary deduction that is reported on page 1 of Form 1065. It is not a separately stated item and is not reported on Schedule K.

Schedule K, Line 18a: Tax-Exempt Interest Income

The tax-exempt interest income was not reported on the draft of Form 1065. However, it should be reported on Schedule K as a separately stated item. While the income is not taxable to the partners, it does increase their bases in their partnership interests.

Schedule K, Line 18c: Nondeductible Expenses

There are two nondeductible expenses for NIU, life insurance premiums ($3,000) and fines ($1,000). The life insurance premiums are not deductible because the policy is owned by NIU. Fines are not deductible since they are due to a violation of public policy.

These expenses were not reported on the draft of Form 1065. However, they should be reported on Schedule K as a separately stated item. While the expenses are not deductible for the partners, they do decrease their bases in their partnership interests.

These errors are corrected as follows.

Tax Item		As Shown On Original Return	Insert Corrected Number If Needed
Form 1065, page 1			
1a	Gross receipts or sales	$100,000	
2	Cost of goods sold	52,000	
6	Net gain (loss) from Form 4797 (recapture)	0	$3,000
8	Total income (loss)	48,000	51,000
9	Salaries	18,000	
10	Guaranteed payments to partners	12,000	
14	Taxes and licenses	6,500	
16a	Depreciation	13,000	0
20	Other deductions	20,500	10,500*
22	Ordinary business income (loss)	(22,000)	4,000
Schedule K			
1	Ordinary business income (loss)	(22,000)	4,000
2	Net rental real estate income	11,000	
4a	Guaranteed payments	12,000	
5	Interest income	6,000	
9a	Net long-term capital gain	9,000	
11	Other income (loss) – Section 1245 recapture	3,000	0
12	Section 179	18,000	
13a	Contributions	6,000	
13b	Investment interest expense	2,000	
13d	Other deductions – supplies	6,500	0
13d	Other deductions – depreciation	0	13,000
18a	Tax-exempt interest income	0	2,500
18c	Nondeductible expenses	0	4,000
19	Distributions of cash and marketable securities	16,500	

**This consists of $6,500 for supplies and $4,000 for advertising. The cash distributions are not reported here.*

Additional Information For Partnership Tax Return

Form 1065, Line 20, Other Deductions

Description	Amount
Advertising	$ 4,000
Supplies	6,500
Total	**$10,500**

21.02 Basis of a Partner's Interest

Basis of a Partner's Interest

Representative Task (Application): Calculate the partner's basis in a partnership for tax purposes resulting from business operations, cash contributions by a partner, cash distributions to a partner and changes in existing partnership liabilities.

Overview

Basis versus Capital Account

A *partner's tax basis* is different from the partner's **capital account** in the P/S. While basis represents one's investment in a partnership for **tax purposes**, the capital account represents the amount a partner should receive when the partnership is liquidated (accounting purposes). Generally, the capital account should represent the FMV of the partner's interest.

Basis and capital account are computed in a similar fashion, except:

- Liabilities of the partnership do not affect the capital account; and
- Contributions to and distributions from the capital account are accounted for at FMV.

Basis: There are two bases: inside and outside basis. Inside basis is the partnership's tax basis in the P/S assets. **Outside basis** (sometime referred to as tax basis) is the **partner's basis in the P/S interest** and is the basis that is used to determine the:

- Deductibility of P/S losses;
- Treatment of distributions;
- Amount of gain or loss on the sale or liquidation of a P/S interest; and
- Partner's basis of property received in a liquidation.

Partnerships: Inside vs. Outside Basis

Inside Basis Partnership's adjusted basis in its assets	**Outside Basis** Partner's basis in P/S interest owned

Each partner "owns" their % share of the assets	• Initially equals amount contributed • Adjusted for % share of P/S income (loss) and P/S liabilities, additional contributions and distributions • Used to limit deductibility of P/S losses and determine tax treatment of distributions

P/S = partnership

Initial Basis

The partner's initial basis in their partnership is determined based on how the interest was acquired:

- If the interest was purchased, the partner has a cost basis equal to the purchase price
- If the interest was acquired in a tax-deferred formation, the partner's basis is equal to the sum of the cash and adjusted basis of property contributed to the partnership
- The adjusted basis for contributions of services is the value included in the income of the partner
- If the interest was received as a gift, generally the partner's basis is the same as the donor's basis in the interest. If the donor had an unrealized loss in the interest, the partner's basis is the lower of the donor's adjusted basis or the FMV of the property
- If the interest was received as an inheritance, the partner's basis is the FMV of the partnership interest on the decedent's date of death

Adjustments to Basis

Since a P/S is a flow-through entity, each partner's basis is adjusted for their distributive share of the P/S income (loss) and separately stated items (eg, capital gains/losses, charitable contributions, dividends, tax-exempt interest). A partner's share of partnership tax items flows to the partner on the last day of the partnership tax year.

Distributive share is determined by the P/S agreement (eg, profits and loss percentages) and must have a substantial economic effect. Generally, unless otherwise stated, the *partner's proportionate interest in the P/S* is used (eg, 25%, 60%).

The items impact basis in a *specific order* to determine whether a partner's distributive share of a P/S's loss is deductible. Therefore, when determining a partner's basis:

- First, increase basis for income and gains;
- Then, decrease basis for distributions; and
- Finally, decrease basis for expenses and losses.

Because basis may **never go below zero**, any nondeductible losses are **suspended** and carried forward until there is sufficient basis.

P/S Debt and Partners

Generally, a partner is liable to pay the P/S debt. Thus, changes in the P/S liabilities affect a partner's basis. The degree to which a partner is liable for P/S debt depends on the type of liability and whether the partner is a *general* or *limited* partner.

Effect on Partners' Basis: Because partners bear an economic risk of loss (ie, are personally liable), their basis includes their share of the P/S liabilities.

- **Increases** in a partner's share of P/S liabilities (eg, accounts payable, loans to a bank) are added to their basis (ie, considered cash contributions); **decreases** are **deducted** from their basis (ie, considered cash distributions to the partner)
- Personal loans to the P/S are allocated 100% to that partner
- A **decrease** in a partner's share of P/S debt is **deducted** from their basis on the last day of the P/S year
- When a P/S assumes a partner's *individual liability*, this is considered a distribution of money to the partner by the P/S (ie, the partner's basis is reduced)
- If a P/S is *cash basis*, then *accounts payable* are *excluded* from a partner's basis

Recourse Debt: If a partner is liable (ie, bears the economic risk) to pay the P/S debt, it is a **recourse** liability. Accounts payable are recourse unless the P/S uses the *cash basis* method of accounting.

- For *general partners*, **all debt** increases the partner's basis for the *basis limitation*, but only **recourse** debt and **qualified nonrecourse** debt (discussed below) are included when determining the *amount at risk* for a partner
- Since limited partners are *not* generally liable for the repayment of debt, recourse liabilities are *excluded* from their basis unless the P/S agreement specifies otherwise

Nonrecourse Debt: If **no** partner is responsible for paying for the P/S debt, it is considered a nonrecourse liability (eg, generally secured by collateral). The lender bears the risk of nonpayment (eg, loan collateralized by the property).

- Nonrecourse debt increases the basis of both general and limited partners. If a basis adjustment was not permitted, there would be no rationale to take P/S deductions (eg, depreciation) on an asset financed with nonrecourse debt
- Partners (general and limited) generally share in nonrecourse liabilities in relation to their profits interest in the partnership. If a profits interest is not stated, the capital interest is used

Qualified Nonrecourse Debt: The IRC allows an **exception** for "qualified nonrecourse debt" to be included in a limited and general partner's basis and at-risk amount.

- Qualified nonrecourse debt is any nonrecourse debt that is collateralized by real property (eg, mortgage) in the activity of holding real property. The *general and limited partners'* share of qualified nonrecourse debt is *included* in their basis

The following chart provides a detailed analysis of the items that impact the partner's basis in the P/S interest:

Calculation of Partner's Tax Basis

Guaranteed payments do **not** *directly* affect basis

Partner's initial contribution (or amount paid, if purchased)

Increased by:

Additional contributions

Share of net increase in P/S liabilities

Share of P/S net income

Share of separately stated income and nontaxable income

Decreased by:

Cash and property distributions

Share of net decrease in P/S liabilities

Share of nondeductible expenses

Share of P/S losses and separately stated deductions

Partner's ending basis (not below zero)

Examples

An individual contributed $20,000 in exchange for a 50% interest in the profits and losses as a general partner in the ABC Partnership. At the time of the contribution, the P/S had accounts payable of $5,000, other recourse debt of $10,000, and nonrecourse debt of $6,000. What is the individual's tax basis in the P/S at the time of the contribution?

Because the individual is a general partner, both the recourse debt and nonrecourse debt are included in their P/S basis.

Cash contribution	$20,000
Share of recourse debt ($15,000 × 50%)	7,500
Share of nonrecourse debt ($6,000 × 50%)	3,000
Tax basis	**$30,500**

How would the basis change if the individual is a limited partner?

Limited partners **exclude recourse** debt from their basis, since they have limited liability. Accordingly, the basis would be **$23,000** ($20,000 contribution + $3,000 nonrecourse debt).

January 4, Year 4, Smith and White contributed $4,000 and $6,000 in cash, respectively, and formed the Macro Partnership. Both individuals are general partners. The partnership agreement allocated profits and losses 40% to Smith and 60% to White. In Year 4, Macro purchased property from an unrelated seller for $10,000 cash and a $40,000 mortgage note. What effect does Macro's liability have on Smith's tax basis?

In this scenario, Smith is a 40% general partner and liable for 40% of the P/S debt. Therefore, the $40,000 mortgage incurred by the P/S **increases** Smith's tax basis by **$16,000** (40% × $40,000).

The XYZ partnership has one general partner (Jon) with a 75% profit interest and one limited partner (Sally) with a 25% profit interest. In Year 3, Jon's beginning basis is $63,000, and Sally's is $21,000. The partnership had the following items for Year 3:

Net ordinary business income	$150,000
Municipal bond interest income	2,000
Short-term capital loss	10,000
Nondeductible fine	6,000
Cash distribution to Jon	35,000
Cash distribution to Sally	15,000

The liabilities at the beginning and end of P/S year are below:

	Beginning of Year	End of Year
Recourse debt	$60,000	$80,000
Nonrecourse debt	300,000	350,000
Qualified nonrecourse debt	150,000	125,000

Determine Jon's and Sally's basis in the partnership at the end of Year 3.

- Jon is allocated 75% of the pass-through items, and Sally receives 25%. However, each partner is allocated 100% of their cash distribution
- The change (increase or decrease) in nonrecourse liabilities is allocated to each partner's basis according to the profit interests. Only general partners are responsible for recourse debt. Therefore, Jon is allocated 100% of the recourse debt

	Jon (75%)	Sally (25%)
Recourse debt ($20,000 increase)	$20,000	$ 0
Nonrecourse debt ($50,000 increase)	37,500	12,500
Qualified nonrecourse debt ($25,000 decrease)	(18,750)	(6,250)
Net increase in partner's basis	**$38,750**	**$6,250**

	Jon's Basis	Sally's Basis
Beginning basis	$ 63,000	$21,000
Net increase in P/S debt	38,750	6,250
Net ordinary business income	112,500	37,500
Municipal bond interest income	1,500	500
Cash distribution	(35,000)	(15,000)
Short-term capital loss	(7,500)	(2,500)
Nondeductible fine	(4,500)	(1,500)
Ending basis	**$168,750**	**$46,250**

Ning is a 40% general partner in LMN Partnership, which has the following tax items this year:

Ordinary business loss	$(50,000)
Qualified dividends	10,000
Net long-term capital gain	12,000
Section 179 expense	18,000
Increase in partnership debt	20,000

Ning's basis in her partnership interest at the beginning of the year is $26,000, and she received a cash distribution during the year of $8,000. Using the ordering rules, Ning's basis is as follows:

Balance at the beginning of the year	$26,000
Increase in partnership debt ($20,000 × 40%)	8,000
Qualified dividends ($10,000 × 40%)	4,000
Net long-term capital gain ($12,000 × 40%)	4,800
Available basis for distributions	$42,800
Cash distribution	(8,000)
Balance	$34,800
Ordinary business loss ($50,000 × 40%)	(20,000)
Section 179 expense ($18,000 × 40%)	(7,200)
Balance at end of year	$ 7,600

What if Ning's share of the net ordinary business loss was $30,000 instead of $20,000?

Because a partner's basis must never go below zero, not all of the loss is currently deductible. The subtractions of $37,200 ($30,000 loss + $7,200 Sec. 179) exceed the basis balance of $34,800 by $2,400. Ning is unable to take the full $30,000 loss. Ning reduces her basis to zero and has a suspended loss and Section 179 deduction that are carried over to future years.

Effect on Partners When Cash Distributions Exceed Basis

The excess of the cash distribution over the partner's basis is reported as a **gain** by the partner. For purposes of determining the tax treatment of distributions, marketable securities generally are treated as cash. Because **reduction in debt** is considered a cash distribution, if a partner's share of the reduction in P/S debt exceeds their basis, the excess is also taxable as a gain.

Gain from a nonliquidating distribution is treated as **capital gain** by the partner since a P/S interest is a capital asset.

Chase has a basis in his partnership interest of $32,000. He receives a cash distribution of $40,000. Because the cash distribution exceeds Chase's basis in his partnership interest, Chase recognizes a capital gain of $8,000 ($32,000 − $40,000). His basis in his partnership after the distribution is $0.

Assume that Chase is a 40% general partner in the partnership. Instead of receiving a cash distribution, assume that the partnership pays off one of its liabilities of $100,000. Chase's share of the debt is $40,000 ($100,000 × 40%). The **reduction** in the debt is treated as a **cash distribution** to Chase. Therefore, Chase recognizes a capital gain of $8,000 ($32,000 − $40,000). His basis in his partnership after the distribution is $0.

REG 22
Limited Liability Companies

REG 22: Limited Liability Companies

22.01 Limited Liability Companies

Classification Choices for Limited Liability Companies

Representative Task (Remembering & Understanding): Recall the tax classification options for a limited liability company for tax purposes.

Overview

Some states, most of which follow the Revised Uniform Limited Liability Company Act (RULLCA), have an enabling statute that allows for the formation of limited liability companies (LLCs). LLCs are hybrid entities that have characteristics of both partnerships and corporations. They are pass-through entities from a tax standpoint, while they provide their owners, referred to as *members*, with *the limited liability protection* of a corporation.

Unlike partnerships, even if a member actively participates in the business, the LLC and not the member is liable. This is one reason why businesses are frequently formed as LLCs. Also, like a corporation, members have no interest in the LLC's assets but only in the LLC itself.

An LLC is a separate **legal entity** that can be formed only in a state that allows their formation and, as a result, can be sued or file suit in its own name.

- Like limited partnerships, LLCs file a certificate with the Secretary of State. The certificate must include the entity's name, which must include the words "limited liability company," "limited company," or appropriate abbreviations
- In addition to the certificate of formation, an LLC may draft an operating agreement used to govern the LLC's operations, which spells out voting rights, profit/loss allocations, and changes in members, for example. This allows LLCs more flexibility than corporations
- The formation of an LLC is usually not a taxable event; however there are exceptions. For example, if an existing C corporation wishes to convert to an LLC, the corporation must first dissolve (ie, liquidate its assets), which would trigger taxation

Characteristics of an LLC	
Formation	• Separate legal entity • Formed pursuant to the requirements of state law • Any person or entity can invest in an LLC • Minimal regulatory compliance
Management	• Member managed or manager managed
Limited Liability	• Members are generally *not* responsible for company debt
Distributions	• Depends on how the LLC elects to be taxed
Taxation	• Can elect to be taxed as a partnership, as a C corporation, or as an S corporation • A single-member LLC that does not elect corporation classification will be taxed as a sole proprietorship
Loss Limitation	• Member's basis + Personal loans to company (if any)
Termination	• Terminates by action of state law or by decision of the members

Members may participate in management (agents) without restriction and owe the same duties of loyalty and care to the LLC as owed to a limited partnership by the general partner.

- Also, like a general partner in a limited partnership, a member cannot freely transfer an interest, and a new member must be admitted upon the consent of the other members
- An LLC may be member managed or manager managed. A member-managed LLC will be bound by the actions of any of its members, who are considered agents of the LLC
- A manager-managed LLC is bound only by the actions of the manager that are either authorized or in the ordinary course of business. In either case, a member or manager who is able to bind the LLC owes it both *a duty of loyalty and a duty of care*. A member of a manager-managed LLC, however, owes no fiduciary duty to the LLC. Under duty of care and loyalty, those who operate the LLC must **not**:
    - Compete with the LLC;
    - Use LLC business opportunities for personal gain;
    - Have a conflict of interest with the LLC; or
    - Sell their control over the LLC (eg, bribes, kickbacks).

Who Owes Fiduciary Duties* to a Limited Liability Company (LLC)

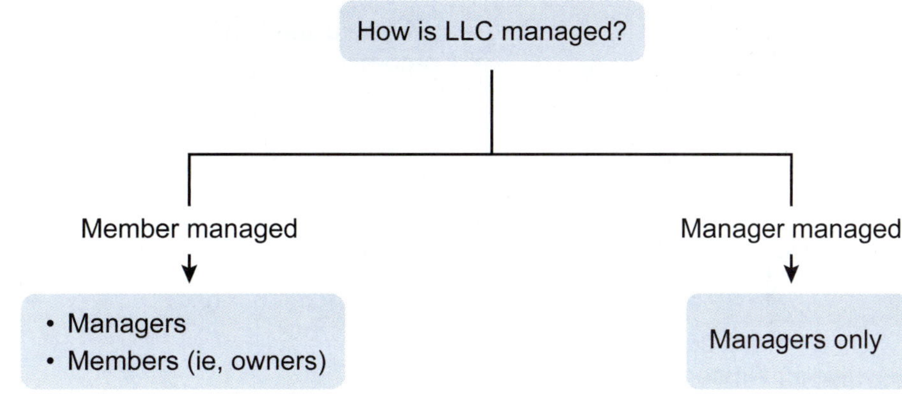

*Duty of care and duty of loyalty

In a manager managed limited liability company, are the duty of care and the duty of loyalty owed by the managers, the members, or both?

An LLC may be member managed or manager managed. A manager managed LLC is operated only by managers who are authorized by the LLC to be managers and is more like a corporation. In a corporation, only properly elected directors and officers are authorized to operate the business and therefore owe fiduciary duties to the corporation. Shareholders of a corporation do not owe any fiduciary duties to the corporation. In a manager managed LLC, **the managers owe fiduciary duties to the LLC**; however, members do not.

Tax Classification

When forming an LLC, one important determination is how the entity will be treated for **tax purposes**. Taxpayers have some flexibility here as the **check-the-box regulations** apply to the LLC. The check-the-box regulations provide **default tax classifications** that can be modified by election. In other words, it allows owners of eligible entities, like the LLC, to choose the entity's tax classification, which may not necessarily align with the entity's legal classification. The options are as follows:

- **Entity classification election**
  Multiple-member LLCs can elect to be treated as a corporation (ie, C corporation, S corporation) or partnership. Single-member LLCs can elect to be treated as a C or an S corporation (if requirements are met and members file an S corp election) or as a disregarded entity (ie, sole proprietorship)
- **No election made** (ie, default treatment)
  - *Multiple members*: If a multiple-member LLC makes no election, the LLC is treated as a partnership for tax purposes. The LLC files a Form 1065 income tax return, and each member of the LLC will receive a Schedule K-1 that flows to their individual tax return (ie, Form 1040, Schedule E)
  - *Single member*: If a single-member LLC makes no election, the LLC is treated as a "**disregarded entity**," and its activities are reported on the individual's tax return, using Schedule C of Form 1040. Disregarded entities are considered to be the same entity as the owner. This means taxes owed by this type of business are paid as part of the owner's income tax return

Tax Classification of a Limited Liability Company

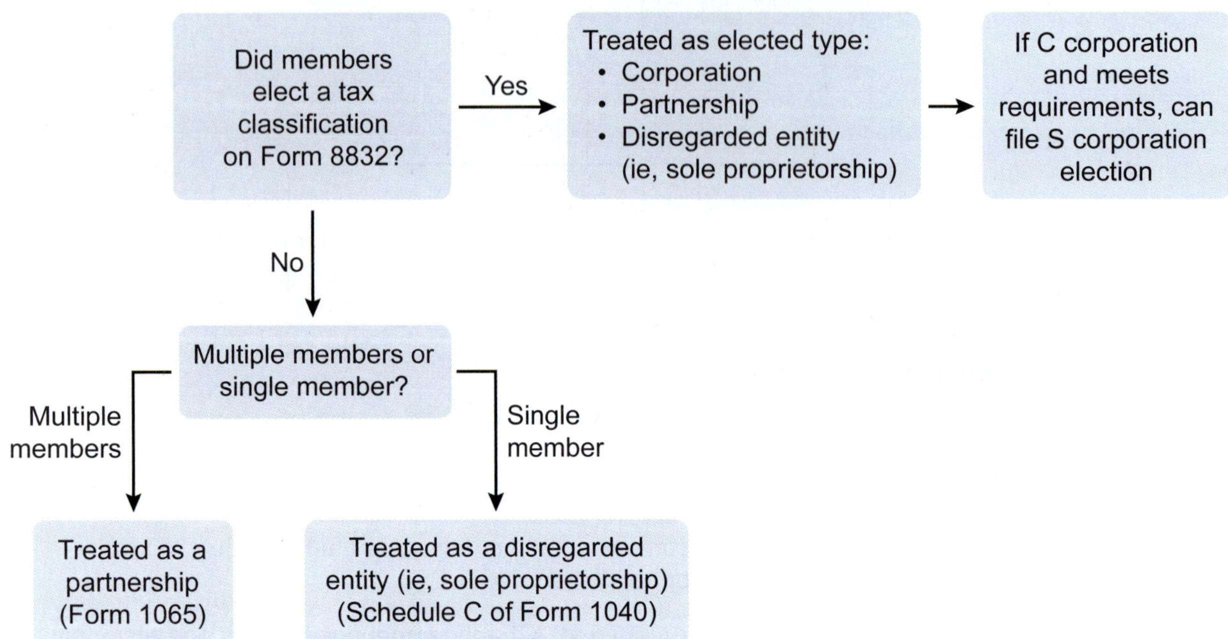

Janice legally forms MLT as an LLC by filing a certificate of formation in her state. If she is the *only member* of MLT, the default classification for MLT is a *sole proprietorship* (ie, disregarded entity) because MLT is unincorporated with one individual member. Janice may elect to have MLT taxed as a C corporation or, if the requirements are met, file an S corporation election.

If Janice allows other individuals or entities to become members of MLT, the default classification for unincorporated entities with more than one member is a partnership. Janice and the other members may elect to treat MLT as a partnership or as a corporation or file an S corporation election if the requirements are met.

A two-member LLC elected classification as an S corporation three years ago. At the beginning of the current year, one member withdrew from the LLC. What is the LLC's tax classification immediately after the member withdraws?

By default, the IRS classifies a single-member LLC as a disregarded entity and a multiple-member LLC as a partnership. However, a single- or multiple-member LLC may file an election with the IRS to be taxed as a C or an S corporation.

In general, once an LLC registers its classification, it must wait 60 months (5 years) to make a new election. Therefore, a two-member LLC that elected to be treated as an S corporation remains an S corporation even if one member withdraws. Once the 60-month waiting period is met, the LLC is eligible to change its classification.

REG 23
Tax-Exempt Organizations

REG 23: Tax-Exempt Organizations

23.01 Tax-Exempt Organizations

Types of Tax-Exempt Organizations

Representative Task (Remembering & Understanding): Recall the different types of tax-exempt organizations for tax purposes.

Organizations formed for the purpose of helping the public as opposed to making a profit, as is the purpose of most businesses, are called *nonprofit organizations*. Certain organizations are designated 501(c) organizations and given exempt status from federal income tax once approved by the IRS.

To be granted tax-exempt status, the organization must be one of those specifically identified in the tax code and must apply for and receive an exemption. The IRS recognizes more than 19 different classifications under IRC Sec. 501(c) that are eligible for tax-exempt status.

Examples of Tax-Exempt Organizations	
Public Charities (501)(c)(3)	**Other 501(c) Organizations**
• Religious organizations • Scientific foundations • Public safety groups • Arts organizations • Amateur sports associations • Child & animal welfare groups	• Social and recreational clubs (eg, fraternities and country clubs) • Civic leagues • Credit and labor unions • Chambers of commerce • Homeowner associations • Cemeteries

- Recognition of tax-exempt status is not automatic. It is instead granted to a qualifying entity upon submission of an application with the IRS (ie, Form 1023). The organization must include articles of organization or incorporation that state the entity's charitable purpose
  - An annual information return (Form 990) is required for most tax-exempt organizations if gross receipts exceed $50,000
- The entity must be operating as a corporation, community chest, fund, charity, labor organization, social club, pension and profit-sharing trust, or private foundation. Partnerships **cannot** be treated as tax-exempt
- The organization may **not** be operated for the benefit of a private interest, and no part of the organization's income or assets may be inappropriately diverted for use by any internal individual (eg, directors, officers) involved in the organization (referred to as inurement)

- An organization does not qualify as an exempt charity if it is merely a feeder organization. A feeder organization is an organization that is operated as a business for profit but that transfers all its net earnings to charitable organizations
- Social clubs must be primarily supported by membership dues and fees; they generally cannot provide their goods or services to the general public

Section 501(c)(3) Private Foundations and Public Charities

Section 501(c)(3) tax-exempt organizations are established to benefit the public interest and are classified by their funding as private foundations or public charities.

501(c)(3) Organizations	
Type	**Example**
Religious organizations	Churches
Public charities	American Red Cross
Educational organizations	Colleges, museums
Scientific/literary organizations	National Endowment for the Arts
Amateur athletic organizations	Little League baseball
Testing for public safety	Insurance Institute for Highway Safety
Private foundations	Bill and Melinda Gates Foundation

Private foundations typically have a single major source of funding, such as an endowment from a family or a corporation, and receive **less than one-third** of their support from members and the general public.

- Their primary activity is using the funds generated from the endowment to provide grants to charitable organizations and individuals
- Private foundations may be subject to penalty taxes on investment income, self-dealing activities, or participation in prohibited transactions. All private foundations must file Form 990-PF annually

Organizations that are publicly supported (ie, public charities) normally receive **at least one-third** of their support from the **general public** and/or **governmental entities**. The donations must be used exclusively for carrying out their exempt purpose. It is important to identify a nonprofit organization as a "public charity" for compliance/reporting requirements and donor deduction limitations. Examples of public charities include:

- Religious organizations, hospitals, and public schools
- Entities actively fundraising and receiving contributions from many sources, including the general public, governmental agencies, corporations, private foundations, or other public charities
- Entities receiving income from the conduct of activities furthering the organization's exempt purposes

Which of the following types of business may not qualify for a 501(c)(3) exemption from federal income taxes?

- A foundation
- A fund
- A corporation
- A partnership

IRC §501(c)(3) includes "*Corporations, and any community chest, fund, or foundation, organized and operated exclusively for religious, charitable, scientific, testing for public safety, literary, or educational purposes, or to foster national or international amateur sports competition…, or for the prevention of cruelty to children or animals*"; thus, a **partnership would not qualify**.

- Section 501(c)(3) organizations are prohibited from directly or indirectly participating in, or intervening in, any political campaign. However, nonpartisan voter education and registration activities are allowed
- An organization may, on a *limited* basis, engage in lobbying activities if directly related to its tax-exempt purpose. However, organizations (other than churches) are subject to an excise tax for excessive lobbying activities

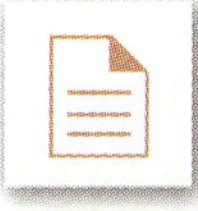

A charitable organization for the prevention of cruelty to animals supports a candidate for town council by allowing a political campaign poster and literature to be displayed in its lobby. Is this a permitted activity by the organization?

No, it is considered political campaigning. Section 501(c)(3) organizations are explicitly prohibited from such activity. However, displaying pamphlets about *how to register to vote* is permitted.

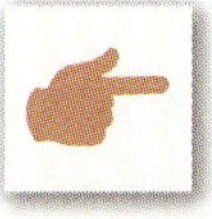

Generally, with few exceptions, only contributions made to organizations that qualify for 501(c)(3) status are tax deductible by the donor.

Other Types of 501(c) Organizations

Generally, nonprofit organizations established for the **benefit of a community** (rather than the general public) are **not** charitable organizations or public charities (eg, civic leagues, chambers of commerce, unemployment benefit trusts, credit unions, cemeteries). Note that some nonprofit organizations under 501(c) may still receive tax-deductible donations (eg, cemeteries) but are not technically "public charities" under 501(c)(3).

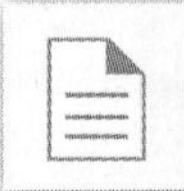

Which of the following types of organizations is considered a public charity for purposes of the charitable contribution deduction?

- The Columbia City Chamber of Commerce
- The National Endowment for the Arts
- The Lions Club Civic League
- The Newberry Unemployment Benefit Trust

Charitable organizations, such as the **National Endowment for the Arts**, are established to benefit the public interest. It is important to identify a nonprofit organization as a "public charity" for compliance/reporting requirements and donor deduction limitations.

Which of the following may not qualify as a tax-exempt organization?

- A credit union
- A country club
- A community savings and loan association that issues common stock
- A local sports association

There are numerous classifications of organizations that are eligible for tax-exempt status. Some examples include religious organizations, country clubs, fraternal societies, credit unions, and amateur sports associations. However, a **community savings and loan association** that **issues stock** (ie, third-party ownership interests) is a for-profit entity and therefore does not qualify as a tax-exempt organization.